Simon Hayes

MONEY
FINANCIAL MAR
AND THE ECON

MONEY
FINANCIAL MARKETS
AND THE ECONOMY

Robert Haney Scott
California State University, Chico

PRENTICE HALL
Singapore   New York   London   Toronto   Sydney   Tokyo

First published 1995 by
Prentice Hall
Simon & Schuster (Asia) Pte Ltd
Alexandra Distripark
Block 4, #04-31
Pasir Panjang Road
Singapore 0511

© 1995 Simon & Schuster (Asia) Pte Ltd
A division of Simon & Schuster International Group

Parts of this book were reproduced/adapted from *Financial Markets and the Economy*, 5th Edition, by Henning, Pigott and Scott, © 1988. Reprinted by permission of Prentice Hall, Englewood Cliffs, New Jersey.

Cover photograph by Dominique Sarraute and The Image Bank

Printed in Singapore

2 3 4 5   99 98 97 96 95

Library of Congress Cataloging-in-Publication Data

Scott, Robert Haney.
   Money, financial markets, and the economy/Robert Haney Scott.
      p.   cm.
   Includes bibliographical references and index.
   ISBN 0-13-192089-8 (pbk.)
   1. Finance.   2. Financial institutions.   3. Money market.
4. Capital market.   I. Title.
HG173.S37 1995   95-22498
332--dc20   CIP

Prentice Hall International (UK) Limited, *London*
Prentice Hall of Australia Pty. Limited, *Sydney*
Prentice Hall Canada Inc., *Toronto*
Prentice Hall Hispanoamericana, S.A., *Mexico*
Prentice Hall of India Private Limited, *New Delhi*
Prentice Hall of Japan, Inc., *Tokyo*
Editora Prentice Hall do Brasil, Ltda., *Rio de Janeiro*
Prentice Hall, Inc., *Englewood Cliffs, New Jersey*

Contents

Preface xi

PART I BANKING AND MONETARY CONTROLS

1 Introduction to Financial Systems 1
Interest Rates and Securities Prices 1
Classification of Financial Markets 5
Financial Intermediaries 7
The Role of Government in Financial Markets 7
The Organization of This Book 8
The Economic Growth of the Four Asian Tigers 8
Summary 9   Key Terms and Concepts 9
Discussion Questions and Exercises 9   References 10

2 The Economic Role of Financial Institutions 12
Saving and Investment in Barter and Monetary Economies 13
Money, Debt, Credit, and Assets 14
The Circular Flow Diagram with a Financial Sector 17
Flow of Funds Analysis 24
Interest Rate Forecasts and Other Applications 32
Gross Domestic Product Data from the Four Asian Tigers 33
Summary 34   Key Terms and Concepts 36
Discussion Questions and Exercises 36   References 37

3   **The Business of Commercial Banking**   38

Commercial Banking as a Business   38

Bank Reserves   48

Contemporaneous and Lagged Reserve Accounting   52

Asset and Liability Management of Reserves   53

Banks and Reserve Maintenance Requirements in Other Countries   54

Summary   59   Key Terms and Concepts   61

Discussion Questions and Exercises   61   References   61

4   **Banks and Other Deposit-taking Financial Institutions**   63

History and Introduction   64

NOW Accounts, ATS Accounts and Money Market Mutual Funds   65

The Court's Reaction   68

Money Creation   70

Money Creation by Thrifts and Money Market Mutual Funds   73

Capital Adequacy Ratios   75

A Bleak Outlook for Commercial Banks   80

Banks in Hong Kong, Korea, Singapore and Taiwan   81

Summary   83   Key Terms and Concepts   84

Discussion Questions and Exercises   84   References   84

5   **Money and Seigniorage: Definitions and Measures**   87

Defining Money   87

Measurement of Money   90

Seigniorage   96

Measuring Money in the Four Asian Tigers   103

Money is Fungible   105

The Case of the Missing Currency   111

Summary   112   Key Terms and Concepts   112

Discussion Questions and Exercises   112   References   113

6   **Commercial and Central Bank Interactions**   114

Correspondent Banking Relations   114

Functions of Central Banks   116

Managing Bank Reserves: The Bank's Viewpoint   118

Reserves   124

Tools of Control over Money Creation   125

A Summary Statement on Tools of Monetary Control   131

Summary   131   Key Terms and Concepts   132

Discussion Questions and Exercises   132   References   133

7   **The Monetary Base and Central Banking Controls**   134

The Monetary Base and the Money Supply   135

Factors Affecting the Reserves of Depository Institutions   140
Monetary Tools of the Federal Reserve System   142
Monetary Tools of France, Germany, and the United Kingdom   143
Monetary Tools of Japan   150
Monetary Tools of the Asian Tigers   152
Summary   156   Key Terms and Concepts   157
Discussion Questions and Exercises   157   References   158

PART II   FINANCIAL MARKETS

8 **The Money Market   160**
Money Market Instruments   161
Interest Rates on Money Market Instruments   176
Money Markets in the Asian Tigers   176
Summary   182   Key Terms and Concepts   182
Discussion Questions and Exercises   183   References   183

9 **Capital Markets   185**
The Long-term Government Securities Market   185
Zero Coupon Bonds   190
Government Agency and Similar Bonds   191
Corporate Bonds   192
Eurobonds   196
Municipal Bonds   197
Corporate Stocks   200
Capital Markets in Asia   201
Summary   207   Key Terms and Concepts   208
Discussion Questions and Exercises   208   References   209

10 **Mortgage and Other Securitized Asset Markets   211**
Deductible Interest and Other Support for Housing   211
Secondary Markets for Mortgage Loans   215
Secondary Markets: Good Economics or Good Politics?   217
Collateralized Mortgage Obligations (CMOs) and Real Estate Mortgage
    Investment Conduits (REMICs)   222
Collateralized Securities: A Growth Industry   225
Summary   227   Key Terms and Concepts   228
Discussion Questions and Exercises   228   References   229

11 **Futures, Options, and Swap Markets   230**
Risk and Uncertainty   230
Hedging Bets   232
Futures Markets   233

Stock Market Index Futures Contracts   239
Options Markets   243
Swap Markets   245
An Exploding Swap Market   246
New Products in Futures and Options   248
Financial Derivatives in the Asian Tigers   249
Summary   250   Key Terms and Concepts   251
Discussion Questions and Exercises   251   References   252

PART III   INTEREST RATE THEORY

12   Determining the General Level of Interest Rates   254

Introduction to the Present Value of Bonds and Stocks   255
Classical and Neoclassical Theories of Interest Rates   258
The Loanable Funds Approach   259
Expected Inflation and the Level of Interest Rates   266
Inflation in the Loanable Funds Model   269
Theory in the Asian Tigers   271
Summary   271   Key Terms and Concepts   273
Discussion Questions and Exercises   273   References   274

13   Interest Rate Theory   275

The Equation of Exchange   276
The Modern Quantity Theory of Money   279
A Theory of the Demand for Assets   283
The Fisherian Time-preference Model   287
Summary   294   Key Terms and Concepts   296
Discussion Questions and Exercises   296   References   297

14   The Term Structure of Interest Rates   298

Yield Curves   299
The Segmented Markets Approach   303
The Pure Expectations Approach   306
Liquidity Premium, Risk Premium, Term Premium   311
The Accuracy of the Market's Forecasts   315
Summary   316   Key Terms and Concepts   317
Discussion Questions and Exercises   317   References   318

PART IV   REGULATION AND POLICY

15   Regulation and Efficiency   320

The Theory of Regulation   320
Regulations to Promote Competition, Stability and Efficiency   325

Efficiency   328
A Formal Statement of the EMH and Evidence against It   330
On the Failure of Banks and Thrift Institutions   333
A New Organizational Structure for Bank Regulation   336
Summary   336   Key Terms and Concepts   336
Discussion Questions and Exercises   336   References   337

16 Formulating and Implementing Monetary Policy   340
Meetings of the Federal Open Market Committee   340
Open Market Operations: Targets and Details   343
Summary Statement of Procedures   349
Open Market Churning of Accounts   350
Intervention in Foreign Exchange Markets   351
Pegging Interest Rates and the "Bills-only" Policy   355
A Broadside Approach to Open Market Operations: A Proposal   358
Debate over Reserve Requirements   361
Monetary Policy Concerns   361
Summary   362   Key Terms and Concepts   362
Discussion Questions and Exercises   362   References   363

17 Implementing Fiscal and Debt Management Policies   366
Fiscal Policy   367
Debt Management Policy   373
Economic Impact of Changes in Debt Structure   376
Effectiveness of Debt Management   377
Holding Interest Cost Down   378
Debt Management Techniques   379
Politics and Debt Management   380
Debt Management Operations and Financial Markets   381
Summary   383   Key Terms and Concepts   384
Discussion Questions and Exercises   384   References   384

18 Monetary Policy in the Asian Tigers   386
Monetary and Fiscal Policies in Hong Kong   386
Monetary and Fiscal Policies in Singapore   397
Monetary and Fiscal Policies in Korea   401
Monetary and Fiscal Policies in Taiwan   403
Summary   406   Key Terms and Concepts   406
Discussion Questions and Exercises   406   References   407

Author Index   411

Subject Index   415

Preface

THIS BOOK STEMS from a felt need for a text about financial institutions and markets that would serve the needs of students in Asia as well as those in America. When I joined the Business Faculty of the Chinese University of Hong Kong as a visiting professor in 1983–84, it was appropriate to use an American text, *Financial Markets and the Economy*, by Henning, Pigott, and Scott (Prentice-Hall, 4th edition, 1983). This text had to be supplemented with readings about Hong Kong's financial institutions and systems. I compiled readings for students about Hong Kong, Korea, Singapore, Taiwan, and other Asian countries with only modest success.

By 1990, when I returned to the Chinese University for two additional years, the situation had improved. More references were available. And, the economies of four Asian countries had grown so rapidly that they had become known as the Four Asian Tigers.

These countries are not big by comparison with major trading nations of the world. Singapore has about 3 million population, Hong Kong about 6 million, Taiwan 21 million, and South Korea, the largest in both area and population, about 45 million. These population figures contrast with those of the United States at 280 million, Japan 120 million, Russia 300 million, and a unified Europe, should it come about, of 330 million.

Nevertheless, the small Four Asian Tigers have each demonstrated an economic prowess that was not foreseen until the late 1970s.

Because America plays such an important role in the world economy, and because its dollar is widely used as a currency for international trade, almost all financial arrangements requiring large sums of money involve the dollar. And, with the dollar as a base for trade, there is a need for familiarity with America's financial system by students in all countries, including the Four Asian Tigers.

Furthermore, it is widely recognized in the United States that there is a great need for American business and economics students to become more familiar with the systems of finance used in other countries. I hope, therefore, that this book will find an audience in Asia as well as in the U.S.

Over the next several years, the number of Asian Tigers will surely increase. On the verge of joining those countries with high growth rates are Malaysia and Thailand. Indonesia's programs for the future of its economy are also promising. Guangdong Province in the south of China next to Hong Kong is an expanding and developing area. Thus, trading nations in Europe and South America and throughout the world will be doing more and more business with nations on the Asian side of the Pacific. Australia and New Zealand already trade extensively with the Tiger countries, so students there may find this text useful.

I wish to express my heartfelt appreciation for all the assistance and guidance I received from my students and colleagues in Hong Kong. My students, too numerous to mention them all by name, were often asked to prepare reports on various aspects of financial markets in the Asian Tigers. Needless to say, I learned a great deal from them through their research efforts and reports. My many colleagues always responded to my questions thoughtfully and with patience. I am very grateful.

I would also like to thank Prentice Hall for permission to use many pages from *Financial Markets and the Economy*, 5th Edition, 1988, by Henning, Pigott and Scott.

To the Instructor

This book begins with institutional detail on financial intermediaries and central banking controls. Following those are descriptions of the many different financial markets and types of securities. Next is a section on the theories, both macro and microeconomic, that economists use to explain the determination of interest rates. Final chapters discuss the regulatory policies and other policy formation activities relating to financial markets. So the text moves progressively from description to theory to policy.

One goal in the writing of this text was to produce a concise book—only half the length of others. Yet the overall makeup of the book, including the references, offers a framework for the most comprehensive course.

One supplement for the text I recommend that students read is *Modern Money Mechanics*, Federal Reserve Bank of Chicago, 1992. Free copies may be ordered from Public Information Center, Chicago, Illinois, U.S.A. 60690-0834, or phone (312) 322-5111.

Professors and students in Asian countries have a close and current interest in their ever-changing world of financial institutions and markets. I invite all users of the text to write to me about items they would like to see included in the text. All suggestions will be very welcome. Write to College of Business, California State University, Chico, California, U.S.A. 95929-0051. I would appreciate your assistance.

Discussion questions and exercises at the end of each chapter can be used very much as they are for exams requiring short essay answers. I use 12 of them for a one-hour exam—four on a page and three pages.

Finally, while describing and explaining institutions and markets, I have also taken the liberty of raising controversial topics and making controversial recommendations for policy changes. At some places, I criticize theory and empirical research. In this I recognize that I have departed somewhat from the typical practice in textbook writing. My reason for doing this is that, by raising controversy in theory and policy, the students may find the material more interesting and challenging. Also, instructors who disagree with my reasoning may take advantage of the opportunities to give students additional readings and lectures so that differing views will be heard. I hope that this text will provide, as well as information, a platform for intellectual discussion and debate.

To the Student

Welcome to the fascinating realm of financial markets! I hope that you enjoy this book. I have assigned parts of it to my classes over the past couple of years along with a published textbook. Everyone said that this new text is superior. Perhaps it is because I have tried my best to write every idea in a straightforward and uncomplicated style.

The discussion questions and exercises at the end of each chapter are intended to provide you with a platform for exam review. I suggest that you write out brief answers to those questions after reading the text. Then your own answers may be used in your review and you will not have to re-read the text, except to refresh your memory of specific topics. Also, the questions can be used when you get together with your friends and ask questions of each other. Good luck!

A Final Word of Thanks

My heartfelt thanks to the editors and others at Prentice Hall, especially Ang Lee Ming, for the efforts devoted to this project. Their assistance was greatly appreciated. Also, I would like to express my deep appreciation to my wife, Joy, for her support.

Robert Haney Scott
Chico, California
July 7, 1995

CHAPTER 1

Introduction to Financial Systems

A HIGHLY DEVELOPED set of financial markets and institutions is one hallmark of a modern exchange economy. These facilitate the efficient production and exchange of goods and services by bringing together those who have funds to lend and those who wish to borrow these funds to finance their expenditure. Through markets that determine interest rates, the *financial system channels a nation's saving into its highest and best uses*. Second, the system *also permits individuals to adjust their holdings of property and securities in order to maximize their utility*. Third, the system *places a price on risk so that it can be assumed by those who are willing to accept it*. This book describes and analyzes these important markets and their contribution to the functioning of an economy.

Interest Rates and Securities Prices

Activity in financial markets involves the exchange of one financial asset for another. In most exchanges, lenders exchange money for other financial assets that provide a future return. In effect, they buy a *claim* against someone's money holdings at a future date— they buy a note, often called an IOU that stands for "I owe you." Notes, stocks, bonds, and other financial assets are called securities. These are traded at prices set in the markets by demand and supply.

   When individuals buy and sell outstanding or newly issued claims, they are "adjusting their portfolios," *portfolios* meaning the groups of financial assets (securities) they hold. Also, they may sell a financial asset because they wish to consume more or to invest in real property such as a home. Thus, financial markets allow individuals to adjust their holdings of assets to suit their preferences.

A person who buys a security is called a lender of funds. The person who "issues" or sells the security is called a borrower of funds. The cost of acquiring funds for temporary use is measured by an interest charge or a required return on equity, and the lender earns an income in the form of an interest return or yield. Such types of returns accrue to those who have let others have *use of their money* for a period of time. *Funds* refers to money available for use. Hence, financial markets may be characterized either as a market for securities or as a market for funds.

Demand and Supply for Securities and Funds

Economists use the theory of "market demand and supply" as the analytical frame of reference when they "explain" the price and quantity of goods and services. This same analytical technique is useful when looking at financial markets.

We express the price or cost of oranges as $1 a pound. Similarly, we express the price or cost of a security as $1,000 for a bond. But, we express the price or cost of *funds* in terms of an *interest rate* or *yield*.

If funds are obtained from selling a bond, those who buy the bond may pay $1,000 now in return for a promise to repay the principal of $1,000 plus interest a year from now if the maturity of the bond is one year. If they receive $60 in interest a year from now, the interest rate is 6 per cent per annum. The sum of $60 can be viewed as the rental cost of the use of $1,000 for a year. The 6 per cent rate is called the *coupon rate*. The maturity date set on new issues of bonds is usually many years in the future, and the coupon payments promised may be for different amounts and are usually paid semiannually.

Buyers of such bonds are lenders. Lenders supply loanable funds to the market when they purchase the security for $1,000. Sellers, or issuers, of the bond are borrowers. They have the use of the funds for one year. In return, they pay the lender a yield of $60.

An interest rate, or yield, is the price of something expressed as a percentage of itself at a later date. If a farmer lends a neighbor ten bushels of corn to use for seed, and is repaid the ten bushels plus one extra bushel after the harvest next year, the lender's "yield" on the loan is 10 per cent. In the bond example, the $60 interest payment at the end of the year represents a 6 per cent yield on the loan of $1,000.

Thus, transactions in financial markets may be looked upon in two ways: (1) lending and borrowing of funds, or (2) purchasing and selling securities. These are simply two ways of describing the same phenomenon and are used interchangeably.

The Demand and Supply for Funds. In Figure 1–1(a), straight, solid lines are used to show demand and supply curves for loanable funds. The supply curve for funds is upward sloping. The rate of interest is on the vertical axis and the quantity of loanable funds is measured on the horizontal axis. The supply curve shows that at higher interest rates lenders will supply more funds in the market.

The demand curve for funds is downward sloping. This indicates that those who wish to borrow funds will borrow larger amounts at lower interest rates.

The interaction of market forces of demand and supply will determine the interest rate and the amount of loanable funds being exchanged in the market. The intersection of the solid demand and supply curves shows the interest rate on funds and the quantity of funds exchanged at the market-clearing interest rate i, where the quantity demanded equals the quantity supplied.

An increase in the demand for funds can be shown by a rightward shift in the demand curve in Figure 1–1(a) as depicted by the dashed demand curve. This curve indicates that, at each and every interest rate (measured on the vertical axis), the quantity of funds demanded is larger (measured on the horizontal axis). That is the meaning of "an increase" in demand. Such an increase in demand might arise from a budget deficit that required the government to borrow more funds, for example.

The new intersection of the demand and supply curves will now indicate that the market rate of interest increased from i to i'. It will be higher than before because of the increased demand for funds.

Figure 1–1
Interest Rates and Securities Prices

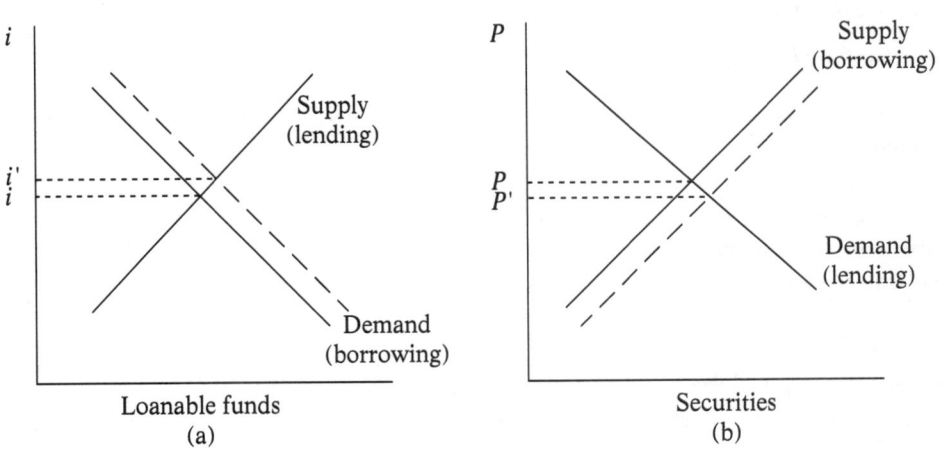

Loanable funds
(a)

Securities
(b)

The Demand and Supply for Securities. Turning to Figure 1–1(b), the price of securities, *not the interest rate*, is measured on the vertical axis, and the volume of securities, *not the volume of funds*, is measured on the horizontal axis. Here, the supply curve represents borrowing by those who offer securities for sale in the market. At higher prices, more will be offered for sale; that is, more funds will be borrowed. Thus the curve showing the supply of securities at various prices in this figure contains the *same* *information* as the curve showing the demand for funds in Figure 1–1(a). Both describe the behavior of borrowers.

An increase in the supply of securities is depicted by the dashed supply curve. If the government offers more bonds for sale in the market, the supply will shift to the right. Securities prices will fall from P to P' as indicated by the new intersection point of the two curves.

In conclusion, both sets of curves in the two diagrams show the same thing. The demand curve for funds on the part of borrowers is described in Figure 1–1(a) as a demand curve, but is described as the supply of securities curve in Figure 1–1(b). Similarly, the supply of funds provided by lenders is described in Figure 1–1(a), but is described as the demand for securities in Figure 1–1(b). The increased demand for funds shown by the dashed line in Figure 1–1(a) describes the same thing as the increased supply of securities shown by the dashed line in Figure 1–1(b).

Only one example of a shift in the curves is described here. Of course, the two graphs can be used to show the direction of changes in interest rates and prices of securities that result from shifts in either direction of either or both of the two curves.

Prices and Yields. The reader should note that the graphs in Figure 1–1 clearly indicate the *inverse relation between interest yield on a security and its price.*

The information presented in the diagrams may also be presented using the present value formula. Consider again the $1,000 bond having a 6 per cent coupon and maturing in one year when the bond holder will receive $1,060. This numerical example can be expressed in a formula:

$$P + Pi = R$$

where P is the face value of the bond, i is the interest rate, and R is the amount to be received in one year.

Using our example, the formula reads, one thousand dollars plus six per cent interest on one thousand dollars equals one thousand and sixty dollars.

By factoring out the P on the left side, the formula becomes $P(1 + i) = R$. Now divide both sides by $(1 + i)$ to have the usual present value formula for a one-period security:

$$P = R/(1 + i) \text{ or } \$1,000 = \$1,060/(1.06)$$

The *present value* of the bond is the same thing as its *price*, $1,000.

If the interest rate on this bond increased to 10 per cent, the price of the bond would fall. To see this, simply use the formula and substitute $1,060 for R and let $i = 0.10$. The formula becomes $P = \$1,060/1.10 = \$963.64$. Thus, when the interest rate increased from 6 per cent to 10 per cent, the price fell from $1,000 to $963.64, demonstrating the inverse relation. If the interest rate were to have decreased, the price would have increased.

Yield and Coupon Rates. It is important to note that the coupon rate on the bond was 6 per cent, and remains 6 per cent throughout the life of the bond. The payment at maturity is for $1,000 as repayment of the principal plus $60 representing a coupon interest payment. But if the lender pays only $963.64 for the bond that guarantees payment of $1,060 in one year, the effective *yield* on the bond is no longer the same as the coupon rate. The effective yield now represents the rate of return, or interest rate, on the security. The coupon rate does not change, but the yield or interest rate does change whenever the price of the security changes.

Prices of most bonds traded in markets change up and down all during the trading day, therefore, their yields change too. When newspapers report yields on bonds, the report is for a certain price established at a given time during trading.

Classification of Financial Markets

Markets exist for many thousands of different securities. There are markets for loans, corporate bonds, shares of stock, mutual funds, and so forth. There are local, regional, and international markets. Although these markets are usually distinct and diverse, they are also closely interconnected. Information on security prices and interest rates flows rapidly and freely in nearly all financial markets.

Because of their great diversity, it is important to establish market classifications into which different financial instruments may be placed.

Primary and Secondary Markets

There are markets for new issues of securities and markets for securities that were issued earlier, that is, for existing claims. The new-issues markets are called *primary* markets, while markets for existing securities are called *secondary* markets.

Primary markets are used by business firms and governments to raise new capital for expanding their operations. Securities are usually purchased by investment bankers and underwriters initially, and then sold to the general public.

Markets for already existing securities are useful because they permit holders to trade and rearrange their holdings to suit their needs. They also add *liquidity* to a security, that is, they make it easier for a holder to obtain cash for the security in case a need arises. We will discuss the concept of liquidity in some detail later on.

Markets for Loans and Markets for Securities

A loan is usually negotiated directly between the borrower and the lender. In contrast, securities are usually traded in impersonal markets, and often on exchanges. Consumer credit is mostly in the form of loans. Mortgage loans are given to purchase homes. Business loans are often made for the purchase of inventories. Large businesses usually rely on both loans and the sale of securities.

Financial institutions such as banks, savings banks, savings and loan associations, credit unions, and others make loans for a variety of purposes. They also borrow funds through the issue of some types of securities such as certificates of deposit. Other financial institutions such as investment banks and merchant banks generally arrange the sale of securities on behalf of businesses rather than making loans themselves.

Although "floor" trading of securities on the stock exchanges in New York, London, Tokyo, Hong Kong, Singapore, and elsewhere around the world gets most of the news coverage, there is actually a larger volume of trading of securities on the over-the-counter markets—that is, the market made up by a network of brokers who trade securities by telephone or computer.

Money and Capital Markets

Money Markets. Money market securities (instruments) are those that mature within a year. Chapter 8 is devoted entirely to the discussion of money markets. A list of principal money market instruments in the U.S. includes *Treasury bills* (T-bills), *certificates of deposit* (CDs), *banker's acceptances* (BAs), and *commercial paper* (CP). A group of contractual arrangements permits banks to lend to each other. These arrangements would be listed under the heading of money market instruments and often mature the day following their issue. That is, the funds are lent overnight—not even for a full 24 hours. These special types of securities are federal funds, repurchase contracts, and Eurodollars.

We will learn a great deal more about these special types of securities in the chapters that follow. *Federal funds* are funds that commercial banks hold on deposit with the Federal Reserve Banks as reserves. *Repurchase agreements* are contracts that specify the sale of a security along with a simultaneous repurchase of that same security on a specific date, often the next day. *Negotiable certificates of deposit* (NCDs or CDs) are issued by banks. Since they are negotiable they may be traded in markets like stocks and bonds are traded. *Banker's acceptances* typically originate from international trade. A banker agrees to guarantee payment for imported goods. In this, the bank has backed the importer with its credit. The importer usually pays a fee for such a guarantee. BAs may be bought and sold. *Commercial paper* consists of IOUs issued by corporations or other businesses and sold to a variety of investors. Other money market instruments are issued by government or by banks, but CP is issued by nonfinancial institutions.

Capital Markets. Chapters 9, 10, and 11 are devoted to discussion of various capital markets. First, there is the market for stocks and second, the market for bonds. The maturity of securities issued in the capital market is greater than one year. Mortgage markets are included under the general heading of capital markets. The property itself is placed as collateral for a mortgage loan. Pools of securities may provide collateral for other securities. For example, managers of mutual funds purchase stocks or other securities and place them in a pool of securities. Then they sell securities to investors—securities that are themselves backed by the pool of securities or mortgages. The mortgage market and the market for collateralized mortgage obligations are the subjects of Chapter 10.

Financial Derivatives. Included under the general heading of capital markets is the market for financial derivatives. These are special types of contracts that are sometimes called securities, but that, in fact, are not securities themselves. They are only contracts that are based upon, or derived from, the underlying security. For example, an *option* on a stock may be a contract that enables the holder to purchase the stock at a set price. The option contract is good until a certain future date. In this case, the underlying stock is the "security" and the option contract is a derivative. However, option contracts may be traded over-the-counter or on exchanges just like the underlying stock is traded. *Futures contracts*, calling for delivery of underlying commodities or securities on a future date, may also be traded on exchanges. The contracts themselves are traded, but not the underlying commodity. Options and futures contracts are the basis of the discussion in Chapter 11.

Financial Intermediaries

Financial intermediaries are business firms that specialize in assisting individuals or other businesses in handling their funds. A prime example is a commercial bank. It accepts deposits and then puts the deposited funds to work by either buying securities or making loans of various types. A depositor receives either some deposit interest or the implicit value of the payment services provided by the bank. Thus, the bank puts the depositor's funds to work. Before the funds go to work, they are channeled through the bank, so the bank is called a financial intermediary.

There are several types of banks: commercial banks, investment banks, merchant banks, saving banks, universal banks, postal savings banks, piggy banks, and so forth— all of which are viewed as places for individuals to put money for safekeeping.

Other firms that participate in financial markets and do part of their business as financial intermediaries include insurance companies, small loan companies, pawn shops, and so forth.

Thus, the activities of financial intermediaries are important in modern exchange economies because they provide liquidity.

Both secondary financial markets and financial intermediaries provide liquidity to asset owners—that is, they provide the owner with the ability to obtain funds readily, should some need arise. Also, they provide the owner with flexibility in arranging the composition of a portfolio of assets to suit his or her preferences.

The Role of Government in Financial Markets

A great deal of this book is devoted to government's role in the management of financial markets. One reason for government's activity is that financial institutions play a role in the creation of money or money substitutes. Governments have assumed the responsibility for controlling money growth in the interest of stabilizing the level of economic activity. The second reason is that individuals need to be able to trust the managers of financial markets and institutions. By placing funds in a bank, the depositor is placing trust in the bank—trust that the bank's managers will exercise great care in handling the funds so that they will not be lost. The bank has a prudential responsibility to the depositor. So, the public demands that government regulate financial institutions—police them—so that the possibility of suffering great loss is reduced. Thus, money control and prudential supervision are the two important reasons that governments regulate financial markets and institutions.

The Organization of This Book

There are three areas of focus in this book. The first is institutional detail, the second is theoretical understanding, and the third is policymaking. Thus, in order to appreciate how financial markets and institutions work to facilitate economic well-being, one must know a great deal about financial institutions—what they do, how they are managed, and how they are regulated. Next, one needs to understand the economic theory of the determination of interest rates, as interest rates are interdependently determined with the level of economic activity and money. So, one needs to know the theory of money and of macroeconomic activity. Finally, armed with an understanding of the institutions in question, and with knowledge of relevant theory, we can examine the policy actions undertaken by government regulators.

The Economic Growth of the Four Asian Tigers

Four communities in Asia (three countries and one colony) showed such strong economic growth and development in the decade of the 1980s that their economies have drawn a great deal of attention from the world community. They are Hong Kong, Korea, Taiwan, and Singapore. (In this book Korea will refer to South Korea in all instances, and not to North Korea, which is still under a communist regime and has not enjoyed significant advancement economically.)

The Asian Tigers of Hong Kong and Singapore have seen financial institutions grow to be strong and resilient. Singapore had an active government policy in place to support the development of its financial sector. This was an integral part of its overall plans for economic development. Hong Kong simply permitted the financial institutions common to it and the United Kingdom to evolve in response to market demand. Taiwan and Korea had very restricted financial institutions until their economies improved, so development of their financial institutions has, for the most part, taken the form of liberalization of financial controls.

The financial systems of the Four Asian Tigers comprise a significant portion of the subject matter of this book.

The Expanding Role of Financial Markets in the World Economy

The financial markets and institutions, which play an important role in the operation of modern exchange economies, were devastated during the Great Depression of the 1930s. However, they have developed rapidly since the end of World War II. Computers and telecommunications have permitted the evolution of internationally interdependent markets. Continued rapid growth is assured for the future because many countries of the world are only just beginning to develop their financial sectors.

Summary

There exist thousands of different types of financial securities. For each there is an interest rate or yield. Interest is a cost to the borrower or a return to the lender. Securities are issued by borrowers and purchased by lenders at market determined prices. Thus, prices for securities are determined in free markets by demand and supply. But demand and supply for funds also determine the interest rate or yield on the securities. Thus, there are two ways of looking at demand and supply related to borrowing and lending—either as demand and supply for funds that determine the interest rate, or as demand and supply for securities that determine their prices. Prices of securities vary inversely with their yields.

There are many different ways to classify securities markets. The principal one is to separate money markets from capital markets. In this case the separation is arbitrary. A security is a money market instrument if it has a maturity of one year or less. It is a capital market instrument if its maturity is longer than one year.

Governments must regulate financial markets because, if they did not, their people would insist that they do. One important reason is that the people want to have their savings kept safely, so the government must police firms that hold savings in trust for others. Another reason is that financial conditions have an important place in the maintenance of economic stability, a matter of utmost importance to government.

Readers are encouraged to examine the textbooks listed below for additional detail on any of the topics raised in the remaining chapters of this book.

Key Terms and Concepts

Funds and securities
Price and present value
Money and capital markets
Financial derivatives

Coupon rate and yield
Primary and secondary markets
Four Asian Tigers

Discussion Questions and Exercises

1. What are the three important functions of financial markets?
2. Use supply and demand curves to indicate the changes in prices of securities and interest rates that would be expected to occur if there were an increase (a) in the supply of funds, (b) in the supply of securities, and (c) in the demand for securities.
3. Use a simple numerical example, such as the one in the text, on a one-year security to demonstrate how the price of a security will increase if the interest rate decreases.
4. What is the present value (price) of a security that will guarantee payment of

$1,100 a year from today when the interest rate is 10 per cent per year? When the interest rate is 5 per cent per year? When the interest rate is 15 per cent per year?

5. Distinguish between the coupon rate on a security and the security's yield. Give a numerical example.
6. Distinguish between primary and secondary markets for securities.
7. Distinguish money markets from capital markets. Give examples of securities traded in each of these types of markets.
8. How does the market for loans differ from other capital markets?
9. What are financial derivatives? Give an example.
10. Why do governments regulate financial markets?

References

Cargill, Thomas F., *Money, the Financial System and Monetary Policy*, Prentice Hall, Englewood Cliffs, NJ, 1991.

Cooper, S. Kerry, and Fraser, Donald R., *The Financial Marketplace*, 3rd Edition, Addison-Wesley, Reading, MA, 1990.

Dufey, Gunter, and Giddy, Ian, *The International Money Market*, 2nd Edition, Prentice Hall, London, 1994.

Evans, John S., *International Finance: A Markets Approach*, Dryden Press, New York, 1992.

Fabozzi, Frank J., Modigliani, Franco, and Ferri, Michael G., *Foundations of Financial Markets and Institutions*, Prentice Hall, Englewood Cliffs, NJ, 1994.

Fraser, Donald R., and Rose, Peter S., eds., *Readings on Financial Institutions and Markets*, 4th Edition, Irwin, Homewood, IL, 1990.

Henning, C. N., Pigott, William, and Scott, R. H., *Financial Markets and the Economy*, 5th Edition, Prentice Hall, Englewood Cliffs, NJ, 1988.

Ho, Y. K., Scott, R. H., and Wong, K. A., eds., *The Hong Kong Financial System*, Oxford University Press, Hong Kong, 1991.

Johnson, Hazel J., *Financial Institutions and Markets: A Global Perspective*, McGraw-Hill, New York, 1993.

Kidwell, David S., and Peterson, Richard L., *Financial Institutions, Markets, and Money*, 4th Edition, Dryden Press, Chicago, 1990.

King, Robert G., and Levine, Ross, "Finance and Growth: Schumpeter Might Be Right," *Quarterly Journal of Economics*, Vol. 108, August 1993, pp. 717–37.

Kohn, Meir, *Financial Institutions and Markets*, McGraw-Hill, New York, 1994.

Madura, Jeff, *Financial Markets and Institutions*, West Publishing, St. Paul, MN, 1989.

Meyer, Paul A., *Money, Financial Institutions, and the Economy*, Irwin, Homewood, IL, 1986.

Nichols, Dorothy M., and Gonczy, Anne Marie, *Modern Money Mechanics: A Workbook on Bank Reserves and Deposit Expansion*, Federal Reserve Bank of Chicago, Chicago, 1992.

Poindexter, J. C., and Jones, C. P., *Money, Financial Markets, and the Economy*, West Publishing, St. Paul, MN, 1980.

Rose, Peter S., *Money and Capital Markets*, 4th Edition, Irwin, Homewood, IL, 1992.

Scott, R. H., Wong, K. A., and Ho, Y. K., *Hong Kong's Financial Institutions and Markets*, Oxford University Press, Hong Kong, 1986.

Scott, William L., *Contemporary Financial Markets and Services*, West Publishing, St. Paul, MN, 1991.

Smith, Gary, *Financial Assets, Markets, and Institutions*, D. C. Heath, Lexington, MA, 1993.

Thygerson, Kenneth J., *Financial Markets and Institutions: A Managerial Approach*, Harper Collins, New York, 1993.

Wilcox, James A., ed., *Current Readings on Money, Banking, and Financial Markets*, Scott, Foresman and Company, Glenview, IL, 1990.

CHAPTER 2

The Economic Role of Financial Institutions

MODERN INDUSTRIAL ECONOMIES of America and Europe rely heavily upon their well-established financial institutions and markets to help guide investment funds to their most productive uses. Japan, now the industrial giant of the Pacific region, rapidly developed its financial sector along with its economy. It is not surprising that Hong Kong and Singapore, two of the Four Asian Tigers, have earned international recognition as world financial centers. The other Asian Tigers, Taiwan and Korea, are liberalizing their financial institutions and markets as rapidly as they can while retaining stability. Eastern European countries and Russia urgently need to develop a strong financial sector as they throw off the yoke of communist control and join the world of modern economies.

The Four Asian Tigers, known as "Newly Industrialized Countries," will be joined within a few years, if present rates of progress continue, by Thailand and Malaysia. China's Guangdong Province, adjacent to Hong Kong, is in the race to become the fifth Asian Tiger, as is Indonesia. Europe's Organization for Economic Cooperation and Development (OECD) now refers to these emerging economic powers as Dynamic Asian Economies (DAEs).

Every developing country needs an efficient financial sector to assist economic growth through investment, the key ingredient to growth. Rising standards of living depend on growth. So, the welfare of the people in every country depends upon the efficiency with which the financial sector operates.

This chapter describes the role of the financial sector in economic activity and the interdependency of the financial sector with other parts of the economy.

Saving and Investment in Barter and Monetary Economies

By definition, barter is trade without the use of money. Goods are exchanged "in kind." Trade takes place directly between two persons or two agencies. Because of inadequate currency arrangements, barter is often still used by Russians and other Eastern Europeans, especially in international trade. For example, Pepsi Cola has worked out barter arrangements where it sells Stolichnaya vodka in the U.S. in exchange for providing cola to Russia. But usually one thinks of barter as the method of exchange in primitive economies. A person trades a chicken for some vegetables, for example.

Yet money has an ancient history. People in antiquity understood that trade worked more smoothly if something, usually some commodity or precious metal, acted as a medium of exchange.

In a barter economy, any decision to save would also be a decision to invest in real capital goods. Taking the time to carve a canoe out of a tree is an investment activity. This activity will produce income, but it is not available for immediate consumption, therefore, carving a canoe also represents saving.

It is clearly difficult to earn an income in a barter economy. For example, patients would have to send along apples for the doctor, other food items, and clothing, in order to pay for medical services. Without doubt, a stable monetary medium facilitates exchange. It reduces transactions costs.

Very high income taxes in some countries lead people to avoid taxation by agreeing to paint the doctor's house in exchange for the services of an operation. Thus, income taxes that are too high can have an adverse effect on a monetary economy.

The Love of Money. Money is a human invention. It surely ranks high among many valuable discoveries. It is sad, therefore, to see it maligned by economists who have a political agenda. Karl Marx often wrote that money was evil. To him, it represented the power of capitalists. Many religious people misquote the Bible and say that "money is the root of all evil." The actual quote is, "*the love of* money is the root of all evil" (1 Timothy 6:10).

Money, like a productive tool, is not something to be loved, but a very valuable something to be carefully maintained to facilitate investment and smooth the operation of a modern exchange economy. *Whenever a monetary system does not work, barter takes over.*

Modern Barter. Computers seem capable of reviving interest in barter. The International Reciprocal Trade Association claims to have 530 barter exchanges worldwide and 250,000 clients—small businesses for the most part. Clients have an account number and they keep track of trades. Their accounts have a "balance" based on the value of what has been traded. The association keeps records and charges membership fees and fees for each trade. Using the computer enables individuals to engage in multilateral trades and avoid the difficulties of finding someone for a one-on-one trade (*Chico Enterprise Record*, March 21, 1993). Notice that the recorded "value" of the trades must be kept in terms of a monetary unit, but the traders skip the use of currency or deposit money.

Money, Debt, Credit, and Assets

Money is used as a medium of exchange. But money can also be lent to someone else to use with the promise that it will be repaid at some later date. Thus, money is often exchanged for an "IOU" (I owe you) signed by the borrower. By signing an IOU the borrower makes a promise to repay the lender at some later date. By issuing deposit receipts to customers, banks give depositors an IOU.

Although paper money had its origin in China in the eleventh century, it has only been in the past century that paper money has replaced gold and silver or other commodities as a medium of exchange. If someone lends gold to another person and receives an IOU signed on a piece of paper, that IOU itself may be acceptable in carrying out exchange. It may circulate as currency. A glance at the paper currency of any country today shows that it is a promise to pay issued by a bank, a central bank, or a government.

Every Debt is an Asset. If you own an IOU, you own a financial asset. This is the point emphasized here: a debt, every debt, or IOU, is also an asset, or credit, to its holder. Thus, *every debt is also an asset*. Debt and credit are two sides of the *same* coin. Keeping this in mind it is strange to find some people disapproving of expansion of debt, when viewing favorably an expansion of credit (see Federal Reserve Bank of Chicago, 1992).

Individuals, firms, and governments may issue debt instruments to finance expenditures for good reasons. Others, of course, may make mistakes in using the funds acquired through debt, and may have difficulty repaying it. But the error made is in the mistake, not in the creation of debt. Debt should not be blamed. In fact, *debt is good*, as it *must* be if credit is good, because for every debt there is a credit.

It is not true, however, that for every asset there is a debt. As we learned from fundamental accounting principles, assets are on one side of the balance sheet, while on the other side both liabilities and net worth are listed. Thus, some portion of the assets of an individual or firm are "free and clear" of debt, so there is no counterbalancing debt to a portion of the firm's assets. However, even equity could be considered as a type of debt or obligation—as a firm's debt to its owner in conjunction with a firm's debt to its creditors.

Debt, Interest and Usury

Nearly all debt, as an obligation to pay, also requires the payment of interest. Nearly all paper dollars in circulation in the United States are Federal Reserve Notes. These are IOUs of a government agency. But the holders of this paper money do not receive interest payments on these notes. As we will learn in Chapter 5, holders of currency subsidize the government by holding its notes without collecting any interest. Holders give the government an interest-free loan. The result is the equivalent of government collecting a tax equal to the amount of interest.

Religious and Cultural Influence in Financial Markets. Through the ages interest has also been considered to be an evil along with money. In the middle ages, Christianity viewed the charging of interest as a sin. Communism adopted Marx's belief that interest was a return to capital and had no place in a socialist economy because *all* return should be paid to labor. And in many regions today, Muslims maintain that collecting interest is an evil activity and is prohibited by the Koran.

Banks in Iran, for example, consider a bank loan to a borrower not as a loan but as a share in the borrower's business activity, and the repayment of interest to the bank along with repayment of principal is viewed as a dividend payment. By this sleight-of-hand banks can satisfy Iran's religious codes and still remain in business. It is simply a matter of substituting one institutional arrangement for another. In substance, both equity participation and debt issuing are simply two means of raising funds for financing productive enterprise. Similar arrangements are undertaken in Pakistan, and some banks in Uzbekistan, for example, also do their best to conform to orthodox interpretations on the prohibition on interest in Islam.

Other Muslim countries have no Islamic banking system as in Iran and Pakistan. And since debt is not generally available to the people in many Muslim communities, the process of funding investment may be greatly constrained. The absence of an efficient financial sector greatly inhibits economic growth in such societies. This is especially the case since nearly all modern banking and international trading arrangements make use of debt instruments of some kind, and as noted, even money is a form of debt. Why would debt be against a religious belief?

One analyst of Islamic Law (see Murvat, 1982) explains that if a creditor lends funds to someone to carry out an enterprise, the capital lent should be productive and provide a return to the borrower of the funds. The lender of capital then has a right to share in the profitability of the investment. However, if the use to which the capital is put turns out not to provide a return, then the creditor is not entitled to demand a fixed (interest) return inasmuch as his capital turned out not to be fruitful. So, the creditor may be entitled to a dividend—that is, a share of the profit—but is not entitled to a fixed return (interest) whether or not the invested capital produced a profit.

The ethical considerations underpinning this position are understandable. Why should someone with funds be able to exact a return from a borrower whether or not the borrower is lucky in investing? Why does the lender not have a responsibility for the success or failure of the use to which funds are put?

Indeed, in U.S. law when a person does not have sufficient resources to repay borrowed funds then he or she may declare "bankruptcy," which means that the creditor can recover only to the extent that the borrower has funds available. Typically, the bankrupt person owes more money to more people than he or she can repay. The bankruptcy courts may take what they can from the borrower, but always leave a home, a car, and wages for living expenses, with the bankrupt person.

Thus, under U.S. law, the creditor is not permitted to take a borrower's livelihood away. This indicates that there is an element of responsibility on the part of the creditor to see that the return demanded under the fixed interest contract can be reasonably expected from the real investment. Lenders at fixed interest go to great lengths to ensure that the borrower is a good "credit risk." However, a person who is a good credit risk can borrow funds at a low interest rate. If the lender of funds were required to assume an equity position in the investment project, as would be the case under orthodox interpretations of Muslim law, the added risk associated with being part owner would lead the lender to require a higher return (share of the profits). Thus, the cost of funds to the borrower will be higher when the contract is for a share of profit rather than a fixed interest payment.

Essentially, a debt means that the creditor has the *first right* to earnings from the project—debt must be repaid before dividends are paid to shareholders. If the project fails, the lender has the right to take over the assets of the firm. This means that, in essence, the owner of the firm holds an option on the firm's assets and will continuously exercise that option so long as the assets are valuable. If the firm's assets remain valuable, then the borrower will willingly repay any loans, and, in an effective sense, this means that the creditor shares in the productivity of the investment—taking a smaller, but more certain and less risky, share of the return.

Viewed in this way, borrowing at fixed interest does not violate the *moral* prescription put forward by orthodox interpretations of Islamic law. Unfortunately, in some communities, too few people understand the principles of finance so that a misinterpretation of the meaning of Muslim standards leads to confusion in both non-Muslim and Muslim communities. Slowly, but surely, better communication will lead to a rapproachment between opposing sides in this unnecessary controversy. Toward this end, Iqbal and Mirakhor's paper on "Islamic Banking" is recommended reading.

An anonymous referee of this book offered the following comment on the preceding section. It is appropriate to quote here in its entirety because it may provide balance to the discussion, however, the opinions expressed are not necessarily shared by the book's author.

> The argument on usury from an Islamic perspective is rather weak and misleading. The author should rewrite that particular section by using more relevant references. The author gives justifications to why interest should be allowed in Islam. Interest is prohibited in Islam for the simple reason that is to make the lender more accountable for his actions. As such, if a person lends money to finance a project and that project fails, then two things can happen depending on the mode of finance and the contractual agreement between the lender and entrepreneur: (1) the financier loses all of his money and the entrepreneur loses his time and efforts under Mudarabah or project financing. (2) The financier loses according to his share in the project under the Musharakah or partnership financing.
>
> According to S. Al-Harran, borrowing at fixed interest violates the Islamic rule: 'you

should not harm or be harmed by others.' Fixed interest is a cost which the entrepreneur must pay to the financier whether the project fails or succeeds. If the project succeeds, then the fixed interest will be transferred to the society in terms of higher prices thus inflicting harm on the society and the entrepreneur. However, if the project fails, then the fixed interest adds to the misery of the entrepreneur and makes his recovery difficult. Therefore, the prohibition of interest makes the lender more accountable for his actions as the lender becomes a partner to the entrepreneur which leads him to study the feasibility of the project and the trustworthiness of the entrepreneur not his creditworthiness. See S. Al-Harran, *Islamic Finance: Partnership Financing*, Pelanduk Publications, Malaysia, 1993.

The author disagrees with the statement "If the project succeeds, then the fixed interest will be transferred to the society in terms of higher prices thus inflicting harm on the society and the entrepreneur," because a successful project will always result in lower real prices to the society even though these include financing costs, and because the cost of debt capital is less than the cost of equity capital. So a successful project using equity capital would mean even higher prices to the society. Otherwise, the concern for social welfare expressed in the referee's comments is well received.

Usury. The biblical Fable of the Talents (St. Matthew 25:14–29) alludes to *usury*, which meant interest in biblical times. According to the fable the master's servants were admonished to put the talents of money to work—if in no other way, to work earning "usury" from the money changers. In this instance there is clearly no sin in the collection of interest. However, elsewhere the Bible urges that one should not charge usury on a loan to a brother. Thus, in Christianity charging of interest on a loan to a stranger is acceptable while charging interest on a loan to a family member is not.

Today the term "usury" is a legal term for "excessive interest" where excessive is defined by law. For example, it is illegal for a pawn shop in Hong Kong to charge interest at a rate greater than 60 per cent per annum. The State of California had a law, similar to laws in other states, that prohibited banks or others from charging interest at a rate greater than 10 per cent a year. Congress suspended all state usury laws on residential mortgages and business and agricultural loans in 1980, after interest rates had risen to levels above 10 per cent and California banks had almost stopped making these loans altogether. Congress ruled that federal law would prevail unless a state passed revised legislation before April 1, 1993. Only a few states did so, and constraints on interest rates imposed by remaining usury laws are much less binding than they were in 1980.

It is clear that cultural, religious, legal, and political factors play significant roles in the development of financial markets and institutions.

The Circular Flow Diagram with a Financial Sector

Figure 2–1 contains the circular flow description often found in principles of economics textbooks to show how production and consumption are related to each other. The middle portion of this diagram shows that consumers, on the left, spend their money income in the consumers' market. Money flows in a clockwise direction up and around

Figure 2–1
Relationship between Consumers and Producers

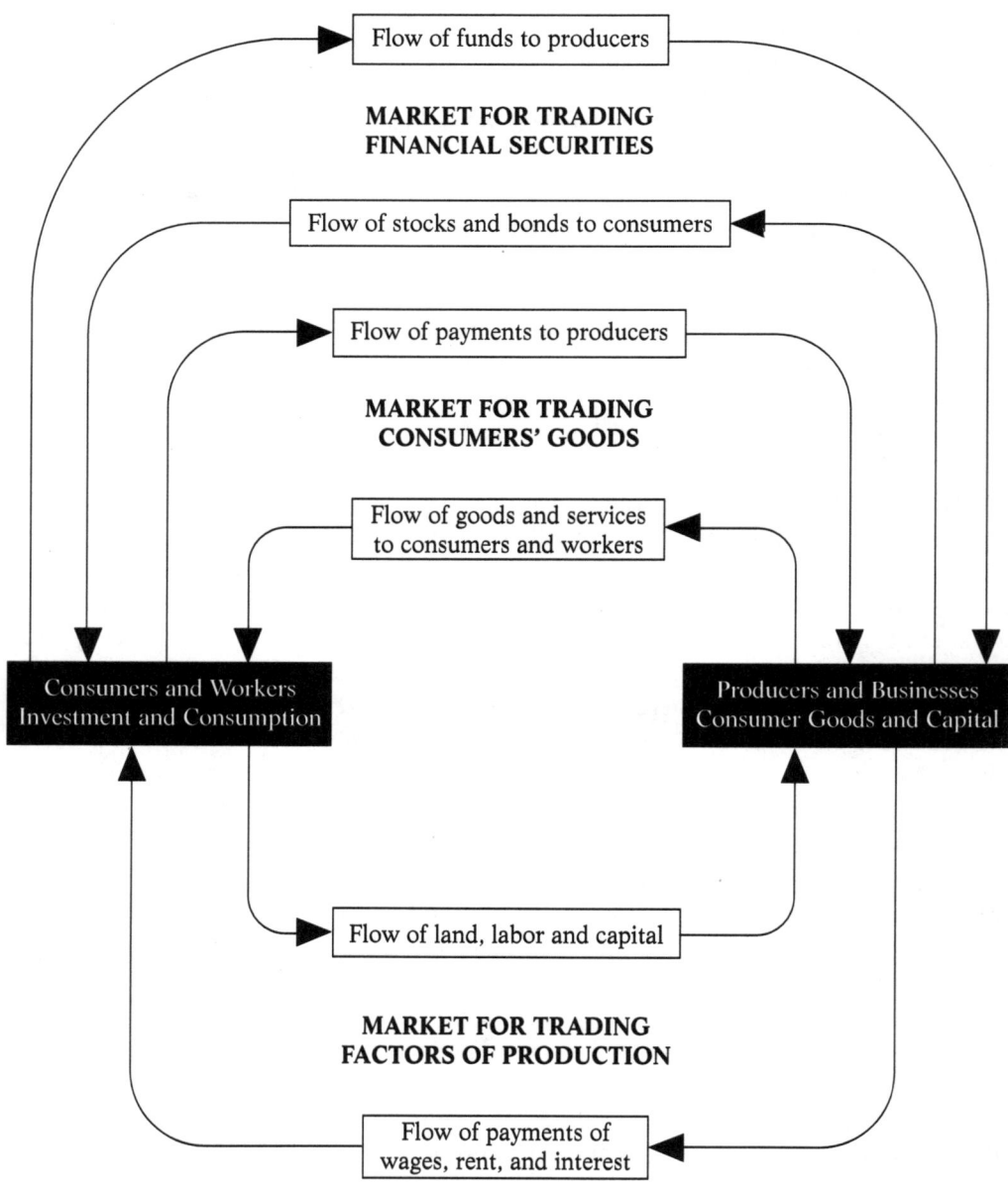

to the consumers' market and from there it passes down into the hands of producers. Goods and services, on the other hand, flow in the opposite direction. The exchange of goods and services for money occurs in the consumers' market.

But money continues to flow in a clockwise direction as producers make payments to owners of factors of production in the producers' market as shown at the bottom of the diagram. Producers need to hire labor, rent land, and obtain the services of capital equipment from consumers in the market for such services. Thus, the money flows back to the hands of consumers and represents their income. Thus, money flows in the clockwise direction, and flows of goods and services including those of factors of production flow in a counter-clockwise direction.

To this basic description of the flows in an exchange economy has been added a surrounding circular flow representing the financial markets. It is placed on the top and outside of the usual circular flow diagram. Consumers, out of their incomes, engage in saving. They do not spend all of their income. Instead they invest it either by lending it to financial institutions, by purchasing securities in the financial markets, or by lending it directly to producers. Thus, money again flows clockwise up to the financial markets where it passes on into the hands of producers. In exchange, securities flow in a counter-clockwise direction as they are sold in the financial markets to consumers. The money again continues to flow on around in a circle.

Producers do not simply hold these invested funds. Instead they use these funds to pay consumers for services of labor, land, and capital in order to create real capital equipment, such as buildings, machinery, and materials in the form of inventories. Part of what producers spend is spent in the form of interest payments to consumers who have bought the securities. Money payments continue to circulate clockwise. Newly created capital is purchased in the market for capital goods as indicated at the bottom of the diagram and money continues its counter-clockwise flow. Capital goods are used by producers. Producers and businesses produce both consumers goods, which are sold in the consumers' market, and capital goods, which are used by producers but that are purchased with funds supplied by consumers.

It is important to note that money simply passes from hand to hand. It does not disappear when it is spent. It is called a circulating medium or medium of exchange.

Of necessity, the diagram is oversimplified. But it depicts quite efficiently the essence of a modern exchange economy. Omitted from the diagram is a huge amount of expenditure that is made for what economists call "intermediate goods." As wheat is sold to a miller, and then flour to a baker, and finally bread to the consumer, the money in use changes hands many times before it reaches the final consumer of the bread.

Also omitted from the diagram is a huge amount of expenditure made to pay for existing capital as it is bought and sold and changes ownership. The continuous trading of existing capital goods, as distinct from the purchase of new capital goods, involves huge exchanges of money. These trades are made because people wish to rearrange their holdings of assets from time to time. To do so they use the services of financial intermediaries or put their funds to use in secondary financial markets.

Finally, the diagram does not show government's spending and taxing, nor does it show international trade that involves exports and imports. These sectors of the economy could be introduced, but to do so would unnecessarily complicate the drawing. Nevertheless, the diagram is useful in that it shows saving and investment, and, by inference, both the role of government in taxing and spending and the role of foreign sector imports and exports can be understood.

Saving, Investment and National Product. Figure 2–1 provides insights into the measures that industrial economies use to talk about their nation's level of economic activity. Like debt and credit, income and output (product), are also simply two sides of the same coin. The value of output created by the producers is the economy's output. And, it also represents income for consumers. Output is produced by factors of production: land, labor, capital, and materials. The value of goods produced and sold in the marketplace is a measure of output. Income is the total of wages, rents, interest and dividends, and profits received by the producers of goods. Because accounts must balance, the total value of output will equal the total value of income received in the form of payments to factors of production. The diagram shows that money received by producers is passed on to consumers in a circular flow.

A nation's output is called Gross Domestic Product (GDP). It is made up of several components as shown in Table 2–1. Let C = consumption, I = investment, G = government spending, Ex = exports, and Im = imports, so that:

$$GDP = C + I + G + Ex - Im$$

Income, consumption, investment, and all the components of the GDP accounts are *flow* concepts as distinct from *stock* concepts. For example, the water in a lake on any given day is a *stock* of water. However, the water that flows into the lake, and out of it, during the day are flows of water. If the inflow exceeds the outflow, the level of the lake rises and the stock of water in the lake increases. There is a *net inflow* of water. A *flow* takes place over a period of time while a *stock* exists at a specific time.

It is important to recognize that: *Net investment is the net addition to the stock of capital.* Some capital is used up in production while other capital is produced. So gross investment is gross capital formation while net investment is gross investment less depreciation and obsolescence.

Capital consists of all of those tools that man produces and then uses in the production of other things—man-made factors of production as distinct from land, for example, which is a factor of production given by nature. Capital consists of buildings, equipment, tools, and inventories of materials. The more capital that people have available to use to produce goods and services, the more goods and services they can produce. The more they produce the higher will be their standard of living.

People who receive incomes will spend some of their money and save the rest. The accumulated savings will usually be invested. Businesses may save some of the profits earned and invest those profits. Indeed, by definition, saving will always equal investment.

Table 2–1

Gross Domestic Product, Disposition of Personal Income, and Prices

	1992	1993	2nd quarter annual rate 1994
	Billions of current dollars		
Gross domestic product	6020.2	6343.3	6685.5
Personal consumption expenditures	4136.9	4378.2	4587.3
Durable goods	497.3	538.0	581.8
Nondurable goods	1295.5	1339.2	1381.0
Services	2348.7	2501.0	2624.5
Gross private domestic investment	788.3	882.0	1031.7
Fixed investment	785.2	866.7	967.5
Nonresidential	561.4	616.1	683.4
Structures	171.1	173.4	181.4
Producers' durable equipment	390.3	442.7	502.0
Residential	223.8	250.6	284.1
Change in business inventories	3.0	15.4	64.2
Nonfarm	−2.7	20.1	60.5
Net exports of goods and services	−30.3	−65.3	−99.8
Exports	638.1	659.1	703.2
Imports	668.4	724.3	803.0
DISPOSITION OF PERSONAL INCOME			
Personal income	5154.3	5375.1	5651.0
Wage and salary disbursements	2974.8	3080.8	3257.6
Proprietors' income	418.7	441.6	467.6
Transfer payments to persons	8602.4	915.4	957.6
Other	900.6	930.3	968.3
Less: Personal tax and nontax payments	648.6	686.4	746.4
Equals: Disposable personal income	4505.8	4688.7	4904.6
Less: Personal outlays	4257.8	4496.2	4713.3
Equals: Personal saving	247.9	192.6	191.3
Personal saving as a percentage of disposable personal income	5.3	4.1	3.9
Index numbers, 1987 = 100	Prices indexes		
GDP	121.9	125.5	128.5

Source: U.S. Dept. of Commerce, Bureau of Economic Analysis.

Saving is a residual concept. Take income and then consume most of it and what is left over is saving:

$$S = Y - C$$

However, total output equals that which was consumed plus that which was added to the stock of capital (investment):

$$Y = C + I, \text{ and by transformation, } I = Y - C$$

Thus, by definition saving will equal investment: $S = I$.

It is astonishing to learn that people who receive income and save are *not* the same people who make investments. And yet, whatever amount of investment is made, the amount of saving that consumers undertake will be equal to that amount of investment.

This statement requires a minor amendment when governments and a foreign sector are introduced. With government we have government spending, G, and taxes T. With foreign trade we have exports Ex, and imports Im. Taxes are a drain on consumer's income, but government spending adds to consumer receipts of money. Thus, in many ways taxes are like saving forced on consumers. Government spending, as an injection of money income to consumers, is somewhat like investment. Thus, allowing for government the equation becomes:

$$S + T = I + G$$

Exports are produced at home, but not available for consumption. Thus, they are somewhat like investment in their effect on spending. Imports are available for use at home, but do not require domestic production activities. Thus, they are somewhat like saving in that consumers save some money income and use some of it to purchase imports. Thus, allowing for both government and a foreign sector the equation becomes:

$$S + T + Im = I + G + Ex$$

If $G = T$, the government's budget is balanced. If $Ex = Im$, the balance of trade with the rest of the world is also balanced, and $S = I$. But if $G > T$, and/or $Ex > Im$, then saving must be greater than investment in order to balance the equation. During the 1980s the United States government had large deficits, that is, G exceeded T every year. At the same time, Im exceeded Ex, and the United States also had a deficit in its trade balance. Thus, foreigners reinvested their earnings from their excess sales of goods in the debt sold by the United States government. In a sense, foreigners helped finance the U.S. government expenditures. In another sense, foreigners had to lend these funds to U.S. citizens so that they could buy the excess of imports from the foreigners. This example is merely to illustrate that at any particular time S need not equal I exactly because of offsetting differences in the other items in the equation.

Financial Investment and Real Investment. *Financial* investment must be distinguished from *real* investment. Real investment consists of additions to those physical pieces of equipment, tools, buildings, and inventories that make up the country's capital stock.

Financial investment consists of pieces of paper or records such as shares of stock, bonds, bank deposit accounts, and so forth.

If a consumer purchases a washing machine or a business constructs a warehouse, such spending for real equipment represents real investment. But if a consumer buys a bond from someone else or a business buys an existing warehouse, these are investments but they are *financial* investments because they involve only the transfer of ownership from one person to another. They do *not* involve the construction of new real physical pieces of equipment.

On some occasions a financial investment can represent directly a real investment. For example, if a company sells a new issue of shares of ownership, collects the money from investors, and uses the money to construct a factory, then the financial investment of those who bought the shares is representative of the real factory that was built. On most occasions, however, when someone buys shares of a company, the shares were originally issued years ago. They are not new shares but merely old shares being transferred to a new owner. Thus, the purchase represents a financial investment of the buyer but does not represent newly created real capital goods. The word "investment" may refer to either real investment or financial investment. Its meaning must be inferred from the context of its use.

Intermediation. This is a term that relates to financial investments. Banks, deposit-taking companies, insurance companies, and other financial institutions are often referred to as *financial intermediaries*. A customer who maintains a savings deposit in a bank, in a very real sense, has not given his money to the bank for safekeeping, but instead has lent money to the bank that then re-lends the money to a business firm to use to purchase additional inventory. Thus, while the funds flow from the bank's customer to the business, the bank plays an intermediary role. If the customer were to lend funds directly to the business, there would be no intermediary.

Sometimes, *disintermediation* occurs. For example, if interest rates on bank deposits are held low, some people will take their money out of the banks and buy securities directly from the issuer. Thus, banks will have less business. So, with disintermediation some financial firms may grow smaller in size.

Not all people buy shares on the stock exchange, but nearly everyone has a bank deposit and nearly everyone buys some investment goods like washing machines and refrigerators and TV sets. So everyone in modern exchange economies makes investments of one type or another.

But many investment goods have very long lives—buildings and heavy equipment. If a consumer lends money directly to a business, the consumer may find that he wishes he had his money back to use for other purposes. Consumers are reluctant to lend money to a business if the funds will not be returned until the end of the life of the investment, many years in the future. That is why financial intermediaries and financial markets are useful.

An active financial market provides *liquidity* to an investment. An investment is said to be *liquid* if it can be sold readily in a marketplace without loss of value—that is, if it can be traded for money. Money is the most "liquid" of all assets. It is said to be perfectly liquid. Other assets are said to be more or less liquid depending upon how difficult it is to sell them. For example, selling a house involves large *transactions costs*. Also, if the seller tries to sell in a hurry, he may have to accept a lower price, that is, he may lose *capital value*. Thus, as an asset, a house is an "illiquid" asset because losses from transactions costs and capital value make it more difficult to sell than a stock or a bond. Shares of stock traded on a stock exchange are said to be very "liquid" assets because they can be sold rapidly and with only the loss of a small handling fee.

Flow of Funds Analysis

Every day consumers spend on goods and services, and producers contribute to the output of goods. The money spent on goods plus the money saved and invested represents a large proportion of the money flows of an economy. But the dollar volume of funds that flows into and out of banks, households and government coffers into real estate or bonds or shares of stock is also huge by comparison. These represent flows of funds to trade existing assets. They are quite large. A single portfolio investment can equal several months' salary for a worker. Thus, in modern exchange economies flow of funds accounting is used to integrate saving, investment, lending and borrowing, and to bring together the real and financial sectors of an economy.

Sectors of the Economy. Although aggregate saving and investment must be equal for the entire economy, it is unlikely that saving will equal investment for a particular sector during a given period. For example, the surplus funds on one sector may have been used to buy securities or to make loans to another sector. If a sector has investment greater than saving, sources other than its own saving will have provided the funds necessary to finance these expenditures. The flow of funds accounts include all the sources and uses of funds for the various sectors of the economy, and by summation, for all sectors.

Preparing a Matrix of Flows. Flow of funds data for an economy are derived for a specific period of time by (1) dividing the economy into sectors, (2) preparing a source and use of funds statement for each sector, (3) summing the sources and uses for all sectors, and (4) placing the sector accounts side-by-side to form a table or matrix. A simple matrix may consist of only a few sectors. For example, the entire economy can be divided into households, business firms, governments, and financial institutions. In a more complex matrix, these sectors may be subdivided with additional categories established for different types of business firms, government units, financial institutions, and so on. And, if foreign transactions are to be considered, it is necessary to include a sector for the rest of the world. The larger the number of sectors, the more likely it is that each sector will be composed of relatively homogeneous units. However, if the economy is divided into too many sectors, the model becomes cumbersome. Too much detail may obscure important relationships. The optimum number of groups depends ultimately on the purpose of the analysis and the degree of disaggregation necessary, on the availability of data, and on the time and effort required to collect and assemble the data. The Federal Reserve maintains data on the 21 sectors in Table 2–2.

The second step in constructing flow of funds accounts is to prepare a source and use statement for each sector. This is done by examining the balance sheets of the various sectors at the beginning and end of a quarter or a year. Net changes are noted in the stock of assets, liabilities, and net worth that occurred during the period. Certain assets holdings may have increased, others declined; some liabilities may be greater and some smaller than at the beginning of the period. The convention is to treat increases in assets as a use of funds and increases in liabilities or net worth as a source of funds.

A simple source and use statement for a given sector shows only intersectoral flows, that is, it does not record intrasector transactions.

For any given sector, and by summing all sectors, for the economy as a whole, the following equalities hold:

$$\Delta \text{ net worth} + \Delta \text{ liabilities} = \Delta \text{ real assets} + \Delta \text{ financial assets}$$

or   Saving + Borrowing = Investment + Lending

It follows that if, in a particular sector, saving exceeds investment, then lending exceeds borrowing. This sector is a surplus sector and a net lender to other sectors. If investment exceeds saving, then borrowing exceeds lending. In this case the sector is a deficit sector and a net borrower from other sectors.

In principle, an account is easily established for each of the several sectors that make up the economic system. Sources and uses of funds are identified as in the case of our hypothetical sector. If we place these statements side-by-side, we form a matrix to describe an interconnected system of flow of funds for, say, a year. As is shown in the hypothetical matrix in Table 2–3, not only does each sector's sources match its uses, but, by summation, total sources equal total uses. Furthermore, whereas $S \neq I$ for any sector individually, for the economy as a whole, $S = I$.

Table 2–2
Sector Structure in Flow of Funds Accounts

Households	Credit unions
Total nonfinancial business	Life insurance companies
Farm business	Other insurance companies
Nonfarm noncorporate business	Private pension funds
Corporate nonfinancial business	State and local government employee
State and local governments	retirement funds
Foreign	Finance companies
U.S. government and credit agencies	Real estate investment trusts (REITs)
Banking system	Open-end investment companies
Savings and loan associations	Money market mutual funds
Mutual savings banks	Security brokers and dealers

Source: Board of Governors of the Federal Reserve System, *Introduction to Flow of Funds*, February 1975, p. 35.

Table 2–3
Flow of Funds Accounts for a Given Time Period (Billions of dollars)

	Sectors									
	Households		Business		Government		Financial intermediaries		All sectors	
	U	S	U	S	U	S	U	S	U	S
Saving (net worth)		60		40		−10				90
Investment (real assets)	10		80						90	
Net change in financial assets, or	50						50		100	
Net change in financial liabilities				40		10		50		100
Total	60	60	80	80	0	0	50	50	190	190
Sector surplus or (deficit), i.e., net changes	50		(40)		(10)		–		–	

U = Uses of funds
S = Sources of funds

Table 2–3 is a simplified, hypothetical flow of funds matrix for an economy that has been divided into four sectors. Items in the cells of the matrix represent dollar flows that occurred during a period of time. In general, U stands for uses of funds and represents acquisitions or additions to assets, while S stands for sources of funds and represents additions to liabilities or to net worth.

The table shows that households saved $60 billion of their income during the period and used $10 billion of this to purchase real investment goods. The remaining $50 billion of this saving was used to purchase financial assets from financial intermediaries. The business sector saved $40 billion but also invested $80 billion during the period. This required business to obtain $40 billion in additional funds from financial intermediaries to have a total of $80 billion for investment spending. The government, by running a deficit in its budget, dissaved $10 billion and had to issue $10 billion of financial liabilities to cover this excess of spending over tax revenues. Finally, financial intermediaries experienced an increase in both assets and liabilities. They accepted deposit liabilities to the households in the economy in the amount of $50 billion. At the same time, they used these deposits to purchase the debt of $40 billion that business offered in the market and $10 billion borrowed by government.

The column totals show equality of U and S for each sector, in keeping with the requirements that flow of funds statements always balance, so that net changes in uses equal net changes in sources for each sector.

The row totals show the overall equality of uses and sources of funds in the aggregate, for all sectors. Saving by households, business, and government totaled $90 billion, since the government actually dissaved $10 billion. This total saving also equals total investment of $90 billion, of which, in this simplified example, $80 billion was undertaken by business firms and $10 billion by households. The government's dissaving figure (–$10 billion) probably results from the fact that government spending is treated as being entirely for goods and services and not as representing additions to the stock of capital. In the United States, the federal government does not maintain a separate set of "capital" budget accounts as some other countries do. This is an arbitrary procedure. If, in fact, the government spent $10 billion on long-lived dams, perhaps it would be more appropriate to replace the –10 under sources with a +10 under uses in the investment row. Then total investment would be $100 billion and again equal to total saving. However, this is not the convention in the United States.

Households increased their holdings of financial assets by $50 billion, and this is reflected in the sources side of the financial intermediaries column, showing a $50 billion increase in financial liabilities. This $50 billion might be, for example, consumer demand or savings deposits at commercial banks or savings deposits at savings and loan associations—liabilities of financial institutions. The $50 billion, under uses, reflects the purchase of government and business securities. Overall, financial assets increased by a total of $100 billion, and liabilities also increased by $100 billion. Thus in the "all sectors" column the total of $190 billion reflects the equality: Saving + Borrowing = Investment + Lending. In our example, saving and investment were both $90 billion, while borrowing and lending were both $100 billion.

Along the bottom of Table 2–3 there is a row indicating the surplus or deficit that each sector realized during the period. Households had a surplus of $50 billion, whereas business firms and government both engaged in deficit financing part of their expenditures, $40 billion and $10 billion, respectively.

From the figures in the flow of funds matrix we can construct a credit market summary table that shows funds raised and advanced by sector. Table 2–4 provides this summary.

In Table 2–3 there is no separate row for money; rather, we pooled money in the row with other financial assets. Furthermore, we did not allow for the fact that business and government borrowed funds directly from the household sector and from each other: all borrowing took the form of loans from financial institutions. We have also assumed that the nonfinancial sectors acquired financial assets or financial liabilities; that is, they loaned or borrowed funds. We know, of course, that they do engage in both borrowing and lending. These simplifying assumptions were made to acquaint the reader with the basic elements of flow of funds accounting.

Federal Reserve Flow of Funds Matrix

The Federal Reserve has published flow of funds data in various forms since 1955. It is too cumbersome to present the data in matrix form, so tables are used to summarize

Table 2–4
Credit Market Summary (Billions of dollars)

Funds raised by sectors (change in financial liabilities)	
Households	0
Business	40
Government	10
Financial institutions	50
Total	100
Funds advanced by sectors (change in financial assets)	
Households	50
Business	0
Government	0
Financial institutions	50
Total	100

the rows and columns. Table 2–5 indicates uses of funds, and Table 2–6 indicates sources.

Table 2–5 shows funds raised by nonfinancial sectors, funds raised by financial sectors, and funds raised by major types of instruments. Of total net borrowing of $628.1 billion in 1993, shown at the top of Table 2–5, some $256.1 billion was borrowed by the U.S. government, while private sector borrowing was the remainder, or $372.0 billion.

The next section of the table shows borrowing by financial sectors, which amounted to $286.1 billion.

Total net borrowing for all sectors in 1993 was $961.2 billion. This amount could be contrasted with total new share issues that raised funds in the equity markets of $436.9 billion in 1993. These figures clearly indicate that, from the point of view of the financing of investment spending activity, the debt markets are far bigger than the equity markets in dollar terms. Although the debt markets are relatively more important to the economy, the stock markets tend to get far more coverage in the news. They seem to provide a bellwether on the economy for the general public.

Data for 1993 direct and indirect sources of funds are found in Table 2–6. Note that the total sources, $961.2 billion, is exactly equal to total uses (borrowing) reported in Table 2–5. But several categories in the two tables differ. One group of accounts relating to deposits in financial institutions is of special interest. There we see that $117.3 billion in funds were supplied to the economy in 1993 in the form of deposits and currency (line 40). These are created by banks and issued by government. Increases in the money supply constitute one of the sources of supply of funds in our analysis of the demand and supply of funds in later chapters.

Table 2–5
Summary of Funds Raised in U.S. Credit Markets, 1990–93 (Billions of dollars)

Transaction category or sector	1990	1991	1992	1993
	Nonfinancial sectors			
1 **Total net borrowing by domestic nonfinancial sectors**	**635.6**	**475.8**	**536.1**	**628.1**
By sector and instrument				
2 U.S. government	246.9	278.2	304.0	256.1
3 Treasury securities	238.7	292.0	303.8	248.3
4 Budget agency issues and mortgages	8.2	−13.8	0.2	7.8
5 Private	388.7	197.5	232.1	372.0
By instrument				
6 Tax-exempt obligations	48.7	68.7	31.1	78.1
7 Corporate bonds	47.1	78.8	67.5	75.2
8 Mortgages	199.5	161.4	123.9	155.6
9 Home mortgages	185.6	163.8	179.5	183.9
10 Multifamily residential	4.8	−3.1	−11.2	−6.1
11 Commercial	9.3	0.4	−45.5	−22.5
12 Farm	−.3	0.4	1.1	0.5
13 Consumer credit	16.0	−15.0	5.5	62.3
14 Bank loans n.e.c.	0.4	−40.9	−13.8	5.0
15 Commercial paper	9.7	−18.4	8.6	10.0
16 Other loans	67.4	−37.1	9.2	−14.3
By borrowing sector				
17 Household	218.9	170.9	217.7	284.5
18 Nonfinancial business	123.7	−35.9	−2.0	21.9
19 Farm	2.3	2.1	1.0	2.0
20 Nonfarm noncorporate	10.1	−28.5	−43.9	−26.0
21 Corporate	111.3	−9.6	40.9	45.8
22 State and local government	46.0	62.6	16.4	65.7
23 Foreign net borrowing in United States	23.9	13.9	21.3	46.9
24 Bonds	21.4	14.1	14.4	59.4
25 Bank loans n.e.c.	−2.9	3.1	2.3	0.7
26 Commercial paper	12.3	6.4	5.2	−9.0
27 U.S. government and other loans	−7.0	−9.8	−0.6	−4.2
28 **Total domestic plus foreign**	**659.4**	**489.6**	**557.4**	**675.0**
	Financial sectors			
29 **Total net borrowing by financial sectors**	**202.9**	**152.6**	**237.1**	**286.1**
By instrument				
30 U.S. government-related	167.4	145.7	155.8	161.2
31 Government-sponsored enterprises securities	17.1	9.2	40.3	80.6
32 Mortgage pool securities	150.3	136.6	115.6	80.6
33 Loans from U.S. government	−0.1	0.0	0.0	0.0

Table 2–5 (Cont'd)

Transaction category or sector	1990	1991	1992	1993
	Financial sectors			
34 Private	35.5	6.8	81.3	125.0
35 Corporate bonds	46.3	67.6	78.5	118.3
36 Mortgages	0.6	0.5	0.6	3.6
37 Bank loans n.e.c.	4.7	8.8	2.2	−14.0
38 Open market paper	8.6	−32.0	−0.7	−6.2
39 Loans from Federal Home Loan Banks	−24.7	−38.0	0.8	23.3
By borrowing sector				
40 Government-sponsored enterprises	17.0	9.1	40.2	80.6
41 Federally related mortgage pools	150.3	136.6	115.6	80.6
42 Private	35.5	6.8	81.3	125.0
43 Commercial banks	−.7	−11.7	8.8	5.6
44 Bank holding companies	−27.7	−2.5	2.3	8.8
45 Funding corporations	15.4	−6.5	13.2	2.9
46 Savings institutions	−30.2	−44.5	−6.7	11.1
47 Credit unions	0.0	0.0	0.0	0.2
48 Life insurance companies	0.0	0.0	0.0	0.2
49 Finance companies	24.0	18.6	−3.6	0.2
50 Mortgage companies	0.0	−2.4	8.0	−1.0
51 Real estate investment trusts (REITs)	0.8	1.2	0.3	3.5
52 Issuers of asset-backed securities (ABSs)	52.3	51.0	56.3	81.5
	All sectors			
53 Total net borrowing, all sectors	**862.3**	**642.2**	**794.5**	**961.2**
54 U.S. government securities	414.4	424.0	459.8	417.3
55 Tax-exempt securities	48.7	68.7	31.1	78.1
56 Corporate and foreign bonds	114.7	160.5	160.4	252.9
57 Mortgages	200.1	161.9	124.5	159.2
58 Consumer credit	16.0	−15.0	5.5	62.3
59 Bank loans n.e.c.	2.2	−29.1	−9.4	−8.3
60 Open market paper	30.7	−44.0	13.1	−5.1
61 Other loans	35.6	−84.9	9.5	4.7
	Funds raised through mutual funds and corporate equities			
62 Total net share issues	**19.7**	**215.4**	**296.0**	**436.9**
63 Mutual funds	65.3	151.5	211.9	316.8
64 Corporate equities	−45.6	64.0	84.1	120.1
65 Nonfinancial corporations	−63.0	18.3	27.0	21.3
66 Financial corporations	10.0	15.1	26.4	38.2
67 Foreign shares purchased in United States	7.4	30.7	30.7	60.6

Source: *Federal Reserve Bulletin*, February 1995.

Table 2–6
Summary of Financial Transactions (Billions of dollars except as noted)

Transaction category or sector	1990	1991	1992	1993
NET LENDING IN CREDIT MARKETS				
1 **Total net lending in credit markets**	**862.3**	**642.2**	**794.5**	**961.2**
2 Private domestic nonfinancial sectors	190.1	−7.5	72.0	6.8
3 Households	157.2	−39.6	70.7	−9.6
4 Nonfarm noncorporate business	−1.7	−3.7	−1.1	−3.2
5 Nonfinancial corporate business	−3.7	6.7	29.2	18.0
6 State and local governments	38.3	29.2	−26.8	1.5
7 U.S. government	33.7	10.5	−11.9	−18.4
8 Foreign	85.5	26.6	100.5	126.0
9 Financial sectors	553.0	612.5	633.9	846.8
10 Government-sponsored enterprises	13.9	15.2	69.0	90.2
11 Federally related mortgage pools	150.3	136.6	115.6	80.6
12 Monetary authority	8.1	31.1	27.9	36.2
13 Commercial banking	125.1	80.8	95.3	142.2
14 U.S. commercial banks	94.9	35.7	69.5	149.6
15 Foreign banking offices	28.4	48.5	16.5	−9.8
16 Bank holding companies	−2.8	−1.5	5.6	0.0
17 Banks in U.S. affiliated areas	4.5	−1.9	3.7	2.4
18 Funding corporations	16.1	15.8	23.5	18.1
19 Thrift institutions	−154.0	−123.5	−61.3	−2.0
20 Life insurance companies	94.4	83.2	79.1	105.1
21 Other insurance companies	26.5	32.6	12.8	33.3
22 Private pension funds	17.2	85.7	37.3	40.2
23 State and local government retirement funds	34.9	46.0	34.4	25.5
24 Finance companies	29.0	−12.7	1.7	−9.0
25 Mortgage companies	0.0	11.2	0.1	0.0
26 Mutual funds	41.4	90.3	123.7	164.0
27 Closed-end funds	0.2	14.7	17.4	10.2
28 Money market funds	80.9	30.1	1.3	12.9
29 Real estate investment trusts (REITs)	−0.7	−0.7	1.1	0.6
30 Brokers and dealers	2.8	17.5	−6.9	9.2
31 Asset-backed securities issuers (ABSs)	51.1	48.9	53.8	80.1
32 Bank personal trusts	15.9	10.0	8.0	9.5
RELATION OF LIABILITIES TO FINANCIAL ASSETS				
33 **Net flows through credit markets**	**862.3**	**642.2**	**794.5**	**961.2**
Other financial sources				
34 Official foreign exchange	2.0	−5.9	−1.6	0.8
35 Special drawing rights certificates	1.5	0.0	−2.0	0.0
36 Treasury currency	1.0	0.0	0.2	0.4
37 Life insurance reserves	25.7	25.7	27.3	35.2
38 Pension fund reserves	165.1	360.3	249.7	304.7
39 Interbank claims	35.4	−3.9	61.7	42.1
40 Checkable deposits and currency	43.3	86.4	113.8	117.3

Table 2–6 (Cont'd)

Transaction category or sector	1990	1991	1992	1993
RELATION OF LIABILITIES TO FINANCIAL ASSETS				
41 Small time and savings deposits	63.7	1.5	–57.2	–70.3
42 Large time deposits	–66.1	–58.5	–73.2	–23.5
43 Money market fund shares	70.3	41.2	3.9	15.8
44 Security repurchase agreements	–24.2	–16.5	35.5	65.5
45 Foreign deposits	38.2	–16.7	–7.2	–22.1
46 Mutual fund shares	65.3	151.5	211.9	316.8
47 Corporate equities	–45.6	64.0	84.1	120.1
48 Security credit	3.5	51.4	4.2	61.9
49 Trade debt	37.0	3.6	41.5	49.0
50 Taxes payable	–4.8	–6.2	8.5	4.6
51 Noncorporate proprietors' equity	–28.3	–3.3	18.4	–10.2
52 Investment in bank personal trusts	29.7	16.1	–7.1	1.6
53 Miscellaneous	135.7	197.2	257.6	302.1
54 Total financial sources	**1,410.6**	**1,530.2**	**1,764.5**	**2,273.0**
Floats not included in assets (–)				
55 U.S. government checkable deposits	3.3	–13.1	0.7	–1.5
56 Other checkable deposits	8.5	4.5	1.6	–1.3
57 Trade credit	9.1	9.7	4.1	16.5
Liabilities not identified as assets (–)				
58 Treasury currency	0.2	–0.6	–0.2	–0.2
59 Interbank claims	1.6	26.2	–4.9	4.2
60 Security repurchase agreements	–24.0	6.2	27.9	81.1
61 Taxes payable	0.1	1.3	14.0	1.0
62 Miscellaneous	–35.4	–45.3	–46.0	–45.3
63 Total identified to sectors as assets	**1,447.2**	**1,541.2**	**1,767.2**	**2,218.5**

Source: *Federal Reserve Bulletin*, February 1995.

These tables are summaries of a large set of tables prepared for each sector as part of the overall data collection process. They are available from the Board of Governors of the Federal Reserve.

The Federal Reserve System also publishes annual tables of total credit market debt outstanding for various types of debt: the U.S. government debt, home mortgage debt, consumer debt, and corporate debt.

Several private institutions—banks, brokerage houses, and insurance companies— also prepare their own statements of sources and uses of funds to focus more directly on those sectors that are of greatest importance to their planning.

Interest Rate Forecasts and Other Applications

One method of forecasting interest rates begins with estimates of the supply and demand for funds in the period ahead. The first step in preparing these estimates is to project the future level of business activity. A useful proxy for this purpose is the nation's GDP and its components: consumer, business, government, and net foreign spending. The economic forecast must then be used to derive estimates of sources and uses of funds. For example, the expected demand for residential construction is translated into a forecast of demand for mortgage loans. To do this one must make assumptions about interest rates in the period ahead since the demand for such loans depends in part on the interest rate charged the borrower.

On the supply side, the same procedure is used to project sources of funds. Expected saving of each sector is converted into estimates of funds available to purchase various types of financial instruments directly or through financial intermediaries. Next, the sources of funds are added together and compared with total uses.

It is highly unlikely, of course, that the totals will balance on the first try when put in matrix form. Funds needed will exceed or fall short of those available. That is, there will be a gap between projected supply and demand for funds. Since the source-use approach to forecasting requires equality of supply and demand, adjustments must be made in these preliminary figures.

Suppose, for example, that when source and use estimates are first compared, uses exceed sources. This implies that credit conditions will tighten and interest rates will rise. Adjustments in interest rates and in estimates of funds supplied and demanded can be made until the gap between the flows is closed. In this way the analyst will obtain reasonable and consistent estimates of financial flows and interest rates.

It is usually supposed that a large part of the adjustment in credit flows will take place on the supply side. A rise in interest rates, for example, will induce interest-sensitive investors such as individuals, foreigners, and others to supply more funds to the market. Individuals may buy additional financial instruments with idle funds, and foreign investors will be attracted to financial markets in the United States. Many analysts classify these purchases by households as a "residual" source of funds. Often foreign purchases are included as well. Some studies show that the "residual" component of supply is highly correlated with the level of rates. Changes in the size of the residual brought about by changes in rates is an important mechanism in balancing supply and demand for funds.

Further, flow of funds data are becoming more widely used in studies of portfolio choices of sectors of the economy. The relative preference of, say, households or business for money versus other financial assets may be studied using these data. More broadly, flow of funds accounts and source-use statements may be used to develop and test hypotheses concerning total spending in the economy.

Gross Domestic Product Data from the Four Asian Tigers

Compilation of estimates of GDP is expensive and requires a commitment on behalf of the authorities. Hong Kong publishes regular estimates of annual GDP, but no flow of funds accounts that are similar to the ones described above. Singapore, Taiwan, and

Korea also publish estimates of GDP. Each country does publish a large volume of economic statistics, however, that can be used to estimate production and trade along with price level changes, and so forth.

Table 2–7 contains a summary statement of GDP estimates from Hong Kong for a selection of years. Noteworthy in these data are the estimates of exports of goods and services. These exceed gross domestic product—a rare situation for an economy. Hong Kong has only about 20 square miles of territory where nearly six million people live. In 1990 the per capita GDP was approximately US$13,000 using an exchange rate of HK$7.8 to US$1. Gross investment as a per cent of GDP was over 25 per cent in 1990 and this reflects a high saving rate. This saving was facilitated by a world class financial sector—by some measures it might rank fourth behind only London, New York, and Tokyo.

Table 2–7
Gross Domestic Product in Hong Kong (Estimates in HK$ millions at current market prices)

GDP components	1980	1985	1990	1993
Consumption spending	84,660	167,483	330,459	509,211
Government spending	8,720	19,787	43,283	71,841
Gross fixed investment	46,011	57,280	153,776	233,723
Change in inventories	3,745	1,469	5,728	2,040
Exports of goods	98,242	235,152	639,874	1,046,250
Imports of goods	111,794	232,617	645,200	1,075,710
Exports of services	22,164	61,050	142,321	223,890
Imports of services	16,952	37,949	87,692	123,631
Gross domestic product	141,796	271,655	582,549	887,614
Change over year	26.9	5.9	11.2	14.0
Per capita GDP in HK$	28,006	47,848	102,121	149,960
Change over year	23.8	4.2	10.7	11.9

Source: Hong Kong, Census and Statistics Department, *Revised Estimates of Gross Domestic Product, 1961 to First Quarter 1994*, August 1994.

A sample of Korea's GDP figures appears in Table 2–8. With a population of about 43 million, its per capita GDP was just under US$5,000 in 1988. Again, a look at the relation between gross investment and GDP indicates a saving rate in the neighborhood of 30 per cent.

Figures for Singapore appear in Table 2–9. Figures for Taiwan appear in Table 2–10.

Summary

Modern exchange economies need a stable money supply to provide a medium of exchange of goods and services. They also need a large supply of interest-earning debt

Table 2–8

Gross Domestic Product in Korea (Estimates in billions of Korean won at 1990 prices)

GNP components	1990	1991	1992	1993
Private consumption	114.6	125.3	133.7	140.8
Government consumption	18.2	19.7	21.2	21.8
Gross fixed capital formation	66.6	74.9	74.4	77.0
Increase in stocks	−270.0	1,147.4	153.2	−2,052.0
Surplus on the current account		−5.1	−1.8	
Exports of goods and services	53.5	59.8	66.4	73.8
Imports of goods and services	54.4	64.9	68.2	72.8
Net factor income from abroad	−1.3	−1.5	−1.6	−1.6
Statistical discrepancy	−0.4	−0.3	−0.5	0.4
Gross National Product	178.3	194.4	204.2	215.6

Source: *Monthly Statistical Bulletin*, Bank of Korea, June 1994.

Table 2–9

Gross Domestic Product in Singapore (Estimates in billions of Singapore dollars)

GDP components	1991	1992	1993
Private consumption	31.6	34.0	38.0
Government consumption	7.3	7.4	8.3
Gross fixed capital formation	27.6	30.9	36.1
Increase in stocks	0.2	1.1	2.3
Net exports of goods and services	6.9	5.7	3.2
Statistical discrepancy	−0.5	−0.0	−0.4
Gross Domestic Product	73.0	79.1	89.0

Source: *Yearbook of Statistics*, Department of Statistics, Singapore, various issues.

Table 2–10

Gross National Product in Taiwan (Estimates in billions of new Taiwan dollars)

GNP components	1990	1991	1992	1993
Private consumption	2,302	2,554	2,899	3,226
Government consumption	744	840	911	945
Gross fixed capital formation	947	1,043	1,208	1,371
Increase in stocks	−1,638	29	51	70
Surplus on the current account				
Exports of goods and services	2,014	2,281	2,313	2,583
Imports of goods and services	1,784	2,043	2,184	2,482
Net factor income from abroad	105	117	103	97
Gross National Product	4,327	4,821	5,301	5,809
Gross Domestic Produce	4,222	4,704	5,199	5,712

Source: *Quarterly National Economic Trends*, Executive Yuan, Taiwan, reprinted in *Economic Review*, International Commercial Bank of China, May–June 1994, p. 32.

instruments and shares of stock that represent equity ownership of properties. Capital needs to flow to its most productive uses and only well-developed financial markets can facilitate capital flows.

In this chapter an economy's circular flows were described along with a description of the flows of funds among the various sectors of the economy.

In the process of providing these descriptions the role of debt was noted, and it was emphasized that for every debt there is also a credit. Financial intermediation and secondary financial markets provide liquidity for asset holders. Examples of flows of funds tables were provided along with examples of the GDP accounts of the Asian Tigers.

Key Terms and Concepts

Barter

Usury

Financial and real investment

Intermediation

Money is the root of evil?

Circular flow diagram

Flow of funds

Liquidity

Discussion Questions and Exercises

1. Does saving always equal investment? Explain.
2. What are the attributes of an asset that impart "liquidity" to it? Give an example of a liquid asset and explain why it is liquid, and an example of an illiquid asset and explain why it is not liquid.
3. Would a country with a high saving rate be expected to have a faster growing economy than one with a low saving rate? Explain your reasoning.
4. Construct a simple flow of funds matrix without looking back at the one provided in the text.
5. Why are prices of factors of production given special names?
6. What is the attitude toward the collection of interest on debt in your community? Can you give any examples of the expression of concern over interest that is evident in government regulations? Discuss.
7. List the major classes of expenditure usually presented in GDP tables. Cite the latest measures of GDP and GDP per capita for your community.
8. Distinguish between financial investment and "real" investment and give a few examples of each.
9. Do you think that any government regulations in your economy inhibit the flow of capital to its highest and best use? Discuss.
10. From the flow of funds tables, compare the extent of financing derived from debt issue with that derived from the sale of equity. Which type of financing seems to be the most important? Discuss.
11. What cultural factors affect the way in which borrowing and lending take place in your community?

References

Effros, Robert C., ed., *Current Legal Issues Affecting Central Banks*, Vol. 1, International Monetary Fund, Washington, DC, 1982.

Federal Reserve Bank of Chicago, *Two Faces of Debt*, 5th Revision, Chicago, 1992.

Federal Reserve Bulletin, various issues.

Hamid, Akhtar, "Addendum on Recent Developments," in Effros, pp. 431–20.

Hong Kong, Census and Statistics Department, *Gross Domestic Product: Quarterly Estimates and Revised Annual Estimates*, August 1991.

Hongkong and Shanghai Banking Corporation, *Business Profile Series*, various countries.

Iqbal, Zubair, and Mirakhor, Abbas, "Islamic Banking," Occasional Paper No. 49, International Monetary Fund, Washington, DC, 1987.

Kahn, Mohsin S., and Mirakhor, Abbas, "The Framework and Practice of Islamic Banking," *Finance and Development*, September 1986, pp. 32–36.

Murvat, Sardad Khan, "The Legal Framework for Islamic Banking: Pakistan's Experience," in Effros, pp. 351–419.

CHAPTER 3

The Business of Commercial Banking

THIS CHAPTER BRIEFLY describes the role that commercial banks play as important financial intermediaries in a modern exchange economy. It should be useful as background reading for students who wish to take complete courses in commercial bank management that focus on the decision-making activities of bank managers. The discussion here begins with a very broad introduction to commercial banking as a business and a look at bank balance sheets and income statements. From there it moves to a discussion of government regulations that relate to money supply control and money supply creation by the banking industry. Chapter 4 extends the discussion to investment banks, merchant banks, universal banks, saving banks, thrifts, credit unions, and other forms of financial intermediaries that accept deposits, make loans, and compete directly with commercial banks for the business of banking.

Commercial Banking as a Business

When placing a sign outside the door of a shop declaring that banking services for consumers are offered inside, a banker assumes a responsibility that goes beyond that of most shopkeepers. A consumer can walk into a grocery or restaurant and exchange money for goods if there is something he wants to buy. But a bank customer is not buying goods.

There are two major types of bank customers. One is a *depositor.* He deposits money with the bank for safekeeping, and the bank guarantees that the money can be withdrawn and spent later. Thus, although throughout history banks have been known for their vaults that hold valuables for customers, in today's modern economies a depositor is someone who *lends* money to banks.

Banks then offer to re-lend the depositor's money to someone else. Thus, the second type of bank customer is a *borrower*. The sign, "bank," outside the door tells customers to "borrow from us." Banks, like nearly all people and nearly all businesses, are both borrowers and lenders.

Because banks presume to serve people by accepting their money for safekeeping, the people generally ask that government intervene to prevent, through regulation, dishonest people from engaging in the business of banking. Government enforcement of contracts, alongside the moral and ethical responsibilities on the shoulders of bankers, make most banks a safe depository for funds.

In performing the safekeeping function, banks are said to exercise *prudential* responsibility, which simply means that they should be very careful in handling other people's money.

Banks offer a variety of other types of services depending upon the permission they have from regulators. Besides renting part of their vault space to people who wish to store valuable papers or jewelry, banks may sell traveler's checks, make wire funds transfers, trade foreign exchange, handle trust arrangements, and so forth.

Banking Corporations

Because they operate like other businesses and seek to make profits for their owners, banks take advantage of limited liability permitted by the corporate form of legal enterprise. In the United States, corporate charters are available from each and every one of the 50 states. In addition, the Congress of the federal government can establish the framework for permitting corporations to be established, as it has in the case of banking. In 1863 Congress passed the National Banking Act that set up the Office of the Comptroller of Currency in the Treasury Department, through which corporate charters were made available to banks.

Banks with charters issued by the Comptroller are called national banks, and originally all of them carried the word "national" in their names. These national banks operate in competition with state-chartered banks.

But, just because they are called "national" does not mean that they operate throughout the nation. Indeed, in some states, such as Illinois and Texas, banks were permitted only one geographical base of operations for many years. Thus, until the law was changed in 1987 in Texas, for example, a bank could not have branch offices in more than one town. Texas had 1,986 commercial banks in 1986 and by 1991 the number had fallen to 1,138 because of mergers. However, the number of branches of banks—bank offices— actually increased during the period. In other states, such as Arizona and California, banks can branch into any town within the state. State laws regarding branching vary greatly. In the State of Washington, for example, a bank can open branches as it likes in the county in which it has its headquarters, but it can have a branch office in a different county only if it acquires an already existing bank that operates in that different county. That is, branching outside of the geographical region of a county occurs only through merger and acquisition.

For many years state banks were not permitted to branch outside of the state in which they were chartered. Later when national banks were first chartered under the National Banking Act of 1863, their ability to branch was unclear. *The McFadden Act* of 1927 was passed to clarify their situation. It gave national banks permission to establish branches in states if states gave permission to allow state banks to branch. That is, it gave national banks permission to do whatever state banks were permitted to do.

But a law that specifies that a bank has *permission* to engage in a certain activity may be interpreted to mean that the bank does *not* have the authority to engage in other activities. So, the McFadden Act is often referred to as the law that *limits* the branching of national banks across state lines. This is not strictly correct. It was, instead, the Glass-Steagall Act that expressly limited nationally chartered banks to branch only to the extent that state law permitted state chartered banks to branch.

The result of branching restrictions for the country as a whole was, in 1980, a system with 14,700 commercial banks of which 10,300 were state chartered and 4,400 were nationally chartered. None were permitted to branch across state borders. In early 1994 there were about 10,888 banks of which about 70 per cent (7,655) were state banks. There were also about 2,300 savings banks and savings and loan institutions competing for deposits and acting as banks in many ways. Because restrictions on branching led to the establishment of thousands of banks in the United States, economists sometimes refer to this country's *unit banking system.*

The large number of banks meant that correspondent banking relations became very strong. In Great Britain, or in Canada, a small number of banks operate nationwide to serve customers who want to do business in many cities. In the United States, due to restrictive branching regulations, banks must have working relations with other banks, especially with those in other states. Furthermore, the clearing of checks among banks all over the country was a bigger problem in the United States than in other countries where most banks operate nationwide.

Interstate Banking. In the 1980s in the United States, the limitations on bank branching across state borders became less strict. Branch banking across state borders may be arranged under provisions of the *Bank Holding Company Act* of 1956 with amendments in 1966 and 1970. Some state legislatures have approved reciprocal arrangements with other states. Thus, the holding company of a bank in a different state could acquire a local bank if the legislature of the other state also permitted local banks to branch into it. Interestingly, the legislatures of the State of Washington and the State of New York, on opposite coasts of the continental United States, established arrangements that would permit a bank holding company to operate banks in either state. As a result, by 1994 Key Bank of New York had established several branches in Seattle. But, on many occasions the reciprocal relations were made regionally by neighboring states. Also many states now permit unrestricted national interstate banking.

It appeared that the unwillingness of the nation's Congress to repeal the McFadden Act and the Glass-Steagall Act meant that interstate banking would develop only slowly, over the years, as across-state-lines branching was arranged by state legislatures. However, in the fall of 1994, Congress passed legislation that extended interstate banking privileges.

Because there are so many thousands of small banks around the country, they comprise a significant political force. Their managements do not wish to compete for the banking business with "big banks from the city." The resulting political situation prohibits more efficient banking arrangements from being put in place. Supermarkets, department stores, the 7-Eleven chain, and McDonald's are corporations that operate nearly everywhere and can compete in any geographical location. (Imagine what it would be like if all the little hamburger shops had gotten Congress to pass laws restricting the branching of McDonald's.) But the special privileges that banks acquire through their corporate charters have led to laws that often hold down competition (see Pozdena, 1991). Political resistance to change is often a fact of life in democracies.

Bank Balance Sheets and Income Statements

Accountants inform us that by reading a balance sheet one should be able to know a great deal about what a particular business firm does. Of course, the more refined the accounts, the more information there is. Also, in a company's annual report there are many items contained in supplementary notes that are highly informative. Here, Table 3–1 contains a composite balance sheet for all commercial banks in the United States. With a broad-brush stroke the items in the composite tell us what banks are up to, generally.

Assets listed at the top of the table include bank holdings of securities, loans to businesses, homeowners, and consumers. Also listed are interbank loans. Cash assets (line 14) includes currency and coin held in bank vaults, deposits at the Federal Reserve banks, and other cash items amounting to $206 billion in June 1994. Vault cash and deposits with the Federal Reserve are counted as legal reserves to meet the commercial banks' reserve requirements imposed by the Federal Reserve. They are important assets that will be the subject of extended discussion below.

Other cash assets include cash items in the process of collection and deposits with other deposit-taking institutions. In this composite balance sheet, interbank deposits are canceled out, but deposits with thrifts, credit unions, and other noncommercial bank financial intermediaries remain.

Cash items in the process of collection simply means the net dollar value of checks that are temporarily held in the clearing process at the end of the day on which the balance sheet is assembled.

Cash items earn practically no interest at all. No interest is earned on vault currency and coin. The Federal Reserve does not pay interest to banks on the deposits that banks

Table 3–1
Assets and Liabilities of Commercial Banks[1] (in billions of dollars)

Account	Wednesday figures 1994			
	June 8	June 15	June 22	June 29
ALL COMMERCIAL BANKING INSTITUTIONS				
Assets				
1 Bank credit	3,195.5	3,209.7	3,200.5	3,215.2
2 Securities in bank credit	960.8	968.4	966.0	972.2
3 U.S. government securities	750.0	756.5	751.6	755.0
4 Other securities	210.9	211.9	214.4	217.2
5 Loans and leases in bank credit[2]	2,234.7	2,241.4	2,234.5	2,243.0
6 Commercial and industrial	605.3	609.7	609.5	609.7
7 Real estate	949.0	949.5	950.6	953.2
8 Revolving home equity	73.9	73.9	74.1	74.2
9 Other	875.1	875.5	876.5	879.0
10 Consumer	411.8	412.5	414.4	417.6
11 Security[3]	79.1	79.8	72.7	74.0
12 Other	189.5	189.9	187.3	188.5
13 Interbank loans[4]	162.9	149.0	160.7	159.4
14 Cash assets[5]	213.6	230.5	215.2	206.0
15 Other assets[6]	228.9	230.8	229.5	227.5
16 **Total assets**[7]	**3,743.4**	**3,762.4**	**3,748.2**	**3,750.1**
Liabilities				
17 Deposits	2,504.3	2,531.9	2,495.1	2,483.6
18 Transaction	806.6	837.0	802.3	791.3
19 Nontransaction	1,697.8	1,694.9	1,692.8	1,692.3
20 Large time	334.8	334.4	332.1	332.1
21 Other	1,362.9	1,360.5	1,360.7	1,360.2
22 Borrowings	567.9	567.4	585.8	591.2
23 From banks in the U.S.	164.2	149.8	155.5	159.5
24 From nonbanks in the U.S.	403.7	417.6	430.3	431.6
25 Net due to related foreign offices	181.9	180.1	192.6	187.9
26 Other liabilities[8]	166.0	164.0	162.5	162.2
27 **Total liabilities**	**3,420.2**	**3,443.4**	**3,436.0**	**3,424.9**
28 Residual (assets less liabilities)[9]	323.2	319.0	312.3	325.2

1. Covers the following types of institutions in the fifty states and the District of Columbia: domestically chartered commercial banks that submit a weekly report of condition (large domestic); other domestically chartered commercial banks (small domestic); branches and agencies of foreign banks; New York State investment companies, and Edge Act and agreement corporations (foreign-related institutions). Excludes international banking facilities. Data are Wednesday values, or pro rata averages of Wednesday values. Large domestic banks constitute a universe; data for small domestic banks and foreign-related institutions are estimates based on weekly samples and on quarter-end condition reports. Data are adjusted for breaks caused by reclassifications of assets and liabilities.

Table 3–1 (Cont'd)

2. Excludes federal funds sold to, reverse repurchase agreements with, and loans to commercial banks in the United States.
3. Consists of reserve repurchase agreements with broker-dealers and loans to purchase and carry securities.
4. Consists of federal funds sold to, reverse repurchase agreements with, and loans to commercial banks in the United States.
5. Includes vault cash, cash items in process of collection, demand balances due from depository institutions in the United States, balances due from Federal Reserve Banks, and other cash assets.
6. Excludes the due-from position with related foreign offices, which is included in lines 25, 53, 81, and 109.
7. Excludes unearned income, reserves for losses on loans and leases, and reserves for transfer risk. Loans are reported gross of these items.
8. Excludes the due-to position with related foreign offices, which is included in lines 25, 53, 81, and 109.
9. This balancing item is not intended as a measure of equity capital for use in capital adequacy analysis.

Source: *Federal Reserve Bulletin*, September 1994.

hold with the Federal Reserve. And, no interest is earned on checks being collected. Therefore, items on the asset side of the balance sheet of great importance to banks as a business are investments in securities and loans (lines 2 and 5). They provide the interest earnings that make a bank a profitable business.

Banks are called commercial banks because they make mostly commercial loans, loans to finance inventories for retail shops. Today, other loans including consumer loans, real estate loans, and the like, are twice the amount of commercial loans. Thus, borrowers from banks are not only business firms, but also consumers and homeowners.

Investments, of course, are a form of loan. Below the item "securities," there appears investments in U.S. government securities. The item "other securities" includes the debt obligations of state and local governments and some corporate bonds, but it does not include shares of stock in corporations. Banks in Europe and Japan are allowed to hold shares of corporate stock as part of their revenue-yielding asset portfolios. But, the tradition in the United States since the Great Depression of the 1930s has been to bar banks from holding "speculative" assets.

Notice that the asset categories do not include holdings of real estate or land. Again, except for its own offices and buildings, regulations prohibit banks from holding such assets, but banks in Greece and Germany, for example, may own apartment buildings and other real estate.

The item, "other assets," does include a very small amount of real estate holdings, namely, the main office building in which the bank is headquartered. In such skyscrapers only a few floors may house the banking business and offices. The remaining floors may be rented out to tenants just like any other office complex in a modern city. So there is some minor flexibility to property ownership by U.S. banks. Also, if a bank has foreclosed a mortgage on a property and taken ownership in order to redeem its claim to an asset, the property will appear on a balance sheet as an asset. But banks operate under regulations that require that such assets be sold within a reasonable time. Bank managers in the United States cannot choose to hold such assets as business investments.

Under the heading of liabilities there is the usual set of deposit items that every holder of a checking account recognizes. There are transaction deposits (line 18) and time deposits and savings deposits under the heading of nontransaction deposits (line 19). It is customary in the U.S. to refer to transaction deposits and other checkable accounts as demand deposits. Demand deposits are called cheque accounts in England, Singapore, Hong Kong and other countries influenced by the British tradition. Savings accounts used to be called passbook accounts. Depositors could withdraw cash from their savings accounts by bringing their book into the bank and filling out a savings withdrawal slip. The fine print on a savings account agreement may indicate that the bank can, at its discretion, take up to 30 days to make a payment out of the account. As a practical matter, however, banks will not require the savings depositor to wait, as evidenced by the ever growing number of ATMs that provide cash withdrawal from savings accounts.

In Taiwan, reported figures on demand deposits include savings account deposits that can be withdrawn if the depositor goes to the bank and demands his money. Thus, Taiwan's figures include not only what would be called demand deposits in the U.S., but also what are called savings accounts in the U.S. The simple fact is that banking terms differ slightly from country to country and this makes translations from one language to another quite difficult.

Time deposits are special in that they can be withdrawn only on or after a specified date, usually in three, six, nine months, and so forth. Typically, a certificate will be issued to a time depositor and will have to be returned to the bank for the depositor to claim his funds. If a time deposit is not withdrawn on its specified date, it changes to a demand deposit and further interest accrues at the savings deposit rate. Thus, in Hong Kong, for example, there is a sizable number of foreign currency demand deposits in banks even though none of the banks offers checking accounts in foreign currency.

Deposits are also classified as individual (personal) deposits, deposits made by partnerships or corporations (business deposits), deposits of state and local governments, of the U.S. Treasury, or deposits of other banks.

In countries in which banks accept deposits in currencies other than those of the country in which the bank is located, deposits are classified as domestic currency deposits and foreign currency deposits. In Hong Kong the money supply figures sometimes include Hong Kong dollars and foreign currency deposits both separately, *and added together*. It is rather like adding apples and oranges, but supposedly one can view both as "fruit."

In Singapore, the official reports further distinguish bank deposits, taking into account whether the deposits are held by Singapore citizens or by foreign citizens.

Chapter 5 discusses further the different types of bank deposit and the implications each type holds for the measurement of the money supply.

The final category of items on any balance sheet is, of course, the capital accounts. These appear here as a residual (line 28). Banks maintain a very small amount of equity or net worth, relative to assets or debt. Table 3–1 shows that capital is about 9 per cent. This high debt/equity ratio indicates a very high degree of leverage. In Hong Kong it is called a gearing ratio as if the banks were speeding in "high gear." A ratio similar to this one is now subject to international standards and regulated as the

Capital Adequacy Ratio. An explanation of this required ratio may be found in the following chapter.

Bank Income and Expenses

Table 3–2 shows some composite data on income and expenses of banks (see Brunner and English, 1993). As financial intermediaries, banks are both borrowers and lenders. They borrow either from depositors or from other banks and then re-lend the funds to businesses or to other banks. As a result, the lion's share of income for banks is interest income, and the lion's share of expense for banks is interest expense. Banks' profit positions are principally determined by the spread they are able to maintain between the lending rates they charge borrowers and the rates they must pay to depositors.

The maturity of bank deposits is, on average, very short. Indeed, a large portion of demand deposits has already "matured." Bank loans, on the other hand, have a somewhat longer maturity. The shorter the maturity of a security, the greater its liquidity, and since liquidity is valuable, short maturities of a given security usually offer lower interest rates than longer maturities. By offering depositors very short maturities, banks can pay a relatively low interest rate. By lending funds to businesses for somewhat longer periods, the interest rate banks receive is usually somewhat higher. The spread results in a profit position for banks and other deposit-taking financial institutions.

In the early 1980s in the U.S., tight monetary policies pushed short-term interest rates up to levels above long-term interest rates. This meant that banks incurred large interest expenses to attract short-term deposits, and that the interest earnings on their longer term loans were low. So, deposit-taking institutions made losses and this situation contributed significantly to widespread failure of banks and thrift institutions. See further discussion in Chapter 15.

In 1992–93 easy monetary policies drove short-term interest rates down while long-term interest rates also declined but not very much. Thus, bank expenses associated with attracting depositor funds declined greatly while interest earned on loans did not decline as much. The result was an increase in bank profits.

Setting Interest Rates

In Hong Kong the government established, by official ordinances, the Hong Kong Association of Banks. This association acts as a cartel to set interest rates on short-term deposits. The existence of such a cartel in what is ostensibly a free enterprise economy is anachronistic. By holding rates of interest paid to depositors low, banks can remain profitable. Some observers contend that such restrictions are necessary to protect the system from experiencing bankruptcies. Surely this is a rationalization for an anti-competitive cartel's operations. In any case, a consumer's interest group launched a noisy campaign against the cartel and it began the elimination of deposit rate ceilings step-by-step in October 1994. If the deregulation goes smoothly the process will be finished by the middle of 1995.

Table 3–2

Report of Income, All Insured Domestic Commercial Banks and Nondeposit Trust Companies, 1990–92 (Millions of dollars)

Item	1990	1991	1992
Operating income, total	**375,729**	**350,140**	**323,366**
Interest income	319,968	289,288	256,356
Loans	238,491	213,879	185,900
Balances due from depositories	12,573	9,067	7,411
Gross federal funds sold and repurchase agreements	12,530	9,120	5,907
Securities (excluding trading account)	50,977	52,552	51,818
Tax exempt	6,282	5,378	4,658
Taxable	44,694	47,174	47,160
Trading account assets	5,398	4,670	5,319
Noninterest income	55,761	60,852	67,010
Service charges on deposits	11,419	12,812	14,116
Other operating income	44,342	48,040	52,894
Operating expense, total	**352,812**	**327,726**	**281,594**
Interest expense	204,647	167,607	122,426
Deposits	161,228	138,684	98,690
Deposits in foreign offices	34,087	25,169	21,431
Deposits in domestic offices	127,141	113,515	77,260
Transaction accounts	9,758	9,719	7,051
Savings (including MMDAs)	33,260	31,063	23,029
Large denomination certificates of deposit	27,844	20,441	11,459
Other time deposits	56,279	52,292	35,720
Gross federal funds purchased and repurchase agreements	22,730	14,370	9,259
Other	20,688	14,552	14,477
Loss provisions	31,965	34,248	26,556
Noninterest expense	116,201	125,871	132,612
Salaries, wages, and employee benefits	52,007	53,513	55,449
Occupancy expense	17,513	17,878	18,137
Other operating expenses	46,681	54,480	59,026
Securities gains	470	2,897	3,951
Income before taxes	23,386	25,311	45,722
Taxes	7,844	8,279	14,505
Extraordinary items	651	686	412
Net income	16,194	17,719	31,630
Cash dividends declared	13,906	14,360	14,244
Retained income	2,287	3,359	17,386

n.a. Not available

Source: *Federal Reserve Bulletin*, July 1993, p. 663.

Prohibition of Interest on Demand Deposits. In the United States the Glass-Steagall Act of 1933 prevented banks from paying interest on demand deposits. Hundreds of banks were failing every month in 1933, the year President Franklin Roosevelt took office. Immediately after his inauguration in March, he declared a Bank Holiday, closed down all the banks in the country for several days, and had Congress pass emergency legislation to permit them to reopen with emergency federal backing. Congress felt that competition for deposits among banks had caused interest costs to rise and had forced many banks into failure. The law was supposed to prevent "cut-throat" competition under which a large "wealthy" bank could offer high rates and induce depositors in other small banks to withdraw their funds, thus leading to runs and the collapse of small banks.

The prohibition on paying interest on demand deposits still exists, but everyone except small businesses can avoid this restriction today because a new set of checking accounts has been created that escapes the restriction.

Regulation Q. The prohibition of interest payments on demand deposits was followed by the imposition of Regulation Q. The Federal Reserve has been given powers to regulate banks, and the regulations are known by the various letters attached to them. For example, Regulation D concerning reserve requirements will be the subject of discussion below. Regulation Q imposed ceilings on the interest rate that banks were permitted to pay savings depositors. Thus, the ceiling was zero for demand deposits under the Glass-Steagall Act, and was often limited on savings accounts to 3 per cent, say, under Regulation Q. The percentage was occasionally changed by the Federal Reserve. Then, thrift institutions were also subjected to similar regulations over the interest that they were allowed to pay on savings accounts.

Usury. Laws that limit interest payments made by banks to depositors constitute strange types of usury laws. Usury laws usually prohibit wealthy creditors from charging too high interest rates on loans given to poor persons. In the case of laws that limit what banks pay to depositors, it is the presumably wealthy banks that are protected from having to pay high interest rates to the greedy depositors. Thus, this type of usury law seems perverse. In the usual usury case it is the creditor who is restricted from *collecting* interest whereas in the case of Regulation Q it is the borrowing bank that is restricted from *paying* a high interest.

Thus, not unlike the banking cartel in Hong Kong, the Congress and the Federal Reserve of the United States introduced the same kind of pricing that a cartel would have set had there not existed stringent anti-trust laws incompatible with cartels. Regulation Q was phased out during the early years of the 1980s. But because of many bank and thrift failures during the entire decade of the 1980s, some economists have recommended a return of Regulation Q and its use as a means to regulate rates in order to prevent bank failures.

Bank Reserves

As businesses in the financial industry, commercial banks must meet their contractual obligations to customers. Also, they must have earnings sufficient to satisfy owners or other suppliers of capital. Finally, they must meet the demands of government regulators. Bank managers must balance not only their balance sheets but the competing demands of customers, shareholders and governments as well.

Perhaps the most important asset on a bank's balance sheet is cash reserves because those reserves are used to pay depositors when they want to withdraw their funds. Failure to pay a depositor is a default on an obligation that will lead to a lack of confidence and a run on the bank.

Every day a banking office will find some depositors withdrawing funds and other depositors depositing funds. If the amount deposited equals the amount withdrawn then the total amount of cash in the bank's vaults will be left undisturbed. Thus, banks monitor the history of their withdrawals and deposits and estimate how much cash to hold to be sure that, when withdrawals exceed deposits, there is enough cash to pay out upon demand.

Depositors must be confident in the bank's ability to pay on demand. If they are not confident, they not only will not deposit funds, but will want to withdraw them. *What a bank banks on is not having to pay all of its depositors at once.* That is, it must maintain the confidence of depositors. It might be said that banking is a sophisticated confidence game for bank managers. Image is often as important as substance.

What applies to cash withdrawals also applies to checks against accounts of depositors that are presented for payment through a clearing house. Some depositors deposit checks drawn on other banks while other depositors make payments by check to people who deposit them in other banks. On any given day (actually, overnight) check clearings may not net to zero. The bank may have to dip into its reserves to meet the obligation it has to pay other banks to bring net clearings into balance.

Thus, it is of the utmost importance for banks to maintain a sufficient amount of vault cash and other reserves needed to adjust check clearing balances.

Bank Runs. A popular gift for Chinese New Year in Hong Kong is a gift certificate. In 1984 a bakery in Hong Kong, Maria's Bakery, sold a large number of gift certificates, each good for one dozen cup cakes. A rumor circulated that Maria's Bakery might go bankrupt and might not be able to deliver a sufficient amount of cup cakes to meet its obligations to redeem its outstanding certificates. Lines began to form outside the many branches of the bakery. Newspapers carried pictures of the bakery's ovens running all night and all day to meet the demand. The bakery did not go bankrupt! It still operates in Hong Kong. It survived a run on cup cakes.

The outcome has been less happy in other instances. In the summer of 1991, Hong Kong's Bank of Credit and Commerce (BCC) was closed down by the authorities. It was associated with the Bank of Credit and Commerce International (BCCI) but had operated independently and seemed not to be tainted in any way with suggestions of illegal activities that had led to the scandals associated with the closing of BCCI. Local authorities had announced on a Saturday that the BCC was solvent, but closed the BCC on the following Monday.

During a bank run, a bank may be forced to close its doors and go into bankruptcy because it has insufficient funds to meet withdrawals *on demand*. In this case, the bank faces a liquidity crisis. The bank may be *solvent* in the sense that its assets exceed its liabilities and its net capital is positive. In other words, given sufficient time to sell its assets, the bank could raise the funds to pay off all of its liabilities and have funds left over to give some return to its shareholders. But many solvent banks have had to close down because of liquidity problems. And, once government regulators take control, the value of a bank's assets may depreciate rapidly.

In the case of BCC in Hong Kong, the estimate is that depositors will receive perhaps 50 per cent of their deposits after the bank is liquidated.

In the month that followed the closing of BCC, there were runs on the local branches of Citibank and also on the Standard Chartered Bank. Other banks came to the rescue and provided plenty of cash to pay off the lines of depositors that had formed, and the runs were short-lived.

Legally Required Reserves. Almost invariably, after an unfortunate incident, one hears the refrain, "there ought to be a law." After a bank run, people clamor for laws that would force banks to maintain sufficient cash reserves to pay off depositors. In most instances, governments tend to accommodate these demands. Britain, followed by Hong Kong, imposes a rather innocuous form of reserve requirement known as a liquidity requirement. Germany, Japan, and the United States have rather stringent reserve requirements.

For U.S. banks the Federal Reserve publishes a thick booklet that spells out *Regulation D*, the regulation of legal reserves. Only a few of the many details spelled out in Regulation D may be described here.

The general structure of legal reserve requirements is quite simple in concept. Let D be the level of deposit liabilities a bank holds, R be the amount of reserves, and r be a minimum legal ratio of reserves to deposits. Then, the law determines $r = R/D$ which may be 0.12 or 12 per cent, and banks must maintain $r \geq R/D$.

Thus, if a bank has $100 million in deposit liabilities it must maintain $12 million in accounts identified as legal reserves. These legal reserves consist of cash in the vault plus deposits with the Federal Reserve. On the surface this is quite a simple concept. Unfortunately, for bankers and regulators it is far more complex and is a costly managerial problem. Let us look a bit deeper into reserve requirements.

First, not all banks have to report their reserve position every week. Small banks must report only on a quarterly basis. How is the distinction between small and large banks determined? It is based on the total amount of reservable liabilities and the total amount of deposits. For example, in 1988, if a bank had less than $3.2 million of reservable liabilities (checking deposits) and less than $40 million total deposits, it need only report quarterly. These deposit limits are subject to change.

Second, under the *Depository Institutions Deregulation and Monetary Control Act* signed into law by President Carter in 1980, all national banks, saving and loan companies, credit unions, state-chartered banks and any institution issuing *transactions* accounts were required to hold legal reserves with the Federal Reserve to back their deposit liabilities. (Incidently, this law may have its title broken in half and be referred to as the Depository Institutions Deregulation Act, and separately, the Monetary Control Act. Here we are discussing provisions in the Monetary Control Act.) Thus, the law covers not only small and large banks, but thrift institutions as well—any institution that offers transactions accounts, that is, checking accounts of one type or another, to the depositing public.

Small institutions, if they like, can ask larger banks to act as agents for them and handle their account with the Federal Reserve. Before the Monetary Control Act, many banks held reserves, as required by state banking law, in the form of deposits with large banks. Such correspondent relations were extensive and large banks became agents for smaller banks and other thrifts and credit unions as well.

Under the Monetary Control Act, small institutions with $25 million or less in transactions accounts had to keep only 3 per cent in reserves. Thus, a 3 per cent reserve requirement applied to the first $25 million of such liabilities for all banks. The 12 per cent applied only to amounts over $25 million. But the Monetary Control Act also had an escalation clause. Each year the total of reservable transactions accounts for all banks is measured in June and the percentage increase from the previous year is noted. Then the $25 million figure is increased by 80 per cent of that percentage. This adjustment represents an attempt to permit growth in the lower amount of reserves required of small institutions. By January 1994 the 3 per cent requirement applied to the first $51.9 million of reservable transactions accounts.

Under the *Garn-St Germain Depository Institutions Act* of 1982, passed just two years after the Monetary Control Act, the first two million of deposits for any size bank was exempted from reserve requirements all together. So, the 3 per cent figure given in the example is not an average and neither is the 12 per cent figure. That is, the percentages apply to the marginal amounts that are added to the level of the specified types of deposits above the exempted amounts.

Furthermore, the initial two million exemption is also subject to an adjustment each year. Thus, just as in the previous case, the board takes the percentage increase in total reservable liabilities of all the banks in the system over a year from June to June, and increases the exemption by 80 per cent of that percentage. Thus, in a sense these escalation clauses represent an attempt to index the exemption to growth in the financial industry. Otherwise, the exemption would continue to decrease relative to inflation, and so forth. It is unfortunate that too few laws, and tax laws in particular, fail to index legislated amounts for exemption. By January 1994 the basic exempt amount had risen to $4.0 million.

Table 3–3 shows the reserve requirement levels as reported by the Federal Reserve. Readers may note that the reserve ratio was reduced from 12 per cent to 10 per cent on December 15, 1992 as part of an attempt to stimulate a weak economy. This made a

Table 3-3

Reserve Requirements of Depository Institutions[1]

Type of deposit[2]	Requirement	
	Percentage of deposits	Effective date
Net transaction accounts[3]		
1 $0 million–$51.9 million	3	12/21/93
2 More than $51.9 million[4]	10	12/21/93
3 Nonpersonal time deposits[5]	0	12/27/90
4 Eurocurrency liabilities[6]	0	12/27/90

1. Required reserves must be held in the form of deposits with Federal Reserve Banks or vault cash. Nonmember institutions may maintin reserve balances with a Federal Reserve Bank indirectly on a pass-through basis with certain approved institutions. For previous reserve requirements, see earlier editions of the *Annual Report* or the *Federal Reserve Bulletin*. Under provisions of the Monetary Control Act, depository institutions include commercial banks, mutual savings banks, savings and loan associations, credit unions, agencies and branches of foreign banks, and Edge Act corporations.
2. The Garn-St Germain Depository Institutions Act of 1982 (Public Law 97–320) requires that $2 million of reservable liabilities of each depository institution be subject to a zero per cent reserve requirement. The Board is to adjust the amount of reservable liabilities subject to this zero per cent reserve requirement each year for the succeeding calendar year by 80 per cent of the percentage increase in the total reservable liabilities of all depository institutions, measured on an annual basis as of June 30. No corresponding adjustment is to be made in the event of a decrease. On Dec. 21, 1993, the exemption was raised from $3.8 million to $4.0 million. The exemption applies in the following order: (1) net negotiable order of withdrawal (NOW) accounts (NOW accounts less allowable deductions); and (2) net other transaction accounts. The exemption applies only to accounts that would be subject to a 3 per cent reserve requirement.
3. Includes all deposits against which the account holder is permitted to make withdrawals by negotiable or transferable instruments, payment orders of withdrawal, and telephone and preauthorized transfers for the purpose of making payments to third persons or others, other than money market deposit accounts (MMDAs) and similar accounts that permit no more than six preauthorized, automatic, or other transfers per month, of which no more than three may be checks. Accounts subject to such limits are savings deposits.

    The Monetary Control Act of 1980 requires that the amount of transaction accounts against which the 3 per cent reserve requirement applies be modified annually by 80 per cent of the percentage change in transaction accounts held by all depository institutions, determined as of June 30 each year. Effective Dec. 21, 1993, for institutions reporting quarterly and weekly, the amount was increased from $46.8 million to $51.9 million.
4. The reserve requirement was reduced from 12 per cent to 10 per cent on Apr. 2, 1992, for institutions that report weekly, and on Apr. 16, 1992, for institutions that report quarterly.
5. For institutions that report weekly, the reserve requirement on nonpersonal time deposits with an original maturity of less than 1½ years was reduced from 3 per cent to 1½ per cent for the maintenance period that began Dec. 13, 1990, and to zero for the maintenance period that began Dec. 27, 1990. The reserve requirement on nonpersonal time deposits with an original maturity of 1½ years or more has been zero since Oct. 6, 1983.

    For institutions that report quarterly, the reserve requirement on nonpersonal time deposits with an original maturity of less than 1½ years was reduced from 3 per cent to zero on Jan. 17, 1991.
6. The reserve requirement on Eurocurrency liabilities was reduced from 3 per cent to zero in the same manner and on the same dates as was the reserve requirement on nonpersonal time deposits with an original maturity of less than 1½ years (see note 5).

Source: *Federal Reserve Bulletin*, September 1994, p. A9.

nice Christmas present for the banks. It meant they were not required to hold such a large amount of non-interest-bearing accounts with the Federal Reserve, a subject that will be discussed further in Chapter 5. A 3 per cent reserve on nonpersonal time deposits was removed on December 27, 1990. A description of the exemption accorded to banks by the Garn-St Germain Act appears in the finely printed notes to the table.

Contemporaneous and Lagged Reserve Accounting

Having decided what the reserve percentages are to be, the next problem concerns the precise periods of time over which they are to be calculated. Reserve accounting rules may seem unnecessarily detailed but these sometimes play a crucial role in understanding the policies implemented by central banks.

Banks prepare a balance sheet at the end of every business day. Central banks do not require banks to maintain reserves every minute of every day nor even every day. Instead they set a reserve maintenance period of a week or so, and take the average of balance sheet items over the seven days of the week. Days of the week that are not business days, such as weekend days, are included by using the balance sheet items for Friday also for Saturday and Sunday.

So the authorities must establish a period for calculating the average level of deposits that the bank had in order to know D in the equation $R = rD$. Next, they need to establish the period for calculating the average level of reserves the bank maintained in cash or deposits with the Federal Reserve, that is, R. They need to know R in order to establish whether or not the bank met the requirement that R exceeded rD.

The periods for calculating R and D are not exactly the same. The period for D must be earlier than that for R because D must be known before the reserve requirement R can be calculated. Banks must be given time to create their accounts.

In Figure 3–1 there is a simple representation of days of the week that will be helpful in understanding reserve requirement calculations. We begin by describing a system of lagged reserve accounting that the Federal Reserve applied from 1968 to 1984.

Figure 3–1
Reserve Accounting

A. Lagged Reserve Accounting

M T W <u>T F S S M T W</u> T F S S M T W <u>T F S S M T W</u> T F S S

Deposits	Reserves
Vault cash	(Deposits at Federal Reserve)

B. Contemporaneous Reserve Accounting

M T W T F S S M <u>T W T F S S M T W T F S S M</u> T W T F S S

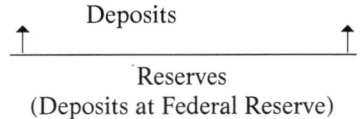

Deposits

Reserves
(Deposits at Federal Reserve)

In part A of the figure, the underlined letters on the left show the days during which the level of deposit liabilities, against which reserves had to be held, were calculated. The underlined letters on the right, the second subsequent week, show the period for which reserves had to be held against the deposits recorded two weeks before. Thus banks knew an entire week in advance just what average level of reserves they would have to maintain during the coming seven days beginning Thursday and ending the following Wednesday.

This calculation presents yet another small complication: There are two accounts that are considered as reserves, one is vault cash and the other is deposits with the Federal Reserve. Because counting cash is cumbersome, the portion of cash attributable to reserves was also made for the earlier week so that the only reserve account being watched for the reserve week two weeks later is the deposit with the Federal Reserve. Reserves were calculated every week in this fashion from 1968 to 1984 in the U.S.

In part B of the figure, the example is of a two-week period that overlaps all but two days. This is called a contemporaneous period but it does have a lag of two days, so it is not exactly contemporaneous.

Both deposits against which banks must hold reserves and those reserves held on deposit with the Federal Reserve are calculated over the respective periods. Banks know every Monday at the close of business just what amounts they have to have in their accounts with the Federal Reserve for the average of two weeks ending on Wednesday evening. Thus, banks have two days to ensure that their reserves are sufficient to meet their legal obligations.

Calculations for vault cash and for any reservable liabilities other than transactions accounts are made for a two-week period four weeks earlier and are not depicted here for the purpose of clarity.

Asset and Liability Management of Reserves

In earlier days banks, if deficient in reserves to meet legal requirements, would sell off an asset for cash. They would manage the other asset accounts and maintain a large holding of very liquid assets such as Treasury bills so that they would be able to obtain reserves as needed.

It is important to note here that when banks must hold legal reserves, those reserves are tied up by the law and are essentially no longer available to meet the demand of depositors for cash in case of a run except for a very temporary period. The law has, to an extent, had a perverse effect on its original intent. The idea was to force banks to hold adequate reserves so they would be able to pay depositors, but under the law they have to hold the cash and cannot use it to pay depositors!

So, what is the effect of reserve requirements and why do we keep them? The answer is that they are designed to limit the extent to which banks create deposit money. Notice that the bill affecting reserves held by all institutions that offer transactions was called the Monetary Control Act. We will discuss monetary control more extensively in the following chapters.

Today, banks manage not only their assets but also their liability accounts. One thing they can do if they need more reserves is sell a supply of certificates of deposit. To do so is a form of borrowing.

Federal Funds. Another form of borrowing is to borrow from other banks in the federal funds market. Large banks are in the market for reserves continuously. They do not wait until the end of the reserve period to start to adjust their reserve position at the Federal Reserve. Instead they enter the *federal funds* market, which is a telephone market in which banks borrow and lend to each other the funds they have on deposit at the Federal Reserve. It is basically an interbank market although some other institutions have access to it as well.

Banks and Reserve Maintenance Requirements in Other Countries

Table 3–4 provides information on the way different industrialized countries manage their reserves. The original source shows 12 per cent for the U.S. because its 1990 publication predates the reduction to 10 per cent in late 1992. Also, the U.S. reduced reserve requirements on time deposits to zero in 1991, illustrating how reserve requirements are subject to frequent change.

Legal reserve requirements are low in Japan at about 2 per cent, moderate in France at about 5 per cent, and higher in Germany and the U.S. In Italy they are 25 per cent, in Spain 18 per cent, in Portugal 15 per cent, in Ireland 10 per cent, and in Greece 7.5 per cent (see *World Financial Markets*, 1988). There are no reserve requirements, or only negligible ones, in the United Kingdom, Belgium, Denmark, Luxemburg, and Switzerland, for the purpose of maintaining a lever on the extent of money creation by bank lending.

Table 3–4
Required Reserve Ratios and Reserve Maintenance Periods for Selected Countries*

	Demand deposits	Time deposits	Computation period	Maintenance period
France	5.5%	3.0%	Last day of calendar month	16th of month to 15th of next month
Germany	12.0%	4.95%	16th of month to 15th of next month	Calendar month in which period ends
Japan	2.5%	1.75%	Calendar month	16th of month to 15th of next month
U.S.	10.0%	0.00%	Two weeks ending Monday	Two weeks ending Wednesday

*Ratios are subject to change and may not be current. Ratios apply at the margin for large banks since lower ratios apply for smaller levels of deposits. There exist a variety of types of accounts against which reserves may be required in each country.

Sources: Batten et al. (1990); Brunner and English (1993).

Switzerland removed its legal reserve requirements in 1988 and bank responses have been watched to see what effects follow this removal (see Pozdena, 1991; Evanoff, 1991). Requirements are subject to change. The question of whether it is appropriate to reduce them to zero is discussed in Chapters 5 and 16.

In every country, with or without legally required reserves, there are liquidity requirements. These require banks to hold highly liquid, but interest-earning, assets as "liquidity reserves" that banks may need to sell in case they are faced with unexpected withdrawals.

Thus, *legally required reserves* are maintained for monetary control, while *liquidity reserves* are maintained for prudential protection of depositor's money.

Reserve Maintenance Periods. France, Germany and Japan each have monthly accounting periods that overlap by two weeks. They could be thought of as half contemporaneous and half lagged. Beginning at the last, the middle, or the first of the month respectively, the banks begin to count up deposits against which reserves are required. Then, approximately 15 days later, they begin counting up reserves. There is a 15-day overlap where reserves are held contemporaneously with deposit liabilities, and this is followed by another 15 days where reserves are held against already known deposit levels— lagged reserve maintenance. This detail will be discussed at some length in Chapter 16. It plays an important role in the implementation of monetary policies.

Korean Banking and Reserve Requirements

Commercial Banks. The central and commercial banking system in Korea today is largely the outcome of the economic rehabilitation program following the Korean War in the early 1950s. The system reflects many of the suggestions put forward by American advisors, and it resembles many American institutional arrangements. There is a central bank, the Bank of Korea, and in 1990 there were 88 commercial banks (see Bank of Korea, 1990). Seven of these commercial banks have branches nationwide. They are called city banks, and they hold about 30 per cent of all deposits of all financial institutions. They have hundreds of branches as well as overseas offices, branches and subsidiaries (see Euh and Baker, 1990: 11). Five of the largest banks were originally owned by the government, that is, the government held ownership shares. One bank was privatized in 1972, and the government sold shares in the other four as part of a financial liberalization program in the early 1980s. It would be called a "deregulation" program in the United States. Now the shares of ownership in the large banks are held mostly by large Korean companies.

There are 48 foreign banks in the group, representing 13 different countries.

Specialized Banks. In the 1960s several specialized banks were established. One of these, the Korean Exchange Bank, helps manage the exchanges among banks and financial institutions. Others assist the agricultural and housing sectors, and small businesses.

Nonbank Institutions. During the 1970s other types of financial intermediaries were established and grew. In 1990 there were 6,551 savings institutions. These included mutual savings banks, credit unions, a postal saving system, 47 investment companies, 29 life insurance companies, one of which is a post office life insurance company, and 117 others, such as securities companies, non-life insurance companies, leasing companies and venture capital companies (Bank of Korea, 1990: 2, 16).

Reserve Requirements. Under the Bank of Korea Act of 1950, a Monetary Board was established to supervise the Bank's activities. The Act provides that the Monetary Board may fix and alter minimum ratios of reserves to each class of bank deposits that are payable on demand and on time deposits. The ratios may be set as high as 50 per cent. As much as 25 per cent of the reserves that banks hold may be in bank-notes of the Bank of Korea held in bank vaults. The remainder may be in the form of deposits with the Bank of Korea payable on demand. If requirements are set to exceed 50 per cent, the Bank of Korea must pay interest on the excess amount over 50 per cent.

From the information in Table 3–5, it is clear that required reserve ratios are applied to both demand and time and savings deposits and that they are held the same for each class. It is also clear that the reserve ratio was very low in 1981–85 but was raised to 11.5 per cent in 1990, and has remained unchanged at least until April 1994. Before 1990, changes in reserve requirements were used frequently by the Bank of Korea as a tool of monetary policy (*Monthly Statistical Bulletin*, Bank of Korea, May 1994: 25).

In Korea, reserves against deposits are calculated twice a month (semi-monthly). Information on the extent to which lagged or contemporaneous accounting applies, is not available at this time.

Hong Kong Banking and Liquidity Requirements

No Reserve Requirements—Only Liquidity Requirements. There are no legal reserve requirements in Hong Kong, following the tradition of the United Kingdom. However, there are requirements for holding "liquid assets." The minimum ratio a bank must maintain is 25 per cent. Basic changes to the accounting rules for liquidity requirements were introduced by the Banking Ordinance of 1986. The ordinance introduces new definitions. Under the ordinance, "liquifiable assets" of all depository institutions must be at least 25 per cent of "qualifying liabilities." The liquid assets may be in the form of interbank deposits, Hong Kong or foreign currency, quality loans coming due within one month, government securities and other debt coming due within one month, gold, and others accepted by the Commissioner of Banking. Qualifying liabilities are the total of liabilities maturing within one month and any net balance of interbank liabilities (see Ho et al., 1991: 103).

In previous years the banks have had liquidity ratios closer to 50 per cent, so the liquidity ratio has imposed no constraints on the extent to which banks in Hong Kong may extend loans or create deposit money.

Table 3–5

Reserve Requirements of Deposit Money Banks[1], Bank of Korea (in per cent)

Effective date	Time and savings deposits		Demand deposits	
	In won currency[2,3,4]	In foreign currency[5]	In won currency[3,4]	In foreign currency[5]
1979. 11.23	20 (17) <15>	1	27 (22) <20>	1
1980. 1.8	11 (8) < 6>	1	20 (15) <13>	1
9.23	10 (7) < 5>	1	14 (10) < 8>	1
1981. 7.1	5.5	1	5.5	1
11.23	3.5	1	3.5	1
1982. 5.23	5.5	1	5.5	1
1984. 9.8	4.5	1	4.5	1
1985. 7.23	4.5	1(20)	4.5	1(20)
1987. 2.20	4.5	1(4.5)	4.5	1(4.5)
11.23	7.0	1(4.5)	7.0	1(4.5)
1988. 12.23	10.0	1(4.5)	10.0	1(4.5)
1989. 5.8	10.0(30.0)[6]	1(4.5)	10.0(30.0)[6]	1(4.5)
1990. 2.8	11.5	1(4.5)	11.5	1(4.5)
1990. 3.8	11.5	1(11.5)	11.5	1(11.5)

1. Applies also to KDB and KLCB.
2. A favorable 3 per cent rate has applied to housing installment dep. included in reserve requirements from Dec. 23, 1988, workman's property formation savings introduced on Apr. 1, 1976, workman's savings for housing loans introduced on Dec. 1, 1987, workman's long-term savings introduced on Jan. 1, 1991 and Mutual installment dep. included in reserve requirements for Feb. 8, 1991 and a favorable 8 per cent rate has applied to household preferential installment savings deposits, time deposits and installment savings deposits for 2 years or more.
3. A portion of uncleared checks and bills was exempt from reserve requirements as a proportion of total deposits as follows: 2 per cent from Jan. 1971; 4 per cent from July 1979.
4. Figures in parentheses and brackets are the preferential rates applied to NACF and NFFC respectively.
5. Figures in parentheses apply to the resident account.
6. Figures in parentheses are marginal reserve ratio applied to the increment of each half-monthly average deposits compared with the first half-monthly average deposits of Apr. 1989.

Source: *Monthly Statistical Bulletin*, Bank of Korea, June 1994, p. 25.

Banks in Hong Kong. Hong Kong has a "Three Tier Banking System," indicating essentially that there are three types of approved institution: Licensed Banks, Restricted Licensed Banks, and Deposit-taking Companies (see Ho et al., 1991: 8).

As of 1990 there were 165 licensed banks in Hong Kong, 134 of which were incorporated outside of Hong Kong and only 31 incorporated in Hong Kong. Thus, the presence of foreign banking institutions is very large.

A Monetary Authority for Hong Kong. It was not until the spring of 1993 that Hong Kong established a Monetary Authority to supervise banks and carry out a role similar to that of a central bank. Previously, monetary policies were in the hands of a government department, the Monetary Affairs Branch. Under it, an Exchange Fund operated and performed many aspects of central banking. The Exchange Fund is now under the Hong Kong Monetary Authority, which is under the Monetary Affairs Branch.

Singapore Banking and Reserve Requirements

The government in Singapore has put out the welcome mat for foreign banks as well. Measured by the number of foreign banking offices, Singapore can claim fifth place in world financial markets, after New York, London, Tokyo, and Hong Kong. As the central location of the Asian dollar market, it is clearly an important international financial center, and will surely become more important after Hong Kong reverts to Chinese rule after June 30, 1997.

In 1989 there were 35 full banks in Singapore, 13 of which were local, and 22 of which were foreign chartered. There were 14 banks with restricted licenses and 86 offshore branches of banking firms (see Tan, 1989: 5).

Asian Currency Units. An Asian Currency Unit (ACU) is not a unit of currency. It is simply a division of a financial institution that keeps a set of accounts separate from its parent bank. There were 190 ACUs in Singapore in 1989. Should you walk into a bank and ask for the ACU, you will be shown to a set of separate offices and told, this is it. ACUs of financial institutions are permitted by government to accept deposits in foreign currencies. Through the ACU a bank keeps its foreign currency operations in the Asian dollar market separate from its domestic operations. The role of the ACU will be touched upon again when the Eurodollar market is discussed in Chapter 8.

The Monetary Authority of Singapore. The Monetary Authority of Singapore (MAS) was established on January 1, 1971 under an Act of Parliament passed in September the year before. It acts as a central bank. One of its responsibilities is to see that banks maintain reserves in accord with statutory requirements. Originally banks were required to maintain a minimum cash balance with the MAS of not less than 6 per cent of total deposits and a minimum of 20 per cent liquid assets against total deposits. These requirements are subject to change (see Tan, 1989: 259).

According to the *Monthly Statistical Bulletin* of the MAS (July 1992: 19) the minimum liquid assets ratio was reduced from 20 per cent to 18 per cent on May 21, 1987. In June 1992, their liabilities base was S$72 billion, liquid assets were S$13.7 billion, for a ratio of 19 per cent. (Evidence on accounting for reserves, whether contemporaneous or lagged, is not available at this time.)

At the same time, banks held assets that included cash of S$527 million and balances with the MAS of S$4,395 million. These were held against deposits of S$76,303. The ratio is about 6.5 per cent, which indicates that the 6 per cent required ratio remains the same as the original ratio set in 1971.

Taiwan Banking and Reserve Requirements

Taiwan's financial intermediaries consist of commercial banks, both domestic and foreign, and specialized banks and credit cooperatives. It also has investment and trust companies, insurance companies, and a significant postal savings system.

In 1990 there were 16 ordinary commercial banks operating nationwide, and 12 of these were government owned (see Chen, 1990: 4). As part of its financial liberalization program, the Taiwan government authorized, and began approving, the establishment of 15 new privately owned commercial banks. Part of the reason for this liberalization was that there were many financial "institutions" operating in the back streets illegally. It was clear that there was a need for more financial services than were provided by a government dominated banking industry.

Taiwan's official name is the Republic of China, and its central bank is called the Central Bank of China. These names should be distinguished from mainland China names, the People's Republic of China (PRC), and the People's Bank of China. The Central Bank of China was originally established in 1928 in Shanghai, but its duties were delegated to the Bank of Taiwan from 1949 when communist control of China was completed, until 1961 when the Central Bank of China was reconvened in Taiwan (Chen, 1990: 8).

Reserve Requirements. The Central Bank of China imposes reserve requirements on banks in Taiwan and uses these along with other monetary tools to control money creation by banks. Table 3–6 shows that the minimum reserve requirement against checking accounts is 15 per cent and the maximum is 40 per cent. Thus, Taiwan would be called a "high legal reserve" country. These ratios must be maintained on a ten-day average basis, that is, three accounting periods each month (Article 42 of the Banking Law). It is not known whether contemporaneous or lagged accounting is used by the Central Bank.

There is also a liquidity ratio requirement (Article 43). It is set at 7 per cent, that is, banks must hold excess reserves, treasury bills, bankers acceptances, and other liquid securities approved by the Central Bank of China, in an amount not less than 7 per cent of total deposit liabilities. These readily salable assets can be made available to meet unexpected withdrawals. The liquidity ratio is reported on a monthly basis. It has remained unchanged since 1978. Individual banks are instructed by the Central Bank to correct any deficiency that appears in the liquidity ratio. For example, the Central Bank will sometimes give the bank three days to make the adjustment.

Summary

Banks are highly regulated financial institutions. The business of banking can be understood by analyzing a bank's balance sheet and income statement. Banks operate as businesses and must meet expenses and earn revenues like other businesses. It is often the case that governments regulate banks in a way that will ensure that they do not go bankrupt. In an effort to prevent failure, many governments have imposed reserve requirements. However, these vary widely from country to country.

Table 3–6

Reserves against Deposits and Liquid Assets, Republic of China (Required reserve ratios of deposit money banks, per cent of deposits)

Kinds of reserves	Commercial banks		Industrial banks*		Savings banks	
	Demand deposits	Time deposits	Demand deposits	Time deposits	Passbook deposits	Time deposits
Guarantee reserve requirements						
Actual requirements						
Effective date of change						
July 1, 1948	15	10	12	8	–	–
May 1, 1953	13	8	10	6	–	–
July 21, 1956	13	5	10	5	–	–
Aug. 1, 1958	10	5	8	5	–	–
Jan. 1, 1959	13	8	10	6	–	5
Feb. 1	15	10	12	8	–	5
Jan. 1, 1966	12	8	10	6	–	5
May 6, 1967	15	10	12	8	–	5
Sept. 30, 1968	15	10	12	8	10	5
May 10, 1969	12	8	10	6	10	5
July 21, 1971	15	10	12	8	10	5
July 11, 1973	15	10	12	8	10	10
Nov. 15, 1974	15	7	12	7	10	7
Legal requirements						
Minimum	10	5	8	5	10	5
Maximum	15	10	12	8	15	10
Payment reserve requirements (Legal requirements)	15	7	12	6	10	5

Effective date of required reserve ratio	Checking accounts	Passbook deposits	Savings deposits		Time deposits	CDS-F.C.
			Passbook	Time		
July 21, 1975	25	23	17	11	13	–
Nov. 21, 1978	30	28	17	11	13	–
May 16, 1979	25	23	17	11	13	–
Aug. 21	25	23	15	9	11	–
June 29, 1982	23	21	14	8	10	–
July 11, 1986	23	21	14	8	10	7
Dec. 11, 1988	25	23	16	9	11	8
Apr. 1, 1989	29	27	20	11	13	10
Legal requirements						
Minimum	15	10	5		7	7
Maximum	40	35	20		25	25

*In respect of reserve requirements, Bank of Taiwan, The Bank of Communications, The Farmers Bank of China, The Central Trust of China, Land Bank of Taiwan, The Co-operative Bank of Taiwan, City Bank of Taipei, and The International Commercial Bank of China were treated as industrial banks.

Source: *Financial Statistics Monthly*, Central Bank of China, July 1993.

Key Terms and Concepts

Asian Currency Units

Reserve accounting (lagged and contemporaneous)

Regulations Q and D

Liquidity reserves

Required reserves

Three Tier Banking System

McFadden Act

Unit banking system

Discussion Questions and Exercises

1. An executive in an overseas bank of American Express fondly tells a story of an elderly depositor who would come to the offices of the bank about once each month and ask to see the money that the bank was holding for her in her deposit. The teller would count it out in front of her. Should she be told that her cash should be put in a safety deposit box if she really wanted them to "hold" it for her? Should she be told that she has lent her funds to the bank for its use? Discuss the ethical issues that bank managers face in these situations.
2. What are the conditions that give rise to the "unit banking system" of the United States?
3. What is the business of banks?
4. Discuss how banks in the United States are restricted from branching, but are able to run their businesses in more than one state nevertheless.
5. Why do governments impose legal reserve requirements on banks?
6. Distinguish between lagged and contemporaneous reserve accounting.
7. Contrast reserve requirement accounting in Germany with that in Japan.
8. Distinguish between asset and liability management of reserve accounts.
9. What are federal funds and why do large banks enter the federal funds market, or other interbank borrowing markets, every day?
10. How is the cartel of banks established by the government in Hong Kong similiar to the regulations imposed by the Glass-Steagall Act in the United States?
11. What is an Asian Currency Unit—precisely?
12. What is unique about the ownership of commercial banks in Taiwan?
13. Briefly discuss the wide range in the percentage of reserves legally required of commercial banks in countries around the world.
14. Explain why governments require banks to hold liquid assets in addition to legal reserves. That is, what do banks bank on, and what happens if they make a mistake?

References

Batten, Dallas S., Blackwell, Michael P., Kim, In-Su, Nocera, Simon E., and Ozeki, Yuzuru, "The Conduct of Monetary Policy in the Major Industrial Countries: Instruments and Operating Procedures," Occasional Paper No. 70, International Monetary Fund, Washington, DC, July 1990.

Brunner, Allan D., and English, William B., "Profits and Balance Sheet Developments at U.S. Commercial Banks in 1992," *Federal Reserve Bulletin*, July 1993, pp. 649–73.

Chen, Mu-Tsai, "The Financial System and Financial Policy in the Republic of China," *Economic Review*, International Commercial Bank of China, Taipei, July–August 1990, pp. 1–19.

Euh, Yoon-Dae, and Baker, James C., *The Korean Banking System and Foreign Influence*, Routledge, London, 1990.

Evanoff, Douglas D., and Israilevich, Philip R., "Productive Efficiency in Banking," *Economic Perspectives*, Federal Reserve Bank of Chicago, July/August 1991, pp. 11–32.

Financial Statistics Monthly, Central Bank of China, Republic of China, various issues.

Ghose, T. K., *The Banking System of Hong Kong*, Butterworths, Hong Kong, 1987.

Ho, Y. K., Scott, R. H., and Wong, K. A., eds., *The Hong Kong Financial System*, Oxford University Press, Hong Kong, 1991.

Korea, Bank of, *The Financial System in Korea*, Republic of Korea, 1990.

Monthly Statistical Bulletin, Bank of Korea, Republic of Korea, various issues.

Monthly Statistical Bulletin, Monetary Authority of Singapore, various issues.

Pozdena, Randall J., "Eliminating Reserve Requirements," *Weekly Letter*, Federal Reserve Bank of San Francisco, September 8, 1989.

———, "Why Banks Need Commerce Powers," *Economic Review*, Federal Reserve Bank of San Francisco, Summer 1991, pp. 18–31.

Srinivasan, Aruna, "Are There Cost Savings from Bank Mergers?" *Economic Review*, Federal Reserve Bank of Atlanta, March/April 1992, pp. 17–28.

Stevens, E. J., "Required Clearing Balances," *Economic Review*, Federal Reserve Bank of Cleveland, No. 4, 1993, pp. 2–14.

Tan, Chwee Huat, *Financial Markets and Institutions in Singapore*, 6th Edition, Singapore University Press, Singapore, 1989.

World Financial Markets, Morgan Guaranty Trust Company of New York, No. 5, September 1988.

CHAPTER 4

Banks and Other Deposit-taking Financial Institutions

ARE BANKS SPECIAL? Commercial banks, that is? Some economists believe they are while others disagree (see Becketti and Morris, 1992; Fama, 1985; Keeley and Furlong, 1986). Banks are held by some to be very special because, unlike other financial institutions, they play a role in the creation of a country's money supply. Others feel banks are not special because they do not create government currency. Therefore, creating bank deposit money is irrelevant because many other financial institutions create credit instruments similar to deposits. So, what is special about a bank?

All economists do agree that governments make banks special by granting them special privileges and often requiring legal reserves. As discussed in the next chapter, the privilege of creating money is valuable. Perhaps banks are special only because government makes them special. Of course, one could also say that people insist that governments make banks special. Thus banks are special because people make them so.

However, special privileges given to banks induce other institutions to try to act like banks, and many competitors have effectively entered the business of banking over the past 20 years or so. Essentially, those who think banks are special will justify regulating them and also justify preventing others from offering banking services. Those who think banks are not special do not believe in regulating them so much, and think other institutions should be allowed to act as bankers if they want.

History and Introduction

After the collapse of the stock market in October 1929, the U.S., and the world at large, started down the road to depression. As the economy faltered, banks began to fail. By the winter of 1932–33 hundreds of banks were failing each month and Franklin D. Roosevelt declared a countrywide Bank Holiday when he took office in March 1933. Banks were closed for several days while emergency legislation was passed by Congress.

By the summer of 1933 Congress had passed The Banking Act of 1933, called the Glass-Steagall Act. It was followed by The Banking Act of 1935. This legislation set the tone for the development of banks and other financial institutions for several decades. Specifically, it separated the business of commercial banking from the business of investment banking. Congress believed that commercial banks should not involve themselves in the stock market as it was too speculative an activity contravening the banks' duty not to take risks with depositors' money.

The act also prohibited commercial banks from paying interest on checking accounts. This law presumably protected banks from "cut-throat" competition, that is, under this law, large wealthy banks would be unable to raise interest paid to depositors and attract depositors away from smaller weaker banks, thereby forcing them into bankruptcy.

Investment banks were told that if they wanted to manage speculative investments they were free to do so. But they had to use their own capital and not the capital of depositors. So investment banks could not solicit deposits.

Basic securities laws—establishing the Securities and Exchange Commission (see Securities and Exchange Act of 1939) to regulate the securities markets, and giving the Federal Reserve powers to require margins for anyone borrowing funds to finance the purchase of securities—are other by-products of the Great Depression. In addition, a program of deposit insurance was established.

A variety of savings and loan associations, both state and federal, and a set of mutual savings banks that were authorized to operate in 17 states retained their status as "thrift" institutions. They accepted savings deposits (or passbook share accounts) and offered mortgage loans on homes. Their business was specialized and they were typically run by a board of trustees and were not taxed as heavily as profit-making corporations. They paid interest to depositors or dividends to shareholders.

Interest rates remained relatively low throughout the 1930s and even through the war period of 1940–45. It was not until 1960 that the Treasury began to pay as much as 5 per cent interest on its notes. Interest rates began to rise above these levels with the onset of the Vietnam War in 1965, and continued to rise through 1980. With a tight money supply and a recession forced upon the economy by the Federal Reserve under the Chairman, Paul A. Volcker, interest rates and inflation rates finally declined.

High Interest Rates and Competition. During the period of rising interest rates, competition heated up between the various types of deposit-taking financial institutions. Slowly, over several years, the lines separating the various kinds of financial institutions have become blurred. Competition has led each type of institution to move into areas of business activity that were formerly the preserve of others. Competition has led to the deregulation of the activities of financial institutions.

In the 1970s banks became impatient while waiting for depositors to provide them with funds and began issuing negotiable certificates of deposit. By introducing the legal arrangements necessary to make these CDs negotiable (transferable by signature just like checking deposits) banks were able to establish a secondary market in certificates of deposit. This meant that, if a bank were short of funds, it could simply sell some of its own CDs in the market.

Under Regulation Q in the late 1970s banks were permitted to pay savings depositors 5 per cent while the equivalent regulation for thrifts permitted them to pay 5½ per cent. Banks argued that thrifts had too much of an advantage with a ½ per cent spread above banks and thus attracted depositors away from banks. Thrifts countered that banks were able to offer checking accounts while thrifts could offer only savings accounts. Each said that competition was unfair and asked for a "level playing field."

Regulations have strange effects. Thrifts argued that they needed ½ per cent spread to keep customers. Thus, they seemed to be asking regulators to hold their expenses of doing business high. They would have liked to be free of regulations that limited the interest they could pay depositors so they could raise it and attract savings deposits away from banks.

In the meantime, banks were expanding into real estate lending and consumer lending. Banks also set up shops to handle mergers and acquisitions (formerly activities of investment banks) and expanded into the credit card business. Under the Bank Holding Company Act of 1956 and amendments in 1966 and 1970, they set up holding companies under which a bank could be owned by its holding company and the holding company could own other banks and engage in other business that was "related" to banking.

Under the 1970 amendment the Federal Reserve was called upon by Congress to regulate bank holding companies and to require all holding companies to register with the Federal Reserve. In general, the Federal Reserve has kept bank activities under restraint. Banks sell traveler's checks but have been denied the ability to operate travel agencies. They are also denied the right to operate armored car services. They can underwrite insurance that covers credit, but not life or casualty insurance. They are permitted to sell insurance in small towns with less than 5,000 population. Otherwise, they are generally not permitted to sell insurance. This restraint may soon be lifted.

NOW Accounts, ATS Accounts and Money Market Mutual Funds

New England refers to the northeastern section of the U.S. comprising the states of Maine, Vermont, New Hampshire, Massachusetts, Connecticut, and Rhode Island. In 1972 these states passed laws that permitted state-chartered mutual savings banks and savings and loan associations to issue Negotiable Orders of Withdrawal—a unique innovation. As a practical matter Negotiable Orders of Withdrawal permitted these thrifts to offer checking accounts without calling them demand deposits.

When writing a check on a demand deposit account one notices that the face of the check reads, "Pay to the order of ..." This is an order, written by the owner of the bank account, addressed to the bank and telling the bank to pay the person to whom the check is made out a specified number of dollars. A thrift institution could also respond to such an order if it gave a book of checks to a depositor. The depositor could order the thrift to pay someone else. But the problem was that the other person would have to take the check back to the office of the thrift on which the check was drawn. The ownership of the deposit could not be transferred to someone else by signing the check on its back. That is, it was not "negotiable." Therefore, it could not pass through a check clearing house where ownership could be transferred through the several steps involved in clearing. Thus, as a check, an order to pay without negotiability is relatively useless. The big breakthrough in allowing checks to be written against savings accounts in thrift institutions was the acquisition of the legal right to make those checks negotiable.

Negotiable orders of withdrawal, NOW accounts, effectively gave customers interest on a demand deposit in direct violation of the provisions of the Glass-Steagall Act. In response Congress passed legislation in 1976 allowing this "violation" to take place in New England and New York, but only there. Banks brought suit against the thrifts in federal court claiming that NOW accounts violated the law!

But banks also decided that they had better compete or the thrifts would take away their customers. So they began offering *Automatic Transfer System* accounts. Under the ATS program a depositor in a bank would own both a demand deposit account and a savings account. He could deposit a paycheck in the savings account and earn interest on its daily balance. However, he could write a check against the demand deposit account, which may have no funds in it, and the bank would agree to, automatically, upon receipt of the check, transfer funds from the savings account into the demand deposit account in order to cover the payment. Effectively, through the offering of ATS accounts banks were paying interest on checking accounts in direct violation of the provisions of the Glass-Steagall Act.

So, the thrift institutions filed suit in federal court claiming that the banks were violating the law by issuing ATS accounts!

Money Market Mutual Funds. Meanwhile, the investment banking community was not just watching its competitors. Instead, it was busy creating financial "products" that would compete for the savings flowing into banks and thrifts.

Money market mutual funds (MMMFs) are short-term investment pools, or large pools of funds made up of the individual contributions of many people and invested in highly liquid securities with very short time period maturities. The pools of funds are managed by investment banks. Interest earned on the funds is, for the most part, passed on to individual fund holders.

A variety of factors make such pools of funds attractive. When they first became popular in the 1970s, short-term interest rates were very high and they offered a return much higher than that obtainable at a bank. The pools of funds are invested in Treasury bills, commercial paper, banker's acceptances and bank certificates of deposit. These securities are not so readily available to small investors. For example, the smallest denomination of a Treasury bill is $10,000, the usual size of a negotiable bank CD is $100,000. Commercial paper is usually traded among underwriters and specialists.

But what made these funds so special and attractive was the alternative method that they offered to someone who wanted to withdraw funds. An investor could withdraw funds by writing a check on a bank account owned by the MMMF. The mutual funds limited the extent to which checks could be written. Sometimes they preprinted the checks in amounts of $500, so that $500 was the minimum size that the holder could write. Also, sometimes the funds limited the number of checks that could be written each month. The idea was that the MMMFs did not want to become involved in providing a direct substitute for a checking account in a bank.

Nevertheless, if anyone had a bill to pay, say a mortgage payment, the holder could write a $500 check and send it in to the mortgage company. Once again, de facto, receiving interest payments from a pool of funds and making such a payment by check on that pool of funds is a violation of the Glass-Steagall prohibition of the payment of interest on demand deposit accounts. MMMFs, just like the thrifts, were moving to compete with banks for depositors' funds.

Commercial Firms in the Banking Business. The intense competition for depositor funds in a period of high interest rates also led commercial firms, such as the department store Sears, to enter the banking business. Sears bought a real estate brokerage firm and a California thrift institution. It runs an insurance company. It has a significant presence in foreign countries, not as a department store, but as a financial institution. Similarly, American Express, which merged with a brokerage firm, runs a credit card company but operates as a bank overseas.

Meanwhile, commercial banks began huge leasing operations through which they bought plants, ships, docks, planes, and so forth, and leased them back to operators under agreements that kept the banks within the law that prohibits them from entering commercial enterprises.

As often as not, the law restricting the activities of banks in other areas of business, and restricting the activities of other firms in the business of banking, can be circumvented by lawyers and accountants hired to find loopholes. Lawyers can find new kinds of contractual arrangements to adjust "ownership" to mean what they want it to mean, and accountants can invent new accounting names and procedures to add legitimate disclosure to an arrangement. Then, if the new process successfully grows as a part of a business, the consuming public suddenly has a political interest in its success. So if a court challenge occurs, there will be a tendency for the successful new enterprise to withstand the attempt to close it out.

The Court's Reaction

In the spring of 1979 a federal judge ruled that both commercial banks and thrifts should *stop* violating the provisions of the Glass-Steagall Act against offering interest on checking accounts! The judge issued an injunction or order to the banks and thrifts, directing them to refrain from engaging in such violations of the Glass-Steagall Act. Most, if not all, injunctions, when they are issued by federal judges, require that the affected party refrain from engaging in a particular act *immediately*, or be found in contempt of court. What was different about this injunction was that the judge ruled that the order would take effect only eight months later, in January 1980!

The reason for the delay was that it was common knowledge that Congressional committees in both the House and the Senate were holding hearings to decide what kind of legislation would be appropriate for the restructuring of the competitive environment for banking as an industry. It was anticipated that some comprehensive legislation would be forthcoming by the end of the year. Thus, the judge's ruling essentially told Congress to get the legislation passed or all the banks and the thrifts would be in big trouble with the judge if they did not stop offering NOW and ATS accounts. January passed. The banks kept right on doing what they were doing. But, sure enough, in March, President Carter signed into law the *Depository Institutions Deregulation and Monetary Control Act* of 1980. This act contained the most comprehensive legislation affecting banking since the Glass-Steagall Act in the early 1930s.

As noted in the preceding chapter, the name of the act can be divided in two. The part of the act that deregulated institutions provided for two principal changes. First, it provided for the phasing out of all kinds of Regulation Q rules by 1986. It also abolished all state usury laws on many types of loans, although it did leave open the possibility that states might reimpose these laws if certain approval requirements were met later on. So, the Act deregulated the setting of interest rate ceilings of most types, but it did not repeal the prohibition of payment of interest on demand deposits! The second principal change was that it permitted any bank and any thrift in the country to issue NOW accounts and it continued to let banks offer ATS accounts. Similar privileges were granted to credit unions. Thus, banks and thrifts had their hands untied in the payment of interest and in the offering of accounts. This was referred to as a *deregulation* measure for depository institutions, and it was thought to provide the competing depository institutions with a "level playing field."

However, the Monetary Control Act, which was a portion of the overall legislation, effected changes in the opposite direction. It added approximately 10,000 state-chartered banks, 6,000 thrifts, and 25,000 credit unions to the cluster of depository institutions already subject to the Fed's reserve requirements. Thus, it deregulated interest rates, but brought over 40,000 institutions under the umbrella of reserve requirements.

At least Congress did not identify this Act as legislation for the protection of depositors. Instead Congress acknowledged that the Act constituted legislation for monetary control. The point is that reserve requirements really do not offer protection to depositors who want to withdraw funds, as was noted in the last chapter. By imposing a legal reserve requirement, the Federal Reserve can limit the extent to which banks can create deposit money.

Thus, although the federal government took steps to deregulate the industry, it did not want to leave banks and thrifts free to create deposit money without control. So if thrifts were to be involved in offering transactions accounts, Congress ruled that they should also participate in the system of required reserves that gives the Federal Reserve significant power to control the extent of money creation.

It was the Monetary Control Act, first mentioned in Chapter 3, that set reserves at 3 per cent for the first $25 million of reservable liabilities and 12 per cent for those reserves above $25 million with provisions to adjust the $25 million figure each year to grow with the overall volume of liabilities.

One other significant aspect of the Monetary Control Act deserves mention. Consistent with earlier practice, Congress gave the Federal Reserve the authority to change the 12 per cent number within a range. The Fed could lower the requirement to 8 per cent, or it could raise it to 14 per cent. (The ratio was lowered to 10 per cent in 1990.) And, it could raise it a further 5 per cent to a total of 19 per cent all together, *provided that the Federal Reserve pay interest on bank deposits with the Fed to the extent that those deposits exceeded 14 per cent.*

Congress added this provision to the Act in response to arguments put forward by the banks reasoning that if banks had to pay interest to all of their customers, the Federal Reserve should pay interest to all the banks on all the deposits that the banks have to maintain with the Federal Reserve. The subject of interest on reserves will be discussed again in the following chapter.

What Happened to Money Market Mutual Funds? MMMFs were not included in the Monetary Control Act. They were not brought under the reserve requirement umbrella along with the other institutions. MMMFs, however, were clearly in competition with banks as long as they permitted their investors to withdraw funds by check. The banks again charged that the playing field was not level, and Congress came to the rescue.

The Depository Institutions Act of 1982, or Garn-St Germain Act. This act permitted small institutions to operate without having to hold reserves if their deposit liabilities were less than $2 million, and this amount was subject to adjustment upward each year as described in Chapter 3.

But the second, and most important, part of the act was that it permitted banks to set up *money market deposit accounts* (MMDs). The purpose of this provision was to level the playing field. MMDs for banks were set up on almost the same basis that MMMFs operated. Writing checks was limited to three per month and additional withdrawals at the bank were limited to another three per month. Funds deposited in MMD accounts were to be invested in various money market securities, and interest earnings were to be passed through to depositors on a pro-rata basis. About the only difference between MMMFs and MMDs is that MMDs at banks carry deposit insurance coverage of up to $100,000 while there is no similar insurance coverage for MMMF accounts.

Third, the act also increased the deposit insurance coverage for banks and for thrifts from $40,000 to $100,000. With the widespread failure of thrifts and banks in the 1990s, insurance funds have failed and Congress has had to appropriate additional funds to meet these insurance obligations. Critics contend that the $100,000 coverage ceiling imposed by Congress was too high and resulted in too great an exposure for the insurance funds.

Thus, in 1982 Congress responded to the banks' complaints, not by changing the law to bring MMMFs under the reserve umbrella, but by allowing banks along with anyone else to engage in money-creating activities, as long as competition prevails. Again, Congress accommodated the commercial and investment banks just as it had accommodated the banks and thrifts in the earlier 1980 legislation. In a democracy there is a tendency for laws to accommodate change if change is viewed as good.

What Happened to Glass-Steagall Restrictions? Nothing. The law that prohibits the payment of interest on demand deposits is still on the books. It seems that it is easier to change a law than it is to repeal a law. Life would be a lot simpler for everyone if Congress had simply repealed the prohibition. Now what we have is a confusing set of names for several types of checking or transactions accounts that banks and thrifts offer in place of what used to be called demand deposits. What's in a name? It depends on what attorneys, accountants, and legislators say is in a name.

One class of bank depositor still gains no interest on its demand deposits—small businesses. The accounts labeled NOW, ATS, and MMD are, legally, limited to personal accounts and cannot be used for business accounts. Thus, a small corporation, for example, with a demand deposit at a bank cannot be paid interest. Of course, a small business can be managed out of an individual's account at the bank. No one would ever bother to check whether the account is truly an individual's account or not. For its part, a corporation must show that it is a corporation on its stationery and checks, so it cannot get around the Glass-Steagall restrictions through the use of an individual's account. Large corporations, however, can deal in repurchase contracts, as we will see in following chapters, and effectively escape Glass-Steagall restrictions.

Money Creation

Nearly every comprehensive textbook on the principles of economics contains a description of the way banks create money. Therefore, the exposition here is brief and focused on certain issues regarding the creation of money.

When a banker agrees to lend funds to a customer, the banker simply enters the amount of the loan into the customer's demand deposit account. Thus, bank deposit liabilities increase. At the same time the banker also has the customer sign a note with the terms of the loan written on it and enters the loan on the bank's books as an interest-earning asset. Both demand deposit liabilities and loan assets increase by the same amount. Since the customer can write checks against the new demand deposit, demand deposit money has been increased.

However, even today some bankers protest that they do not create money. They claim that all they do is re-lend money that depositors place on deposit with them. The bank manager has a point because the bank needs to have some excess cash or other reserves on hand if the loan is made. The reason is that customers almost never borrow money unless they want to spend it on something. They want money to use to discharge a debt of one sort or another. So the banker who makes a loan must be prepared to have the borrower either withdraw cash, or spend the money by writing a check. The person who receives payment by check may deposit the check in a different bank and when the check clears the lending bank's reserves will decrease.

Thus, when making loans, banks must be prepared to have reserves drawn down, so they usually make loans only to the extent that they have excess reserves. An individual bank acquires excess reserves when depositors bring in cash, or checks drawn on other banks, for deposit. So, the individual bank needs to acquire funds from depositors in order to expand its own loans. It is perfectly appropriate, therefore, for an individual bank to view its ability to make loans as dependent upon the extent to which other people deposit funds with the bank.

None of this, however, negates the fact that banks create deposit money in the process of making loans. The question of greater interest is whether the newly created deposit money represents a net addition to the supply of money in circulation in the economy as a whole. The answer to this question depends upon the reserve position of banks.

In the previous chapter there was a lengthy discussion of bank reserve requirements. If a bank must maintain legal reserves then it is unlikely to make a loan unless it has reserves in excess of the legally required amount. But even if there is no legal reserve requirement, banks will voluntarily hold some cash reserves to ensure that they can meet any likely demand for withdrawals. Thus, in a *fractional reserve* banking system, the fraction of reserves to deposits held by the banking system, whether legally required or voluntarily held, will limit the overall extent of deposit creation by the banks in the system.

Explaining Money Creation by Banks. There are two accounting approaches that can be used to explain the creation of money by banks. These approaches use sample balance sheets, often called "T Accounts" because they resemble the t-accounts of the accounting profession. As expected, the two approaches lead to the same conclusion.

Under a legally required reserve ratio, the limit to an expansion of money on the basis of an increase in the volume of reserves is principally determined by the required reserve ratio. Thus, as mentioned in Chapter 3, when r is the required reserve ratio, R is total reserves, and D is deposits, then $R = rD$. Thus, the maximum volume of deposits is:

$$D = (1/r)R$$

If $r = 0.12$, $D = 8.33R$. So, if the reserve ratio is 12 per cent, then an expansion of R by \$100 will lead to an eightfold increase in deposits to \$833. It is useful to think of a deposit multiplier of $1/r = 8.33$ in this example.

As we will learn in Chapter 6, this deposit multiplier is greatly exaggerated because of certain leakages. These are examined in Chapter 6 under the topics relating to the "monetary base."

Let us look at a simple example. Assume Mr. Jones makes a *primary deposit* in a bank of $100 (item 1). The bank now has cash of $100 (item 2). Then the bank lends $88 to a borrower by giving him or her a deposit (item 3) while the bank records the loan (item 4). If the borrower writes a check for $88 and it is either used to withdraw cash or is deposited in a different bank, the first bank loses $88 in reserves (item 5) and the deposit that the bank created for the borrower is down by $88 (item 6). However, it has $12 left in cash to cover the new deposit, or 12 per cent.

Assets		1st Bank	Liabilities	
Cash	+ $100 (2)		Deposit	+ $100 (1)
	− 88 (5)			
Loans	+ $ 88 (4)		Deposit	+ $ 88 (3)
				− 88 (6)

Now assume that the second bank receives the deposit of $88. We can call this a *derivative* deposit. This second bank has similar entries (items 7 through 10) as shown. We have simply left out the two steps shown as items (3) and (6) above because they cancel each other out. After all, a borrower will spend the money he or she borrows. The second bank has kept $11 in cash reserves. (The loan amount should be $77.44 if the reserve requirement is 12 per cent, but the number has been rounded to keep the presentation simple.)

Assets		2nd Bank	Liabilities	
Cash	+ $ 88 (8)		Deposit	+ $ 88 (7)
	− 77 (9)			
Loan	+ $ 77 (10)			

With the process now started we can imagine the rest, as a $66 loan is made to a third bank, and so forth. The result of a long series of loans will be that the banking system as a whole will keep all of the primary deposit of $100 in cash reserves spread out among many banks. And, the total volume of deposit liabilities in the set of all banks will equal $100 + $88 + $77... = $800 if we round off the odd dollars.

When the banking system has just exactly the right amount of reserves to meet its reserve requirements, we say that *the banking system is fully loaned.* That is, the system as a whole has no excess reserves. In this case one bank can expand its lending only if some funds are transferred either from other banks or from currency that is taken out of circulation and deposited with a bank. In this sense a bank only "lends out funds that depositors have lent to us." But, banks have created $800 of deposit money nevertheless.

The second approach often used to explain money creation by banks is simply to construct a composite balance sheet of all the banks in the system like the one examined in Chapter 3. Pooling all of the accounts of all of the banks is like treating the economy as if it had only one bank. The accounts would look as if banks one and two, and so forth, in our example were all *the same* bank. Thus, the initial borrowing of $88 would be placed back in the same bank, and so would the $77, and all the rest of the loans. The entire $100 primary deposit would be held as reserves, and the entire amount of loans and deposits would be $800 including the primary deposit of $100.

The next big question to ask is, where do primary deposits come from? In Chapter 6 this question will be answered. We will find that there are many sources of primary deposits, but one principal source is Federal Reserve purchases. For now let us look at the question of the role played in creating money by various thrift institutions. Such institutions often make loans but do not often create a deposit for the borrower like banks do, so some observers question whether or not they create money. They do create money just like banks do, and the following balance sheet items may help explain why.

Money Creation by Thrifts and Money Market Mutual Funds

Before the 1980s when thrifts could not offer *checkable* accounts, professors would point out that banks could create money and thrifts could not. In the "T accounts" above, the first bank made a loan and created deposits, simultaneously. The second bank could have represented a thrift that received deposits but only lent out cash. And the deposit in the second bank would have been a savings account and not spendable money. So we would say that the thrift had to attract deposits and would re-lend the funds, but that its actions did not create any new money. So, do thrifts create money or not?

The proposition to be explained is that thrifts, such as savings and loan associations (S & Ls), now *create money* on the basis of a fraction of reserves, legally required, just as banks do. This remains true even if thrifts still lend out cash when making loans. Money includes all checkable deposit accounts.

The Treasury pays a soldier with newly issued greenbacks. The soldier returns home and deposits his $100 in an S & L (item 1). The S & L has cash (item 2). No money is created since deposits are exchanged for currency. Now the S & L makes a loan (item 3). It pays out cash to the borrower (item 4). (Of course, the loan would not be the full $100 because of some fractional reserve that would be retained in cash, but this detail is ignored here and will be discussed further just below the example.)

	Assets	S & L	Liabilities	
Cash	+ $100 (2) − $100 (4)		Deposit	+ $100 (1)
Loan	+ $100 (3)			

Now the currency in circulation is back up to its previous level. *And*, there is still $100 in the soldier's account that represents $100 of checkable money "created" by the S & L. The money supply, measured by currency in circulation plus checkable deposits, is up by $100.

The net effect is exactly the same as it would have been if the cash had been deposited in a commercial bank and the bank had lent out cash.

But what if a bank did not lend out cash, but only created a deposit? Then, currency in circulation would not return to its earlier level. Instead, the bank's newly created deposit when making its loan merely represents a *replacement* for the currency that had been withdrawn from circulation. Thus, the net effect on the total money supply, currency in circulation plus checking accounts, would be exactly the same whether in cash or by deposit creation.

The conclusion is that *all* financial institutions offering checking accounts—deposit money—are playing a role in the money creation process in a fractional reserve banking system, and it is misleading to emphasize the "creation" of deposits by banks in a narrow sense of giving a borrower a deposit instead of cash or a check on a bank. Offering a loan in the form of a checkable deposit is only a single step in a process. Individual banks must attract primary deposits just as the S & L did in this example in order for *new* money to be created on the basis of fractional reserves.

An alternative process leads to the same conclusion. Begin with a bank creating deposit money (item 1) when making a loan (item 2) to Mr. A.

	Assets	**Bank**	**Liabilities**	
Loan A	+ $100 (2)	Deposits A	+ $100 (1)
			− $100 (6)
		Deposits S & L	+ $100 (5)
			− $100 (10)
		Deposit B	+ $100 (9)

	Assets	**S & L**	**Liabilities**	
Dep./Bank	+ $100 (4)	Deposit A	+ $100 (3)
	− $100 (8)		
Loan B	+ $100 (7)		

Now let Mr. A make a deposit in the S & L with a check on his account at the bank (item 3) which the S & L takes as an asset (item 4). The S & L deposits the check in its account in the bank (item 5) and the bank reduces Mr. A's deposit account (item 6).

Now let the S & L give a mortgage loan of $100 to Ms. B (item 7) by giving Ms. B (or the person from whom Ms. B bought a home) its check on its account in the bank (item 8). Assume Ms. B (or the person to whom the S & L gives the check, say the seller of a home) deposits the check in the bank (item 9) and the bank reduces the S & L's account (item 10).

Now let us review. The $100 deposit originally created by the bank is still outstanding. It has changed hands several times. But *now* the S & L has outstanding checkable deposits, too. Mr. A has a $100 deposit in the S & L *and* Ms. B has $100 in the bank. There are now $200 in deposits outstanding, whereas there had originally been only the $100 the bank "created." The extra $100 was created by the S & L.

What does the term "create" mean? If the S & L did *not* "*create*" the extra $100, then where did it come from? Certainly the bank did *not* "*create*" this extra $100. Too narrow a version of the meaning of "create" gives a misleading impression of the way deposit money is created by a fractional reserve banking system.

This same analysis applies to Money Market Mutual Funds and other depository institutions offering checkable accounts that can be used by their holders to discharge debts.

Money Market Mutual Funds as Creators of Money. Let us assume that a depositor decides to transfer funds from a bank into a money market mutual fund. In the examples above the S & L can be replaced with MMMF. All of the same results apply again. So long as a person can write a check and discharge a debt using a NOW account in an S & L, or using a check drawn on a MMMF, these institutions create part of the money that circulates in an exchange economy.

There is one important difference, however. Under the Monetary Control Act of 1980, all S & Ls must hold reserves with the Federal Reserve. If reserve requirements of 12 per cent had been included in this example, there would have been a limit on the expansion of loans and deposits like that in the preceding example of money creation. But, MMMFs are *not* required to hold reserves. The absence of the requirement that a fractional reserve be held with the Federal Reserve allows MMMFs to create money as they wish.

From a prudential point of view, MMMFs must hold certain types of securities that are outlined in their descriptions and, if someone does not steal the securities, the depositor's (fund holder's) funds are presumably safe from bankruptcy.

But, from the point of view of money control, there may be a problem. And, as we noted above, with the passage of the Garn-St Germain Act in 1982, banks can now also create MMD accounts as they wish. Should MMD and MMMF accounts be treated as money? This question is discussed at some length in the following chapter.

Capital Adequacy Ratios

Like other businesses, banks can raise capital by selling long-term bonds as well as by selling shares and accumulating surplus funds as net worth. The composite balance sheet of commercial banks in the United States presented in Chapter 3 shows that the equity capital accounts that represent net worth, or assets minus liabilities, are approximately 7.9 per cent of assets. Banks are required by regulators to maintain a certain ratio of capital to assets where capital includes equity along with some types of debt. For many years the minimum ratio in the United States was 6 per cent. But this 6 per cent capital standard had several flaws. Principal among the flaws was its failure to distinguish between high-risk and low-risk assets. Second, there were no provisions for the risk attached to off-balance sheet items, such as standby letters of credit that expose banks to risk. Third, capital is defined differently in different countries around the world, which makes international comparisons difficult or impossible.

The Basle Agreement

After discussing the topic for years, in 1987 representatives from 12 countries met in Basle, Switzerland as guests of the Bank of International Settlements to discuss uniform capital adequacy requirement standards for all countries. An 8 per cent minimum risk-weighted capital requirement was recommended at that time. By 1993 all countries that wished to maintain an international banking presence required banks within their jurisdictions to comply with the 8 per cent rule. However, each country is unique and each considered the suggested rules and amended them to fit with their individual domestic institutions. The suggestions from Basle were used as guidelines to establish rules for the items to be included as capital and for the items to be included in the variety of asset categories.

The Capital Base. What accounts should represent the base capital of a bank? The new regulations specify two "tiers" for base capital.

Tier I is called core capital. It includes capital stock and surplus that make up equity. It may also include perpetual noncumulative preferred shares. It must make up at least 50 per cent of the total capital base.

Tier II is called supplementary capital. It includes other preferred shares along with some debt if the debt is completely subordinated to the interests of depositors. It also includes so-called "inner reserves."

Banks in the United States and the United Kingdom do not have any "inner reserves" because regulations require full disclosure. But in other places, Hong Kong and Japan for example, banks are not required to disclose all of the reserves that they have accumulated in the past. They do not tell the public how much these reserves are or what they consist of. They can change their reported profit in any year by transferring money to and from inner reserves. Presumably, by keeping secret inner reserves, banks can better sustain an air of confidence among depositors.

Banks that have shares listed on stock exchanges may be required by regulators to disclose inner reserves. In the spring of 1992 the Hongkong and Shanghai Banking Corporation announced its inner reserves because it wanted to have a dual listing of shares in London and Hong Kong, and that it was bidding for the takeover of Midland Bank in Great Britain. Hong Kong law does not require the disclosure, but other jurisdictions do, so it was just a matter of time before the bank would have had to disclose its accounts. In early September 1984, the Hong Kong Monetary Authority, the Securities and Futures Commission, and the Stock Exchange announced that listed banks would have to disclose any transfer to or from inner reserves. The Monetary

Authority began a review of the question of full disclosure of inner reserves in 1995. Since the Hongkong and Shanghai Banking Corporation has to disclose its reserves, it will not resist the proposal to impose the disclosure requirement on its competitors.

Some assets, such as shares of stock in holding companies or subsidiaries, or in other banks, are deducted from total capital in calculating the capital base.

Weighting Risky Assets. Some assets held by banks are more risky than others, so under the Basle agreement each of a bank's assets is subjected to a weighting scheme. It was suggested that there be five categories of assets, with weights applied to each category. The U.S. regulators adopted only four categories.

An Outline of Capital Adequacy Ratio Requirements Using Five Categories*	
Assets	Liabilities and net worth
Risk-weighted asset categories	Capital adequacy accounts Two tiers of base capital
Category Weight in %	

I   0%
Cash, gold, government debt
	Tier I Core capital
	   Common stock
	   Surplus

II 10% Short-term liquid securities	Noncumulative preferred shares

III   20%
Longer-term securities and
high quality loans
	Tier II Supplementary capital
	   Preferred shares
	   Subordinated debt

IV 50% Residential mortgages and mortgage-backed securities	Inner reserves At least 50% of base capital must be Tier I.
V 100% Business and consumer loans	

With a capital adequacy ratio of 8 per cent, at least 4 per cent must be held in Tier I capital accounts while the remaining may be in Tier II.

For example, assume that the bank has total assets of $500 made up of $100 in each of the five categories. The $100 in category I would not require any dollars of capital to back it. The $100 in category II would be weighted at 10 per cent to make up assets of $10 that would require capital. The $100 in category III would be weighted at 20 per cent or $20. The $100 in category IV would add $50, and the $100 in category V would add a full $100. Weighted assets would total $180. Required capital would be 8 per cent of $180 or $14.40. At least half of this, $7.20, would have to be in core capital items. This bank, with $500 in assets, would have to hold only $7.20 in equity capital, or about 1.4 per cent of its total assets. Banks are highly leveraged businesses.

---

*The U.S. adopted four categories.

Category I carries a weight of 0 per cent because it consists of cash and gold bullion and securities issued by governments of developed countries. These are often called risk-free assets.

Category II carries a weight of 10 per cent. Assets in this category consist of nearly risk-free short-term securities.

Category III carries a weight of 20 per cent. Long-term securities and loans to certain other institutions are included here.

Category IV carries a weight of 50 per cent. Residential mortgage loans and mortgage-backed securities are in this category.

Category V carries a weight of 100 per cent. Most of the business of commercial banks is represented in this category. It includes consumer loans and loans to private businesses along with the bank's buildings, equipment and real estate. These are considered to be the riskiest of all bank assets.

By classifying all the assets into appropriate categories and applying a weight to the amount in each, a total amount is calculated. The requirement is that base capital be at least 8 per cent of this total.

Off-Balance Sheet Items. These items are contingent liabilities of banks and do not appear in the balance sheet but in footnotes to the balance sheet. The first step in requiring capital behind these is to convert them to an equivalent of some risky asset already on the balance sheet. This requires the establishment of conversion factors so that an equivalence with other assets can be established and capital required accordingly. U.S. banking agencies had used such procedures in their bank examinations.

U.S. banking regulators know how to create a lot of new work for accountants, attorneys, and other regulators. The specifics of the implementation in various countries will vary somewhat because accounting standards and practices vary.

Concerns over the New Capital Adequacy Ratios (CARs). First, why are inner reserves part of Tier II capital when they are kept secret?

Second, what conversion factors should be given to off-balance sheet items such as lines of credit and banker's acceptances outstanding?

Third, the new CAR standards address the question of *credit risk*, that is, the risk that borrowers will default on their bank loans and bank assets will lose value or become worthless and have to be written off as bad debts. This is the most damaging type of risk that banks face, and the type of risk that most often leads to bankruptcy. However, another very important type of risk for financial institutions is *interest rate risk*. If interest rates rise, the market price of many bank assets declines. In 1993 the Federal Accounting Standards Board issued rules that require banks to mark-to-market the values of securities (Government Securities, for example) that banks hold instead of treating their value at cost. However, bank loans to businesses are not traded in markets so there is no market-based dollar values against which a bank can value its portfolio of business loans in the wake of changes in interest rates. Besides the interest rate risk that arises from fluctuations in the *level* of interest rates, there is another kind of interest rate risk related to the pattern of interest rates on short- and long-term maturities. Bank liabilities to depositors are very short-term. Bank loans have a longer term. If short-term interest rates rise above long-term rates, as happens when the Federal Reserve engages in tight monetary policy, the banks face a high cost of borrowing funds from depositors. This high cost is not offset by higher interest returns on outstanding assets. Not only that, but higher interest rates mean a decline in the market value of existing securities that banks hold. Therefore, banks are likely to be faced with higher costs and capital losses at the same time. The reverse is also true. As interest rates fall, the rates banks pay depositors fall, too, so bank costs decline. At the same time the value of bank securities rises and banks profit from capital gains and the low cost of funds. This happened in 1992 as banks reported high profits (see Levonian, 1994b).

The new capital adequacy rules concern credit risk and do not address the question of interest rate risk. However, the Federal Deposit Insurance Corporation Improvement (FDICI) Act of 1991 requires that regulators include some allowance for interest rate risk within the context of capital adequacy requirements. Initial proposals include evaluating the maturity, or duration, of bank assets and liabilities. The closer the match between the duration of assets and liabilities, the less is the interest rate risk bank managers face. Thus, the proposals for meeting the directive of the FDICI Act require that banks report on measures of maturity and then tie these in with existing capital adequacy requirements. The new regulatory measures are due to be in place by the end of 1993.

Fourth, many banks, and all large banks, are actively engaged in foreign exchange markets. Again, the new rules do not address the risk questions that arise from foreign exchange trading.

Fifth, the weights are arbitrary and will be subject to frequent changes. It is a certainty that over the years the banking industry will develop methods to change what would have been a normal loan to a business for maintaining inventory, into a residential real estate loan in order to have it qualify for the lower category. It would then release some capital for investment elsewhere while still meeting the letter of the law. For example, consider a line of credit that is backed by a second mortgage on a home. The interest rate paid on any loan extension is lower than it would be on any usual consumer loan, and there is some tax exemption on the interest paid. Given the inventiveness of accountants and attorneys, very few loans will remain in Category V with a weight of 100 per cent after several years of adjustments are arranged. Also, if there are only five categories now, why should there not be ten in a few years?

Sixth, governments have a way of protecting themselves from legislation that might impinge on their privileges. Notice that in the case of CAR there is a zero per cent weight placed on bank holdings of government securities. This is to ensure that there is a continuous demand for securities issued by governments and that interest rates will remain low for government as a borrower.

Seventh, when these rules took full effect in January 1993, the banks of the country had, for many months, been rearranging their portfolio of assets by discarding business loans and acquiring more government securities. This was in 1991–92 when the U.S.

economy was in a recession and banks were being asked to expand their loans to businesses—not cut back on them! Thus, the CAR regulations made holding government securities more desirable for banks and made business loans less desirable so that the net effect was to make the recovery from the recession more sluggish and hesitant than it otherwise might have been (see Breeden and Isaac, 1992).

Will all the burden of new Basle requirements make banks a safer place to keep your money? Will the benefits exceed the costs? Is there a less expensive way to keep bankers in line and protect depositors?

A Bleak Outlook for Commercial Banks

From the above description of the evolution of legal arrangements regulating financial institutions, it is clear that institutions other than banks are now big players in what used to be the sole preserve of the commercial banking industry. Part of the reason for this change is that the banking industry no longer provides as many convenient services as it once did.

Check Cashing. There are now about 5,000 check cashing stores in the U.S. These stores charge fees for cashing checks, providing for money transfers, writing money orders, offering private postal boxes, and paying phone bills (see Marino, 1993). The national average is about 5,000 persons per bank branch in the U.S. But in some areas there are over 20,000 per branch. As savings and loan institutions have failed and merged, and as banks have consolidated operations, many branches have been closed. The market for services has opened where banks used to operate.

As could be expected, bills have been introduced in Congress to license these outlets, set maximum fees for cashing checks at $0.50 or 0.85 per cent of the check amount, and require that these outlets cash government checks. Thus, Congress wants to restrict free-market banking activities. At the same time other bills have been introduced to require banks to offer low-cost checking account and government check-cashing services.

Electronic data transmission services offered by AT&T, British Telecom, IBM, and others, are now offered by about 700 banks. These services complement electronic payments that replace checks. Banks are still special. Government protects them from competition and at the same time tells them what to do (see Tyson, 1994).

Regulation. From 1970 to 1990 the share of commercial bank assets fell from 40 per cent to 25 per cent of all financial assets in the U.S. Eugene Ludwig, Comptroller of the Currency, reportedly said, "Government has layered on banking a mountain of regulations that are often duplicative, superfluous or otherwise wasteful" (see Bacon, 1993). At the same time, deregulation efforts have let other institutions compete with banks for basic depositor business. In the case of Money Market Mutual Funds, they engage in money-creating activities as banks do, but are not regulated by the Federal Reserve. The overall result is a weakened commercial banking sector. Some economists believe that banks should be deregulated so they can act more like securities firms, while others believe those securities firms that now act like banks should be regulated and made subject to the same reserve requirements, deposit insurance requirements, and capital adequacy standards that banks must meet.

In July 1993 a National Commission reported on its study of the Savings and Loan wave of bankruptcies in the 1980s. It recommended many sweeping changes in the way in which financial institutions are regulated. Along with death and taxes, one more thing is certain—change in regulations over financial institutions and markets! Regulation is the subject of Chapter 15.

Technology and Risk. Record keeping by computer has made it possible to do away with all the handwritten and "hands-on" dealing with customers of banks. You do not need to know your banker any more, all you need is a telephone with appropriate computer access. If the interpersonal relations have largely gone out of the banking business, why not substitute a mutual fund for your banker? The only reason is that you may wish to write lots of checks and/or withdraw small amounts.

Technology makes it easy for an individual investor to make changes in a portfolio of assets and thus to handle his own risk position. Banks and thrifts recommend variable rate mortgages and these transfer interest rate risk to the borrower, whereas under fixed rate loans the bank or thrift used to bear all the risk. Mortgage markets are discussed in Chapter 10.

Banks in Hong Kong, Korea, Singapore and Taiwan

In Hong Kong the commercial and merchant banking system continues to be strong and predominate. Saving flows go to properties with the use of mortgages from banks. Mutual Funds called Unit Trusts thrive. And banks handle foreign investments routinely since there is no constraint on the free flow of foreign exchange.

The other three Asian Tigers each have a considerable history of intervention in financial markets to suit national objectives. Korea has followed in the footsteps of Japan. Its Ministry of Finance played a powerful role in directing the lending by banks to selected industries at subsidized interest rates as part of a National Industrial Policy. Both Japan and Korea have taken important measures to liberalize their banking sectors. In Taiwan, as noted in Chapter 3, the government actually owned 12 of the country's 16 commercial banks until 1993 when the solution was to charter more private banks. Again, the government's direct role in the banking industry there has been in line with tradition.

Japan, Korea, Singapore, and Taiwan have large and important *postal savings systems*. These support their respective governments by attracting funds from the saving public. For example, in Singapore at least half of the assets of the system must be held in the form of government securities. In Japan the system funnels its funds through the Ministry of Finance.

In Singapore the POSBank (Post Office Savings Bank) focuses on small accounts and is not permitted to hold large business deposits. It even pays a lower interest on larger deposits than it pays on small deposits. It maintains ATM machines for customer convenience. Customers can purchase shares on the Singapore Stock Exchange directly through their POSBank account.

In Hong Kong, there is no unique set of thrift institutions nor a postal savings system. Hong Kong's powerful banks have not permitted other types of institutions to evolve.

The Giro System of Money Transfer

The giro system is a system of paying bills in which an institution, such as a postal service, will take an order (similar to a money order that can be purchased at U.S. post offices) designated as a payment to someone else. For example, if you purchase something at a store and take it home, then you have an obligation to pay the seller. You go to the post office and ask that funds be transferred from your account to the seller's account. The post office does this for you and sends you a receipt to indicate that your debt has been discharged.

The giro system is contrasted with a checking account system. In the case of the use of a checking account you would buy something and write out an order for your bank to pay the seller. Then, the seller will take the check to the bank to collect his payment. See Figure 4–1.

Figure 4–1

(a) Checking Payments System

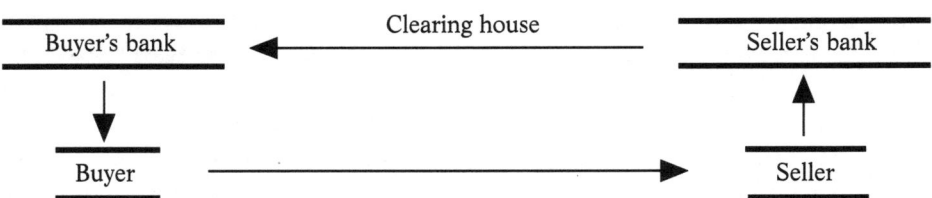

Payment order to bank is written by buyer and given to seller. Arrows indicate the path of the check. It may go through a clearing house or it may simply be cleared between buyer's and seller's bank.

(b) Giro Payments System

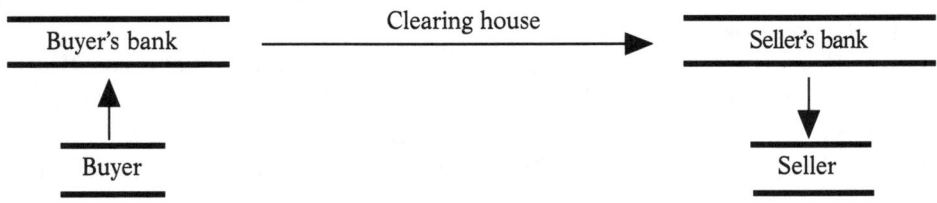

Payment order to bank is given directly to bank. It may be cleared through a clearing house, or be exchanged by the two banks directly. Then the seller receives payment.

The final result of the two systems is the same. However, in the case of the checks, the seller is uncertain about whether you have sufficient funds in your account. In the case of a giro system, the seller is uncertain about whether you can be trusted to instruct the post office to transfer the funds. Thus, checks are most often used for payments for such utility items as gas, electric, water, telephone, and so forth. In these cases the seller knows its customer, or where to find him. Cash is used where the seller does not know the customer.

Giro systems are used between businesses in many European countries. They are used by individuals to pay bills through the postal systems of Japan and the Asian Tigers. Giro services are offered by commercial banks in Uzbekistan, for example, a community in which checking exists but is rarely used. Giro transfers are used to discharge debt, along with cash.

In the U.S. some bank deposit accounts allow a customer to pay utility bills by telephone. Also, some grocery stores now have point-of-sale machines that take bank cards and let the customer tell the bank to pay funds into the store's account. These systems are funds-transfer giro systems.

Thus, one way or another, institutions will evolve to provide the payments services that modern economies require. (For a complete description of payments networks and clearing systems, see Summers, 1994.)

Summary

This chapter contains an outline of major changes in the banking and thrift industries in the 1980s. Commercial banking had been protected by the provisions of the Glass-Steagall Act in the early 1930s, but by 1980 other depository institutions had begun to break down the protective walls and had become significant competitors with banks for the depositor's dollar.

A new competitive structure for the industry was established by the Depository Institutions Deregulation and Monetary Control Act of 1980 along with the Garn-St Germain Act of 1982. Essentially, these acts gave thrift institutions, such as savings banks, savings and loan societies, mutual savings banks, and credit unions, the power to create money.

Money creation occurs in a fractional reserve system of banking when money circulates. Money is created not only by banks and thrift institutions, but by money market mutual funds as well, when they permit holders of funds to write checks against their accounts.

The 1980s were also a period of widespread failures of thrift institutions and banks. These failures led banking regulators to institute a new set of rules regarding the capital that banks must hold—Capital Adequacy Requirements. These requirements include a risk-based weighting scheme that encourages banks to hold fewer risky assets. However, the new system also has its disadvantages. Indeed, making banks avoid risk-taking amounts to taking away one of the principal functions of banks—the provision of risk capital to local businesses.

Other countries rely heavily on giro payments systems, such as those provided by postal savings systems. Under a giro system the buyer submits a payment order to the bank and asks the bank to pay the seller. This system differs from the checking account system under which the buyer gives the seller a check and the seller must seek collection from the bank.

Key Terms and Concepts

Glass-Steagall Act of 1933

Securities and Exchange Commission

Bank Holding Company Act of 1956

Money Market Mutual Funds (MMMFs)

Garn-St Germain Act of 1982

Automatic Transfer System accounts

Derivative deposits

The Basle Agreement

FDIC Improvement Act of 1991

Thrift institutions

Certificate of deposit

Negotiable Order of Withdrawal

Depository Institutions and Monetary
   Control Act of 1980

T accounts

Capital Adequacy Ratio (CAR)

Check cashing stores

Giro system of money transfer

Discussion Questions and Exercises

1. What were the major provisions of the Glass-Steagall Act? Should any or all of its major provisions be repealed by Congress?
2. What are money market mutual funds? What did Congress do when commercial banks complained about competition from MMMFs?
3. Do banks create money? Explain your answer using balance sheet entries.
4. Do thrifts create money? Explain with "T accounts."
5. Compare Money Market Mutual Funds with Money Market Deposit Accounts.
6. What is "cut-throat" competition? Do you believe there should be laws preventing it in a free market economy?
7. Under the capital adequacy rules, of what does the capital base consist?
8. Briefly explain the risk-weighting procedure for assets in the new capital adequacy requirements.
9. List and discuss briefly each of the seven weaknesses of the new capital adequacy requirements mentioned in the text. Can you think of others?
10. Should MMMFs be required to hold reserves against their checkable liabilities? Discuss reasons for and against.
11. What are the functions of a typical postal savings system?
12. Distinguish between a giro payments system and a checking account system.

References

A classic booklet on *Modern Money Mechanics* was first published in 1961 by the Federal Reserve Bank of Chicago and most recently revised in June 1992. It is available for student use and is free of charge.

Other excellent texts contain comprehensive historical information on the evolution of the financial industry. Interested students should examine: David S. Kidwell and Richard L. Peterson, *Financial Institutions, Markets, and Money*, 5th Edition, Dryden Press, Chicago, 1990.

Avery, Robert, and Berger, Allen, "Risk-based Capital and Deposit Insurance Reform," *Journal of Banking and Finance*, Vol. 15, pp. 847–74.

Bacon, Kenneth H., "The End of Banking as We Know It," a series, *Wall Street Journal*, July 7–9, 1993.

Banking Regulators' Report on Capital Standards, Hearing before the Committee on Banking, Housing, and Urban Affairs, United States Senate, 101st Congress, 2nd Session, September 10, 1990.

Becketti, Sean, and Morris, Charles, "Are Bank Loans Still Special?" *Economic Review*, Federal Reserve Bank of Kansas City, 3rd Quarter 1992, pp. 71–84.

Berger, George S., "What Should Banks Really Do?—Comment," *Contemporary Policy Issues*, Vol. 11, October 1993, pp. 71–84.

Breeden, Richard C., and Isaac, William M., "Thank Basle for Credit Crunch," *Wall Street Journal*, November 4, 1992.

Caskey, John P., "Check-cashing Outlets in the U.S. Financial System," *Economic Review*, Federal Reserve Bank of Kansas City, November/December 1991, pp. 53–67.

Clarke, Robert L., "Statement," before the Committee on Banking, Housing, and Urban Affairs, U.S. Senate, in *Banking Regulators' Report on Capital Standards*, pp. 10–18.

Fama, Eugene F., "What's Different about Banks?" *Journal of Monetary Economics*, January 1985, pp. 92–93.

Haubrich, Joseph G., and Wachtel, Paul, "Capital Requirements and Shifts in Commercial Bank Portfolios," *Economic Review*, Federal Reserve Bank of Cleveland, 3rd Quarter, 1993, pp. 2–15.

Holder, Christopher L., "FYI—Competitive Considerations in Bank Mergers and Acquisitions: Economic Theory, Legal Foundations, and the Fed," *Economic Review*, Federal Reserve Bank of Atlanta, January/February 1993, pp. 23–36.

Kane, Edward J., "Incentive Conflict in the International Regulatory Agreement on Risk-based Capital," in S. G. Rhee and R. P. Chang, eds., *Pacific Basin Capital Markets Research*, Vol. 2, Elsevier, Amsterdam, 1991, pp. 3–21.

Keeley, Michael, and Furlong, Frederick, "Are Banks Special?" *Weekly Letter*, Federal Reserve Bank of San Francisco, July 18, 1986.

Keeton, William R., "The New Risk-based Capital Plan for Commercial Banks," *Economic Review*, Federal Reserve Bank of Kansas City, December 1989, pp. 40–60.

Laderman, Elizabeth S., and Pozdena, Randall J., "Interstate Banking and Competition: Evidence from the Behavior of Stock Returns," *Economic Review*, Federal Reserve Bank of San Francisco, Spring 1991, pp. 32–47.

Levonian, Mark E., "Market Risk and Bank Capital," Parts 1 and 2, *Weekly Letter*, Federal Reserve Bank of San Francisco, January 7 and 14, 1994a.

————, "Bank Capital Standards for Foreign Exchange and Other Market Risks," *Economic Review*, Federal Reserve Bank of San Francisco, No. 1, 1994b, pp. 3–18.

Lewis, M. K., and Davis, K. T., *Domestic and International Banking*, MIT Press, Cambridge, MA, 1987.

Marino, Vivian, "Check-cashing Outlets Offer 'Fringe Banking' for Many," *Chico Enterprise Record* (Associated Press), July 21, 1993.

Marriott, Dean, "Statement," before the Subcommittee on General Oversight and Investigations, Committee on Banking, Finance and Urban Affairs, U.S. House of Representatives, in *Risk-based Capital Requirements for Banks and Bank Holding Companies*, April 21, 1988, pp. 50–65.

Newberger, Jonathan A., "Risk-based Capital Standards and Bank Portfolios," *Weekly Letter*, Federal Reserve Bank of San Francisco, January 10, 1992a.

————, "Interest Rate Risk and Bank Capital Standards," *Weekly Letter*, November 6, 1992b.

————, "On the Changing Composition of Bank Portfolios," *Weekly Letter*, March 19, 1993.

Summers, Bruce J., ed., *The Payment System: Design, Management, and Supervision*, International Monetary Fund, Washington, DC, 1994.

Tyson, James L., "Banks Are Getting Squeezed in Lucrative Check-Handling Business," *Christian Science Monitor*, April 29, 1994.

White, Lawrence J., "What Should Banks Really Do?—Reply," *Contemporary Policy Issues*, Vol. 11, October 1993, pp. 111–13.

CHAPTER 5

Money and Seigniorage: Definitions and Measures

SINCE EVERYONE USES money nearly every day, it may seem strange to devote an entire chapter to an explanation of just what money is. Indeed, the role of money flow and the flow of funds were introduced in Chapter 2. Although everyone has a general understanding of money and its function, this chapter is devoted to the refinement of the concept of money.

The chapter begins with a definition of money. On the basis of this definition, money is distinguished from other assets that are highly liquid. After defining money carefully, we take a look at the process of measuring money. Next, we present an analysis of the way governments are able to obtain revenue from their monopoly control of money supplies. This analysis provides a rationale for a great deal of government involvement in money creation and control.

Defining Money

Measuring things is a very important part of scientific endeavor. Before scientists measure something, they need to know precisely what it is that they are measuring. Of course, one can observe something and then give that something a name. In such cases naming and measuring occur simultaneously. But naming is not defining. According to *Webster's New Collegiate Dictionary,* to define means "to mark the limits or boundaries of; to make distinct or fix in outline or character." A definition is an explanation of the meaning of a word.

Definitions are often expressed in terms of functions. For example, an automobile is a four-wheeled motorized vehicle designed to provide transportation. But what about a dune buggy? Is it or is it not an automobile? What about a three-wheeled automobile? The point is an automobile is difficult to define—"to make distinct." Any customs agent can provide thousands of examples of items that are difficult to define precisely.

But money is a subject of great importance to economists as scientists, so its definition needs as much precision as we can muster. However, as is always the case, some imprecision remains.

The Definition of Money. The most precise definition of *money* is that it *is what people in an exchange economy can use to discharge debt.*

While money is used as a medium of exchange, that is, it is used to pay for goods and services, these payments amount to a discharge of debt to the suppliers of goods and services. For example, after you eat in a restaurant, the waiter will give you a bill. A bill is an order to pay the cashier for the debt you have incurred to the restaurant. If you pay with cash the debt is discharged.

What if you pay with a credit card? Have you discharged your debt? The answer is no, you have only transferred the debt that you still owe to the credit card company. You only discharge the debt when you write a check on your bank account and mail it to the credit card company. By this process the company takes ownership of part of your bank deposit, and your debt is finally discharged. Thus, bank deposits are also used to discharge debt and, as such, are part of the money supply along with currency. But credit cards are not money.

However, credit cards substitute for cash in that a person needs to carry less cash if he or she has credit cards. Because credit cards exist, there is less demand for currency than there otherwise would be, but there is also more demand for checking accounts in banks so that payments by check can be made to the credit card companies. Thus, credit cards affect the composition of the demand for money and they may reduce the total amount of money demanded in the form of currency and demand deposits.

Four Functions of Money

Besides serving as a *medium of exchange*, money also serves other functions. For example, it serves as a *store of value*, that is, a person may hold wealth in the form of money. Since most money is not interest-earning, it is not productive to hold much wealth in the form of money. Money is certainly not unique as a store of wealth; gold, gems, bonds, stocks, savings deposits in banks, real estate and other items can also function as stores of wealth. Some of these items may earn interest for their holders.

Others may require expenditure for maintenance, such as storage charges for keeping gold in vaults and repair expenses for the upkeep of real estate.

The monetary unit, such as the dollar in the U.S., Taiwan, Singapore, and Hong Kong, the won in Korea or the yen in Japan, serves as a *unit of account*. These unit values are used by accountants in keeping books. Such units have legal connotations. Settlements of contracts must be made in amounts of money based on the unit of account. Before the United States abandoned the gold standard in 1934, it was common for legal contracts to require payment in gold. Afterwards, laws were passed to eliminate the requirement for gold payment in all outstanding contracts so that settlement could be made in dollars. Gold coins were retired from circulation so that gold could no longer serve directly as a medium of exchange within the country.

As a unit of account, the monetary unit may also serve as a *standard for deferred payment*. The concept of a standard for deferred payment is important in monetary economics. It refers to contracts for future payments. Unlike payment for a meal in a restaurant, many payments are deferred under the terms of a contract to a later date. All bonds, notes, and other securities carrying interest payments involve deferred payments. The unit of currency used as a standard for these payments may not be a very constant standard. The inch is a standard of measurement, but how easy would it be to measure a table if inches varied in length from place to place and from time to time?

The problem of monetary units being used as standards in contracts requiring deferred payments is that inflation reduces the purchasing power of the monetary unit. If the inch became smaller year after year, a carpenter would find it difficult to construct a table to specifications. When the unit of currency fluctuates in value, it is difficult for businesses to make rational financial decisions. That is one very important reason for countries to manage money supplies in a manner that keeps price stability as an achievable goal.

It is often noted that money serves four functions: (a) as a medium of exchange, (b) as a store of value, (c) as a unit of account, and (d) as a standard for deferred payments. But money has one principal function: *it serves to discharge debt*. Its function of discharging debt gives money its distinguishing characteristic.

What people use as money depends upon the circumstances. Gold and silver coins have been around for thousands of years. Cattle, salt, and beads have been used as money. Cigarettes were used as money among war prisoners during World War II. The prevalence of paper money and bank account money is a relatively recent development. It is largely the result of technological advancement in transportation and communication. It is far easier to collect payment in the form of a deposit to a London bank than it is to ship gold around the world.

What people use as money will undoubtedly change over time. But a clear definition of money is needed so that money can be recognized for what it is, whatever its form. Too much money leads to inflation. To prevent inflation, it is important to keep track of the growth of the money supply and not let it grow too rapidly. Authorities need to know exactly what it is that needs to be controlled if they are to do their job.

Money and Gross Domestic Product

Hundreds of articles and books in the literature of economics focus on the relation between money supplies, gross domestic product, and inflation. Correlations of money, measured as currency and checking deposits, with GDP, and with inflation, are not usually very high. That is, fluctuations in the money supply do not usually explain a large proportion of changes in income or inflation except over a period of several years. This lack of evidence has led economists to broaden their measures of money to include some additional highly liquid assets that provide better correlations over shorter periods of one or two years.

But, a fundamental problem arises: if your thesis is that control over money means control over GDP, and if money does not correlate, then your thesis is weak. But if you find a broader monetary aggregate that does correlate rather well with GDP and then choose to define that aggregate as money, instead of testing your theory you have simply chosen the aggregate that supports your thesis best. The manipulation of evidence to support your theory is an improper scientific procedure. It is referred to as empiricism.

If some broader monetary aggregate than money itself proves to be a better explanatory variable for movements in GDP and inflation, and if better control of that aggregate provides the economy with greater economic and price level stability, then someone should build a theory around the relation between that aggregate and the economy. There exists no theory that holds that some unique combination of money and non-monetary liquid assets determines GDP.

Measurement of Money

It is not easy to measure the money supply and keep track of how it changes in economies with complex financial systems. Nor is it any easier in backward economies where much barter still takes place. In this section the measures of money published by the Federal Reserve System in the United States will be examined in some detail. Toward the end of the chapter the money measures published by the Four Asian Tigers will be examined briefly.

Measures Published by the Federal Reserve System. Each Thursday the Federal Reserve publishes a statistical release on "MONEY STOCK, LIQUID ASSETS, AND DEBT MEASURES." Data in the release are also summarized in the *Federal Reserve Bulletin*. A recent set of such data appears in Table 5–1. Both seasonally adjusted data and nonseasonally adjusted data are published, but here only the seasonally adjusted data are presented. There are five measures, three of which are identified as *M*1, *M*2, and *M*3, and two others which are labeled *L* and Debt.

The first item of the table, labeled *M*1, contains the measure of money that best fits the definition of money as anything that can be used to discharge debt. The footnotes to the table are required reading. They contain more specific information on what is in each item. In the footnotes we see that *M*1 includes currency, traveler's checks issued by nonbank institutions, demand deposits, and other checkable deposits at banks and thrift institutions.

Currency means all coins and paper money issued by the Treasury and the Federal Reserve *less* any amounts held in bank vaults or held by the Treasury after having been issued. The net amount is called "currency in circulation" or "currency in the hands of the public." Amounts of currency held by the Federal Reserve, by the Treasury or in bank vaults are not counted because such vault cash is *not* available for spending. It was mentioned earlier that what is used as money changes over time. A few years ago a statistical release suddenly appeared one day with traveler's checks included in the total. The statistical staff at the Federal Reserve was right to include these because they can be used to discharge debt.

Demand deposits are *private* demand deposits *adjusted*. Private means that federal government deposits in banks are not included, because federal government spending does not depend on the amount of such deposits, but on the federal budget. Adjusted means that interbank deposits and checks in the process of being collected are excluded. A deposit by one bank in another bank is an asset for one bank but a liability for the other; for all banks, these items offset each other. Checks being collected are those deposited but not yet collected from banks on which they were drawn. When checks are deposited, depositors' accounts increase. Checks still in the process of collection have resulted in increases in some depositors' accounts, but have not yet resulted in decreases in the deposits of those who wrote the checks. Thus, counting checks that are being collected would count some deposits twice: for the depositor and for the writer of the checks. Thus, interbank deposits are excluded.

In this analysis it is clear that those who attempt to measure the money supply are trying to measure all items that can be used to discharge debt. But here is an interesting case in point. What is to be done about cash in the vaults of thrift institutions? Some of it is simply held by these companies and, like the cash held by other businesses, is available for spending. Another part of it is held specifically to service the other checking accounts that make up a portion of the money supply. If they are held to service other checking accounts, then they should be excluded as part of the supply of "currency in circulation" just as bank vault cash is excluded.

For a time the Federal Reserve simply made an estimate of that portion of thrift vault cash that is used for servicing demand deposits and excluded that amount from its measure. Now it appears that all vault cash of depository institutions, including thrifts, are excluded. The footnotes do not provide sufficient detail for the reader to know for sure. Such estimated exclusions are clearly imperfect, but measurement problems being what they are, this is the best that can be achieved.

Other checkable deposits include negotiable orders of withdrawal (NOW) accounts, automatic transfer service (ATS) accounts, and credit union share draft accounts. Checks may be written against these accounts. They also pay interest.

Components of the $M1$ measure also appear in the table in the appropriate rows. The broader measure $M2$ contains $M1$ plus other items. The other items are overnight repurchase agreements (RPs) at banks, certain overnight Eurodollar deposits, certain

Table 5–1

Money Stock, Liquid Assets, and Debt Measures[1] (Billions of dollars, averages of daily figures)

Item	1990 Dec.	1991 Dec.	1992 Dec.	1993 Dec.	1994 Mar.	1994 Apr.	1994 May	1994 June
					Seasonally adjusted			
Measures[2]								
1 *M1*	826.4	897.7	1,024.8	1,128.4	1,142.4	1,141.3	1,143.2	1,146.9
2 *M2*	3,353.0	3,455.3	3,509.0	3,567.4	3,582.7	3,590.0	3,591.3	3,582.3
3 *M3*	4,125.7	4,180.4	4,183.1	4,230.0	4,214.5	4,222.9	4,216.7	4,213.5
4 *L*	4,974.8	4,992.9	5,057.2	5,132.5	5,139.5	5,157.7	5,153.3	n.a.
5 Debt	10,669.5	11,144.2	11,722.1	12,317.3	12,485.3	12,530.8	12,575.0	n.a.
M1 components								
6 Currency[3]	246.7	267.1	292.2	321.4	332.4	334.8	337.6	340.3
7 Traveler's checks[4]	7.8	7.7	8.1	7.9	8.0	8.1	8.1	8.1
8 Demand deposits[5]	277.9	290.0	339.6	384.8	390.0	388.9	385.9	386.6
9 Other checkable deposits[6]	294.0	332.8	384.9	414.3	411.9	409.5	411.6	411.8
Nontransaction components								
10 In *M2*[7]	2,526.6	2,557.6	2,484.3	2,439.1	2,440.3	2,448.7	2,448.1	2,435.4
11 In *M3*[8]	772.7	725.2	674.1	662.6	631.8	632.9	625.4	631.2
Commercial banks								
12 Savings deposits, including MMDAs	582.1	665.5	754.6	785.3	790.2	788.2	784.2	779.4
13 Small time deposits[9]	611.3	602.9	508.7	468.5	462.6	461.6	464.0	466.7
14 Large time deposits[10,11]	368.6	342.4	292.8	277.1	270.0	269.3	273.7	273.7
Thrift institutions								
15 Savings deposits, including MMDAs	338.3	375.6	429.0	430.2	431.7	432.5	431.7	428.1
16 Small time deposits[9]	563.2	464.5	361.8	317.1	308.6	307.0	305.2	303.9
17 Large time deposits[10]	120.9	83.4	67.5	61.8	60.9	61.2	59.8	60.1
Money market mutual funds								
18 General purpose and broker-deal	355.5	370.4	352.0	348.8	348.4	361.5	365.1	359.3
19 Institution-only	135.0	181.0	201.5	197.0	177.4	177.0	169.3	169.5
Debt components								
20 Federal debt	2,490.7	2,763.8	3,068.4	3,327.6	3,375.4	3,383.6	3,395.4	n.a.
21 Nonfederal debt	8,178.8	8,380.4	8,653.6	8,989.7	9,109.9	9,147.2	9,179.7	n.a.

1. Latest monthly and weekly figures are available from the Board's H. 6 (508) weekly statistical release. Historical data are available from the Money and Reserves Projection Section, Division of Monetary Affairs, Board of Governors of the Federal Reserve System, Washington, DC 20551.

Table 5–1 (Cont'd)

2. Composition of the money stock measures and debt is as follows:

*M*1: (1) currency outside the U.S. Treasury, Federal Reserve Banks, and the vaults of depository institutions, (2) traveler's checks of nonbank issuers; (3) demand deposits at all commercial banks other than those owed to depository institutions, the U.S. government, and foreign banks and official institutions, less cash items in the process of collection and Federal Reserve float, and (4) other checkable deposits (OCDs), consisting of negotiable orders of withdrawal (NOW) and automatic transfer service (ATS) accounts at depository institutions, credit union share draft accounts, and demand deposits at thrift institutions. Seasonally adjusted *M*1 is computed by summing currency, traveler's checks, demand deposits, and OCDs, each seasonally adjusted separately.

*M*2: *M*1 plus (1) overnight (and continuing-contract) repurchase agreements (RPs) issued by all depository institutions and overnight Eurodollars issued to U.S. residents by foreign branches of U.S. banks worldwide, (2) savings (including MMDAs) and small time deposits (time deposits—including retail RPs—in amounts of less than $100.000), and (3) balances in both taxable and tax-exempt general-purpose and broker-dealer money market funds. Excludes individual retirement accounts (IRAs) and Keogh balances at depository institutions and money market funds. Also excludes all balances held by U.S. commercial banks. money market funds (general purpose and broker-dealer), foreign governments and commercial banks, and the U.S. government. Seasonally adjusted *M*2 is computed by adjusting its non-*M*1 component as a whole and then adding this result to seasonally adjusted *M*1.

*M*3: *M*2 plus (1) large time deposits and term RP liabilities (in amounts of $100,000 or more) issued by all depository institutions, (2) term Eurodollars held by U.S. residents at foreign branches of U.S. banks worldwide and at all banking offices in the United Kingdom and Canada, and (3) balances in both taxable and tax-exempt, institution-only money market funds. Excludes amounts held by depository institutions, the U.S. government, money market funds, and foreign banks and official institutions. Also excluded is the estimated amount of overnight RPs and Eurodollars held by institution-only money market funds. Seasonally adjusted *M*3 is computed by adjusting its non-*M*2 component as a whole and then adding this result to seasonally adjusted *M*2.

L: *M*3 plus the nonbank public holdings of U.S. savings bonds, short-term Treasury securities, commercial paper, and banker's acceptances, net of money market fund holdings of these assets. Seasonally adjusted *L* is computed by summing U.S. savings bonds, short-term Treasury securities, commercial paper, and banker's acceptances, each seasonally adjusted separately, and then adding this result to *M*3.

Debt: Debt of domestic nonfinancial sectors consists of outstanding credit market debt of the U.S. government, state and local governments, and private nonfinancial sectors. Private debt consists of corporate bonds, mortgages' consumer credit (including bank loans), other bank loans, commercial paper, banker's acceptances, and other debt instruments. Data are derived from the Federal Reserve Board's flow of funds accounts. Debt data are based on monthly averages. This sum is seasonally adjusted as a whole.

3. Currency outside the U.S. Treasury, Federal Reserve Banks, and vaults of depository institutions.

4. Outstanding amount of U.S. dollar-denominated traveler's checks of nonbank issuers. Traveler's checks issued by depository institutions are included in demand deposits.

5. Demand deposits at commercial banks and foreign-related institutions other than those owed to depository institutions, the U.S. government, and foreign banks and official institutions, less cash items in the process of collection and Federal Reserve float.

6. Consists of NOW and ATS account balances at all depository institutions, credit union share draft account balances, and demand deposits at thrift institutions.

7. Sum of (1) overnight RPs and overnight Eurodollars, (2) money market fund balances (general purpose and broker-dealer), (3) savings deposits (including MMDAs), and (4) small time deposits.

8. Sum of (1) large time deposits, (2) term RPs, (3) term Eurodollars of U.S. residents, and (4) money market fund balances (institution-only), less (5) a consolidation adjustment that represents the estimated amount of overnight RPs and Eurodollars held by institution-only money market funds.

9. Small time deposits—including retail RPs—are those issued in amounts of less than $100,000. All IRAs and Keogh accounts at commercial banks and thrift institutions are subtracted from small time deposits.

10. Large time deposits are those issued in amounts of $100,000 or more, excluding those booked at international banking facilities.

11. Large time deposits at commercial banks less those held by money market funds, depository institutions, U.S. government, and foreign banks and official institutions.

Source: *Federal Reserve Bulletin*, September 1994.

money market mutual funds (MMMF) deposits, money market deposit accounts (MMDAs) at banks, and savings accounts and small time deposits.

We will look more carefully at these items just below. But first the table shows that $M3$ includes more items, and L includes $M3$ plus a variety of government securities and other money market securities. Debt includes L plus a variety of debt issued by non-financial institutions, state and local governments and corporate bonds, mortgages, and so forth. The extensive detail given in L and Debt need not detain us. But a close look at $M2$ is useful because it is currently the most widely watched measure and is subject to target setting by the Federal Reserve. For several years prior to 1985, $M1$ was also targeted by the Federal Reserve. But after $M1$ growth and GDP growth parted company, the $M1$ target was abandoned.

Money and Liquidity Measures

There are two points about measures of money that need consideration. First, there are some items that are *not* included in the measure of $M1$ that should be included, for example, Money Market Mutual Fund deposits. Second, there are items included in measures of $M2$ and $M3$ that are *not* money and should be excluded from any measure of money.

It would surely be better, therefore, to have *one* money measure, M, and several liquidity measures, $L1$, $L2$, $L3$, and Debt because the measures, as presently compiled, do *not* in fact provide three measures of money. It is simply misleading to identify them as three measures of money. Other than money proper, the other measures provide measures of money plus other nonmonetary liquid assets. It is clear that this is the case because, in Table 5–1, one heading by the $M2$ measure reads "nontransaction components." By stating that some of the items in $M2$ are nontransaction items the record shows that these are not items of money because they cannot be spent.

It is safe to say that no one ever bought an ice cream cone with a savings deposit. To spend a savings account it is necessary to withdraw cash from it first. Then you can spend your cash. It is true that some savings accounts permit some account holders to pay certain regular bills such as utility bills by telephone. To the extent that debt can be discharged in this way, the savings account should be counted as money. This is true of postal system savings accounts which, under the *giro* money transfer system described in Chapter 4, can be used to discharge a debt.

As mentioned before, it is not easy to measure money. But as more and more electronic transfers of funds can be made by home computers with direct links to bank accounts, it is clear that such accounts need to be added to measures of the money supply.

Surveys to Measure Money. One suggestion for measuring money might be to simply ask a sample of people how much they have, that is, measure it by survey in the same way unemployment and the price indexes are measured. A person, if asked how much money he or she had, would probably include savings accounts in banks in the answer.

But it would be easy to persuade him to separate out that type of "money" from the rest. This is simply an example of the distinction between a formal definition of "money" and the meaning that the term carries in the mind of the public.

Besides Money Market Mutual Funds, $M2$ contains some other items that would probably best be included in $M1$. Specifically, Money Market Deposit Accounts that banks hold for their customers can be used to pay some bills. These accounts should be in $M1$. Also, consider the item mentioned above, overnight repurchase agreements. Let us assume that a corporation has an account at a bank and decides at 3:00 P.M. to put the funds into securities overnight, under a repurchase agreement with the bank. The money in the account can certainly be spent the following day, because the bank automatically repurchases the securities and puts the funds back into the company's deposit account when the bank opens for business the next day. In essence, the funds remain spendable.

Banks routinely offer RPs to their corporate customers these days. RPs allow a business to earn one day's worth of interest on what would otherwise be non-interest-bearing accounts. Regulations in the U.S. put in place in 1934 still prohibit the payment of interest on business deposits in banks. If the law were repealed, banks would offer some interest on these deposits just as they now offer on personal accounts. Thus, deposits removed overnight under RP agreements are not effectively divorced from their ability to be spent any more than all the other deposits and checkable accounts cannot be spent because the bank is closed at night.

Does deposit money disappear because the bank is closed? The answer is surely no. To be consistent, then, a measure of M should include overnight RPs. The same analysis applies to overnight Eurodollar deposits.

Money market mutual funds and money market deposit accounts with banks are also spendable, but within some limits. Checks can be written against these accounts, but usually only three in a month. Additional funds can be withdrawn from MMDAs if the deposit holder goes to the bank. So, MMDAs are partly checkable deposits and partly savings accounts. Analysts say that they are not really held for spending, but as invested savings, so they are not part of $M1$, only of $M2$.

But, the purpose of holding an item of money has nothing to do with whether or not it is money. Indeed, as noted at the outset of this chapter, one of the principal functions of money is to store wealth. Lots of money is not held for the purpose of spending it, but for the purpose of holding it. As mentioned earlier, people do not spend hundred dollar bills in the United States very often. But a hundred dollar bill is still money. There are lots of things you cannot buy with a hundred dollar bill, such as a newspaper from a paperboy, because he does not carry sufficient change. But, does its inability to be spent on every occasion keep it from being money? No.

The only reason that MMMF checkable money is not included in $M1$ is that the investment banking industry would then have to admit that it participates in money creation when it accepts "deposits" to a fund. This would mean that MMMFs would have to be regulated by the Federal Reserve and would have to register as banks and hold reserves at the Federal Reserve.

One factor contributing to the profit deficiencies in bank operations today in the U.S. is that MMMFs have eaten into the competitive position of the banking industry. Thus, because the Federal Reserve would be in an awkward regulatory position if it were to acknowledge MMMFs as money, it chooses to ignore the monetary content of such accounts and places them in *M2*.

Seigniorage

First, some definitions. *Brassage* is a fee that was charged for minting bullion into coin. Usually, the bullion was gold or silver. Except for the brassage, the gold content of a coin was equal to its value as a circulating medium. Such coins were called "full-bodied" coins as distinct from token coins. Token coins were "debased" by adding other less valuable metals to the alloy. Their value was greater in the marketplace than the value of the metals in the coin.

A "seignior" is the lord of a manor who has jurisdiction over a territory. *Seigniorage* is a claim over something arising from the exercise of sovereign prerogative; but more specifically "it is the difference between the value of a coin and the cost of the bullion and the minting" (*Webster's New Collegiate Dictionary*).

By controlling the minting of coins, a seignior could issue token coins and profit by the difference in cost and value. The issue of paper money permits the seignior, or government, to make a profit from the difference between the value of the money and the cost of printed paper. In the case of a one dollar coin costing 5 cents to make, the government makes 95 cents. A $1 paper bill costs only 1 to 2 cents so the profit is 99 cents. A $100 dollar bill gives a $99.99 profit.

But if governments issue too much currency, the purchasing power of the monetary unit will fall with inflation. So there is a limit to the seigniorage that a government can collect in the manner just described. Nevertheless, so long as non-interest-bearing notes circulate as currency, the government continuously earns the interest that it would otherwise have to pay if it borrowed the money. It earns this interest steadily and continuously in a non-inflationary environment. Thus, today seigniorage is earned in the form of interest.

It is useful to use Hong Kong or Singapore as an example to illustrate how governments earn seigniorage from the consuming public. The seigniorage can be observed directly in the accounts that governments there keep. Seigniorage in the U.S. can also be tracked through a series of accounts, but it is not directly observable in the U.S. Thus, the Hong Kong example comes first and will be followed by the more complex example of the U.S.

Note Issuing Banks in Hong Kong. The Hong Kong government issues coin in Hong Kong, and it permits the Hongkong and Shanghai Banking Corporation (HSBC) and Standard Chartered Bank to issue paper notes. About 85 per cent of the notes in circulation are those of the HSBC while 15 per cent are those issued by Standard Chartered. The proportion issued by each of the two banks is not set by the government, but simply reflects the volume of business each bank has and the public's willingness to accept the different notes. In May 1994 the local branch of the Bank of China (BOC) began issuing notes as well. The BOC handles China's foreign banking relations and is supervised by the People's Bank of China, the PRC's central bank. One of the several branches of the BOC, the Hong Kong BOC, was established in 1917.

Media reports say the Bank of China plans eventually to be the issuer of 20 per cent of the currency in Hong Kong. However, such a percentage is pure speculation because the people may choose to hold much more of the BOC's currency and much less of HSBC's currency. If people should prefer one over the other, the pure substitutability of one currency for the other will permit them to choose, and the resulting relative amounts issued by the three banks will be the result of those choices. It is not possible for a bank to set a percentage on the currency that it will issue, although it may offer an estimate as to the percentage that it expects to issue. Such estimates might be based on the proportionate share of the volume of business the BOC has.

Government spokesmen say that the BOC's move to issue currency indicates a forward look to a smooth transition of power over Hong Kong from Britain to China at the end of June in 1997. However, any bank in Hong Kong may apply to be a note-issuing bank. The move is purely symbolic.

All note-issuing banks must comply with rules that require that they place a type of collateral for the outstanding notes with the government's Exchange Fund. These rules result in the earning of seigniorage for the Hong Kong government. Let us see how the system works in Hong Kong.

Seigniorage in Hong Kong

Seigniorage is a revenue that can be collected by government because it has a monopoly over the issue of currency. This revenue can now be observed directly in Hong Kong.

Exchange Fund Holdings. The Exchange Fund is Hong Kong government's official holder of foreign exchange reserves. It operates under the direction of the Monetary Affairs Branch of the Hong Kong government. The Exchange Fund is now under the Hong Kong Monetary Authority which began operation in the spring of 1993.

It was only in the summer of 1992 that the Exchange Fund first published figures on its holdings of interest-earning foreign exchange for 1991. In July of 1993 it published figures for 1992—the second year for which the Financial Secretary revealed the Exchange Fund's figures. As reported in the *South China Morning Post Weekly* (July 17–18, 1993) the U.S. dollar value of the fund increased from $29 to $35 billion (HK$236 to HK$287 billion) from 1991 to 1992. Earnings on the fund added just over $1 billion (HK$8 billion) to accumulated earnings. About half of this $1 billion (HK$4 billion) in earnings represents seigniorage. By January 1995 it held $49 billion.

With a population of about six million, the fund has about $6,000 for every person in Hong Kong, the second highest per capita value for official foreign exchange reserve holdings of any country in the world—second only to Singapore's $14,500 per capita holdings.

Note-issuing Banks. Let us clarify how seigniorage is earned by looking at sample balance sheet items of one of the note-issuing banks in Hong Kong along with the balance sheet of the Exchange Fund.

A	Exchange Fund		L	A	HSBC		L
Assets	+100	CIs	+100	CIs	+100	Notes	+100
				Assets	−100	Deposit	−100

On the far right side of these balance sheet accounts, the two entries show that an individual, Mr. A, goes to the Hongkong and Shanghai Banking Corporation (HSBC) and withdraws $100 in currency from his account. His deposits show a reduction and the bank issues notes—currency that Mr. A now carries in his wallet.

Certificates of Indebtedness. Ordinances in Hong Kong require that the HSBC acquire from the Exchange Fund (EF) certificates of indebtedness (CIs) by giving the EF certain assets. In earlier days these consisted of gold and silver and other items such as United Kingdom Gilt-edged Securities, but now the requirement has been simplified to require that the HSBC give U.S. dollars or U.S. Treasury securities. The reduction in HSBC assets and the increase in its CI holdings appear under the asset side of the HSBC balance sheet.

The EF's balance shows that it has issued a liability in the form of a certificate of indebtedness to HSBC, and it now has the assets that it was given in exchange. It can invest these assets in whatever interest-earning securities it wants. So the EF recognizes the "deposit" of assets with it and issues a certificate of indebtedness, as shown.

The Exchange Fund now earns interest on accumulated assets. The value of the assets equals the value of the bank notes that have been issued and are in circulation. Mr. A now carries a non-interest-earning asset in his wallet, while the EF holds an interest-earning U.S. Treasury security.

Many historical details have been omitted from this example, but in mid-1992 the amount of bank-issued currency in circulation was about HK$50 billion. If the EF earns 8 per cent on its assets, it collects HK$4 billion every year because of the way it exercises its monopoly over the issue of currency. The Exchange Fund holds other assets as well. It holds the government's surplus and earns interest on it as well as interest on that portion of the assets pledged to back the outstanding issues of bank notes.

It has been estimated that 16 per cent of Hong Kong's currency is circulating in Guangdong Province in China. If so, this means that the Exchange Fund has issued paper that now circulates as money in the streets of towns in Guangdong. The people of Guangdong are not paid interest on the Hong Kong banknotes they hold. However, the Exchange Fund of Hong Kong is earning interest on the foreign exchange that the banks gave it in order to issue these paper notes. The net result is as if the people of Guangdong are paying a tax to the Hong Kong government in exchange for the use of Hong Kong's money.

The story of seigniorage is fundamentally the same for every issuer of currency everywhere in the world. The details differ and usually the accounting is covered up in order to avoid disclosing that governments collect a seigniorage tax from the public without declaring the collection openly—taxation without representation.

Seigniorage on Checking Accounts in Banks

Banks earn seigniorage, too, as Figure 5–1 illustrates. Governments, through their sovereign powers, have allocated to banks some of the monopoly power they have to create money by permitting banks to offer demand deposit accounts. Banks create deposit money when they accept a customer's cash deposit. Then they use the cash money they have received to make interest-earning loans. To the extent that banks pay interest on deposits, the bank customers receive the seigniorage rather than the banks themselves. In any case the banking industry and its customers are subsidized by the government's regulatory structure over banking.

Figure 5–1 provides a simple demand and supply framework for bank reserves that illustrates the receipt of seigniorage on the part of banks. Interest rates paid and collected by banks in general in the economy are represented on the vertical axis, and the volume of demand deposit money supplied by the banking industry is measured on the horizontal axis.

Figure 5–1
Demand and Supply for Demand Deposit Money

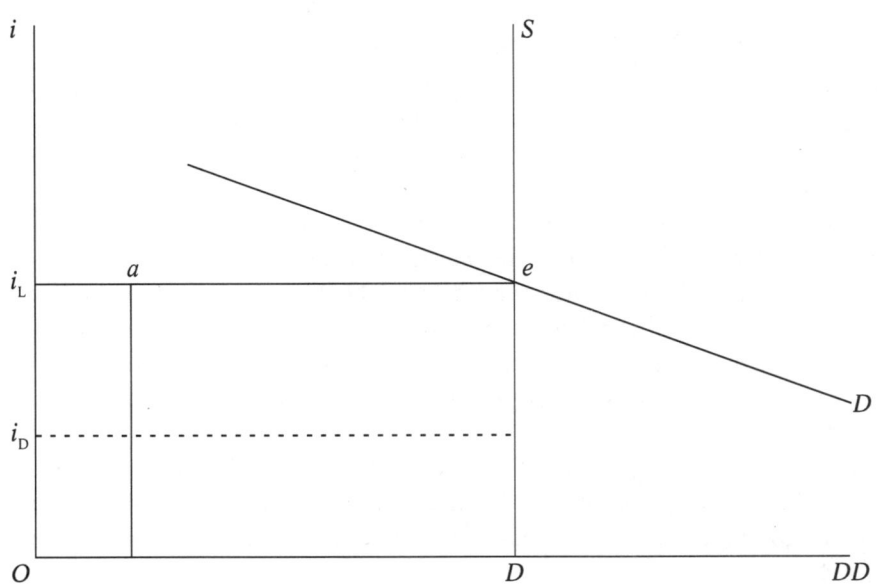

The demand curve shown has its usual downward slope. Just as there is a demand and supply for vehicles that can be separated into a demand and supply for each cars and trucks, it is presumed that it is possible, for analytical purposes, to separate the demand and supply for money into a demand and supply for each currency and demand deposits. Here the figure represents the demand and supply for demand deposits. These are "industry" demand and supply curves, not those representing the demand and supply for a single banking firm in the industry.

The supply curve is drawn as if it extends along the horizontal axis from the origin up to point D and then rises vertically. The reason that it is horizontal up to point D is that the marginal cost of creating another dollar's worth of deposits is zero. The only cost of creating a dollar's worth of deposits is the value of the time that it takes to make a book entry into a computer to provide a bank customer with additional funds in his checking account. But the supply curve rises steeply at point D, approximated by a vertical line, because under a fractional reserve system banks must maintain a supply of cash in the vault to handle the inflow and outflow of cash on a routine daily basis. In many instances there are legal reserve requirements that prevent the system from expanding the supply of deposit money beyond a certain limit. These were discussed in detail in Chapter 3.

In equilibrium there will be an interest rate that banks charge on loans shown here as i_L. At this equilibrium, point e, the demand for deposit money by borrowers just equals the supply that banks are able to create. The box created from i_L to e to D to O represents the interest earnings of banks on their loan portfolios. The narrow portion on the left of the box represents the non-interest-earning reserves that banks must hold as reserves.

The dashed line from i_D to the supply curve represents the interest earnings paid to depositors when they receive an interest rate of i_D on *current,* or *checking, accounts.* Thus, the box, except for the narrow portion at the left, represents the seigniorage that is earned by banks and/or the depositors because they have been given the privilege of issuing part of the country's money supply. A license to bank is a license to receive these funds from the consuming public. Counterfeiters do not have such a license but banks do. Counterfeiters are called thieves because they steal in competition with governments and their agents, the banks.

In April 1992, demand deposits of Hong Kong banks amounted to about HK$80 billion. The interest charged on loans was near 9 per cent. Thus, seigniorage to the industry was about HK$7.2 billion for the year. The interest paid depositors on savings and time deposits was about 4 per cent, but *no interest* was paid on current checking accounts. Thus, banks received the entire amount of seigniorage noted, and, needless to say, they reported very hefty earnings in their annual reports published in March and April of 1992.

Similar estimates of seigniorage earned by banks can be made for any economy, but institutional details make it difficult. Politically, it is not convenient for governments to focus on seigniorage because it amounts to an undeclared subsidy to an industry.

Seigniorage in the United States

In the case of Hong Kong, one could directly observe the amount of seigniorage earned by the government if the Exchange Fund published its accounts. In the case of the United States, the government has borrowed money from the public by issuing interest-earning securities. So, unlike in Hong Kong, seigniorage from currency issue appears indirectly through a reduction in the interest payments the Treasury must make on its debt. The following accounts illustrate the essence of the case.

A	Federal Reserve	L		A	Bank	L	
Treasury debt	+100	Notes payable	+100	Cash	−/+100	Demand deposit	−100
		Bank deposits	−100	D/Fed	−100		+100
.			+100		+100		

On the right side of the bank's balance sheet, the withdrawal of $100 in Federal Reserve Notes by Mr. A appears. The cash is paid out of the bank's vault, but the bank needs to replace it to be sure it has enough to meet withdrawals generally. So the cash account shows a decline at first and then an increase as the bank asks the Federal Reserve (the Fed) to issue replacement notes. On the balance sheet of the Fed, the increase in the Notes Payable account shows the issue of currency to the bank, and below it a decline in bank deposits reflects the bank's decision.

The Federal Reserve notices that bank reserves have fallen. It wants to keep the money supply from declining so it chooses to replenish the bank's reserves by buying government securities from the public. Mr. B sells his securities to the Fed for $100. The Fed gives B a check for $100 and B deposits it in the bank so that demand deposits rise again. The bank sends the check for deposit to its account at the Federal Reserve so D/Fed rises. The books of the Fed now show an increase in bank deposits and an increase in the holdings of securities.

The Federal Reserve now earns interest from the Treasury on these securities while Mr. A holds non-interest-earning Federal Reserve Notes in his wallet. But, the Fed does not spend the interest it earns. Instead it returns 85 per cent of the earnings back to the Treasury. Thus, the Treasury saves 85 per cent of the interest that it would otherwise have had to pay to the public. Indirectly, the Treasury "earns" interest by reducing its interest cost through the issue of currency with the help of the Federal Reserve.

Some estimates say that half of the US$340 billion in currency is held by people living outside of the United States. Assuming an interest rate of 5 per cent is applicable, this implies that foreigners are providing the United States with about $8.5 billion in implicit taxes every year.

Seigniorage in Hong Kong

Seigniorage is a revenue collected by government because it has monopoly over the issue of currency.

Exchange Fund				HSBC		

A	L
Assets +100 (6)	CIs +100 (5)

A	L
CIs +100 (4)	Notes +100 (2)
Assets −100 (3)	Deposit −100 (1)

(1) Mr. A withdraws $100.
(2) HSBC issues paper note.
(3) HSBC gives assets to EF.
(4) HSBC receives a certificate from the EF.
(5) EF now has a liability of CIs
(6) EF now owns interest-earning asset.

Seigniorage in the United States

In the case of the United States, the government has borrowed money from the public by issuing interest-earning securities. So, seigniorage from currency issue appears indirectly through a reduction in the interest payments the Treasury must make on its debt.

Federal Reserve

A	L
Treasury debt +100 (10)	Notes payable +100 (5)
	Bank deposits −100 (6)
	Bank deposits +100 (9)

Bank

A	L
Cash −100 (2)	Demand deposit −100 (1)
Cash +100 (3)	Demand deposit +100 (7)
D/Fed −100 (4)	
D/Fed +100 (8)	

(1) Mr. A withdraws cash from his demand deposit.
(2) The bank's vault cash is down.
(3) The bank replenishes cash.
(4) It obtains the cash by reducing its deposit with the Federal Reserve.
(5) The Federal Reserve issues more cash to the bank in the form of Notes.
(6) The bank's deposit with the Federal Reserve is reduced.
(7) The Federal Reserve buys securities from Mr. B and B deposits the check.
(8) The bank sends the check to the Federal Reserve for deposit.
(9) Bank deposits are now higher at the Federal Reserve.
(10) The Federal Reserve now holds interest-earning Treasury debt but gives 85 per cent of the interest back to the Treasury.

Measuring Money in the Four Asian Tigers

Circumstances unique to each country lead it to choose its own set of monetary measures. However, most measures published today reflect a general approach.

Money Measures in Hong Kong

Table 5–2 is a copy of the tables regularly published by the Monetary Affairs Branch of Hong Kong. These tables may change now that a new Hong Kong Monetary Authority has been established.

There are two problems with Table 5–2 that would be easy to correct. One is that the money supply is subjected to three "definitions," whereas these should be called three "measures." Second, under the heading of money supply, there is no statement telling the reader what "definition 1" consists of, or "definition 2" and so forth. So, to decipher what is meant the reader may start at the top of the column labeled HK$.

Down the column are listed the dollar value of bank notes that the issuing banks have placed in circulation. This should equal the dollar volume of certificates that the Exchange Fund has issued to the banks. To this amount, add the dollar volume of coins that the government has issued. From this sum, *subtract* the amount of vault cash held by banks because this money is not in circulation. Then we have the "legal tender notes and coins in the hands of the public."

Just below this figure is definition 1, which should read measure 1, of the money supply. What is this measure? To arrive at the sum, one must add to the currency figure shown in the table the amount of demand deposits of licensed banks, which is found in a different table (not included here) with banking statistics. The combination of currency in circulation and demand deposits of licensed banks adds up to the $M1$ measure of money.

Official definitions published in the *Hong Kong Monthly Digest of Statistics* read as follows: "Money supply definition 1 (Total): Notes and coins with the public, plus customers' demand deposits with licensed banks. Money supply definition 2 (Total): $M1$ plus customers' savings and time deposits with licensed banks, plus negotiable certificates of deposit issued by licensed banks and held outside the monetary sector. Money supply definition 3 (Total): $M2$ plus customers' deposits with restricted licence banks and deposit-taking companies plus negotiable certificates of deposit issued by restricted licence banks and deposit-taking companies held outside the monetary sector."

The Hong Kong government chooses to add foreign currency to domestic currency balances for a "Total" figure on Hong Kong's money supply. Therefore, there is a Hong Kong dollar total and a foreign currency total and a combined total. These three sets of data are reported even though foreign currencies are not used to make purchases in Hong Kong, and adding them together with local currency is like adding apples and oranges. It might be called the "fruit" measure of money for Hong Kong.

Tables 5–2
Currency in Circulation and Money Supply*, Hong Kong ($ million)

As at end of year/month	Legal tender notes and coins in circulation			Authorized institutions holdings of legal tender notes and coins HK$	Legal tender notes and coins in hands of public HK$
	Commercial bank issues HK$	Government issues HK$	Total HK$		
1988	31,826	2,262	34,087	4,210	29,877
1989	37,286	2,384	39,670	5,478	34,192
1990	40,886	2,375	43,261	5,568	37,693
1991	46,506	2,671	49,177	6,569	42,608
1992	58,226	2,931	61,157	8,985	52,172
1993	68,896	2,978	71,874	8,520	63,354
1994: Jan.	75,736	3,214	78,950	11,665	67,284
Feb.	73,746	3,052	76,798	8,102	68,695
Mar.	74,796	2,971	77,767	9,963	67,804

As at end of year/month	Money supply definition 1			Money supply definition 2			Money supply definition 3		
	HK$	Foreign currency	Total	HK$	Foreign currency	Total	HK$	Foreign currency	Total
1988	79,257	9,577	88,834	355,065	469,583	824,648	389,052	504,291	893,342
1989	85,183	9,675	94,858	403,987	584,849	988,836	434,376	625,831	1,060,207
1990	91,826	15,683	107,509	471,934	738,116	1,210,050	503,482	784,546	1,288,028
1991	111,769	16,728	128,497	595,808	775,182	1,370,990	619,882	817,460	1,437,342
1992	139,479	16,078	155,557	668,302	850,475	1,518,777	691,586	882,679	1,574,265
1993	168,440	19,168	187,608	850,618	911,252	1,761,870	867,692	952,871	1,820,562
1994: Jan.	187,940	20,280	208,219	954,095	926,992	1,881,087	970,698	966,517	1,937,215
Feb.	178,903	21,081	199,984	876,229	916,932	1,793,161	893,075	958,136	1,851,211
Mar.	171,558	19,051	190,609	950,529	835,787	1,786,315	967,405	878,513	1,845,918

*Unadjusted for foreign currency swap deposits.

Source: *Hong Kong Monthly Digest of Statistics*, April 1994.

Money Measures in Korea, Singapore, and Taiwan

Money measures in Korea follow U.S. money measure types (see Table 5–3). Money measures in Singapore and Taiwan are shown in Tables 5–4 and 5–5 respectively.

Money is Fungible

In order to better appreciate the importance of money as a medium of exchange, its usefulness in discharging debt, its enhanced value as the "perfectly liquid asset," and the extent to which its role in the economy is misunderstood by government officials and others, it is useful to provide an example from the law.

In the following discussion, it is shown that food stamps, issued to about 20 million persons in the U.S. as part of the nation's welfare safety net, should be included in measures of the money supply. It is also shown that because of money's fungible quality, welfare recipients should be given money instead of food stamps to economize on costs of managing two currencies side by side. Let us begin by looking at the obscure legal term, fungible—a useful term to know in this context.

Legal Term—Fungible

Webster's New Collegiate Dictionary defines the legal term fungible as "of such a nature that one part or specimen can be used in place of another in the satisfaction of, or discharge of, an obligation, e.g., money, food, etc."

Assume that your crop-duster plane flew over your neighbor's rice field by mistake and laid down a herbicide. Because of the negligence of your agent, the pilot, your neighbor lost a field of crop. You have a field of rice too, but his was planted with long-grain rice and yours is planted with short-grain rice. You offer to settle the dispute by giving your neighbor your short-grain rice crop. Is short-grain rice fungible for long-grain rice? That is what the judge has to decide. Instead of making reimbursement for the loss with a different kind of rice, perhaps you could just figure out what the dollar value of the field's rice would have been and offer a monetary payment. If it is acceptable, then money is the fungible item.

Money is so very fungible that it is even substitutable for losses in the form of human suffering according to some judges and juries.

Food stamps are in practice substitutable for money. Although food stamps are supposed to be used only to purchase food, a person can purchase nearly anything with food stamps, including such items as used cars and the services of a prostitute. Such uses are prohibited by law, but are common practice.

Food Stamp Example

As a perfect substitute for money in nearly every situation, food stamps are fungible. Table 5–6 provides an example of what studies have shown typically happens to expenditures when a family is a recipient of food stamps. Studies suggest that families

Table 5-3
Money Supply, Korea

		Bank notes and coins issued				Reserve money[1]				Money supply (M1)[2]			
		End of		Averages		End of		Averages		End of		Averages	
		Billion won	Change (%)	Billion won	Change (%)	Billion won	Change (%)	Billion won	Change (%)	Billion won	Change (%)	Billion won	Change (%)
1991		9,102.3	10.6	7,547.4	18.0	16,321.7	18.2	13,742.7	17.4	21,752.4	36.8	15,620.3	16.1
1992		9,807.7	7.7	8,353.2	10.7	18,107.3	10.9	15,286.7	11.2	24,586.3	13.0	20,672.2	32.3
1993		13,883.5	41.6	10,849.0	29.9	p23,079.8	27.5	p18,467.2	20.8	p29,266.0	19.0	p25,248.6	22.1
1993	1	9,667.8	0.3	9,744.1	14.9	17,264.1	10.0	17,359.9	12.9	23,948.2	7.8	24,602.0	25.4
	2	9,893.3	19.8	8,996.7	1.6	17,245.5	16.9	16,382.1	5.8	24,897.4	17.6	23,351.1	17.6
	3	10,252.8	22.8	10,113.9	22.1	17,509.3	13.1	17,553.5	16.4	23,734.7	20.5	23,592.0	21.0
	4	10,181.1	26.2	10,221.3	26.2	17,787.6	20.7	17,597.9	17.8	24,704.0	23.5	23,901.2	24.6
	5	10,164.9	29.8	10,140.8	27.2	17,702.6	17.2	17,565.1	18.4	23,923.5	13.9	24,081.0	22.2
	6	10,107.0	27.8	9,920.5	27.8	18,127.4	22.6	17,542.6	20.5	24,170.1	12.4	23,614.0	20.2
	7	10,232.1	27.9	10,045.5	27.6	18,691.4	23.4	17,755.4	20.0	24,249.5	11.7	24,360.4	18.9
	8	11,678.9	44.5	10,785.3	34.4	18,819.6	25.1	18,540.8	24.6	26,251.2	20.8	25,072.0	23.3
	9	15,712.4	83.4	12,446.4	36.2	22,424.1	39.1	19,946.8	24.9	30,643.8	38.8	27,396.1	25.4
	10	12,301.5	46.6	13,064.3	55.8	20,372.6	32.0	20,828.3	36.4	27,429.6	17.2	27,324.3	24.6
	11	12,369.8	42.7	12,136.9	43.4	20,105.8	33.2	20,032.6	28.4	27,448.1	19.1	27,333.2	21.6
	12	13,883.5	41.6	12,571.9	41.1	p23,079.8	27.5	p20,501.6	22.9	p29,266.0	19.0	p28,355.7	20.9

Table 5-3 (Cont'd)

	Money supply (M2)[3]				M2Λ[4]				M3[5]	
	End of		Averages		End of		Averages		End of	
	Billion won	Change (%)	Billion won	Change (%)	Billion won	Change (%)	Billion won	Change (%)	Billion won	Change (%)
1991	83,745.9	21.9	73,024.0	18.6	58,836.5	20.6	50,797.9	15.0	243,955.9	23.3
1992	96,258.6	14.9	86,491.7	18.4	66,819.7	13.6	59,356.7	16.8	294,843.7	20.9
1993	p112,447.1	16.8	p102,583.3	18.6	p76,211.3	14.1	p70,074.7	18.1	–	–
1993 1	96,590.9	14.1	96,780.4	17.5	66,547.2	12.1	67,217.7	17.1	299,697.9	20.6
2	97,999.5	15.9	96,106.3	15.9	67,765.0	15.2	65,886.2	14.4	305,281.7	21.7
3	97,500.2	16.3	97,559.5	16.7	66,612.6	15.4	66,669.8	15.3	307,308.6	21.0
4	99,312.9	18.1	98,470.1	17.9	67,889.1	17.6	67,515.7	17.3	311,895.3	21.0
5	99,612.8	16.2	99,756.3	18.6	67,703.7	15.0	68,215.7	18.2	314,422.1	19.9
6	100,760.5	16.9	100,266.7	18.9	68,222.2	15.8	68,316.8	18.8	319,984.3	20.9
7	102,285.8	17.1	102,164.2	18.9	69,101.4	16.0	69,455.2	18.7	325,426.0	21.2
8	105,184.3	20.5	103,849.9	20.6	71,732.5	21.0	70,594.1	20.8	330,646.1	21.7
9	111,387.6	24.7	107,609.3	21.5	77,087.5	26.6	73,748.7	22.1	338,282.8	21.9
10	108,949.0	18.5	108,775.9	20.8	74,110.1	17.7	74,318.6	21.1	339,024.2	19.8
11	108,828.8	17.2	108,904.7	18.4	73,164.8	14.9	73,814.7	17.3	344,360.0	19.5
12	p112,447.1	16.8	p110,756.7	17.4	p76,211.3	14.1	p75,142.8	15.5	–	–

1. Reserve money = Bank notes and coins issued (excludes commemorative coins from March 1986) + Reserve deposits of DMB
2. M1 = Currency in circulation + Deposit money (Demand deposits at monetary institutions)
3. M2 = M1 + Quasi-money (Time and savings deposits and resident's foreign currency deposits at monetary institutions)
4. M2 Λ = M2 – Long-term time and savings deposits at deposit money bank
5. M3 = M2 + OFI deposits + Debentures issued + Commercial bills sold + CD + RP

Source: *Monthly Statistical Bulletin*, Bank of Korea, January 1994.

Table 5-4
Money Supply, Singapore (S$ million)

End of period	M1	M2	M3	Currency in active circulation	Demand deposits	Quasi-money				Net deposits with nonbank financial institutions	
						Total	Fixed deposits	S$ NCDs	Savings and other deposits	Finance companies	POSB
	1=4+5	2=1+6	3=2+10+11	4	5	6=7+8+9	7	8	9	10	11
1988	11,957.7	42,087.6	52,823.5	5,996.7	5,961.0	30,129.9	20,898.1	846.8	8,385.0	5,092.9	5,643.0
1989	13,744.6	51,545.5	64,007.8	6,609.9	7,134.7	37,800.9	27,207.8	1,138.7	9,454.4	6,709.2	5,753.1
1990	15,260.9	61,845.1	75,792.4	7,108.5	8,152.4	46,584.2	35,965.9	1,160.3	9,458.0	7,419.4	6,527.9
1991	16,430.0	69,542.3	84,199.7	7,497.1	8,932.9	53,112.3	40,852.0	921.8	11,338.5	7,557.3	7,100.1
1992	18,515.6	75,728.5	91,082.1	8,279.2	10,236.4	57,212.9	43,176.4	741.1	13,295.4	8,060.9	7,292.7
1993 Jan.	18,733.0	74,968.6	90,735.2	8,624.1	10,108.9	56,235.6	41,987.9	753.8	13,493.9	8,157.4	7,609.2
Feb.	18,433.1	74,577.2	90,240.6	8,290.3	10,142.8	56,144.1	41,774.0	740.3	13,629.8	8,243.8	7,419.6
Mar.	18,769.6	75,738.3	91,464.6	8,302.5	10,467.1	56,968.7	42,543.3	740.3	13,685.1	8,143.7	7,582.6
Apr.	19,240.5	76,019.3	91,975.8	8,397.5	10,843.0	56,778.8	42,337.2	721.8	13,719.8	8,236.1	7,720.4
May	19,226.6	77,011.5	92,919.2	8,415.5	10,811.1	57,784.9	43,007.1	721.5	14,056.3	8,436.1	7,471.6

Note: Discount houses ceased operations in May 1987. Prior to this, discount houses were treated as part of the banking system.
Column 4 figures exclude commemorative, numismatic and bullion coins issued by the Board of Commissioners of Currency, Singapore, and cash held by commercial banks and other financial institutions.
Columns 10 and 11 refer to deposits of finance companies and the Post Office Savings Bank less their deposits with banks and discount houses which have been included in M2.

Source: *Monthly Statistical Bulletin*, Monetary Authority of Singapore, June 1993, p. 7.

Table 5–5
Money Supply, Taiwan (NT$ million)[1]

End of month	Net foreign assets[2]	Claims on gov't[3]	Claims on gov't enterprises[4]	Claims on private enterprises & others[4]	Total assets (net) = Total liabilities (net)	Money supply			Quasi-money[6]	Gov't deposits[7]	Presettlement requirements for imports	Other items (net)
						Sub-total	Net currency	Demand deposits adjusted[5]				
1984 Dec.	771,643	70,459	288,211	1,507,225	2,637,538	669,619	168,160	501,459	1,464,601	161,939	20,985	320,394
1985 Dec.	1,168,732	79,440	279,922	1,625,500	3,153,594	751,469	182,808	568,661	1,881,673	175,505	27,233	317,613
1986 Dec.	1,649,092	87,018	278,308	1,732,244	3,746,652	1,137,863	231,046	906,817	2,160,999	215,170	27,002	205,618
1987 Dec.	1,981,963	92,791	236,933	2,110,203	4,421,890	1,568,225	284,964	1,283,261	2,606,796	318,752	31,199	103,082
1988 Dec.	2,062,840	157,942	237,243	2,982,934	5,440,959	1,950,473	320,624	1,629,489	2,970,331	474,191	31,978	13,986
1989 Dec.	2,005,653	402,567	270,191	3,718,895	6,397,306	2,068,975	347,998	1,720,971	3,600,390	620,422	35,391	71,067
1990 Dec.	2,152,901	393,140	331,886	4,322,370	7,200,297	1,929,991	353,628	1,576,363	4,298,072	618,710	40,101	313,423
1991 Dec.	2,242,937	509,180	406,423	5,243,433	8,401,973	2,165,299	387,740	1,777,559	5,230,956	554,347	47,543	403,828
1992 Dec.	2,183,645	723,434	422,599	6,751,144	10,080,822	2,434,475	436,139	1,998,336	6,430,216	687,521	46,680	481,930
1993 Dec.	2,301,148	896,327	453,055	8,033,398	11,683,928	2,806,390	470,387	2,336,003	7,399,188	745,377	43,128	689,845
1994 Jan.	2,308,459	922,874	468,715	8,104,393	11,804,441	2,883,592	503,570	2,380,022	7,390,033	754,011	43,297	733,508
Feb.	2,361,767	939,167	461,284	8,188,784	11,951,002	2,835,293	525,625	2,309,668	7,575,226	745,612	44,874	749,997
Mar.	2,368,697	962,388	457,891	8,290,938	12,079,914	2,772,229	489,577	2,282,652	7,707,231	770,613	43,201	786,640

1. This table is a consolidated balance sheet of the accounts of monetary institutions, comprising the Central Bank of China, domestic banks, local branches of foreign banks, medium business banks (prior to February 1979, including mutual loans and savings companies), credit cooperative association and credit departments of farmers' and fishermen's associations.
2. Represents net foreign assets of monetary institutions.
3. Includes government securities (but excluding holdings of Treasury bills B), unfunded public debts and loans to government agencies.
4. Includes loans, discounts and investments.
5. Includes checking accounts, passbook deposits and passbook savings deposits held by enterprises and individuals with monetary institutions.
6. Includes time deposits, NCDs, time savings deposits (including deposits replaced by the Postal Trust Fund and CDs in foreign currency held by enterprises and individuals. In addition, the bank debentures and savings bond issued by CBC and held by the public were included (the balance of bank debentures and savings bonds and Treasury bills B were NT$690 million, NT$136,951 million and NT$16,691 million respectively at the end of Nov. 1988).
7. Includes general treasury deposits, ordinary treasury deposits and foreign currency deposits held by government agencies, and Sino-American Development Fund Deposits, but excludes the outstanding balance of Treasury bills B.

Source: *Economic Review*, International Bank of China, May–June, 1992.

would buy the same package of goods whether given food stamps or money. Therefore, one can argue that it is a waste to spend extra resources maintaining and managing a second money supply along with the principal currency used in the economy (see West and Price, 1976).

The typical family unit in Table 5–6 receives supplementary purchasing power in the form of food stamps worth $100 toward the purchase of food. Housing costs remain unchanged. The other four categories of spending increase by $25 each as a result of having $100 of food stamps available to use at the grocery store. The net change in spending applied to each category represents, in fact, what the food stamps were used to purchase. Thus, only $25 of the stamps were used to purchase food. The remaining $75 was used to buy other things.

Notice that the pattern of consumption, if given $100 in cash instead of $100 in food stamps, would have been *identical* to the pattern of actual consumption using stamps, so long as the family has complete freedom of choice in the way it spends its stamps. By 1994, a handful of communities had begun making cash payments in lieu of food stamps. This switch to cash will doubtless be copied by other communities.

Because food stamps are in practice fungible for money, food stamps in circulation should be included in measures of the money supply under the present arrangements. Moreover, in view of the fungible nature of food stamps, it would be simpler to give money to poor people and avoid the many problems associated with having a dual currency in circulation. On a more political note, to say that "food stamps can only be used to buy food," is to lie to the public. If the voting public would not approve a program to give money to poor people, but does approve a program to give stamps that "can only be used to buy food," then the public is being misled by the food stamp program run by the U.S. Department of Agriculture since food stamps, in spite of negligible differences, are *perfect substitutes for money in a consumer's budget*. Finally, it is wrong for the Department of Agriculture to print what is effectively part of the money supply when such activities should be the responsibility of the Federal Reserve System.

Table 5–6
Sample Budget for a Consumer (Family) Unit

Spending categories	Without food stamps (Income $400)	With $100 worth of food stamps (Income $500)	With $100 more in cash (Income $500)
Housing	$150	$150	$150
Transportation	50	75	75
Clothing	50	75	75
Food	100	125	125
Miscellaneous	50	75	75

The student loan program is in many ways similar to the food stamp program. A student comes to campus with $5,000 for the year. Tuition is $1,000. He comes across a used Dodge pick-up truck that he would like to use to carry kegs of beer on weekend picnics. He borrows at a subsidized interest rate to pay his tuition, and uses $1,000 of his own funds to buy the pick-up. If money is fungible, what did he really buy with his student loan? If, without the loan, he would have paid tuition and made it through the year without the pick-up, it is clear that the loan money was spent on the pick-up and *not* on tuition. Therefore, governments that subsidize student tuition are wasting their money because money is fungible and so are student loans. If students are poor and want government support, government should give them money and not hide behind the facade that they are "paying for (subsidizing) student tuition."

Many more examples of this kind abound. Business firms pay for employee's health insurance. Should such payments be a business expense or employee income? If the employee would have bought the insurance anyway, then having it paid for by the employer simply frees up dollars that provide additional income to the employee. If the employee would not have bought any insurance, then it should be treated as a business expense. Payments that others make on your behalf are fungible for the money that you have available. Private contractual payments recognize fungible payments, but government programs often fail to consider them.

The Case of the Missing Currency

A huge amount of the U.S. dollar paper currency outstanding is unaccounted for, that is, surveys do not reveal where it is being held. Currency amounts to about 30 per cent of the nation's money supply, say $300 billion in 1993. But about 80 per cent of this, or $240 billion, was not uncovered by surveys according to C. M. Sprenkle (1993).

Surveys of currency holdings did not include (a) persons under 18 years of age, (b) foreigners, and, quite obviously, (c) underground holders. Holders of illegally obtained currency will not report their holdings to survey takers.

A large increase in the currency component of the U.S. money supply occurred in the aftermath of the opening of Eastern Europe in November 1989. As a significant component of the money supply, this led to an increase in the rate of growth of money and could have been interpreted as inflationary. But this money was not used for spending in the U.S. Instead, it was used to purchase the services of taxis and other items from suppliers in Eastern Europe and in countries in the former Soviet Union. This contributed to the inflation in those countries as the dollars began to be used as money in those places.

One should note that real commodities were provided to those who supplied dollars to the Eastern Europeans. Thus, for the Eastern Europeans to obtain a supply of dollars to use as a currency, they had to give up commodities. Like the Chinese province of Guangdong, mentioned earlier, Eastern Europeans or their people pay seigniorage to the U.S. and other developed countries, whose currencies circulate in Eastern Europe. If those countries had strong currencies then the seigniorage would be earned by the local government instead. So long as they continue to have dollars circulate in their countries, they will be paying seigniorage to the U.S. and other more developed countries whose currencies they use in their transactions.

Summary

In this chapter money was defined to be anything that can be used to discharge debt. A detailed analysis of the measuring of monetary aggregates was presented and measures of money in the U.S., Hong Kong, Korea, Singapore, and Taiwan were briefly described.

It was suggested that measures of money, the perfectly "liquid" asset, should be distinguished carefully from measures of liquidity that include money and other highly liquid assets.

Brassage and seigniorage represent ways in which governments can effectively collect a tax from the general public because governments have taken the right to control the money supply. If money is thought of as a commodity, then one might say that government has instituted a monopoly over the supply of money and collects a monopoly rent in the form of seigniorage. In the case of Hong Kong and Singapore, seigniorage is easy to recognize and measure. It is simply the interest earnings on the holdings of foreign exchange reserves.

Seigniorage is not so readily observable in countries that have outstanding debt in the form of government securities. There, the seigniorage takes the form of a saving in the interest that the government has to pay because non-interest-bearing debt in the form of currency is in circulation.

Key Terms and Concepts

Money	Four functions of money
Brassage	Seigniorage
Measures of money	Fungible
Food stamps as money	

Discussion Questions and Exercises

1. What are the four functions of money? Give an example of each.
2. Why is currency in the vaults of banks not considered part of the money supply?
3. Why are interbank deposits excluded from the money supply measures?
4. What proposal was made for giving money supply measures different labels?
5. What is seigniorage? How is it different from brassage?
6. If all of the traveler's checks outstanding in the U.S. were issued by American Express, roughly how much seigniorage does American Express earn annually? Make your assumptions clear.
7. How much seigniorage does the government in Taiwan, Singapore, and Korea each earn from issues of currency?

8. How much seigniorage is earned by banks in the United States assuming that the typical checking account earns 2 per cent, that banks can lend at 8 per cent, and that reserve requirements average 10 per cent?
9. Some economists recommend that governments permit money creation by private citizens and eliminate government involvement in the process. Discuss the merits of this proposal.
10. Are credit cards money? Explain their relation to the money supply.
11. Should the outstanding supply of food stamps circulating in the U.S. be included in measure of money, $M1$? Discuss.
12. Many former republics of the U.S.S.R. have begun to issue their own currencies. Is there any good reason for them not to simply use U.S. dollars as a medium of exchange? Explain.

References

For a detailed analysis, comprehensive references, and interesting empirical estimates, students should refer to Neumann's "Seigniorage in the United States: How Much Does the U.S. Government Make from Money Production?" He concludes that fiscal seigniorage on average over 1950–1990 contributed about 2 per cent of the financing of real federal expenditures. He does not discuss the question of seigniorage accruing to the deposit-money creating industry.

An exposition of how banks earn seigniorage may be found in Scott and Johnson, "Rent-Seeking in U.S. Banking and the Optimal Quantity of Money."

Neumann, Manfred J. M., "Seigniorage in the United States: How Much Does the U.S. Government Make from Money Production?" *Review*, Federal Reserve Bank of St. Louis, Vol. 74, March/April 1992, pp. 29–40.

Roberds, William, "Changes in Payments Technology and the Welfare Cost of Inflation," *Economic Review*, Federal Reserve Bank of Atlanta, May/June 1994, pp. 1–12.

Russell, Steven, "The U.S. Currency System: A Historical Perspective," *Review*, Federal Reserve Bank of St. Louis, September/October 1991, pp. 34–61.

Scott, Robert Haney, and Johnson, Dudley W., "Rent-seeking in U.S. Banking and the Optimal Quantity of Money," *Hong Kong Economic Papers*, No. 15, 1984, pp. 67–78.

Sprenkle, Case M., "The Case of the Missing Currency," *Journal of Economic Perspectives*, Fall 1993, No. 4, pp. 175–84.

Webster's New Collegiate Dictionary, G. & C. Merriam & Co., Springfield, MA, 1949.

West, Donald A., and Price, David W., "The Effects of Income, Assets, Food Programs and Household Size on Food Consumption," *American Journal of Agricultural Economics*, November 1976, pp. 725–30.

CHAPTER 6

Commercial and Central Bank Interactions

AS WE SAW in Chapter 4, the distinction between commercial banks and other types of deposit-taking institutions has changed greatly since 1980. In other countries with universal banking, institutions may operate as investment or merchant banks as well as acting as thrift institutions and commercial banks. In the following presentation, references made to commercial banks should be interpreted to mean all banks and other deposit-taking institutions generally.

Bankers are no exception to the rule that persons in the same trade will tend to meet with each other to discuss matters of common concern. Typically their meetings are held to share information and assist each other in solving problems common to their trade. Sometimes, when only two or three persons dominate a trade, strong rivalries form. But when many persons engage in the same trade, close friendships often form and trade associations or unions are a result. These associations or unions provide political representation in the halls of government to pursue the private interest of the group.

Correspondent Banking Relations

Efficient functioning of the unit banking system in the U.S. requires that each bank maintain a network of correspondent banks. A country bank in Oregon may have a customer who wants to travel to New York on business and wants to be sure that checks on the Oregon bank will be accepted. Correspondent banks will prearrange check-cashing services for the customer.

Regulations applying to most banks in the U.S. limit the size of a loan that a bank can make to any single customer. The limit is often 10 per cent of the bank's capital and surplus. Thus, a small country bank with a million dollars in capital could only arrange a loan for $100,000. If a local farmer comes into the bank offices to arrange for the purchase of $500,000 of equipment, the local bank will agree to make the loan because it has relations with a large nearby city bank that will agree to take up the other $400,000 portion. The larger the loan required, the more likely it is that a large number of banks will participate in a consortium.

A correspondent banking relation may also encourage one bank to come to the assistance of another in the event of a run by depositors. A small country bank may maintain a sizable deposit with a city bank and, if a run begins, it will call upon its larger associate to deliver cash to pay depositors and also lend the extra cash needed to ward off the run.

But what if a large city bank runs into difficulty meeting a run on its deposits? Where can it go to get a loan? It must go either to the government or to other large banks. In such an instance, other large banks would be happy to let the government handle the problem. If the government were to set a precedent, that would help solve the confidence problem that banks often run into.

In a typical case, the government might go to a large bank that was in sound financial condition and prevail upon it to take action to assist the troubled institution. It might ask the sound bank to buy out the failing bank. The sound bank would request guarantees from the government regarding liability for some of the bad loans that the failing bank might have on its balance sheet. Involved and complex negotiations between the government and the banks would ensue. In Hong Kong, in 1991, the Bank of East Asia offered to buy up the failing Bank of Credit and Commerce, conditional upon receiving some guarantee from the government that it would cover the possibility of bad assets. No accommodation was reached, and the bank remained closed and was eventually "wound up."

Governments faced with repetitions of such events will want to make arrangements so that they need not deal with each individual case on an ad hoc basis. What better solution than to establish a central bank as an arm of the government? Hong Kong moved to establish a central monetary authority in 1993. Many other countries took similar steps many years ago. Each central bank has its own history, and many evolved out of their role as large correspondent banks whose functions were commandeered by government.

The Bank of England, however, originated in the 1690s as a private bank chartered by the government of England with the express purpose of handling the government's banking business. In the years that followed the bank took over the business of lending to other banks and became famous as the world's first lender of last resort—"the little old lady of Threadneedle Street," as it was called.

Thus, in the evolution of central banking, one of the principal functions of a central bank was to act as "lender of last resort" to banks that faced bankruptcy.

Functions of Central Banks

Several interrelated functions are carried out by full-fledged central banks in modern exchange economies. The single broad overall objective of a central bank is to *protect money holder's wealth*. It attacks this problem by *regulating*, examining, and monitoring activities of individual banks in order to prevent fraud and bad loans that lead to bank runs and failures, and monetary losses to depositors. It also attacks this problem by *controlling* the extent to which banks are able to *create money*. If banks create too much money, there will be inflation and an erosion in the purchasing power of money—hence a decline in the money holder's wealth.

Central bank functions can be broken down into more numerous interrelated parts in order to provide a more informative overview. All the while we must remember that no two central banks function in the same way. In general, a look at a specific central bank's balance sheet indicates the functions of that particular central bank, just as an examination of a commercial bank's balance sheet informs the reader about its activities. The following ten accounts, five asset and five liabilities accounts, typically appear on the balance sheet of a central bank—in this case the Federal Reserve System's accounts are representative of most central banks.

Liabilities

A. Central banks issue currency. Usually, the currency is issued to commercial banks, which then pay bank-notes out to the public in response to the demand for cash withdrawals.

B. Central banks play the role of banker to commercial banks. Commercial banks use the central bank in a manner analogous to the way that a citizen uses a local bank. That is, commercial banks bank with the central bank—keeping funds on deposit and occasionally asking for loans. The central bank also clears checks between commercial banks in the absence of other clearing houses in the same way a commercial bank clears checks through a citizen's checking account.

C. Central banks play the role of banker to governments. As a government's fiscal agent, the central bank will accept deposits of the Treasury and help the government issue and redeem securities. When the Treasury spends by writing checks, those checks are cleared through its account at the central bank.

D. Central banks play banker for other central banks and official or authorized institutions of foreign governments. They swap currencies with other governments and arrange for other governments to invest their foreign exchange reserves in interest-earning securities.

E. Central banks often clear checks for commercial banks just as commercial banks will clear customer's checks. However, when a commercial bank gives a batch of checks to the Federal Reserve, the Fed will not give all the funds to the bank immediately. (This is the same as when a customer goes to his or her bank to deposit a check on a different bank and finds that the funds will not be available until after a few days have passed.) While the Fed holds the bank's checks it records them as a liability called *deferred availability items*. After a delay, determined by a set time schedule of a day or two at most, the deferred availability account is reduced and the bank that deposited the checks receives the funds in its reserve account.

Having looked briefly at the liabilities on the right side of Table 6–1, now let us glance at the assets on the left.

Table 6–1
Outline of the Federal Reserve System Balance Sheet

Assets	Liabilities
A. Gold	A. Notes payable
B. Loans to banks	B. Deposits of banks
C. Government securities	C. Treasury deposits
D. Foreign securities	D. Foreign deposits
E. Items being collected	E. Deferred availability items

Assets

A. Central banks hold gold, or in the case of the Federal Reserve, gold certificates issued by the Treasury. The certificates represent the nominal value of the gold held by the Treasury and stored mostly in Fort Knox. It also holds "paper gold" in the form of Special Drawing Rights with the International Monetary Fund. Both of these accounts form the U.S. government's "reserves" in some sense, but, since the world has not been on the gold standard since 1973, it is not clear just how these gold holdings should be viewed.

B. Central banks make loans to commercial banks and on rare occasions to others. The Banque de France acts as France's central bank as well as acting as a commercial bank making loans to depositors, and the like. In 1993 it was proposed that the Banque de France be privatized so it would no longer be dependent on the government. But the 12 Federal Reserve Banks no longer engage in any commercial banking activities nor do they make loans to industry, except on rare occasions in the past when justified by special circumstances.

C. Central banks hold government securities whether issued by the Treasury or other federal agencies. Sometimes central banks will hold securities of private corporations or perhaps even shares of stock traded on exchanges. The Bank of Japan has held stock. But, basically, the Federal Reserve holds only government securities.

D. Central banks hold foreign exchange in the form of securities denominated in the currency of other countries. The Federal Reserve added a considerable sum to the volume of its holdings of foreign exchange in 1991 as it attempted to hold down the value of the dollar on foreign exchange markets by buying foreign currencies. Germany's central bank, Bundesbank, was very active in the foreign exchange markets several years ago.

E. A central bank notifies depositing banks before reducing their central bank accounts due to check clearing. When a bank sends checks to the Fed for clearing, the Fed credits the deferred availability item and then records the value of the deposited checks as the asset: *cash items in the process of collection.* Here, these items are simply called items being collected. Thus, the bank against which the checks are being collected does not have its deposits with the Fed reduced until such time as transportation services can deliver the checks to it. In other words, the Fed tries not take funds out of the bank's reserve account before the bank is informed. After the bank knows the checks against it are being collected, the Fed reduces its deposit account on the liability side and reduces the account cash items in the process of collection at the same time.

F. Central banks monitor the float. The *float* is the difference between cash items in the process of collection and deferred availability items (Float = Cash items − Deferred items). Because the Fed always releases the deferred availability items to depositing banks before it collects the funds from the banks against which the checks were drawn, the float is always positive and is an asset of the Fed. When this asset increases, bank deposits at the Fed increase as well, adding reserves to the banking system. In the early 1980s, Congress instructed the Federal Reserve to install a system for charging banks fees for its clearing services and thus reduce the size of the float. This system is now in place, and each bank now has a *separate clearing balance with the Federal Reserve* through which checks are cleared, along with its usual deposit known as its reserve balance.

In broad summary, therefore, balance sheets of typical central banks have these five asset classifications and five classes of liabilities along with other items not listed here, such as buildings and equipment, capital stock, clearing accounts, and so forth. By watching changes in each of the balance sheet items one can interpret the actions taken by managers of central banks and discern the role that a central bank plays in the economy. The role played by central banks as examiners and auditors of commercial banks is not so evident in the balance sheet items.

Managing Bank Reserves: The Bank's Viewpoint

In order to understand how central banks operate, it is useful to begin by taking the view of the manager of a commercial bank who is faced with regulations that require the bank to carefully meet the reserve requirements as described in Chapter 3. Legally required reserves must be in the form of deposits with the Federal Reserve, in sufficient amounts, especially on Tuesday and Wednesday because on Tuesday morning each bank knows what its required reserves for the two-week reserve accounting period will be. The manager has the opportunity to lend out any excess reserves, and also the opportunity to acquire any reserve deficiencies.

Table 6–2
Outline of a Commercial Banking Balance Sheet

Assets	Liabilities

A. Reserves
    Cash
    *Deposits with Federal Reserve
	A. Demand deposits
	    Individual, corporate, government,
	    banks, etc.
	    Other transaction deposits

B. Government securities	B. Saving and time deposits Negotiable CDs
C. Mortgage loans	C. Treasury deposits (TT&L)
D. Business loans and consumer loans	D. Treasury Notes (TT&L Note) E. Borrowing from Federal Reserve F. Repurchase agreements (RPs) G. Net Federal Reserve funds purchased

*See main text for explanation.

In discussing the alternatives open to the bank manager it will be helpful to keep in mind the balance sheet items shown in Table 6–2.

On the liability side of the bank's balance sheet, items A, B, and C are those against which legal reserves are, or may be, required. For many years there was a 3 per cent reserve required against time and savings accounts. These were removed on personal accounts in 1980, and in December 1990 the remaining 3 per cent reserve against nonpersonal time deposits and Eurodollar liabilities was phased down to zero. Thus, as a practical matter, reserve requirements are effectively 10 per cent at the margin on all transactions deposits (not including Money Market Deposit Accounts on which check-writing is usually restricted to six withdrawals per month, no more than three of which can be checks).

On the asset side, legal reserves comprises Cash and Deposits with the Federal Reserve and are shown in item A. However, as noted in Chapter 3, cash in vaults is accounted for with a lag of two weeks. So, when it comes to the last two days of the two-week reserve maintenance period under contemporaneous accounting, it is only the reserves held in the form of deposits with the Federal Reserve that can be adjusted to bring the bank's reserve in line with legal requirements. The importance of this account is indicated by the asterisk preceding it. It is the *target variable*.

Slack Variables Used to Meet Target Variables

In the 1920s many business loans were "call" loans. That is, the loan was made on the condition that the borrower would be willing to pay it off whenever the bank called for repayment. Many call loans were made to investors in the stock markets with the shares of stock behind them as collateral. Thus, the bank figured that, if it wanted its money, the investor could always sell the shares on the stock exchange and pay off the loan immediately with the proceeds from the sale of the stock. The *call loan account* was considered by many bank managers to be the *slack variable*, that is, the account that could be used to pick up any slack in the supply of reserves.

One big problem arose, however, if the stock market took a nosedive, as it did in October 1929. A decline in the market led worried bankers to call loans that led to sales of shares and further erosion of share prices. Some attribute the stock market collapse of 1929 to this malfunctioning of the call loan market.

Another way that managers obtained reserves to meet legal requirements after World War II was to sell government securities. During the war, bank reserves increased greatly and, since consumer and business loans were restricted by regulations governing the production of war materials, the banks simply used excess reserves to purchase government securities. Thus, each bank in the country had a huge portfolio of these. The government securities specialists organized a nationwide telephone market so that banks from anywhere in the country could call in, sell government securities, and the funds could be transferred by wire through the Federal Reserve. The *government securities* account was another example of a bank's *slack variable*.

Targets and Slack Variables. At this point it is useful to note that if the target or goal is to obtain an increase in the level of deposits with the Federal Reserve then the manager has the choice of selling off some other asset. That is, if a plus is needed in deposits with the Fed, this can be obtained with a minus in some other asset such as call loans or government securities. The beauty of double entry accounting assures this result.

Instead of acquiring reserves by selling some other asset, the manager may decide to acquire a liability. An increase in any item on the liability side will result in an increase in the bank's reserves.

Thus, one way a bank can deal with a need for more deposits with the Fed is to induce someone to deposit more funds in the bank. An increase in customer deposits can be sent along for deposit at the Fed. But it is not easy to attract deposits on the spur of the moment.

However, in the early 1970s banks had reduced their holdings of government securities to low levels and they hesitated to rely on these holdings as a slack variable. So they invented *negotiable certificates of deposit* as a *slack variable*. Banks helped establish a secondary market in these certificates. Thus, whenever a bank needed extra funds it could simply print up these certificates, deliver them to a trader and sell them in a market like any other over-the-counter security. The effect was the same as if deposits had been made to the bank.

Below-the-Mark Items

The reader will please note the short line on the liability side of the balance sheet that separates the deposits from items D, E, F, and G. The dividing mark is placed there to separate accounts against which the Federal Reserve might require that reserves be held from those liability items against which no reserves are to be required. Each of these items have special operating relevance to both the Federal Reserve and the commercial bank. Let us examine each in some detail.

Liability Item D. TT&L stands for Treasury Tax and Loan accounts. These appear above the mark and below the mark as well as a TT&L note account. A short history may be useful. During World War I the Treasury issued Liberty Bonds as part of its financing operations. It encouraged the sale of these to the general public by setting up accounts in banks so that banks could sell the bonds and simply transfer the funds from depositor accounts into the Treasury's TT&L account. Arrangements were also made for some tax payments to be made directly into the TT&L account. Hence, the name Treasury Tax and Loan account. Then banks were classified as A, B, and C banks with the A banks being the small ones and the C banks being the large ones. The Treasury would then require that A banks send funds from the TT&L accounts in to the Treasury's account with the Federal Reserve on a set schedule at the end of each month, for example. Banks with the B class would be able to keep the funds for perhaps two weeks, and then send them in to the Treasury's account. Finally, the C banks were subject to call any day of the week. For example, the Treasury might send a notice to all C banks and request that 60 per cent of TT&L account funds be wired in to its account in the Fed.

In each case the bank would reduce its TT&L liability and also reduce its deposit at the Federal Reserve. This means that a call for TT&L balances by the Treasury results in the bank having less reserves at the Federal Reserve. Looking back at the Federal Reserve's balance sheet liability items there are Bank Deposits (item B) and Treasury Deposits (item C). When the Treasury collects funds from the banks, the Treasury's deposits at the Federal Reserve increase (item C) while banks' deposits at the Federal Reserve decrease (item B).

This process came under review in the late 1970s because the Treasury was not earning interest on tens of billions of dollars kept in TT&L accounts in banks. So the Congress told the Treasury to send their funds in directly to the Fed as they arrived at the bank. When bank reserves are down, the Fed buys government securities to replenish them. This was described in the discussion of seigniorage in Chapter 4. Then the Treasury pays interest to the Fed, but the Fed only uses a small fraction of this interest to meet its expenses and returns the excess to the Treasury. In 1990 the amount returned to the Treasury was $23.6 billion and is considered to be a payment of interest on Federal Reserve Notes (with the green seal) that now comprise almost all of the paper currency issued by the U.S. government.

Thus, the Treasury receives the seigniorage on the circulating currency in this indirect fashion.

But a problem arose out of this procedure. Treasury receipts and payments were often erratic and made in sizable amounts, especially on quarterly tax dates. This made it difficult for the Fed to control banks' overall reserve position. So a new arrangement was made under which commercial banks created the TT&L note account, item D, and the old call system with A banks, B banks, and C banks was re-instituted. Money coming into the regular TT&L account stays there for one day and is then transferred below the mark to the TT&L note account on which the bank pays interest to the Treasury. It remains in that interest-earning account until called in to the Fed. In this fashion the disturbances to bank reserve positions are greatly reduced. In addition, banks charge the Treasury service fees for selling bonds and accepting tax payments to make up for the earnings that the banks formerly realized from investing the funds deposited into non-interest-bearing TT&L accounts. So the banks now pay interest but the Treasury pays service fees, and presumably the Treasury saves some money for the taxpayer under these arrangements.

Liability Item E. This item, Borrowing from the Federal Reserve, represents the "lender of last resort" function of the central bank. It increases after the bank requests a loan from the Fed and gives it full collateral in the form of government securities. Then the Fed accepts the loan as an asset and credits the bank's deposit account with the Fed.

Liability Item F. Repurchase agreements are contracts in which a customer of the bank agrees to buy a security held by the bank and hold it overnight. The bank agrees to repurchase the security from the customer when the bank opens the following morning. Thus, the bank has a repurchase agreement with a depositor. Bank deposits are reduced (liability item A) while repurchase agreements are increased. Notice that this activity permits depositors with large sums of money to earn interest for one day without giving up their ability to use their checking account. These RPs, or REPOs, are used to avoid the laws that forbid banks to pay interest on demand deposits (see Glass-Steagall Act). Banks are not required to hold reserves against these RP contracts, yet in practice they represent funds that are simply removed from the deposit category only overnight when the bank is closed. They continue to be, de facto, a deposit liability subject to reserve requirements, but the inventiveness of accountants and attorneys has led to the creation of a special type of contract and a special set of accounts to avoid the legal constraints. Small businesses cannot take advantage of these special contracts to earn interest on their accounts with banks. Only depositors with large sums can avail themselves of these special arrangements.

Liability Item G. This item comprises Net Fed Funds Purchased. Sometimes banks record two accounts, Fed Funds Sold as an asset and Fed Funds Purchased as a liability. When combining these two accounts on the liability side, the result is *Net* Fed Funds Purchased. This account is perhaps the most interesting account in the world of banking today. All large banks have these accounts. As mentioned in Chapter 3, federal funds, for the most part, are simply those funds that banks hold on deposit with the Federal

Reserve. Such deposits are legal reserves in the United States. Thus, this account is now *the slack variable* used by all banks to adjust their reserve positions.

Net Fed Funds Purchased

Assume that First Bank in Seattle finds that it has $16 million more deposits with the Fed than it needs to meet its legal reserve requirement for the current reserve maintenance period. First Bank's manager came to the office on Wednesday morning thinking that there was an extra $20 million in the account at the Fed. But the overnight clearings went against First Bank to the tune of $4 million, leaving $16 million free to be invested overnight. Around noon the manager calls Los Angeles to talk with the Los Angeles branch of Pacific Bank (LA/Pac) and asks if LA/Pac would want to purchase the excess funds. LA/Pac replies that it will buy the funds for an interest rate of 3.75 per cent.

First Bank's manager agrees to sell the funds to LA/Pac at this annual rate for one day, and then puts several copies of a form in the out-box. A runner picks up the forms and takes copies to the local Fed branch where the Fed reduces First Bank's account and increases LA/Pac's account by $16 million. The next day LA/Pac sends a form to the Fed branch in Los Angeles and orders the Fed to reduce its account by $16 million plus interest for one day at an annual rate of 3.75 per cent. (Interest amounts to about $1,600.)

The result is that First Bank has earned interest on the reserves it held in the Fed that were in excess of the amounts required to meet its legal reserve obligations.

Was the LA/Pac bank in need of additional reserves? Perhaps and perhaps not. These federal funds are traded continuously throughout the working day in bank trading rooms. The trader in Los Angeles may have had another call at the same time it received a call from First Bank from a different bank that wanted to buy fed funds. Thus, LA/Pac may have, fundamentally, only played a dealer's role, buying funds from First Bank and re-lending them in the market for, say, 3.825 per cent. Before finishing trading for the day LA/Pac managers will watch their net position to ensure that it too, is in compliance with Federal Reserve legal reserve requirements.

Large banks playing the fed funds market continuously every business day sometimes are in net overdraft positions with the Federal Reserve. This situation aroused the concern of the regulators who worried that a bankruptcy situation could occur before the bank was able to reverse its position. Thus, in 1993, provisions were made to levy charges that amount to the equivalent of an intra-day interest charge on overdraft positions. These regulations are designed to dissuade banks from allowing their fed funds positions to swing so widely in intra-day trading.

Net Fed Funds Purchased represent borrowing of funds from other banks. Yet no reserve requirements are levied on these debt obligations. Also, interest is paid on this overnight money by one bank to the other. If this kind of borrowing had been in the form of a deposit by First Bank into an account of LA/Pac, interest payments to First Bank would have been prohibited by the Glass-Steagall Act and LA/Pac would have had to maintain reserves against the deposit. De facto, two banking regulations are being bypassed. Again, "creative accounting" and "legal construction" play a big role in what we see happening in the financial industry.

To see the irony in this situation, consider the following situation: the LA/Pac manager takes a friend to dinner that night and calmly declares over martinis that he had *purchased $16 million* of federal funds that day. The friend will really be impressed. $16 million! Would it not be great to be a banker and have all that money to buy things—just think, the bank manager spent $16 million to purchase federal funds.

Contrast this response with the one that would have followed if LA/Pac's manager had told the truth—namely that LA/Pac had *borrowed* $16 million from a bank in Seattle. What? Borrowed all that money from Seattle? My God, is LA/Pac about to go broke? Why would it need to borrow so much money? Are its loans going bad? Should I withdraw my deposits?

Sometimes what something is called does make a difference, and Juliet's observation, "That which we call a rose, by any other name would smell as sweet:" may not always hold true (Romeo and Juliet, act 2, sc. 2).

Reserves

Individual banks operating day by day, count on some depositors to provide an inflow of funds roughly in equal amount to the funds that other depositors withdraw. Since precise equality of deposits and withdrawals does not exist, however, it is necessary for banks to hold vault cash or currency in ATM machines in sufficient amounts to meet withdrawals, that is, to hold some cash reserves. Banks must hold some reserves in order to do business every day, whether required by law to do so or not. Indeed, many countries do not have legal reserve requirements like those of the United States, as will be mentioned later in this chapter.

Because legal reserves play an important role in the management of the money-creating activities of banks, it is important to define certain terms.

Legal reserves are the accounting items that may be used to meet legal reserve requirements. In the United States, these are vault cash and deposits with the Federal Reserve Banks. *Total reserves* are the *amount* of reserves held by a bank or banks. *Required reserves* are those dollar amounts of reserves that must be held according to computations using the legal reserve ratio. *Excess reserves* are those dollar amounts held in excess of required reserves. *Borrowed reserves* are the funds that a bank or banks have borrowed from the Federal Reserve. *Nonborrowed reserves* (or unborrowed reserves) are simply total reserves minus borrowed reserves. The following summary may be helpful:

Total reserves	Total reserves
less *Required reserves*	less *Borrowing from Federal Reserve*
= Excess reserves	= Nonborrowed reserves
less *Borrowing from Federal Reserve*	
= Net free (or borrowed) reserves	

The reserve position of an individual bank determines whether it can make loans or not. The reserve position of the banking system overall determines whether, by making loans, banks can create additional money. Thus, whether the Federal Reserve is tightening up on the extent of money creation, or relaxing the reins on banks and encouraging them to create money, depends to a large degree on what actions the Federal Reserve takes with respect to bank reserve positions.

For many years the Federal Reserve reported total reserves and calculated net free reserves in its weekly statement on bank reserve positions. The calculation is shown on the left side of the summary above. Some economists complained, however, that net free reserves did not mean that money was "easy" because the money supply could not be growing at all while free reserves were still large. Similarly, free reserves could be negative when the money supply was growing rapidly. It would be a mistake to interpret net borrowed reserves as a "tight" money condition, if the money supply were growing rapidly. Because of this debate with economists, the Federal Reserve stopped interpreting the net free reserve position for the public.

However, if the data show over several weeks that the extent of excess reserves is diminishing and that banks are being forced by a scarcity of reserves to go to the Fed for funds, then net borrowed reserves will be rising and this indicates a "tight" monetary posture on the part of the Fed. That is, while the level of net free reserves may not disclose the current policy posture of the Federal Reserve, *changes* in the level of net free reserves over time will indicate the Fed's plan. Therefore, although the Federal Reserve does not publish nor interpret the free reserve figure, it does publish excess reserves and borrowing figures so that anyone is free to calculate the free reserve figure from the numbers in Table 6–3. The free reserve data are published by financial analysts and reported in major newspapers along with the other measures of reserves. But the Federal Reserve, stung by the criticism of academics, publishes everything but the free reserve figure in its principal data source, the *Federal Reserve Bulletin.*

Tools of Control over Money Creation

Central banks are charged with the responsibility of controlling the growth in the money supply. They should not let it grow too rapidly in order to prevent inflationary spirals, and they should not let it contract and contribute to deflation and depression. Many central banks seem to honor their responsibilities, "... more in the breach than in the observance." But those that take their responsibilities seriously generally exercise controls by taking actions that affect the reserve situation that banks face.

There are four major ways that central banks go about controlling money growth: open market operations, regulation of borrowing by banks, changing required reserve ratios, and moral suasion. Each will be discussed briefly here. The implementation of monetary policies will be discussed more extensively in later chapters.

Table 6–3

Aggregate Reserves of Depository Institutions and the Monetary Base (Adjusted for changes in reserve requirements[1]; averages of daily figures, seasonally adjusted unless noted otherwise; in million of dollars)

Date	Reserves of depository institutions					Monetary base[6]	Borrowings of depository institutions from the Federal Reserve, NSA		
	Total[2]	Nonborrowed[3]	Nonborrowed plus extended credit[4]	Required	Excess NSA[5]		Total	Seasonal	Extended credit[4]
1994 Jan.	60,554	60,480	60,480	59,106	1,448	389,563	73	15	0
Feb.	60,736	60,666	60,666	59,597	1,140	393,890	70	15	0
Two weeks ending									
1994 Feb. 2	60,729	60,684	60,684	59,462	1,267	391,720	45	18	0
16	60,737	60,642	60,642	59,625	1,112	393,344	95	15	0
Mar. 2	60,737	60,692	60,692	59,586	1,151	394,887	45	15	0
16p	60,624	60,586	60,586	59,562	1,063	396,377	39	17	0
30pe	60,226	60,159	60,159	59,399	827	397,759	68	32	0

1. Reserves and monetary base figures incorporate adjustments for discontinuities, or "breaks," associated with regulatory changes in reserve requirements.
2. Seasonally adjusted, break-adjusted total reserves equal seasonally adjusted, break-adjusted required reserves plus unadjusted excess reserves.
3. Seasonally adjusted, break-adjusted nonborrowed reserves equal seasonally adjusted, break-adjusted total reserves less unadjusted total borrowings of depository institutions from the Federal Reserve.
4. Extended credit consists of borrowing at the discount window under the terms and conditions established for the extended credit program to help depository institutions deal with sustained liquidity pressures. Because there is not the same need to repay such borrowing promptly as there is with traditional short-term adjustment credit, the money market impact of extended credit is similar to that of nonborrowed reserves.
5. Excess reserves NSA equals unadjusted total reserves less unadjusted required reserves.
6. The seasonally adjusted, break-adjusted monetary base consists of (1) seasonally adjusted, break-adjusted total reserves plus (2) the seasonally adjusted currency component of the money stock plus (3) for all quarterly reporters on the "Report of Transaction Accounts, Other Deposits and Vault Cash" and for all those weekly reporters whose vault cash exceeds their required reserves, the seasonally adjusted, break-adjusted difference between current vault cash and the amount applied to satisfy current reserve requirements.

p   preliminary
pe preliminary estimate

Source: *Federal Reserve System*, Board of Governors, March 31, 1994, p. H.3(502).

Open Market Operations

Open market operations are the major means of controlling the money supply. The Fed regularly uses its government securities account, often called the open market account, as a *slack variable* to be used to ensure that a targeted level of bank reserves is available to banks. On the basis of reserves there is a volume of deposit money that banks in the system can create.

When the Fed buys securities, it pays for these with a check drawn on the Fed. The Fed is in a very fortunate position. It can, unlike the rest of us, write a check on itself without having any money! When the person who receives the check deposits it in his bank account, the bank sends the check in to be deposited with the Fed. The Fed then records a deposit for the bank, and in the swipe of a pen (nowadays, the tap of a computer key) the bank has reserve money that the Fed has simply created. Although it may seem like magic to most people, it is simply a human act carried out in accordance with institutional procedures that humans have devised.

Open market purchases of securities (or purchases of anything else) create bank reserves. Open market sales of securities (or sales of anything else) destroy bank reserves.

For example, if the Fed sells a security to an individual, that person gives the Fed a check on a bank to pay for it. The Fed collects the check by reducing the bank's reserve deposit with the Fed, and bank reserves are down. The bank is notified that its reserves are down and it then reduces the deposit account of the individual who bought the security. Actually, wire transfers are used in place of checks, but it simplifies the explanation to imagine checks passing from hand to hand.

Thus, the Fed, using its portfolio of government securities as a slack variable, can increase or decrease the total level of bank reserves at will.

Defensive and Dynamic Open Market Operations. If a snowstorm delays forwarding of deposited checks to the banks on which they were drawn, the Federal Reserve float will increase. An increase in the float will increase bank reserves. The manager of the open market account may sell government securities to absorb the reserves created by the float. Such an open market operation would be called defensive because it is taken to defend the system against an unwanted change in reserves brought about by the snowstorm.

Other defensive operations may be undertaken to offset changes in other accounts. For example, at Christmas time there are outflows of currency into circulation that reduce bank reserves. At tax time there are inflows of Treasury money that may reduce bank reserves. Foreign deposits may change. Managers of the open market account try to anticipate all of these changes. They may simply offset each other. But more likely they will leave some net impact on bank reserves, and defensive open market operations will be used to negate this net impact.

When the Federal Reserve reduces the required reserve ratio and increases the volume of excess reserves, it may need to absorb these excess reserves through open market operations. In other words, sometimes defensive open market operations are used to defend against other Federal Reserve policy actions! This actually happened in December 1990 and January 1991 after the Federal Reserve reduced the 3 per cent reserve requirement on nontransaction deposit accounts to zero and released $13 billion in reserves which it then absorbed. Thus, the net effect of the offsetting actions was simply to permit banks to earn more seigniorage.

Defensive operations stand in contrast to offensive, or dynamic, operations. These are the net purchases or sales of government securities designed expressly for the purpose of encouraging banks to increase the money supply in periods of recession, or to restrain growth in the creation of deposit money by banks in an inflationary environment. Thus, dynamic (offensive) open market operations are taken for the express purpose of changing the level of bank reserves in line with monetary policy dictates.

The distinction between defensive and offensive open market operations is more clearly understood in theory than in practice. When random factors affect the level of bank reserves, some increasing them and some decreasing them, the net result may be an increase of 3 per cent, which, in turn, may just happen to be exactly the amount that the policy authorities set as the target for growth in bank reserves. In this case, to achieve dynamic goals, no operations need to take place at all! This is merely to say that one cannot easily distinguish whether a certain trade is taken for defensive or offensive purposes.

Discovered by Accident. When the Federal Reserve Act was passed by Congress in 1913 there was no discussion about the possibility of its using open market operations as a tool for monetary control because the idea had not yet occurred to anyone. Instead, the 12 regional Federal Reserve Banks were supposed to be independent and, as banks, earn their own money to pay operating expenses. Congress would not appropriate taxpayer's money for that purpose. Thus, like other banks, the 12 regional Federal Reserve Banks could lend money, especially in the form of the purchase of securities, and use the interest earnings on those securities to pay expenses.

A huge volume of debt was issued by the Treasury during World War I, and the 12 regional reserve banks bought U.S. Treasury securities when they needed earnings. Persons in research departments noticed a high correlation between additions to the government securities portfolio and increases in bank reserve positions. It dawned on them that this correlation was the direct result of their purchases of securities in the open market. It was an easy next step to see that the government securities portfolio could be a slack variable in managing the volume of bank reserves for monetary policy purposes.

The 12 regional reserve banks organized a committee, independently of the Board of Governors, to oversee their purchases and sales of government securities. The following year the Board of Governors of the Federal Reserve System exercised its authority over the 12 regional reserve banks and reorganized the regional reserve banks' "Open Market Investment Committee," over strong objections. The Board insisted that it must give formal approval to the Committee's policy recommendations. The policymaking arm of the Federal Reserve today, the Federal Open Market Committee, evolved from this early arrangement. Its activities today will be the subject of further discussion in later chapters on monetary policy implementation.

Borrowing from the Federal Reserve (Central Bank)

When the Federal Reserve wants to tighten monetary conditions, it engages in open market sales of securities. But, when banks find themselves short of reserves, interest rates in the interbank lending market—the federal funds market—rise. Since the discount rate is an administered price, set by Federal Reserve Banks, it does not change immediately. Thus, the difference between the federal funds rate and the discount rate, $i_f - i_d$, increases. The larger this difference becomes, the greater the incentive for banks to obtain funds from the discount window.

Banks must apply to the discount window for loans, and loans are made on a discretionary basis. For example, a single bank is not expected to borrow too frequently. So, when the incentive to borrow becomes great, as when the federal funds rate rises, many banks will apply to use their privileged borrowing rights and the volume of borrowing rises. There is a clear positive correlation between the level of bank borrowing from the Fed's discount window and the interest differential $(i_f - i_d)$. (Actually, there is no window as such borrowings are negotiated in an office.)

This situation means that the bank that obtains the borrowed funds from the Federal Reserve obtains them at a lower price than other banks pay when they borrow funds from the federal funds market. Borrowing provides a subsidy in the form of low priced funds to the borrowing banks. Not only that, but when the discount window makes additional funds available, it is often, in a sense, undoing the tightening effect that open market sales were supposed to bring about. Since discount window borrowing subsidizes some banks and also helps undo the policies of the open market desk, many economists believe that borrowing should be eliminated. However, there is still a felt need for a "safety valve," for the lender of last resort, to assist temporarily those institutions caught in a justifiable, difficult situation.

Types of Borrowing. In 1973 Regulation A, the Fed's regulation relating to discount window borrowing, was revised to allow about 2,000 small banks in agricultural and resort areas to borrow from the discount window on a seasonal basis. These banks had routinely come to the Federal Reserve at harvest time and asked for reserves. In a sense, the Fed decided to give these banks a "line of credit" for 90 days if they could offer proof of seasonal demand for an eight-week (56-day) period. The institution of this *"seasonal" borrowing* privilege indicates that discount window activity will remain strong as a subsidy to many small banking institutions that carry many voting voices to the political powers in Washington.

In distinguishing seasonal borrowing from other borrowing, the Fed called the other borrowing *"adjustment" borrowing.* Thus, adjustment borrowing is that done for the usual temporary period for purposes of tiding a bank over a liquidity problem.

There is, however, a third type of borrowing—*"extended credit" borrowing*. This type of borrowing is used when a bank is in big trouble and likely to fail if not given extended support. In 1984 the Continental Illinois Bank in Chicago got into trouble, and the Fed ended up lending about $5 billion to it for more than a year. Other instances of extended credit occurred frequently during 1990–93 when many bank failures took place.

A problem arose in connection with the occasional willingness of the Federal Reserve to offer extended credit support to a bank that was "too big to fail." Although a central bank is charged with performing as a lender of last resort, it is *not* charged with responsibility to prevent bankruptcy nor to insure depositor's funds. Instead, the Federal Deposit Insurance Corporation (FDIC) is charged with that responsibility.

However, because the Federal Reserve has the ability to create funds, it could save any bank from bankruptcy if it chose to do so. Congress has not clearly defined Federal Reserve responsibilities in all such cases, but under the Federal Deposit Insurance Corporation Improvement Act of 1991, it did instruct all supervisory agencies, including the Federal Reserve, to monitor institutions whose capital fell below adequate levels, to limit their activities, and to place them in receivership after three quarters of undercapitalized status. The subject of bank failure will be raised in subsequent chapters.

Changing Required Reserve Ratios

A legally required reserve ratio may be changed by a central bank. The ratios imposed by the Federal Reserve were described in Chapter 3. The ratios were set anew with the Monetary Control Act of 1980. Ten years later, during December 1990, the 3 per cent reserve requirement against nonpersonal time deposits was reduced to zero. Two years later, in April 1992, the percentage of net transactions accounts that was required to be held as reserves was reduced from 12 to 10 per cent.

On both of these occasions a huge volume of reserves was released. Because of this, the Fed undertook open market operations to prevent a wholesale expansion of deposit money on the basis of this increased capability of banks to create it.

A change in the required reserve ratio is a cumbersome way to control bank deposit creation. It has been appropriately called a "blunt" instrument of policy.

However, with the development of modern communications, it is now possible to implement very small changes in reserve requirements, frequently, and sharpen the tool for regular use. For example, the Fed could instruct banks that, next period, the reserve ratio will be 10.1 per cent instead of 10 per cent. In this fashion it could avoid such a heavy volume of open market transactions and still invoke a reserve growth policy.

Many countries do set zero legal reserve ratios. For example, Belgium, Denmark, and Luxembourg have zero reserve requirements while the United Kingdom and the Netherlands have nearly zero reserve requirements. Other European countries, however, have requirements ranging from 5 per cent in France to 25 per cent in Italy. Many economists in the United States believe that reserve requirements should be abolished. Switzerland reduced its reserve ratio to zero at the beginning of 1988. Further discussion of the appropriateness of reserve requirements will be presented in Chapter 16 on the implementation of monetary policies.

Moral Suasion

Central bankers are powerful. In most countries a mere suggestion by the central bank authorities that banks should behave differently is taken as a directive. Central banks may simply announce that it would be appropriate for banks to limit their loan expansion by about 10 per cent in the coming year. Moral suasion is used less often in the U.S. However, the Chairman of the Board of Governors of the Federal Reserve System has, at times in the past, openly encouraged banks to reduced foreign lending, expand their capital to asset ratios, assist other banks, permit adjustments in banking practices to ease the problems of customers in cases of natural disasters, and so forth. For example, in the aftermath of the great earthquake that struck Los Angeles in January 1994, the banking regulators offered support for banks that assisted those who suffered property losses.

A Summary Statement on Tools of Monetary Control

Open Market Operations affect the *volume* of bank reserves.

Borrowing induces banks to change the volume of reserves voluntarily in response to changes in the discount (bank) rate that the Federal Reserve charges. The tool used by the central bank is the discount rate itself.

Changes in required reserve ratios do *not* change the *volume* of reserves, only the extent to which money can be created on the basis of a given volume of reserves.

Moral suasion has no direct effect on volumes of reserves or rates of interest or reserve ratios. "Arm twisting" might sometimes better be called "immoral suasion" on those rare occasions when ignoble governments choose to use their central banks as an instrument of oppression.

Summary

The focus of this chapter has been on the interaction between governments and their central banks with the commercial banks in an economy.

Banks that operate on a fractional reserve system are subject to bank runs and bankruptcy. They obtain assistance from larger correspondent banks, and the lender of last resort is a large bank that government may establish for the task, or may assign the task, of acting as lender of last resort.

To understand interactions between central banks and their commercial counterparts, it is useful to use balance sheets. A liability of the central bank, such as bank deposits with the central bank, is also the asset of a commercial bank and part of its reserves. Commercial banks have set up huge financial markets in which banks lend and borrow reserves to each other. In the U.S. this market is called the federal funds market.

Central banks also intervene in the market for bank reserves by using open market operations, that is, by buying or selling short-term securities so that the volume of bank reserves is altered as the transaction takes place. These activities are the most important source of changes in financial conditions in major exchange economies today.

Key Terms and Concepts

Correspondent banks

Float

Slack variable

Negotiable certificates of deposit

Repurchase agreements

Reserves (legal, required, total, borrowed, nonborrowed, excess)

Moral suasion

Central banks (functions of)

Commercial bank's balance sheet (principal items)

TT&L accounts

Net Fed Funds Purchased

Borrowing (seasonal, adjustment, extended credit)

Open market operations

Discussion Questions and Exercises

1. Make a list of the functions of central banks. Does the central bank or monetary institution carry out all of these functions in your country?
2. Without looking it up in the chapter, can you list the five major categories of assets and the five major liabilities of central banks? Briefly describe what is represented by these ten accounts.
3. Distinguish those liabilities against which banks are usually required to maintain reserves and those that do not require reserve backing. Why are special exemptions given for certain liabilities?
4. Explain what the typical bank's *slack variable* is. Why does a bank want to have a slack variable?
5. How are Treasury accounts with commercial banks handled?
6. Explain clearly what the federal funds market involves. What are federal funds and what is their price?
7. Distinguish between legal, total, required, excess, borrowed, free and nonborrowed reserves.
8. Explain how open market operations work as a tool of monetary control. What is the difference between defensive and dynamic (offensive) open market operations?
9. Explain how banks arrange to borrow from the Federal Reserve in the United States. Do the same procedures apply in your country?
10. Evaluate the use of changes in legally required reserve ratios as a tool of monetary control.

References

Federal Reserve Bank of Chicago, *Modern Money Mechanics*, Chicago, 1992.

Gilbert, R. Alton, "Payments System Risk: What Is It and What Will Happen if We Try to Reduce It?" *Review*, Federal Reserve Bank of St. Louis, January/February 1989, pp. 3–17.

Goodhart, Charles, *The Evolution of Central Banking*, MIT Press, Cambridge, MA, 1988.

Johnson, Verle B., "The Great Discovery," *Weekly Letter*, Federal Reserve Bank of San Francisco, March 7, 1986.

Singapore, Monetary Authority of, *The Financial Structure of Singapore*, 1989.

Stevens, E. J., "Removing the Hazard of Fedwire Daylight Overdrafts," *Economic Review*, Federal Reserve Bank of Cleveland, 2nd Quarter, 1989, pp. 2–10.

CHAPTER 7

The Monetary Base and Central Banking Controls

UNDER THE FRACTIONAL reserve banking system, a change in the volume of bank reserves, or in the legally required reserve ratio, will lead to a change in the volume of deposit money that banks can create. There was a lengthy discussion of the way central banks might influence reserves in order to stabilize monetary growth in the previous chapter.

In this chapter the concept of the *monetary base* is used to modify appropriately our understanding of the multiplier effect on bank deposits of a given increase in banks' legal reserve supplies. In a nutshell, when the Federal Reserve buys securities and bank reserves increase, the multiple creation of deposits is constrained by "leakages." For example, as banks make loans some individuals withdraw cash and this withdrawal reduces banks reserves—offsetting partially the original increase in reserves. Because of such leakages the multiplication of deposit money and the money supply generally is much smaller than it otherwise would be. Thus, the monetary base concept, since it allows for all the leakages, is a superior accounting concept than simpler forms of reserve accounting. It deserves thorough development here.

After examining the monetary base in the United States, some monetary tools used by other countries will be examined. It will be shown that although the names of the accounting items used by central banks around the world differ greatly, there is a certain uniformity in the central banking activities used to control money.

The Monetary Base and the Money Supply

Let us begin by defining some variables:

R = bank reserves (vault cash plus deposits in the Fed)
C = currency in circulation
D = demand deposits and other checkable accounts
T = time deposits including savings accounts
G = government deposits
M = the money supply, $C + D$
B = the monetary base, $R + C$
m = the money "multiplier"

Using these variables begin by noting that the objective is to uncover the relation between changes in the monetary base and changes in the money supply. Begin with the equation:

$$M = mB$$

This equation says that the money supply, consisting of *currency* in wallets, purses, cash registers and drug dealer's briefcases, and *deposits* that individuals and businesses hold in banking accounts, is some multiple of the monetary liabilities created by the Treasury and the Federal Reserve when they issue currency and provide reserve deposits to banks. In other words, the government, through its agencies, creates the monetary base, B, which consists of Treasury currency in the hands of the public, and bank reserves consisting of bank vault cash that the Treasury also issued and bank deposits held with the Federal Reserve.

If the monetary base is increased by government actions, then the money supply will increase. But, by how much? The amount that M increases with an increase in B depends on the value of m, the "money multiplier."

The Money Multiplier

The value of m is the result of decisions taken by depository institutions and the public, as well as those taken by the Federal Reserve and the Treasury.

Consider four ratios:

1. *The r-ratio:*

$$r = R/(D + T + G), \text{ or}$$
$$R = r(D + T + G)$$

The r-ratio is the ratio of reserves to total deposits. Principally, the value of r depends upon the legal reserve ratio. Of course, the ratio is a weighted average figure because legal reserve requirements differ between time and demand deposits and between institutions with different amounts of deposits. It is also affected by the voluntary action of depository institutions when they establish their excess reserve position and their borrowing from the Fed.

2. *The k-ratio:*

$$k = C/D, \text{ or}$$
$$C = kD$$

The k-ratio is the ratio of currency to demand deposits and other checkable accounts. It reflects the desire of the public to hold money in one or the other of the two forms. Seasonally, the k-ratio varies considerably. At Christmastime shoppers need more currency than usual and so do retailers. Similar currency needs arise at Easter and during the August vacation season. In recent years it has increased because of drug dealing and because U.S. currency is being used in Eastern bloc countries that have opened their markets to the use of foreign currencies.

3. *The t-ratio:*

$$t = T/D, \text{ or}$$
$$T = tD$$

The t-ratio is the ratio of time deposits to demand and other checkable accounts. Again, this ratio is determined by the preferences of the consuming public to hold their deposits in one of two forms—as checkable accounts or as time deposits. If interest rates on time deposits rise, for example, the public may wish to hold more time deposits and less in checking accounts that pay lower rates of interest.

4. *The g-ratio:*

$$g = G/D, \text{ or}$$
$$G = gD$$

Government deposits are not part of the money supply as it is currently measured. However, reserves must be held against some of these deposits. Thus, the g-ratio is the ratio of government deposits to demand deposits and other checking accounts. It is determined by Treasury decisions to hold amounts of funds with banks until the funds are needed and sent on to the Federal Reserve.

Four Ratios or Five or Six? The r ratio has always been included and so has the k ratio. Notice, however, that deposits have been broken into three types: demand, time, and government. A larger number of ratios could be created by simply breaking out a larger number of categories of various items on the liability side of a bank's balance sheet and treating them as ratios to D.

Deriving the Money Multiplier. Now let us derive the money multiplier m:

$$M = mB, \text{ or}$$
$$m = M/B$$

By substitution:

$$m = \frac{D + C}{R + C}$$

$$= \frac{D + kD}{r(D + T + G) + kD}$$

$$= \frac{D(1 + k)}{D[r(1 + t + g) + k]}$$

Since the Ds cancel, we have

$$m = \frac{1 + k}{r(1 + t + g) + k}$$

The money multiplier is not a constant, but a variable, determined by all the factors, other than B, that affect the money supply. In Table 7–1, the check marks indicate which sectors' decisions directly affect the determinants of the money supply. The monetary base, B, is affected by Treasury and Fed actions. The portfolio decisions of depository institutions are reflected in the value of r, which depends on the legal reserve ratio and the willingness of depository institutions to hold excess reserves. The value of t reflects the willingness of banks to attract time deposits. Portfolio decisions of the public are reflected in both k and t, which indicate preferences for holding money in the form of currency and holding time rather than demand deposits. Treasury decisions are reflected in g, reflecting treasury preference for holding deposits in banks rather than at the Fed.

The formula for the money multiplier depends upon which measure of money one uses. For example, if $M2$ money is the focus, then money includes not only currency and demand deposit and other checkable accounts but time deposits as well. Thus, $M = D + C + T$ will be used in the formula for $m = M/B$, and $m = (1 + k + t)/[r(1 + t + g) + k]$ where m becomes much larger.

Many different breakdowns of m are used by financial analysts, and each depends upon the measure of money chosen and the number of different types of bank accounts that are designated for ratios to be included in the formula.

Table 7–1
Sectors that Affect Determinants of m and $M1$

Determinants of $M1$	Sector			
	Depository institutions	Nonbank public	Treasury	Federal reserve
B			✔	✔
r	✔			✔
k		✔		
t	✔	✔		
g			✔	

Both the Federal Reserve Bank of St. Louis and the Board of Governors publish monthly data on the monetary base. These two sources present slightly different data because the two use slightly different adjustment processes. When economic data are monthly, they are often *seasonally adjusted,* and in the case of estimates of the monetary base the data must also be adjusted whenever there is a change in legal reserve requirements. This later adjustment is called a *break adjustment*—an adjustment for a break in the continuity of the data. Research staff at the St. Louis Bank and at the Board use slightly different adjustment procedures, and this accounts for slightly different values of the monetary base published by the two sources. The Board publishes both adjusted and unadjusted series of data in table form in the *Federal Reserve Bulletin,* and the St. Louis Bank publishes a chart along with its series of data on the monetary base as shown in Figure 7–1(a).

Empirical Values of the Base and Multiplier

Figures 7–1(a), (b), and (c) show data for the monetary base, the multiplier, and the money supply. At the end of March 1994, the base was $436.8 billion, the multiplier was 2.62, and the money supply was $1,143 billion. The figures show how the values of these variables changed over a 15-month period.

Looking at additional data sources to find bank reserves and deposits, values for the chief factors determining m (r, k, t, and g) were derived from the respective ratios:

$$r = 0.03, k = 0.41, t = 2.87, g = 0.01$$

Some analysts keep track of changes in these ratios over time in order to see where changes in m are coming from.

The Variable m. In the formula $M = mB$ it is important to emphasize that m *is not a constant.* It is a variable made up of at least four other variables.

If the letter m standing for multiplier were not the same letter as the letter M standing for money the possibility of misinterpretation could be significantly reduced. For example, if the reader saw a formula $X = YZ$, it would be interpreted as a three-variable equation. So it would be best if the formula for the base would be $M = XB$, where X represents a variable and replaces the variable m.

In addition, not only is m not a constant, it is not an independent variable. Indeed there are interdependencies between m and B. For example, if B increases when the Fed buys securities and yields on these fall, the public may shift its portfolio into higher yielding time deposits. This could increase t and reduce m. So, B and m would not be independent. The rise in B would be offset by a decline in m. Furthermore, the other ratios used in determining m are not independent of each other either.

Thus, the formulas for the monetary base and its multiplier should be looked upon as a convenient frame of reference, that is, as a way of putting the pieces of a puzzle together. Many economists and a large number of monetarists like to treat m as a constant because they believe that the Federal Reserve should simply control the

Figure 7–1

(a) Adjusted Monetary Base (Averages of daily figures, seasonally adjusted)

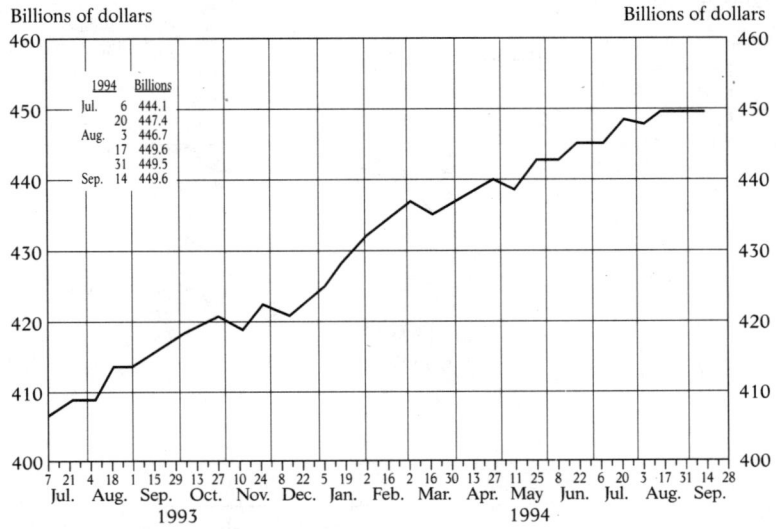

Lastest data plotted reserve maintenance period ending: September 14, 1994

The adjusted monetary base is the sum of reserve accounts of financial institutions at Federal Reserve banks, currency in circulation (currency held by the public and in the vaults of all depository institutions) and an adjustment for reserve requirement ratio changes. The major source of the adjusted monetary base is Federal Reserve credit. Data are computed by this bank. A detailed description of the adjusted monetary base is available from this bank.

Recent data are preliminary.

(b) Money Multiplier (Averages of daily figures, seasonally adjusted)

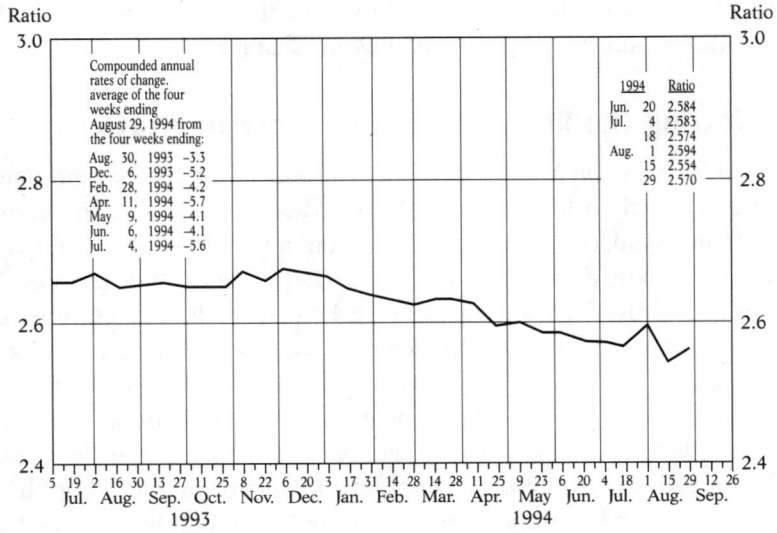

Latest data plotted two weeks ending: August 29, 1994

Figure 7–1

(c) Money Stock (*M*1) and Total Checkable Deposits (Averages of daily figures, seasonally adjusted)

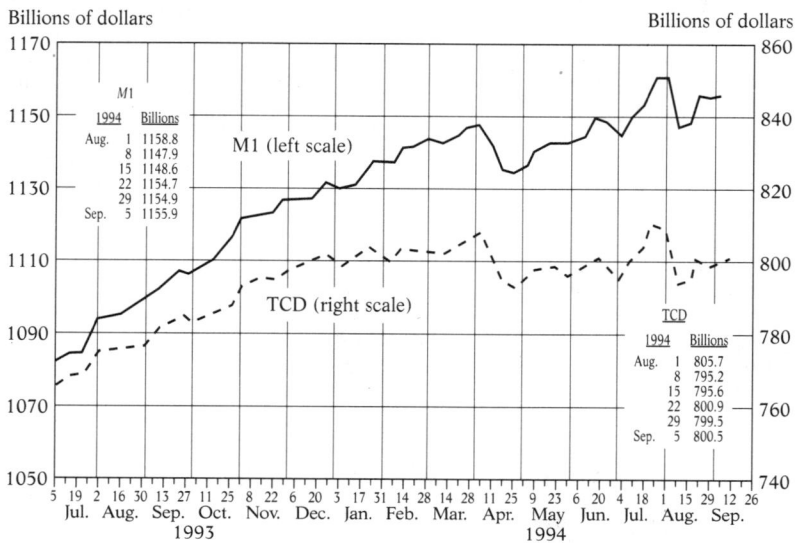

Latest data plotted week ending: September 5, 1994

Current data appear in the Federal Reserve Board's H.6 release.

*M*1 is the sum of currency held by the nonbank public, demand deposits, other checkable deposits and traveler's checks.

Total checkable deposits is the sum of demand deposits and other checkable deposits at depository institutions.

monetary base and let *M* grow steadily. Thus, if *m* were a constant, their suggestion for Fed policy makes sense. It makes much less sense if *m* is viewed as a variable. There will be more discussion of policy procedures in Chapter 16.

Factors Affecting the Reserves of Depository Institutions

At the close of business on Wednesday, banks around the country send data on their deposits, reserves, and so forth, to the Federal Reserve. The data are compiled and released to the newspapers on Thursday afternoon in time to make the Friday morning paper. A sample of these data appear in Table 7–2. The items show sources (Supplying Reserve Funds) and uses (Absorbing Reserve Funds) of the monetary base.

Increases in any of the items on the left, the sources, will give rise to an increase in bank reserve deposits at the Federal Reserve. The first item under the heading of Federal Reserve credit is the holdings of government securities. The second item represents borrowing by banks from the Fed, and the third is the float. All of these have been described earlier. On the right are the two items that make up the monetary base, bank reserves, and currency held by the public, along with other factors that absorb reserves of the banks.

Table 7–2
Reserves of Depository Institutions and Reserve Bank Credit (Millions of dollars)

Factor	Average of daily figures for week ending on date indicated		
	1994		
	June 15	June 22	June 29
SUPPLYING RESERVE FUNDS			
1 Reserve Bank credit outstanding	385,440	388,362	387,367
U.S. government securities			
2 Bought outright—System account	348,867	350,769	348,221
3 Held under repurchase agreements	0	0	1,705
Federal agency obligations			
4 Bought outright	3,955	3,952	3,938
5 Held under repurchase agreements	0	0	129
6 Acceptances	0	0	0
Loans to depository institutions			
7 Adjustment credit	13	84	107
8 Seasonal credit	192	242	278
9 Extended credit	0	0	0
10 Float	300	962	526
11 Other Federal Reserve assets	32,112	32,353	32,463
12 Gold stock	11,052	11,052	11,052
13 Special drawing rights certificate account	8,018	8,018	8,018
14 Treasury currency outstanding	22,489	22,503	22,517
ABSORBING RESERVE FUNDS			
15 Currency in circulation	378,639	378,545	379,136
16 Treasury cash holdings	358	357	355
Deposits, other than reserve balances, with Federal Reserve Banks			
17 Treasury	4,826	7,064	7,561
18 Foreign	176	172	182
19 Service-related balances and adjustments	5,839	5,926	5,871
20 Other	300	314	274
21 Other Federal Reserve liabilities and capital	10,756	10,712	10,758
22 Reserve balances with Federal Reserve Banks	26,106	26,844	24,817

Source: *Federal Reserve Bulletin*, September 1994, p. A5.

The mechanics of the tools of monetary control in the United States have been described above and in previous chapters. A brief review of the way monetary policies are carried out will provide a basis for comparison with other countries—first with other major industrialized countries and second with the four Asian Tigers.

For simplicity, assume that the Fed's or any central bank's goal is to dampen inflationary spending and achieve a return to price stability. Of course, it is often the case that a central bank wants to stimulate a weak economy instead. If so, the procedures nearly always involve reversing those used to halt inflation. Thus, by looking at one side of the problem only, one can project the use of opposite procedures to correct a situation that represents the other side of this problem.

Monetary Tools of the Federal Reserve System

If the Federal Open Market Committee decides that a tighter monetary situation would be helpful in reducing inflationary pressure on the economy, it will have its open market desk sell securities from its portfolio. These are usually U.S. Treasury bills. Thus, there is a money market security, the Treasury bill, that is the conduit for the Federal Reserve. By selling these bills, the Fed receives a check from whoever buys these bills in the open market. And the Fed will collect the payment for the bills by reducing the reserve account of the bank on which the check was written. Thus, the process by which bank reserves are reduced involves entering the money markets, in this case the market for Treasury securities.

Since bank reserves are part of the monetary base, the base is reduced.

As banks find the supply of reserves reduced, they enter the federal funds market and bid up interest rates on this huge interbank market. Yields on fed funds traded throughout the day are carefully watched. As they rise a signal is given to the market that the open market desk is assuming a tightening position. As we noted before, sometimes the operations are defensive. Occasionally a tightening will occur without deliberate action by the Fed as the open market desk copes with an unexpected drain on reserves. But market participants become used to some variation and can usually sense when the Federal Reserve's desk is at work draining reserves and pushing the federal funds rates up.

With the bellwether federal funds rate up, banks find they will have to charge higher interest rates from borrowers, and as they, as individual banks, compete for depositors' money to try to hold their reserve positions intact, they will find that they must pay depositors higher interest rates. Thus, higher interest rates on federal funds soon spreads through the banking system to raise both lending and deposit rates. Finally, since interest rates on deposits are more attractive, issuers of commercial paper and other short-term money market instruments that are good substitutes for deposits will find that they must offer their customers higher rates as well. In this way, tighter monetary conditions are spread throughout the world of money markets.

Four Steps in Monetary Policy

In summary, (a) the Federal Reserve enters the money markets and trades securities to affect bank reserve positions, (b) the interbank funds markets respond to the new reserve position, (c) banks compete for funds from depositors and ration funds to borrowers, (d) competition for money market funds leads all money market rates to change. This, in a nutshell, is how monetary policy works, and the same four steps may be found not only in the major industrial countries of the world but in the banking systems of the Asian Tigers as well.

Monetary Tools of France, Germany, and the United Kingdom

Batten et al. (1990) provide readers with an excellent summary of the way in which monetary policies are carried out in major industrial countries. Of course, monetary authorities constantly change their rules and procedures. Therefore, some of their descriptions may no longer strictly apply. However, their paper is highly recommended.

France and the Bank of France

From about 1985 to 1987, France overhauled both its financial markets and its central banking operations. The old engine of monetary controls and regulations had developed into a bureaucratic maze. Monetary growth depended upon rules governing the extension of credits by the Bank of France, and interest rates that it administered. The Bank operated both as a central bank and as a commercial bank in competition with other commercial banks. Conflicts of interest lurked around every corner, and regulations to ensure fairness became oppressive. France should be congratulated for its bold move into a new system that substituted market mechanisms for bureaucratic ones.

Before it could develop a mechanism for engaging in open market operations, it needed a market for securities in which such operations could be carried out without disrupting the prices of marketable securities. So it set about purposefully to establish markets for money market instruments: treasury bills, commercial paper, and certificates of deposit. All businesses and individuals were invited to participate in these markets whereas under previous arrangements they were forced to go directly to banks for credit for the most part.

After secondary markets for these money market securities developed, another layer of trading in these markets was structured so that access to it was limited to banks and major financial institutions. This market was designed to emulate the federal funds market in the United States. It is like a wholesale market for funds as contrasted with retail markets for money market securities.

On January 1, 1987, the old credit allocation system was abandoned. The new system works mostly through market determined interest rates.

Legal Reserve Ratios. Having developed domestic money markets to tolerable levels of activity and sophistication, France took the next step and established the position of the Bank of France as a participant in open market operations designed to have an effect on the reserve position of banks. It seemed that a legally required fractional reserve ratio was needed, so this was initially set at 5.5 per cent on demand deposits. In addition, there was a 3.0 per cent reserve required against time deposits.

Defensive Open Market Operations. The Bank of France uses its open market trading to stabilize interest rates in the market intermittently during the day. In general, French open market operations could be viewed as "defensive" as are most of the Federal Reserve's open market operations.

Repurchase Agreements. However, unlike the Fed, which implements offensive open market operations to regulate the creation of monetary aggregates, the Bank of France moves to a different mode of operation when it wishes to influence market interest rates in order to implement its policies. It entertains offers by financial institutions that have a temporary need for credit. They obtain funds by "selling" acceptable securities to the Bank under an agreement whereby the securities are repurchased the following day (or, occasionally, within a very few days). The securities that are "acceptable" as collateral for the agreement include those treasury bills, quality commercial paper, and other paper subject to an evaluation by the Bank of France.

Repurchase Contracts as Borrowing. In this repurchase program, the rate of interest charged to banks is similar in many respects to the rate on *discount window borrowing* for banks in the United States. French banks in need of liquidity contact the Bank of France, just as banks in the U.S. approach the Fed for loans on a collateralized basis.

The rate of interest on these repurchase agreements in France is held low, and the rate, called the *rate on tender for repurchase agreement,* is believed to be like a floor to interest rates in the market.

As in the U.S., where market rates of interest rarely fall below the discount rate administered by the Fed, the French discount rate is a "floor." Lending to banks at these below-market rates acts as a subsidy to those institutions that avail themselves of funds acquired through discount window borrowing in the U.S., and through these repurchase contracts in France. In this respect the supply of funds acquired by banks through this program is administered and represents the way the Bank of France handles its responsibility as a lender of last resort.

Repurchase Contracts as Offensive Money Management in France. A second type of repurchase contract is also offered to banks by the Bank of France. This is the contract that provides funds on terms set by the Bank and that indicates whether the Bank is changing its policy stance. It is called a *repurchase tender offer.* It is the Bank's principal tool of monetary policy, and tender offers are usually invited each week.

Under a repurchase tender offer, the Bank of France notifies the banks that it will accept tender offers for repurchase contracts at various interest rates. By bidding at this auction-like event, the banks indicate the amounts they would like to borrow at several different interest rates. That is, a typical bank will set several rates it is willing to pay to acquire funds through repurchase contracts, and also indicates amounts for each rate.

The Bank of France then exercises control over market interest rates by the extent to which it accepts the tender-offers. It holds monetary conditions tight by accepting only a few bids for reserve funds at high rates, thus adding only marginally to the volume of bank reserves. It can signal a lower interest rate condition by accepting a larger volume of tenders for funds at lower interest rates.

Summary. The Bank of France uses open market operations as a defensive instrument of policy. It enters the newly created money markets and affects interest rates in the wholesale market for these securities, which is primarily an interbank market for funds. Then it sets overall monetary conditions (takes offensive action) by affecting bank reserves through its weekly *repurchase tender offers*. Again, the impact on bank reserves initially affects interest rates on money market securities as banks enter the restricted wholesale market for those securities. In the meantime, the Bank of France offers a type of lending to banks as a safety valve at a subsidized rate viewed as a floor, called a *rate on repurchase agreement*. Repurchase agreements are made at the request of banks. Repurchase tender offers are under the control of the Bank of France. Although the language is completely different, today there are fundamental similarities between the system operating in France and that of the United States and other major industrial countries. For example, Table 7–3 shows the different types of financial instruments that different countries use to carry out open market operations.

Germany and the Deutsche Bundesbank

The Federal Republic of Germany has instructed the Bundesbank to maintain the purchasing power of the currency, that is, to hold money creation to a rate consistent with zero, or near zero inflation. It uses a concept similar to the U.S. monetary base as a guide to monetary expansion—the central bank money stock. This stock includes currency in circulation, as does the monetary base, but instead of including *all* bank reserves, the Bundesbank money stock includes only minimum required reserves, and, of the required reserves, it includes only those reserves required against domestic deposits and not those held against nonresident (read "foreign") deposits.

The Bundesbank is a federal bank and there are regional Land Central Banks that play a role somewhat similar to that played by regional federal reserve banks in the

Table 7–3
Financial Instruments Used in Central Bank Operations

Country	Outright purchase and sale	Other
France	Government securities Foreign exchange	Commercial paper
Germany	Government securities Foreign exchange	Central bank bills
Japan	Government securities Central bank bills	Commercial paper Private bills Certificates of deposit Central bank bills
U.K.	Government securities	Commercial paper
U.S.	Government securities	

Source: Batten et al. (1990).

Federal Reserve System. The Bundesbank uses all the tools of monetary policy: open market operations, legal reserve ratios, and lending to banks through discount window operations.

There are many technical differences in its procedures however. For example, in its open market operations, it has sometimes used purchases and sales of foreign currencies instead of always using purchases and sales of long-term government bonds. But principal differences in procedures are concerned with lending to banks. Some aspects are similar to the repurchase contract tender offers used by France. Let us take a glance at these differences.

Discount Rates. The discount rate is the floor rate in Germany. Banks can borrow at this rate and receive funds at lower cost than in the open market. Thus, just as described in the case of the Federal Reserve, banks borrowing at the discount rate are receiving a subsidy.

The Federal Reserve exercises administrative discretion when it loans to banks so that banks cannot simply borrow as much as they want whenever they want. In Germany, to solve the problem of borrowing too much at the subsidized discount rate, the Bundesbank simply imposed quotas on lending to each bank. The result is that each bank borrows its full quota routinely so as to obtain the largest possible subsidy.

Although the discount rate is moved up and down from time to time by the Central Bank Council of the Bundesbank, such changes are simply signals from the central bank indicating its attitude toward monetary policy. Such changes have little relevance to monetary policy itself since the volume of reserves supplied to the banks is governed by a set of quotas. Nor does it play a role in central bank actions as the lender of last resort. That role is played by the Lombard rate.

Lombard Rates. If banks need extra reserves, they can approach the Bundesbank for assistance from the Lombard facility, which is something like the discount window in the U.S. The rate of interest that the Bundesbank charges a bank is called the Lombard rate. This rate is *higher* than market rates for reserves that banks charge each other in the *call money* market. The call money market is an interbank borrowing market similar to the *federal funds* market in the U.S. Thus, the Lombard rate is more like the rate that the Federal Reserve charges for what is called "extended credit" borrowing as described above in the context of seasonal credit, adjustment credit, and extended credit. Rates charged for extended credit, like those charged for Lombard facilities, are *penalty* interest rates. That is, they are higher than market interest rates. If a bank must go to the Bundesbank or to the Federal Reserve, to ask for serious help, the rates of interest they pay will not be the subsidized discount rate, but will be instead a negotiated rate higher than the interbank borrowing rate.

Thus, the Lombard Rate is known as a ceiling rate—a counterpart to the floor rate set as a discount rate. Both rates are administered, and the Bundesbank sends a signal to the markets when it announces changes in either or both administered rates. A wide variety of securities are accepted as collateral for Lombard borrowing.

Market rates of interest on money market instruments are influenced by the Bundesbank—by the volume of reserves it provides through its repurchase tender offers, which are similar to those of the Bank of France, and by the rates it sets on these offers.

Repurchase Rates. The rate that is kept in between the floor discount rate and the ceiling Lombard rate is the repurchase rate.

The Bundesbank asks banks to bid for the right to sell it certain securities with an agreement that those securities will be repurchased from it on a date usually four or five weeks in the future (28 to 35 days).

There are two types of tender offers. One is a volume tender, and the other is an interest rate tender.

Under a *volume tender*, the Bundesbank sets a rate of interest, and banks submit bids for the volume of securities they wish to sell to the Bundesbank under a repurchase contract. The Bundesbank can control the total volume of bank reserves created by the tender offer. For example, it may accept around 50 per cent of the bid amount.

Under an *interest rate tender*, the Bundesbank sets a minimum repurchase rate and then asks banks to bid for the volume they would like to have at that rate. They can also indicate additional volumes of funds that they would be willing to obtain if they had to pay higher interest rates. This interest rate tender is similar to the one used by the Bank of France. The Bundesbank may accept 50 per cent of the volume of tenders, and it will allocate to the banks the amounts for which they were willing to pay the highest interest rates. Thus, banks offering higher rates receive the funds they bid for, and then the banks bidding lower rates also receive funds, and finally the Bundesbank cuts off the supply at a certain interest rate with a certain volume. So the Bundesbank can influence both the volume and the rate that clears the bidding for funds. The bids at higher interest rates (prices of funds) could be construed as an attempt to construct the market demand curve for funds. The Bundesbank sets the supply at will, and determines the price of funds, or what is called the repurchase rate.

Other Actions. In its open market operations the Bundesbank acts as a defensive agency. It also sometimes acts defensively using foreign exchange markets. In addition it has the authority to shift government funds from the Bundesbank to banks or back. That is, the government maintains deposits with the Bundesbank, and if a large amount of funds are paid in because of tax collections, for example, the Bundesbank has the authority to shift them back to the banks in order to replenish the reserves that the banks lost as a result of tax payments.

In the U.S., the Treasury and the Federal Reserve cooperate and the Treasury has a system for calling in funds to the Federal Reserve in a way that does not create too much disturbance for the reserve position of banks. By comparison, in Germany, tax payments go directly into the Bundesbank's government accounts, so the Bundesbank has the problem of putting them back into the banks. In any case, it is important to note that the transfer of government deposits into or out of accounts with a central bank can affect the reserves of the banking system. Both the Fed and the Bundesbank acknowledge this, although the system works in opposite directions in the two countries.

Summary. Influencing the repurchase rate is the dominant tool used by the Bundesbank to establish its offensive monetary policy position. By supplying reserves to banks through this mechanism, it indirectly influences the interbank call money rate, which is similar to the fed funds rate in the U.S. It also uses a variety of open market operations during the day. It has a penalty Lombard rate that it charges banks as a lender of last resort, and a rather meaningless discount rate under which banks routinely borrow their quota each period.

As in the other countries, via the volume of reserves, the central bank affects interest rates in the interbank call market which, in turn, affects interest rates on other money market securities, such as commercial paper, certificates of deposit, and so forth. The German government does not issue treasury bills, and the Bundesbank has only experimented with the issue of central bank bills.

The United Kingdom and the Bank of England

Being the world's oldest central bank, the Bank of England and its monetary activities are steeped in tradition. It began operating in the 1690s after being chartered by the government as a private bank with the specific understanding that it would be the government's banker and handle the Exchequer's accounts. Its role as the government's bank soon provided it with authority, and with this authority came responsibility. It continued to act unofficially as the United Kingdom's central bank until after World War II when a newly elected labor government nationalized it—a symbolic act, not one of substance.

Many countries of the world established their own central banking institutions along guidelines set by the Bank of England. Congressmen in the United States called on it for advice when the Federal Reserve Act was being prepared in 1913. At that time the discount rate was believed to be the best tool to use for monetary policies, and it was the principal tool used by the Bank of England.

London's Discount Houses. Members of the London Discount Market Association are private discount houses that have a role to play in carrying out monetary policies. These discount houses are unique financial institutions. They could be called agents of the Bank of England, or they could be called agents of commercial and merchant banks in the U.K., or they could be called dealers in government securities. Indeed, they do play all three roles.

No Legal Reserve Requirements. Banks in England are not subject to a legally set reserve requirement, but they do maintain some "cash" with the Bank of England.

Lender of Last Resort. The Bank of England is, de facto, the lender of last resort, but in practice banks with a need for reserves go to the discount houses for accommodation. Discount houses act as brokers by bringing together banks that are short of funds and banks that have excess funds. There is an interbank market for funds as well, but the discount houses play an important role in that market.

One could say that the discount houses play a principal role in a market like the federal funds market in the U.S. The reason is that all of the commercial banks maintain what are essentially deposit accounts with the discount houses, and these resemble the reserve accounts that banks maintain with central banks to ensure that they will have funds available to meet unexpected withdrawals. That is why, when banks need to borrow funds, they go to the discount houses and not to the Bank of England.

But, when there is a general shortage of funds for the system of banks, the discount houses themselves may go to the Bank of England for support. The Bank of England may also entertain offers from banks directly rather than through discount houses, if banks offer Treasury bills. It will also engage in repurchase contracts in order to provide funds in exchange for temporarily holding Treasury bills—funds that are needed because of a general shortage of bank reserves.

Discount Houses as Dealers. The Bank of England handles sales of treasury securities for the government. But the discount houses underwrite all Treasury bills that are issued. They tender offers for all bills that the Bank sells under prearranged agreements to allocate the bills proportionally among the discount houses. Subsequently, the discount houses take an active stance in the secondary market for treasury securities just as the 40 or so government securities dealers make markets in the U.S. and also trade with the Federal Reserve when it engages in open market operations.

Defensive Open Market Operations. The Bank of England watches the cash position of the banking system routinely throughout the day, and will respond with open market purchases of securities if there appears to be a shortage of funds. In case, for example, tax payments cause banks to lose reserves, the Bank of England will supply reserves to offset those losses just as the Federal Reserve would. If there appears to be a glut of reserve funds, the Bank will ask the discount houses to bid for some treasury bills, and since settlement takes place during the day, the banks will find their supplies of funds lowered.

Offensive Open Market Operations. The Bank of England can readily tighten or ease monetary conditions. It can tighten by providing too few funds to the banks so that the discount houses are forced to come to the Bank for accommodation. And the terms of the accommodation—the Bank of England's dealing rate—will be set at a higher than going interest rate. When this occurs, interest rates throughout the money markets rise.

Summary. There are no formal reserve requirement ratios set for U.K. banks, so the monetary tool used by many central banks—changing legal reserve ratios—is not used in the U.K. However, through its agents, the discount houses, the Bank of England carries out open market operations in order to influence the tightness or ease of banks' reserve positions. It enters the markets for money market securities, principally Treasury bills. Also, indirectly through the discount houses, the Bank makes funds available to individual banks. Although the institutional structure of these activities is unique, the three tools exercised by the Bank in carrying out its monetary policies are open market operations, borrowing agreements (indirectly with discount houses for the most part), and moral suasion.

Monetary Tools of Japan

Japan and the Bank of Japan

The Bank of Japan has a Policy Board that manages monetary policy. Although the Bank is formally under the Ministry of Finance (known as the notorious MOF), it operates with considerable independence. However, consistent with Japan's national industrial policy, credit allocations through the discount window and moral suasion characterized the Banks operations for many years.

For example, if a particular business firm had the blessings of the MOF, it could go to a bank and ask for a development loan of significant amounts. The bank might be reluctant to make the loan and would approach the Bank of Japan's discount window. The Bank would make a loan of reserves to the requesting bank at below-market interest rates—the discount rate.

This behavior pattern was part of the overall structure of government-business relations that enabled the MOF to coordinate business operations and guide the industrialization of Japan in the postwar period.

But by 1980, in the wake of substantial liberalization of financial markets and institutions, the Bank of Japan changed its operating system to reflect those systems in other countries more closely.

Money Market Securities. The Bank of Japan intervenes in the money markets for a variety of instruments. Years ago it intervened in the stock markets. In the late 1980s it began to intervene in certificates of deposit and in commercial paper. Before that it routinely intervened in call markets and bill markets. Call loans are short-term loans in the interbank market for reserves, and bills traded at discount rates in the bill market include those issued by corporations, promissory notes, export and import bills, and others. There is also a supply of short-term government bills that are similar to U.S. Treasury bills, but the market is small and not used frequently by the Bank of Japan for open market operations.

The call market is an interbank market similar in scope to the federal funds market in the U.S., or the call market in Germany. In Japan, the Bank of Japan will intervene directly in the call market. The Federal Reserve never intervenes directly in the federal funds market.

Defensive Open Market Operations. The Bank monitors the net cash flows expected to lead to shifts of funds into and out of bank reserves and takes operations that will stabilize the volume of bank reserves. It has an extensive monitoring program known as the *reserve progress ratio*. The reserve maintenance period in Japan is a month, not like the U.S. period of two weeks. Even though the legally required reserve ratio is quite small, around 2.5 per cent, the Bank of Japan monitors day by day the extent to which banks are maintaining their required reserve position. Over a 30-day month, the daily average maintenance should be 3.33 per cent, in order to reach 100 per cent by the end of the month. This holds not only for each bank individually, but for the system as a whole.

In order to smooth daily fluctuations in bank reserves the Bank of Japan may rely on its old mechanism, the discount window. It can do this because when the Bank of Japan lends to banks, the loans are made on a call basis, that is, the reserves lent to banks a day or two ago may be called back today. Thus, the Bank's overall lending can be adjusted and bank reserves either increased or decreased through the discount window operations. In contrast, the Federal Reserve's open market operations are undertaken with the assumption that the volume of bank borrowing of reserves is a given, while in Japan both open market operations and borrowing can be adjusted in combination. The Japanese system has a certain flexibility in this regard that the Federal Reserve does not have.

Offensive Open Market Operations. If the Bank of Japan wishes to implement a tight monetary policy, in addition to its management of cash flows into and out of reserves for defensive purposes, it will supply too few reserves for banks to maintain the 3.33 per cent growth in the reserve progress ratio. This will force banks into the interbank call and bill markets to demand funds. The increased demand for reserve funds will drive up the interest rates in those markets.

Repurchase Agreements. Unlike Germany and France, countries in which central banks make extensive use of repurchase agreements, the repurchase market is not actively used by the Bank of Japan as a monetary tool. However, the so-called *Gensaki market*, which is a repurchase market usually involving government securities, was developed in the 1970s.

Summary. There was a period in U.S. history in the early 1900s before World War I in which there was a dearth of government securities to provide a financial instrument on which to base trade and expansion. Japan had very little government debt until the 1970s and its government securities markets did not develop. In contrast, U.S. debt exploded in the 1918 war period, again during the Great Depression of the 1930s and in the 1940–45 period. Now, in the 1990s we have a glut of government debt. Thus, because there is a high active secondary market for government securities, it is easier for the Federal Reserve to intervene in the market for U.S. Treasury bills, when it wants to implement a monetary policy than it is for Japan to act in similar fashion.

So, Japan uses a variety of tools to implement its monetary policy. A major portion of its activities involves defensive operations, sometimes directly intervening in the interbank call and bill markets. For its offensive monetary policies, it will act to influence the movement of rates in those markets by adding or withholding reserves in line with its monitoring of the reserve progress ratio, which reflects the reserve position of banks. Again, the process involves intervention in money markets to affect reserves, and then to affect interest rates in interbank markets, which will spread monetary conditions throughout the remainder of the financial markets.

Monetary Tools of the Asian Tigers

The phenomenal economic advancement of the people of Hong Kong, Korea, Singapore, and Taiwan since about 1980 has captured the imagination of all the world's less developed countries, and has astonished the developed countries. Thailand, Malaysia, Indonesia, and others, wish to emulate the successes of the newly industrialized countries.

As noted in earlier chapters, Hong Kong established the Hong Kong Monetary Authority in the spring of 1993, Korea has the Bank of Korea, Singapore has its Monetary Authority of Singapore, and Taiwan has the Bank of Taiwan.

Singapore was a British Colony until it became independent in 1965. Hong Kong is also a British Colony and will revert to control by China in mid-1997, although it is supposed to retain some independence and be self-governing to an extent after 1997.

Long years of British influence in these two colonies have left their marks on the way in which financing and management of monetary controls have been carried out. Financial arrangements in Korea were influenced by the U.S. because of U.S. involvement there in the wake of World War II. Korea's occupation by the Japanese from about 1910 ended when Japan surrendered in 1945. The U.S. stayed on in Korea through the Korean War and afterwards. Advisors on all aspects of financial controls from the U.S. were used by Korea, but its institutions retain their own uniqueness, too. Taiwan's financial system was also influenced by American methods.

The four Asian Tigers have all developed institutions for the control of money supplies that operate in ways very similar to those of the major industrialized countries. A very brief look at the four systems is in order here, while further discussion is postponed until later chapters on monetary policy.

Hong Kong's Money Control System

The Hongkong and Shanghai Banking Corporation (HSBC) is a private bank that acted as the government's bank in Hong Kong. In some ways the situation was like that of the Bank of England: since the HSBC acted for the government, it also, to be fair, had to assume responsibilities involving the support of government's policies over money and credit. Over the years the HSBC has assisted the government in many ways. It often acted as the lender of last resort and even assumed management of failed banks. Indeed, its power was such that it could have turned itself into the central bank for Hong Kong.

But, it chose not to because its managers and shareholders felt it would be more profitable as a private, profit-maximizing institution—an eminently reasonable position.

Therefore, the Monetary Affairs Branch of the Hong Kong government exercised whatever monetary policies it could implement through its charge, the Exchange Fund. (The reader was introduced to the Exchange Fund in Chapter 5 under the discussion of seigniorage.)

In the spring of 1993 the Hong Kong government established a new Monetary Authority. The establishment of a central bank was debated for many years and from time to time the Exchange Fund would take on additional responsibilities in the wake of various pressures.

In March 1991 the Exchange Fund began to sell 91-day bills. At that time the government continued to have its usual revenue surplus. In other words, the government did not borrow funds to finance a deficit in its budget. Instead it borrowed funds and issued these bills for the sole purpose of establishing a money market security to be traded along side trading in the interbank market for bank reserves. The Exchange Fund wanted to establish a security that it could issue and buy and sell in an open market. When it sells bills, it can require payment through an account that represents the net reserve balance of the banks in Hong Kong.

When it borrows funds by selling securities it obviously cannot use the proceeds to pay down outstanding debt simply because it has no outstanding debt. So the funds may be invested by the Exchange Fund in foreign exchange, say, in U.S. Treasury securities where it earns interest that can be used to pay interest on the Hong Kong securities. However, the act of selling the bills and investing the proceeds has the immediate effect of drawing down bank reserves. This means that, in the process of building up the volume of outstanding amounts of government securities to create a money market instrument, the Exchange Fund must regularly replenish bank reserves by supplying liquidity to the interbank funds market in some other way. It can do this by adjusting its holdings of government deposits, that is, it can switch its holdings of government deposits over to the banks. Presumably, after a time, by balancing its accounts carefully, a regular market in government securities will evolve that can be used as a medium for open market operations.

A description of Hong Kong's monetary policy will be presented in Chapter 18. For now, all that is needed is a general description of the government's operating techniques. The government has given the Exchange Fund several responsibilities: (a) maintaining foreign exchange reserves backing the issue of Hong Kong dollar notes, (b) maintaining an account that represents the net clearing balance of banks in Hong Kong, where the balance represents the reserves of banks, (c) keeping track of a balance of the government's funds—the government banks with local banks, but some of its funds are held with the exchange fund (incidently, as in Germany, the Exchange Fund can shift funds either into or out of commercial banks and such shifts will affect the banks' reserve positions).

As described in Chapter 5, in Hong Kong the bank notes that represent most of the money in circulation are issued by two banks, the Hongkong and Shanghai Banking

Corporation and the Standard Chartered Bank. And, a third bank, the Bank of China, began issuing bank notes in May 1994. So the Exchange Fund does not issue notes. Instead, it will issue Certificates of Indebtedness to the three note-issuing banks in exchange for foreign exchange or other suitable funds to use as reserves for the note issue. Thus, unlike other central banks the Exchange Fund does not issue notes directly, only indirectly by requiring the issuing banks to purchase noncirculating CI's from it whenever they issue bank notes.

Therefore, except for the note issue, the new Hong Kong Monetary Authority will continue to operate the Exchange Fund accounts and indirectly control note issues. In addition it will enter the market using open market purchases and sales to tighten or ease "liquidity" in the interbank market. They do not use the term reserves because Hong Kong, like the U.K., has no legal reserve ratio. Instead it has a very loose liquidity ratio. Changes in the liquidity of the interbank market immediately affect interest rates in the money markets and subsequently interest rates in other parts of the financial markets as well.

Thus, Hong Kong has just recently changed its monetary institutions and adopted nearly all of the same tools of control that major industrialized countries now use. However, its application of those tools is different. It uses them to maintain a fixed exchange rate against the U.S. dollar. Further discussion of monetary policy in Hong Kong is found in Chapter 18.

Korea's Money Control System

The Bank of Korea has the same set of monetary tools that the Federal Reserve has. It sets a legal reserve requirement against deposits (about 11 per cent in 1990). It will also make loans to banks and re-discount various financial instruments that banks wish to sell to it in order to obtain additional reserves. It engages in open market operations and it continues to set maximum interest rates, and exercises some direct controls over the extension of credit. However, during the 1980s Korea's financial system went through a significant liberalization and expansion.

The call money market in Korea is a functional equivalent to the federal funds market in the U.S. A restricted number of banks and other institutions have a formal call market among themselves that is in some ways similar to the dealer market in the U.S. The Bank of Korea enters this market for the purpose of open market operations to adjust bank reserves. There is also a secondary call market, which is over-the-counter and in which the investing public in general can participate. The current arrangements were put in place in 1989.

During the 1980s there was a tremendous expansion in the volume of important monetary instruments. Corporate bills, like commercial paper, expanded 10 times, repurchase agreements expanded 16 times, certificates of deposit issued by banks expanded 364 times, and a special bond issued by the Bank of Korea—*the Monetary Stabilization Bond*—along with other government securities, expanded 5,408 times. That decade saw the establishment of a huge market for money market instruments.

The Bank of Korea's Monetary Stabilization Bond is quite unique. The Bank issued these bonds so that it would have a financial market instrument that it could trade when it wanted to engage in open market operations. In some ways the bonds are like the Exchange Fund bills issued in Hong Kong. They were issued to establish a money market instrument and not to raise funds for purposes of spending them on some project.

The Bank of Korea is under Korea's Ministry of Finance. In this respect the system of Korea is similar to that in Japan. Also, Korea expanded its industrial output by exercising a national industrial policy similar to that in Japan. However, it is generally acknowledged that industrial development was plagued by errors and inefficiencies. The liberalization of financial markets was, in part, undertaken to establish conditions appropriate for market-determined expansion of industry as a replacement for Ministry of Finance and Bank of Korea guidance.

Singapore's Money Control System

Singapore became an independent and sovereign republic in 1965. Prior to that it had been a Crown Colony like Hong Kong, and its financial institutions have a great deal of similarity to those in the United Kingdom. It does not have a central bank as such, but its monetary affairs are under the direction of the Monetary Authority of Singapore (MAS).

Singapore has a well-developed financial sector with many banks and money market instruments such as treasury bills, interbank funds, repurchase agreements, commercial paper, banker's acceptances, and so forth. For many years the MAS followed the style of the U.K. and dealt through a group of discount houses. This group handled bank requests for funds by offering to discount various securities for them. The discount houses themselves underwrote the government's issues of debt, and the MAS influenced the extent to which the discount houses provided funds to the banks. However, under a variety of financial reforms introduced in 1987, specialized discount houses were done away with. Today the MAS influences interest rates in the interbank market for funds, and whatever pressures on interest rates occur in the interbank market extend into the various markets for money market instruments.

The MAS does not use open market operations in treasury bills, but it does enter the foreign exchange markets to buy or sell U.S. dollars to stabilize the exchange rate. Since the trading of foreign exchange also affects the volume of bank reserves, policies on foreign exchange rates and on the money supply must be coordinated.

As in Hong Kong, the MAS does not issue currency. Instead there is a Currency Board that receives foreign exchange and issues and redeems currency and coin in circulation. Unlike in Hong Kong where banks issue bank-note currency and the Exchange Fund issues certificates of indebtedness to the banks, in Singapore the Currency Board issues currency and coin. Otherwise, the MAS operates as the government's banker and regulates banking and other financial institutions for the purpose of controlling monetary conditions.

Taiwan's Money Control System

Taiwan's economy, like Korea's, grew rapidly in the 1980s. This growth was accompanied by huge increases in the amounts of money market instruments outstanding. Except for 1987, treasury bills, commercial paper, banker's acceptances, and certificates of deposit grew from year to year at rates of 10–90 per cent.

In Taiwan there is the Executive Yuan that oversees the Ministry of Finance and the Central Bank of China. (In Taiwan, the Bank of China is a commercial bank, and should not be confused with the Central Bank of China.) Thus, unlike Japan and Korea, the central bank does not take direction from the Ministry of Finance. Instead, the Ministry regulates banks and finance while the Central Bank of China issues currency, regulates finance and credit, and acts as banker to the government. It also exercises controls over interest rates and other conditions for the extension of credit. But the official policy of the Taiwan government is to move slowly and surely to liberalize their financial system. In 1989 the Central Bank introduced an interbank market in U.S. dollars. (One item that is worth drawing attention to is that many official documents state that it is the year 78 when it is 1989. This is because the Taiwan calendar starts 11 years after the calendar most of us use. When looking at past data, be careful to see that the proper year is correctly understood.)

As mentioned in Chapter 3, before 1992 the number of ordinary banks in Taiwan was approximately 16, and all but four of these were government owned. In 1992 the government began to charter an additional 15 private banks. The idea was to increase competition.

The Central Bank of China sets discount rates and reserve requirements and engages in open market operations. Since 1983, open market operations have become the most important tool of monetary policy. The legal reserve ratio, as noted in Chapter 3, changes infrequently, but is quite large on average since its minimum is 15 per cent, and maximum is 40 per cent according to law.

By 1993 Taiwan had acquired US$85 billion of foreign exchange reserves. This is larger than that of any other country including all of the major industrial countries. The local people have a saying in Chinese that they are "up to their knees in money." There are plans to spend much of this on infrastructure projects, but any rapid expenditure would be highly inflationary. This is a problem that the Central Bank of China will face—how to handle an abundance of riches.

Summary

The focus of this chapter is on monetary controls. Understanding these technical operations by monetary authorities around the world will be helpful in later chapters in which the actual implementation of monetary policies will be discussed in greater detail.

The chapter began with a description of the concept of the monetary base—the base upon which money is created—and its sources and uses. The base consists of bank reserves along with currency in circulation. Since currency in circulation depends heavily upon fairly predictable spending patterns and varies considerably over seasons of the year, that part of the base consisting of bank reserves is the focus of central banks. By engaging in activities that affect the availability of reserves to banks, the central bank can move interbank interest rates. Movements in these rates spread throughout the money markets in the economy, and later may also affect long term interest rates.

Very brief descriptions of the financial markets through which central banks operate were given for five major industrial countries as well as for the four Asian Tigers. In all instances it appears that monetary policy actions of the central banks are very similar in approach. Countries have established active secondary markets in money market instruments. The central bank trades in these markets, either directly or indirectly through repurchase agreements. As a transaction with the central bank occurs, the aggregate reserves of banks in the system will change.

For example, the volume of bank reserves increases when the central bank buys securities. Interest rates in money markets will decline both because of the central bank purchase itself, and also because additional reserves increase the monetary base and give banks increased ability to enter the markets for short-term money market instruments as well. Buying pressure pushes up prices of these securities and simultaneously pushes down interest rates. Lower interest rates are consistent with an expansion of the quantity of money created by banks.

By understanding these operating techniques of monetary control one can more easily analyze the theory and policy of financial markets and institutions.

Key Terms and Concepts

Monetary base
Factors determining money multiplier
Four steps in implementing monetary policy
Lombard rates in Germany
London Discount Market Association
Monetary Stabilization Board in Korea
Currency Board of Singapore

Money multiplier
Federal Open Market Committee
Repurchase contracts in France
Gensaki market in Japan
Hong Kong Exchange Fund
Monetary Authority of Singapore
Taiwan's U.S. dollar reserves

Discussion Questions and Exercises

1. What is the formula for the money multiplier, m, in the equation for the monetary base, $M = mB$? What items make up M and what items make up B? What ratios are used in constructing the formula for m?
2. Should the money multiplier be interpreted as a constant? Explain.
3. See if you can identify the institutions that affect the variables in the monetary base as noted in Table 7–1.
4. Briefly discuss each of the major tools of monetary policy used by central banks.
5. What are the four steps involved in the implementation of monetary policy?

6. Distinguish defensive from dynamic (offensive) open market operations.
7. Briefly describe the way in which monetary policies are carried out in France, Germany, Japan, and the U.K.
8. How do different governments use auctions for repurchase contracts to control bank reserves? Distinguish a volume tender from an interest rate tender.
9. In which countries is the discount rate a penalty rate, and in which is it set below market rates? Explain.
10. Explain how the Bank of Japan uses the "reserve progress ratio" as a guide to open market activities.
11. What are "discount houses" in London and Singapore, and what role do they play in the banking system of these countries?
12. Does a country need to impose a legal reserve ratio on banks in order to control the creation of money by banks? Discuss.
13. How is money controlled in Hong Kong, Korea, Singapore, and Taiwan?
14. Did any of the four Asian Tigers employ a national industrial policy like that of Japan? Discuss the issue of such a policy and explain the role of central banks in implementing it.

References

Batten, Dallas S., Blackwell, Michael P., Kim, In-Su, Nocera, Simone E., and Ozeki, Yuzuru, "The Conduct of Monetary Policy in the Major Industrial Countries: Instruments and Operating Procedures," Occasional Paper No. 70, International Monetary Fund, Washington, DC, July 1990.

Chen, M. T., "The Financial System and Financial Policy in the Republic of China," *Economic Review*, July–August 1990, pp. 1–10.

Chen, S. M., *The Financial System of Taiwan*, Cheng Ching Book Co., Taiwan, 1989.

Drake, P. J., "The Evolution of Money in Singapore since 1819," *Papers on Monetary Economics*, Economics Department, Monetary Authority of Singapore, ed., Singapore University Press, Singapore, 1981.

Economic Review, International Commercial Bank of China, Taipei, Taiwan, various issues.

Espinosa, Marco, "Are All Monetary Policy Instruments Created Equal?" *Economic Review*, Federal Reserve Bank of Atlanta, September/October 1991, pp. 14–20.

Euh, Yoon-Dae, and Amsden, Alice H., "Korea's Financial Reform," *Journal of Management*, College of Business Administration, Korea University, Vol. 33, 1990, pp. 45–84.

Euh, Yoon-Dae, and Baker, James C., *The Korea Banking System and Foreign Influence*, Routledge, London, 1990.

Garfinkel, Michelle R., and Thorton, Daniel L., "Alternative Measures of the Monetary Base: What are the Differences and are They Important?" *Review*, Federal Reserve Bank of St. Louis, November/December 1991, pp. 19–35.

Ho, Y. K., Scott, R. H., and Wong, K. A., eds., *The Hong Kong Financial System*, Oxford University Press, Hong Kong, 1991.

Kasman, B., "A Comparison of Monetary Policy Operating Procedures in Six Industrial Countries," *Quarterly Review*, Federal Reserve Bank of New York, Summer 1992, pp. 5–24.

Kim, Wang-Woong, "Recent Interest Rate Liberalization in Korea," *Monthly Review*, Korea Exchange Bank, December 1988, pp. 3–13.

Kneeshaw, J. T., and Van den Bergh, P., "Changes in Central Bank Money Market Operating Procedures in the 1980's," Economic Paper No. 23, Bank for International Settlements, January 1989.

Korea, Bank of, *The Financial System in Korea*, Republic of Korea, 1990.

Lee, S. Y., and Jao, Y. C., *Financial Structures and Monetary Policies in Southeast Asia*, Macmillan, London, 1982.

Lee, Wan Deok, "Korea's Call Money Market," *Monthly Review*, Korea Exchange Bank, December 1990, pp. 3–12.

Monthly Review, Korea Exchange Bank, various issues.

Shieh, Samuel C., "The Role of the Central Bank in Economic Development—The ROC's Taiwan Experience," *Economic Review*, November–December 1990, pp. 1–19.

Stevens, E. J., "Comparing Central Banks' Rulebooks," *Economic Review*, 3rd Quarter, 1992, pp. 2–15.

Tan, Chwee Huat, *Financial Markets and Institutions in Singapore*, 6th Edition, Singapore University Press, Singapore, 1990.

CHAPTER 8

The Money Market

AS NOTED IN the first chapter, the distinction between a money market and a capital market is set arbitrarily: money market securities (or instruments) are those with maturities of a year or less, while capital market securities have maturities longer than one year.

If a capital market security issued several years ago has less than a year left to maturity it is, conceptually, a money market instrument and competes directly with other money market instruments. However, because pricing of money market instruments is often on a discount basis whereas pricing of bonds is not, the bonds are listed separately. Also, quoted yields are not strictly comparable.

The principal characteristic of money market instruments is that they have a very low risk of default. The Treasury bill is called the (default) "risk-free" asset, and its yield is used as the risk-free rate of return when comparing risky and risk-free assets. Furthermore, because money market securities have very short maturities their prices do not fluctuate widely during the time that they are held. Thus, the risk of capital loss from the early sale of money market assets is very low.

Money markets are important because money market instruments are highly liquid—they have a low risk of capital loss and a low default risk. They are also markets in which central banks operate to influence the level of bank reserves and the money-creating activity of the banking system.

Most trading of securities in money markets is between governments, banks, other financial intermediaries such as money market mutual funds, and large businesses. Individuals rarely participate directly in money markets. They purchase certificates of deposit and money market deposits from banks, and they invest indirectly by purchasing money market mutual fund shares. But the large exchanges of funds in money markets are made between financial institutions.

Payments of money to settle money market dealings are made in "immediately available" funds that are sent by wire to the seller of securities. So, if you sell $1 million in Treasury bills, for example, the money proceeds from the sale may be placed in your bank account before the trading day is over.

Money Market Instruments

Securities exchanged in money markets are principally liabilities of governments or their agencies, central banks, and banks or other financial intermediaries. The principal money market instrument issued by corporations is commercial paper.

The non-interest-bearing note liabilities that the Federal Reserve issues, that is, paper currency of the U.S., are not money market instruments—they are money itself. Money is a perfectly liquid asset because it can be used to discharge debt.

If a corporation has idle money, it can earn interest by using this money to purchase an interest-bearing money market security and holding it for a short period. Then, when the money is needed for operations or other spending, the money market instrument can be sold and, through wire transfers, again be made available for spending or paying bills. Thus, in the money market, large sums of money can be turned into interest-earning assets for one or more days or several weeks. This temporary placing of funds into interest-earning securities is the principal activity of money market participants.

Now let us examine briefly some of the more important money markets.

Treasury Bills

In both the United Kingdom and the United States, a large portion of government debt is in the form of Treasury bills. T-bills, as they are often called, were first issued in 1887 in England at the suggestion of a famous journalist and economist, Walter Bagehot. He was editor of *The Economist* magazine, and the Columbia University School of Journalism sponsors a program of study in his name. It was not until 1929 that the U.S. government began issuing T-bills as a regular activity.

In the U.S., T-bills are routinely issued at weekly auctions with maturities of three months, six months and one year. The 3-month bill is a 13-week bill with 91 days until maturity, except in an unusual circumstance when there is a business holiday and the maturity may be 90–92 days.

The Treasury has experimented with several special types of T-bills. These include *tax anticipation bills*, or TABs. TABs are scheduled for maturity on quarterly tax dates and are thought to be attractive to corporations that are holding funds for the purpose of making tax payments. By holding TABs, corporations can use the maturing securities to make payments and earn interest up until the date that taxes are due. The Treasury may also issue *cash management bills.* These may have a maturity of only 30 days or 60 days and are offered by the Treasury when it needs some funds for a month or two to cover anticipated expenditures, and when the Treasury does not want to change the number of bills regularly issued at its auctions by a sizable sum.

Treasury bills are sold on a discount basis. The bills are worth face value at maturity so the difference between the purchase price and face value is the discount and represents the interest earned by the buyer if held to maturity. For example, if a $10,000 T-bill sold for $9,900, the buyer would gain $100 at maturity. If the bill were a three-month bill, the equivalent annual yield would be $400 and would be expressed as a 4 per cent discount rate. More specifically, the formula for the discount rate on T-bills is based on a 360-day year. Where d is the discount rate, P is the price of the security, and n is the number of days to maturity the formula is:

$$d = \frac{360}{n} \frac{10,000 - P}{10,000}$$

The Treasury bill rate is a *discount rate* based on *par* value, or $10,000, using a *360-day* year. In contrast, *bonds* have a bond *yield* based on the *purchase price* and a *365-day* year. When i is the yield on a bond, the comparable formula becomes:

$$i = \frac{365}{n} \frac{10,000 - P}{P}$$

Formerly, the smallest unit in which bills were sold was $1,000, but high yields on bills in the late 1960s led many individuals to withdraw savings from bank accounts and invest directly in bills. This disintermediation led banks to protest the competition from the Treasury for depositor's funds, so the Treasury raised the minimum purchase to $10,000 to exclude small investors and prevent funds from being diverted away from the mortgage and housing markets. After buying the minimum $10,000 bill, the investor can purchase additional amounts in multiples of $5,000.

Investors send in the face value amount at the time of purchase and the Treasury returns the amount of discount on the issue date of the security (on the Thursday following the Monday auction in the case of T-bills). So the interest on bills may be viewed as being paid at the time of purchase in the form of a discount from the face value. An alternative view of the discount rate as an interest rate is that the investor actually lends the government the discounted amount and earns interest in the form of the accrual of value as the bill approaches maturity, at which time the investor receives the face value.

Treasury notes have maturities from two to ten years. They are sold in denominations of $5,000, $10,000, $100,000 and $1,000,000. Notes with maturities of four years or longer are available in $1,000 face value amounts. Treasury bonds are securities issued with maturities of more than ten years and are sold in the same denominations as the notes are sold. Semiannual interest payments are made on bonds.

Government securities dealers, about 40 altogether, bid for new issues and make a market for all outstanding issues of T-bills and other government securities the Treasury sells. The Federal Reserve acts as the Treasury's agent in handling the auctions of government securities.

The Treasury announces the dollar amount that it wishes to borrow at its auctions every Thursday and invites bids to be submitted the following Monday. Bids must be submitted to the Treasury, or to a Federal Reserve Bank or branch, by 1:00 P.M. New York time. Dealers wait until the very last minute to submit bids, and there is a rush of bidders at 12:59 P.M. for the billions of dollars of bills offered at auction.

Competitive bids will state the dollar amount wanted and a bid price. Dealers may submit several bids for different prices. The Treasury accepts bids at the highest prices offered. It takes amounts offered at lower and lower prices until the dollar amount accepted equals the amount the Treasury wants to borrow.

Investors may also submit *noncompetitive* bids for a certain dollar amount, not to exceed $1 million, and stand willing to purchase the securities at the average price paid by those whose competitive bids were accepted. Noncompetitive bids must be submitted an hour before those of competitive bids.

One-year T-bills are auctioned only once each month whereas the three- and six-month bills are auctioned each week. To separate the auctions, two-year or five-year notes may be auctioned on Tuesday and Wednesday and one-year bills may be auctioned on Thursday. Routinely, competitive bids must be submitted by 1:00 P.M., and non-competitive bids an hour earlier. Treasury announcements for auctions appear in the newspapers a few days before the auctions take place. Longer maturities are auctioned quarterly. With weekly, monthly, and quarterly auctions, the Treasury holds hundreds of auctions every year.

In the 1970s the Treasury Department began to issue all of its marketable securities in registered form. With computerized accounting and record keeping, it makes a great deal of sense to save the costs that are associated with issuing securities printed on paper.

Treasury bills are probably the single most important type of money market instrument for several reasons. First, as a risk-free asset, they are used in constructing optimal portfolios of risky and risk-free assets to attain a desired degree of trade-off between risk and return. Second, they are the principal security that the Federal Reserve uses when it engages in open market operations, that is, when it undertakes to purchase or sell government securities in order to implement a monetary policy. Third, banks and other financial institutions hold large quantities of T-bills as "liquid" reserves to meet certain capital adequacy or liquidity requirements (as distinct from legal reserve requirements) insisted upon by regulators in some jurisdictions. Fourth, T-bills are used as a basic investment medium in a variety of arbitrage activities and hedging operations.

Just as every country should maintain a steady money supply to support market exchanges, every country should also maintain an outstanding supply of T-bills in order to provide business and the financial industry with a base for building stable financial arrangements. Most large countries do. However, a major exception is Germany where government debt is never issued with a maturity of less than one year. However, the Bundesbank issued Bulis (Bundesbank liquid securities) in 1992 and then stopped issuing them in September 1994. It may try again.

Other Government-backed Money Market Instruments

A large variety of government agencies sell short-term money market securities. These may or may not be directly guaranteed by the government, but in all cases they are government supported to a considerable degree. Such support means that they are nearly risk-free. However, yields on these securities are slightly higher than those on Treasury bills. Studies seem to indicate that the higher yield is the result of a slightly lower marketability. They are issued in smaller amounts, are less well-known than T-bills, and are slightly less easy to sell at a moment's notice.

The Federal Financing Bank. In 1974 the Federal Financing Bank was established. This is an intra-government bank that loans funds to a variety of federal or federally supported agencies. Because federal agencies must pay slightly higher interest rates for funds than the Treasury does, and because the need for funds on the part of individual agencies was modest, the Federal Financing Bank was formed to consolidate the borrowing of a group of agencies.

Essentially, the Treasury issues securities and then lends the proceeds to the Federal Financing Bank. The bank then lends the funds to the separate agencies. In this fashion the agencies were supposed to be able to get funds on approximately the same terms granted to the Treasury. All of this was supposed to permit agencies to borrow at lower costs.

Also, many of the agencies are now considered to be privately owned even though they have considerable government backing. So their debt is no longer considered to be part of the outstanding federal debt. The agencies, through the Federal Financing Bank, are in debt to the Treasury, so the funds raised by the Treasury are part of the national debt, but, since they are given to the Federal Financing Bank, they represent an offsetting asset held by the Treasury. The net result is that agency debt is removed from the sum of the outstanding federal debt by this sleight of hand. Reducing the national debt by privatizing some government agencies and then setting up an in-house Financing Bank to handle the paperwork involving borrowed funds for agencies is surely one way to fool the public.

The system worked quite well, that is, to the satisfaction of the agencies, until early 1993 when the Post Office got into a flap with the Federal Financing Bank. Interest rates had fallen in 1992 and into 1993. The Post Office wanted to refinance its loan from the Federal Financing Bank at the new lower rates, but the Bank was reluctant to accommodate the Post Office. The Post Office then announced that it was going to issue its own securities in order to obtain lower interest rates, and the matter became one of interpreting the legal rights of the Post Office and whether or not it was forced by law to borrow from the Federal Financing Bank under the terms set by law. After months of controversy, a compromising agreement was reached between the Bank and the Post Office.

State and local government units also issue some money market securities to meet temporary cash needs and in anticipation of bond sales, and so forth.

Floating Rate Notes. The Treasury does not now issue a floating rate note of the type that is prevalent in European and Asian markets. However, it is studying a proposal to offer one that would be tied to an index of yields on T-bills.

Federal Funds and Repurchase Agreements

The federal funds market was the subject of extensive discussion in earlier chapters. Primarily, it is an interbank market for funds. Of course, correspondent banks had a long history of lending funds to each other. But the development of the market was facilitated by changes in banking rules in the 1960s. In 1970 the Federal Reserve's Regulation D, the regulation that specifies the details of reserve requirements, was changed to permit borrowing of federal funds. It specified that these borrowings (purchases) would not be subject to reserve requirements. Lenders of federal funds would be those that had access to the Fedwire transfer services and thus could make *immediately available funds* transfers. Thus, borrowers and lenders included not only commercial banks but also savings and loan associations, mutual saving banks, and agencies of foreign banks.

Federal Reserve open market operations affect the volume of legal reserves available to the banking system and therefore determine the availability of federal funds. An increase in the supply of federal funds leads to a decline in the interest rate called the federal funds rate. A decline in the federal funds rate is thus considered to be a signal that the Fed has either eased its monetary policy or is permitting market conditions to lead to an easier monetary policy. Thus, since the 1970s the federal funds rate has become the bellwether rate of interest.

Repurchase agreements have also developed into a significant money market instrument since the 1970s. A repurchase contract is one in which the holder of a security, usually a Treasury bill or bond, agrees to sell the security to someone under a contract that provides for the repurchase of the security at a set price either the following day or within a short time period. The seller of the security is essentially borrowing funds temporarily from the buyer. The difference between the price the seller receives and the price paid to repurchase the security represents the interest return on the temporary use of funds. Such interest yields are negotiated between the contracting parties, and they typically range slightly above the yield on federal funds.

In a typical example, a large business firm may have funds in a demand deposit account on which it wishes to earn interest for a few days over a weekend. It will call the bank and negotiate to purchase a government security that the bank owns, hold it over the weekend, and sell it back on Monday morning when the bank opens. Thus, the firm can write checks on its account and withdraw funds on Monday. Essentially, it earned interest on its demand deposit account at the bank by simply entering into a contract with the bank.

The firm entered into a repurchase contract—it agreed to buy a security under an agreement that the bank would repurchase it later. The firm lent its funds to the bank.

The bank entered into a matched sales-purchase agreement (or a reverse repo agreement)—it agreed to sell some securities and buy them back at a set price on a set date. The bank borrowed funds from the firm.

Another common example in the repurchase contract market is the case of a government securities dealer. Such dealers maintain large inventories of government securities of all maturities. They have a unique way of obtaining funds to finance their large inventories that involves using repurchase contracts. In this case the bank enters into a repurchase agreement. It agrees to buy the dealer's inventory, hold it overnight and sell it back the following day. The bank has effectively lent funds to the dealer so the dealer can pay for the securities that were purchased from the Treasury. The dealer has entered a matched sales-purchase agreement with the bank under which the dealer sells the inventory of securities to the bank for a temporary period. The dealer can then sell these securities to a client the following day having given up control of the ownership of the securities only for the contract period.

The Federal Reserve Bank of New York's open market desk often enters into repurchase contracts with government securities dealers instead of buying or selling securities "outright." It does so when it wishes to make temporary adjustments in bank reserve balances.

Certificates of Deposit

Banks may accept deposits into several different types of accounts: demand deposits, other checkable accounts, Money Market Deposits, time deposits, savings deposits, and certificates of deposit. Time deposits differ from checking accounts because the depositor agrees to leave the funds on deposit until a specified future date. For example, in Hong Kong there is no arrangement for withholding taxes from salaries paid to workers. Therefore, banks have begun accepting deposits for a period of time before the approximate due date of an individual's tax payments. Thus, the depositor can earn interest on the funds that are being laid aside in anticipation of taxes. (In America, the Internal Revenue Service does not pay interest on funds withheld saying that the tax is effectively due each month.) Thus, individuals who anticipate a need for funds on or about a specific future date can use the time deposit. Interest paid on a time deposit is slightly higher than that paid on demand deposits and other checkable accounts.

In addition, time deposits usually pay higher interest than that paid on savings accounts. Savings accounts may, in practice, be withdrawn on demand. Indeed, many people keep funds in savings accounts and withdraw funds from them by using the Automatic Teller Machine. However, in earlier days, and still today in many countries, individuals with savings deposits in banks must approach the bank with a passbook and request a withdrawal. The bank usually pays out the money immediately, but it does have the right to delay payment for, say, up to 30 days. Such delays were legal in order to help protect the bank from bank runs by giving some extra time for the bank to arrange to have more cash on hand.

Certificates of deposit are merely time deposits for which a certificate is prepared and given to the depositor. Certificates are typically offered for one, three, and six months and one, two, three, and five years, or other periods for which there is a customer demand. Interest rates on such certificates typically reflect the yield curve as the longer-dated certificates typically pay higher interest rates than the shorter-dated ones.

It was not until the 1960s that large banks in the United States, led by Citibank (earlier named First National City Bank of New York), established a secondary market for large ($100,000) *negotiable certificates of deposit*. Small certificates of deposit that individuals buy at a bank are not negotiable. They are issued to a single individual and that individual is responsible for returning them to the bank for collection on or after the maturity date. In the case of NCDs, or simply CDs as they are now called, the holder turns them in to the bank, and they can be sold or traded. Ownership changes with a signature, and that legal provision over property rights is what makes the certificate *negotiable*.

It is the negotiable CD that is now one of the most important money market instruments in the world of finance. All large banks issue CDs and many thrift institutions also issue them. Branches of foreign banks operating in the U.S. issue *Yankee CDs*. The rating agencies, Moody's and Standard & Poor's, now rate not only the banks themselves, but specific issues of CDs.

The creation of a secondary market for CDs was very important to banks because CDs permit a bank to manage their liabilities actively. Suppose that a bank was in need of some extra funds to make a business loan. To acquire additional deposit funds the managers do not have to go out on the street and solicit from potential depositors—instead all they do is print up the certificates and distribute them to brokers in the secondary market. They simply sell time deposits to investors in the same way that investment banks sell bonds to investors, and so forth. Secondary markets in CDs would not have developed without the CDs negotiability.

Occasionally, the opportunity to acquire deposited funds by the sale of CDs can prove to be a mixed blessing. The usual view of a bank is that it builds a deposit base and accepts deposits from individuals and businesses in its community. This is especially true of banks in unit-banking states, such as Illinois and Texas, that permit banks to have only one location. For example, the Continental Illinois Bank of Chicago with only one building, built up into a huge financial institution, not on the basis of local people and business, but on the basis of the sale of large volumes of CDs to investors from all over the country *and* in Europe. In 1984 when rumors circulated that Continental Illinois might be in financial difficulty, many European investors permitted their holdings of CDs to mature and did not buy new ones. The bank came under strain and had to be rescued by regulators. Some observers thought that it was unfortunate that the bank had not been more conservative and built its deposit base in the local community rather than in the international money markets where there is little loyalty to a local business or bank.

Banker's Acceptances

In commercial law, there are two major types of negotiable instruments: *promises to pay* (notes and bonds) and *orders to pay* (drafts or bills of exchange). Checks are orders to pay drawn on banks by people who have deposits. They may be called drafts, which is a general term for orders to pay.

To explain the concept of a banker's acceptance in very simple terms, let us begin with an example. Assume that it is September 1, and you write a check to pay for something you bought. But you will not have the funds until September 30. So you postdate the check for October 1, 30 days into the future. Since you have postdated the check, the bank is not obligated to honor the check until October 1. The seller of the goods that you have bought will question whether or not your check is "good." So the two of you may go to the bank and explain your situation.

After visiting with you, the bank is assured that you will have the funds in your account by October 1, and agrees to "accept" the obligation to pay on that date. In order to place its credit behind your check, the bank places a stamp on it that says "Accepted" and the cashier of the bank signs on the dotted line. Your check has become a banker's acceptance.

The bank has guaranteed payment of your check at a future date, so the banker's acceptance becomes a liability of the accepting bank as well as your own liability. Because the bank's credit is now behind your check, the seller of goods is willing to accept your check for payment.

But the seller of goods may not want to wait until October 1 for payment. He or she may ask the bank to cash the check now. But the bank will only "buy" the check at a discount from face value. If the check is for $1,000 the bank may pay only $990 for it today. By paying this amount for the check, the bank will earn $10 (1 per cent per month) interest on a discount basis for providing funds to the seller one month before it is able to collect the $1,000 from your account. If the bank does not buy your "accepted" check, there are other money market dealers who will buy it from the seller at a discount from face value.

This highly oversimplified example shows how a bank's credit is substituted for a depositor's credit when an acceptance is created. Notice that the bank does not have to pay out any cash, but the bank does have a liability. It has lent its credit, but there is no record on the bank's balance sheet. Instead, banks are required to note the volume of acceptances outstanding in the footnotes accompanying a balance sheet.

A slightly more complicated example of the creation of an acceptance will be sufficient for our purposes here. Texts on international finance and trade and bank brochures will provide more information on the subject. Anyone engaging in international trade will need the services of persons who specialize in letters of credit.

Assume that you plan to visit a foreign country to arrange for the importation of some goods that you will sell at home. Before you leave you will visit your banker and arrange for a letter of credit. This letter will specifiy what you want to buy and an amount of money you may want to spend, and so forth. When you go abroad and talk to the seller, you will provide him or her with copies of the letter that indicates that you have arranged a line of credit with your bank. The seller agrees to export the commodities to you by ship, with the shipment arriving in 30 days. The seller then takes *your* letter of credit to *his or her* bank. The seller-exporter then writes an order to pay that is just like a check and the order cites the terms of your letter of credit. So, the exporter asks for payment from the local bank and the local bank then asks your bank to "accept" the order to pay and a banker's acceptance is created. Either bank may discount the acceptance in order to make a payment to the exporter. After 30 days you cover the payment that your bank makes on your behalf.

Thus, international trade is financed largely by interbank payments under credit arrangements out of which banker's acceptances are created. In this example, the exporter, not the importer, wrote the bank draft that ordered payment in 30 days—a time draft.

There are many variations in this process. Banker's acceptances have been around since ancient times, but they have not been prevalent in many countries. For example, a market for banker's acceptances in Japanese yen opened only in mid-1986. Acceptances denominated in U.S. dollars dominate the international markets.

Commercial Paper and Finance Paper

Commercial paper consists of short-term unsecured promissory notes issued by industrial firms, public utilities, bank holding companies, finance companies and other institutions. Finance paper is issued by finance companies. The maximum maturity is 270 days. This limit is imposed because longer-dated securities require registration with the Securities and Exchange Commission. The registration process is long and expensive. It requires the issue of a prospectus and full disclosure. Commercial paper has been exempted from this time consuming registration process.

Commercial paper is often sold either directly or through dealers in denominations of $100,000 or multiples thereof. Dealers charge fees for the sale of paper and maintain a network of clients. The largest dealers are investment banks. Over half of all commercial paper sold is issued by nonbank financial companies such as General Motors Acceptance Corporation, General Electric Capital, and Ford Motor Credit. These companies make loans to people who want to buy their products. To finance their loans, they borrow funds in the commercial paper market.

About $200 billion of the $600 billion in commercial paper outstanding in 1993 is held by Money Market Mutual Funds. Bank trust departments also purchase large amounts of commercial paper. However, since 1983 the volume of commercial and industrial loans by banks has fallen relative to the volume of commercial paper. It is clear that banks have been losing many of their best loan customers.

Credit Enhancement. In the early 1990s banks generally cut back in their lending to businesses, partly because businesses found that they could raise funds just as easily in the commercial paper market. Issuers of commercial paper often arrange backup lines of credit with banks in order to provide liquidity and marketability for it. Like letters of credit, such backing lends the bank's credit without it appearing as a loan directly on the bank's balance sheet.

Beginning in 1983 many issues of commercial paper have been "asset-backed." Special companies are established for the sole purpose of buying receivables from producing companies and issuing commercial paper using the receivables as collateral. Credit card receivables are often handled this way. They are bought by a special company that uses them as collateral, so the special company's credit risk, rather than the risk of the originating firm, is the base for establishing a risk premium. The default rate on commercial paper has been very low (see Hahn, 1993).

Rating agencies provide investors with ratings on issues of commercial paper. Interest rate swaps, described in Chapter 11, are often used by issuers of commercial paper.

Eurodollars

The last money market to be discussed in this chapter is called the Eurodollar market. In both size and importance it is undoubtedly the most important money market in the world. It is an international market, and every large bank in every country of the world participates in it. The best way to learn about the workings of the Eurodollar market is to review the history of its beginnings and then to imagine how it came to grow to its present size.

In 1948, three years after the end of World War II, the Cold War began. In a speech Winston Churchill gave in Fulton, Missouri, he declared that the U.S.S.R. had dropped an iron curtain that had turned relations with the Western Allies into a cold war. During World War II, American policies in support of its Allies, including the Soviet Union (no distinction will be made here between the U.S.S.R. and Russia—at the time the terms were used interchangeably), had provided it with dollar funds to use to purchase many goods. Also, Russia sold gold to the U.S. in order to acquire dollars to use later to purchase wheat. Thus, the Russian government had large dollar deposits in American banks. With the Cold War declared, Russian authorities began to worry that their bank deposits might be blocked or confiscated by American authorities. Dollar deposits were very valuable, and the Russians did not want to lose their dollar holdings. No other currency of the world had retained its strong standing so well as the American dollar. Indeed, in the wake of the war's devastation, the dollar was the only really hard currency left, although the British pound remained a key currency in international trade alongside the dollar. The reason, of course, was that only the American economy had avoided wartime destruction.

So Russian authorities approached British and French banks and asked that these banks accept their dollar deposits and hold them in dollars instead of in pounds or francs. Before this time, if someone brought dollars into a bank in London, the bank would buy them with pounds and then the pounds could be put into a bank account. One could not bring dollars into a London bank and open a bank account in dollars. Essentially, the Russians asked, "Why not?" The London bank had only to stand ready to repay the depositor with dollars (instead of with pounds). If the deposit was a time deposit, the London bank could arrange its holdings of dollars so that it could pay out dollars when the time came. The U.S. would not confiscate dollar deposits in London banks and Russian dollar holdings would be safe. So London and French banks began holding dollar deposits alongside their pound deposits and franc deposits. The idea caught on and the volume of dollar deposits grew rapidly.

Now it is easy to understand the answer to the question, "What is a Eurodollar?" It is a U.S. dollar deposit in a European bank.

No American authorities exercise control over deposits of dollars in European banks, nor do they impose reserve requirements on the volume of Eurodollar deposits created by European banks, nor is deposit insurance required, nor do European banks have to contend with any other regulatory restrictions or examinations by U.S. authorities. In other words, since dollar deposits were not British pounds, the British authorities had little interest in regulating them, and, since the dollar deposits were outside of the jurisdiction of the United States, U.S. authorities could not regulate them. Eurodollar markets have expanded exponentially largely because they are essentially not regulated by anyone. This lies in sharp contrast with the heavy regulation of banking that is typical of most nations.

Eurocurrencies. It would be more correct, technically, to refer to a Eurocurrency market in Europe than to a Eurodollar market. The reason is that, after London banks began accepting deposits in dollars, it was rather easy for them to accept deposits in German marks, French francs, Swiss francs, and eventually Japanese yen, and so forth. Similarly, French banks could accept deposits in these currencies including the British pound. And, in Hong Kong and Singapore, for example, banks can accept deposits in other currencies. The market there is usually called the Asian dollar market. For example, the Hong Kong dollar is accepted by banks in Singapore, but the term dollar in both places usually refers to the U.S. dollar and not the Singapore dollar or the Hong Kong dollar. Besides, how can yen be called a Eurocurrency? Thus, the Eurodollar or Eurocurrency market is just a name for a market in which banks located physically in one country accept deposits in currencies of other countries. (A U.S. dollar deposit in a branch of Chase Manhattan bank located in Europe is a Eurodollar deposit.) Meanwhile, the Federal Reserve has authorized U.S. banks to establish International Banking Facilities within the United States! These subsidiaries of U.S. banks are physically located in the U.S. but operate in the Eurodollar market *as if* they were in Europe! It saves on phone bills.

Eurodollars in the U.S.? A *Wall Street Journal* article, written by Alan Murray and Paul Duke, Jr., appeared in the January 4, 1989 issue, with the headline "Fed Ruling Will Allow Banks to Take Foreign Currency Deposits." It indicated that the Federal Reserve, which had previously declined to permit U.S. banks to accept deposits in foreign currencies, would review favorably a request for such permission. To the date of this writing, however, the author knows of no U.S. bank that accepts such deposits. If any reader should happen to know of such a bank, please inform the author.

If American banks begin accepting German mark deposits, British pound deposits, and so forth, perhaps these deposits will be called the Merimarks, the Meripounds, the Meriyen or the Mericurrency market. It would hardly be consistent to call it the Eurocurrency market, now would it?

Eurodollar Creation

Does a European bank that accepts a U.S. dollar deposit as a liability end up creating U.S. dollars? The answer is clearly yes, but many economists say no, or sometimes, or not always, or not very often. Economists who work for commercial banks tend to deny that banks create U.S. dollars even in the U.S., let alone abroad. Of course, if banks admit that they create money, then they are asking to be regulated because money control is supposed to be government's job. So banking spokesmen are reluctant to admit that European banks are creating billions of U.S. dollars right under the nose of the Federal Reserve, which is supposed to control the creation of U.S. dollar supplies. They have a lucrative banking business, and they do not want to lose it.

Taking a step-by-step approach to money creation, it is clear that banks in Europe do create U.S. dollars in precisely the same way that banks in the U.S. create U.S. dollars. The only questions of interest that remain are: in what form and how many dollars do they create?

Begin with Knudsen's, the makers of fruit juice in Chico, California, an American company with a deposit in a U.S. bank. Having already established markets for their juices in Asia, they decide to begin distributing their products in England. The company officers go to England to set up their shop and open a bank account with Barclays bank. (This story is fictitious, only the names of companies and banks are real.) The officers go to Barclays and write a dollar check on their account in Bank America and deposit it. Knudsen's may decide to sell some of its dollars for pounds, but it may also keep most of its funds in U.S. dollars. So, Barclays gives Knudsen's an account in U.S. dollars for $100. This is item (1) in the balance sheet accounts below. Barclays takes the Knudsen's check and sends it to its account with Bank of America (B.A.) so it now has a dollar asset in the U.S. shown as item (2). Meanwhile, in the U.S., B.A. receives Barclays' deposit and increases its account, item (3). At the same time it reduces Knudsen's balance in its account, item (4).

	Assets	Barclays	Liabilities	
Deposit in B.A.	+$100 (2)		Deposit Knudsen's	+$100 (1)

	Assets	Bank of America	Liabilities	
			Demand deposit Knudsen's	−$100 (4)
			Demand deposit Barclays	+$100 (3)

Now, stop and see, after four entries, just exactly what has happened. Does Knudsen's still have its $100? Yes. Was the $100 on deposit in Bank America transferred out of B.A. to Barclays? No. The $100 is *still deposited in* B.A. However, Barclays owns that $100 now instead of Knudsen's. Has Knudsen's lost its money? No. Does Barclays have $100? Yes. Does Knudsen's have $100? Yes. So there is clearly $200 where there was only $100 before Knudsen's made its deposit. Thus, without a doubt, $100 of U.S. money has been created by Barclays bank.

Has the money supply in the U.S. declined by $100? Should Barclays' $100 in B.A. be counted as part of the U.S. money supply? As we saw in Chapter 5, interbank deposits in banks are not included in measures of money. So, perhaps the U.S. money supply should be reduced by the amount of Barclays' deposit. But this would not correctly reflect the $100 that Knudsen still has unless Eurodollars are included in the U.S. measures of money. This exclusion of interbank deposits in measures of money is appropriate in the case of domestic banks, but it may not be appropriate when the banks in question are foreign banks. In looking at the process of money creation in Europe, we will see that more and more U.S. dollars are created.

To continue. Barclays will not want to hold idle demand deposits in the U.S. bank. Thus, assume that someone from France walks into Barclays' lobby and asks if it has any U.S. dollars for lending. Having just received Knudsen's deposit, Barclays says it has $100. So a loan of $100 is arranged and the French borrower walks out with a check that Barclays has written on its account in B.A. See items (5) and (6) on Barclays' balance sheet below.

Assets		Barclays	Liabilities	
Deposit in B.A.	+$100 (2)		Deposit Knudsen's	+$100 (1)
	−$100 (5)			
Loan to French	+$100 (6)			

In Paris, the U.S. dollar check is deposited in a U.S. dollar account in Banque de France, item (7) in the balance sheet below. It is then sent to B.A., item (8), as shown below. Upon reaching America, the Banque de France account in B.A. shown above is increased, item (9), and Barclays' account is reduced, item (10).

Assets		Banque de France	Liabilities	
Deposit B.A.	$100 (8)		Deposit French	$100 (7)

Assets		Bank of America	Liabilities	
			Demand deposit Knudsen's	−$100 (4)
			Demand deposit Barclays	+$100 (3)
				−$100 (9)
			Demand deposit Banque de France	+$100 (10)

After ten entries on the balance sheets of banks in different countries, what has occurred? The person in France has $100, Knudsen's still has $100, and the Banque de France has $100. There now exists $300 whereas before this process started there was only $100 in Knudsen's account at B.A. European banks have created $200.

Every time the same $100 that is on deposit in B.A. is lent out and deposited in another bank, there is another $100 created. All that happens to the $100 in the U.S. in the form of a deposit at B.A. is that it changes hands from bank to bank to bank. This $100 deposit in the B.A. could be called the "Eurodollar base"—the base upon which a multiple of U.S. dollar deposits in European banks is created by those banks.

Now let us turn to the interesting questions mentioned above: in what form are these dollars created, and how many dollars are created?

Table 8–1(a) contains the last data provided by the Federal Reserve Bank of St. Louis in its *International Economic Conditions* (April 1989: 8). The January 1990 issue simply reported, "Data on Eurocurrency market size are currently not available in this publication" (1990: 8).

As the table indicates, gross liabilities in Eurocurrencies had grown to $4.561 trillion by March 1988, 67 per cent of which were in U.S. dollars and the remainder other currencies. Foreign central banks held $144 billion. And, interbank Eurocurrency liabilities amounted to $3.577 trillion. This left only some $839 billion of deposits held by nonbanks such as Knudsen's, the French borrower, and others.

As we saw in Chapter 5, interbank deposits are not counted as part of a money supply. Neither are deposits held by central banks. So 67 per cent of the $839 billion, or about $562 billion is the estimated extent of the creation of U.S. dollars by European banks and Asian banks—banks outside of the U.S. itself. This amount was approximately 75 per cent of the money supply in the U.S. at the time.

But there is another concern. What form do these deposits take? Most of them are time deposits on which interest is earned. Only a small proportion is in the form of demand or call deposits. Thus, the estimate of $562 billion should be added to *M2* money rather than *M1* money. It was only about 25 per cent of *M2* money.

So, after considering other factors, it appears that the gross volume of Eurocurrency deposits may not be so large after all. But the volume of demand deposits of foreign banks held in large commercial banks in the U.S.—the base upon which Eurocurrency credit is created—was about $5 billion or less than 1 per cent of the total credit in U.S. dollars created by banks outside of the U.S.

In other words, the reserves in U.S. dollars voluntarily held against Eurodollar creation are very small, and it is reasonable for banks to hold as small a level of reserves as possible. Why? Because the volume of interbank Eurocurrencies that banks hold is a very large sum. This means that the markets for Eurocurrencies are very large, and when any given bank needs a few more dollars, it need only call a correspondent bank in the market and borrow some! The interbank market operations in Eurodollars are almost identical to the Federal Funds market in the U.S. Banks are in constant contact, borrowing and lending Eurocurrencies.

LIBOR is the London Interbank Offered Rate that is set on such borrowing and

Table 8-1

(a) Eurocurrency Market Size (Billions of dollars at end of period)

	1980	1981	1982	1983	1984	1985	1986	1987 Sept.	1987 Dec.	1988 Mar.
Gross liabilities to:										
Nonbanks	$ 278	$ 372	$ 432	$ 479	$ 497	$ 585	$ 699	$ 780	$ 814	$ 839
Central banks	128	112	91	88	96	112	105	144	151	144
Other banks	1,172	1,470	1,645	1,711	1,793	2,149	2,879	3,319	3,544	3,577
TOTAL	1,578	1,954	2,168	2,278	2,386	2,846	3,683	4,243	4,509	4,561
Eurodollars as per cent of total gross liabilities in all Eurocurrencies	76%	79%	80%	81%	82%	75%	71%	70%	66%	67%
Dollar liabilities of foreign branches of U.S. banks as per cent of total gross liabilities in all Eurocurrencies	20%	19%	18%	17%	15%	12%	9%	8%	8%	8%

Based on foreign liabilities of banks in major European countries, the Bahamas, Bahrain, Cayman Islands, Panama, Canada, Japan, Hong Kong, and Singapore.

Source: *International Economic Conditions*, Federal Reserve Bank of St. Louis, April 1989, p. 8.

(b) Eurocurrency Market Size for BIS Reporting Banks, Summary of Reporting Positions, March 1993 (in billions of U.S. dollars)

Gross external liabilities	$6,181.2
To nonbanks	1,358.3
To banks	4,822.9
Local liabilities in foreign currency	$ 996.2

Source: *International Banking and Financial Market Developments*, Bank of International Settlements, Basle, August 1993, Table 1.

lending (or should we say purchasing and selling of Eurocurrencies) at a given time each day. It is used as a basis for many floating rate contracts.

Large Borrowers and Lenders in the Eurodollar Market

All large borrowers go to the Eurodollar market for funds. The reason is clear. Eurodollar market interest rates are lower than those available on dollar loans in the U.S. Yet they are not much lower, so, for small amounts of money, it is better to deal with one's friendly neighborhood banker. But if the amount involved is in the hundreds of millions, then a few basis points difference in interest costs on borrowing means a lot of cash.

All large lenders go to the Eurodollar market to lend their funds. The interest they earn from lending their extra cash is slightly higher than what they would earn in the U.S. It is only a few basis points higher, but this means a lot if the size of the Eurodollar deposit is large.

As a result, the situation can be expressed in terms of the spread between borrowing and lending rates in the Eurodollar market: it is smaller, and in between, the spread between borrowing and lending rates in the U.S. Thus, basis points can be shaved off borrowing costs and can be added on to deposit returns in the Eurodollar market.

The reason that the spread can be smaller is that the market is not regulated: principally (a) there is no requirement that banks hold legal reserves against Eurodollar deposits, and (b) there is no requirement that deposits be insured by the Federal Deposit Insurance Corporation.

Interest Rates on Money Market Instruments

The Federal Reserve regularly publishes interest rates on money market instruments along with the federal funds interbank rate and the discount rate that the Federal Reserve charges for loans to banks. Except for discount window borrowing, the rates are quoted for a 360-day year, and, except for the federal funds rates, the quotes of interest rates on all of the money market instruments are on a discount basis.

Figures 8–1(a) and (b) show the pattern of short-term interest rates that are regularly tracked by financial analysts. As noted in Chapter 7, nearly all countries implement monetary policy by entering money markets and affecting bank reserves. Thus, the federal funds rate and the discount rate are shown alongside the rate for Treasury bills, for certificates of deposit, and so forth.

Money Markets in the Asian Tigers

Banks tend to play the largest role in developing economies because financial markets require the evolution of accounting standards, trading rules, legal arrangements, and so forth. Bankers tend to have the ear of government and, as described in the previous chapter, banks are often owned by government or are given cartel privileges. But as development progresses business enterprises look to other sources of capital—debt or equity markets. Only after debt and equity markets develop are the money markets

Figure 8–1

(a) Yields on Selected Securities (Averages of daily figures)

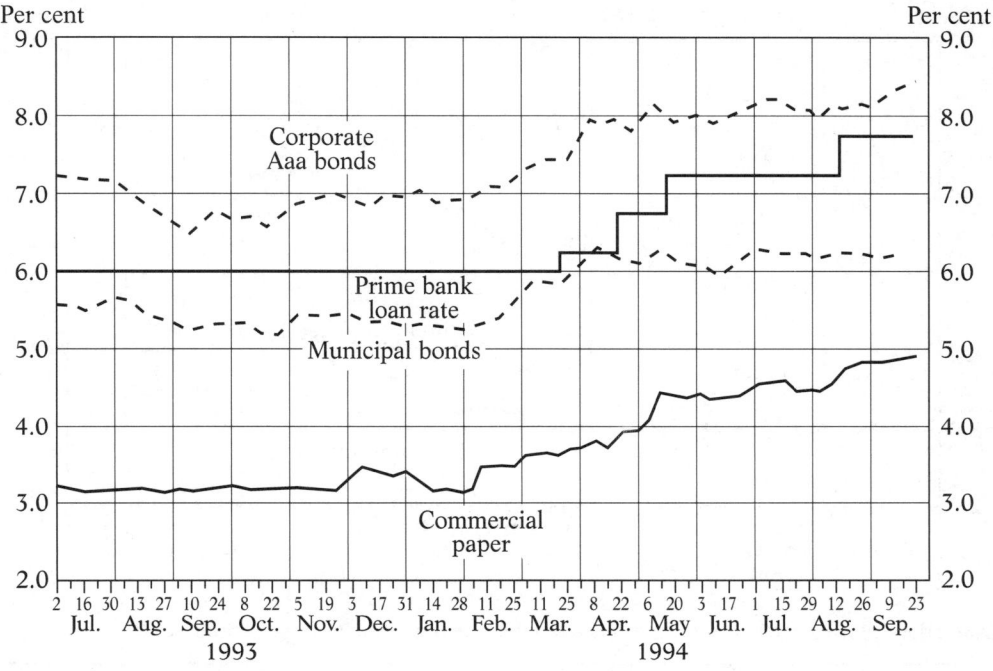

Latest data plotted are averages of rates available for the week ending: September 23, 1994

1994	30-day commercial paper	90-day CDs	90-day banker's acceptances	Corporate Aaa bonds	Corporate Baa bonds	Municipal bonds**
Jul. 1	4.47	4.71	4.64	8.11	8.80	6.28
8	4.53	4.78	4.72	8.18	8.87	6.27
15	4.55	4.78	4.69	8.17	8.86	6.22
22	4.44	4.65	4.59	8.06	8.75	6.22
29	4.46	4.70	4.61	8.05	8.74	6.22
Aug. 5	4.45	4.68	4.61	7.96	8.64	6.16
12	4.54	4.79	4.71	8.12	8.79	6.25
19	4.74	4.86	4.80	8.07	8.73	6.22
26	4.79	4.87	4.79	8.13	8.79	6.21
Sep. 2	4.80	4.88	4.81	8.09	8.76	6.16
9	4.82	4.89	4.81	8.22	8.88	6.18
16	4.87	4.96	4.88	8.32	8.97	6.24
23*	4.90	5.02	4.95	8.40	9.03	N.A.

Current data appear in the Federal Reserve Board's H.15 release.

*Averages of rates available.

**Bond Buyer's Average Index of 20 municipal bonds, Thursday data.

N.A. — Not available.

Figure 8–1

(b) Selected Interest Rates (Averages of daily figures)

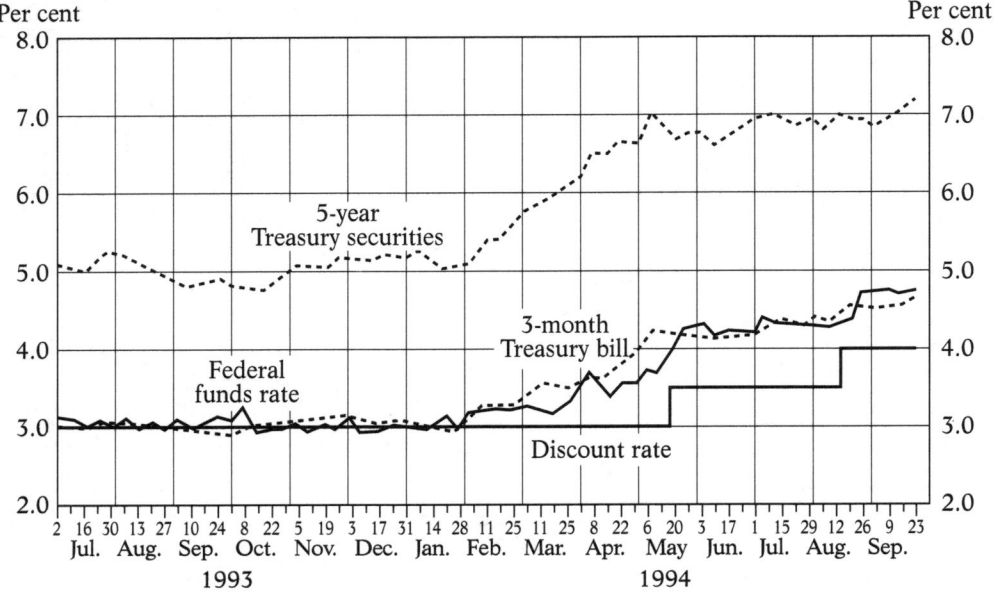

Latest data plotted are averages of rates available for the week ending: September 23, 1994

1994	Federal funds**	3-month Treasury bill	1-year Treasury bill	5-year Treasury securities	10-year Treasury securities	Long-term Treasury securities
Jul. 1	4.19	4.16	5.18	6.89	7.27	7.57
8	4.38	4.28	5.19	6.95	7.34	7.64
15	4.30	4.37	5.18	6.97	7.36	7.65
22	4.30	4.30	5.10	6.83	7.23	7.52
29	4.28	4.39	5.22	6.89	7.26	7.52
Aug. 5	4.28	4.34	5.12	6.77	7.15	7.41
12	4.26	4.40	5.29	6.96	7.31	7.58
19	4.35	4.56	5.30	6.90	7.24	7.53
26	4.66	4.55	5.31	6.92	7.27	7.58
Sep. 2	4.72	4.56	5.26	6.83	7.21	7.52
9	4.74	4.56	5.30	6.95	7.33	7.65
16	4.70	4.59	5.38	7.05	7.44	7.76
23*	4.73	4.66	5.51	7.15	7.53	7.83

Current data appear in the Federal Reserve Board's H.15 release excluding long-term Treasury securities which are computed by this bank. Treasury bill yields are on a discount basis.

*Averages of rates available.

**Seven-day averages for week ending two days earlier than date shown.

Source: *U.S. Financial Data*, Federal Reserve Bank of St. Louis, September 23, 1994.

brought into the game. Money markets are used not so much as a source of capital (only a source of working capital) but as a supporting market for banks, stock exchanges, business, international trade, and so forth. The players in the money markets tend to be large institutions and not individuals or small businesses. Money markets act as grease on the wheels of the financial industry that enables financial markets to run smoothly.

Hong Kong

Interbank Funds. Hong Kong has an active interbank funds market. Interest rates in that market are watched by the Monetary Authority for indications of tightening of funds or major changes in the market environment in case some support should be needed from government. HIBOR is Hong Kong's Interbank Offered Rate—the rate observed at a certain time each trading day that sets the terms of floating rate financial instruments.

Exchange Fund Bills. As stated in Chapter 7, the Hong Kong government first issued bills in March 1990 when it initiated a program of bill auctions in order to support the development of a market for this money market instrument (see Culp, 1991 for an early analysis of this new market).

The Exchange Fund announced its plans on March 3, 1990, and auctioned HK$300 million of 13-week bills on March 10. Bills have a face value of HK$500,000 (US$64,000). These bills are now auctioned every week. Six-month bills (26 weeks) are auctioned every two weeks, and one-year bills are auctioned every four weeks. Ownership records are kept in registered form.

A group of "recognized dealers" may bid directly for the issues. When they purchase bills their clearing accounts with the banks are debited directly for the purchase sum.

Initially, a subgroup of 20 of the recognized dealers were chosen to provide a secondary market in bills. Eleven of these were retail banks and the remaining nine were merchant banks. This composition reflects somewhat the relative power of the banking industry in Hong Kong. These dealers have the authority to operate a repurchase market for bills, and to make short-sales. At the close of business each day a dealer may be short in one issue of bills, but must be sufficiently long in other issues so not to be "net-short."

In addition, there are tax advantages provided to the holders of bills. These make the interest return especially advantageous to banks. For the first couple of years, nearly all of the Exchange Fund bills were held by banks (see Culp, 1991 for more detail).

Negotiable Certificates of Deposit. NCDs, or CDs, for short, are issued with a maturity greater than one year in Hong Kong. So discussing this instrument in a chapter on money markets may violate our classification scheme that says that a money market instrument is one with a maturity of one year or less. However, these are issued with maturities of just over one year but are traded in secondary markets when they have less than a year to maturity. The reason they are issued with a maturity greater than one year is that the banking cartel in Hong Kong, the Hong Kong Association of Banks, sets the interest rates that banks may pay depositors. The only way to avoid this constraint on the market was to issue securities dated longer than one year (see Lui, 1991).

Floating Rate Notes. These were first issued in Hong Kong by the Mass Transit Railway Corporation in 1986. These proved very popular and more issues followed. The rate is adjusted periodically according to changes in HIBOR.

Commercial Paper. The Mass Transit Railway Corporation issued the first commercial paper in Hong Kong in 1977. It was not until 1984 that the government ruled that the sale of commercial paper was not the equivalent of the "taking of public deposits." After all, only banks were permitted to take public deposits, so business firms should not be permitted to enter the banking business in this indirect way. Between 1977 and 1984 every issue of commercial paper required that the issuer obtain specific permission from government (see Lui, 1991).

Nearly all commercial paper issued in Hong Kong is placed by dealers even though, by direct placement, the issuing firm might save 0.125 per cent on the commission. The issue may be underwritten fully by the dealer or sold on a "best effort" basis. It is popular to establish a RUF, a *revolving underwriting* facility, so that firms can tap the market for funds routinely as needs arise. Because credit risk is very important in the case of commercial paper, it is common for the issuer to obtain support from credit rating agencies.

The secondary market for money market instruments is not yet well developed in Hong Kong. A number of instruments exist, but are not actively traded for a variety of reasons. The interbank market for funds is active, but it is a banker's world. The powers that be dictate that any new money market instrument must support banking activities first. So long as policy does not interfere with the profitability of banks, the people are free to do what they want, or so it seems in many instances.

Korea

Important money market instruments including the *Monetary Stabilization Bond*, issued by the Bank of Korea since 1961, along with *Treasury bills*, issued since 1967, provided a base for the Bank of Korea to use as instruments of monetary policy as described in Chapter 7. The *call money market* was an interbank market for funds in which banks transacted with each other on an individual basis. However, in 1975 the Bankers Association of Korea established a Call Transactions Center to mediate the transactions like a clearing house. Banks, other financial institutions, and the Bank of Korea all engage in transactions in the call market.

In 1972 the Short-Term Financing Business Act became effective (see Roh, 1989). This Act permitted the creation of Investment Finance Companies (IFCs).

Investment Finance Companies. Between 1972 and 1983 there were 32 IFCs formed. The government stopped licensing IFCs at that time under the argument that there was a need to prevent excessive competition. These companies may issue their own securities, deal in commercial paper, underwrite issues of securities, offer a kind of money market mutual fund called Cash Management Accounts, and so forth. In many respects they resemble investment banks in the U.S. Their trading activities dominate the money markets in Korea.

Merchant Banking Corporation. In 1976 the Merchant Banking Corporation Act was passed. Under this act a handful of joint ventures with foreign banks registered as Merchant Banking Companies. The goal was to import expertise and also provide a mechanism for the easy importing of capital. These institutions participate in the local money markets.

Negotiable Certificates of Deposit. NCDs were first issued by banks in Korea in 1974. However, they were abolished in 1977, started up again in 1978, abolished in 1981, and started again in 1984. The problem was that interest rates on bank deposits in Korea were regulated. In 1986 the rates were set at around 2 per cent above rates on bank time deposits (see Roh, 1989: 11). A secondary market cannot function well in an environment of dictated rates. Liberalization of financial institutions continues in Korea. In 1989 interest rates on CDs, short-term government securities, commercial bills, commercial paper, and trade bills were allowed to float.

Commercial Paper and Commercial Bills. IFCs and MBCs are the exclusive dealers in what has become a large and well-developed commercial paper market. Commercial bills are purchased by banks and may be resold to the Bank of Korea.

Trade Bills. These bills are the equivalent of *banker's acceptances*. They were introduced in 1989.

When viewed against a background in which government regulated nearly all interest rates in order to "direct" investment, the progress toward market determined rates has been quite rapid in Korea.

Singapore

Singapore has well-developed markets for Treasury bills and other government securities. Six-month, nine-month and one-year T-bills were first issued in 1974. In 1975 banks in Singapore began issuing negotiable certificates of deposit denominated in Singapore dollars.

It also has a market for *bills of exchange*. A bill of exchange is an order to pay. One example is a check. Most checks are dated the day they are written and called a sight draft. Others may be drawn for a time period as indicated by the date in the future written on the bill. Such bills may be discounted and traded in markets. A bill may be *bank endorsed*, that is, a bank may add its guarantee of payment to the bill. The reader should note that this bank guaranteed bill is a *banker's acceptance* in American terminology.

The interbank market for funds is large in Singapore, along with the Asian dollar market, which is the equivalent of the Eurodollar market, and involves several major currencies of the world. SIBOR is Singapore's Interbank Offered Rate.

Taiwan

The money market in Taiwan has five major financial instruments. They are Treasury bills, commercial paper, banker's acceptances, commercial acceptances and negotiable certificates of deposits.

Organized money markets, in contrast to markets where individuals transact with each other, came into existence in May 1976 with the establishment of the Chung-Hsin Bills Finance Corporation. Subsequently two additional corporations, International Bills Finance Corporation and Chung-Hua Bills Finance Corporation were established. These three corporations have expanded their organized trading of money market instruments at very high annual rates. The volume of instruments has also expanded rapidly. For example, the volume of commercial paper expanded at annual rates of about 40 per cent throughout 1980–88 (see Chen, 1990).

Summary

The principal money market instruments held and traded in the United States are Treasury bills, federal funds, repurchase agreements, certificates of deposit, banker's acceptances, commercial, paper and Eurodollars. All of these securities are very liquid and billions of dollars worth are traded every day. They have low risk and carry low interest rates. Indeed, the U.S. Treasury bill is considered to be *the* risk-free asset.

Eurodollars are unique. They are "created" in Europe by European banks, and in Asia by banks in Asian financial centers.

Each of the Asian Tigers has several money market instruments. These tend to facilitate the development of financial markets that support not only the business growth of the Tigers, but their infrastructure as well.

Key Terms and Concepts

Money vs. capital markets
T-bills
Discount rate
Repurchase agreement
Yankee CD
Creation of Eurodollars
HIBOR
Banker's acceptance
Net-short position

Risk-free asset
Tax anticipation bills (TABs)
Federal Financing Bank
Certificate of deposit (CD)
Eurodollar
LIBOR
SIBOR
Commercial paper
Korean trade bills

Discussion Questions and Exercises

1. Should a bond that has less than a year remaining to maturity be considered a money market instrument or a capital market instrument? Discuss.
2. Payment in the money markets is usually made by "immediately available funds." What does this mean?
3. Briefly describe the auction of Treasury bills.
4. What does it mean, precisely, to say that Treasury bills are sold on a discount basis?
5. What makes Treasury bills the single most important money market instrument?
6. Briefly describe the function of the Federal Financing Bank.
7. What is the federal funds market a bellwether for?
8. Briefly describe how the market for negotiable certificates of deposit evolved.
9. Did Continental Illinois Bank get into trouble issuing CDs? Explain.
10. Do buyers or sellers usually make out drafts on banks that turn into banker's acceptances? Explain.
11. How was the Eurodollar market started?
12. Explain how Eurodollars are created.
13. Explain why the Eurodollar interest spread between borrowing and lending rates is smaller than the same spread in the U.S.
14. Write a descriptive paragraph on the market for commercial paper in the U.S.
15. Explain why Hong Kong's government issues debt even though it has a surplus in its budget from tax revenues.
16. What are the unique characteristics of Korea's money markets?
17. What are the unique characteristics of Singapore's money markets?
18. What are the unique characteristics of Hong Kong's money markets?
19. What are the unique characteristics of Taiwan's money markets?

References

Over the years the Federal Reserve Bank of Richmond's research department has kept a running stream of articles devoted to descriptive material on the various money markets in the U.S. It has published several volumes such as *Instruments of the Money Market*, the latest version of which appeared in 1986. But each issue of its *Economic Quarterly* is likely to have an article such as those by Hahn and LaRoche cited below.

Carmichael, Jeffery, and Harper, Ian R., "Implementing Monetary Policy in a Deregulated Financial System: A Study of the Australian Short-term Money Market," in *Proceedings of the Second International Conference on Asian-Pacific Financial Markets*, City Polytechnic of Hong Kong, September 12–14, 1991, pp. 78–87.

Chen, M. T., "The Financial System and Financial Policy in the Republic of China," *Economic Review*, July–August 1990, pp. 1–10.

Chen, Mu-Tsai, "Development Issues of Money Markets in the Republic of China," in

Proceedings of the Second International Conference on Asian-Pacific Financial Markets, City Polytechnic of Hong Kong, September 12–14, 1991, pp. 222–33.

Culp, Christopher, "An Analysis of the Exchange Fund Bills Programme: Market Microstructure and Performance," *Asian Monetary Monitor*, November–December 1991, pp. 8–25.

Emery, Robert F., *The Money Markets of Developing East Asia*, Praeger, New York, 1991.

Hahn, Thomas K., "Commercial Paper," *Economic Quarterly*, Federal Reserve Bank of Richmond, Spring 1993, pp. 45–67.

Kavanagh, Barbara, Boemio, Thomas R., and Edwards, Gerald A., Jr., "Asset-backed Commercial Paper Programs," *Federal Reserve Bulletin*, February 1992, pp. 107–16.

LaRoche, Robert K., "Banker's Acceptances," *Economic Quarterly*, Federal Reserve Bank of Richmond, Winter 1993, pp. 75–85.

Lui, Y. H., *The Hong Kong Financial System*, Commercial Press, Hong Kong, 1989.

———, "Money and Capital Markets," in Y. K. Ho, R. H. Scott, and K. A. Wong, eds., *The Hong Kong Financial System*, Oxford University Press, Hong Kong, 1991, pp. 161–86.

Post, Mitchell A., "The Evolution of the U.S. Commercial Paper Market since 1980," *Federal Reserve Bulletin*, December 1992, pp. 879–91.

Roh, Choong-Hwan, "The Money Market Development in Korea," *Monthly Review*, Korea Exchange Bank, December 1989, pp. 3–15.

Yamashita, Takeji, *Japan's Securities Markets: A Practitioner's Guide*, Butterworths, Singapore, 1989.

CHAPTER 9

Capital Markets

IN THIS CHAPTER *capital markets* refers to markets for financial securities and not markets for capital equipment such as buildings and machinery. Capital markets differ from money markets because the original maturities of the securities that are issued and traded are greater than one year. This is an arbitrary distinction, of course. This chapter contains brief discussions of markets for government notes and bonds, corporate bonds, Eurobonds, municipal securities and equities. The discussion begins with federal government securities.

The Long-term Government Securities Market

Government securities are "default free." This fact stems from government's monopoly over the creation of money. Paper money in the U.S. consists almost entirely of Federal Reserve Notes. These are non-interest-bearing debt obligations of the Federal Reserve—an agency of the federal government. The federal government can always pay off any maturing bonds by printing money, although Congress would have to approve such action. Under current arrangements, Congress insists that the Treasury borrow the funds needed to make up for an excess of spending over tax revenues—that is, to pay for the deficit. A deeper discussion of deficits, debt, and its management by the Treasury department appears in Chapter 17. Here, the market for this debt is the focus of concern.

Who Owns the Government's Debt? Table 9–1 shows the holders of government debt. (Here the reference to government debt is to the debt of the U.S. federal government and excludes the debt of state and municipal governments.)

Table 9–1
Holders of Government Debt at End of 1992

Holder	Per cent
State and local governments	18.0
Foreign investors	16.6
Federal Reserve system	9.9
Individuals	9.4
Commercial banks	9.0
Private pension funds	7.2
Insurance companies	6.2
Corporations	6.0
Mutual funds	4.8
Money market funds	2.6
Other	10.4

Source: *Congressional Budget Office Report*, May 1993.

Of the 1993 gross public debt of over $4 trillion, about two-thirds is marketable. Nonmarketable debt includes savings bonds and some issues to other government units and foreign agencies. About one-fourth of the marketable debt is in Treasury bills, one-fifth in bonds and just under one-half in notes.

Trading in this huge dollar volume of securities is extensive. An individual may purchase these securities through a broker in the over-the-counter market. Most banks will sell some of their own securities holdings to service a customer's needs. But the really large dollar trades are undertaken by government securities dealers.

In the past the Treasury has issued callable bonds, but it did not call any bonds between 1962 and 1991 because interest rates generally rose from the 1960s through the 1980s. In 1985 the Treasury quit issuing callable bonds, and in 1991 it called a bond due to mature in 1993. About $80 billion of callable bonds is still outstanding and due to mature after the year 2000.

The Dealer Market

The number of officially approved government securities "dealers" changes from time to time but there are about 40 all together. They are at the core of the market. They have been approved to engage in trading with the Federal Reserve Bank of New York, which carries out the open market operations recommended by the Federal Open Market Committee. They apply for inclusion in this privileged group, and the Federal Reserve Bank evaluates their reputation, financial situation, ability and willingness to make a market in government securities. About a dozen of the dealers are large commercial banks, several are investment banks, and several are financial firms that specialize in the sole business of dealing in government securities. About ten of the firms are owned by foreign interests.

Unlike brokers, who place orders and receive commissions from bringing buyers and sellers together, dealers maintain inventories of various issues of securities and make a market by buying and selling securities for their own account. Dealers need to finance their large inventories of government securities and make use of the repurchase markets as described in the previous chapter.

Depth, Breadth, and Resiliency

Capital markets originate as new issue markets where dealers engage in competitive bidding for new securities. But most trading takes place in the secondary market, which is designed to add marketability to these securities, that is, to permit holders to sell them easily and without great expense. In many countries the markets for capital instruments is "thin." They cannot be sold quickly and easily at little cost. In the U.S., in contrast, the dealer market makes the markets for government securities (a) *deep*, that is, there are both buy and sell orders below and above the current market price, (b) *broad*, that is, orders to buy and sell come from many different groups, such as commercial banks, insurance companies, corporations, state and local governments, and so forth, and (c) *resilient*, that is, new orders to buy and sell enter the market in large volume whenever prices fluctuate.

In the secondary market for notes and bonds, dealers price securities by using bid and asked spreads. Prices are quoted in $\frac{1}{32}$ of a point, for example, "101 : 3 bid 101 : 5 asked" means the price is 101 and $\frac{3}{32}$ bid and $\frac{5}{32}$ asked. Spreads usually are $\frac{2}{32}$ but will increase to $\frac{4}{32}$ when a particular issue is going through significant price changes during the trading period. The larger movements in prices mean that dealers are forced to protect themselves with higher spreads. With the extension of electronic payments systems in the 1980s, however, spreads have fallen to $\frac{1}{32}$, or even $\frac{1}{64}$, as all dealers are quickly aware of bid and offer prices throughout the market. Government bonds carry semiannual coupons, and interest accrued since the last coupon date is added to the price of the security.

The Treasury now issues marketable securities only in registered form, so it is not necessary to wait for the issue of a piece of paper in order to buy, sell or trade securities. Such transactions are now handled electronically.

Auctions

In earlier years the Treasury sold securities on a subscription basis. It attempted auctions in the 1930s and again on a couple of occasions in 1963. By the 1970s auctions had replaced subscriptions. As in the case of Treasury bills, the auctions of securities are on both a competitive and noncompetitive basis. Competitive bids for new issues are based on yields, such as 7.31 per cent or 7.25 per cent, even though in the secondary market trading is based on thirty-second's of a point. The coupon rate attached to the bond is set by the Treasury after the allotment has been made to all noncompetitive and competitive bidders. Noncompetitive bids may be up to $1 million. The Treasury conducts many auctions of securities every year.

For five days prior to the sale of an issue of Treasury bonds, dealers are allowed to trade securities on a "when issued" basis. Settlements of trades are made on the date of issue. Prices set in the "when issued" market help dealers narrow price ranges on issues for which they submit bids at the auctions.

Dutch Auctions. At the usual auction a bidder pays the bid price. This means that the bidder who bid the highest price has his bid accepted and that those who bid lower prices also have bids accepted down to the lowest accepted price. The Treasury keeps lowering the price until the full amount of the offered securities is taken up. Other bids at even lower prices are not accepted. Noncompetitive bids are accepted at the average of bid prices. This means that, when the secondary market opens for business, some holders of the securities have bought them at higher prices than the accepted bid price and others have bought them at lower prices than the accepted bid price. This is fair only because bidders were free to bid what they chose to bid.

Dutch auctions are different. At a Dutch auction, all bidders receive allotments of securities at the lowest of all bid prices that are accepted. That is, every buyer of the security pays the *same* price and receives the amount he bid for, so long as his bid price was as great as, or greater than, the lowest accepted bid price. Thus, when entering trading in the secondary market after the auction, every player has purchased his inventory of securities at the same average cost per bond.

Under the regular auction, the Treasury receives a higher price for part of the issue of securities it sells than it does for another part of the issue. In a sense the Treasury saves interest expense because it is able to capture a higher price from all but the lowest price bidders.

However, some potential bidders may be afraid to bid because they may mistakenly bid too high a price. Immediately after the auction, a bidder may find the value of his investment is down. Fear of making such mistakes may keep bidders away.

If the Dutch auction technique were used, however, every bidder would feel more comfortable bidding because he has the assurance that his cost will be no higher than that paid by others. With more participants encouraged to bid, the overall average price paid for Treasury securities may be higher. If so, the Treasury would realize higher prices on average and a lower interest cost on the funds it needs to raise.

Could the Treasury save on its interest costs if it used the Dutch auction technique? The markets for government securities are already highly competitive, and data generated from actual attempts at Dutch auctioning are very difficult to interpret. In late 1972, the Treasury announced 6¾ per cent, 20-year bonds for sale under the Dutch auction technique. There were additional bidders but mostly from the New York area. And the price of the security sold several thirty-second's of a point below the accepted bid price the first day of trading in the secondary market. This discouraged bidders, so the Treasury turned back to its usual auction technique.

However, an extended test of the Dutch auction technique was started in 1992 as a result of an unfortunate chain of events.

The Trading Scandal at Salomon Brothers. Under the bidding rules established by the Treasury, no one dealer is permitted to submit bids for more than 35 per cent of the issue of a single security. This rule is to prevent one dealer from cornering the market for a single security. Most dealers make arrangements with customers to supply some amounts of certain securities after they are issued, and if the supply is scarce those commitments must be met by going into the market and paying higher prices for them. The holder of a large proportion of a single issue can ask for higher prices and realize significant profit. In February 1991 the Treasury discovered that traders at Salomon Brothers had bid for a five-year note under their own name and under the name of a corporate customer as well. The corporate customer did not know its name was being used. The total bidding exceeded the 35 per cent limit set by the Treasury.

In May 1991 a "squeeze" occurred in the two-year note market just after it had been auctioned. It appears that Salomon Brothers and its customers had bid more aggressively for the note than expected. Finally, on August 9, in response to investigative actions of the Treasury and the Justice Departments, Salomon admitted to the violation of the 35 per cent rule in the two-year and five-year note auctions as well as in one previous auction of four-year notes in 1990.

Did Salomon Brothers corner the market for the five-year note? Other dealers, looking to satisfy their commitments had to pay premium prices to Salomon Brothers and suspicion surrounded the markets. This is a *classic case of a cartel in operation*. The cartel was formed by the government when it licensed a group of dealers (39 were licensed at the time) to bid competitively for Treasury securities at auctions. The typical cartel is always in an unstable equilibrium because, if one member cheats, it can gain at the expense of other members. Did Salomon cheat?

In May 1992 Salomon made a $290 million settlement of charges brought by the Securities and Exchange Commission. Out of these funds it paid $54.5 million to investors who bought Salomon's own stock and bonds at prices that were higher than they would have been if information about the firm's illegal activities had not been withheld (see Siconolfi, 1993). The result was great damage to a reputable financial giant. The Treasury imposed fines. The firm was saved only through extensive restructuring of its personnel and operations. But still remaining in the summer of 1993 was a set of suits brought against Salomon by other Treasury market participants who will claim that they paid excessive prices for the securities they purchased because of Salomon's illegal activities.

A debate ensued over what might be done to prevent such occurrences in the future. Milton Friedman published an article in the *Wall Street Journal* (September 3, 1991) arguing that a Dutch auction, a technique that he had recommended in 1959 would have prevented this problem from arising. The Dutch auction technique was tried when George Schultz was Secretary of the Treasury in 1972, but when William Simon, a former bond trader, was made Secretary in 1974, the experiment with Dutch auctions was canceled. Remember that, under a Dutch auction, competitive bidding is open to all bidders, not just government securities dealers.

The Treasury's Response. The *Treasury Bulletin* carried an analysis of debt management concerns in December 1991, but expressed no enthusiasm for Dutch auctions. The analysis was written by Jerome H. Powell, then Assistant Secretary for Domestic Finance of the Treasury Department (see Powell, 1991). Then, on July 29, 1992, investment banker Michael E. Basham, former deputy assistant secretary of the Treasury, wrote in the *Wall Street Journal* saying that trading in the "when issued" market in which securities are actively traded for five days prior to the actual sale of the securities was the most relevant activity and concluded that the Dutch auction was largely irrelevant to the market-cornering strategy that Salomon pursued. However, in spite of objections from dealers and resistance from Treasury officials, the Treasury announced that it would attempt Dutch auctions of its securities for a year and evaluate the result. In September 1992 it began Dutch auctions of its two-year notes each month. In October it used the Dutch auction on its five-year notes. The results of these auctions will be forthcoming.

Zero Coupon Bonds

Traditional bonds are contracts that provide for a stream of payments over a fixed period and a return of principal at maturity. Typical textbook examples are for annual payments of coupons attached to the bonds. However, most corporate bonds and U.S. Treasury bonds provide for semiannual coupons. Before the age of computers, bonds were printed and coupons were attached and arranged so that they could be clipped off with scissors and turned in for cash when coupon payments came due. Federal Reserve Banks had teller windows to pay out cash to Treasury bondholders in exchange for their clipped coupons.

Zero coupon bonds simply have no coupons attached. Instead the bond is a contract that provides for redemption of its face value at the bond's maturity on some date several years in the future. These bonds are sold at a discount from face value. The price of the bond today is its present value (*PV*), and its future value (*FV*) is its face value. The discount of its future value to present value determines its implicit yield to maturity (*i*) on a date *n* years in the future by the simple formula, $PV = FV/(1 + i)^n$. By entering *PV*, *FV* and *n* on a hand calculator one can find the implicit yield, *i*, the annual interest yield from holding the bond to maturity. No periodic payments are made.

Originally, some issuers and some buyers of zero coupon bonds believed that they could have a lower tax on interest income by treating all of the implicit interest earnings as capital gains that were subject to a lower tax rate. This occurred in the 1970s, but the Treasury soon closed what would have been a tax loophole (see Glick, 1992). The Treasury now requires that holders of such bonds use a method of estimating the appreciation in value of such bonds each year and pay taxes annually on that appreciation. The years to maturity at the time of purchase are divided into the difference between the purchase price and the face value of the bond, so the appreciation is an equal amount for each year. It could be called a "straight line appreciation" method.

But the concept of the zero coupon bond is very appealing, and such bonds have gained great favor since the early 1980s.

TIGRs, CATS, and STRIPS

In the early 1980s two investment banks, Merrill Lynch and Salomon Brothers, placed large volumes of government bonds in trust and then sold certificates against their coupon interest payments and principal payments separately. For example, a certificate might be sold to an investor. The certificate might give the investor the right to the interest payment of $5,000 that will be made on a specific $1 million Treasury bond on January 1 some ten years from now. This $5,000 coupon payment might represent a semiannual coupon payment on a bond yielding 10 per cent on par of $1 million. Similarly, another investor might purchase a certificate giving the right to receive the $1 million principal payment in 20 years. Thus, the certificates essentially strip the coupons off of the Treasury securities and permit the rights to them and to the principal to be sold separately. Such stripping made both the interest payments and the principal payments into zero coupon bonds.

Merrill Lynch called its certificates Treasury Investment Growth Receipts (TIGRs) and Salomon Brothers called their issues Certificates of Accrual on Treasury Securities (CATS).

The certificates became very popular and other investment houses followed suit. Finally, the Treasury agreed to assist the development of the market for these securities. The Treasury sells its marketable securities only on a registered basis so it keeps all records of ownership in computers. So the Treasury agreed to separate the registration of the ownership of rights to coupons from rights to principals. Thus, the investment firms no longer had to handle all of the bookkeeping required to manage changes in ownership of different parts of different Treasury bonds. So the Treasury called its new program of assistance to the securities industry, Separate Trading in Registered Interest and Principal of Securities (STRIPS).

Interest Spreads. Interest yields on zero coupon stripped securities run about half a percentage point (50 basis points) higher than those on identical underlying bonds that have been stripped. There are two factors that may contribute to this difference in yields: (a) zero coupon bonds maturing on a given future date have a duration equal to the length of time to maturity, which is longer than the duration on a regular bond because coupon payments shorten the duration, and (b) the volatility in price of the zero coupon bond is greater than the volatility of price in a coupon-paying bond when both bonds mature on the same date, so the capital risk (not the default risk) is greater on the zero coupon bond. Of course, since duration may be used as a measure of volatility, the two factors describe the same phenomenon.

Government Agency and Similar Bonds

There exists a bewildering variety of securities issued by agencies of the federal government and other governmental institutions. Some agencies have been "privatized" and now often referred to as sponsored by government. In some cases the question of whether or not the U.S. Treasury would come to the rescue of a bankrupted agency has no clear answer.

One type of note issued by a government agency that is never mentioned under the heading of government agency securities is the Federal Reserve Note—the non-interest-bearing notes that are the principal part of U.S. currency. Other countries, such as Korea, have central banks that do issue interest-bearing securities.

Usually, under the heading of government agency securities, there are issues of such institutions as the Tennessee Valley Authority (TVA), the Federal Farm Credit Bank, the Banks for Cooperatives, the Federal Intermediate Credit Banks, the Export-Import Bank, the Student Loan Marketing Association (Sallie Mae), Federal Land Banks, and others.

World Bank bonds, which are bonds issued by the International Bank for Reconstruction and Development, represent bonds of a governmental type of organization that is an international agency and not a U.S. government agency.

The most important type of government-backed or sponsored agency securities are tied to the market for mortgages on housing. These are the well-known Government National Mortgage Association (Ginnie Mae), the Federal National Mortgage Association (Fannie Mae), the Federal Home Loan Mortgage Corporation (Freddie Mac), the Veterans Administration Mortgage Corporation (Vinnie Mac), and the Farm Home Administration (FmHA). These housing agencies operate through financial intermediaries. They issue bonds and then use the proceeds of the sale of these bonds to buy packages of mortgages from financial institutions. In many instances the packages of bonds are converted into so-called pass-through certificates or collateralized mortgage obligations. These special types of mortgage-backed securities are the subject of discussion in the following chapter.

The Student Loan Marketing Association (Sallie Mae) handles the government-backed student loan portfolio and operates in a manner similar to the housing program.

Spreads. Yields on government agency bonds run between 10 and 25 basis points higher than those of U.S. Treasury bonds of the same maturity, even when backed by the Treasury. One reason may be that if an agency ran into financial difficulty there would be a delay in the recovery of the bond's value while the government figured out how to handle the problem. A potential delay in the time of payment makes the bond slightly more risky.

Another reason may be that state income taxes are not levied on income received in the form of interest on U.S. Treasury securities, but are levied on agency securities. Thus, to residents living in states that have income taxes Treasuries are a better investment than agencies.

Corporate Bonds

When issuing a bond, the borrowing corporation signs a contract to make payments to the lender. Corporate bonds are usually issued in denominations of $1,000 or larger, they may be in bearer or in registered form, and they usually have call provisions. In addition they usually provide for semiannual coupon payments. A bond covenant or indenture—a written statement that contains all the terms and conditions under which the bond is sold—may contain many variations.

There may be provisions for converting the bond into shares of stock in the company—*convertible bonds*.

Or, a bond may have a *warrant* attached that gives the holder the right to purchase shares of stock in the company at a set price during, say, the next two years. A warrant is a type of option.

Linked Securities. Equity-linked Securities (EKLs) appeared in the summer of 1993 when Salomon Inc. issued $60 million of three-year notes that paid an interest rate of 6.75 per cent. However, the repayment of principal at the end of three years depends upon what happens to the price of the stock of a company, Digital Equipment Corporation, that has no involvement in the arrangement. If the stock price falls by 10 per cent, the principal repayment will be 10 per cent lower. If the stock price rises, the principal will also rise, except a cap on the rise is set at 35 per cent. Other types of links can also be made. In Hong Kong several bond issues have been linked to movements in the Hang Seng Index of stock prices. These are noted as bull and bear bonds and are described later in the chapter.

A typical bond is "in default" if the company misses payment of any of the interest payments when due, however, a company may issue *income bonds* that provide for the company to miss an interest payment if the company's income falls short without going into "default." Income bonds are rarely issued even though issuers should find them attractive. Perhaps buyers of these bonds feel that such bonds are too risky to hold and have demand yields that are too high to suit the borrowers.

Bonds may have sinking fund provisions under which the bonds may be paid off periodically. Funds are accumulated over time and earmarked for use to repay bondholders.

There is really no limit to the terms that issuers can place in a bond covenant, although there is a certain uniformity that the market expects.

A bond may be *subordinated* to an earlier bond issue of the company. That is, in case of bankruptcy, the holder of a subordinated bond will not receive payment until holders of the original bond issue have been paid all amounts of interest and principal due.

Corporate bonds are usually issued for a period of 10 years or longer. In 1993 when long-term interest rates fell to lower levels from the highs of the 1980s, some corporations issued 40-year bonds. Reports indicated that Time Warner, Inc., had some difficulty in issuing its $1 billion in 40-year bonds (*Wall Street Journal*, July 13, 1993). Then, a week later, Walt Disney isssued $150 million of 100-year bonds (*Wall Street Journal*, July 21, 1993). Coca-Cola issued another $150 million ten days later. This phenomenon is reminiscent of the 1860s to 1900s when railroad companies issued very long-term bonds to finance the construction of railroads across America.

Rating Services. Corporation bonds are rated by Moody's Investor Service and by Standard & Poor's. Some bonds are secured by collateral that may consist of airplanes, trucks, railroad cars, ships, piers, or other real assets. Others may be secured by collateral in the form of stock or bonds of other companies. When there is no collateral, the bond is also called a debenture—simply a debt of the company itself. The rating services have a great deal to look into in putting a grade on a company and its bonds. Table 9–2 presents a general description of the rating classifications and what they mean. Securities that are rated below the Ba and BB ratings are sometimes said to be below investment grade.

Table 9–2
Investors' Services Rating Classifications*

Moody's	General description	Standard & Poors
Aaa	Highest quality	AAA
Aa	High quality	AA
A	Upper-medium grade	A
Baa	Medium grade	BBB
Ba	Lower-medium grade	BB
B	Speculative	B
Caa	Poor standing	CCC, CC
Ca	Often in default	C
C	Lowest grade (in default)	DDD, D

*The rating services also provide common stock rankings, and ratings on preferred stock, short-term debt, money market funds, and so forth.

Because of the variety of types of collateral that may be available, and because of the credit ratings established by the issuing companies, the yields on corporate bonds of the same maturity have a wide range. The very highest rated bonds carry yields that run around half a percentage point above yields on Treasury bonds. The lower the rating, the higher the yield will be because of the higher probability of default according to the judgment of the rating companies.

For example, in late December 1993, Moody's Investors Service downgraded Hong Kong dollar debt—the debt of the local Mass Transit Railway Corporation—from triple A to double A. At the same time it raised ratings on certain China-owned enterprises operating in Hong Kong. In 1995 lower ratings were placed on five banks in China.

Selling Bonds. Bonds may be placed directly by the borrowing corporation, or may be sold with the assistance of an investment or merchant bank that underwrites the issue. An underwriting bank will, in essence, purchase the bond issue and then sell it to various investors through a network of customer contacts.

The largest proportions of outstanding corporate bonds are owned by three groups: (a) individuals and foreign investors, (b) pension funds, and (c) insurance companies.

Mutual funds, commercial banks and thrift institutions also purchase corporate bonds in significant amounts, but hold smaller proportions of outstanding issues.

Leveraged Buy-outs and High-yield Bonds ("Junk Bonds")

"Junk bonds" are bonds that have received below investment grade ratings. Over a long period in the late 1980s the term took on a new meaning. It was then that investment bankers became very well-known and very rich for arranging financing for *leveraged buy-outs* of companies.

A leveraged buy-out takes place in the following way. Some managers look at their company's capital structure and find that the debt to equity ratio is very low. The company has small amounts of debt outstanding. Everyone knows that interest costs on debt are deductible from income for tax purposes so that a higher leverage ratio—more debt and less equity—should provide a greater return to shareholders. In Great Britain, leverage is called gearing and the debt/equity ratio is the gearing ratio.

So these managers may offer to buy the shares of the stockholders at a price considerably above the current market price of the shares. They make a leveraged buy-out offer to the shareholders. In order to acquire the funds needed to pay the shareholders off, they go to banks and arrange financing and eventually may issue bonds to repay the banks. With all of the arrangements in place, the stockholders receive a high price for their shares and are happy, and the managers become the firm's owners. The firm prospers with lots of interest expense written-off against its income for tax purposes.

Everybody wins—almost, that is. One group that does not win is the existing bondholders. Because of the new high debt/equity ratio, the firm's credit rating sinks. There is little cushion left to pay the bondholders in case the firm should become financially strapped. Thus, the firm's debt is downgraded by the rating companies.

In this example, those who did the buying-out were the managers of the firm. However, in many instances those doing the buying-out are outsiders who are hostile to the management of the firm, and the "leveraged buy-out" becomes a "hostile takeover."

Tobin's Q. James Tobin, whose contributions to economic theory are described at greater length in Chapter 13, defined a variable Q to be the ratio of the market value of a firm measured by the price of its shares to the replacement cost of the firm's assets. When Q rises above one, it indicates that management is doing a good job in raising stockholder's wealth. A ratio greater than one for industry as a whole indicates the need for new investment activity. A ratio less than one indicates that something is wrong. The stock is less valuable than the value of the firm's assets and the firm would be a good candidate for a takeover (see Baumol, 1991).

Insider Trading

The loss to bondholders resulting from leveraged buy-outs is not the principal cause of concern. The big concern stems from the accusation of *insider trading* by those engaged in arranging the leveraged buy-outs. Prior to the announcement that buy-out arrangements had been made, insiders would know that the prices of the shares of stock were about to rise. They would buy shares and profit from the announcement. There are laws against insider trading, so some issuers of "junk bonds" became known as associates of greedy white collar criminals.

Just who are "insiders"? Under the law insiders refers to officers, directors, and major shareholders. These people are all required to disclose their trades and are prohibited from short selling, and so forth. If they breach these laws they are subject to prosecution. However, insider trading is viewed by the civil courts as covering a much broader range of activities that leaves insiders of all sorts subject to legal suits.

To protect the property rights of shareholders from being manipulated by fraudulent activities in securities markets, the law has relied strongly on *disclosure*. Thus, the Securities and Exchange Commission has stringent disclosure requirements for issuing and trading securities. However, another requirement is the prohibition of trading on inside information. This illegal activity is very difficult to define and almost impossible to enforce.

It is regrettable that it is impossible to have disclosure cover all aspects of the information needed to assure that stockholders are treated fairly. If all information, including inside information were made public, there would no longer be any inside information by definition. Restricting trading on information of any kind is a very undesirable activity for government. Insider information trading laws are very inefficient, and someday sufficiently effective disclosure laws will make it appropriate to drop laws against insider trading. After all, every doctor, lawyer, and professor earns profit (economic rent) for insider information each has by charging fees to those who do not have such information. It is simply not good to have laws that prevent persons from acting upon information available to them.

However, protecting shareholders from unscrupulous behavior is also desirable. The issue of illegal insider trading is a difficult and perplexing one (see Gillis and Ciotti, 1992).

Eurobonds

Eurobonds, as the name implies, are bonds issued in Europe. Their distinctive feature is that they are not denominated in the currency of the country in which they are sold. Instead, they usually are sold for U.S. dollars and require coupon and principal payments in dollars.

Some Eurobonds have currency options, that is, the holder may request payment of interest and principal in any of several currencies. They are usually structured by and sold with the assistance of a syndicate of merchant banks in several countries in bearer form.

Global Bonds. There now exist a large variety of global bonds. These are structured precisely so that they meet the regulations of different countries. For example, they may be sold in bearer form in Europe but be registered in the U.S.

Municipal Bonds

The term "municipal" refers to an internal self-governing unit of authority and responsibility. The term "municipality" generally refers to the governing unit of an urban area. But a municipal security refers to securities issued both by state governments *and* by any of its subdivisions such as counties, townships, cities, municipalities, parishes, and any authorities created by these governing units.

Each state has its own set of rules regarding the activities of political subdivisions and, in this instance, it establishes the conditions under which such political units may borrow funds for the financing of various projects. While details differ among the many different political units, there is general uniformity.

There are two general classes of municipal bonds. First, there are *general obligation* securities, sold with backing in the form of the "full faith and credit" of the issuing governmental unit—that is, on the signature of the managers of that unit who promise to repay the debt with tax revenues. The ability to repay out of tax revenues depends, of course, on the taxing authority and the tax base available to the local governmental unit. The rating agencies that grade debt instruments from AAA to BBB and so forth will examine the tax base of the community when setting grades.

Second, there are *revenue* bonds. By issuing these bonds, a state or local government raises the funds needed to finance the construction of a special project, such as a toll bridge. After the bridge is constructed, the collection of tolls is used to pay the interest on the bonds when due and to repay the principal of the bonds at maturity. The governing unit pledges to pass special revenues (from tariffs, taxes, levies, tolls) on to the bondholders as those collections are made. In grading revenue bonds, the rating agencies will evaluate the likely success in collecting the required revenues. Such revenue bonds may also be used, for example, when a local improvement district (LID) is created, such as a residential area where all of the power lines are to be placed underground in order to improve the visual character of the area. Bonds are sold to raise the funds needed to finance the construction work. Property owners pay additional tax levies for a given number of years, and payments of interest and principal to the bondholders are made from levies. These are but two examples of many situations in which municipal bonds are issued.

Taxes on Interest on Municipal Bonds

In 1818, the Maryland Assembly passed a law that would have required the local office of the Bank of the United States to pay a $15,000 annual fee and to buy stamped paper from the state. The fine for using unstamped paper for its notes was set at $100 per note. James W. McCulloch, the Bank's local cashier, refused to abide by Maryland's law. Finally, in a Supreme Court case [*McCulloch* v. *Maryland,* 17 U.S. (4 Wheat.) 316 (1819)] it was held that a state could not levy a tax upon a bank established by the federal government, because "the power to tax is the power to destroy." Thus, states cannot tax the federal government nor its property, and the federal government cannot tax state government nor its property, in general. States and local governments do not levy property taxes on federal government land. However, when the federal government comes into a community to undertake a major construction project that will require bringing in or importing many families, who will live on federal property, and so forth, the local community will negotiate with the federal government for a support payment to be made to the local schools so that the children of the new families in the area will have teachers. So there is a great deal of intergovernmental contracting going on.

Today, interest income from investments in U.S. Treasury securities is not subject to state income taxes in those states that have income taxes. Similarly, interest income from investments in municipal securities is not subject to the federal government's income tax. The principle maintains that these two types of government should not be taxing each other. The taxation of interest incomes from the bonds these governments issue is viewed as an indirect form of tax on the issuing governmental unit itself.

For example, if the federal government imposed its income tax on interest income from municipal bonds, the local government would have to pay a higher interest rate. Thus, the federal government would be adding to the local government's cost of borrowing. It would be as if the federal government were imposing "costs" on the local government, according to the reasoning now applied in the law.

When Does the Exemption Apply? Local governments might decide to issue bonds to pay for housing and rent the housing for revenue. Would interest on these "commercial" activities be exempt from the federal income tax? The courts say no. What if the state government sells bonds at the lower tax-exempt interest rate and then simply invests the proceeds in higher yielding bonds? It does not have to pay an income tax to the federal government so it could simply pocket the revenue and make a net "profit." Again, the courts say no, local governments cannot do this. Thus, tax exemption provisions apply only to "legitimate" state and local government activities. For example, if a state agency, say a state university, receives funds from the general revenue, then that agency may invest in higher yielding taxable securities because the source of funds was not directly from the sale of securities. In this case the investment is "legitimate." These distinctions become very confusing very rapidly.

How are Yields Affected? Individuals who have incomes that are high enough to require payment of a marginal tax of 40 per cent need to calculate whether or not they should invest in municipals. For example, assume that the yield on an Aaa rated corporate bond is 10 per cent. If the individual invested in this bond, the after-tax return would be 6 per cent or 40 per cent less than the interest received. Thus, if the nontaxable market return on an Aaa rated municipal bond were above 6 per cent, the after-tax return to the investor would be greater if the investment were in municipals rather than corporates. People are supposed to take the exemptions and deductions that the law allows. Thus, the prudent investor would choose the option that leaves the largest after-tax income.

Thus, prices of municipal securities will be driven up, and yields driven down below the 10 per cent on corporate securities (to, say, 6.25 per cent in the example) until the difference in yield is slightly smaller (here, 37.5 per cent) than the marginal tax rate (of 40 per cent) levied on income receivers who have federal tax liabilities. The maximum difference in yield would be the marginal tax rate itself, that is, if the difference were that size or greater, there would be no reason for investors to choose municipal bonds. Thus, a difference that is slightly less than the top marginal tax rate would induce investors to purchase the available supply of municipal securities and realize a slightly larger after-tax take home income than they would have if they invested in corporate securities. [Let Cy be the corporate yield, My be the municipal yield, and t be the marginal tax rate. Then, to express the limit to the difference in corporate and municipal yields, in percentages, $Cy - My < t$, or alternatively expressed in ratios, $My/Cy > (1 - t)$.]

Do Investors Who Buy Municipals Pay Taxes? Yes, they do pay taxes. They pay taxes indirectly by receiving a much smaller return on their investment than they would have received if they had bought the corporate bonds yielding 10 per cent. They may pay only 30 per cent tax on their interest income instead of 40 per cent, but they do pay taxes because their interest income is smaller. It is misleading and wrong to characterize such investors, as some politicians do, as paying no taxes, although they pay somewhat lower taxes, indirectly and in an opportunity cost sense.

Sometimes television ads wrongly promote municipal bond sales by reporting that holders, "Don't pay a penny in taxes." Also, profitable insurance firms which purchased large amounts of municipal securities, and therefore paid smaller amounts in taxes, were wrongly accused of profiting from tax loopholes in the discussion leading to a reform of taxes in 1986 in the U.S. It is wrong for such widespread false information to go unchallenged.

Who Receives the Taxes if Investors Pay Them? The federal government does not receive the tax payments, but the state or local government does. Again they receive the tax payments in an indirect or opportunity cost sense. The state and local governments borrow funds at a lower interest than other equally rated borrowers must pay. By saving money on borrowing as a result of the exemption from tax on interest income, the local governmental unit is, in effect, receiving the benefit that the taxpayers give up when they buy lower yielding municipal securities.

To the extent that the federal government does not tax interest on municipal securities the implicit subsidy is, therefore, divided between wealthy holders of municipals and state and local governments that pay lower yields.

Does Anyone Lose in This Situation? Only the federal government loses in this situation. Interest income payments are made to the investors, but the federal government does not collect taxes on that income whereas it would have collected tax revenues if the exemption did not apply. Thus, investors do pay taxes, state governments receive benefits from them, and the federal government is left out in the cold.

Who Sells and Who Buys Municipals?

Locally issued securities need the support of investors in the local community. Local politicians want to give their business to local people. Thus, local banks play a big role in underwriting and holding securities issued by local governmental units. Property liability insurance companies also participate heavily in the municipal bond markets.

The market for municipal securities is characterized somewhat as an "old boys club." There are a few people who specialize in the trading of these securities and it is a "thin" market generally, however, this condition is changing as trading has become computerized.

Banks are allowed to underwrite local general obligation bonds and some revenue bonds, and local investors are encouraged to participate in holding them.

Are Municipals Safe Investments? When some very large projects are underway, sales of bonds are made throughout the country. Perhaps the most notorious experience in municipal securities in history was the failure of the Whoops bonds, an appropriate name for the Washington Public Power Supply System (WPPSS) bonds issued to construct nuclear power plants to produce electricity in the State of Washington. The System sold $800 billion of bonds, but by 1983 cost overruns and the slow growth of demand for electricity made it clear that the system would fail, and the System defaulted on $2.5 billion of bonds—a huge default by any standards. These bonds had been rated highly by the rating services and had been touted by many investment bankers. Legal claims are still being pursued. Municipal bonds are not free of default risk, and today everybody knows that.

In order to raise the value of an issue of municipal bonds it is possible to arrange for insurance coverage so that an insurance company guarantees payment in case of default.

Corporate Stocks

In Great Britain the term "stock" refers to shares of ownership in a firm as well as to corporate bonds and even government bonds. In the U.S. the term stock refers to shares of ownership, or "equity," while bonds mean instruments of indebtedness to the firm. A firm's creditors including bondholders have a prior claim to the assets of a firm in case the firm defaults on its debt.

An alternative view of the bondholder-shareholder relation that has become popular in recent years is that shareholders really hold an option on the firm's real assets. Each day (or periodically) the firm's shareholders decide whether or not to exercise their option to own the firm's plant and equipment and organization, or to abandon their option and give the assets over to the firm's bondholders. From this point of view the valuation of a share of ownership involves a process like that used in the valuation of an option to own the firm's assets.

Any valuation scheme, of course, looks at the firm's earnings prospects. If earnings come forth, then dividends can be declared. Alternatively, earnings can be reinvested in additional plant and equipment and the firm can expand. Additional assets held by the firm should result in a rise in the prospect for earnings and a higher price for the stock.

Thus, returns for investors accrue either in the form of dividends or through appreciation in the value (price) of the existing shares of stock traded on the secondary market.

The Stock Market's Popularity

Wall Street is the standard-bearer for capitalism and the focus of criticism by socialists. The stock market's performance, especially in the secondary markets in which issues of shares are traded on the New York Stock Exchange and the American Stock Exchange, is a bellwether for all things economic and political. Bad news from Bosnia or the Persian Gulf causes stock prices to decline. But the big bond houses are located on Wall Street, too. And political bad news elsewhere in the world means bond prices will rise when investors move their funds to the "safe haven" of the U.S. and thus push up bond prices. Socialists find capital markets and ownership of capital despicable. Capitalists do not love or hate capital, they simply find capital very useful in directing resources to productive uses, and therefore, in raising the standards of living of the wealthy, and poor as well. As a resource, capital is "good" like its team members, land and labor. Labor, after all, can earn high wages when it has lots of capital in the form of tools to work with. So labor needs capital and land, and capital needs land and labor, and land needs labor and capital! Progress is based on the mutual support supplied by each to the others.

Interest in the world of capital is focused on Wall Street and the stock exchanges. Our interest in the stock exchanges is fed by the press and the media generally. So long as investors recognize that a great deal of media hype is applied to Wall Street and the antics performed there, it is appropriate to note Wall Street's importance and the importance of the market for shares of ownership. However, it is also perhaps even more important to note that the bond markets, the money markets, the mortgage markets, the funds provided by financial intermediaries, and the international financial markets are far larger in terms of dollar volumes of trading than the stock exchanges. These other markets are not nearly so well-known.

For example, 1993 was a big year for the sale of new stocks and bonds in the U.S. as the dollar value of 6,602 securities exceeded a trillion dollars—a record. However, just over $900 billion was in bonds while the remaining $100 was in stock. Thus, while $100 billion is nothing to sneeze at, the bond market is about nine times the size of the stock market when it comes to raising new funds for investment purposes.

Capital Markets in Asia

There are 27 Asian countries if former Soviet central Asian countries are included. Stock exchanges operate in 18 of these countries (see Selwyn, 1992). Other countries of the region are also contemplating the establishment of stock exchanges as economic growth has led to the lowering of barriers to foreign influence. Space limitations permit mention of only selected observations about markets in some countries. Table 9–3 provides information on the market capitalization of six of the regional exchanges in August 1993—an indication of relative size.

Table 9–3

Market Capitalization of Six South East Asian Stock Exchanges, August 1993 (in billions of U.S. dollar equivalents)

Hong Kong	$243.7
Indonesia	17.3
Philippines	14.7
Malaysia	125.0
Singapore	65.0
Thailand	68.7

Source: *South China Morning Post Weekly*, August 28/29, 1993, p. B5.

China

The People's Republic of China officially restarted stock exchanges in 1991 in Shenzhen, a city in the southern province of Guangdong near Hong Kong, and in 1990 in Shanghai. The Shanghai stock market had been closed when communists took control of China in 1949, and Shenzhen was not a commercial center then. Other financial markets are being established in other cities as China moves to an open economy. In December 1990 China opened trading in government bonds on a Securities Trading Automated Quotations System (STAQS). But government bonds were also traded on the Shanghai Stock Exchange.

It is not easy for former communist countries to move from government owned enterprises to private ownership. In China's case the government decided to give selected enterprises permission to issue stock. The government routinely kept 50 per cent or more of the stock for itself under the theory that the "people" deserved to retain control because they "owned" the existing assets of the enterprise, and the sale of shares of stock represented a means of raising additional funds for expansion.

The demand for enterprise shares was so large that lotteries were established and only those winning the lotteries could purchase shares. Riots occasionally broke out among the people waiting in line to buy the lottery tickets.

After meeting certain standards and receiving permission from the People's Bank of China, the shares of an enterprise could be listed on an exchange.

The Shanghai Stock Exchange was founded on November 26, 1990 and opened for trading on December 19 in the refurbished ballroom of a hotel built in 1860—originally the Astor House Hotel, and later renamed the Pu Jiang Hotel, at No. 15 Huang Pu Road.

The exchange is a nonprofit institution with 24 members on a board of directors and managed by a president, vice-president and general manager. It exists to:

1. provide a place for organized trading
2. manage the trading in listed securities
3. provide for clearing of trades and transfer services
4. provide storage and delivery services
5. provide information services on the securities market

Dividends declared by companies are first paid to the exchange and then distributed to shareholders by the exchange. At that time, companies paid a fixed dividend of 12 per cent annually.

Bonds also paid a specified interest annually according to the covenant, however, the exchange did not collect and distribute interest payments. This is because no interest was to be paid until maturity at which time the principal and all of the accumulated interest was to be paid in a lump sum. This turned bonds traded on the exchange into zero coupon bonds with the effective yield being calculated on the basis of the difference between what one paid for the bond and the total dollar amount to be received at maturity a number of periods later. The stated coupon yield on the face of the bond lacked meaning. (It was unclear to the author, a visitor to the exchange in 1991, whether the interest stated on the bond was accumulated periodically and compounded to arrive at the total due at maturity, or whether the interest calculation was simple interest.)

As of June 1991 trading took place on 6 government bonds, 9 financial bonds, 13 corporate bonds, and 8 corporate stocks, for a total of 36 securities comprised of 28 bonds and 8 stocks.

Foreigners were not permitted to buy shares on the stock exchanges until a special class of shares called B shares was issued. By January 1993 there were 23 stocks—A shares—traded on the Shanghai Stock Exchange along with 9 B shares, and 18 stocks traded on the Shenzhen Stock Exchange along with 9 B shares. However, these stock exchanges are growing rapidly. The number of listings doubled by 1995.

China published a new set of laws covering the securities industry in mid-1993. These new regulations were published in full in Hong Kong's *South China Morning Post Weekly* (June 12–13, 1993: B4-5). Also, in August 1993 eight foreign brokerage houses were permitted to buy special seats on the Shenzhen Exchange and to trade B shares. On the first day the turnover of B share trading ballooned. It appears the industry will expand dramatically, but will experience many growing pains.

In May 1993 the Securities and Exchange Commission in the U.S. decided not to prevent U.S. investment companies from buying B shares. Under its regulations, all investment companies must buy shares only where there are adequate clearing and custodian facilities for shares. These were finally developed as clearing systems in China improved and ten custodian banks began operating.

The Chinese government often borrows money by the issue of government bonds, and these are sold to workers through enterprises. They are given a quota of bonds to sell and often the workers resent having to buy them. The program resembles a system of forced saving.

Yankee Bonds. In July 1993, a Chinese investment firm sold $250 million of ten-year bonds in the U.S. market at a yield that was only about 1 per cent above that on U.S. Treasury securities. It was the first sale in the U.S. since before the communists took over in 1949. Thus, a Yankee bond is a bond sold in the U.S. by a foreign borrower and denominated in U.S. dollars. If the Chinese had borrowed British pounds in London the bond would be called a *Bulldog bond*. Then there is a *Samurai bond*, issued in Japan and denominated in yen. These are *foreign bonds*, that is, bonds issued in the currency of a foreign country. They differ from *Eurobonds*, which are issued in a foreign country but denominated in a currency other than that of the country in which they are sold—such as when a bond is sold in Europe or Japan but denominated in dollars.

Japan

The Tokyo Stock Exchange began operations in 1947 and is patterned after those in the U.S. There is a JASDAQ over-the-counter market similar in most respects to the NASDAQ market in the U.S.

Hong Kong

Hong Kong's money markets, stock markets, banking institutions, and foreign exchange markets are very well-developed and, in isolated cases, even surpass those of developed western countries. Its money markets were described briefly in Chapter 9. On a handful of occasions, the Hong Kong government has issued five-year bonds, but as a practical matter there is, as yet, no active market in government bonds. Corporations issue a variety of bonds on occasion, but it is generally recognized that there is, as a practical matter, no active secondary market for bonds. Thus, bonds lack liquidity. Furthermore, the uncertain outlook for Hong Kong after 1997 when China takes over leads to a reluctance to make loans further into the future.

However, by 1994 several issues of ten-year bonds were made in Hong Kong. The government has an active policy to promote the issue of debt securities in order to enhance Hong Kong's reputation as a financial center.

Linked Securities. Although the bond market is undeveloped in Hong Kong, the local people have shown great innovative ability. In July 1987, Paribus Investment (Asia) issued "Fixed Rate Indexed *Bull and Bear* Bonds." By 1991, there were two index linked, two gold price linked, and one currency linked, bonds issued (see Lui, 1991). In the case of the Bull and Bear bonds, the redemption price of the bond is tied to the change in the Hang Seng Index of stock prices. The base value of the Index is set at the time of issue. For a bull bond, the redemption value on the Paribus issue was set to rise above the face value of the bond by HK$7.5 for every one-point rise in the Hang Seng Index, but the redemption value would also fall the same amount on each point if the index declined. The situation faced by the Bear Bond holders was precisely the opposite. Thus, by selling an equal amount of Bull and Bear bonds, the issuer would be perfectly hedged—the total repayment to be made would equal the face value of all outstanding bonds. At the time of issue, the demand for the bull bonds was greater than that for the bear bonds. Thus, the issuer placed a fixed interest rate of 4 per cent on the bull bonds and, to encourage more demand, a 10 per cent interest rate on the bear bonds. An equal amount of each bond was issued—HK$75 million.

Stock Market. The stock market in Hong Kong dominates the business news. Although formal stock trading began in 1891, it became an important source of funds only after 1970 (see Wong, 1991). The market is known to be more volatile, and therefore, more risky than the market in the U.S. It took a fall in 1973–74, another in 1982, and another in 1987. It rose to very high levels over the next few years. For example, the Hang Seng Index rose from around 6,000 to over 12,000 in 1993. Then it fell to 10,000 during the first two weeks of January 1994, and moved on down to near 8,000 by May, and back up to near 10,000 in September. The boom from 1987 through 1993 was accompanied by a persistent annual inflation rate of nearly 10 per cent. With 1997 approaching, stock market volatility will doubtless continue.

Much of the volatility in the Hong Kong market has been attributed to insider trading. Prompted by the crash of 1987 and charges that the market was a "club of insiders," the authorities introduced ordinances restricting the ability of insiders to take advantage of their positions in September 1991 (see Zuckerman, 1991). Tougher fines and penalties were also set under the ordinance, but it stops short of making illegal trading a criminal offense. Large shareholders must disclose holdings of more than 10 per cent of the shares in a company, and must disclose their trading whenever their holdings move across a percentage point. This is an odd rule. If holdings increase from 12 per cent to 12.9 per cent no disclosure is required, but if it increases from 12.9 to 13.1 per cent then disclosure is required.

Korea

Typical of Korea's extensive government control over financial institutions, the government owned 70 per cent of the Korea Stock Exchange from 1956 when it opened until 1988 when the government sold out to member firms. The exchange played an insignificant role in the mobilization of savings for corporate financing for many years.

Although the Korean economy was basically capitalist, the planning activities of the government in the post-Korean War period resembled those of a socialist government. The flow of financial resources was largely directed by the Ministry of Finance as interest rates were regulated and financial markets were controlled. Korea's successful economic development occurred in spite of such controls.

Korea launched a "liberalization and internationalization" plan in the early 1980s that was to have four stages. By the 1990s financial markets were to be opened. The Korean Stock Exchange grew rapidly in the late 1980s and in terms of capitalization it became the world's largest exchange that was closed to foreign participation.

In August 1991 another four stages of liberalization were announced. Then it was announced that foreigners would soon be permitted to purchase up to 10 per cent of the stock of some Korean companies as part of a program to open the market to international investment. After considerable criticism, the limit was raised to 25 per cent in December, but the limits were set much lower on some companies believed to be strategically important (see Yun, 1991).

Korea also started an over-the-counter stock market in 1987. Overall, government is slowly relaxing controls over Korean capital markets.

Singapore

The Malaysian Stock Exchange in Kuala Lumpur had its stocks automatically listed on the Stock Exchange of Singapore prior to January 1990, when it withdrew the listings. Malaysia wanted to promote trading on its own exchange. The move was successful for Malaysia as the Kuala Lumpur Composite Index rose from 600 to 1,300 during 1993. Prior to the withdrawal, over half of the companies listed on the SES were Malaysian, and they represented over half of the capitalization of the SES at the time. But the SES was the dominant exchange nevertheless.

The SES survived the split and opened its exchange to foreign brokers later in 1990. It offered full member seats on the SES to seven foreign firms in 1992. The SES maintains one of the most, if not the most, modern computerized trading systems in the world. It maintains an over-the-counter market for regional firms. It also has a second board referred to as SESDAQ that trades smaller companies. Trading in depository receipts was begun in 1992.

Over the years the government has had a strategic policy to make Singapore an international financial center. Singapore decided to privatize Singapore Telecom beginning in October 1993. One of the reasons for this action was to encourage its listing on the Stock Exchange of Singapore in order to increase the exchange's capitalization (see Stewart, 1993).

Singapore introduced a government securities market with regular auctions patterned on the U.S. market in 1987. It established a set of authorized dealers who would bid for the securities, and closed the four discount houses that had acted as the intermediaries for the Monetary Authority of Singapore. These four houses were either absorbed by banks or became subsidiaries of banks and remained active as newly appointed government securities dealers.

Taiwan

The Taiwan Stock Exchange (TSE) opened in 1961. It had 18 companies listed in 1962, and 212 listed by 1992. Prices are volatile. The TSE weighted stock index was about 1,000 in 1986, and with intermittent setbacks rose to 12,000 in late 1989. It fell to below 3,000 by the end of October 1990. Now that's volatility! During 1993, the index fell from 5,000 to 3,000. It was back up to 5,000 at the beginning of 1994.

In an attempt to support trading activities on the exchange the financial authorities promoted the trading of government bonds. In November 1992, trading began. Each of about 30 authorized dealers was given a specific bond and required to offer quotations through the exchange daily.

About 85 per cent of government securities outstanding are held by banks, and the secondary market has rarely been active. However, a stock market crash in February

1990 left many investors looking for a safe haven for funds, and the government bond market surged. This led authorities to believe that trading on an organized exchange would be appropriate. (There is little in the way of a long-term corporate bond market in Taiwan.)

The Securities and Exchange Law in Taiwan is patterned after American law. Taiwanese law establishes a Securities and Exchange Commission. Recent years have seen a variety of amendments to that law, including amendments strengthening disclosure requirements along with amendments deregulating securities firms. In June 1989 the SEC issued a set of new regulations that permit foreign securities firms to set up branches in Taiwan (see Hsu, 1991). However, there are a large number of restrictions, and only very large firms can meet the hurdles to entry that have been structured.

There are similarities in the extent of control over the financial industry in Taiwan and Korea. In both countries the institutions are patterned after those in the U.S. Also, both countries reflect Japanese institutions in that both have Ministries of Finance that act to guide investment funds. The Taiwanese authorities seem determined to liberalize their financial markets albeit at a deliberately slow pace. The Korean authorities appear to want to liberalize but find that giving up control to markets is difficult.

Summary

Capital markets differ from money markets simply because of the arbitrary line of demarcation limiting securities in money markets to those that have a year or less to maturity. Thus, capital markets concern bonds and stocks.

The market for U.S. Treasury bonds is very large and very well regarded. It is a dealer's market, however, and has recently been the subject of investigation. The Treasury is experimenting with the Dutch auction method of selling its bonds.

Treasury securities are sold in registered form in the U.S., and both the coupons and principal may be sold separately to make both into zero coupon bonds. They are called STRIPS—Separate Trading in Registered Interest and Principal of Securities.

Corporate bonds, municipal bonds, and Eurobonds each have large markets and unique characteristics.

Corporate stocks are popular with the press. In 1993 there was a large increase in the volume of funds raised by businesses through IPOs—initial public offerings of securities by smaller corporations.

Stock markets have been established in the Asian Tiger countries and in other emerging markets. (See Park and Van Agtmael, 1993, for descriptions of exchanges in 18 different countries. The exchanges described do not include the many exchanges that have been re-established in Eastern Europe and former republics of the Soviet Union. A directory with a list of 56 exchanges is included in an appendix.) It seems clear that the establishment of exchanges for the trading of ownership in capital, symbols of capitalism often subject to derision by socialists, provides the basis for the economic development expected for the twenty-first century.

Key Terms and Concepts

Government securities
Dutch auctions
Cartels
Sallie Mae
Fannie Mae
Warrants
Rating services
Levereged buy-out
Eurobonds
Bull and Bear bonds
Yankee bonds

Dealers
Zero coupon bonds
Salomon Brothers
Ginnie Mae
Convertible bonds
Income bonds
Junk bonds
Insider trading
Municipal bonds (general
    obligation, revenue)
Equity-linked Securities

Discussion Questions and Exercises

1. Who are the principal buyers of federal debt and why would these buyers find it attractive as an investment?
2. When dealers in government securities refer to "depth, breadth, and resiliency" what do they mean, precisely? Is the dealer market a cartel? Explain.
3. What reasons might be offered in support of using the "Dutch auction" technique for selling government securities? Discuss.
4. Explain how to calculate the "rate of return" on a zero coupon bond. What is the income tax status of such returns?
5. What are STRIPS, and why did the U.S. Treasury start issuing them?
6. Why would zero coupon bonds carry higher yields than conventional bonds of the same maturity? Why would government agency bonds carry higher yields than Treasury issues even when both are backed by the government?
7. Explain precisely what it means for a corporate bond to be "in default." What would be the answer if the bond were an income bond? What is a "linked" bond? Give an example.
8. What is a leveraged buy-out and why would it likely lead to the issue of "junk bonds"?
9. Explain "Tobin's Q" and discuss how it might be related to the takeover of a company.
10. Briefly compare the purposes and processes of laws requiring disclosure of information with laws against trading on inside information.
11. Distinguish between general obligation bonds and revenue bonds routinely issued by state and local governments.
12. Analyze the economic impact of laws that exempt interest income on municipal bonds from calculations of income for tax purposes. How does the exemption affect: the investor, the local government, and the federal government?
13. What is likely to happen to stock exchanges as we know them with the advent of computerized trading such as that on NASDAQ?

14. Briefly describe the markets for stocks and bonds in Shanghai, Hong Kong, Korea, Singapore, and Taiwan.

References

Bae, Kee Hong, "Market Segmentation and Time Variation in the Price of Risk: Evidence on the Korean Stock Market," Technical Report No. 93–4, Asia-Pacific Financial and Forecasting Research Centre, City Polytechnic of Hong Kong, September 1993.

Basham, Michael E., "The Dutch Auction, a Bogus Solution," *Wall Street Journal*, July 29, 1992.

Baumol, William J., "Enterprising Pursuit of Rents and the Case of Takeovers," *Applied Financial Economics*, No. 1, 1991, pp. 1–10.

Booth, Richard A., "Insider Trading, Better Markets," *Wall Street Journal*, June 28, 1991.

Cheng, Yan-leung, and Wong, Kai-tai, "An Assessment of Risk and Return: Some Empirical Findings from the Hong Kong Stock Exchange," in *Proceedings of the Second International Conference on Asian-Pacific Financial Markets*, City Polytechnic of Hong Kong, September 12–14, 1991, pp. 512–22.

Cheung, Y. L., and Ho, Y. K., "The Intertemporal Stability of the Relationships between the Asian Emerging Equity Markets and the Developed Equity Markets," *Journal of Business Finance and Accounting*, January 1991, pp. 236–54.

Dawson, Steven M., "IPO's, the Singapore Authorities and the Asian Wall Street Journal," in *Proceedings of the Second International Conference on Asian-Pacific Financial Markets*, City Polytechnic of Hong Kong, September 12–14, 1991, pp. 581–90.

Euh, Yoon-Dae, and Amsden, Alice H., "Korea's Financial Reform," *Journal of Management*, College of Business Administration, Korea University, Seoul, Vol. 33, 1990, pp. 45–84.

Friedman, Milton, "How to Sell Government Securities," *Wall Street Journal*, September 3, 1991.

Gillis, John G., and Ciotti, Glenn J., "Insider Trading Update," *Financial Analysts Journal*, November/December 1992, pp. 46–51.

Glick, Steven L., "More on STRIPS," Letters to the Editor, *Financial Analysts Journal*, November/December 1992, pp. 14–15.

Gregory, Deborah, and Livingston, Miles, "Development of the Market for U.S. Treasury STRIPS," *Financial Analysts Journal*, March/April 1992, pp. 68–94.

Hsu, Paul S., and Liu, Lawrence S., "Recent Developments in Taiwan's Capital Market," *Economic Review*, International Commercial Bank of China, Taiwan, March/April 1991, pp. 12–25.

Jegadeesh, Narasimhan, and Titman, Sheridan, "Contrarian Profit Opportunities in the Korean Stock Market," in *Proceedings of the Second International Conference on Asian-Pacific Financial Markets*, City Polytechnic of Hong Kong, September 12–14, 1991, pp. 322–31.

Kopcke, Richard W., and Rosengren, Eric S., "Are the Distinctions between Debt and Equity Disappearing? An Overview," *New England Economic Review*, Federal Reserve Bank of Boston, March/April 1990, pp. 3–10.

Lui, Y. H., "Money and Capital Markets," in Y. K. Ho, R. H. Scott, and K. A. Wong, eds., *The Hong Kong Financial System*, Oxford University Press, Hong Kong, 1991, pp. 161–86.

Mayer, Martin, *Nightmare on Wall Street*, Simon & Schuster, New York, 1993.

Miller, Sam Scott, "Every Market Player Deserves to be an Insider," *Wall Street Journal*, November 29, 1988.

Park, Kieth K. H., and Van Agtmael, Antoine W., eds., *The World's Emerging Stock Markets*, Probus Publishing, Chicago, IL, 1993.

Powell, Jerome H., "Auction Violations Lead to Closer Scrutiny of the Government Securities Market," *Treasury Bulletin*, December 1991, pp. 4–13.

Reinhart, Vincent, "An Analysis of Potential Treasury Auction Techniques," *Federal Reserve Bulletin*, June 1992, pp. 403–13.

Scott, Robert Haney, ed., *Manual of the Securities Industry*, Stock Exchange of Hong Kong, 1992.

Selwyn, Susan M., "Asian Stock Exchanges," Remarks before the Hong Kong Financial Executives Institute Regional Conference, 1992.

Siconolfi, Michael, "Salomon to Pay $67 Million to Settle Suit," *Wall Street Journal*, June 11, 1993.

Simons, Katerina, "An Assessment of Financial Market Volatility: Bills, Bonds, and Stocks," *New England Economic Review*, Federal Reserve Bank of Boston, November/December 1989, pp. 29–38.

Stewart, Ian, "Telecom Float to Buoy Singapore Exchange," *South China Morning Post Weekly*, August 28/29, 1993, p. B5.

Stowe, David W., "The Interest Rate Sensitivity of Stock Prices," *Economic Review*, Federal Reserve Bank of Atlanta, May/June 1991, pp. 21–29.

Terpstra, Robert H., ed., *Manual of the Hong Kong Securities Industry*, 2nd Edition, Stock Exchange of Hong Kong, 1994.

Wong, Kie Ann, "The Hong Kong Stock-market," in Y. K. Ho, R. H. Scott, and K. A. Wong, eds., *The Hong Kong Financial System*, Oxford University Press, Hong Kong, 1991, pp. 215–34.

Yamashita, Takeji, *Japan's Securities Markets: A Practitioner's Guide*, Butterworths, Singapore, 1989.

Yun, Yuo-Jin, "Seoul's Heavy Hand Smothers Financial Markets," *Asian Wall Street Journal*, October 10, 1991.

Zuckerman, Laurence, "The Cleanup in Hong Kong: Rules on Disclosure and Insider Trading Take Effect," *International Herald Tribune*, September 2, 1991.

CHAPTER 10

Mortgage and Other Securitized Asset Markets

LIVING SPACE DOES not come cheap. Americans, especially, invest a great deal of wealth in housing. One reason is that Congress has, on repeated occasions, indicated that it would like to support a nation of homeowners by passing laws that favor homeownership. Probably the most important law in this regard is the tax law that permits homeowners to deduct interest payments on home mortgages from their income for tax purposes. This law, in effect, subsidizes homeownership. In the 1960s, legal arrangements were made that paved the way for a wave of changeovers from apartments to condominiums so that condo owners would have this same subsidy available to them.

Deductible Interest and Other Support for Housing

Like all subsidies, the deductibility of interest on mortgages tends to distort the allocation of resources in favor of home and condo ownership. When tax laws were revised extensively in 1986, there was a great deal of debate about removing this subsidy, but it was not removed because such action would have been very unpopular, politically. There now exist far too many people who benefit from the subsidy.

If one thinks of buying a home as a form of business investment, and of interest on a mortgage as an expense, then it is true that expenses should be deducted from the rental return in order to calculate net income. This is the appropriate mode of calculation when someone owns a residential rental property. However, the difference between owning a rental and living in one's own home is that, in homeownership, there is no measure of the rental value. To make the "business-like" deductibility of a legitimate business expense, one needs to deduct the expense from the rental income. So, if the "rental income" received by a family from living in a housing unit that it owns were included in the family income, then deducting mortgage interest would be a proper expense.

Implicit Rental Income. In some countries, for example, in Greece, when a taxpayer fills out an income tax form, there is a space in which is placed a dollar (drachma) figure estimated to be the amount of rent that the homeowner would have to pay if the dwelling unit were being rented. This amount is *added* to the family income for income tax purposes. In an opportunity cost sense, it is perfectly appropriate to add this amount to a family's income because it represents the value of real services in the form of shelter, and so forth, that the family receives from the dwelling unit, and thus, it represents real income. Thus, a change of tax policy that kept the deductibility of mortgage interest but that added the value of housing services to a family's total income would be the most appropriate way to eliminate the subsidy to housing from an economic point of view—keep the deduction but tax what is now an untapped source of income. However, in a nation of homeowners, such a change in law will not occur in the near future. Yet many previously sacrosanct changes are being looked at because of the community's desire to eliminate the federal budget deficit.

Savings Associations. Banks now make a huge number of mortgage loans. Savings and Loan Associations and other thrift institutions were formerly called by such names as Building and Loan Societies. In Louisiana some are still called Homestead Societies. These and other mutual savings banks and institutions specialize in providing a place for small investors to earn interest on savings and also borrow funds against the collateral of their dwellings and land. Because of their activities in promoting homeownership, such mutual associations were given other favorable tax treatments.

The Federal Housing Administration. The Great Depression of the 1930s led to declining property values and defaulted mortgages. In response, Congress established the Federal Housing Administration (FHA) in 1938. This federal government agency provided backing to housing by providing guarantees on mortgage loans that met certain criteria. Because of the government's guarantee, FHA approved loans carried lower interest rates than those that banks and thrifts charged on their conventional loans. An FHA-approved loan also involved a smaller down payment toward the ownership of a home. Beginning in 1944, the Veterans Administration (VA) also provided guarantees on mortgage loans taken out by veterans of World War II. Guarantees have been extended to other veterans as well.

Types of Mortgages

Fixed Rate Mortgages. The devastation of financial institutions during the Great Depression led to many changes in the way in which financial institutions did business. The business of generating mortgage financing for homeowners was given to the thrift industry. Fixed rate mortgages (FRM) were the order of the day. Today this fixed type of mortgage is still the mortgage most people prefer. The typical FRM is a contract that provides for the amortization of a mortgage loan over 30 years with fixed monthly payments being applied to cover interest on the unpaid balance of the loan and the remainder to the balance of the principal. Since the principal declines by only a small amount with each payment at the outset, most of each payment in the first years of the mortgage is applied to interest. As the unpaid balance declines, later interest payments are smaller and smaller as a proportion of the fixed payment. In the last years of the amortization process, most of the payment is applied to the unpaid balance of the principal so the unpaid balance declines very rapidly. Numerical examples of this interesting process are found in all textbooks dealing with principles of finance.

Adjustable Rate Mortgages. In 1965 the escalation of the Vietnam War began in earnest. At the same time President Lyndon Johnson declared a Great Society program that would correct the ills of America by treating the problems of the poor in a land of plenty. Federal spending on both war and society's problems led to an unprecedented inflationary period in American history. Throughout the nineteenth century wage rates in America remained in the neighborhood of one to two dollars per day. These wage rates grew in the 1920s but growth was halted during the Depression of the 1930s. After World War II the rate was about four dollars per day. Since inflation was very low, except for wartime periods, interest rates remained low as well. During World War II, long-term interest rates on government bonds remained at $2\frac{1}{2}$ per cent while mortgage rates were in the 3–3½ per cent range. Interest rates on Treasury bills were in the range of ⅜–⅞ per cent.

After World War II, there was a gradual escalation of interest rates. In 1960 interest rates on FRMs were around 7 per cent. But the rise during the Johnson administration of the mid-1960s was remarkable. America had bitten off more spending than it could chew. Fiscal deficits and escalating inflation brought on high interest rates.

Victims of High Interest Rates. The biggest victim of high interest rates and inflation was the thrift industry, and next biggest was the banking industry. Why do we say that these financial intermediaries were victims? Banks and thrifts have long-term fixed rate mortgages as assets with yields that are fixed over many years. But the deposit base of these intermediaries is liabilities that are very short-term in maturity or duration—they can be withdrawn either on demand or as time deposits, perhaps within a year. So when interest rates rise in line with inflation, banks and thrifts must pay high rates to attract deposits while the yields on outstanding mortgages do not change. Interest expenses rise and interest receipts do not. This combination means bank profitability declines, losses occur, and capital becomes inadequate, especially in a highly leveraged industry like banking. Thus, banks and thrifts fail.

Risks. The risk associated with variation in interest rates is assumed by the banks and thrifts in the case of FRMs. So, *Adjustable Rate Mortgages* (ARMs) were introduced and spread widely in the 1980s as one way that managers of banks and thrifts could deal with their exposure to risk. An ARM places the risk of interest rate changes on the shoulders of the borrower and takes it away from the lender. The interest rate that the borrower pays is adjusted periodically. Adjustments were originally made yearly or every three years, but now there are ARMs that provide for adjustments as often as twice a year or as infrequently as every five years. Thus, when interest rates rise, the lender usually finds that the cost of borrowing funds from depositors also rises. But the rate that the lender receives on the mortgages held also rises because of the adjustable rate contract. As long as the spread between the rate received and the rate paid remains more or less unchanged, the bank or thrift has a margin of difference that it can use to earn a positive return on its intermediation business.

The adjustment of rates is made on set dates, and is tied to an established time series of interest rates that is set by an independent authority and approved for use in such contracts. For example, if the mortgage rate set in the contract was 1 per cent above the rate on a one-year Treasury bill, then each year it may be adjusted. If the one-year T-bill rate rises and is 2 per cent higher on a certain day a year later, then the interest charged on the mortgage rises by 2 per cent, too. The base series for adjustments may also be an index of cost of funds to savings and loans as calculated by the Eleventh District of the Federal Home Loan Bank, or it may be a National Cost of Funds, or the rise may be attached to an index of mortgage rates being charged by banks and thrifts known as the average of Federal Home Loan Bank Contract Rates. Adjustments are made automatically and not at the discretion of the lender.

However, borrowers understandably fear that interest rates might rise to very high levels—levels so high that monthly payments would rise beyond their ability to pay. So various *caps* were placed on adjustments. Caps may be on (a) the interest rate, or (b) the monthly payment, or both. Caps may, for example, limit the annual rise in interest rates to 2 per cent, with a 6 per cent rise the maximum over the lifetime of the mortgage. However, if there is a cap on the monthly payment, there may be provision for the underpayment to be added on to the principal so that the result would be *negative amortization* until interest rates fell again. Terms and conditions for caps must be looked at carefully.

In order to induce lenders to take on the added risk, financial intermediaries must offer borrowers an interest rate that is attractive in comparison with the interest rate on an FRM.

Other Mortgage Types. Space does not permit examination of all the various types of mortgages that lenders have created to protect their businesses from bankruptcy because of the vagaries of interest rates. To mention a few, there are *Roll Over Mortgages*

(ROMs) that provide for the terms of the mortgage contract to be renegotiated after, say, five years. There are *Graduated Payment Mortgages (GPMs)* that start with low monthly payments that rise when new home buyers are expected to receive higher wages after gaining experience in business, and so forth. There are *Reverse Payment Mortgages (RPMs)* that permit an older individual with a home as an asset to receive funds from a lender on a regular payment basis—the lender does not lend a lump sum but lends in the form of an annuity for a given period. Then, the lender is repaid when the property is sold or when a new mortgage is negotiated. The net effect of this type of mortgage is that the homeowner is able to sell a home in exchange for an annuity—a stream of payments. But there is no necessity for the home to be sold out from under the owner. By living at home and using it as an income, too, the homeowner is merely reducing the inheritance that otherwise might have accrued to heirs.

Secondary Markets for Mortgage Loans

Imagine that someone comes in the front door of a bank or thrift institution and wants to arrange for a mortgage on a home. Assume that the bank had just lent out its last dollar. How can it acquire funds to meet the request of its new customer? It could raise additional capital, it could beat the bushes for more depositor money or sell certificates of deposit, or it could sell some of its existing mortgages. That is, it could either increase the liabilities and net worth on the right hand side of the balance sheet, or it could sell some of its assets on the left side in order to increase its cash account, then lend that cash and hold a new mortgage in place of the old one. A bank can do this and earn extra fees because it continues to service the old mortgage that it sold. It collects the payments and keeps the necessary records on the old mortgage as well as the new one.

Facilitating the sale of old mortgages requires a secondary market for mortgages. Before FHA guaranteed mortgages were readily available, it was difficult to find buyers for mortgages, but, after the FHA began guaranteeing them, many investors became interested in them, including insurance companies, pension funds, private mortgage bankers, and even other financial intermediaries.

In 1938, the *Federal National Mortgage Association (FNMA or Fannie Mae)* was established under the sponsorship of the federal government. Its purpose was to establish and support a secondary market for the mortgages guaranteed by the FHA. To achieve this goal, it issued bonds and used the proceeds of the sale of bonds to purchase mortgages. Its bonds were guaranteed by the government.

At one point FNMA took advantage of its authority to sell stock as well as bonds. An interesting question arises when stockholders own shares in a government agency— since shares of stock supposedly represents ownership do stockholders own the agency or does the government "own" its own agency? (Incidently, the Federal Reserve was established on capital raised by requiring all national banks to subscribe to shares of stock. But few would view the Fed as owned by the banks in any but a figurative sense.)

Over several years the situation evolved and Fannie Mae was restructured as a "privately owned" institution in 1968. Part of the reason for its privatization was to remove the Treasury's liability for the FNMA's huge debt from the Treasury's books in order to reduce the size of the federal debt. Direct backing of FNMA's bond issues was replaced with a guarantee that it could borrow from the Treasury if it ran into financial difficulties. It is unclear to what extent this borrowing privilege constitutes a government guarantee of its debt. Its debt is considered to be government "backed" but not government "guaranteed," and it is called a government "sponsored" agency.

In 1970, the Federal Home Loan Bank, which supports savings and loan institutions, was given authority to establish the *Federal Home Loan Mortgage Corporation (FHLMC or Freddy Mac)*. Its job was to support a secondary market for conventional mortgages—mostly those issued by savings and loan associations. In 1968, the *Government National Mortgage Association (GNMA, or Ginnie Mae)* was formed, again for the purpose of facilitating the raising of funds to be passed through into mortgages, and thereby supporting the market for housing. Unlike Fannie Mae, Ginnie Mae is an agency of the federal government and operates from within the Department of Housing and Urban Development (HUD).

But Ginnie Mae was based, not on the selling of bonds and later purchase of mortgages, but on a pool of new mortgages from which securities were sold. These securities carried the government's guarantee that the mortgage interest and the principal repayments that homeowners make into the pool would be *passed through* to the investors who hold the securities. When bonds are sold by Fannie Mae, the mortgages are treated as collateral for the bonds. In contrast, in Ginnie Mae, when "pass-through" securities or "participation certificates" are sold, the rights to the interest and principal payments to the pool of mortgages are sold to the bondholder. Essentially, the overall impact of both types of arrangements is to support the creation of home mortgages and support the housing industry. This support is provided through government guarantees and the creation of bonds by government agencies (GNMA) or government-sponsored agencies (FNMA and FHLMC). These agencies support mortgage liquidity, first, by buying pools of mortgages from banks and thrifts, and second, by supporting secondary markets for mortgage-backed bonds.

From 1970 to 1983 Ginnie Mae pooled mortgages that were government guaranteed and were fixed rate mortgages on one to four family homes. In 1983 it began a second program in which the pool was constructed with adjustable rate mortgages, ARMs, that are adjusted annually. Capped ARMs are also pooled by Fannie Mae to provide for the issuing of its pass-through securities. And Freddie Mac's pass-through securities are called participation certificates (PCs). It has two programs—a cash program and a guarantor/swap program. Under the cash program, it sells PCs as usual, but under the guarantor/swap program, it buys a pool of mortgages from a thrift, then sells the pool's PCs back to the same thrift from which it bought the mortgages. This permits the thrift to have a guarantee from Freddie Mac added to its assets.

Pass-through securities may be issued against any pools of mortgages that are not associated with government sponsorship or guarantees. But to sell such privately arranged pools, the organizing firm must obtain permission from the Securities and Exchange Commission. Because of their private nature and lack of government guarantee or sponsorship, issuers need to reduce the risk to the investor by a program of bond insurance, or some other type of guarantee from a highly rated independent company or bank. The pass-through issues can then obtain higher ratings from Moody's and Standard & Poor's.

Another method of increasing the credit rating of bonds is to issue more than one class of certificates against a given mortgage pool. For example, A/B certificates may be issued, and the A certificates are "senior" while the B certificates are "subordinated" in the same fashion that corporations may issued subordinated bonds. In cases of default, holders of senior certificates are paid before holders of subordinated certificates. Senior certificates will receive a high rating and can be sold for higher prices. Risk-takers, including the originator of the pool, may buy/hold the more risky subordinated certificates.

It is easy to see that the world of mortgage financing becomes very involved and complicated the deeper one looks into it. Later, Collateralized Mortgage Obligations (CMOs) will be described. The reader will find that the complications have only just begun. At this point let us interrupt the description of the securities in this market and reflect briefly on how a market that should have remained simple has become so complicated.

Secondary Markets: Good Economics or Good Politics?

Thirty years ago buying a home was a pretty straightforward proposition. Managers of banks and thrifts knew their community. They raised funds from depositors and lent to people who had good credit reputations. They knew which areas had the best homes and could judge the quality of the collateral behind a mortgage. If the demand for loans was great, they looked for some way to expand their capital base in order to meet demand. Then Congress, with good intentions, decided to expand support for family homeownership and expanded guarantee-loan programs. These have developed into financial market monsters that now take trillions of dollars of funds out of markets for bonds and stocks that corporations need to issue in order to raise funds for business development and productivity growth.

Try to imagine that a different course of events took place. Imagine that, instead of offering support through government guarantees of loans, the government simply created and maintained continued support for banks and thrifts throughout the country. Those financial intermediaries would have continued to grow with roots in local housing offices throughout the country. Savers would have found an outlet for savings as thrifts offered interest rates that were high enough to attract savings away from the bond markets. By loan guarantees and other programs designed to attract money into housing mortgages indirectly, there has occurred a huge *disintermediation* of funds flows out of financial intermediaries and into bond markets run by investment banking institutions. If the government had not supported the banks and thrifts by guaranteeing mortgage loans, the banks and thrifts would not now be pooling and selling their mortgages. Instead they would be expanding as intermediaries and collecting the funds that local people now invest in mortgage-backed securities. Local lenders would look after local mortgage borrowers. The garden of homeownership would be cultivated.

Making it easy to buy homes has made it more expensive for businesses to acquire capital for expansion. With less capital expansion, labor productivity stagnates along with wage rates. With relatively slow-growing wages it now takes a two-income family to buy a home. And, making it easy to buy homes with subsidized guarantees makes demand rise and home prices rise. Add a little inflation to this and home prices skyrocket.

Nowadays, homeownership has evolved into a very complicated way of renting living space with a tax break attached. Today, young people rightly ask in despair, why does it take a two-income family to afford a home? One big reason may be that government has interfered, with good intentions but not necessarily good results, as usual. Tax breaks and other subsidized lending programs drive up the demand for housing and home prices. Capital flows away from business so neither productivity nor wages increase. Surely, this is yet another classic example of the way in which government's good intentions may go awry.

The insidious aspect of government assistance is that, at each step of the development of a government's program, it appears that government is helping. Then like a disease that slowly progresses and becomes entrenched before it becomes apparent, government's assistance becomes a burden. Some readers may disagree with the views expressed here about the impact of subsidies on housing in the U.S. However, there is merit to the logic used in the analysis and it should provide food for thought. The U.S. League of Savings Institutions has often expressed concern that FNMA and GNMA may be usurping the role of their members and that the mortgage interest deduction for tax purposes is controversial.

The Prepayment Problem With Pass-through Securities

If you lend your money to the bank by making a deposit that you can withdraw anytime you like, you have made the equivalent of a "call" loan to the bank. If a bank makes a loan to your firm, it may include a clause that enables the bank to ask you to repay your loan whenever the bank wants its funds back—a "call" loan. In both of these examples, the lender has the right to ask the borrower to repay the loan at any time. Sometimes, the opposite sort of situation arises in which the borrowers rather than the lenders can "call" the agreement. For example, if a corporation issues a ten-year bond, it may include a call provision that enables the borrower (issuer of the bond) to call the bond back at the end of five years, that is, to pay off the loan early. Similarly, in the case of a mortgage, the borrower (homeowner) usually has the right to pay off the balance of the mortgage at any time, after a couple of years, without penalty. As in the case of the corporation issuing a callable bond, the borrowing homeowner has signed a callable mortgage—it can be paid off in full at any time. It is continuously callable, not just callable at a certain date. In the case of the callable corporate bond and the callable mortgage, the borrowers rather than the lenders get to call the shots on the time of repayment.

The yield on a bond is calculated by comparing its price with the cash flows that it is expected to provide. When estimating the current yield on a bond that has a call date, it is conventional for cash flows to be estimated to the first possible call date and not the maturity date. Yields differ depending on which date is used. Imagine that you wanted to examine the yield on a bond that did not specify a single call date but that permitted the corporation to call the bond on *any* date in the future. How could an investor estimate the yield?

Essentially, this is the puzzle that investors in pass-through securities must try to solve every day—it is called the *prepayment* problem. Out of a pool of mortgages, there will be some that will be prepaid from time to time as people move to take new jobs and want to sell their present home in order to raise funds to buy a different home in a different community. Also, interest rates may fall and investors will want to refinance their mortgage in order to take advantage of the lower rates. So the funds flowing into a pool of mortgages will vary as some principal payments are made early. There is no good way to predict just when the early payments will be made. It would be like a bond that is callable at any time, and investors would have to guess when corporations would decide to call them in order to estimate the yield on the bond.

Prepayment Assumptions. In order to sell collateralized securities in the bond market, the securities need to be as much like bonds as possible. Otherwise, they would not be competitive. To place a value on a bond, the seller needs to make an assumption about the prepayments that the underlying pool of mortgages will experience—*the prepayment assumption*. The simplest assumption to make is that prepayments will be made at a constant rate each month. This prepayment is called a constant prepayment rate (CPR). Remember that a monthly mortgage payment is broken into interest on the unpaid balance and on a portion of repayment of principal. So, if CPR is stated as an annual rate, say 5 per cent, the monthly percentage decline in the outstanding balance is $1 - (1 - 0.05)^{1/12} = 1 - (0.95)^{0.08333} = 1 - 0.9957 = 0.0043$.

This factor is multiplied with the unpaid balance at the beginning of the period after whatever already scheduled principal payment is subtracted. In other words, the scheduled principal payment may be $100 and the mortgage balance may be $30,000. So applying the monthly rate of 0.0043 to $30,000 - $100, or $29,900 gives $128.57 as the estimated prepayment for the given month according to the 5 per cent annual CPR assumption.

Please note that this 5 per cent figure is an assumption and remember that nobody knows what the rate will turn out to be. Remember, too, the assumption means that the estimated cash flow will be affected month by month throughout the life of the mortgage.

Monthly Payments and Prepayments. Without computers it would be extremely difficult to analyze the yield on, or value of, a pass-through security. Let us look first at the task that a real estate agent has when explaining to a buyer the allocation of monthly payments to principal and interest over the life of a 30-year mortgage loan. Assume a loan for $100,000 with a fixed annual interest rate of 8 per cent. There will be 360 monthly payments with the first due in 30 days.

Month	Beginning balance	Payment	Interest	Principal	Ending balance
1	$100,000.00	$733.76	$666.70	$67.06	$99,932.94
2	$ 99,932.94	$733.76	$666.44	$67.32	$99.865.61
3	$ 99,865.61	Etc.			
⋮					
360					

The left hand column houses the months numbered 1–360. The table would need to be several pages long to reach line 360. The balance of the loan at the beginning of each month is in the second column. The payment remains the same until the very end. The interest is calculated by applying the monthly interest rate, 8%/12 = 0.6667%/month, to the beginning balance that starts out at $100,000. Since the principal balance declines each month the interest will also decline—only by a small amount over several years and then rapidly in the last years of the mortgage. The next column is made by subtracting the interest from the payment to arrive at the residual that is applied to the principal balance. This residual gets larger month by month—very slowly in the first years and rapidly in the last years of the mortgage. Finally, the far right column is calculated by subtracting the payment toward the principal from the beginning balance. This ending balance is used as the beginning balance for the second month, and the calculations start over again and are repeated for each successive month. With computers, spreadsheets, and printers available, a real estate agent will provide a printout of this entire set of numbers to a customer upon request.

Space does not permit an explanation of all the calculations needed to introduce prepayment assumptions. Readers may refer to the references at the end of the chapter. However, in order to obtain an intuitive appreciation of the added complication, consider the following:

1. With the prepayment assumption, the monthly constant prepayment rate must be applied to the beginning balance as described above, requiring an additional column.
2. With the prepayment into the mortgage pool, the monthly payment will not remain the same every period—it will decline over time.
3. Scheduled interest and principal amounts will be affected too, for each month, because the prepayment means the beginning balance changes.
4. A servicing fee of perhaps 50 basis points will be taken out of the payments, and the amount of the fee will diminish over time. Interest and principal payments represent the cash flow to the holder of the mortgage, but the cash flow to the mortgage pass-through security holder is less because of the service fee.

5. After adding the mortgage payment (no longer a constant sum each month) and the prepayment, and then subtracting the service fee, a column can be constructed that shows the *cash flow* that will be paid on through to the holder of the pass-through security.

Making these calculations means adding another four columns to the six columns already there. Constructing the table requires a financial engineer!

Instead of being constant over time, the mortgage payments decrease as mentioned, and the cash flow to the holder will decrease steadily if the CPR remains constant. However, if the CPR increases for several periods and then remains flat, the *cash flow* to the holder of the security will increase because of the prepayments, but then will drop off later. So the pattern of cash flows varies over time, depending on the prepayment assumptions made.

Now for a truly complicating factor, *the prepayment assumption usually applied is not a constant rate.* The industry was under pressure to devise some estimate of what prepayment rates might be, and the FHA's historical experience with actual prepayments was used as a basis for estimating prepayments. Of course, the historical experience changed with each new month of payments, so the FHA's rate was constantly changing. However, it was roughly 6 per cent, so 6 per cent became a basic reference rate and was called the 100 per cent prepayment assumption base. Faster rates would be designated as, say 200 per cent of the FHA experience, which would mean a constant prepayment rate assumption of 12 per cent. A slower rate might be 50 per cent of the FHA base and indicate a 3 per cent CPR. But the *Public Securities Association*, an industry group, decided to establish a basic reference rate schedule because experience showed that prepayments in the early years of a mortgage were lower than a few years later. Its basic reference, or benchmark, assumption was that prepayments would be only 0.2 per cent the first month and rise by 0.2 per cent each month for 30 months (in the thirtieth month prepayments would be 6.0 per cent). Then the PSA assumed that a 6 per cent rate would continue for the remainder of the 330 months of the mortgage. Thus, the current industry standard is to refer to the PSA prepayment of 100 per cent. This benchmark standard, *the PSA standard prepayment assumption*, consists of the assumption of the pattern of prepayments of 0.2 per cent up to 6.0 per cent and then constant after that. That is what a PSA of 100 means. Now if the PSA assumption is assumed to be 200 per cent of the PSA, it means that rates assumed for each of the months doubles to 0.4 per cent each month for 30 months, and so forth, and if the rate is 50 per cent in means that the prepayments are assumed to be 0.1 per cent at the outset, rising to 3.0 per cent after 30 months, and so forth. PSA assumptions are routinely referred to in offerings of pass-through securities. The PSA benchmark prepayment assumption is not much different from 6 per cent except for the first 30 months (2½ years).

Cash Flow Yields. Recall now that the *cash flows* predicted from the investment depend upon the PSA assumption. What is called the *cash flow yield* can be calculated if the current price of the security is known. The cash flow yield is simply the internal rate of return—the discount rate that will make the present value of those uneven flows equal to the current price of the security. If an investor has a required rate of return, then that rate can be applied to the cash flows and the present value of the security can be estimated. In summary, if the price of the security is observable in the market, then the cash flow yield can be calculated. But if the price is not known because of lack of trading, then the value of those flows (an appropriate price) can be calculated only by assuming some yield as a basis for the calculation. It is not easy to determine the value (price) of these securities. Their price depends on what those cash flows are worth to the investor.

Different investors may have different opinions about what PSA assumption should be made. Should it be 100, 150, 200? Sellers of the securities will present cash flow yields for different PSA benchmarks in order to let the investor use a self determined opinion. Sometimes the PSA benchmarks are referred to as PSA or CPR *speeds*.

Collateralized Mortgage Obligations (CMOs) and Real Estate Mortgage Investment Conduits (REMICs)

In the mid-1980s the CMO became a significant security in the bond market. In 1986 tax laws were changed to establish an appropriate tax treatment for interest payments on CMOs. For example, if you set up a company and agree to pass interest payments through it, does your company have to declare income taxes on the interest it receives and passes through? As another example, in the case of real estate, if you form a corporation to hold real estate and agree to pass through rental payments, does the corporation have to pay taxes on rentals only to have the receiver of the passed-through rents also pay tax? Congress passed laws permitting the creation of *Real Estate Investment Trusts* (REITs) in the 1970s and, if the trust paid through at least 90 per cent of its rental payments, the trust could avoid double taxation of rents. Similarly, in 1986 Congress passed laws permitting the creation of *Real Estate Mortgage Investment Conduits* (REMICs), which permitted the establishment of trusts that would hold pools of mortgages, as well as pass both interest and principal payments through to final holders and avoid double taxation of mortgage interest payment income. Today most CMOs are sold through REMICs and the terms are often used interchangeably.

Every pool of mortgages has cash flows coming in and the securities require that cash flows go out. Instead of paying out the funds as a participation certificate, those in charge of constructing the securities that are backed by the pool of mortgages can write any type of contract they like. So, for example, they can sell a certain amount of securities that are paid off first, and guarantee first rights to the cash flow to those securities. A second pool will take subordinated rights, and so forth.

What are CMOs and REMICs?

Today's CMOs and REMICs are special types of mortgage-backed securities. They are formed on the basis of estimates of the cash flows that come into the pool and that can be paid out according to design. Some securities are constructed to be as much like bonds as possible. These are often Planned Amortization Classes (PACs). They are like a bond with a sinking fund that provides for payments when due. Thus, the pool of mortgages is carved up into "tranches." Some non-PAC tranches are left over and these, usually called the Z-class, are used to absorb risk so the PAC tranches can be sure to perform like a bond. Z-class tranches accrue interest and principal but do not begin payments of interest and principal until after the all other classes have been paid off. Next there are Targeted Amortization Classes (TACs) that have slightly less stability of cash flow than PACs.

Interest payments are sometimes separated out from the principal payments to create a security that has characteristics similar to those of zero coupon bonds. Tranches are formed to make interest only (IO) and principal only (PO) securities that carry no interest. Also, sometimes IO and PO securities are created from an entire mortgage pool.

Within some tranches are certificates called "floaters" and the interest they pay are tied to floating rate indexes such as the London Interbank Offered Rate (LIBOR). For hedging purposes they are always issued along with a counterpart called an "inverse floater."

CMO tranches are formed both from pools of fixed rate mortgages and pools of adjustable rate mortgages.

The expertise of financial engineers is needed to construct these CMO securities given the complications involving prepayment assumptions, cash flow yields, portions or *tranches* of the pool that are given certain characteristics with respect to life of the investment, and so forth. These financial engineers use computers a lot. Many financial engineers should be called financial architects.

For example, a prospectus and offering circular and supplement on $300 million of Federal Home Loan Mortgage Corporation Multiclass Mortgage Participation Certificates, Series 1450, dated May 1992, is 85 pages of small print that presents details on 20 classes of certificates complete with a great deal of information on PSA assumptions, and so forth.

The Government National Mortgage Association first issued pass-through CMOs after it started in 1968, but did not get into the business of carving up their pools into REMIC tranches until 1994.

The CMO Market Today

We are not talking about peanuts here. By 1990 there were about $1 trillion in mortgage-backed securities outstanding. By 1992 the total value of residential mortgages in the U.S. were estimated at $3.25 trillion and about $1.3 trillion were securitized— a $300 billion increase in two years. Investment bankers have a large and growing business in the CMO world.

What are CMO's Worth? They are often sold on the basis of their yield as a percentage spread against a Treasury security of the same maturity. The spread is 25–125 basis points higher in the one-to-five-year range. The collateral behind the CMO is very, very good. For the Ginnie Mae issues, of course, there is 100 per cent U.S. Treasury backing, and other nongovernment-backed issues carry triple-A ratings because they are over-collateralized. However, the residual class of securities is much more risky because prepayments are uncertain.

Raising the Red Flag of Risk. For example, inverse floaters go in the opposite direction of the market. When interest rates fall in the marketplace, the rate of return on inverse floaters goes up! These are great for risk lovers to buy when they think interest rates are going down. They lose big if rates actually go up.

The managers of the mortgage pool may issue equal amounts of floaters and inverse floaters in order to hedge their own position. If they want to issue more floaters than inverse floaters, for example, they may do so. For example, they may issue four times the volume of inverse floaters and still be fully hedged if they tie the floater to LIBOR and make the inverse floater adjust by four times LIBOR in the opposite direction. This greatly magnifies swings in the return on floaters. Sometimes the multiple is nine instead of four. The demand for floating rate CMOs is especially heavy on the part of international investors and may be used in hedging against floating rate liabilities as part of international swap arrangements. In general, inverse floaters are for speculators.

The interest-only securities, IOs, are for speculators too, but they have shocked many unsuspecting buyers who did not realize their riskiness. The IOs are government guaranteed securities so that they are free of default risk. What investors fail to realize is that when the pool of mortgages is prepaid and the principal is paid off, the *interest payments on the mortgages stop altogether*. Monthly payments of interest are no longer paid on mortgages that no longer exist. This came as quite a shock to many holders of IO securities in the summer and fall of 1993 when prepayments reached a peak as individuals took advantage of low interest rates to refinance their homes. Large investment banks as well as individuals have incurred losses on IOs. Lawsuits were filed against Hyperion Capital Management, Inc. (HCM, Inc.) by holders of Hyperion 1999 Term Trust—a publicly traded bond fund that HCM, Inc. manages. The fund's shares had dropped by 30 per cent and shareholders claimed they had been misled about the quality of the fund's investments (see Jereski, November 1, 1993; Pulliam, 1993).

After carving up pools of assets the bits and pieces that are left are thrown in as backing for the remaining issues of bonds. This last assortment of backing has led to the creation of the term "kitchen sink" bonds—those backed with everything but the kitchen sink (see Jereski, November 18, 1993).

During 1993 about $18 billion of *commercial real estate mortgages* were securitized. Banks and insurance companies pool commercial loans into performing and non-performing categories. Then they create an A-rated CMO with the good loans, and issue what are called B-pieces with the rest. Then they retain a batch of the A-pieces on their balance sheet and sell the remainder. This takes the risk away from the banks and insurance companies and shifts nearly all of it to those investors who purchase the B-pieces. This also helps banks and insurance companies meet more stringent regulatory capital adequacy requirements.

Banks are also willing to sell off corporate loans in an expanding secondary market. These are nearly always floating rate loans and are backed by collateral. However, they are not yet placed into pools from which CMOs and REMICs are constructed (see Haubrich and Thomson, 1993).

Simulations of Prepayment and Interest Rate Experience. Investment banking houses have devoted a great deal of attention to the problem of determining the value of various CMOs. For example, Fitch Investor Services of New York has established a volatility rating service that is similar in some respect to Moody's and Standard & Poor's. They make a V-rating for each tranche of a pool with V-1 to V-5 as the measures. These ratings are designed to provide a summary statement of a complex system of analysis. The analysis takes into consideration prepayments, interest rate scenarios and various aspects of the CMO structure itself.

One problem for academics is that the large investment firms have hired special financial engineers to construct analytical structures, but these structures are not made generally available. Researchers at the Wharton School of the University of Pennsylvania have developed what is called MOSES, standing for a Mortgage Simulation and Evaluation System. Prepayments of mortgages are like call options, as noted earlier, so the analysis requires a combination of bond and option valuations and how these valuations change over time under different assumptions about the future path of interest rates. The calculations required to simulate the experience are enormous. They are used to compute either a price of a CMO or an "option adjusted" spread above the return on a Treasury security.

Prepayment Experience. Managers of the underlying pool of mortgages provide updated information on the weighted average coupons (WACs) and weighted average maturities (WAMs) for the remaining mortgages in the pool. In this way CMO holders are provided with some current prepayment experience.

Collateralized Securities: A Growth Industry

In America the success of collateralized mortgage markets has led to expansion into types of collateral other than mortgages. In particular, automobile loans have been packaged and established as backing for bonds. Also, credit card receivables have been used as collateral for bonds. In 1993 banks began pooling business loans so they could be used as collateral for bonds that could be sold in the market. According to the new Capital Adequacy Requirements discussed in Chapter 4, business loans are weighted 100 per cent whereas bonds are weighted much lower. Thus, if a bank makes a pool of its loan portfolio and then buys the bonds that are sold against it, it can effectively hold its loans in securitized form and reduce its capital requirements.

However, it seems that collateralization of bonds, also called securitization, has been less successful in Europe. While such securities have been issued there, there has been no boom in activity there to reflect the pronounced boom in America beginning about 1988. European firms do not maintain computer banks of information to track performance as American counterparts do, and there are as yet no regulations or guidelines to follow. For example, the Accounting Standards Board in the U.K. plans to issue standards in 1994 (see Sharpe, 1993).

A conference was held in Hong Kong in 1991 to encourage the establishment of a CMO market there. Banks in Hong Kong hold hundreds of thousands of mortgages on condominium units that are between 350 to 650 square feet in size in 30-storey high-rise buildings with eight units on each floor. With an average family size of three, a single building houses 720 persons. By 1993, perennial inflation in Hong Kong finally drove prices of such units to levels that exceeded those in Japan. However, mortgages are generally set at 15 years and extend beyond the 1997 turnover date for Hong Kong to revert to Chinese control. Uncertainties about the future of bonds in this case would require that any such collateralized bonds would have to have some externally guaranteed, very expensive insurance in order to induce investors to purchase them. This is unfortunate because surely banks in Hong Kong would find that the ability to sell a huge part of their mortgage portfolios into a trust would free up their capital and reserves for other purposes. However, it may also be fortunate that local banks still deal with local people in matters of housing. Indeed, in the summer of 1993 banks raised effective down payments on housing loans to 40 per cent of the loan in an effort to stem speculative pressures on prices and to favor first-time buyers with plans to live and raise a family in a home.

In Singapore, the government's *Central Provident Fund* (CPF) is the medium for the acquisition of housing by nearly everyone. It is a compulsory saving scheme for salaried employees that was established in 1955. When it began, all salaried employees paid 5 per cent of their salary to the CPF. This payment was matched by their employer. Limits were set on the amounts that low-paid persons had to pay. Over the years until 1984, the amounts required were raised to 25 per cent by both employer and employee. However, ceilings on monthly payments were also set at S$3,000 per month for the combined amounts. The government reduced the payments required of employers to help stimulate the economy in 1986. It announced that the target would be to stabilize payments at 20 per cent each, for employer and employee, over the long-run. The payments collected by the CPF are invested principally in government securities.

The normal retirement age in Singapore is 55, and individuals may begin collecting from the fund when they reach that age. However, in 1968 various schemes for early withdrawal of funds for use in purchasing public housing for low and middle income persons, and for purchasing private housing generally, were initiated. Thus, the people of Singapore find it advantageous to use their CPF credits to buy housing. What essentially happens is that the government sells bonds to the CPF, uses the proceeds to build public housing, and offers the housing for sale to the people who bought the bonds in exchange for their bonds. Singapore's program ensures that the government gets to decide what kind of housing is appropriate. But, as acknowledged at the beginning of the chapter, governments almost everywhere have long had policies to guide its people's housing. In Hong Kong, the government still owns the land, leases most of it, and actively regulates the construction of housing development projects and all land use. Hong Kong may be an example of capitalism and private property generally, but in the housing and land use area it has a governmentally directed system of control.

Summary

Governments set up laws regarding ownership of property. The ownership of property is necessary if individual liberties are to exist. Thus, property ownership is an essential ingredient of a free and democratic society, and it is also a necessity for a free market economy. But the rules for property ownership itself must be provided by government. Hence, government regulation, which balances ownership of property and the uses to which property is put, exists in every modern exchange society.

In the U.S., government has supported homeownership by individuals through an important tax incentive: the law permits homeowners with mortgages to deduct the mortgage interest from income in calculating the income on which income tax must be paid. Thus, homeowners are encouraged to borrow money to use to buy a home. Yet they are also discouraged from paying off the mortgage in order to own the home without legal encumbrance. The result is, nearly every homeowner also has a mortgage.

Mortgages are offered by highly regulated financial institutions. Thus, the interaction between government, property ownership, and financial institutions is extensive.

Financial institutions offer many different types of mortgage contracts. Most are fixed rate mortgages. The interest rate is fixed for the entire life of the loan. Of course, the loan can be paid off prior to maturity in most cases. The second most important type of mortgage contract is called the adjustable rate mortgage. It provides for the interest rate applied to the unpaid balance to change periodically.

Government agencies support the housing market by purchasing mortgages, forming pools, and issuing securities like bonds with the pools of mortgages as collateral. These are called Collateralized Mortgage Obligations.

The mortgage interest income and principal can be separated when dealing with a pool of mortgages. Thus, financial engineers may carve up the cash flows from the pool into a variety of different securities that can be tailor made to meet investor demand.

Many sections of the carved up mortgage pool are very risky. For example, someone may purchase an interest only security and be told that it is backed by the government. But they are not told that to the extent that borrowers decide to prepay the mortgages in the pool, the interest will stop flowing. This has shocked many investors. Their income streams simply dried up. They should have anticipated this possibility, but may not have been adequately informed.

The Asian Tiger countries have not yet developed collateralized mortgages or other types of securitized assets. But as the financial sectors of these economies grow one would expect such mortgages or other types of securitized assets to be introduced.

Key Terms and Concepts

Adjustable rate mortgages

Graduated payment mortgages

Freddie Mac

PSA standard payment assumption

Planned Amortization Classes (PACs)

Interest only securities (IOs)

Weighted average coupons (WACs)

Central Provident Fund

Roll over mortgages

Reverse payment mortgages

Participation certificates

Real Estate Investment Trusts (REITs)

Targeted Amortization Classes (TACs)

Principal only securities (POs)

Weighted average maturities (WAMs)

Discussion Questions and Exercises

1. Should interest expenses on mortgages be deducted from income for tax purposes? Should imputed income from living in one's own home be included in income for tax purposes? Discuss.

2. Clearly distinguish between fixed rate mortgages and variable rate mortgages and give an example of each.

3. Explain why banks and thrifts might find that profits go down when interest rates go up and *vice versa*.

4. What are graduated payment mortgages, roll over mortgages and reverse payment mortgages, and why might different borrowers prefer each to the others?

5. What was the government's goal in creating FNMA? GNMA?

6. Economic theory suggests that subsidies distort the allocation of resources and such distortion leaves everyone worse off than they might otherwise be. Do housing subsidies in the U.S. leave people with less housing in the long run? Discuss.

7. Sometimes borrowers can call a loan, that is, repay it early. Sometimes lenders can demand repayment of a loan on call. Explain the concept of "call" with respect to lending and borrowing.

8. Explain the Constant Prepayment Rate assumption as applied to mortgages.

9. Using the amortization schedule for a fixed rate mortgage as a base, what additional columns of calculations need to be included if one wants to look at prepayments to a pool of mortgages and calculate cash flows each month?

10. What is the benchmark prepayment schedule referred to as PSA of 100 per cent?

11. "To calculate cash flow yield you need a market price and to find a market price you have to assume a yield." Explain.

12. What is a Collateralized Mortgage Obligation? What is an REMIC? Discuss the differences if any.

13. Discuss other types of assets that are, or might be, "securitized."

14. What are the prospects for the issue of collateralized assets in other economies such as Hong Kong? Discuss.

References

Anderson, Gary A., Barber, Joel R., and Chang, Chun-Hao, "Prepayment Risk and the Duration of Default-free Mortgage-backed Securities," *Journal of Financial Research*, Vol. 16, Spring 1993, pp. 1–9.

Becketti, Sean, "The Role of Stripped Securities in Portfolio Management," *Economic Review*, Federal Reserve Bank of Kansas City, May 1988, pp. 20–31.

_____, "The Prepayment Risk of Mortgage-backed Securities," *Economic Review*, Federal Reserve Bank of Kansas City, February 1989, pp. 43–57.

Bhattacharya, A. K., and Chin, H. W., "Synthetic Mortgage-backed Securities," *Journal of Portfolio Management*, Spring 1992, pp. 44–54.

Bykhovsky, Michael, and Hayre, Lakhbir, "Fact and Fantasy about Collateral Speeds," *Journal of Portfolio Management*, Summer 1992, pp. 63–66.

Cagan, L. D., Carriero, N. J., and Zenios, S. A., "A Computer Network Approach to Pricing Mortgage-backed Securities," *Financial Analysts Journal*, March/April 1993, pp. 55–62.

Derosa, Paul, Goodman, Laurie, and Zazzarino, Mike, "Duration Estimates on Mortgage-backed Securities," *Journal of Portfolio Management*, Winter 1993, pp. 32–38.

Fabozzi, F. J., *Bond Markets, Analysis and Strategies*, 2nd Edition, Prentice Hall, Englewood Cliffs, NJ, 1993.

Freer, Jim, "REMICs' First Year," *Banker,* November 1987, pp. 44–54.

Gilkeson, James H., and Smith, Stephen D., "The Convexity Trap: Pitfalls in Financing Mortgage Portfolios and Related Securities," *Economic Review*, Federal Reserve Bank of Atlanta, November/December 1992, pp. 14–27.

Haubrich, Joseph G., and Thomson, James B., "The Evolving Loan Sales Market," *Economic Commentary*, Federal Reserve Bank of Cleveland, July 15, 1993.

Hueglin's Bond Market Report, Gabriele, Hueglin & Cashman, Vol. 10, No. 3, 1989.

Jereski, Laura, "Ohio Case Signals Backlash Against Exotic Mortgages," *Wall Street Journal*, November 1, 1993.

_____, "Kitchen-sink Bonds May Offer Everything but Stability," *Wall Street Journal*, November 18, 1993.

Konstas, Panoz, "Derivative Mortgage Securities and their Risk Return Characteristics," *FDIC Banking Review*, Fall 1983, pp. 28–33.

Peek, Joe, and Wilcox, James A., "A Real, Affordable Mortgage," *New England Economic Review*, Federal Reserve Bank of Boston, January/February 1991, pp. 51–66.

Pulliam, Susan, "Firms Face Big Losses on IO Investments," *Wall Street Journal*, October 28, 1993.

Sharpe, Antonia, "Securitization: Flexible Friend for Lenders," *Financial Times*, October 28, 1993.

Smith, D. J., "The Arithmetic of Financial Engineering," in Don Chew, Jr., ed., *The New Corporate Finance*, McGraw-Hill, New York, 1992, pp. 401–10.

CHAPTER 11

Futures, Options, and Swap Markets

FINANCIAL MANAGERS HIRE financial engineers to mix investments and construct portfolios with many different characteristics in order to meet the preferences of borrowers and lenders. The "tools" used in constructing these portfolios often include what are called "financial derivatives." These "derivative" investments involve contracts that are not the stocks or bonds or mortgages or collateralized bonds themselves but are investments in contracts that have those money and capital market securities as their reference. Such derivative financial instruments have been formed to provide investors with a way to hedge various risks.

The discussion in this chapter begins with risk, uncertainty and hedging, and is followed with brief descriptions of various derivative markets.

Risk and Uncertainty

When thinking of a "risky situation" people usually think of a risk of *loss*. However, most risky situations involve the possibility of *gain*, too. Risk is not just about losing, it is about winning or losing. In general, then, the term "risk" refers, to the *outcome* of an action; if the outcome is *certain*, then taking the action involves no risk, if the outcome is uncertain, then the action involves taking risk.

However, mathematicians have refined the concept of risk by developing the concept of probable outcomes. Their theorems on probability are often based on gambling situations—the probability of getting a heads in a coin toss, or the probability of drawing an ace from a deck of cards. The concept of probability is based on *repeated* events. Thus, the probability of drawing an ace is $\frac{4}{52}$ ($\frac{1}{13}$) since there are four aces in a deck of 52 cards. What is the probability of drawing an ace? The answer is that, out of many repeated random draws, the ratio of aces to other cards drawn will approximate $\frac{1}{13}$. What is the outcome of a single draw? Will it be an ace? The answer is that the outcome is uncertain. There is no such thing as a probability applied to a single draw. One cannot draw $\frac{1}{13}$th of an ace. A single draw will always either be an ace or not be.

A great deal of information about the probability of outcomes can be obtained from experience. Insurance companies rely on mortality tables that describe the probability of surviving life through, say, age 25, and so forth. Such probabilities determine insurance premiums.

The concept of probable outcomes is now applied in business everywhere and especially in finance. Business is, by nature, risky. Business decisions can be made less risky if one knows the distribution of probable outcomes and can estimate the standard deviation of that distribution. *Degrees of risk can be measured using standard deviations* of outcomes. If one may win a little or lose a little, the range of outcomes is narrow and the risk is small. But when the range, measured by a standard deviation, is larger, the risk is greater. The outcome of any single action is uncertain, but through repeated actions the probability of the outcome may be well established. Then, managers can take action based on measures of risk. However, in many instances, there are no measures of risk to rely upon. In such situations, the outcome is *uncertain*.

Thus, there is a difference between risk and uncertainty. Since degrees of risk can be measured, a risky situation is one with an estimate of riskiness. If degrees of risk have not been, or cannot be, measured, then the situation should be called *uncertain*.

Types of Risks in Finance

There are many different types of risk and here only a few types related to financial matters are described briefly.

Default Risk. What is the probability that a company will default on its bonds? To default is the failure to meet the terms of an agreement, usually the failure to make interest payments on schedule or failure to repay principal when due.

Inflation Risk. Even if the debtor does make interest and principal payments on time according to the contract, it is possible that inflation will have reduced the purchasing power of the funds used to repay the debt. This results in a loss to the lender. Or, a decline in inflation may leave the borrower with heavy interest payments that were agreed to under the expectation of higher future rates of inflation. Thus, unanticipated changes in inflation rates can result in gains or losses on bond contracts.

Capital Risk. While a piece of property or a security is being held, its price will fluctuate.

If it falls a great deal, and if the holder wishes to sell, the holder will absorb a loss of capital. Thus, homeowners may gain or lose from the sale of their house or from the sale of their stocks or bonds. Holding an asset is risky; the outcome may be a gain or a loss.

However, if you are certain that you will hold a bond to maturity, does it matter to you if the price varies a great deal in the interim? There is a sophisticated debate over this question. Some advisors recommend that investors, when investing for the "long haul," should buy shares. Historically shares fluctuate more in price than bonds do, so shares are more "risky" than bonds, by measures of standard deviations of returns. However, bonds yield less over long periods on average than shares. Therefore, should advisors tell investors, even risk-averse investors, to buy stocks for a long period in order to gain the higher return and to ignore the greater risk associated with stock investments? Risk-averse investors watching stock prices fluctuate wildly may be very unhappy. Should investors just refuse to read the news about the stock market and adopt the attitude of "don't worry, be happy"? Ignorance is bliss, but can it tell us the truth? The assumption of capital risk, which each of us assumes every day, is difficult to analyze.

Reinvestment Risk or Interest Rate Risk. Some people are worried about possibilities of gain or loss from holding capital; others are worried about gain or loss from having interest income go up or down. For example, should an elderly person put funds in short-term securities yielding 10 per cent, or put them in long-term securities yielding 7 per cent? If the short-term interest rates fall from 10 to 4 per cent, and the person has to reinvest at 4 per cent, he or she will have a big drop in annual income. Would it be better to be assured of a steady 7 per cent yield over many years? Interest rate fluctuations mean gains and losses to many people.

Foreign Exchange Risk. If one is engaging in trade with another country, there is the risk of loss or gain from changes in the rate of exchange between the currencies of the two countries.

There are many other specialized types of risks associated with changing prices of all sorts. Those listed here are of great concern to financial managers.

Hedging Bets

A bookie in a small town may have only $1,000 of capital to operate with when taking bets on a ball game. Assume a person comes in and bets for Team A, and by "taking the bet" the bookie is betting on Team B. As long as bets are roughly equal on both teams, the bookie can simply use money from one set of betters to pay the other set, keeping a percentage for profit. Now assume the betting is about equal for both teams, but just before the game, someone comes in to place a *big* bet, say $10,000, on Team A. The bookie would be exposed to the risk of a big loss or gain. And if he loses $10,000 and has free capital of only $1,000, he may get into big trouble with the gambling world by being unable to pay.

Should he refuse to take the bet? No. Instead, immediately after taking the bet, he should call Las Vegas and place the same bet on Team A with a big-time bookie who has lots of funds. Then, if Team A wins, the local bookie will collect from Las Vegas, and pass the winnings on to the local winner. If it loses, he takes the money from the local better and sends it to Las Vegas.

The local bookie "hedged" his position by laying off the risk. By hedging fully, he will neither win nor lose. As to the uncertain outcome of the game, the hedger has, in essence, not bet on the game at all because he made offsetting bets. He could have decided to lay off only part of the bet and then would be only partly hedged.

Throughout each day, hedging of risks "protects" literally trillions of dollars of financial investments by use of various markets for financial derivatives.

Futures Markets

There are two broad classes of futures markets: (1) commodities futures markets and (2) financial futures markets. *Commodities futures markets* for wheat, coffee, plywood, orange juice, pig iron, pork bellies, tin, petroleum, and the like are very well-known among the farming community and the foreign trade community.

Financial futures markets can be broken into two types: (1) *foreign exchange futures markets* for Canadian dollars, German marks, Japanese yen, the British pound, and so forth, and (2) *interest rate futures markets* for Treasury bills, Treasury bonds, certificates of deposit, and futures contracts on a stock market index.

Commodity futures are similar to foreign exchange futures—if you are American, just think of German marks as a "commodity" being traded like coffee. Also, interest rate futures are like commodities too, except in this case the "commodity" in question is a Treasury bill or bond, and these securities are being sold for a dollar price. The reason these futures are called "interest rate" futures is that when locking in the price of a Treasury bill you also lock in the yield or interest rate on the bill. These futures could just as well be called security futures instead of interest rate futures, and one could think of the price of a security as being like the price of coffee, orange juice, and so forth.

Thus, all futures markets have basically the same structure. In this chapter we will use the futures markets for Treasury bills as the basic example.

Treasury Bill Futures Markets

First, it is useful to distinguish between a *spot* market and a *forward* market, and then to take the next step to draw the contrast between a forward market and a *futures* market.

A spot market is simply a market where trades of goods or securities take place "on the spot." The transaction is completed at the instant goods or securities are exchanged for money. A forward market exists when people who trade agree to make the exchanges of goods or securities, not instantly, but at some date in the future, at a price agreed upon when the trade is agreed upon. The price is set in a certain currency and that monetary unit is used as the "standard for deferred payments."

For example, it is common for an importer to want to have foreign exchange available at some date in the future in order to pay foreign suppliers. Rather than buying deutschemarks on the spot market today, the importer may go to a bank and draw up a contract with the bank to buy a certain number of deutschemarks for a specified price in dollars on a specific future date. The dollar price of the foreign exchange is locked in as part of the contract. These kinds of forward contracts make up the *forward market* for deutschemarks. Banks offer forward contracts regularly. One can shop among banks for the best price. Just as there is a market for bread, there is also a forward market for foreign exchange.

The distinction between a forward market and a futures market can now be clarified: a futures market in marks is not a market where marks are traded on future dates; it is instead a market where *contracts* to trade marks in the future are themselves traded. A reference to "futures" is a shortened reference to "futures contracts." Futures contracts are bought and sold on a futures exchange in a futures market. The people who buy and sell contracts usually have no foreign exchange and only occasionally end up delivering or buying foreign exchange on the terms of the contracts. A diagram may help explain how a futures exchange operates.

Trading on the Floor of a Futures Exchange. Figure 11–1 lets us imagine that we are looking directly down onto the floor of a futures exchange. There are steps all around the edges of the trading floor with telephones and desks for traders' use. The circles represent traders. The floor is crowded with them, and they use hand signals as they make trades with each other. Assume that a runner takes a phone call from a client,

Figure 11–1
Diagram of a Futures Exchange Floor

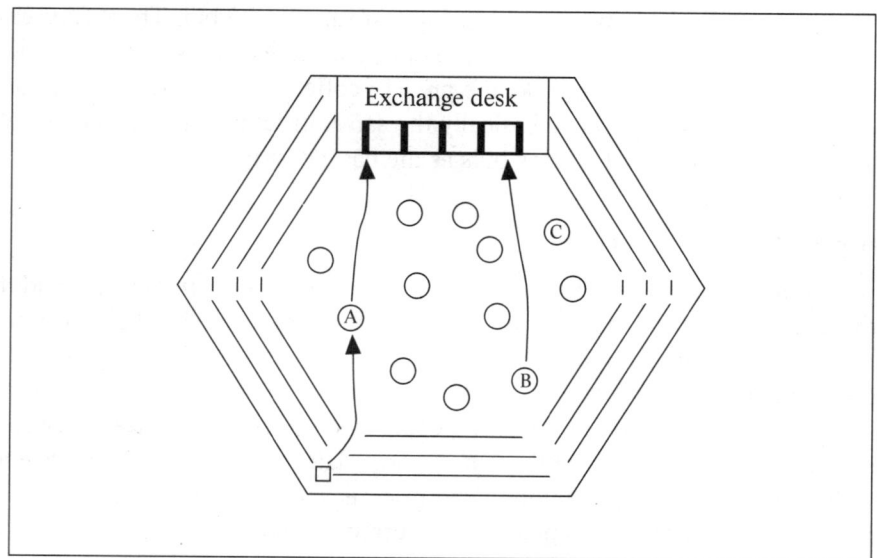

writes the order to buy ten futures contracts (each providing for the delivery of a $1 million Treasury bill on a certain future date), and then runs across the floor and hands the contract to trader A. The trader yells and signals around the floor showing that he wants to buy ten contracts at a certain price. The basic denomination of a T-bill is $10,000, so the price may be $9,850 for a discount of $150. This is 150 basis points, or the equivalent of $1.50 on $100.00 or 1.5 per cent. A basis point is $\frac{1}{100}$ of a per cent or 0.01. All traders know that the first two digits are 98 so they need only yell out basis points like 50 or 52.

The term "open interest," reported in the press, refers to the number of futures contracts that are outstanding on a particular day and on each specific contract being traded. It is a measure of trading volume.

Trader A gets a signal from trader B who agrees to sell ten contracts to A at the proposed price. At this point an interesting thing happens. Trader A makes note of the agreement to buy ten contracts and has the runner take it to the *desk of the exchange*. Trader B *also* makes a note of the sale of ten contracts and has a runner take it to the desk of the exchange. *Each of the traders has now made a contract, not with each other, but with the exchange.* The exchange's position is perfectly hedged. It holds offsetting buy and sell contracts in equal number. (The hedge is in some jeopardy, however, simply because in the hectic trading environment, the delivery to the exchange desk is sometimes sidetracked. The members of the exchange establish strict procedures to take when, at the end of the trading day, there is some disparity between numbers of contracts bought and sold. The exchange is, for the most part, a self-regulating institution.)

The buyer of the contracts, for whom trader A acted, may have been a corporation that sold equipment and would receive payment of $10 million in about two months. It knew that it wanted to invest the receipts in default-free securities for three months until it worked out additional uses for the funds, but it wanted to make sure that interest rates available on T-bills would not fall below those currently specified in the futures contracts. Thus, by buying the futures contracts, it could "lock in" the price of the bills and also the yield that it would receive from owning them.

About two months later the corporation would call trader A again. This time it would ask the trader to sell ten futures contracts. A runner would take the phone order to trader A on the floor and the signals would begin again. This time trader A is able to sell the contracts to trader C. There is no need for A to try to find B, the other trader in the original trade. Any trader will do. With the sale completed, both A and C send their notes to the exchange. With that action the corporation has cleared its position with the exchange, and it takes the money it receives from its equipment sale and goes directly to the market to buy T-bills. By the sale of T-bill contracts the corporation has offset the earlier purchase of contracts and there is no delivery or exchange of T-bills themselves by anyone. (Sometimes delivery does take place because not all of the buyers and sellers of contracts end up clearing their positions. Basically, it is not the best idea to take delivery. An acquaintance of the author forgot to clear a purchase of 3,000 dozen eggs and had to take delivery. The problem was that, before they could be sold to a supermarket chain, they had to be candled again, at considerable expense.)

Has the corporation won or lost from the initial purchase and later sale of the contracts? If the price of T-bills rose during the two months that the corporation held the bills, then it bought the contract for a low price early on, and sold it later for a higher price and made a profit. It won on the futures market. The futures price and spot price converge on the date the contract expires. So when the corporation bought the bills it wanted in the market it had to pay a higher price. Thus, what was won on the futures contract trades, was lost in the actual purchase of the bills. If the hedge were perfect, the gain and loss would exactly offset each other. The corporation hedged its position against interest rate risk.

What about trader B? For whom was he acting when he agreed to sell ten T-bill contracts? To expand this example assume that, in some other part of the country, there was a property development company that had a $10 million loan with a bank at 2 per cent above the prime rate of interest, which was 6 per cent at the time. The developer knows that in about two months the loan will need to be rolled over because it will take about five months before the property can be sold and the bank repaid. When the rollover takes place, the developer may end up having to pay higher rates than the then current 8 per cent. A higher borrowing rate would make a big dent in the developer's profit position because the development company is highly leveraged. Indeed, a 2 per cent rise might wipe out its profit altogether.

The financial manager of the development company knows that the prime rate of interest varies directly with the Treasury bill rate at about 3 percentage points above the T-bill rate. So, if that relation stays constant, it would be possible to enter the market for Treasury bill futures contracts and hedge against the interest rate risk in the form of a change in the prime rate of interest. If it sells ten contracts, and prices of the contracts fall, then it will make a profit two months later when it buys the contracts back. But the fall in price means higher interest rates, so when the development company rolls over its loan at the bank, it will have to pay the higher rates, and this will cause a loss. However, the loss should be nearly the same as the gain from the futures contract trades. So the developer can hedge using the futures exchange.

How convenient. The corporation just happens to need to buy some T-bills and the developer just happens to want to sell some at the very same time! In reality, the matching of hedgers on one side with hedgers on the other side, is very unlikely. That is why futures exchanges invite speculators to be traders on the exchange floor. Speculators are not risk averse. They tend to like risk. They tend to like gambling, too, and some of them dress like they just came from the race track. But they are willing to trade on the floor, and take positions of their own in contracts on either the buy or sell side. They help "make" the market when there is little demand for hedges on either side. It is said that they add "liquidity" to the futures markets.

Gambling and Speculation. Remember, please, that there is a big difference between speculators and gamblers. In gambling, the risky situation is created by the players. They structure a race or game or toss of coins or machine, or whatever, so that a risk, that did not exist before, is created. People who gamble do so because they get the "thrill" produced in everyone's brain by an endorphin that gives people under stress a feeling of exhilaration. Speculators on the floors of futures exchanges have the same experience, but they are providing a public service by enabling risk-averse people to hedge and avoid risk that exists naturally in the world of business and finance. If the speculators did not assume risk, businesses would have to. No one creates the risky system that speculators deal with. A person who likes to gamble, can achieve the same result by becoming a speculator and perform a public service at the same time.

Futures markets are socially productive because they may reduce risk for hedgers on both sides of the transaction, and if speculators are involved in a trade, the result is a reduction in risk for the hedger and an increase in utility to the "risk-preferring" speculator, so again both parties benefit. Speculators who might otherwise create nonsocially productive gambling situations have their energies directed to a productive form of risk-taking—taking risks that others wish to avoid.

Margins. The Exchanges require that investors in futures contracts put up margins to cover their positions. The amounts vary but are very small relative to the dollar value of the securities themselves. For example, a margin requirement for the $1 million T-bill may be $2,000. This is held by the exchange and if the contract's value declines, the exchange will ask the holder to add to the margin. The margin account is updated each day with the gains or losses registered at the end of the day's trading. This is to ensure that day by day funds will be available to absorb losses. Exchanges often permit margins to be held in the form of interest-earning securities such as T-bills or bank certificates of deposit. Thus, the risk-free rate of interest can usually be earned on a margin account balance.

The Basis

In our example, the developer had a successful hedge so long as the *basis—the difference between the T-bill rate and the prime rate*—remains unchanged. In the example, it was 3 per cent. If the prime rate rises during the two-month hedging period, but the T-bill rate does not, the basis increases. Then, the developer will have to pay a higher rate on his rollover loan with the bank, but will not realize any gain from his futures market trades to offset that loss. Thus, there will be no hedge. Of course, it is also possible that the basis might decrease. The T-bill rate could rise and give a profit on trades, while the prime rate remained the same, so the extended loan at the bank would not be more costly. Then, the developer will make profit from the hedge. The overall result is that the hedge is incomplete because the program of trades may result in either loss or profit for the developer.

The Reason for a Basis. Futures contracts are constructed to be uniform. They are not "tailored" to fit the needs of every investor. They specify:

1. the commodity or "product" or security being traded (the T-bill in this example)

2. a fixed dollar amount of face value per contract ($1 million in the case of T-bills)
3. fixed quarterly dates of expiration (March, June, September, and December)

There is not a large number of investors who deal strictly in this commodity on these terms. The contractual terms must be simple and uniform in order to permit an exchange to function on a sufficiently large scale. To get *perfect* hedges, the hedger must be dealing in $1 million T-bills and want one on exactly the expiration date. However, the market serves many hedgers whose needs may be similar, but not exactly the same as the contract specification. For example, some may wish to hedge $1.5 million. Should this person buy one contract or two? Also, in the example above, the developer hedged a prime loan with a T-bill contract. This was a case in which the product being hedged was not exactly the same as the product on which contracts are traded on the exchange. Others wish to hedge but may want to cancel the contract a month before the expiration date instead of just the day before. Others may wish to hedge only $900 thousand instead of a million. In other words, the contract is close enough to provide hedges, but not perfect hedges, in a variety of contexts. Thus, a *basis* should be identified for any differences between what the customer wants and the underlying contract. Analysis of the basis will lead to estimates of the likely success of a hedge.

Options on Futures Contracts. Many potential users of futures contracts may prefer to buy an *option* to buy a futures contract, or an option to sell one, rather than buying the futures contract itself. For example, a hedger may face a basis risk and an option enables him to hedge against it. The markets for options will be discussed in more detail later in this chapter.

Can You Believe It! A thrift institution in Kansas (The Franklin Savings Association of Ottawa, Kansas) began using interest rate hedging (called risk-arbitrage) as a device to protect itself from losses from unanticipated changes in interest rates. Then, in the hedging itself, the thrift made a loss. The Office of Thrift Supervision took over the thrift on February 15, 1990. Of course, in a hedge, the idea is to lock in a return, so a loss on the one hand will be offset with a gain on the other. "Nevermind," said the regulators, "You were engaging in *speculative* futures markets transactions that resulted in losses, so your management is bad and we are closing you down!" This really happened. After several years of legal maneuvering, an appeals court ruled that the regulators were within their right to set the standards they applied in making their ruling, *even though the managers were doing the right thing to protect the thrift's profit position!* So now, the Resolution Trust Corporation has brought suit against the former officers and directors of the thrift (see McCartney, 1993).

Do not believe everything you read in the papers about crooks being responsible for all the bank and thrift failures. There are a few crooks among bank and thrift managers, of course, as in any walk of life, but the *vast majority* of bank and thrift managers are thoughtful, responsible members of the community. Government regulations and regulators who do not understand risk management should take a measure of responsibility upon their own shoulders for the failure of so many deposit-taking institutions.

Taxes on Gains and Losses on Futures Contracts. The Internal Revenue Service (IRS) won a case in the Supreme Court in 1988. The Supreme Court held that Arkansas Best Corporation had to treat losses on hedging in the futures markets as capital losses, and could not deduct them as expenses against income. In October 1993 the IRS shifted its position because, in June, a tax court had ruled in favor of the Federal National Mortgage Association in a similar case involving hedging losses. The new rulings of the IRS include the requirement that the players identify the hedge being undertaken up front so that the nature of the offset in gain and loss can be identified (see Wartzman and Jereski, 1993).

Dates of Interest

Futures contracts are useful when dealing with commodities, whose prices fluctuate a great deal, or with foreign exchange. During the period of more or less fixed exchange rates, from 1944 into 1971–73, the U.S. followed the Bretton-Woods Agreement and kept the dollar convertible into gold at a fixed price of $35 per ounce when dealing with official institutions of other countries in settling payments balances. Most other countries, most of the time, then kept their exchange rates fixed in relation to the dollar. Because the prices were administered and held fixed, there was no need for futures markets for foreign exchange. There simply was too little variability in exchange rates, except for periodic devaluations by some countries. Those who favored abandoning gold and adopting freely fluctuating exchange rate systems were told that fluctuations in exchange rates would discourage trade because every business would face foreign exchange risk. Proponents of freely fluctuating exchange rate systems replied that futures markets would develop to enable business to hedge foreign exchange risk. They were right. In 1972 the Chicago Mercantile Exchange (CME) opened its International Monetary Market (IMM) and began trading futures contracts in several foreign currencies.

In 1975, the first interest rate futures contracts were offered by the Chicago Board of Trade and tied to Government National Mortgage Association (GNMA) mortgage backed securities. In 1976, the IMM began trading T-bill futures. Each year saw the addition of contracts based on other securities, and the opening of futures exchanges around the world. In 1982, the London International Financial Futures Exchange (LIFFE) opened. Australia, Singapore, Hong Kong, New Zealand, Japan, and other countries now have futures exchanges. There is even a fledgling futures exchange operation in China. It was in 1982 that a totally new type of financial futures contract was first traded, the stock market index futures contract.

Stock Market Index Futures Contracts

The Kansas City Board of Trade introduced a new type of futures contract in February

1982, and the concept has caught on all over the world. The contract is not based on a commodity such as wheat, deutschemarks, T-bills, and so forth, but on an index number that tracks a group of stock prices. The Kansas City Board chose the Value Line Stock Index, which measures average movements in the price of about 1,700 different stocks. Shortly thereafter, the Chicago Mercantile Exchange offered contracts on the Standard and Poor's 500 Index (S & P 500). There is also a New York Stock Exchange Composite Index, and the Chicago Board of Trade offers a Major Market Index.

Foreign Stock Index Futures Contracts. Stock exchanges around the world have indexes. In Japan there is the Nikkei Index on 225 stocks, and one in Osaka on 50 stocks. There is the Financial Times Stock Exchange 100 Index, and a Barclay's Share Price Index on 40 shares in New Zealand, and numerous others.

The Hang Seng Index Futures Contract in Hong Kong

The Hang Seng Bank is a large commercial bank in Hong Kong. Since November 24, 1969 its research department has published an index of the prices of stock traded on the Hong Kong Stock Exchange. It is a value weighted index of 33 stocks. Hang Seng stock index futures contracts are traded on the Hong Kong Futures Exchange (HKFE). The HKFE started in 1977 and traded commodities. It added the Stock Index futures contract in 1986. Let us use this index as an example of an index futures contract.

Contract Specifications

1. Contract Size: The Hang Seng Index (HSI) times HK$50. If the HSI is 7,000 then the contract would be worth HK$350,000 or about US$45,000.
2. Quotation: Index Points, that is 7,001 or 7,002, and so forth.
3. Minimum Fluctuation: One index point.
4. Maximum Fluctuation: 300 points per trading session above or below the last closing quotation and no limit on the spot month.
5. Trading Hours: 10:00–12:30 and 14:30–15:45.
6. Delivery Months: Spot month, the next calendar month and the next two calendar quarter months. (This differs from the usual March, June, September, and December months.)
7. Last Trading Day: The business day preceding the last business day of the month.
8. Settlement Day: The first business day after the last trading day.
9. Final Settlement Price: An average of quotations for the Hang Seng Index taken at five-minute intervals during the last trading day rounded down to the nearest whole number.
10. Settlement Method: Cash.
11. Margins: Initial margin HK$22,500, maintenance margin HK$18,000 (subject to change).

For example, on June 9, 1993, the Hang Seng Index rose from 7,260 by 79 points to end at 7,339 (rounded to nearest whole number).

For the sake of simplicity let us assume these figures also represented the settlement prices of a specific index futures contract, the contract value of HK$50 × 7,260 = HK$363,000, which increased to HK$50 × 7,339 = HK$366,950 for a gain of HK$3,950 for those who bought a contract and a loss of the same amount for those who had sold a contract. Gains and losses are settled every day. About $4,000 (a little over US$500) gain on a $22,500 margin would be a return for the day of about 18 per cent.

Arbitrage and Limits on Futures Contract Prices

Buying a futures contract is like speculating on changes in the index of stock prices. But the value of a futures contract has limits, which are set by stock dividends and the risk-free interest rate. The price of futures contracts will not rise to unlimited heights simply because arbitrage is possible between the futures markets and a portfolio of stocks that are the basis of the index. Consider the following example (see Terpstra, 1992).

Let:

I_t = $7,000, the Hang Seng Index price at time t
d = 0.02, the dividend yield on the index
r = 0.06, the risk-free interest rate
$F^e_{(r,T)}$ = the theoretical or equilibrium futures price at time t for a contract that expires T days in the future

Then,

$$F^e_{(r,T)} = I_t(1 + r - d)^{T/365}$$

This is the formula for the theoretical price. Putting the assumed values in the formula gives

$$F^e_{(r,T)} = \$7,000(1 + 0.06 - 0.02)^{365/365} \text{ when } T = 1 \text{ year or } 365 \text{ days}$$
$$= \$7,000(1.04)$$
$$= \$7,280, \text{ the theoretical futures contract price}$$

This price of $7,280 may not be the actual price of a futures contract. On the floor of the futures exchange the price moves up and down all during the day. Let us assume the price moves $100 above the theoretical price to $7,380. Traders would then say, "the contract is overpriced by $100." This overpriced contract would attract the attention of arbitrageurs. Their strategy would be as follows:

1. Borrow at 6 per cent, the risk-free rate (bankers can come very close to borrowing at such a low rate).
2. Use the borrowed funds to buy the index portfolio, that is, buy a weighted package of all the stocks used to make up the index and that are traded on the Stock Exchange of Hong Kong—the index portfolio. (This can be accomplished most easily by buying shares in a mutual fund that holds the index portfolio.

For example, such a fund was organized, and is managed by, Barclays de Zoete Wedd Investment Management Limited in Hong Kong on Taiwan's stock exchange. It is called The Taiwan Tracker Fund, Limited.)

3. Sell an equal dollar amount of futures contracts.

(These first three steps should be taken simultaneously.)

4. One year from today, sell the portfolio and pay off the loan with interest.

The arbitrageur, seeing that futures contracts were overpriced, sold a number of them. Will he or she make a profit? To learn the answer, consider what happens to a single contract at these prices. Assume that a year from today the market index is right at the level of $7,280, up from $7,000 as predicted. He or she will have dividends of 2 per cent or $140. On the shares of stock bought with borrowed funds, he or she will have capital gains of $280 because that is the rise in the index portfolio's value. Paying interest of 6 per cent on the purchase price of the stocks, at $7,000 means $(1 + 0.06)\$7,000 = \$7,420$, the amount that must be repaid. This uses up the returns in capital gains from the sale of stock and the dividends. But $100 is received on each futures contract that was overpriced! The arbitrageur should sell as many of these overpriced contracts as possible.

The arbitrageur is fully hedged because he or she has the contracts to sell outstanding contracts and owns an equal amount of the underlying collateral in the form of shares in the mutual fund. So, if the market index goes higher than that predicted by the theoretical price, the gain on market holdings will be larger, but he or she will earn less, or even lose if the index rises far enough, on the futures contracts. If the index does not rise to the theoretical value, he or she will not make capital gains on share holdings, but will make more on his futures contracts. So the arbitrageur is hedged against changes in the market index but has earnings from arbitrage activities because the futures contracts were overpriced.

The interest rate being charged on borrowed funds may also be thought of as the opportunity cost of investing in the stock index fund.

This example uses a one-year contract for simplicity. If the contract is for less than a year, the formula needs to be adjusted for the number of days left in the contract.

Transactions costs are ignored here, but must be estimated when money is on the line. The existence of such costs means that there is a narrow range of prices above the theoretical price that may exist before the arbitrage is profitable enough to cover all attendant fees and costs of carrying out the contracts. One of these involves the interest lost on the funds required to be deposited as a margin against the futures contract. On some exchanges in the U.S., the exchange permits margins to be maintained in interest-earning T-bills rather than in non-interest-earning cash. This factor would affect the cost of the futures transaction, too.

Under-priced Contracts. Remember that the theoretical price in the example was $7,420. Any price lower than this theoretical price would be under-priced. If the contract were under-priced on the market, instead of overpriced, the arbitrageur would want to take a set of opposite steps. Instead of selling overpriced contracts he or she would want to buy under-priced contracts. And, instead of buying shares in an index portfolio he or she would want to sell them. This, however, presents a problem. How do you sell these shares if you do not have them? It does not help to buy them and then sell them.

Short Sales Required. In the example of overpriced contracts, the arbitrageur borrowed money to buy the shares, and to do the opposite he would want to borrow shares and sell them to get the money. The only solution is to borrow the shares from someone and sell them—that is, sell them "short"—make "short-sales." A problem sometimes arises in this regard because stock exchanges often have rules that inhibit short-sales. Such rules interfere with the arbitrage mechanism that governs futures prices in the case of an under-priced contract. In Hong Kong short sales were restricted to those required in clearing and settlement activities until January 1994 when rules were changed to permit them. Short selling is permitted in Japan, and there are plans for it to be introduced in Singapore and Malaysia.

For brochures describing all types of futures contracts and other information the reader may contact, Public Affairs and Education, National Futures Association, 200 West Madison Street, Chicago, Illinois, U.S.A. 60606-3447, or phone 1-800-621-3570.

Options Markets

An option is a contract. Individuals often find it appropriate to use options. For example, you see a home that you think you would like to buy, but for some reason you are not in a position to make a final decision, perhaps you have not yet had the opportunity to see all the market has to offer. You might ask the seller to hold it for you at the asking price until you decide. That is, you ask the seller to give you an option to buy. If it is only a matter of a day or two, the seller may simply say, "o.k., I'll hold it for you," and according to law his word is a contract. In this case, where the time period is very short, the option if not worth very much, so the seller may give you the option as a gift. However, assume that you decide that you do want to buy the home, but it will take a month to make appropriate financing arrangements. Every home purchase requires such a wait in order to complete all of the required documentation. Why should the seller wait? What if someone else wants to buy the house in the interim and is even willing to pay more for it? This situation requires an earnest money agreement under which you give the seller $1,000, which the seller keeps if you decide not to buy the house. The seller has "written" a type of option and you have bought it for $1,000. This is an earnest money agreement and the $1,000 is applied to the purchase price of the house if everything goes as planned. In some cases involving long periods, the seller will ask to keep the $1,000 even if you do buy the house. This is like charging a fee for giving you something valuable. The date of expiration of the contract must be specified, and the price at which the potential "exercise" of the contract's terms must also be specified.

An option to buy a share of stock from someone is called a "call" option. An option to sell a share of stock to someone is called a "put" option. A person buys both types of options—you buy a call and you buy a put. The seller of the option is called the "writer" of the option. He or she writes the option—writes a call or writes a put. You buy an option and the writer sells you an option.

The writer of a call option sets a price, called a "strike price," and an expiration date. Under the terms of an *American option*, the buyer of the call option has the right to purchase the stock any time before the expiration of the contract. Under the terms of a *European option*, the buyer has the right to buy *on* the date of expiration only. The buyer of a call option pays a fee to the writer. In the case of put options, the contract terms are simply the mirror image of the terms for a call option.

A call option is used to hedge against the possibility of loss from buying a stock whose price might fall, but permitting a gain to occur if the price of the stock should rise above the strike price. Thus, assume you want to buy a stock and you think it will rise in price. But what if you guess wrong? To protect yourself from possible losses, you purchase an option to buy the stock instead. But you must pay something for the option—a fee to the writer. The fee is the cost of your hedge against a loss. You give up a certain loss in the form of a fee in exchange for a possible gain from an increase in price.

If you hold some shares of stock and think that their price is going to fall you may want to buy a put. It gives you the right to sell at a certain price. If the price does fall, you can sell to the writer at the higher strike price. Then, if you like, you may repurchase shares you want at the lower market price, make a profit, and still have your shares. However, if the price rises instead, you will have lost the fee you paid for the option, but you still hold your higher valued shares of stock. So, for a limited cost you have hedged your position against a potentially damaging decline in the price of the shares you hold while not eliminating the potential for gain.

Call and put options provide buyers with a hedge against either an upward or downward movement in price in exchange for a cost in the form of a fee. In contrast with using a futures contract, in which the hedge is against any change in price, options can be used to hedge a change in either one direction or the other.

Markets for Options. Options can be written and sold individually, or they can also be written with uniform terms so they can be traded on an exchange. Options on individual stocks are traded on the Chicago Board of Options Exchange, on the American Stock Exchange, the Philadelphia Stock Exchange, and the New York Stock Exchange. Then there are stock index options, options on stock index futures contracts, options on interest rate futures contracts, options on foreign exchange and on foreign exchange futures contracts. The Philadelphia Stock Exchange has specialized in currency options. Then, of course, there are London, Amsterdam, Singapore, and other exchanges, that permit 24-hour trading.

The Value of Options. Of the several factors that make an option valuable, three are important:

1. An option is more valuable, with a longer time to the date of expiration. Obviously, there remains a greater chance for prices to move in the longer time horizon.
2. The option is more valuable with a greater variation in expected price. Options are valuable when prices gyrate, but when they are stable no one needs an option.
3. The call option has more value with a *lower* exercise price set on the option by its writer.

Swap Markets

In Middle English, *swappen* meant "to strike" as in the process of striking hands in sealing a business deal. To swap is to hit hands together. High-fives, the swapping of teamplayers' hands high in the air, is a symbol of exuberance for having made a good play. A few hundred years ago, traders used the slap of hands to signal more than exuberance; it was a sign that a contract to trade assets with one another had been completed. If trade is freely arranged, then both parties to a contract are, presumably, satisfied. So there is a measure of exuberance in the signing of a contract with a swap of hands, too. Not until 1625 did the meaning of the term swap extend from the swapping of hands to also mean the exchange of goods.

If you were to travel to the west of Ireland today, and stop at a farm house to buy an Irish Wolfhound pup, after bartering—"50 pounds. I'll give you 40. No, 45. Done!"—there will be a swap of hands to seal the deal. Then, the seller, after receiving the 45 pounds, will give the buyer back a pound as "luck money"—a wish that the pup will turn out to be a good dog when it grows up.

Today, to swap one good for another is called barter. To swap money for a good is to buy it, or to purchase it. But when someone exchanges an asset, such as a bond, debt, or foreign exchange, for some other person's asset, it is still called a "swap," even today. However, today's bankers are not well-known for swapping hands, only for signing contracts with lots of fine print.

Typically, in today's swap markets, investors exchange, not assets themselves, but streams of interest payments that are derived from those assets (*interest rate swaps*). They also swap the currencies in which those streams or assets are denominated (*currency swaps*). Often, the swap agreement involves both different currencies and different interest payments.

A Fake-U.S. Dollar Swap Market in Hong Kong. In the mid-1980s banks in Hong Kong set up a program under which they offered to swap U.S. dollar deposits for Hong Kong dollar deposits, and then to repurchase those U.S. dollar deposits at a set price. They paid interest on the U.S. dollar deposits. They offered this U.S. currency swap because Hong Kong laws established the Hong Kong Association of Banks, a cartel that permits the banks to set interest rates that banks can pay depositors. There is no interest ceiling on U.S. dollar denominated deposits. So, to attract customers, the banks agreed to take Hong Kong dollar deposits, swap them for U.S. dollar deposits, and pay the higher interest on them. Then they swapped back to Hong Kong dollar deposits when the swap matures, and the customer has HK dollar deposits plus interest back. Of course, the customer never actually owns the U.S. dollar deposit. The bank never has a liability denominated in U.S. dollars. So people refer to the bank contract for deposits as fake U.S. dollars. The entire contract is simply a means for some banks to avoid the limitations set on them by the cartel; it is a means of violating the cartel agreement. But this is not a significant swap market by world standards. Besides, as noted in Chapter 3, the interest rate rules will be phased out by 1996, presumably.

An Exploding Swap Market

Starting in the early 1980s banks began to arrange parallel loans under which one business would swap an interest payment flow with another business. The two businesses were *counterparties*. The banks would broker the arrangement and charge fees. They would also arrange to handle the payments for both sides and act as the collector and payer of interest. It was a profitable business. Banks were soon joined by investment banks and insurance companies in providing what are now called swap services, and more complicated contracts evolved.

By 1992 the estimated dollar volume of swap contracts signed was a huge $4 trillion over the year.

In March 1992, the International Swap Dealers Association met in Paris. The dealers were told that financial institution regulators were worried about this very complex and sophisticated, but unregulated, market.

The "Plain Vanilla" Interest Rate Swap Contract. Basic swap contracts, whether in currencies or in interest rates, are not terribly complicated, and people in the world of finance call them "plain vanilla." The most popular swap agreement provides for one party to trade a fixed interest rate stream of interest payments for a floating rate stream of payments. It can be illustrated by a diagram. Let a jagged line represent a stream of payments subject to variation in size because it is based upon a floating interest rate that is adjusted quarterly. Let a straight line represent a stream of payments that is constant over time because it is under a fixed rate contract. Then Figure 11–2 indicates the balance sheet situation faced by firms A and B.

Figure 11–2
Streams of Fixed and Floating Interest Payments

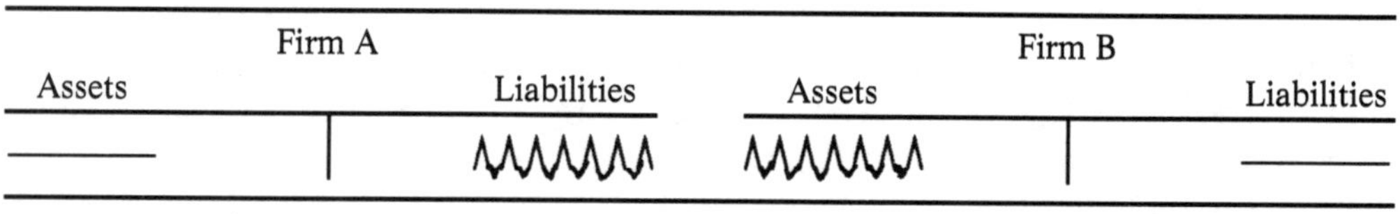

Firm A		Firm B	
Assets	Liabilities	Assets	Liabilities
———	⋀⋀⋀⋀⋀	⋀⋀⋀⋀⋀	———

As noted in the figure, Firm A realizes a steady stream of returns on its assets as indicated by the straight line. However, it has outstanding liabilities that require payments that rise and fall, period by period. Because of these varying interest payments, the firm faces "interest rate risk." These varying rates will be reflected in the firm's profit position. However, Firm B faces the opposite situation. It has a steady stream of interest payments to meet on its outstanding liabilities, but its interest earnings are variable. From period to period it may not have sufficient earnings to meet the required stream of payments on its liabilities.

Both firms can reduce risk by swapping streams of interest payments to be made on liabilities, and the result of this swap is shown in Figure 11–3.

Figure 11–3
After Swapping Fixed for Floating Interest Payments

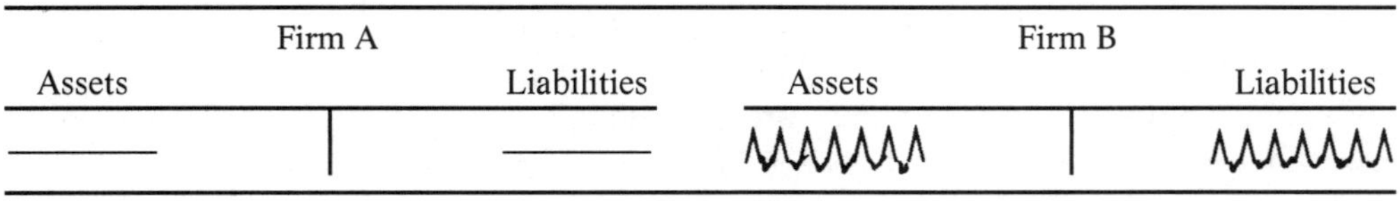

Firm A		Firm B	
Assets	Liabilities	Assets	Liabilities
———	———	MMMM	MMMM

Firm A now has matching fixed rate assets and liabilities, and Firm B has matching variable rate assets and liabilities. To arrive at this new position, Firm A now agrees to make B's interest payments on its floating rate loan, and B agrees to make A's interest payments on its fixed rate loan.

Notice that the two firms could have swapped streams of payments on assets instead of liabilities and arrived at the same result, except it would be Firm A that would have the variable receipts and payments (the jagged lines) while Firm B would end up with the steady streams of receipts and payments (the straight lines).

Also, notice that the liabilities themselves are not swapped—only the interest payments on those liabilities. The value of the liabilities is called the *notional principal* of the swap.

Brokers and Dealers

Brokers have a tendency to turn into dealers when given the opportunity. A broker has to go out and find a buyer for a seller. If buyers are hard to find, the broker is often tempted to become the buyer himself when the price is low. Bankers, too, can become impatient, and begin to deal in swaps. That is, instead of simply acting as brokers they stand ready to agree to provide a variable stream of interest payments in exchange for a fixed stream themselves. They become the counterparty to any firm that wants to swap. Instead of making arrangements with each other, Firms A and B would both go to a bank and make the same arrangements.

Dealers are taking risks. But if the banks, as dealers, carefully monitor their exposure by ensuring that they have roughly the same variable as fixed rate obligations, they reduce or hedge their own risk.

The Many Types of Swaps. The example above could have reflected many kinds of differences besides simply the fixed rate versus floating rate difference. There are zero coupon swaps in which a single payment to maturity is swapped for a stream of payments. There are basis swaps in which two floating rate liabilities are exchanged for each other because they are tied to two different indices. There are swaps that are based on amortized loans like mortgages, and special ones dealing with Collateralized Mortgage Obligations discussed in the previous chapter. There are swaptions, which are options on swaps. The list goes on and on.

The Beginnings. The first big swap arrangement that caught everyone's attention was one in which IBM and the World Bank exchanged currencies as counterparties in 1981. IBM provided the World Bank with German marks and Swiss Francs, and the World Bank provided IBM with dollars. IBM had a presence in Europe and could borrow in Swiss and German markets at low interest rates. The World Bank could borrow at lower rates in the U.S. than IBM. By essentially borrowing on behalf of each other, both could pay lower interest rates for the currencies they wanted than either would have to pay if they borrowed on their own. Salomon Brothers arranged the swap. The market expanded rapidly and moved to interest rate swaps the same year.

Prior Arrangements. Swaps are used not only to hedge but to lower interest costs. Many are arranged *before* any borrowing is done. For example, think of Firm A as one that can borrow in London at a very low floating rate. Firm B, on the other hand, may be a utility that can borrow at a very low fixed rate for a long period. Both firms want to borrow funds. They find that, when each arranges loans in its own best market and simultaneously arranges to swap interest payments on the loans, both can save on interest expenses. Essentially, they borrow on each other's behalf.

New Products in Futures and Options

The Chicago Board of Trade (CBOT) is the world's largest commodities exchange. In March 1993 it began auctions of sulfur dioxide emission allowances that have been allocated by the Environmental Protection Agency of the U.S. government. These "pollution rights" have now become a tradable commodity. Also, a Recycling Advisory Council, with members from government, business and the CBOT, is setting up a formal market for recyclable materials such as glass, paper, garbage (for reuse as feedstock), and some kinds of plastic. The new markets are expected to be operating in the 1990s.

These new kinds of tradable commodities represent the market's response to pollution, as government regulations are put into place. It is government's job to establish "pollution rights" as a form of "property rights" that make it possible for markets to be established. If government establishes the rules of the game and provides "ownership," then markets will form to handle the allocation problem.

Eventually, the CBOT intends to create and trade futures contracts in such things as pollution rights, recyclable glass and paper, and so forth—contracts that specify the amount and price of a commodity at a future date.

Financial Derivatives in the Asian Tigers

Financial markets are highly regulated by governments everywhere. However, in Singapore government policies have promoted active development of the financial sector of the economy. In Hong Kong financial markets are less regulated and have been permitted to develop rapidly. Thus, markets for financial derivatives are very active in Singapore and Hong Kong. This is much less true in the less liberalized markets of Korea and Taiwan, although current trends point to development of such markets in the near future. Australia has financial futures markets and so does New Zealand. In 1987 Japan permitted its banks and other businesses to engage in futures and options trading directly in the U.S. partly to allow Japanese firms to hedge positions in U.S. government debt.

Hong Kong

Futures contract trading in commodities, such as soy beans, sugar and gold was introduced in Hong Kong after the Commodities Trading Ordinance was passed in 1976 to permit such trading on the Hong Kong Commodity Exchange Limited. Its location in Hong Kong permitted traders to be active 24 hours a day using markets in London, New York, Hong Kong, London, and so forth.

The commodity exchange was reorganized in 1984 and renamed the Hong Kong Futures Exchange Limited. In 1986 the Hang Seng Index futures contract was introduced—the first financial futures contract in the territory. Examples from Hong Kong's financial futures market were used above. However, the financial futures market there has not developed extensively. The Hong Kong Futures Exchange (HKFE) opened trading contracts on the Hang Seng Index in 1986. When the Hong Kong exchange was started one of the contracts was supposed to be based on the three month Hong Kong Interbank Offered Rate (HIBOR) but the contract was not offered until 1989. One reason for the delay was that the October 1987 crash of stock markets around the world spelled disaster for the futures contract on the Hang Seng Index. The HIBOR contract is still on the books, but there is little or no trading in it.

Korea and Taiwan

Banking and foreign exchange activities have been tightly regulated by government authorities in both Korea and Taiwan. With the rapid development of their economies in the 1980s, they have initiated significant and far reaching liberalization of their financial sectors. However, the development of stock exchanges and expansion of financial services on the part of depository institutions has not yet led to the development of markets for futures contracts or other types of financial derivatives in these two Asian Tigers.

For example, since October 1987 a foreign exchange market has been operating in Korea, but the government permits Korean residents to trade futures and options only if the trading is conducted through foreign exchange banks. Independent trading is not permitted and contracts have to be based upon bona fide trade transactions.

Singapore

Singapore became an independent republic in 1965. In November 1978 the Gold Exchange of Singapore, a futures exchange, began operations. Rules of the exchange provided for settlement in U.S. dollars in order to attract international participation.

When today's freely fluctuating exchange rate system evolved in the early 1970s and currencies around the world started to fluctuate in value on foreign exchange markets, the Chicago Mercantile Exchange (CME) developed several currency futures contracts for trading and subsequently developed several interest rate futures contracts as well. The time difference between Singapore and Hong Kong is only one hour, and around the clock trading from Chicago, Singapore, London, Chicago, and so forth, is possible in Singapore as well as Hong Kong. It was recognized that this 24-hour trading of futures contracts in Singapore would be identical to those in Chicago, so futures positions taken on in Chicago could be closed in Singapore and/or later in the 24-hour period in London. Thus, Singapore used its Gold Exchange as a foundation for the development of what is now the Singapore International Monetary Exchange (SIMEX) established in December 1983.

In Singapore the term SIMEX is pronounced with a long "i" as in bilateral, not as a soft "i" as in the words Singapore and International.

Several currency futures contracts and interest rate contracts are traded on SIMEX on terms that reflect those on the CME. Options on futures contracts are also traded.

The Monetary Authority of Singapore has regulatory authority over SIMEX, but the emphasis is on self-regulation by the exchange itself. The exchange has been successful.

Summary

Securities that represent either ownership or claims against ownership of assets, such as stocks (equity) and bonds (debt) are traded in financial markets. Other types of trades in financial markets involve contracts to trade securities rather than the securities themselves. Such contracts are referred to as "financial derivatives." They include futures contracts, options contracts, and swap contracts under which an agreement is made to trade streams of interest payments instead of an agreement to trade securities themselves.

Derivatives are useful financial instruments because they provide investors with the opportunity to hedge and/or reduce various types of risk associated with holding assets.

Both futures and options markets have existed in many forms for many centuries. In contrast, some types of derivatives are very new, such as stock market index futures contracts and swaps.

Arbitrage is possible between the securities markets and the markets for derivatives.

The newly developing countries have established securities exchanges, but the development of markets for various financial derivatives is slow because there needs to be a large and well-functioning market in fundamental securities before derivative contracts can become functional.

Key Terms and Concepts

Risk vs. uncertainty
Spot, forward, and futures markets
Gambling vs. speculation
Basis
Chicago Mercantile Exchange (CME)
Chicago Board of Trade (CBOT)
Arbitrage
Swaps markets
Singapore Gold Exchange

Five types of risk
Types of financial futures markets
Margin
Financial derivatives
International Money Market (IMM)
Index futures
Options (American, European)
Plain vanilla
SIMEX

Discussion Questions and Exercises

1. Explain clearly what a "financial derivative" is in the context of a discussion of financial markets. Give clarifying examples.
2. Distinguish between "risk" and "uncertainty."
3. How do probability measures enable people to evaluate risk?
4. Distinguish between the four types of risk: default, capital, inflation, and interest rate.
5. What are the two broad classes of markets for financial futures contracts? Are they fundamentally different from, or fundamentally the same as, commodities futures markets?
6. Explain why there is almost no delivery of goods under contracts traded on futures exchanges.
7. What does "open interest" refer to when it is used in press reports about futures exchanges?
8. How can a business hedge a risk using a futures contract? Give an example.
9. Could a futures exchange operate without speculators? If so, why are they invited to trade?
10. Distinguish between gambling and speculation.
11. Explain the concept of "basis" as it applies to futures contracts.
12. Why did financial futures contracts become popular in the early 1970s?

13. Explain the purpose of having futures trading in a Stock Exchange Index. Give an example.
14. What is the "theoretical price" of a futures contract? Explain each of the terms in the equation. Calculate the theoretical price if $d = 0.04$, $r = 0.03$, and the index today is at 5,000. Explain what actions the arbitraguer would take if the actual futures contract price on the market were "overpriced" by $50. Discuss the problems related to borrowing stock and short selling in the case of an "under-priced" futures contract.
15. Explain the concept of an option contract and why such contracts are valuable.
16. Why was Hong Kong's bank contract for deposits called "fake U.S. dollars"?
17. Give an example of a plain vanilla fixed for a floating rate swap contract.
18. Who engaged in the first prominent swap agreement?
19. Would businesses in the Asian Tigers find financial derivatives useful? Why?

References

Abken, Peter A., "Beyond Plain Vanilla: A Taxonomy of Swaps," *Economic Review*, Federal Reserve Bank of Atlanta, March/April 1991, pp. 12–29.

———, "Globalization of Stock, Futures, and Options Markets," *Economic Review*, Federal Reserve Bank of Atlanta, July/August 1991, pp. 1–22.

Anderson, Torben Juul, and Hasan, Rikky, *Interest Rate Risk Management*, IRF Publishing, London, 1990.

Becketti, Sean, "Are Derivatives Too Risky for Banks," *Economic Review*, Federal Reserve Bank of Kansas City, 3rd Quarter, 1993, pp. 27–42.

Becketti, Sean, and Roberts, Dan J., "Will Increased Regulation of Stock Index Futures Reduce Stock Market Volatility?" *Economic Review*, Federal Reserve Bank of Kansas City, November/December 1990, pp. 33–46.

Chan, David Y. K., "The Gold and Commodity Markets," in Y. K. Ho, R. H. Scott, and K. A. Wong, eds., *The Hong Kong Financial System*, Oxford University Press, Hong Kong, 1991, pp. 252–70.

Cheung, Yin-Wong, and Ng, Lilian K., "The Dynamics of S&P 500 Index and S&P 500 Futures Intraday Price Volatilities," *Review of Futures Markets*, Chicago Board of Trade, Vol. 9, No. 2, 1990, pp. 458–97.

Damodaran, Aswath, "Index Futures and Stock Market Volatility," *Review of Futures Markets*, Chicago Board of Trade, Vol. 9, No. 2, 1990, pp. 442–56.

GAO Report to Congressional Requesters, *Financial Derivatives: Actions Needed to Protect the Financial System*, U.S. General Accounting Office, May 1994.

Gilbert, R. Alton, "Implications of Netting Arrangements for Bank Risk in Foreign Exchange Transactions," *Review*, Federal Reserve Bank of St. Louis, January/February 1992, pp. 3–16.

Ip, Y. K., and Ng, Linda F., "Term Structure of Bases and Basis Risk of Stock Index Futures in Australia," in *Proceedings of the Second International Conference on*

Asian-Pacific Financial Markets, City Polytechnic of Hong Kong, September 12–14, 1991, pp. 600–608.

Knight, Frank H., *Risk, Uncertainty, and Profit*, Houghton Mifflin, New York, 1921.

Kwag, Dae-Hwan, "Foreign Exchange Market in Korea," *Monthly Review*, Korea Exchange Bank, September 1989, pp. 3–13.

Marshall, John F., and Kapner, K. R., *The Swaps Market*, 2nd Edition, Kolb Publishing, Miami, FL, 1993.

Mayer, Martin, *Markets: Who Plays... Who Risks... Who Gains... Who Loses...*, 1st Edition, W. W. Norton, New York, 1988.

McCartney, Scott, *Wall Street Journal,* February 18, 1993.

Morris, Charles S., "Managing Interest Rate Risk with Interest Rate Futures," *Economic Review*, Federal Reserve Bank of Kansas City, March 1989, pp. 3–20.

Niederhoffer, Victor, "The Speculator as Hero," *Wall Street Journal*, February 10, 1989.

Scarlata, Jodi G., "Institutional Developments in the Globalization of Securities and Futures Markets," *Review*, Federal Reserve Bank of St. Louis, January/February 1992, pp. 17–30.

Simmons, Katerina, "Interest Rate Structure and the Credit Risk of Swaps," *New England Economic Review*, Federal Reserve Bank of Boston, July/August, 1993, pp. 23–34.

Singapore, Monetary Authority of, *The Financial Structure of Singapore*, 1989.

Terpstra, Robert H., "The Stock Index Futures Market," in Robert Haney Scott, ed., *Manual of the Securities Industry*, Stock Exchange of Hong Kong, 1992, pp. 123–42.

Wartzman, Rick, and Jereski, Laura, *Wall Street Journal*, October 19, 1993.

Wong, Gordon W., "The Hong Kong Financial Futures Markets," in Y. K. Ho, R. H. Scott, and K. A. Wong, eds., *The Hong Kong Financial System*, Oxford University Press, Hong Kong, 1991, pp. 235–51.

CHAPTER 12

Determining the General Level of Interest Rates

IN PREVIOUS CHAPTERS the focus of discussion has been on the institutions and markets of the world of finance. In this, and the following two chapters, the focus shifts to the theoretical models that are used to analyze and interpret how interest rates are determined. Then, on this foundation of institutional detail and theoretical understanding, the remaining chapters are devoted to discussions of policy. It is important to understand both institutions and theory if one is to make good policy.

The focus of this chapter is on the forces that tend to make the general level of interest rates rise and fall. There are literally thousands upon thousands of different explicit and implicit interest rates at work in modern economies. These tend to be tied together. For example, if government bond yields fall, the interest costs attached to long-term mortgages will typically fall, too. Sometimes, of course, such rates do move in different directions, but it is useful to construct models to interpret the impact of macroeconomic forces on the *general level* of interest rates while taking care to remember that movements in individual interest rates sometimes do not follow the general trend.

For the most part, macroeconomic forces and variables are interdependently determined with the level of interest rates. Microeconomic factors tend to influence the interest return on specific securities. Of course, macro and micro factors are interrelated, too, and both are important to the financial analyst.

This chapter begins with a brief introduction to the present value formula, moves on to discuss the classical and neoclassical views of interest rate determination, and interprets changes in interest levels using the supply and demand for funds model. Finally, there is an analysis of the influence of inflation expectations on interest rate levels.

Introduction to the Present Value of Bonds and Stocks

Readers who have worked through a text on principles of finance will find the following section to be a brief review. Some readers, however, may have had only a limited background in finance, and they may find the equations difficult to follow. The purpose of including this brief introduction is to focus attention on the meaning of the theory to follow, namely the theory of interest rate determination.

Interest rates are prices of a special type—they are prices that express the rate of exchange of one item for itself at a different time. Usually, the item of concern is a monetary unit such as the dollar. Thus, in order to induce you to lend me a dollar today, to keep for a year, I may have to provide you with $1.10 a year from today. Today's dollar is exchanged for a dollar and 10 cents in a year's time. The price of "the use of a dollar for a year" is 10 cents. It is usually expressed as 10 cents per annum—an annual rate of 10 per cent.

As illustrated in Chapter 1, prices of securities can be analyzed using graphs of supply and demand for quantities of securities. Graphs of the supply and demand for funds provide identical information, except that they show the determination of interest rates on securities rather than prices of securities. The interested reader may want to review the appropriate section in Chapter 1 before proceeding.

Definitions and Relations of Yields and Prices

Interest is a term that is often used in a very special way. Interest on a bond may be 10 per cent as reflected in the $10 annual coupon itself when the par value of the bond is $100. However, this "coupon interest" is different from the *yield* on the bond whenever the price is not the same as the par value. In other words, the term *yield* is the most generic term, but, in its general sense, interest is identical to yield and the two terms may be used interchangeably along with the terms *rate of return* and *discount rate*—all refer to interest rates.

The Inverse Relation between Bond Prices and Yields. Bond prices and bond yields vary inversely. If a bond's market price rises, its yield declines; if the price declines, its yield rises. The formula for a *perpetuity*—also called a perpetual bond or consol, the contract for which equal coupon payments (a return of R dollars) need to be made annually forever—is:

$$PV = \frac{R}{i} \qquad i = \frac{R}{PV}$$

In this formula, *PV* stands for present value, or the dollar price of the bond, and *i* stands for interest rate or yield.

The inverse relation between *PV* and *i* is obvious in the formula. The formula is definitional. The interest rate, or yield, is defined to be *R/PV*. If the annual return is $30 and the price or *PV* of the bond is $1,000, the bond's yield is 0.03 or 3 per cent. If the price of the bond fell to $500, the yield would rise to 6 per cent. When the price is cut in half, the yield doubles. If the price doubled the yield would be cut in half, and so forth.

The formula for a perpetuity, and infinite stream of income over time, may be derived from the mathematics of infinite series, however, it is readily understood intuitively—if you pay $1,000 and get $30 each year forever, then your annual return is, indeed, $30 or 3 per cent. The term *consol* is derived from the word consolidated. It refers to the consolidation of a number of outstanding British securities after World War I into perpetual bonds. As should be expected, they are still outstanding!

Bond Formulas

Most bonds are not perpetuities. Instead, they provide for a stream of payments followed by a return of principal on the date of maturity. The stream of cash flows from the coupons on the bond can be considered as an annuity. To this set of payments is added the cash flow that represents the return of principal. The formula for the present value of a bond of *n* periods to maturity with coupons payable at the end of each period is:

$$PV = \frac{R_1}{(1 + i)} + \frac{R_2}{(1 + i)^2} + \dots + \frac{R_n}{(1 + i)^n} + \frac{F}{(1 + i)^n}$$

Consider a two-year bond with *R* = $30 and face value of $1,000. Then:

$$\$1,000 = \frac{\$30}{(1 + 0.03)} + \frac{\$30}{(1 + \$30)^2} + \frac{\$1,000}{(1 + 0.03)^2}$$

Now assume that an increase in the demand for loans occurs, so the comparable bonds yield 4 per cent. What price would one be willing to pay for this bond to realize a 4 per cent return? That is, what would *PV* be if *i* were 4 per cent?

$$PV = \frac{\$30}{(1.04)} + \frac{\$30}{(1.04)^2} + \frac{\$1,000}{(1.04)^2}$$
$$= \$28.85 + \$27.74 + \$924.56 = \$981.15$$

When interest is paid semiannually, as in the case of most corporate and government bonds, the $30 payment would be halved to two $15 payments each year, and the interest rate would also be cut in half to 0.015 or 1.5 per cent. But the number of payments would be doubled, so that *n* in the equation would be replaced by 2*n* or 4 payments over the two years plus the return of principal as the final payment. If payments were to be quarterly, coupons and rates would be divided by four, and *n* would be multiplied by four, and so forth. If payments were made daily, the divisor and multiplier would be 365.

Bond tables provide information to users. Also business-oriented hand calculators will do the calculations. It is important to recognize that in the bond formula there are five variables: PV, i, R, n, and F, the face value to be repaid at maturity. There are three steps to the calculation of the present value of a bond. First, calculate the present value of an annuity using PV, i, R, and n, where R represents a fixed payment each period for n periods. On a hand calculator enter any three of the four variables and it will give you the fourth. Next calculate the present value of the future payment F using PV, i, F, and n. Finally, add the two present values together.

Each of the five variables plays a role in interpreting the meaning of the special term "interest."

Stock Formulas

In principle, the yield on shares of stock is the same thing as the yield on bonds, or the yield on a piece of capital equipment, or any other yield. In the final analysis, yields are determined by what the investor pays for an asset or a security and what cash inflows occur over time as a result of the investment. It is only because of legal arrangements about ownership, in the case of stock, and because of contracts, in the case of debt, that different markets have developed for the two classes of securities.

A share of stock has no maturity date. And a corporation is treated as if it were a person with no limit on life expectation. Thus, a share of stock is very much like a perpetuity. The principal difference between them is that debt has fixed coupons that specify cash flows to the owner in the contractual document. Stock, on the other hand, has no fixed yield.

If cash flows take the form of dividends, these dividends may be similar to the returns labeled R in the bond formula above. Then the present value of shares of stock is the same as the perpetuity, $PV = R/i$, where R is expected to be the annual dividend every year from here on.

However, the dividend may be changed by the corporation's board of directors. Thus, holding a share is more risky than holding a bond. Dividends are not set by contract, but depend upon the profitability of the corporation.

Furthermore, prices of stock change while it is being held, and most investors have a time horizon called a *holding period*. During a perceived holding period, the company may declare some dividends. Also, corporations do a great deal of saving that is recorded as *retained earnings*. These are funds that the corporation uses for investment on behalf of the shareholders. If the investments financed from retained earnings are profitable then the price of the stock will rise because profitable investments mean that larger cash flows are expected in the future. The formula for the present value of a share, therefore, looks very much like that for a bond. The annual payment (or semiannual payment), R, for the bond is replaced by an annual dividend (or quarterly dividend), if any. The return of principal at maturity for a bond is replaced by the expected price of the stock at the end of the holding period at which time the owner plans to sell the stock. Returns to shareholders, therefore, take the form of dividends plus any increment in the price of shares in the market—dividends and capital gains. Projections of these cash flows are fundamental determinants of the yield on stock and the present value of stock.

Many other factors besides those fundamental ones already mentioned must be considered by security analysts. Among those are risk, taxes, management, and so forth. The list is almost endless. Explicit consideration of risk as a factor in the valuation of a security is the principal purpose of the famous Capital Asset Pricing Model. Readers are referred to books on investments for examination of these issues in greater depth.

Classical and Neoclassical Theories of Interest Rates

Classical Theory

Adam Smith, often called the Father of Economics because of his 1776 book, *An Inquiry into the Nature and Causes of the Wealth of Nations*, addresses the relation between saving (parsimony), investment (an increase in capital), and interest rates in the following paragraph:

> Capitals are increased by parsimony, and diminished by prodigality and misconduct. Whatever a person saves from his revenue he adds to his capital, and either employs it himself in maintaining an additional number of productive hands, or enables some other person to do so, by lending it to him for interest, that is, for a share of the profits. As the capital of an individual can be increased only by what he saves from his annual revenue or his annual gains, so the capital of a society, which is the same with that of all the individuals who compose it, can be increased only in the same manner (Smith, 1937: 321).

For a society to accumulate real wealth and capital, capital goods must be produced. Resources devoted to production of capital goods cannot be devoted to production of consumers' goods at the same time. Thus, people must save if society's stock of wealth is to expand. Saving is turned into investment either directly or through lending.

Notice that Adam Smith made no distinction between interest and dividends when he wrote "... by lending it to him for interest, that is, for a share of the profits." Lending can be for interest (debt) or for a share of the profits (dividends or capital gains). Inasmuch as Smith saw no distinction between the two types of financing of an investment, he would have had little concern with the issues raised by Islam regarding the ethics of charging fixed interest as opposed to the sharing of profit.

Along with thrift, there must be productivity. Eugen von Böhm-Bawerk stressed the concept of the "period of production" and "roundaboutness" in the production process in his 1922 book, *Capital and Interest*. As an example, imagine living in the wilderness as Henry Thoreau once lived near Walden Pond. One could walk to the lake for water whenever it was needed. Or one could devote the time and effort to construct a bucket and thus reduce the number of trips required to collect water. Or one could spend even greater time and effort and construct a trough from a spring, running it past the cabin door so that water would be readily available whenever it was desired. Thus, water for consumption can be produced directly or in a roundabout way. Roundaboutness requires investment of time and effort. The productivity of the investment is reflected in greater production and in higher living standards. The productivity of capital gives rise to business demand for it.

Supply and demand functions had not been recognized when Smith wrote. They were first published in 1890 in Alfred Marshall's *Principles of Economics*. But the supply and demand for funds framework, showing that the market interest rate is determined by the supply of saving and the demand for investment (capital) fits well with Smith's prescription for the wealth of nations.

Saving rates in the Asian Tigers are very high—an estimated 20–40 per cent of income by some measures—far exceeding the estimated rate of 6–16 per cent in other countries by some measures. High economic growth rates in countries with high saving rates reflect well on Adam Smith's teachings.

Neoclassical Theory

Neoclassical theory differs from classical theory only in that it includes significant amendments developed by later economists. Thus, today the theory of consumers' choice includes choice between saving today and consuming more in the future. So now the theory of saving behavior is more complete.

The theory of investment and productivity has been improved as well.

Also, in neoclassical theory, the role of money in determining interest rates has been developed extensively. Additional funds for investment may be made available by increasing the money supply. However, too much money will cause inflation, and interest rates will rise. These concerns are discussed below.

Today's theory of saving recognizes that, along with interest rates, income is also an important variable in the determination of saving.

The Loanable Funds Approach

The loanable funds approach simply uses the supply and demand for funds as the basis of forecasting and analyzing changes in interest rates. As presented here it is neoclassical in that it describes business investment demand, consumer choice, changes in the money supply and government spending. It is widely used by financial analysts.

In Figure 12–1 the general level of interest rates is measured on the vertical axis while the volume of loanable funds flows is measured on the horizontal axis. The reader may recall from Chapter 1 that the supply of funds curve represents willingness to lend, principally by people who have savings to lend. The curve slopes upward indicating that higher interest rates induce savers to provide a larger volume of savings into the market.

The demand for funds curve represents borrowing. The interest rate, to borrowers, represents the cost of borrowing. The higher the cost, the less funds borrowers will want, and the lower the cost, the greater the quantity of funds borrowers will want. So the demand for funds curve slopes downward.

Figure 12–1
The Loanable Funds Theory of Interest

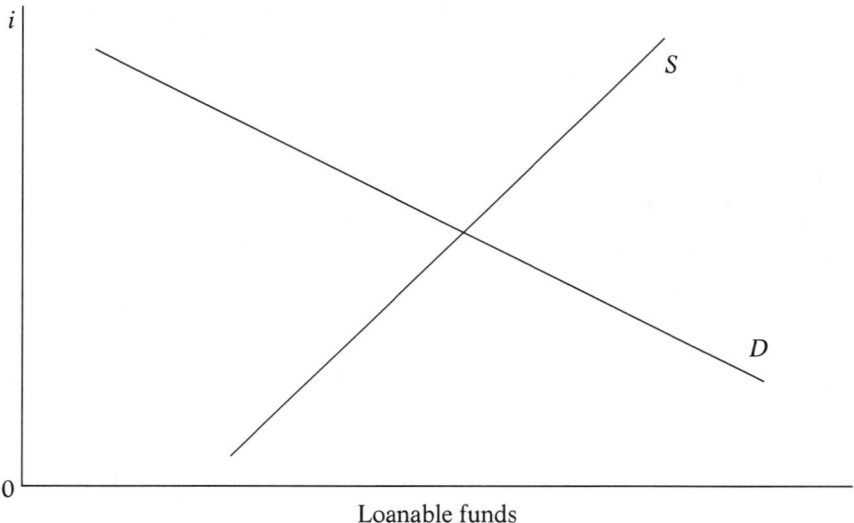

Borrowers and lenders meet in the marketplace to obtain and supply funds. Competition among borrowers for the scarce supply of funds will lead to a market-determined interest rate that represents both the cost of funds to borrowers and the return on saving to lenders. The market clears when the quantity of lending equals the quantity of borrowing, and scarce saving is allocated to borrowers with the greatest demand for funds.

In the following paragraphs the supply and demand curves will be separated into sub-categories, three each, for the purpose of illustrating the use of this analytical framework.

Three Sub-categories of the Supply of Funds

In Figure 12–2 there is a breakdown of the supply of funds curve into two of its three parts.

The first part, on the left side, shows a vertical supply of funds that arises from central bank action that increases the money supply. Central banks provide reserves to banks, which then have an enlarged capacity to make more loans—that is, to provide more funds to borrowers. So the change in the supply of money outstanding, ΔM, adds to the supply of funds. It is assumed that changes in the supply of money are independent of the rate of interest. This makes the curve a vertical line. In more elaborate models that include an analysis of bank behavior, the curve may slope slightly upward to the right.

The second part shows the supply of saving and how it responds to interest rates. The curve, labeled S, slopes upward to the right and is believed to become steeper as interest

Figure 12–2
Components of Supply

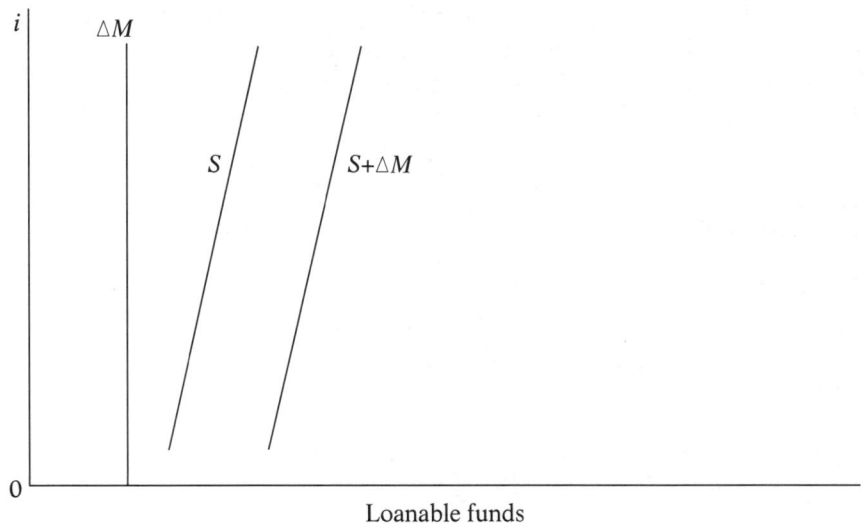

rates rise to high levels. It may bend backward at very high levels for reasons explained in Chapter 13.

By adding the two curves together in a horizontal direction the third line in the graph shows the sum of the two components of the supply of funds.

In Figure 12–3, the third component of the supply of funds curve is introduced. It shows the impact of hoarding and dishoarding behavior on the part of money holders. This particular upward sloping curve is a little more complicated than the others. Here, the curve moves up and to the right to indicate that higher interest rates will induce some holders of money to *dishoard* their money stocks. They do this by using their idle money to purchase securities. By dishoarding they supply funds to borrowers. However, when interest rates fall, many people will find that they would rather keep funds in idle money balances than bother to invest them. So they reduce the supply of funds to borrowers when they *hoard* money. Thus, from any point on this curve, a movement up to the right represents more dishoarding and an increase in the quantity of funds supplied, while a movement back down the curve to the left represents less dishoarding or more hoarding and a decrease in the quantity of funds supplied. So the curve is labeled on both ends—D on the upper end standing for dishoarding, and H on the lower end standing for hoarding.

The overall market supply of funds is, therefore, made up of three categories: the supply of saving function, the increment in the money supply, and dishoarding/hoarding as a function of interest rates.

In combining the three categories to arrive at a market supply of funds curve, the saving function and the change in money are simply added together horizontally, as shown in Figure 12–3. Then, at some level of interest rates such as i_0, there is neither any hoarding nor dishoarding of funds. However, at the higher level i_1 there is dishoarding that adds the interval a–b to the supply of funds so the supply curve, inclusive of dishoarding, slopes up to the right as shown. At rates below i_0 there is hoarding, such as indicated by the interval c–d, and the supply curve continues down to the left as shown. Thus, the market supply curve is the curve labeled $S + \Delta M - H$ in that range of the curve.

Figure 12–3
Components of Supply

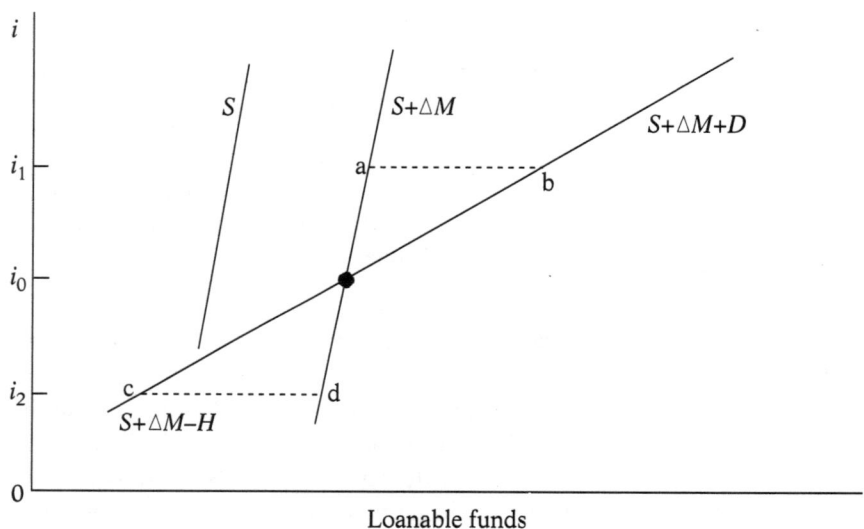

Loanable funds

Three Sub-categories of the Demand for Funds

Having broken the supply of funds into three sub-categories we now shift to the demand for funds and break it into three sub-categories as well. There is *no* direct connection between the supply sub-categories and demand sub-categories. It just happens that it is convenient to have three in each case.

The first component is the demand for funds on the part of the federal government. The federal government borrows a huge amount of funds each year. It borrows these to meet the short-fall of tax revenues over government spending—the federal budget deficit. Indeed, the volume of borrowing is a good measure of the deficit. The government's demand for funds is represented by a vertical line that indicates its borrowing is independent of interest rate levels—it must borrow to meet its obligations whatever the interest rate.

A second component of a demand for funds is a downward sloping demand for funds on the part of business and consumers—funds used to purchase equipment for investment purposes, or consumer durables for household use. When this component of demand is added to the deficit, the curve is labeled $G + B$, and appears in Figure 12–4. At lower interest rate levels, businesses will want to borrow more. So will consumers. This gives the curve its negative slope in accord with the law of demand—people will buy more the lower the price. Here, the price is the cost of funds as measured by the level of interest rates.

A third component of the demand for funds in the U.S. is the demand exercised by state and local governments. These governments borrow great amounts of funds for many different projects. They do not call their borrowing "deficits," a name with bad connotations, instead they call it "debt financing," which sounds perfectly reasonable. If the federal government would adopt a capital budget along with an operating budget, instead of simply running everything on an operating budget, it, too, could classify a large portion of its spending under the heading of "debt financing."

The demand for funds on the part of state and local governments has a flat portion near the interest rate level of 8 per cent as indicated in the figure by the curve labeled $G + B + SG$. The reason for this flat portion is that many states have constitutions that limit the interest rate that government officials may commit their communities to pay on debt. For example, the limit in the State of Washington is 8 per cent. In the 1970s the people of King County voted to sell $50 million in bonds and to use the funds to purchase the development rights to farms and other "green areas" in the county for the purpose of retaining some rural atmosphere and preventing everyplace from being paved over into shopping centers. However, as the program was being put into place, interest rates on municipal bonds rose above the 8 per cent constitutional ceiling. Thus, the bonds were not sold until years later. This borrowing was canceled and the demand on the part of state and local governments for funds was curtailed. The flat portion of the curve is placed there to represent this institutional phenomenon.

Figure 12–4
Components of Demand

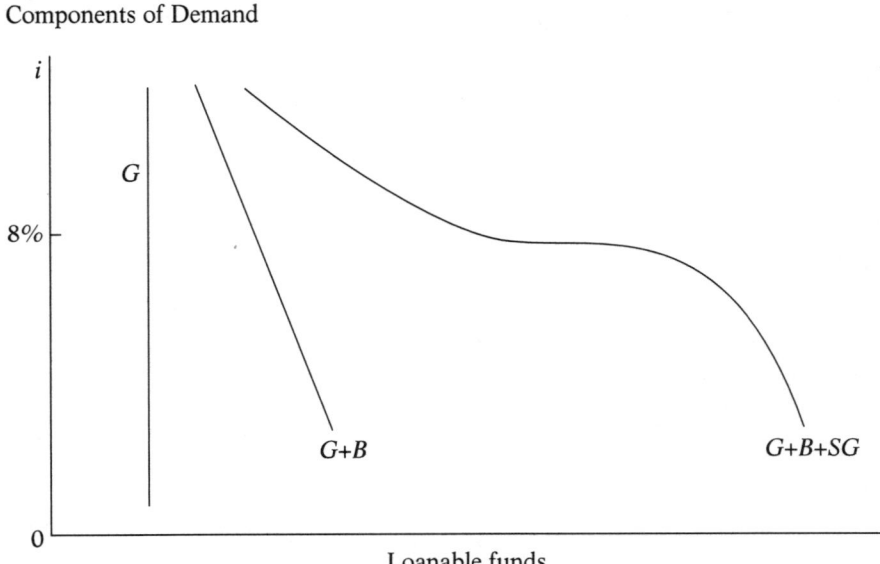

Adding the three components of the demand for funds horizontally gives the market demand for funds curve labeled $G + B + SG$. The market supply curve and the market demand curve, including all components, are shown in Figure 12–5. Their intersection point indicates the level of market determined interest rates in this supply and demand for funds model.

Market Demand and Supply for Funds. Readers often get the mistaken idea that the purpose of demand and supply curves is to determine the price (interest rate) and quantity (of funds) that the curves describe. However, demand and supply curves are seldom, if ever, used for this purpose. They are used as a framework *to predict how forces that shift the curves will affect the price and the quantity*. They are used for this purpose repeatedly, and usually subconsciously, by nearly everyone. So they are very useful as a guide in everyday life.

Examples can be constructed using every one of the six sub-categories described above. The reader may imagine shifts of the curves in the examples.

Shifts in the Demand for Funds. The federal government's demand for funds is directly related to the budget deficit—a larger deficit implies that the government demand will shift to the right. This means the demand curve in Figure 12–5 would shift to the right. A new equilibrium interest rate would be determined by the intersection of supply and demand at a higher level of market interest rates. The quantity of funds supplied would also increase to meet the new level of demand.

If the outlook is for a reduction in government borrowing, the demand curve would shift to the left and interest rates will be expected to fall. Thus, financial analysts

Figure 12–5
Components of the Supply and Demand for Funds

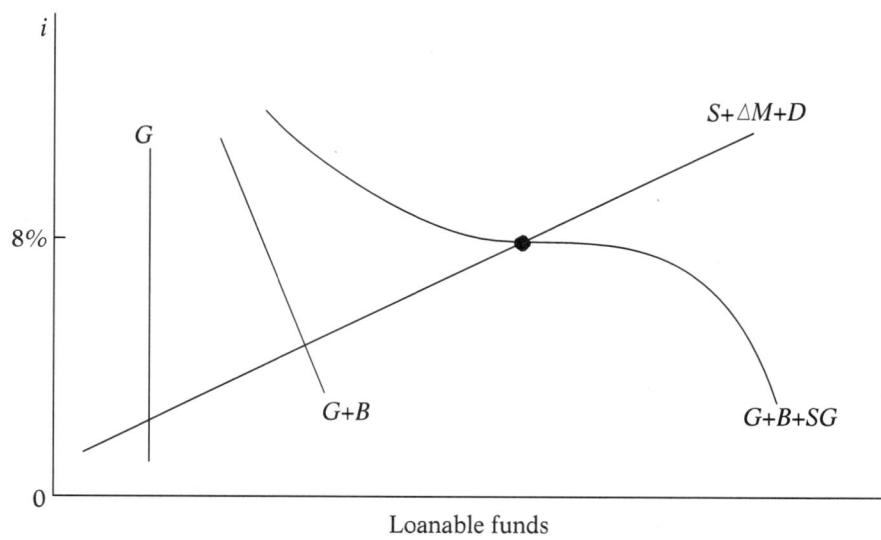

respond to federal budget projections. When Congress passes a tax increase to reduce the deficit, the prices of securities generally rise in anticipation of lower interest rates because of the reduced demand for funds on behalf of government.

If unemployment rises, business and consumer demand for funds should fall, that is, the demand curve should shift to the left. Interest rates should fall.

If state tax revenues fall off, the demand for funds curve might shift to the right as states are required to debt finance some projects that otherwise would have been paid for out of revenues.

When one looks at all of the data that are reported on a variety of factors that affect interest rates, and the announcements related to macroeconomic conditions, one can attempt to predict how interest rates will change as a result of changes in those conditions. The model of supply and demand is used implicitly every day.

Shifts in the Supply of Funds. Factors that cause shifts in the supply curve also give rise to predictions of changes in interest rates. For example, if the Federal Reserve increases the money supply, the supply curve will shift to the right and interest rates will fall. Analysts watch very closely every move the Fed makes in order to be sure that they are not surprised by some monetary policy change.

Tax laws may affect saving rates. Neither interest income nor dividend income, nor capital gain income is taxed in Hong Kong. If these changes in taxes were introduced in the U.S., there would be a large shift to the right in the supply of saving curve, and in the market supply of funds curve. Interest rates would fall, saving rates would increase, investment in modern equipment would rise, and so forth.

A Few Words of Caution

Here is a brief list of things to be wary of when using forecasted shifts in supply and demand curves for funds to predict changes in interest rates or funds flows as in the examples above.

1. More than one shift is likely to occur. For example, a forecast of an increase in the money supply will imply a decline in interest rates as the supply of funds curves shifts rightward, but a simultaneous forecast of an increase in the federal deficit and an increase in the demand for funds by government will imply an increase in interest rates. Then, to predict interest rate changes, one needs to predict the *net change* resulting from the two opposing pressures on the level of interest rates. Indeed, at any time there may be several forces at work and that would require netting out all of them. That is why, in considering the outlook for changes in interest rates, there are many factors to be considered simultaneously.

2. Predictions of interest rate changes based on supply and demand for funds curves should be considered as *a first approximation*. The reason is that supply and demand show only *partial equilibrium*. A full and complete model

shows *general equilibrium*. Supply and demand curves are "partial" because they do not, by themselves, allow for "feedback" effects of changes in variables. For example, if an increase in the money supply results in the predicted decrease in interest rates, lower rates will stimulate investment spending and generate income that will lead to greater saving and shift the supply of funds to the right again so that interest rates will fall even further than first predicted. Also, the increased income may lead to greater tax collections and a reduced federal deficit and a leftward shift in the demand for funds so that interest rates would fall even more. However, if the initial increase in money occurs when the economy is already operating at capacity, the stimulus to investment, income, saving, tax collections, and so forth, may result in inflation, which may push interest rates back up. These feedback effects on interest rates may take some time to come about. In other words, predictions using supply and demand should be supplemented with further analysis involving scenarios of events that might be expected to follow over time.

3. A few economists have different views about the interpretation of the supply and demand for funds as presented above. For example, is it possible that an increase in the federal deficit that pushes the demand curve to the right will lead consumers to believe that they will have to pay more taxes in the future in order to pay off the increased debt? Will consumers prepare for that eventuality by increasing their rate of saving, causing the supply of funds curve to shift to the right? If savers behave this way, the level of interest rates would not rise when the federal deficit rises. This concept is known as *Ricardian Equivalence* and is accepted by some economists. However, evidence of a response of consumers to changes in the size of government deficits is, so far, elusive. Nonetheless, financial analysts should be cognizant of the fact that different economists offer different interpretations of the models from those presented here.

Expected Inflation and the Level of Interest Rates

The supply and demand for funds model includes no reference to inflation and the impact it can be expected to have on interest rates. It is clear that price level changes affect the "real" return that lenders receive from their loans and that borrowers must pay for their loans. If a contract is made under which a lender receives a return of $8 on a $100 loan at the end of one year, the nominal interest rate i is 8 per cent. However, if on the date of maturity of the loan, the price level is found to have risen by 5 per cent, then the "real" rate of earnings on the loan, r, would be only 3 per cent. The borrower repays the lender with dollars that are 5 per cent less valuable in terms of purchasing power than the ones he or she borrowed a year earlier. The equation is:

$$i = r + \dot{p}/p$$

where $\dot{p}$ stands for dp/dt, or the derivative of the price level with respect to time, and p is the price level, so that $\dot{p}/p$ is the percentage rate of change in the price level (see the

Note near the end of this chapter). This formula holds by definition in every *after-the-fact* investment situation.

The "Fisher Effect"

Irving Fisher used this formula as a basis for what is known as the "Fisher effect" in his 1930 book, *The Theory of Interest*. He argued that uniform expectations on the part of borrowers and lenders about future rates of inflation would affect the current nominal rate of interest. If borrowers believe that 5 per cent inflation will occur during the year, they willingly pay this premium to borrow their funds, and if lenders believe that 5 per cent inflation will occur, they require a 5 per cent premium to induce them to lend their funds. Thus,

$$i = r + (\dot{p}/p)^e$$

where the right-hand term no longer describes the results of *after-the-fact* past inflation but rather the *expected future rate of inflation* as indicated by the superscript e.

If one assumes that r is relatively constant, then variation in inflation rate expectations would be the prime determinant of variations in i.

From early 1930 to the mid-1960s, economists in the United States had little interest in the problem of inflation. But, in the late 1960s and in the 1970s, inflation proved to be a problem. Numerous studies have been made that have focused attention on the "Fisher effect."

The equation appears to be valid, but, upon closer examination, use of it in economic forecasting is fraught with pitfalls.

First, when prices fell rapidly, as in 1930–32, recent experience would have led to expectations of deflation, and if the real rate were constant, then, according to the formula, the nominal rate might have been negative, but it was not, and indeed it cannot be, negative, for lenders would simply retain cash holdings rather than lend at negative rates.

Second, if current expectations about inflation are based upon past inflation, a proxy for expected inflation can be constructed. However, a period of recent past experience without inflation could be upset by an outbreak of war so that current expectations of future inflation would fail to be formed on the basis of past experience alone. Hence, the proxy variable for expected future inflation fails to predict significant turning points in expectations.

Third, in Fisher's view the real rate of return, r, is roughly constant over time since it results from the productivity of capital. But what if the real rate does vary over time? If the "real" rate is defined to be the rate of return to investments or the rate of return on capital instead of being based on the purchasing power of the monetary unit—inflation— then it is a variable like other price variables, and it is surely affected by economic conditions.

Fourth, it is questionable whether, "expectations of inflation" can ever be measured in a scientific way. By scientific, of course, we mean capable of being confirmed or refuted by reference to experience. If, for example, we asked everyone to declare his or her expectations, and if we observed the true i in the marketplace and the true r by looking at the technology of production and markets for commodities, and if the difference between i and r did not equal our observed $(\dot{p}/p^e)$, would we say the evidence refuted the theory? Probably not. Instead we would presume that our measures were wrong—that we had not actually observed the true expected rate of price change. What set of observations could one collect that would make it possible for an experiment to refute the validity of the equation itself? No one has ever constructed such an experiment.

After interest rates rise, financial analysts often simply rationalize this rise by reporting that investors are now expecting an increase in the rate of inflation. That is, *they use the rise in rates to indicate a change in expected inflation.* They have placed the cart before the horse. They explain changing expectations by inferring from the rise in rates how expectations must have changed.

To use expected inflation appropriately as part of a theory to predict future changes in interest rates, one must be able to observe changes in expected inflation and test to see if these changes do lead to the theoretically predicted changes in rates. Until this happens, expectations can only be a rationalization rather than a causal force in explaining changes in interest rates.

The nature of the fundamental problem in dealing with the "expected inflation" approach to explaining nominal interest rates can be uncovered by rearranging the terms in the equation. For example, placing the expectations variable on the left and moving the nominal interest rate to the right side, we have:

$$(\dot{p}/p)^e = i - r$$

Here, the equation is in "implicit" form. The difference between i and r in this equation "implies" a value for expected inflation. It should be obvious that if the implicit form of the equation is used to measure expected inflation, it cannot also be used to explain or predict movements in i—circular reasoning.

In some research proxy variables are used as estimates for $(\dot{p}/p)^e$ and the equation

$$r = i - (\dot{p}/p)^e$$

is then used to estimate r. Again it should be obvious that the equation cannot then be used to explain i, since i was already used to measure r. To the author's knowledge, all research has either focused on these two implicit forms of the equation or has simply used the assumption that r is constant.

Thus, the equation showing the "Fisher effect" may be challenged because (1) it may not work at all in periods of deflation, (2) proxies for expectations are unreliable, (3) the assumption of a constant real rate may be false, and (4) direct observation of changing expectations through surveys of opinions, while tempting, gives us an untestable theory in a scientific sense. The most disquieting feature of this equation, however, is that people use this equation to rationalize and sometimes even to deceive others about the role of policy. This will be explained in Chapter 14 in conjunction with another theory containing an expectations variable.

It is tautologically true, for all investors who purchase a contract in which the unit of account (the dollar, say) is variable in real value, that their realized rate of return will differ from the nominal rate:

$$r \equiv i - \dot{p}/p$$

where r is their ex post "realized" rate of return. But to proceed from this and attempt to explain i, and variation in i, through observation of $(\dot{p}/p)^e$, is quite another matter. Finally, to predict future i—the purpose of a theory of interest rate determination—one must observe not only changes in the inflation rate, but also changes in r.

An Example of the Problem of Expected Inflation. Most economists would agree that the assertion "i will rise by the rate of inflation" is empirically true in the long-run (readers should notice that the term "expected rate" of inflation does not appear in this sentence). Indeed, many would say that short-run fluctuations in i are explained by recent changes in the rate of inflation.

But the markets hardly support this view. For example, on Thursday, March 18, 1993, the *Wall Street Journal* reported that consumer prices were up 0.3 per cent in February. This amounts to an annual rate of 3.6 per cent and this is above the 2.9 per cent for the year 1992. In the "C" section of paper a headline read "Stocks Drop on Report for Inflation." This response would be consistent with the idea that yields rise with higher inflation. However, the sub-headline read, "But Bonds Advance After Early Decline."

So, which is it? Why did the headline not say, "bond prices rise and yields fall on news of higher inflation?" Because the results did not fit the journalist's theory that, "... bond traders, apparently deciding inflation is still leashed, pushed bond prices up a little" (see Levingston, 1993: Cl).

The trick to understanding this confusion is that when the prices moved in the opposite direction of that predicted by the theory, the analyst infers that bond traders changed their expectations in a manner appropriate to fit the theory. Readers of the news will always find that analysts use changes in inflation rates to infer what market makers expect rather than using changes in expectations to predict the movements in yields. Such implicit testing of a theory is fundamentally flawed and nonscientific.

Short-run fluctuations in yields are best explained by examining the variety of forces of supply and demand for loanable funds in the context of an operationally meaningful theory of interest rate level determination. They are not explained by changes in expected inflation or by changes in expectations of any other sort.

Inflation in the Loanable Funds Model

We can use supply and demand for loanable funds to analyze the impact of inflation on financial markets. Assume that inflation is fully anticipated by both borrowers and lenders. Then an expected proportional rise in all prices of p will mean that businesspersons will expect a return on their investments equal to $i = r + \dot{p}/p$. Thus, the demand for funds will shift upward by precisely $\dot{p}/p$ as shown by the demand curve of Figure 12–6 shifting from D to D'. Without anticipated inflation, $i = r$ and demand curve D obtains; with inflation, $i' = r + \dot{p}/p$ and the demand curve becomes D' as borrowers are willing to pay the inflation premium. Similarly, lenders, anticipating inflation, will supply less to the market, and their changed willingness to supply will cause the supply curve to shift to the left from S to S'. Lenders "require" a higher nominal yield to induce them to part with their funds. Thus, both demand and supply curves shift up by the full amount of the uniformly anticipated inflation rate. This characterizes the "Fisher effect" in graphical form. The nominal interest rate has risen by the full amount of anticipated inflation, and the quantity of loanable funds remains unchanged at Q. Therefore, the real rate of interest remains at r, even though i has risen.

However, this scenario of the actual effects of inflation differs significantly from reasonable alternatives proposed by other economists (see Jackson, 1976). In the figure there is a dashed demand curve labeled D'' that has shifted to the right, but not so far rightward as D'. First, federal deficit spending that creates federal demand for funds is not responsive to inflation. Indeed, if prices rise, taxes may increase, and the deficit might actually be less if no offsetting increases in spending occur. Second, when the nominal interest rate rises above legal maximum rates paid by some state and local governments, their demand for funds is restrained. Thus, the demand curve may shift only to D''.

The supply curve may not shift so far to the left as in the Fisher theory, but only as far as described by the dashed curve labeled S'' in the figure. First, wealth holders will try to reduce their balances of money when they anticipate inflation. This dishoarding increases the supply of funds; that is, it shifts the supply curve to the right. Second, anticipated

Figure 12–6
Inflation and the Loanable Funds Theory of Interest

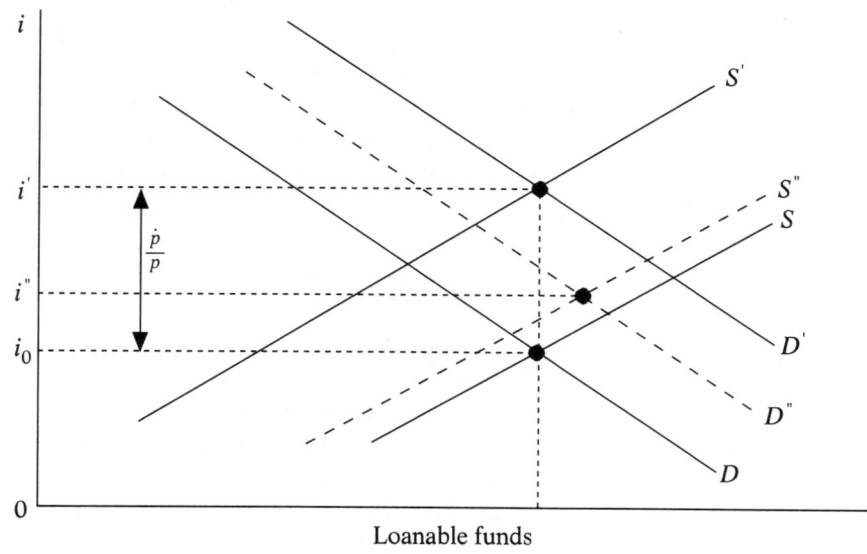

Loanable funds

inflation lowers consumer confidence in their ability to consume in the future. They feel that prices and taxes will rise while their income will not rise by as much; or at least they are uncertain. Therefore, consumers will reduce their expenditures and save more. Third, institutions that collect funds on a steady basis, such as life insurance companies, supply these funds to the market and do not reduce their willingness to lend because of anticipated inflation, so the supply of funds for many investors does not move left. Thus, it would appear that the S curve may only move left to S'' in the short run.

The actual result of inflation is likely to be one in which S'' and D'' curves determine a rate of interest i'' which is lower than i'. With p/p inflation, this means that the real interest rate falls and the amount of funds traded in the market increases. In a sense one could say that in the short run there is "incomplete adjustment" to the inflation. Only in the very long run would the "Fisher effect" occur fully.

Theory in the Asian Tigers

In most chapters of this book, there has been explicit mention of some items of institutional detail in the Asian Tiger economies that are relevant to the topics under discussion. However, this chapter is devoted to theory and in this author's opinion there is little need to mention any specific economy because, for the most part, economic theory, if it is good theory, works in all economies, just as good physics, chemistry, biology, and mathematics "work" well in all economies. Science and technology know no political boundaries. They may work differently in different economies, however, because the institutional details differ. That is why so much of this book is devoted to items of institutional detail that are unique to the Asian Tigers and other countries that are active in the financial markets of the world today.

Summary

This chapter introduces the reader to the theory of interest rate determination. It begins by explaining the formulas that are used to estimate the prices of bonds and stocks and that relate interest rates or yields to prices of securities.

Within the context of the concept of returns to investment and saving, the classical ideas of the value of thrift and the value of investment to society are explained. Neoclassical theory introduces the interest rate as a type of price that rations the supply of saving among those who demand funds for investment.

The supply and demand for funds model provides analysts with a first approximation of the impact that a variety of forces affecting supply or demand may have on interest rate levels. To set the stage for interpreting changes in supply and demand for funds, the supply of funds was broken into three sub-categories: the supply of saving, the increase in the money supply, and dishoarding. The demand for funds was also broken into three sub-categories (not related to the three supply sub-categories): the demand by business and consumers, the demand by the U.S. Treasury and the demand by state and local governments.

The supply and demand for funds model is not a complete model because it does not explain the various interactions between the supply curve and the demand curve. It is called a partial equilibrium model. In contrast, the complete Keynesian model of the macroeconomy is a general equilibrium model because, in it, all of the interactions are accounted for.

Does inflation affect interest rates? Do expectations of inflation affect interest rate? These questions provide the basis of considerable discussion in this chapter.

Note

If prices increase from 100 to 110 in one year, then dp/dt is approximately $\Delta p/\Delta t = 10/1 = 10$. If the original price level p were 100, then $10/100 = 0.10$, or 10 per cent, the rate of increase in p expressed in percentage terms so as to be consistent with the mode of expression for i and r. If $\Delta p/\Delta t = 30$ when the original p was 200, then the percentage rate of increase of p would be only 15 per cent. A more exact formulation of the equation for discrete changes in i, r, and p would be

$$(1 + i) = (1 + r)\left(1 + \frac{\dot{p}}{p}\right)$$

or

$$1 + i = 1 + r + \frac{\dot{p}}{p} + r\left(\frac{\dot{p}}{p}\right)$$

or

$$i = r + \frac{\dot{p}}{p} + r\left(\frac{\dot{p}}{p}\right)$$

The last term on the right-hand side is the interaction term and is usually very small so that it is ignored in most discussions. If, for example, $i = 26$ per cent, $r = 20$ per cent, and $\dot{p}/p = 5$ per cent, then

$$(1.26) = (1.20)(1.05) = 1 + 0.20 + 0.05 + 0.01$$

Omitting the interaction term would have made $i = 25$ per cent instead of 26 per cent. Thus, the error in omitting the term becomes significant if r or $\dot{p}/p$ or both are large. In the case of continuous functions rather than the discrete changes, the interaction terms drop out altogether. To illustrate, assume i = nominal rate of interest, r = real rate of interest, p = price level, V_n = nominal value of an asset, V_r = real value of an asset, and

$$V_n = pV_r$$

i = the percentage change in $V_n = \dfrac{1}{V_n}\left(\dfrac{dV_n}{dt}\right)$

r = the percentage change in $V_r = \dfrac{1}{V_r}\left(\dfrac{dV_r}{dt}\right)$

Solving for i, find

$$i = \frac{1}{pV_r} \frac{d(pV_r)}{dt} = \frac{1}{pV_r} \left(p \frac{dV_r}{dt} + V_r \frac{dp}{dt} \right)$$
$$= \frac{1}{V_r} \frac{dV_r}{dt} + \frac{1}{p} \frac{dp}{dt}$$

and, therefore,

$$i = r + \frac{\dot{p}}{p}$$

for an infinitesimal unit of time.

Key Terms and Concepts

Interest rates as prices
Alfred Marshall
Loanable funds approach
Debt financing
Fisher effect

Adam Smith on saving
Saving in the Asian Tigers
Dishoarding
Partial vs. general equilibrium
Ricardian Equivalence

Discussion Questions and Exercises

1. Price and cost mean the same; a "price" charged by a seller is the same as a "cost" to the buyer. What is an interest rate the price and cost of? Explain by example.
2. Write down the formula for the present value of a bond; for a perpetuity; and for an annuity. Define each variable used.
3. What changes in the bond formula are required to estimate the present value when coupon payments are made semiannually instead of annually?
4. In some sense a share of stock is like a perpetuity, but there are important differences. What are they?
5. Did Adam Smith consider saving through the purchase of stocks and bonds to be more or less equivalent forms of financing investments? Why is saving good for the economy?
6. Capitalist economies use roundabout methods of production. Explain.
7. Explain briefly each of the three sub-categories of the supply of funds and each of the three of the demand for funds.
8. Why does the demand curve for funds have a flat range in it?
9. How would the removal of taxes on interest and dividend income be expected to affect (a) the level of interest rates, (b) investment, (c) economic growth; (d) prosperity?
10. What are three important considerations to keep in mind when using the supply and demand for funds model to predict interest rate level changes?
11. Does inflation affect the return on an investment? Explain.

12. What problems arise when trying to use the Fisher Equation to predict interest rate changes?

13. How can the supply and demand for funds curves be used to explain the Fisher effect?

14. Review the reasons that the supply and demand curves might shift as shown in Figure 12–6.

15. Check recent issues of newspapers to see if you can uncover implicit statements about investor expectations of inflation that are inferred from movements in market prices or yields on securities. Explain the faulty nature of such interpretations.

References

Fisher, Irving, *The Theory of Interest*, Macmillan, New York, 1930, reprinted by Augustus M. Kelley, New York, 1961.

Jackson, William D., "Federal Deficits, Inflation and Monetary Growth: Can They Predict Interest Rates?" *Economic Review*, Federal Reserve Bank of Richmond, September–October 1976, pp. 13–25.

Levingston, Steven E., "Stocks Drop on Report for Inflation," *Wall Street Journal*, March 18, 1993.

Smith, Adam, *The Wealth of Nations*, Modern Library, New York, 1937.

Von Bohm-Bawerk, Eugen, *Capital and Interest*, trans., G. D. Huncke, South Holland, IL, 1959.

CHAPTER 13

Interest Rate Theory

CHAPTER 1 CONTAINED two graphs—one of the supply and demand for securities and a second of the supply and demand for funds. These were used to show that borrowers are suppliers of securities and demanders of funds while lenders are demanders of securities and suppliers of funds. The price of securities was determined by the interaction of the demand and supply of securities, while the interest yield was determined by the interaction of the demand and supply of funds. Both graphs show the *same information*, albeit in different forms. The graphs illustrated the inverse relation between prices of securities and the interest yields on securities.

Similarly, the present value formula was used in Chapter 12 to illustrate the inverse relation between prices of securities and interest yields.

Understanding this inverse relation comes as second nature to those who study and work in the field of finance. It is not easy for others, however. For example, you come home after a day at work and report that, "Securities lost value in the market today as yields rose." Your spouse, sympathetic in response, replies, "I'm sorry they lost value. But, didn't you tell me that a higher yield on a security makes it more valuable? How in the world could they lose value when their yields rose?" How would you try to explain this anomaly? Sidney Homer, often called the dean of the bond market after publishing *The History of Interest Rates*, wrote a charming dialogue in one of his articles (1939) along this line of reasoning. It seems that having a martini helps in such a situation.

In this chapter attention shifts away from the supply and demand for funds and shifts to the supply and demand for assets, such as money, stocks, bonds, and tangible assets (property, buildings, houses, materials, and so forth). Interest rate theory has developed around a function called the demand-for-money function. This will be introduced shortly. First, a very brief history of its evolution beginning with the Equation of Exchange.

The Equation of Exchange

The equation of exchange is used to illustrate the well-known proposition that inflation is caused by "too much money chasing too few goods." If goods become more scarce, and/or, money becomes more plentiful, then prices of goods will rise. For example, goods will become more scarce if there is a crop failure. Food prices will rise, and the average level of prices will rise even if the supply of money remains constant. On the other hand, if output remains constant and money is dumped into the economy, then prices will rise. These propositions stem directly from the equation of exchange.

MV = PT. David Hume published a book of essays, *Political Discourses*, in 1752. His writings influenced Adam Smith. One of the essays was entitled, "Of Money." In this essay he identified the necessary equality between the flow of money spending and the monetary value of sales of goods in an exchange economy. Although he did not use equations, his thoughts were organized into equation form with the now famous equation of exchange.

Let:

M = the amount of money in circulation
V = the "velocity" of money, that is, the average number of times each monetary unit changes hands in a given period
P = the average price paid in all transactions of goods
T = the number of transactions taking place in a given period

Then,

$$MV = PT$$

In this equation the equal sign could be replaced by an identity sign because the two sides measure exactly the same thing—what is paid for goods bought equals what is received for goods sold. The equation must hold because of the definitions of the variables. Nevertheless, the equation has provided a basis for a great deal of insightful analysis.

A Theory of Inflation

By making two simplifying assumptions, the equation of exchange becomes a theory of the cause of inflation. First, assume the variable V is determined by the institutional structure of the payments system. Wages may be paid weekly, or salaries monthly, and checks for bills may be written at the end of the month. There is more or less a steady flow of payments from consumers to businesses to income earners and back again as described in Chapter 2 in the circular flow diagram. Thus, the turnover of money, or its "velocity," is viewed as a constant.

Second, assume the variable *T* is also viewed as a given, or a constant, because it is subject to agricultural production that depends in turn, largely on the vagaries of nature, and on the output of other goods produced more or less steadily in an exchange economy. Of course, neither *V* nor *T* are really constants, but assuming them to be is an approximation.

If V and T are constants, then changes in money must be reflected entirely in changes in prices. More money means higher prices; less money means lower prices. Money "explains" inflation.

In an economy that is growing, *T* may grow at some steady rate. Changing the equation into logarithmic form simplifies the analysis. The equation becomes $\log M + \log V = \log P + \log T$, where logarithms represent rates of change in the variables. Thus, if *T* grows by 3 per cent reflecting a growing economy, and if *V* does not change, then a 3 per cent growth in *M* is consistent with no rise in *P*; a money growth rate that is equal to the growth rate of transactions is consistent with zero inflation. However, if *M* grows at a rate of 5 per cent, then *P* should grow at a rate of 2 per cent.

The Quantity Theory of Money. Several alterations in the basic equation have led economists to a theory of the demand for money called the Quantity Theory of Money.

First, *T* was changed to *Q* where *Q* does not represent all intermediate transactions or those involving the exchange of existing assets, but only those representing final payments for newly produced goods. That is, *Q* represents the real output or production of an economy and *PQ* represents its monetary value, or Gross Domestic Product. Thus, if the money supply is $1 trillion and GDP is $6 trillion, then on average each unit of money is spent about six times a year on final products. It is probably spent about five times that often if all transactions were included, or about 30 times a year, only six of which were spent on final products. So, the income velocity of money, V_Y, is about one-sixth the transactions velocity of money, V_T.

Thus, the equation became $MV_Y = PQ =$ GDP at current prices. Let us recognize that GDP is a widely used proxy for national income. The letter most economists use to represent national income is *Y*. Thus, let $PQ = Y$ which is a measure of money income. Real income $Q = Y/P$, or nominal national income divided by a current index of prices set against some base period average of prices.

Second, the income velocity of money was moved to the right-hand side of the equation. To do this let $k = 1/V_Y$, so that $M = kPQ = kY$. The purpose of this change is to focus attention away from the emphasis on why and how people make transactions with money toward an emphasis on why people demand money to hold. Hence the Quantity Theory of Money is a theory of the demand for money.

If *V* is a constant, so is its reciprocal, *k*. Now, however, when *M* rises the impact can be on either *P* or *Q*. When the money supply is increased there may be, if some resources are unemployed, an increase in national output *Q* without any increase in *P*. There may be time lags in the response to a change in *M*. *Q* may increase in the short run while *P* may increase only much later. If increases in *Q* are limited by the growth in productivity and existing supplies of resources, then a continuous increase in M above real growth will eventually be followed by inflation. Thus, over the long run it is still certain that "too much money chasing too few goods" causes inflation. But over periods of a year or two, or even three or four, the connection between money growth and inflation is less direct and more uncertain.

Interest as a Connecting Link between Money and Prices. *Knut Wicksell* published a book, *Interest and Prices*, in 1898. In it, he spelled out what has become known as "the transmission mechanism." Imports of gold would become bank reserves, and banks would compete with each other to lend out excess reserves. Competition would cause interest rate levels to fall, investment spending would be stimulated because the cost of funds would be below the returns on business investments. Soon business activity would increase and price increases would follow. So increases in money (gold in this case was money) would be transmitted into inflated prices via lower interest rate levels. Wicksell soon faced criticism. According to his theory price inflation and low interest rates go hand in hand. But, everyone knows that interest rates rise to high levels with inflation. The evidence simply did not support the idea that low interest rates brought on inflation. This was a simple matter to correct, which Wicksell soon did. He changed the idea of returns on business investment to "expected" returns on business investment.

This is a perfect illustration of the way that an economist can add an "expectations" variable to accommodate a theory. Since "expected returns" cannot be observed, those who brought the original evidence on inflation and interest rates could no longer bring evidence to refute the theory. This occurred a decade before Irving Fisher explained how inflation caused nominal interest rates to rise as explained in Chapter 12. Of course, this was also about the time that philosophers of science were just beginning to understand that theories, to be scientific, need to be refutable, that is, to be operationally meaningful—capable of being refuted by experiment.

John Maynard Keynes. Keynes was an active participant in securities markets. He also published a two-volume, *Treatise on Money*, in 1932, as well as the famous pathbreaking work in macroeconomics, *The General Theory of Employment, Interest, and Money*, in 1936. He broke the demand for money into three parts, transactions demand, speculative demand, and precautionary demand. In general, transactions demand depends on the level of income—the need to hold money for the purpose of engaging in transactions. Speculative demand for money holdings is related to interest rate levels. People hold money in anticipation of using it to purchase securities. Finally, some money is held in a reserve to meet unexpected contingencies. At very low interest rates, people hold large volumes of "idle balances" of money because security prices are so high. People have a "preference for liquidity" at low interest rates. The opportunity cost of holding idle money balances is very low when interest rates are low because interest given up, when holding non-interest-bearing bank balances, represents the opportunity cost of holding the idle balance. If interest rates are high and the money supply increases, the result would be a decline in interest rates and greater investment, just as Wicksell had suggested. But if interest rates are already very low, increases in money to stimulate a depressed economy would simply be added to idle balances without resulting in a stimulated economy.

The idea of *liquidity preference* eventually became synonymous with the idea of demand for money. The idea is encompassed in the reasoning behind the supply of funds curve in Chapter 12 that represents the willingness of money holders to dishoard their idle balances as interest rates move up. William J. Baumol and James Tobin pointed out that transactions balances as well as speculative balances were affected by interest rate levels. They observed that consumers would economize on transactions balances when interest rates rose because the opportunity cost of holding money also rose.

Milton Friedman. Professor Friedman is famous for his work on the demand for money in a battery of books and articles too numerous to list. Other economists have also made important contributions to the concept of the demand for money. Yet it was Milton Friedman who stressed the idea that the Quantity Theory of Money was best viewed as a Theory of the Demand for Money. The following represents a simplified version of the Modern Quantity Theory of Money.

The Modern Quantity Theory of Money

According to this theory, the level of interest rates is determined by the demand and supply of money. Most of the emphasis is on the demand for money. The supply of money is believed to be essentially given by the decisions of monetary authorities. However, several economists argue that it would be best to have privately issued money, and, if money were to be privately issued, the supply curve would doubtless have an upward slope to it. The demand for money is believed to be downward sloping, as shown in Figure 13–1.

As in the case of the demand and supply of funds examined in Chapter 12, the variable representing the level of interest rates, i, is measured along the vertical axis. However, what is measured along the horizontal axis is *not* funds, as in Chapter 12, but the quantity of real balances of money, M/P, that is, nominal balances of money divided by an index of the level of prices.

The variables are:

M = the nominal amount of money in circulation, where subscripts to M indicate quantity of money demanded or supplied
P = an index of the level of prices
Q = the quantity of goods and services produced (output)
i = the general level of interest rates
X = a vector of several other factors that may affect holdings of real balances of money

Figure 13–1
Money Demand Function

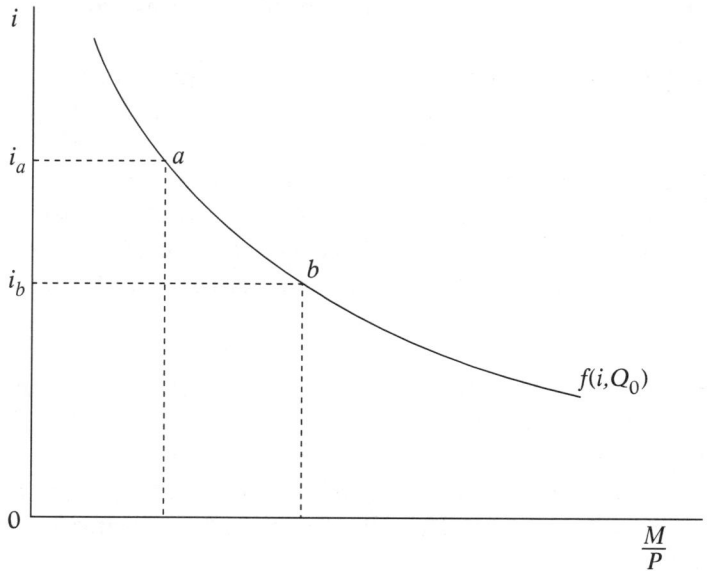

The model of demand and supply contains two equations and a constant term:

$M_S/P = M_D/P$, the equilibrium between quantity supplied and quantity demanded
M_S/P = a constant where M_S is determined by the monetary authorities
$M_D/P = f(i, Q, X)$, the demand-for-money function

Because this function contains the macroeconomic variables of interest, it is the basis for interpreting forces that may lead to changes in interest rate levels. It reads as follows: the quantity of real money balances that people wish to hold depends upon interest rate levels, income as represented by Q, several other variables, and of course, the quantity of money supplied. The two equations serve to determine the two dependent variables in the model, M_D/P, and the focus of our attention, i. Thus, i is a dependent variable and it is interdependently determined with the other variables in the model. Let us see how it works with a few graphs.

Changes in Q. In Figure 13–2 the demand curve slopes downward indicating that at lower interest rates people will willingly hold a larger money supply. The opportunity cost of holding money is low. The curve shows a hypothetical relation between i and M/P *for a given level of Q*. The equation has three variables, but there are only two axes. Thus, a level of Q must be assumed in order to draw the curve in two-dimensional space. One way to see how Q enters the model is to assume two (or a few) different values for Q and see how the curve changes position. An increase in Q from an initial level Q_0 to Q_1 indicates that the curve shifts upward. For, when output increases, there

Figure 13–2
Shift in Money Demand

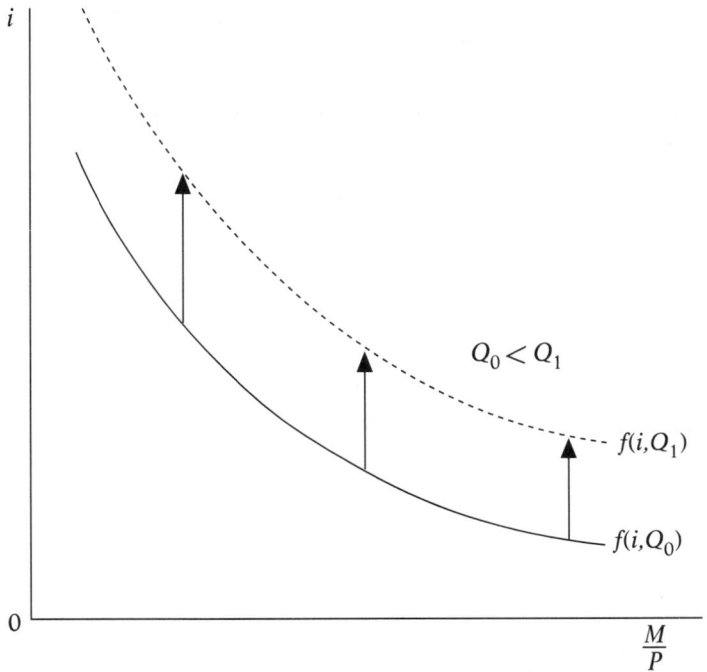

is an increase in the quantity of money that will be needed to handle the expanded volume of transactions. *For any given level of real money balances, interest rates will have to be higher to induce people to dishoard their idle balances and accommodate the increased need for transactions balances of money.* One could say that the demand for money curve shifts up or to the right when output increases. It would shift down or to the left when output decreases.

Financial analysts constantly watch factors indicating whether the output might increase or decrease. If a strong increase in output is projected, interest rates will tend to rise even before the actual increase takes place because investors will anticipate the higher rates and act accordingly. (They will sell securities and push prices down.)

Changes in X. Here we must reintroduce factor X that represents several other important forces. For example, what if credit cards are introduced where none existed before. Credit cards are not money, but they reduce the traveler's need to carry precautionary amounts of currency on trips. So they act as a substitute for money. The expansion of money substitutes leads to a reduction in the demand for money, that is, it leads to a leftward shift in the curve. If the quantity of real money balances stays the same, interest rates will fall.

Similarly, if Treasury bills are sufficiently liquid to act as a substitute for money, an increase in their supply may reduce the demand for money just as credit cards do.

Readers may think of other factors that may increase or decrease the quantity of money that people wish to hold. The impact of changes in such factors may be depicted by shifts in the position of the money demand function. For example, how might a deterioration of political stability in the rest of the world affect the demand for a country's currency?

Thus, the model may be used as a basis for predicting how the interest rate level will respond to various shocks from independent variables, similar to the model of the supply and demand for funds in Chapter 12.

Changes in M. In Figure 13–3 the vertical money supply function shifts to the right to show an increase in the money supply from M_0 to M_1 as indicated by the subscripts attached to M. The interest rate would fall as indicated by the lower point of intersection of the new money supply line with the demand for money curve. This illustrates how action taken by central banks or other monetary authorities to expand M can be expected to lead to a decline in the general level of interest rates. The curve will shift to the left if the money supply is reduced. How might a country's currency supply be affected if other countries start to use it for their own supply?

Figure 13–3
Increase in Money Supply

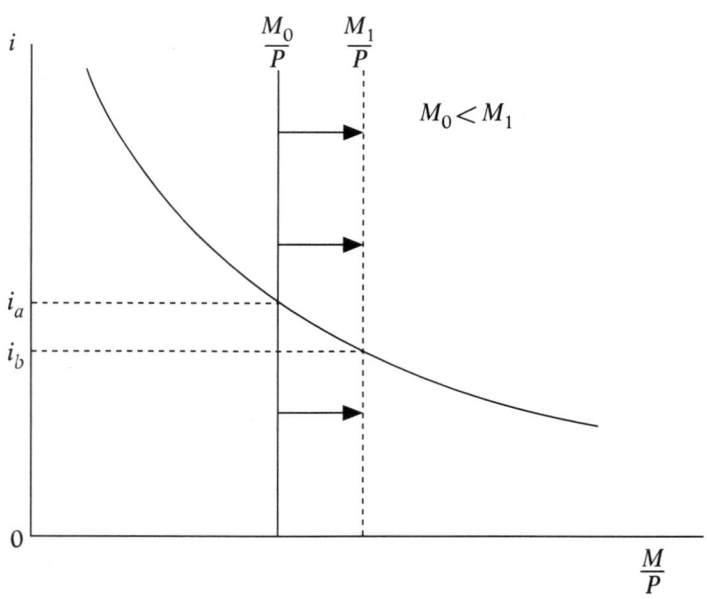

Changes in P. As was noted above, there is reason to believe that inflation will follow if too much money is created. Thus, if P increases from P_0 to P_1 then the value of M/P decreases because P is in the denominator. When the denominator rises, the ratio falls. A decline in real money balances occurs because higher prices mean that an existing nominal amount of money will not buy as many goods as previously. The result is as if the supply of real money balances declines, and this is shown as a leftward shift in the vertical supply of money function, as indicated by the subscripts attached to P in Figure 13–4.

Figure 13–4
Increase in the Price Level

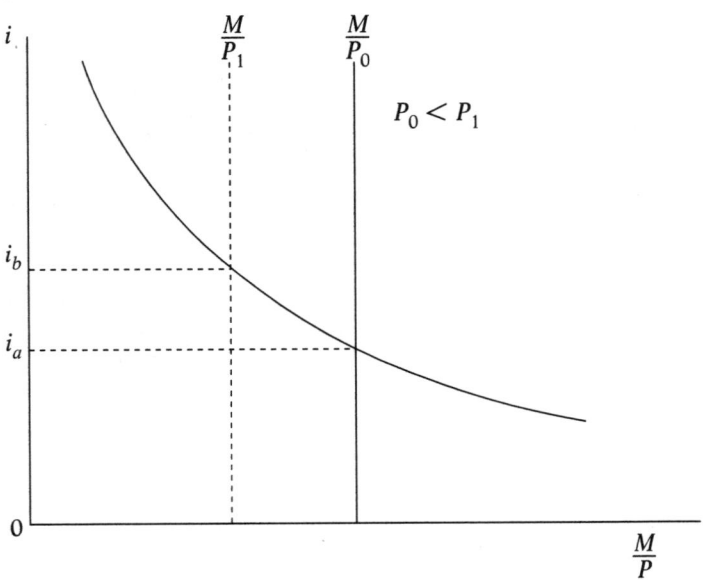

$P_0 < P_1$

Partial Equilibrium Analysis

Analyzing changes in the variables, as in the graphs, should be viewed as making first approximations. The reason is that the demand and supply for money model is a partial equilibrium model just as the demand and supply for funds model was in Chapter 12. There are feedback effects that are not explicitly accounted for. For example, increased money will bring lower interest rates, but these can be expected to raise investment spending and stimulate income and output, and the rise in output will shift the money demand curve to the right and shift interest rates back up again. A shift in one function leads, eventually, to a shift in the other function. These feedback effects are accounted for in the full Keynesian model.

A Theory of the Demand for Assets

The focus of the theory of the demand for money is on the asset "money." However, hidden in this analytical world is an interest-earning asset known as bonds. The reason we know this asset is hidden somewhere is that there is an interest rate, and therefore, there must be some security on which this interest is paid. When the interest rate or yield is described as rising, this implies that the price of some representative bond must be falling. So *the demand for money model has two asset classes, money and all other assets represented by bonds.*

James Tobin. Professor Tobin uncovered some very important concepts when he expanded the number of assets in a theory of demand for assets. The following is a brief summary of the theory.

A Liquidity Continuum

There are, of course, literally billions of distinct observable assets in the world economy. To each of these, one might assign some degree of liquidity. Then each may be placed in its proper position along a continuum. Let the horizontal line represent this continuum. At the very left there is the *perfectly liquid asset* we call money. It is perfectly liquid because it is, indeed, the very stuff used to discharge debt.

Asset:	Money	Bonds	Stock	Tangibles

Returns on assets _____ Increasing direction →
← Increasing direction _____ Liquidity

The return on assets increases as we move along the continuum to the right as indicated, while liquidity increases as we move along from right to left. Returns must rise on assets with less liquidity in order to induce investors to accept the more risky assets.

Money and good substitutes for money would be placed on the far left, followed by money market securities and then bonds. After this would be preferred stock and further right would be common stock. Next would be properties, houses, furniture and last, your son's used motorcycle, assuming that it still runs.

A Four Asset Model

Simplify by dividing the continuum into four classes of assets with money, bonds, stock, and tangibles represented by M, B, S and T. Assume that people receive utility from holding a portfolio of these four classes of assets. The individual's utility function may be written as:

$$U = U(M, B, S, T)$$

This equation simply says tht utility depends upon the amounts of money, bonds, stocks and tangibles that an individual holds.

An individual's wealth consists of the value of these assets. Thus, wealth becomes:

$$W = P_M M + P_B B + P_S S + P_T T$$

where Ps refer to the respective prices, and the variables refer to the number of units of each type of asset held in the portfolio. The sum of the items gives wealth W, the amount that could be consumed at once if all assets were sold. Wealth is the sum of the present purchasing power one holds. Of course, the price of money is simply a dollar, but the prices of bonds, stocks, and tangible assets are all market prices per unit of each. One should remember, too, that as the price of an asset rises, its effective yield falls if there is no change in the revenues it produces. Price and yield are inversely related.

Given the utility function for wealth and the definition of wealth, it is possible to calculate necessary conditions for maximization of utility (see the Note near the end of this chapter). Let us begin with this equation:

$$\frac{MU_M}{P_M} = \frac{MU_B}{P_B} = \frac{MU_S}{P_S} = \frac{MU_T}{P_T}$$

This equation says that the ratio of the marginal utility of money to its price will be equal to the ratio of the marginal utility of bonds to their price, which will equal ... and so on, for each asset held by an individual, if the individual is maximizing to his or her satisfaction. This equilibrium position follows from this theory of asset choice.

Assume that a helicopter drops money and now people hold more money. If the marginal utility of money falls when people have more of it, the ratio MU_M/P_M will fall, so that now

$$\frac{MU_U}{P_M} < \frac{MU_B}{P_B} = \frac{MU_S}{P_S} = \frac{MU_T}{P_T}$$

This inequality means that the individuals are less satisfied with the portfolios of money, bonds, stocks, and tangible assets than they could be. By giving up money, they lose some utility, but they gain even more utility than they lose by using money to buy bonds and other assets, as indicated:

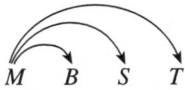

This switching of asset holdings drives up the prices of the other assets and higher prices mean that MU_B/P_B and the other ratios fall, since prices are in the denominators of the ratios. These ratios continue to fall until the inequality in the equations is removed and market equilibrium is restored. A rising price of a bond, of course, implies a falling yield or interest rate; therefore, an increase in the money supply leads to lower interest rates. This result is consistent with macroeconomic theory.

To see Tobin's contribution more clearly, we may use a different example. Let us assume we start from equilibrium and let the government debt increase—U.S. Treasury bonds are dropped from a helicopter. People will find they are holding more bonds that they want, relative to other assets. Now an inequality is introduced:

$$\frac{MU_U}{P_M} > \frac{MU_B}{P_B} < \frac{MU_S}{P_S} = \frac{MU_T}{P_T}$$

Therefore, people will attempt to trade bonds for other assets, as indicated:

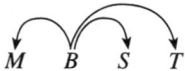

$$M \quad B \quad S \quad T$$

In this case, since the price of money cannot change, all that happens as bondholders sell off bonds for money is that the price of bonds falls and the yield on bonds rises. But if they trade bonds for stocks, the price of stocks may rise, and so may the prices of tangible assets if bonds are sold and tangible assets are purchased. The rise in the price of stocks implies a lower yield on stocks for those buying the stocks after the price has risen. However, if stock prices rise, the ratio MU_S/P_S falls and becomes less than the ratio MU_M/P_M. Because of this disequilibrium, some people may sell stocks to acquire money. Thus, on the one hand, some pressures come into play that would lower the yield on stocks and, on the other, there are pressures that would raise the yield on stocks. Therefore, interest rates on bonds will surely fall while yields on stocks may fall, or may *rise*. Tobin pointed out this indeterminancy.

Another way to view it is to consider the six price ratios that can exist among the four types of assets:

$$\begin{array}{cccccc}
(1) & (2) & (3) & (4) & (5) & (6) \\
\dfrac{P_B}{P_M} & \dfrac{P_B}{P_S} & \dfrac{P_B}{P_T} & \dfrac{P_S}{P_M} & \dfrac{P_T}{P_M} & \dfrac{P_S}{P_T}
\end{array}$$

The first three ratios show the price of bonds in the numerator. With a larger supply of bonds, their prices will fall relative to the other assets, so these ratios will decline. But what will happen to the fourth and fifth ratios? The price of money is a dollar and cannot change, but the money prices of stocks and of tangible assets may either rise or fall. Nor do we know how the sixth ratio will change. The way these ratios change will depend in general upon asset holders' tastes.

One would normally think that an increase in borrowing by the Treasury, with Treasury issue of more debt, would lead to a stock market decline. But if P_S/P_M should rise, as it might, more debt might lead to rising stock prices and lower yields on stocks. This possibly occurred in 1982–87 and 1988–95.

One final example. Assume that the Treasury issues a large volume of Treasury bills. T-bill prices will fall and yields rise. But T-bills are close substitutes for money. Therefore, people may try to hold less money and more stocks. This pushes stock prices up and yields down. Higher stock prices should lead to increased investment spending. Thus, the increased volume of Treasury short-term debt outstanding may actually exert an expansionary influence on economic activity. This result of Tobin's analysis would not exist in the Keynesian world of only two assets, money and "bonds."

Both the liquidity preference model and the Tobin model focus on demand for certain types of assets.

The Fisherian Time-preference Model

In neoclassical economic theory, the pricing system allocates scarce resources among alternative uses. All prices are interrelated, and all are relative, indicating the rate at which one commodity will exchange for another at a given time. An interest rate is a unique form of price.

It indicates the rate at which a commodity can be exchanged for itself at two points in time. If I gave you 10 bushels of wheat today and you return 11 bushels to me one year from today, the real rate of interest is 10 per cent. Therefore, interest rates serve to determine the time pattern of resource allocation. Individuals have preferences with a time dimension. Students may dissave now in anticipation of a higher income when they begin their careers and earn income out of which they can repay their indebtedness. Middle-aged people may save today in anticipation of an income decline when they enter retirement. In these cases, the individuals prefer to even out the time flow of their consumption. Furthermore, people may wish to borrow now to bring out productive investment.

To describe in a general way the forces giving rise to saving behavior, economists use "indifference curves." These are shown in Figure 13–5, which is called Irving Fisher's two-period diagram (see Fisher, 1930). An individual is assumed to have a time horizon of two periods. Income of the initial period, Y_0, is measured on the horizontal axis, and income of the subsequent period, Y_1, is measured on the vertical axis. The three indifference curves represent three levels of satisfaction that an individual may acquire

Figure 13–5
Time-preference Curves for Two Periods

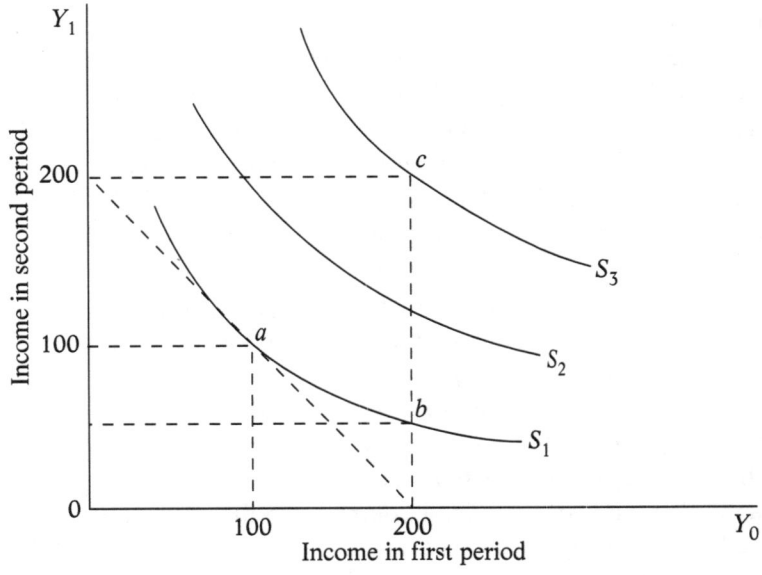

from consumption during the two periods. If a person consumes 100 each period, the person will reach the same level of satisfaction (reach the same indifference curve) as would have been reached had he or she consumed 200 this period and only 50 next period (points *a* and *b*). But the individual would reach a higher level of satisfaction if he or she could consume 200 each period (point *c*). There is, at any point on an indifference curve, a slope of the curve. At point *a* the slope of the curve S_1 is equal to the slope of the tangent to the curve (dashed line). The slope is defined to be $\Delta Y_1/\Delta Y_0$, and at *a* this is −1.

The slope of the indifference curve is called the marginal rate of time preference. At *a*, the individual is just willing to exchange a dollar's worth of this period's consumption for a dollar's consumption next period. However, if the individual is at point *b* the curve is flatter. If we measured $\Delta Y_1/\Delta Y_0$ it would be, perhaps, −1/4. This indicates that the individual's present consumption of 200 is high relative to next period's consumption and that he or she would be happy to give up $4 of this year's consumption if he or she could only have another dollar's consumption next period.

Assume that the individual is at point *a*, where Y_0 and Y_1 both equal 100. Assume also that the interest rate is zero. Then the dashed line represents the variety of ways in which the individual can consume his or her income of 200. The individual could consume all of it this period and none next period, or he or she could consume equal amounts each period, or all next period and none this period. Indeed, any point on the dashed line represents a possible pair of consumption amounts. We could call it the consumption possibility curve. At *a* the individual is on his or her highest indifference curve.

Now assume that the individual faces a positive interest rate. The consumption possibilities will now be different. They are reflected in the straight solid line in Figure 13–6.

The slope of the solid line is −(1 + *i*), where *i* is the market rate of interest. If *i* = 20 per cent, the slope is −1.20. The horizontal intercept is $183.33, indicating that, if the individual borrowed $83.33 today, he or she could repay this amount along with $16.67 interest a year from today, by using his or her next period's income of $100. The intercept of the vertical axis is $220, indicating that the individual might save all his or her $100 and regain it with $20 interest and receive next period's $100 income as well. Thus, with a positive interest rate the individual's possibilities have changed and he or she can now reach a higher indifference curve at point *b* by lending some of this period's income and receiving his or her income and the repaid principal, along with earned interest, in the next period. A positive interest rate has induced the individual to save and lend, as noted in the Figure 13–6.

Another individual might have a preference map with a tangency point somewhere along the possibility curve below and to the right of point *a*, and that person would be a borrower. In the economy as a whole, all the lenders would supply saving to the economy, and all the borrowers would compete for this saving. The market rate of interest would be determined by competition among those who supply saving and those who demand loanable funds. In equilibrium the rate set in the market would be such

Figure 13–6
Current Saving and Lending

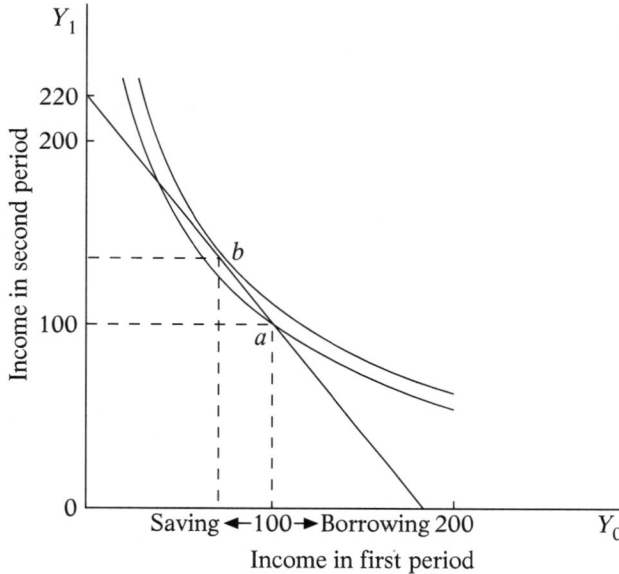

that for each and every individual, his or her marginal rate of time preference would equal $-(1 + i)$; that is, the slope of his or her indifference curve would equal the slope of the possibility curve. Every borrower and lender would be better off (in the sense of being on a higher indifference curve and realizing a higher level of satisfaction) when a market for saving and dissaving could be freely entered than they would be if such a market did not exist.

To illustrate these propositions in greater detail, assume that there are two individuals in an economy, each with a two-period time-preference function as suggested by Figures 13–7(a) and 13–7(b). In Figure 13–7(a), individual A's income is given at point X, that is, the individual has income this period, but unlike the case of Figures 13–5 and 13–6, he or she has none next period. Individual B has income next period but none this period. Using the Edgeworth box diagram technique, rotate individual B's axes by 180° and superimpose the Xs. This appears in Figure 13–8.

The indifference curves of A and B have points of tangency that, if connected, form what is called a contract line; that is, the set of all points for which A's marginal rate of time preference equals B's marginal rate of time preference. The size of the box represents total income of the two individuals in the two periods. At point a the marginal rate of time preference is the same for both A and B and also equals the slope of the line from the X point representing the original incomes of the two individuals to point a. *The slope of the line equals $-(1 + i)$. Individual A lends to B the amount of current income as noted. This reduces B's next period income by an amount noted by "repayment of loan," and it increases A's second-period income by this amount as well.*

Figure 13–7
Time-preferences Curves for Two Persons

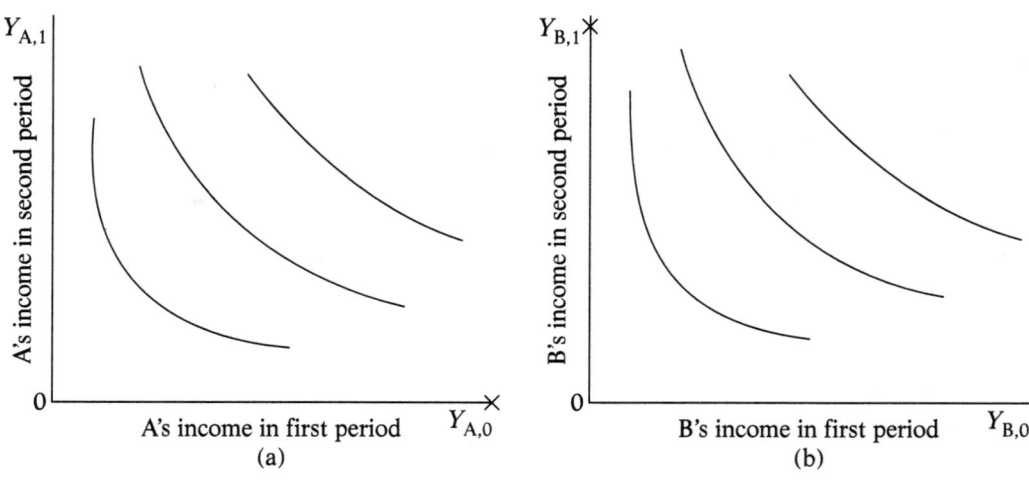

$Y_{A,1}$

A's income in second period

0

A's income in first period $\quad Y_{A,0}$

(a)

$Y_{B,1}$

B's income in second period

0

B's income in first period $\quad Y_{B,0}$

(b)

Figure 13–8
The Two-person Market for Borrowing and Lending

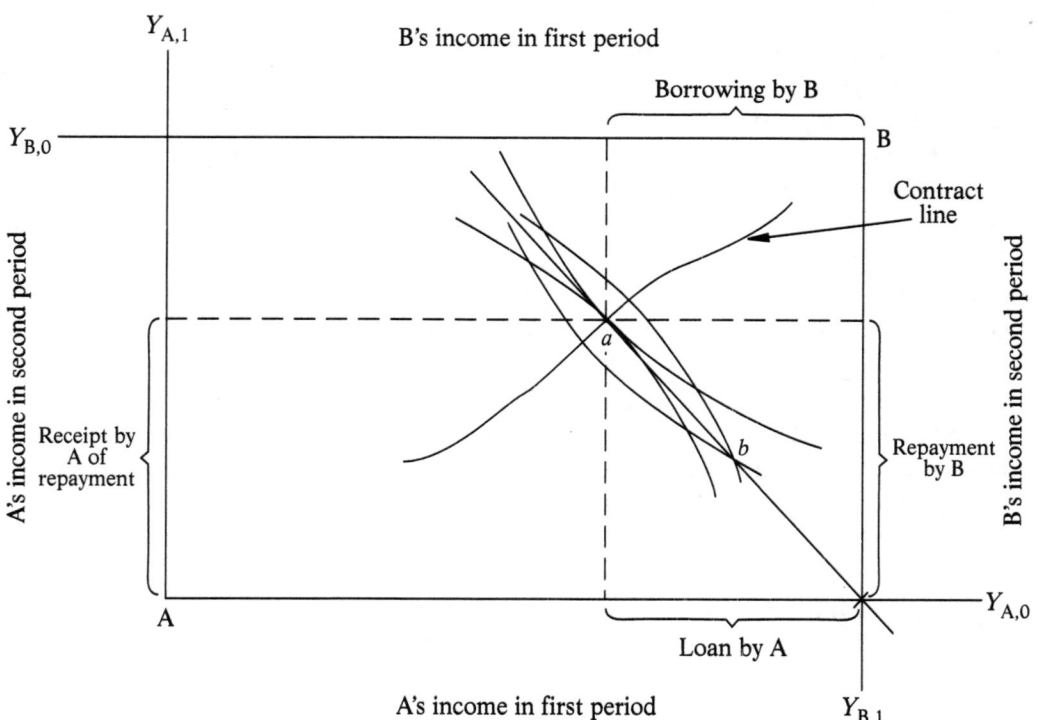

$Y_{A,1}$

B's income in first period

Borrowing by B

$Y_{B,0}$

B

Contract line

A's income in second period

Receipt by A of repayment

Repayment by B

B's income in second period

A

a

b

Loan by A

$Y_{A,0}$

A's income in first period

$Y_{B,1}$

If the amount of the loan were represented by point *b*, for example, at this point A's marginal rate of time preference (the slope of his indifference curve) would be less (flatter) than would be B's marginal rate of time preference. This indicates that, at this rate of interest, B would be on a higher indifference curve if he or she should borrow more from A and also that A would be on a higher curve if he or she could lend to B. Both A and B are better off if they move toward point *a*.

We can avoid thinking of A and B as particular individuals, but rather as representative groups of borrowers and lenders, who meet in the marketplace and supply and demand funds. This competitive interaction determines the market rate of interest at any given time. Thus, the interest rate, which is a market clearing price for loanable funds, is determined, like other prices, by forces of supply and demand.

From Figures 13–4 and 13–5, we can see how a supply curve of loanable funds can be generated. A supply curve shows the interest rate on the vertical axis and the quantity of funds supplied on the horizontal axis. This appears in Figure 13–9.

In Figure 13–5, at point *a*, the individual supplies no funds when interest rates are zero. This point is reflected in point *a*, Figure 13–9. From Figure 13–6, we find the lender willing to move to point *b*; this is reflected as point *b*, in Figure 13–9, which shows a positive amount of saving at a positive interest rate of 20 per cent. (In this frame of reference we are making the simplified assumption that saving is the only source of supply of loanable funds.)

The demand for loanable funds on the part of borrowers can also be derived in a similar way to that used to derive the supply curve. However, the demand for loanable

Figure 13–9
Supply of Saving and Loanable Funds

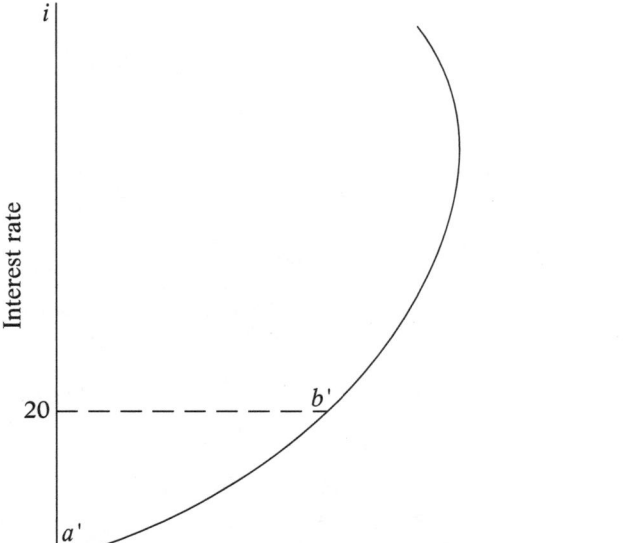

funds is affected not only by the desires of different individuals to even out their income streams, but also, and more important, the demand for loanable funds arises because there exist real investment opportunities that provide a yield in the form of increases in income in the future.

Assume, for example, that the individual whose time-preference curves we are studying believes that by purchasing a $10 machine with a life of one year he or she can earn a 100 per cent return. That is, in a year's time the individual will realize an addition to profits of $10 beyond the $10 that he or she pays in costs for the machine. The machine earns $20 so that at the end of year the individual receives back $10 in "real" interest. This "real" interest rate is often called the "internal" rate of return. Now assume that a second machine, when employed along with the first, will yield a return of 50 per cent. Finally, let a third machine yield a return of 20 per cent. Thus, on the individual's two-period diagram, note the line from the X origin sloping up to the left in Figure 13–10. The lower part of the curve shows the 100 per cent rate on the first $10 machine, then the next segment of the curve shows the 50 per cent return on the second $10 machine, and so forth. The curve is called an investment opportunity (IO) curve. The slope of the IO curve is $-(1 + r)$ where r is the internal rate of return. It falls as investment expands. For simplicity, assume that the curve is smooth and superimpose it on the individual's map of indifference curves as in Figure 13–11.

Figure 13–10
The Investment Opportunity Curve

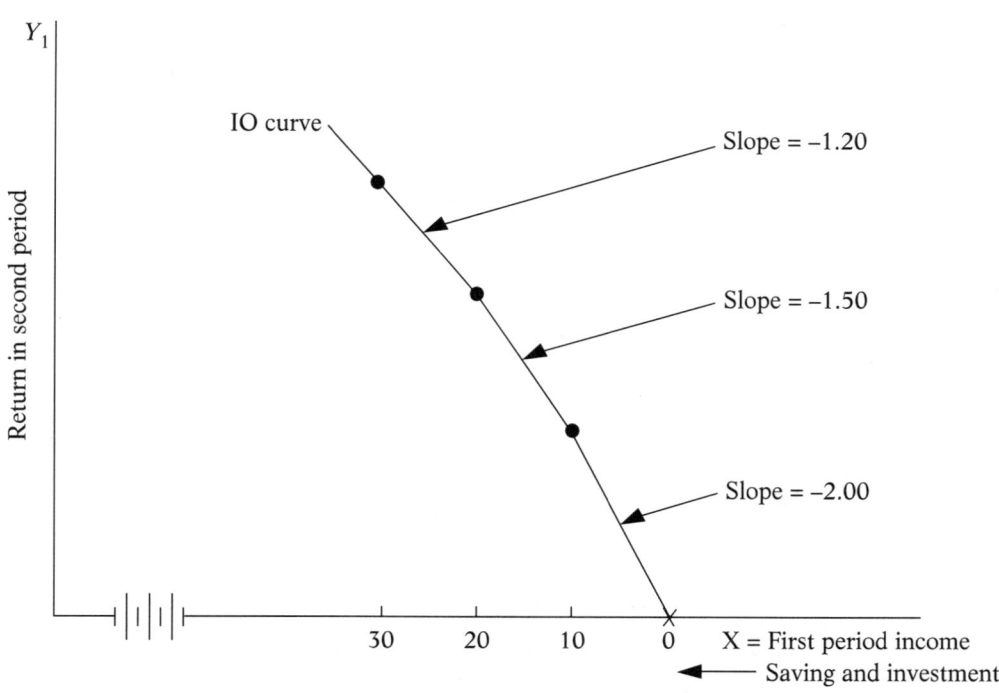

Figure 13–11
Individual Saving and Investment

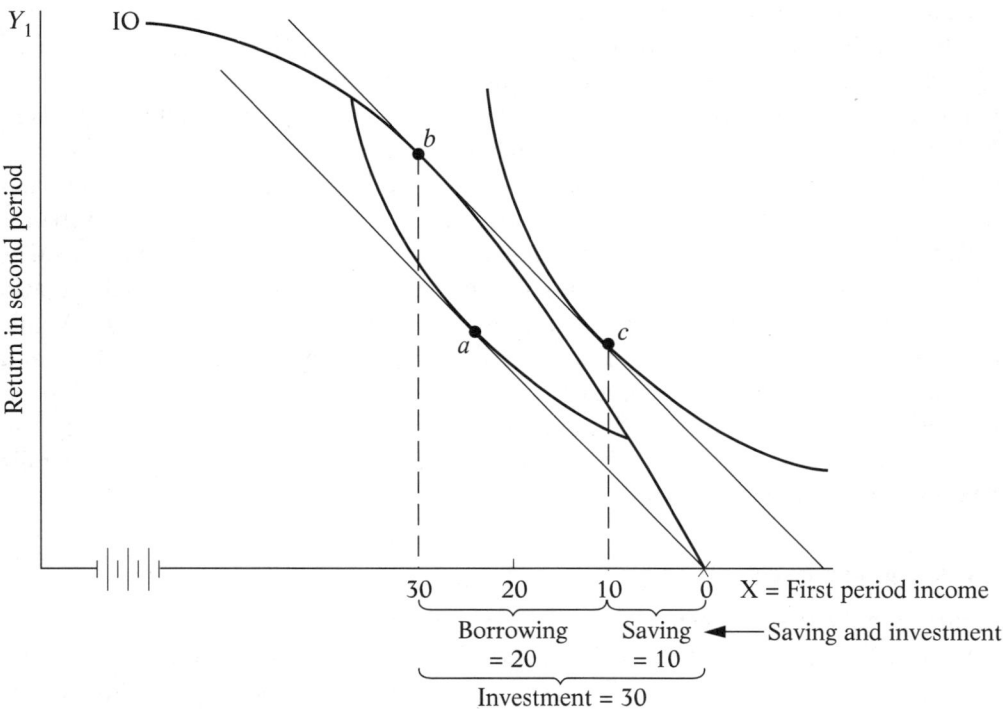

In the absence of investment opportunities, this individual could move along the line from X to point a and reach a higher indifference curve than he or she would be on at point X. The individual could do this by saving part of his or her income and lending it at the interest rate of 20 per cent. This line represents a set of possible options open for dividing his or her income between the two periods. With the IO curve the individual now expands his or her opportunities. The individual can move along the IO curve to point b and reach a higher indifference curve because the investments will give him or her more income in period 1. But, if the market rate of interest is still 20 per cent, the individual may invest in the three machines a total of $30, but then borrow $20 at the going interest rate of 20 per cent and move down along the new straight line to reach point c, a point on the highest indifference curve. Thus, the individual may invest (save) and borrow at the same time to raise his or her own money and borrow the other $20 to make the $30 investment. This is essentially what homeowners do with their "down payments." At b, $-(1 + r) = -(1 + i)$ and the cost of capital i equals the internal rate of return r. At c these both equal the individual's marginal rate of time preference.

Economic growth, in the sense of raising income and consumption levels of the people, follows from investment. From the diagram, it is clear that lower interest rates lead to higher rates of investment spending and to higher income next period. Of course, new technology leads to investment opportunity and is undoubtedly the root source of economic growth. But investment made feasible by low interest rates is the proximate source of higher living standards.

Thus, the neoclassical economical description of the saving-investment process rests upon certain assumptions: (1) that people have time preferences from which appropriate indifference curves may be derived, (2) that there exists a technology such that investment will provide a positive return (that is, a higher real income in the future than would be possible without it), (3) that a competitive, free market exists where borrowers and lenders can meet, and (4) that competitive forces will drive the rate of exchange between present and future income (the interest rate) to an equilibrium position where $-(1 + i)$ equals the marginal rate of time preference for each individual and also equals the marginal rate of return on current investment opportunities $-(1 + r)$. At this equilibrium the market clears. The analysis turns on the concepts of "thrift" and "productivity." If government imposes ceilings on interest rates or other constraints on the freedom of individuals to engage in borrowing and lending and saving and investing, then the competitive equilibrium cannot be attained and welfare (utility) will generally be lower than otherwise (see Scott, 1979).

Expanding the Model

In this simplified analytical model, there is one individual, one type of machine, and one market interest rate representing the cost of funds. In the real world, there are many individuals, each with a set of indifference curves. There are many types of investment opportunities, and there are many interest rates that reflect the riskiness of different investments. In these cases, the model can be expanded to accommodate the increased complexity. Instead of having to construct such a complicated model to direct investment allocations as would be necessary in a regulated economy, the working of free market forces leads to an efficient solution.

Summary

The Equation of Exchange, presented by Hume, provides the foundation for the analysis of inflation in a market economy. A rearranged equation provided the basis for the Quantity Theory of Money showing that money, output, and inflation are related. The interaction of these variables with interest rate levels was described by Wicksell and elaborated upon by Keynes in developing his theory of national income and employment. The general level of interest rates is an important dependent variable in a complete macroeconomic model of income determination.

Stress was placed on the Quantity Theory of Money as a theory of the demand for money by Friedman. Movements in interest rate levels can be interpreted using demand and supply functions for money.

Tobin pointed out that including only the two assets, money and bonds, in the model left open the possibility of error in an analysis of changes in the supplies of money, debt, equity, and tangible assets. A theory of asset choice provided the basis for an enhanced macroeconomic model of interest rate determination.

On the microeconomic side, Fisher developed the idea of interest as a price affecting the saving and consumption decisions of a consumer. This model gives rise to an understanding of the fundamentals of consumer choice regarding the time preferences each consumer has. The model can be elaborated to handle the many different individual interest rates that exist in the economy, including those that describe returns attributable to real machines and equipment. Thousands of individual interest rates are determined in a market economy, along with thousands of individual prices, by the interaction of supply and demand for funds that are used to invest in machines with the market prices of those machines.

Thus, in this chapter, the discussion moved from the macroeconomic theory of the determination of the general level of interest rates to the microeconomic theory of the determination of thousands of individual interest rates. In a free market, these interest rates reflect consumers' decisions to purchase capital goods. Interest rates serve as prices that ration scarce capital among individual uses.

Note

The Lagrangian multiplier method is used to do this. Assume $U = U(M, B, S, T)$ and that $W = P_M M + P_B B + P_S S + P_T T$. Let prices of assets be given. Form a new function using a nonzero constant, λ. Multiply λ by the equation as follows: $\lambda(W - P_M M - P_B B - P_S S - P_T T)$. Notice that the sum of items in the parentheses is zero. Now simply add this term to the utility function to form a new function

$$L(M, B, S, T) = U(M, B, S, T) + \lambda(W - P_M M - P_B B - P_S S - P_T T)$$

Taking partial derivatives of L with respect to each of the four variables gives

$$\frac{\partial L}{\partial M} = \frac{\partial U}{\partial M} - \lambda P_M$$

$$\frac{\partial L}{\partial B} = \frac{\partial U}{\partial B} - \lambda P_B$$

$$\frac{\partial L}{\partial S} = \frac{\partial U}{\partial B} - \lambda P_S$$

$$\frac{\partial L}{\partial T} = \frac{\partial U}{\partial T} - \lambda P_T$$

By setting each of these four partial derivatives equal to zero, and recognizing that $\partial U/\partial M$ is the marginal utility of money, $\partial U/\partial B$ is the marginal utility of bonds, and so forth, one can establish that

$$\frac{MU_M}{P_M} = \frac{MU_B}{P_B} = \frac{MU_S}{P_S} = \frac{MU_T}{P_T}$$

This is a set of necessary conditions for the maximizing of utility from wealth holdings.

Key Terms and Concepts

David Hume

Quantity Theory of Money

Wicksell

Friedman

Theory of asset choice

Two-period diagram

Supply of saving curve

Equation of exchange

Theory of the Demand for Money

Keynes

Tobin

Irving Fisher

Marginal rate of time preference

Investment opportunity curve

Discussion Questions and Exercises

1. What is the equation of exchange? Define each of its variables clearly.
2. What two assumptions can be made to turn the equation of exchange into a theory of inflation?
3. How is the equation used to describe the quantity theory of money? Define each of the terms in the equation carefully.
4. What is the contribution to the theory of inflation for which Knut Wicksell is known? Describe it briefly.
5. According to Keynes what are three important reasons that people hold money?
6. Explain the concept of "liquidity preference" using the concept of "idle money balances" in relation to interest rate levels.
7. Explain why the demand function for money is downward sloping.
8. Use a graph of the demand and supply for money to explain how interest rate levels may change when a crop failure leads to a decline in Q.
9. What happened to the demand curve for U.S. dollars when Eastern European countries found they were no longer isolated from the West?
10. Is the Theory of the Demand for Money a partial equilibrium theory or a general equilibrium theory? Explain.
11. How does Tobin's theory of the demand for assets differ from the theory of demand for money? Explain.
12. In the theory of demand for assets, individuals are presumed to maximize utility from a portfolio, if they are constrained by wealth. Restate this clearly using a utility function and a wealth constraint.
13. If money were dropped from a helicopter, explain what would happen to the demand for bonds, stocks, and tangibles and their prices.
14. If real resources, such as barrels of oil, were freely distributed in a community, what would happen to the demand for money, bonds, and stocks?
15. Draw indifference curves for an individual using a two-period diagram to illustrate the case of a borrower and of a lender.
16. Draw a box diagram showing the determination of the interest rate when competition among borrowers for loans from lenders clears the market of the available supply of loans. Use the box to describe how much lending takes place.

17. How is an investment opportunity curve constructed?
18. Explain why both lending and borrowing is typical for individuals who maximize their utility.

References

Aiyagari, S. Rao, "Explaining Financial Market Facts: The Importance of Incomplete Markets and Transaction Costs," *Quarterly Review*, Federal Reserve Bank of Minneapolis, Winter 1993, pp. 17–31.

Baumol, W. J., "The Transactions Demand for Cash: An Inventory Theoretic Approach," *Quarterly Journal of Economics*, November 1952, pp. 545–56.

Dickey, David A., Jansen, Dennis W., and Thorton, Daniel L., "A Primer on Cointegration with an Application to Money and Income," *Review*, Federal Reserve Bank of St. Louis, March/April 1991, pp. 58–78.

Fisher, Irving, *The Theory of Interest*, Macmillan, New York, 1930.

Homer, Sidney, "How (not) to Explain the Bond Market to Your Wife," in Charles D. Ellis and James R. Vertin, eds., *Classics: An Investor's Anthology*, Institute of Chartered Financial Analysts, Charlottesville, VI, 1989, pp. 375–81.

Scott, Robert Haney, "A Paradox in the Relation of Wealth to Utility," *Nebraska Journal of Economics and Business*, Autumn 1979, pp. 65–71.

Smith, Bruce D., "The Relationship Between Money and Prices: Some Historical Evidence Reconsidered," *Quarterly Review*, Federal Reserve Bank of Minneapolis, Summer 1988, pp. 18–32.

Tobin, James, "The Interest-elasticity of the Transactions Demand for Cash," *Review of Economics and Statistics*, August 1956, pp. 241–47.

_____, "Money, Capital, and Other Stores of Value," *American Economic Review*, Papers and Proceedings, May 1961, pp. 26–37.

_____, "A General Equilibrium Approach to Monetary Theory," *Journal of Money, Credit and Banking*, February 1969, pp. 15–29.

Wallace, Neil, "Some of the Choices for Monetary Policy," *Quarterly Review*, Federal Reserve Bank of Minneapolis, Winter 1984, pp. 15–24.

CHAPTER 14

The Term Structure of Interest Rates

"ARE INTEREST RATES likely to go up this fall?" This question is often heard in the board rooms of businesses everywhere. The questioner implicitly assumes that if the general level of interest rates rises, those rates relevant to a borrowing decision by the board will rise as well.

Factors affecting the level of interest rates were discussed in Chapter 12. Interest rate theory, the subject of Chapter 13, extended the discussion of factors affecting the level of interest rates and then introduced a liquidity continuum and the idea that interest yields are higher on less liquid assets. Depending on consumer preferences, all yields need not always move up and down together. The theory of consumers' choice helps explain saving decisions and consumption over time, and it can be expanded to accommodate choices among the large variety of assets available.

The focus of this chapter is on the term to maturity of bonds, and on why a bond's yield depends on its maturity. The yield on a one-year bill is different from the yield on a six-month bill even when both have the backing of the U.S. Treasury and both are sold on the same day at the same auction under the same procedure. The only discernable difference is that the two bills have different maturity dates. What is it about different maturity dates that leads to different yields? Possible answers are discussed here.

Yield Curves

In Figure 14–1 yield to maturity is measured on the vertical axis and the period of time remaining to maturity is measured on the horizontal axis. This hypothetical figure is drawn to resemble those published in the *Treasury Bulletin* for many years before 1991. The crosses are plots of the returns on securities that mature on specific dates. Because Treasury securities are similar in most respects, the set of yields described in such a graph resembles an experiment in which a set of observations is taken in a laboratory so that results are isolated from many random forces in nature. For example, a mixture of yields on corporate bonds and Treasury bonds would cloud the picture of the relation between yield and maturity because the two types of bonds have quality differences. Treasury bonds are default-free and because of this they are of higher quality than corporate bonds.

Any specific yield curve is for a set of yields as of a certain time and day. The line drawn through the points as closely as possible is drawn by free-hand. It is not statistically calculated, although it could be and has been by academics who were interested in attempting to refine the drawing process. However, a statistical drawing does not seem to provide any superior illustration of term structure relations than that obtained by squinting the eyes to make the picture a blur and then taking a pen and drawing a line through the middle of the blur as best as one possibly can.

A Variety of Presentations of Yield Curves. In 1991 the *Treasury Bulletin* changed its presentation of the yield curve and today's *Bulletin* shows only the curve and not the points through which it is drawn—thus, today's drawings have lost flavor.

Newspapers also report yield curves, but in a variety of different formats. The horizontal axis needs to extend out to 30 years, but a huge number of securities are in the range of money market instruments—within one year. So, to simplify the presentation

Figure 14–1
The Yield Curve

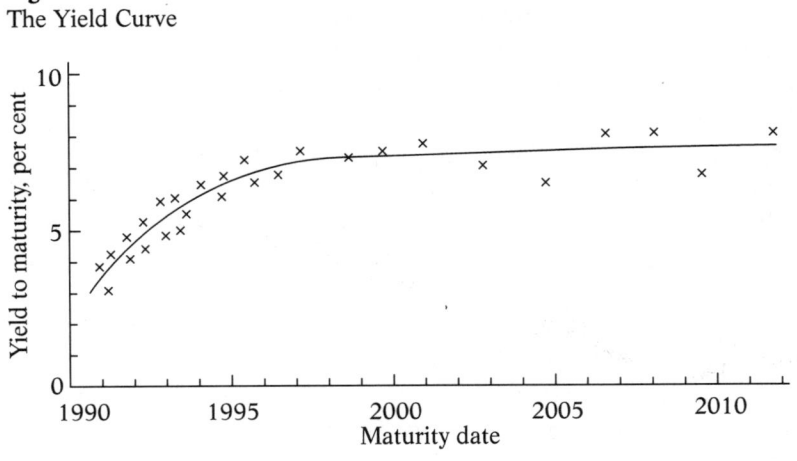

for the reading public, the scale of measurement on the horizontal axis may be distorted. For example, there may be a large horizontal distance representing the range of securities that mature within one year and then smaller intervals presented for longer maturities. This distortion of the horizontal axis also distorts the appearance of the curve and may give a misleading impression of the nature of the relation.

Investment bankers also simplify their presentations of the yield curve in their newsletters. They often refer to yield spreads rather than to a curve itself. For example, they may trace changes in the one-year to thirty-year spread over a recent period. They may also examine yield spreads on different maturities of instruments other than Treasury securities.

Yield Curves in Different Countries. The pink newspaper, the *Financial Times* from London, regularly publishes yield curves taken from securities markets in different countries in a set of graphs placed side-by-side for easy comparison. Newsletters published by investment banks also provide yield curve information from different countries for their clients.

Changing Yield Curves

The yield curve moves up and down over time within a fairly distinct range and set of patterns in response to changing business conditions. Figures 14–2 and 14–3 illustrate the variety of shapes that yield curves may take.

A normal yield curve is believed to be one with a positive slope in the range of shorter maturities and that flattens out in the long-maturity range. The lower four curves shown in Figure 14–2 have a "normal" shape. Such a pattern presumably reflects the extra liquidity short-term low-risk securities have. This premium can be thought of as a premium on the price of a short-term security—people pay a higher price to have greater liquidity so the yield is lower on the short-term security. Or it can be thought of as an interest rate premium, that is, a higher yield on longer securities that borrowers must pay to induce lenders to purchase the longer-dated, less-liquid, more risky long-term securities. With either interpretation the result is a liquidity premium that imparts an upward slope to the curve. And, for very long-dated maturities, the premium is not much affected by an extra year's maturity, so the curve flattens out to the right.

An inverted yield curve is downward sloping from left to right, that is, short-term yields are higher than long-term yields. The curve drawn for August 30, 1974 in Figure 14–2 has this shape. So do all of the curves drawn in Figure 14–3. This shape usually occurs when an economy is overheated and inflationary and is being reined in with tight monetary policies and high interest rates. For example, in Figure 14–2 the scale of interest rates on the vertical axis shows a range of from 4 to 10 per cent. In contrast, interest rates in Figure 14–3, showing inverted yield curves, range from 9 to 18 per cent. If the two graphs were presented together the second figure would be placed on top of the first one and the combined figure would show the range of yield curve shapes occurring between 1974 and 1986. This period was one in which interest rates were

Figure 14–2
Yields on U.S. Government Securities

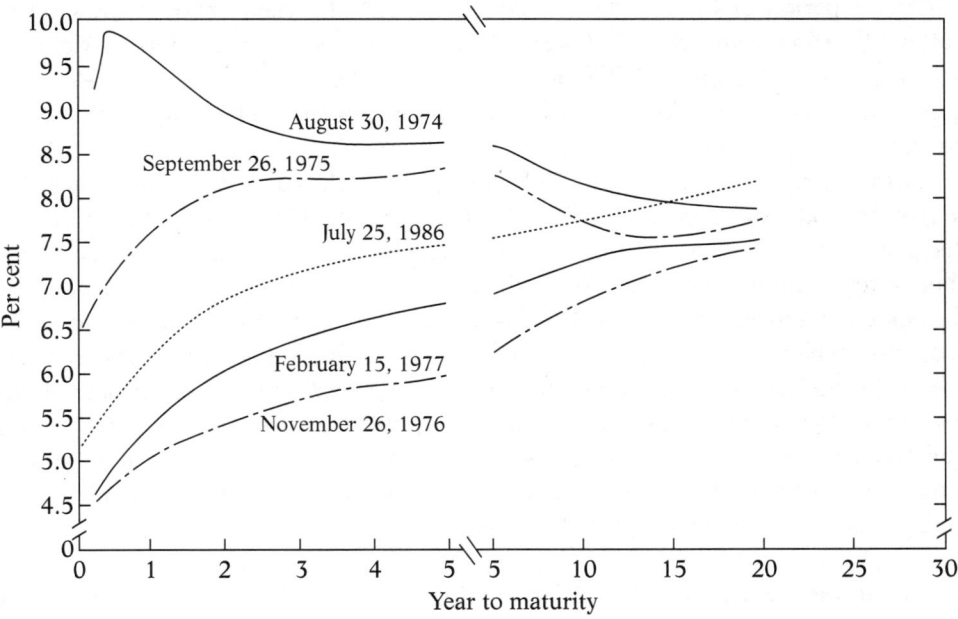

Figure 14–3
Yields on U.S. Government Securities

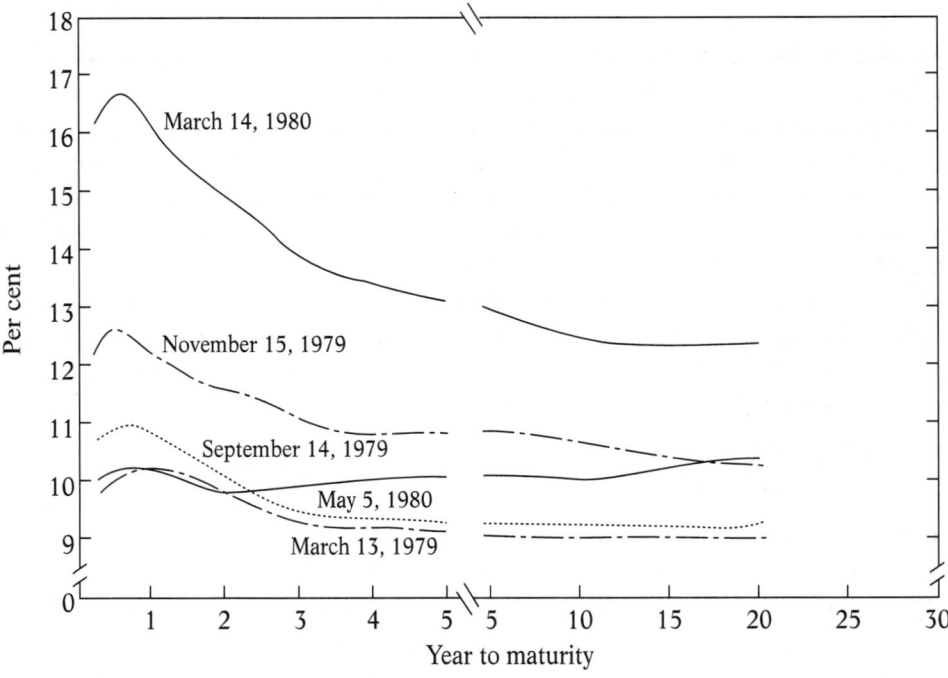

Source: Federal Reserve Bank of St. Louis.

quite volatile so the full set of yield curves provides a good illustration of how they fluctuate over time.

Over a period of fluctuation in business activity the yield curve follows a rough pattern. Starting from a period of weak economic activity, the characteristic yield curve will slope upward and then flatten out. In an extended period of recession, yields will be quite low. Short-term yields may be 1 per cent or even less while long-term yields may be from 2 to 4 per cent.

As the economic recovery proceeds, the entire yield curve will shift upward and short-term and long-term yields will rise to 6–8 per cent. The spread between them will disappear. With further inflation accompanied by restraint from monetary policies, short rates climb to 12–15 per cent while long yields climb to 10–11 per cent, putting the curve in an inverted position. Then as the tight monetary policies take hold, and the economic expansion starts to wane, short-term yields fall. Long-term yields are slow to follow. So the yield curve becomes positively sloped even when all yields are still quite high by historical standards. After short-term yields fall, there is slowly a downward pull exerted on the long yields to fall as well. During the decline the short-long spread is quite large. If the economy enters a recession and stays there for an extended period, long yields will gradually fall to 2–4 per cent again.

A Hump in the Yield Curve. The reader will note that when the maturities are very short term the curve is still positively sloped even though the remainder of the curve is inverted. This simply reflects the continued existence of a noticeable liquidity effect in securities that have only a few months to maturity.

Yield Fluctuations vs. Price Fluctuations. The reader will notice that the amplitude of the fluctuation in short-term *yields* exceeds that of the long-term yields. If we took a look at *price* fluctuations, however, it would show that prices on long-term securities fluctuate with greater amplitude than prices of short-term securities. If the curves were drawn with prices instead of yields on the vertical axis, the picture would be a mirror image, with a narrow band of fluctuation near the axis and wider fluctuations to the right where the maturities are farther in the future.

The reason for these patterns can be found in the present value formula itself. Consider, for example, what happens to the *price* of a $1,000 very long-term security, a perpetuity, when its *yield changes* from 5 per cent to 6 per cent, a 1 percentage point increase or a 20 per cent increase in yield:

$$PV = \frac{R}{i} = \frac{\$50}{0.05} = \$1,000 \qquad\qquad PV = \frac{\$50}{0.06} = \$833.33$$

The equation shows that the price declines by $167 when the yield increases by a percentage point.

Now consider the equation for a short-term security, a one-year bond:

$$PV = \frac{R + F}{(1 + 0.05)} = \frac{\$1,050}{(1 + 0.05)} = \$1,000 \qquad\qquad PV = \frac{\$1,050}{(1 + 0.06)} = \$990.55$$

In this case the price declined only by $10.45 in contrast to the $167 price decline in the case of the very long-term security. Thus, *for a given change in yield, the price of a long-term security changes more than the price of a short-term security*. The mirror image of this proposition is that, *for a given change in the price of a security, the yield on a short-term security changes more than the yield on a long-term security*. The interested reader can use the equations, let the price change by $100, and then see what happens to the yield in each case.

The volatility of the price of a bond is also affected by the coupon rate: the lower the coupon rate, the greater the price change for a given change in yield. The smaller the quantity represented by R in the equation for the one year security shown above, the larger will be the change in PV for a given change in i. Also, zero coupon bonds will have price changes that are larger than coupon bonds when the yield changes by a given amount.

Thus, the mechanics of calculations using the present value formula lead one to believe that the pattern remaining in the diagrams by shifting yield curves can be attributed to the formula itself. However, the pattern may also be explained by theory. There are two principal theories that economists employ: the segmented markets approach and the expectations approach.

The Segmented Markets Approach

Under the segmented markets approach, the approach almost universally used by financial analysts, securities in different maturity ranges are considered to be imperfect substitutes. An increase in the supply of securities in one maturity range will lead to a decline in prices (rise of yields) of those securities. An increase in demand will lead to an increase in their prices. That is, we simply apply the usual supply and demand analysis we use in discussing determination of prices of commodities. Of course, "segmented" does not mean totally separate or independent. Indeed, all analysts recognize that the various markets for securities of different types may be highly interdependent. Three-month bills are very good substitutes for six-month bills, and six-month bills are good substitutes for nine-month bills. Also, 19-year bonds are good substitutes for 20-year bonds. But three-month bills are not good substitutes for 20-year bonds. Thus, the more distant different securities are from each other in the maturity range, the less they can be substituted for each other.

There is a tendency for firms to match the maturity of their assets with the maturity of their liabilities. Commercial banks have short-term liabilities; hence, for liquidity purposes, they hold large amounts of short-term assets. Insurance companies, on the other hand, have liabilities that extend into the distant future, and they hold large numbers of long-term securities to be sure that the revenues they need will be available when the time arrives. Businesses with large inventories borrow short-term to finance their activities, perhaps by pledging accounts receivable against commercial bank loans. Manufacturing firms constructing plants with an expected life of 20 years may sell 20-year bonds to finance the construction. This tendency to match assets with liabilities is tantamount to "hedging" on a bet to avoid the risk of sizable loss.

A lender purchasing a short-term security knows that its price will not change greatly while he or she holds it; that is, there is little risk of being forced to assume a capital loss in case they might wish to sell the security prior to maturity. Thus, short-term securities minimize the risk of capital loss. However, lenders who purchase long-term securities have greater certainty of a steady income flow over the extended period than do those who make repeated purchases of short-term securities over the years. Thus, long-term securities minimize the possibility of income variation. Persons wishing to avoid capital loss will buy short-term securities, and those wishing to avoid income variation will buy long-term securities.

Furthermore, short-term securities are more "liquid" than are long-term securities. They are "closer" to money because they are (1) more readily marketable, and (2) subject to less price variation because they are closer to maturity. Hence it is generally assumed that lenders will be willing to pay a premium price for short-term over long-term securities, thereby pushing the yield on short-terms below those of long-terms. This "liquidity premium" exists because lenders have a positive preference for liquidity, other things being equal.

Besides these institutional preferences for certain maturity ranges because of liquidity and risk preferences, there also exist certain legal restrictions that make securities of different maturities poor substitutes for each other. Formerly, some state-chartered commercial banks were allowed to count certain short-term securities as part of their legally required reserves, but long-term securities were not eligible for this purpose. A variety of other legal restrictions affect the demand for securities on the part of savings banks, insurance companies, and the managements of pension funds.

To summarize, the segmented markets approach treats securities of different maturities as being related, but with unique characteristics. Short-term securities have liquidity and provide certainty of capital value, even for very short periods. Long-term securities have certainty of income flow. Legal restraints on investment activity also affect demand in the various maturity ranges. Therefore, different buyers have preferences for different maturities so that yields respond to changes in conditions of supply and demand in the different maturity ranges.

To see how the segmented markets approach works, let us refer to Figure 14–4. In this figure the yield curve may be divided into four maturity ranges for illustrative purposes: within one year, one to five years, five to ten years, and over ten years to maturity. The lines of segmentation are chosen arbitrarily to suit the analyst's needs.

This type of segmentation is routine in economic analysis. For example, an agricultural economist may wish to study the supply and demand for food. More likely, however, the food category will be broken arbitrarily into various segments. Basic categories include meat, grain, vegetables, and fruit. There are many types of fruit, one of which is citrus fruit. The market for citrus fruit may be divided into oranges, grapefruit, and lemons. Finally, the agricultural economist may wish to narrow the inquiry to the market for oranges, which is simply a market that is segmented from other markets. All supply and

Figure 14–4

A Change in the Yield Curve

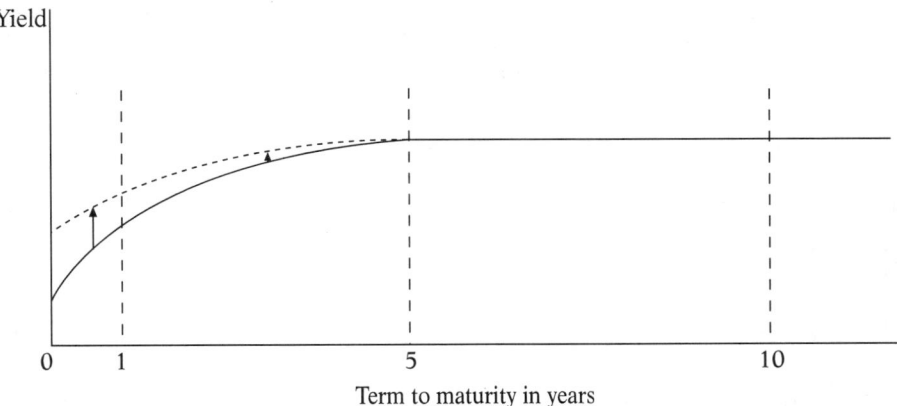

demand analyses require segmentation. But when the market is segmented in this way, it is not separated. The analyst will observe that the demand for oranges depends upon the price of oranges and also upon the price of grapefruit because grapefruit is recognized to be a close substitute for oranges.

The analogy is straightforward. First, we have chosen to look at a special category of securities—those issued by the U.S. Treasury—to draw yield curves. Some of these securities are money market securities, and some are capital market securities.

In Figure 14–5 there are two graphs of supply and demand. One is for securities within one year to maturity. The other is for securities with maturity in the range of one to five years. Assume that the U.S. Treasury decides to sell an increased volume of T-bills. The supply of securities in the within one-year segment of the market will increase. The increase is shown as a shift to the right from initial position S_0 to subsequent position S_1. This increased supply of short-term securities leads to a decline in price. The decline in price implies a concomitant increase in yield on securities in this range. The increased yield is shown by the dashed portion of the curve back in Figure 14–4.

But does this mean no change in the market for securities in the one- to five-year maturity range? Not at all, because the securities in the two ranges are substitutes for each other. The new lower price of the within one-year securities will make those securities attractive. Some investors will switch out of the market for one- to five-year securities to buy the higher-yielding (lower priced) securities in the within one-year segment. That is, there will be a reduction in demand for securities in the one- to five-year segment of the market. This reduction is shown by a leftward shift in the demand curve from the initial demand D_0 to the subsequent demand D_1. The prices of these securities decline from initial position P_0 to the lower level P_1. Again, the lower price is reflected in a higher yield.

Figure 14–5
Effects of Changes in Supply and Demand for Different Maturities

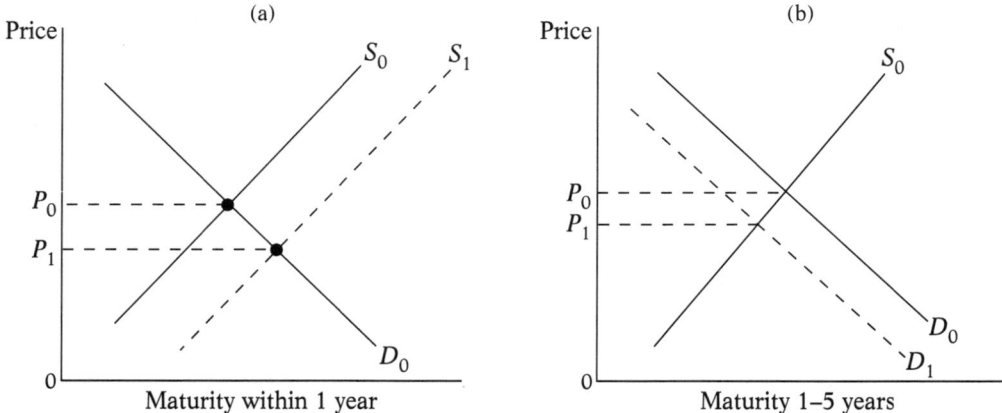

Back in Figure 14–4 the higher yield in the one- to five-year maturity range is shown. Because of substitutability of securities along the maturity spectrum, the yield curve is pushed up in the short end of the market but shows little or no response in the long end. The yield curve changes its shape toward a flatter position as maturity increases.

Think of the supply and demand graphs in Figure 14–5 as graphs for oranges on the left and grapefruit on the right. Assume a bumper crop of oranges and an increase in supply. This lowers the price of oranges. Because they are good substitutes for grapefruit, the demand for grapefruit falls and so does the price of grapefruit. From your microeconomics course, you may recall the concept of cross-price elasticity of demand. Here it is positive, indicating substitute goods.

Similar considerations apply if the Treasury were to issue a big block of 20-year bonds. Long-term yields would rise. So would intermediate-term yields. But yields on securities in the within 1-year range would be little affected, and the yield curve would assume a steeper positive slope in the short maturity segments.

Thus, to apply a segmented markets approach to the analysis of the term structure of interest rates is simply to apply the usual supply and demand approach that is a mainstay of all applied economic analysis.

The Pure Expectations Approach

In this approach to the explanation of the term structure, expectations alone determine the structure of yields. Expectations concerning future interest rates determine the demand for securities, which in turn determines their yields. However, changes in supplies of securities in different maturity ranges do not affect their yields on securities with different maturities as suggested by the segmented markets approach.

Simplifying Assumptions

The pure expectations theory of the term structure is based upon a number of simplifying assumptions:

1. that a large enough number of financial investors (or a smaller number who are well-financed) hold uniform expectations about future values of short-term interest rates
2. that no transactions costs exist, so that investors may enter and leave the market frequently without cost
3. that no market imperfections inhibit interest rates from moving to their competitive level
4. that investors wish to maximize their holding period yield; that is, they wish to obtain the maximum income (profit) available over a given period of time

In a world in which these assumptions hold, the long-term rate will equal the average of short-term rates expected to prevail over the long-term period. To maximize holding-period yield, an investor may invest in, say, either a two-year security or in one-year securities in two successive years—reinvesting at the end of each year. If a two-year security gives a higher return at the end of the two years than the same amount invested in two successive one-year securities, then, to maximize his or her income, the investor will purchase the two-year security. But, if higher income will result from two successive one-year investments, then this is the investment that he or she will make to maximize the return over the two-year investment period.

For example, if an investor can purchase a current one-year security for a 3 per cent return, and then a second one-year security for a 5 per cent return, over the two years the investor will earn approximately 4 per cent (the two-year average of 3 per cent and 5 per cent).

If R_1 is the current market rate of interest on a one-year security, R_2 is the current market rate on a two-year security, and r_1 is the market rate on a one-year security that is expected to prevail one year from today, then in our example, $R_1 = 3$ per cent, $r_1 = 5$ per cent, and

$$R_2 = \frac{(R_1 + r_1)}{2} = \frac{(3 + 5)}{2} = 4\%$$

This is the same as:

$$(1 + R_2) = \frac{(1 + R_1) + (1 + r_1)}{2}$$

or

$$1.04 = \frac{(1.03) + (1.05)}{2}$$

From these formulas it is clear that, if a two-year bond is selling at a price to yield greater than 4 per cent, the lender will choose it. But if the two-year security is selling to yield less than 4 per cent, the lender will choose to invest in the current one-year security and reinvest at the end of the year in another one-year security to obtain a 4 per cent yield over two years.

The crucial element in the decision about which investment to make is the value of the one-year rate that investors expect to exist one year from today. Whether their expectations prove to be right or not, they will invest in a way that will bring the maturity pattern of rates into line with their expectations according to the pure expectations approach. (It should be noted here that this statement is operationally meaningless as will be emphasized later in the chapter.)

The slope of the yield curve is said to reflect expectations held by investors about what the yield on a one-year security will be one year from today. This is shown in Figure 14–6(a), in which today's yield curve is upward sloping, and in which yields on one-year and two-year securities today are 3 and 4 per cent, shown with crosses and labeled R_1 and R_2. If these R values are placed in the formula $R_2 = (R_1 + r_1)/2$ and if the formula is solved for r_1, r_1 turns out to be 5 per cent. This value is shown in Figure 14–6(a) and is designated by a small zero to distinguish it from the observations of today's yields.

The r_1 in the graph is, presumably, the one-year yield that investors expect to prevail next year. It is called the implied forward rate; that is, current spot yields R_1 and R_2 imply that investors expect r_1 to be the one-year yield next year. In this case, r_1 is simply calculated from the formula by inserting the current values of R_1 and R_2. In this example the yield curve is upward sloping, and the implied forward rate is greater than the current rate R_1 and also greater than the current rate R_2.

Thus, when the yield curve slopes upward, some economists say that this implies that investors expect one-year yields to rise over the coming year. Indeed, from the calculation, they could even say that investors expect one-year yields to rise to a level above the current two-year yield. Not only are short-term yields expected to rise, but they are expected to rise by a considerable amount. A belief in rising short-term yields is implied by the current upward-sloping yield curve.

A belief that yields will fall is implied when the current yield curve is downward sloping. This is shown in Figure 14–6(b). Here the spot rate on a one-year security is 10 per cent, and on a two-year security it is 9 per cent. Using these rates as values of R_1 and R_2 in the formula $R_2 = (R_1 + r_1)/2$ and solving for r_1 gives a value of 8 per cent for r_1. When today's yield curve is downward sloping, the implied forward rate is below the spot rates. Investors are presumed to believe not only that yields will fall over the coming year, but also that one-year yields will fall to levels below the current yields on two-year securities.

In these examples the arithmetic mean of two short-term rates are used to find the long-term rate; however, the geometric mean is the correct one to use. Thus,

$$(1 + R_2) = [(1 + R_1)(1 + r_1)]^{1/2}$$

The exponent 1/2 means that we take the square root of the product of the two rates, which is the correct procedure.

Figure 14–6
Today's Yield Curve
(a) Upsloping curve

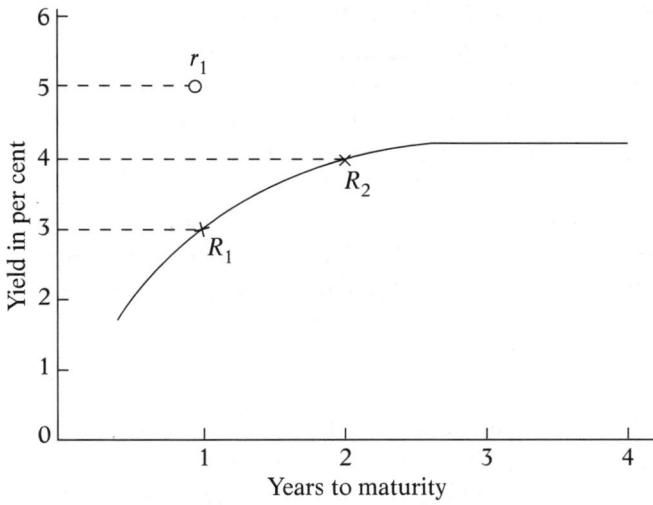

(b) Downsloping curve

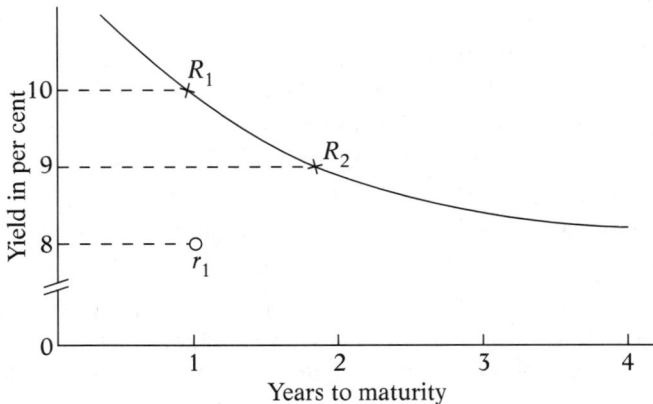

Formal Statement of the Theory

To generalize and formalize the theory, it is necessary to introduce additional notation to set the time dimension of investment. Attach prescripts t, $t + 1$, $t + 2$, and so on to the variables R and r to indicate the dates on which the variables are observed or are expected to be observed. Let $_tR_1$, $_tR_2$, ... represent the current yields on securities of 1, 2, ... periods to maturity existing at a moment in time t, and let $_{t + 1}r_1$, $_{t + 1}r_2$, ... represent the yields on securities of 1, 2, ... periods to maturity that are expected to prevail in the future at time $t + 1$. R's represent current or spot rates and r's represent forward rates, the rates expected to prevail in the future at time $t + 1$. The prescript to the R tells us at what point in time we are observing current rates, the subscript tells the length of time to maturity of the security being observed. Because r represents forward rates, the prescript indicates the future date on which we expect the forward rate to become the spot rate; the subscript, as in the case of R, represents the length of time to maturity. Thus, if t = January 1, 1996 and the rate on one-year bills on that date is 5 per cent, then $_tR_1$ = 5 per cent, or 0.05; and, if on this same date t, the forward rate, which is the rate that will exist on the future date $t + 1$ (or January 1, 1997), on a one-year security is 6 per cent, then $_{t+1}r_1$ = 0.06.

This notation is complex, but it becomes less confusing as we interpret the formula. Making the simplifying assumption that all coupon payments are accumulated and paid out upon maturity, then in the case of a two-period holding period:

$$(1 + {}_tR_2) = [(1 + {}_tR_1)(1 + {}_{t+1}r_1)]^{1/2}$$

This formula says that the yield on a two-year security will equal the geometric mean of the current (spot) rate on a one-year security and the forward one-year rate. As in our earlier example, if the spot one-year rate is 3 per cent ($_tR_1$ = 0.03) and the one-year forward one-year rate is 5 per cent ($_{t+1}r_1$ = 0.05), then the spot two-year rate may be found from $[(1.03)(1.05)]^{1/2}$ = 1.039+, or $_tR_2$ = approximately 0.0399.

As an investor, one has two choices: One may purchase a two-year bond that yields 3.9 per cent; alternatively, one may purchase a one-year bond that yields 3 per cent and reinvest the proceeds at the end of one year at the forward rate of 5 per cent so as to obtain an overall yield of 3.99 per cent. Thus, if one plans to hold bonds for a period of two years (the holding period) and if one wishes to maximize the holding period yield, then either course of action will give the same yield. If the current two-year rate happened to be above 3.99 per cent, the investor would buy the two-year securities, and other investors would also buy them until the prices rose and the yield fell into line with the 3.99 per cent. That is, anytime that the rates in question were out of line with the formula, investors with sufficiently large sums to invest would bid for securities in a way that would return them to balance.

Use of the simple arithmetic average of two percentages, 3 and 5 per cent, in our first example gave an average of 4 per cent. The geometric mean was only slightly different, 3.99 per cent. This difference seems small, but it is significant; in many cases, the difference would not be small. It is important to remember that we used a simple arithmetic average of percentages only to present an intuitively understandable example. In real-life situations, one must use the geometric mean to obtain correct results.

All the examples provided thus far have used rates for only two periods: today's rates and rates expected to prevail one year from today. The formula can easily be extended several periods in the future. An investor may consider purchasing a ten-year bond at today's current yield, $_tR_{10}$, or a one-year security with current yield $_tR_1$, knowing the expected one-year yields for each of the following nine years, $_{t+1}r_1$, $_{t+2}r_1$, ..., $_{t+9}r_1$. On the basis of these actual and expected values, an investor may choose either to buy the ten-year security or to make ten successive annual investments in one-year securities.

The relevant formula, for N periods into the future, is

$$(1 + {}_tR_N) = [(1 + {}_tR_1)(1 + {}_{t+1}r_1)(1 + {}_{t+2}r_1) \dots (1 + {}_{t+N-1}r_1)]^{1/N}$$

Thus, the current or spot yield on a bond of N years to maturity is equal to the Nth root of the product of the current one-year rate and all of the remaining forward one-year rates (the geometric mean). Also, $(1 + {}_tR_N) = [(1 + {}_tR_{N-1})^{N-1}(1 + {}_{t+N-1}r_1)]^{1/N}$.

A Statistical Test of the Theory

Statistical equations appropriate for testing the empirical validity of the expectations model take several forms. One of these is:

$$_{t+1}R_1 - {}_tR_1 = a + b({}_{t+1}r_1 - {}_tR_1) + e_t$$

On the left the dependent variable is a record of the actual change that takes place in the one period interest rate. On the right are the statistical coefficients, a and b, that are estimated by using historical data, where a is the intercept and b is the coefficient of the independent (explanatory) variable. Here, this variable is the difference between the forward rate as predicted by the model and the actual rate on a one-period security next period. That is, on the left is the actual change in yields and on the right is the predicted change in yields. Also, on the right, is a statistical error term.

   If the model does predict changes in yields, then the coefficient a should be zero and the coefficient b should be one. That is, if the forward rate calculated by the model turns out to be the actual rate next period then b will equal one. However, data for three-month and six-month rates were used to estimate the forward rate expected on a three-month security and were put into the equation for the U.S. for 1981–86. The estimated coefficient for b was not +1 as predicted by the theory, but was –0.26, a value significantly lower than +1 and even negative in sign. Rejections of the model appeared, using data from Germany and Switzerland, but the model was not rejected by data for Japan and the United Kingdom. (See Belongia and Koedijk, 1988. The conclusion was that the results were generally negative and that further tests should apply more general models. There was no conclusion that the expectations hypothesis be rejected as false.)

Liquidity Premium, Risk Premium, Term Premium

These three types of premia are very similar. They are more or less part and parcel of the same thing. Liquidity is the more general term. As defined earlier it includes two factors—whether the asset is easy to sell and whether its value will change during the time it is held. It is just as easy to sell a government bond as it is a government bill. But the bond is less liquid than a bill because it is more risky, and it is more risky because its value is subject to swings in value over the holding period. So risk is a big part of liquidity. A risky security sells for a lower price (higher yield) than a risk-free security. This means that the yield on a bond should be higher than the yield on a bill, that is, a bond's yield should include a risk premium. Since a bond has a longer term to maturity, this premium is now called a term premium by professors who engage in econometric studies of the term structure of interest rates.

Liquidity (Term) Premium in the Segmented Markets Approach. The segmented markets approach incorporates the concept of a liquidity, or term, premium in the analysis of the demand for a security. If investors are generally risk averse, and if one security is less risky than another, then investors will demand the less risky security, so its price will be higher and its yield will be lower. The Treasury bill carries the lowest yield and is called the "risk-free" security. Short-term yields generally lie below yields on longer-term securities because differences in risk affect their demand curves. Riskiness is simply one quality, albeit a very important quality, that must be considered in every decision to purchase an asset.

A Term Premium in the Expectations Approach. According to the pure expectations approach, as outlined above, there exists no liquidity or risk premium. The reason is that the emphasis is entirely on the *holding-period yield*. It is easy, and intuitively pleasing, to say, as the expectations approach does, that an investor with a holding period of ten years might choose to roll over one-year securities rather than buy a 10-year bond. However, to say an investor with a holding period of one year might buy a 10-year bond and hold it for one year invokes a strong sense that investors with short holding-period horizons are not willing to do this unless they prefer risky to riskless investments. However, under the pure expectations approach, if an investor's holding period is for one year, the investor would be indifferent about buying a 30-year bond and selling it at the end of the year, or buying a one-year bill and holding it to maturity— the expected return should be the very same on different maturities when markets are efficient.

Let the holding period yield on a security be represented by H, and the expected holding period yield on an N-period security to be held for one year be E_1, then according to the pure expectations approach $E_1(H_N) = {_1}R_1$ and the expected yield from holding a long-term security for a year is the same as the yield that exists on a one-year security today. The theory is that the one-year holding period yield should be the same on any and all securities. Since most economists find this formulation to be a sticky wicket, those who do research simply add a term premium Ψ, to it to form:

$$E_1(H_N) = {_1}R_1 + \Psi$$

"O.K.," they say, "if there is a term premium we will just add it on."

Notice that the psi (pronounced "sigh" in America, but "psee" in Greece) has no time subscript attached to it, indicating that it is viewed as a constant.

Complexities. Several complexities arise in any attempt to test the expectations approach statistically. For example, the holding period yield on a long-term security will be the result of the change in that security's price plus any coupon payment. The equation would be similar to that on a stock that pays a dividend. Thus, $E_t(H_N) = [C + E(P_{t+1} - P_t)/P_t]$, which says that the expected holding period yield equals the coupon plus the change in price (based on the price expected next period) during the holding period divided by today's purchase price.

As explained earlier, when the long-term rate is above the short-term rate, the yield curve slopes upward and, according to the pure expectations approach, this slope portends an increase in short-term interest rates next period. (If there is a term premium, then the long-term rate must remain greater than the short-term rate by more than the amount of the term premium. Let us ignore the term premium for the moment.) When the yield on the long, N-period, security is high and a holder buys it and holds it for one period, then there must be a capital loss on the sale of the bond in order for the holding period yield to equal the lower yield on today's one-year security. In other words, the capital loss must partially offset the coupon payment for the two holding period yields to give the same yield. Note that the capital loss means higher interest rates on long-term securities next period, as the expectations theory predicts.

The problem is that the facts do not support these results. The predominant behavior is that when short-term rates fall, making the yield curve positively sloped, the decline in short-term rates tends to be followed by declines, not increases, in yields on bonds, that is, they tend to be followed by capital gains, not capital losses. These gains make the yield on long-term bonds even greater and even farther above the yield on the one-year security. Thus, the expectations theory predicts higher interest rates from the positive shape of the yield curve, but actual events show the opposite. The evidence is regarded by some as a failure of the expectations model.

For example, in one paper, statistical regressions were made of the difference between the holding period return on a long-term security, H, and today's one-period rate, $_tR_1$, on the spread between the long rate and the short rate:

$$H - {_tR_1} = a + b({_tR_N} - {_tR_1}) + e_t$$

In this case, on data from 1961 to 1984 the coefficient b was greater than one in each of four countries: U.S. 4.99, Canada 3.40, U.K. 1.51, and Germany 1.87 (see Mankiw, 1986: 79–80). What does the expectations theory predict? It predicts that the holding-period yield will equal the short-term rate.

What do the data show? They show that, when the spread is positive, the holding-period yield will rise even further above the current short-term rate. This suggests that the investor should be advised, when long-term rates are significantly above short-term rates, to buy the long-term bonds and realize both a higher return and a capital gain.

For example, if the long-term rate is 7 per cent and the short-term rate is 3 per cent, the difference is 4 per cent. If the investor believes that the term premium should be only 2 per cent then the long–short difference is greater than the term premium. Data indicate that the investor with a short-term holding period should probably buy the long-term security. He should not expect a capital loss as the expectations theory suggests because history shows he should expect a capital gain instead. However, this does *not* mean to imply that such an investment strategy is without *considerable* risk. Also, there is no objective way, as yet, of determining the value of the term premium.

Time-varying Term Premiums. As indicated, studies have shown that treating the term premium as a constant leads to a rejection of the expectations hypothesis. Therefore, researchers infer that one reason the statistical data do not fit the theory may be that the psi in the equation:

$$E_1(H_N) - {}_1R_1 = \Psi$$

actually varies over time. So, some current research is focused on "the time-varying term premium."

One interpretation of the statistical results of the equation above is as follows: the spread between long and short rates does well in predicting excess holding returns; if the expectations approach is not rejected, then the implication is that the term premium varies over time and is positively related to the spread. The problem with this interpretation, however, is that there is no explicit theory of the term premium, let alone a theory of its variation over time.

Again, the data suggest the expectations theory is false, but it is not rejected. People simply search for other reasons that the findings fail to support it. The essence of an operationally meaningless hypothesis is that it cannot be refuted by empirical evidence. To believe it is true, people must accept it on faith. Once it is accepted on faith, no one even bothers to try to refute it with evidence because, in principle, it is recognized to be non-refutable.

For example, one study is based on surveys of interest rate expectations found in the newsletter, *Bond and Money Market Letter*, published by the Goldsmith-Nagan consulting firm in Washington, D.C. A group of about 30 persons who are considered experts in financial markets are asked to submit their forecasts of a variety of interest rates that they expect to prevail three and six months ahead. Then averages of the forecasts are calculated and published. It might appear that surveys of expectations would be good measures of market expectations. However, these forecasters have been found to do very little better than the market or than a naive forecast, which is simply that there will be no change in yields. The study uncovered the same statistical results as those described just above. However, the author's conclusion was that the term premium, while varying on short-term securities, did not vary on long-term securities (see Froot, 1989).

An Opinion on Empirical Tests of the Expectations Hypothesis

When Einstein published his theory of relativity, he was commenting on an experiment by Michaelson and Morely, who were trying to see how light waves were slowed down by ether. Ether, unfortunately, was defined to be that tasteless, weightless, invisible mass of stuff that filled up all of the empty space between all of the molecules in space. In other words, it could not be measured or observed. It *was* empty space—just that, empty. So, one should not expect light to be slowed down by ether. Of course, just because no one found any ether does not *prove* that it does not exist. However, continuously searching for nothing seems a bit of a waste of time. Einstein looked to gravitational forces, and we all know the result. No one talked about ether after that.

Analogously, the "market's forecast of future interest rates" is a tasteless, weightless, mass of empty space about which everyone can and does speculate but no one will ever be able to observe. Since the expectations approach is operationally meaningless, research should ignore it and proceed in areas in which some fruitful results might be forthcoming. If only economics were as simple as physics, perhaps an Einstein would appear. Alas, the outlook of the dismal science remains dismal, given the penchant for economists to accept such principles based on operationally meaningless expectations, rational or otherwise, without question.

The Accuracy of the Market's Forecasts

Proponents of the pure expectations approach correctly point out that the theory itself cannot be rejected just because the implied forecasts of market investors turn out to be wrong a significantly large part of the time. All the theory implies is that investors do hold those expectations at the time the yield curve is drawn. Is this an adequate defense of the theory?

To consider this question, let us draw some implications about the accuracy of market forecasts calculated from the expectations equations. First, over time, interest rates rise and fall as the result of macroeconomic conditions. When interest rates rise over time, it is usually the case that both long and short rates rise. When they fall, both fall. Second, when the level of rates rises generally, short-term rates rise more than long-term rates, and the yield curve often becomes downward sloping. When rates fall, short-term rates often fall more than long-term rates and the yield curve becomes positively sloped. To see this in an abstract example, let us glance at Figure 14–7.

Assume that we begin in an initial period when the yield curve is horizontal. The yield curve is labeled 0. Assume that rates rise generally in subsequent periods 1 and 2. The yield curves of periods 1 and 2 assume steeper downward slopes as interest rates rise in two subsequent periods. Consider now period 1 when the one-period rate is $_tR_1$ and the two-period rate is $_tR_2$ as shown. Using these rates to calculate the implied forward one-period rate, $_{t+1}r_1$, gives the lower rate as shown. The downward slope implies that investors expect short-term rates to fall. But, if rates rise generally during the time from period 1 to period 2, the actual one-period rate in period 2 will be $_{t+1}R_1$. It will not be $_{t+1}r_1$. The actual rate would be higher, whereas the presumed expected rate would be lower. The market's forecast of the direction of movement in rates turns out to be incorrect. The market was forecasting a decline, and an increase occurred instead.

Using the same reasoning but starting with the top downward-sloping yield curve labeled 2, and moving downward to curves 1 and 0, gives the opposite conclusion. The market's forecast of a decline in short-term yields next period turns out to be in the correct direction, as a decline actually takes place.

Figure 14–7

Hypothetical Movements in Yield Curves over Time

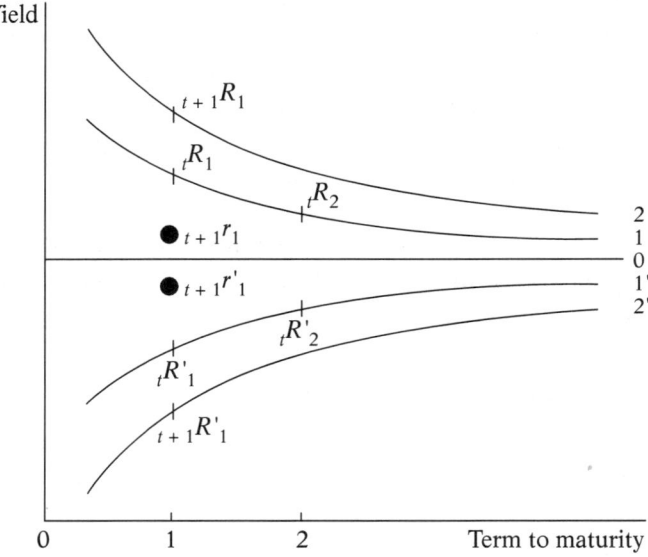

Starting from the horizontal yield curve again and assuming that yields fall to 1' and 2' in subsequent periods, the reasoning implies that when yield curve 1' exists, the market's forecast is for higher short-term rates next period. But when period 2' arrives, the actual yield turns out to be lower, not higher, and the direction of the forecast was incorrect. As the yield curve returns to its horizontal level, the market's forecast will be in the correct direction.

Thus, as the level of yields departs from the horizontal, forecasts will be in the wrong direction. And as yields return to the horizontal level, forecasts will be in the right direction. Forecasts will be in the wrong direction half of the time, and in the right direction half of the time.

Consider yield curve 1 again. According to the theory, market investors expect short-term yields to fall. But why would they expect yields to fall if experience has shown that half of the time yields fall and half of the time they rise? The rational expectation would be that yields will not change from their current structure and level.

Statistical evidence indicated that one could *not reject* the hypothesis that the market's forecast of the *direction of change* in yields *is wrong 50 per cent of the time*! (see Scott, 1990).

Summary

Interest accrues over time, so the time dimension looms large in any theoretical analysis of the determination of interest rates. Thus, the yield curve that shows different interest rates on securities, which reach maturity on different dates, is used in many ways by financial analysts. It is also the basis of a great deal of theoretical discussion.

Yield curves change their positions and shapes as business conditions change. They are usually upward sloping and may become downward sloping as short-term rates become high.

The segmented markets approach to the relation of long-term to short-term rates is not about separated markets but about interrelated markets. These interrelated markets have been placed into different maturity ranges for the purpose of analyzing how interest rates might change if subjected to changes in supply and demand.

The expectations approach to the theory of the determination of the relation between interest rates on securities of different maturities is analyzed in this chapter. Its intuitive appeal is very strong, but its predictive power is weak or nonexistent.

The principal use of the expectations approach is to provide an implicit way to estimate the forecast of future rates being made by the market. The forecast is said to be implicit in the term structure of rates. But implicit forecasts are not refutable and, rather than being enlightening, they may be the source of much confusion.

Key Terms and Concepts

Yield curve

Segmented markets approach

Liquidity premiums

Term premium

Departures from a horizontal yield curve

Inverted yield curve

Expectations approach

Risk premium

Interest rate forecasts

Discussion Questions and Exercises

1. How is a yield curve constructed?
2. Does "segmented markets" mean "separated markets"? Explain your answer.
3. What is the normal shape of the yield curve? Explain why that particular shape is believed to be "normal."
4. Describe the shapes of yield curves in different countries.
5. Over time, the yield curve fluctuates up and down. Describe how its shape changes in the process. Explain why.
6. Use the present value formula to show how a given change in yield affects prices of long- and short-term securities and how a given change in the price affects yields on long- and short-term securities.
7. If there is a sudden increase in the demand for long-term securities, what happens to their price? Their yield? What happens to the demand for short-term securities if the price of long-term securities increases? What happens to the price of short-term securities? Their yield?
8. What are the four assumptions in the pure expectations approach to the yield curve?

9. Explain the "holding-period yield." Explain "efficient markets would make the holding-period yield the same on all assets because of the potential for arbitrage if holding period yields differed."
10. Use a two-period horizon and one-period and two-period spot rates to explain the simple formula for the "implied forward rate."
11. Explain how today's spot rate structure over all maturities contains implicit forecasts of all rates of interest in the future.
12. In statistical tests do the predicted changes in yields based on forward rates implied by today's spot rates predict changes in spot rates from this period to the next? Explain using the equation in the text.
13. Explain why the coefficient b in the equation should take a value of one. What value did it take? What does this imply about the expectations model of the term structure?
14. Is there any difference between a liquidity premium, a risk premium and a term premium? If so, why? If not, why not?
15. Explain how the holding-period yield on a long-term security requires an estimate of the change in price of the security.
16. Describe how the equation on holding-period yields is adjusted when the term premium is included.
17. Explain the terms in the statistical equation showing how the spread in yields affects the excess holding-period yield.
18. What is your opinion on the usefulness of the expectations approach to explaining the term structure of interest rates?
19. Why is it reasonable to expect that the implied forward rate will lead to forecasts of changes in rates that are in the wrong direction half of the time?
20. As interest rates move upward away from the horizontal level, will the implied forward rate give correct signals? Explain.

References

Abken, Peter A., "Innovations in Modeling the Term Structure of Interest Rates," *Economic Review*, Federal Reserve Bank of Atlanta, July/August 1990, pp. 2–27.

Baum, C. F., and Thies, C. F., "On the Construction of Monthly Term Structures of U.S. Interest Rates, 1919–1930," *Computer Science in Economics and Management*, August 1992, pp. 221–46.

Belongia, Michael T., and Koekijk, Kees G., "Testing the Expectations Model of the Term Structure: Some Conjectures on the Effects of Institutional Changes," *Review*, Federal Reserve Bank of St. Louis, September/October 1988, pp. 37–45.

Bernanke, Ben S., "On the Predictive Power of Interest Rates and Interest Rate Spreads," *New England Economic Review*, Federal Reserve Bank of Boston, November/December 1990, pp. 51–68.

Ferson, Wayne E., "Treasury Bill Futures as Unbiased Predictors: New Evidence and Relation to Unexpected Inflation—A Discussion," *The Review of Futures Markets*,

Chicago Board of Trade, Vol. 9, No. 2, 1990, pp. 498–503.

Froot, Kenneth R., "New Hope for the Expectations Hypothesis of the Term Structure of Interest Rates," *Journal of Finance*, Vol. 44, June 1989, pp. 283–305.

Hafer, R. W., and Hein, Scott E., "Comparing Futures and Survey Forecasts of Near-term Treasury Bill Rates," *Review*, Federal Reserve Bank of St. Louis, May/June 1989, pp. 33–42.

Mankiw, N. Gregory, "The Term Structure of Interest Rates Revisited," *Brookings Papers on Economic Activity*, January 1986, pp. 61–110.

Mankiw, N. Gregory, and Miron, Jeffrey A., "The Changing Behavior of the Term Structure of Interest Rates," *Quarterly Journal of Economics*, May 1986, pp. 211–28.

Mougoue, M., "The Term Structure of Interest Rates as a Cointegrated System: Empirical Evidence from the Eurocurrency Market," *Journal of Financial Research*, Fall 1992, pp. 285–96.

Pesando, James E., and Plourde, Andre, "The October 1979 Change in the U.S. Monetary Regime: Its Impact on the Forecastability of Canadian Interest Rates," *Journal of Finance*, Vol. 43, March 1988, pp. 217–39.

Russell, S., "Understanding the Term Structure of Interest Rates: The Expectations Theory," *Review*, Federal Reserve Bank of St. Louis, July/August 1992, pp. 36–50.

Scott, Robert Haney, "On the Forecasting Content of the Implied Forward Rate," *Managerial Finance*, Vol. 16, No. 6, 1990, pp. 40–46.

Seater, John J., "Ricardian Equivalence," *Journal of Economic Literature*, March 1993, pp. 142–90.

Shiller, Robert J., Campbell, John Y., and Schoenholtz, Kermit L., "Forward Rates and Future Policy: Interpreting the Term Structure of Interest Rates," *Brookings Papers on Economic Activity*, January 1983, pp. 173–217.

Yip, Ying K., "The Predictive Power of the Term Structure of Interest Rates—The Australian Evidence," in *Proceedings of the Second International Conference on Asian-Pacific Financial Markets*, City Polytechnic of Hong Kong, September 12–14, 1991, pp. 166–74.

CHAPTER 15

Regulation and Efficiency

PREVIOUS CHAPTERS CONTAIN descriptions of financial institutions and markets involved in the allocation of funds. These are heavily regulated by government in every economy.

There are two broad reasons for government involvement. First, the financial position of an individual is very important to that individual. Therefore, individuals demand that government protect their finances—*government monitors and regulates the exercise of prudential responsibilities assumed by financial institutions.* Second, macroeconomic stability depends on government control over money, and sometimes credit. Again, individuals will demand that *government monitor and regulate money and credit conditions.* Some economists believe that people would be better off if monetary and financial systems could be free of government controls (see Selgin, 1988). But, so long as people demand that their governments exercise such controls, those controls will remain.

Thus, this chapter begins with a discussion of the theory of government regulation and then moves on to discuss some current developments in regulatory structure. It concludes with a discussion of the concern over the efficiency of financial markets.

The Theory of Regulation

At first glance, it appears that there are two ways to run an economy, either let the market operate or have government run it under a set of rules. But a market system cannot be left to anarchy. A market system requires that government establish and maintain property rights and enforce contracts. To do this it must have a police force and a judicial system.

It is easy enough to say that this is mine and that is yours, but in the case of real estate, just exactly where is the property line? Before surveying became an applied science, land could not be divided up for individual ownership because property lines could not be drawn clearly enough. Today, in the U.S., everybody's property is a matter of record kept at the county courthouse. Recently, a friend of the author had to move a fence two inches because an official survey indicated that it was on his neighbor's property.

The invention of Loran navigation systems permits any ship on the ocean to determine within a square meter just exactly where on the earth's surface it is. Before its invention, it was impossible for any country to claim a distance from its shoreline as being within its coastal waters. Nowadays it is typical for coastal nations to claim ownership 200 miles off their coastline. Before World War II the claim was for only 3 miles offshore.

In June 1993 the U.S. Defense Department launched the twenty-fourth satellite to complete the Global Positioning System (GPS). This will enable anyone with a receiver to pinpoint latitude, longitude *and altitude*. The system is three dimensional. It works like the ancient sextant. Radio signals sent simultaneously from each satellite tell the receiver exactly where the satellite is and, by reading the position of a couple of satellites, the holder of the receiver can compute a position on earth with precision of a few feet. Receivers can now be purchased for a few hundred dollars. Without doubt, this new system will lead governments to carve up space for ownership whether public or private.

How much of the air space above a lot is owned by the owner of the land space? It is government's job to establish the rules of ownership of air space.

Governments do their job when they act to establish and maintain property rights, which they should do in order to permit the market to function.

Viewed in this way, those economic difficulties often referred to as "market failure" are better characterized as "government failure." Externalities that result in social costs require that government establish ownership rights to pollution, which it is doing slowly but surely. As we noted in Chapter 12, pollution rights are being auctioned on the Chicago Board of Trade. Air pollution is widely said to be a result of market failure. On the contrary, the market works in a clearly predictable way when government fails to establish and maintain property rights to clean air. Markets lead to the least-cost production method, which may mean that firms will pollute the air. If there is air pollution, it means that government has failed to establish property rights to air as it has to the ocean. But, as we see, government is moving forward on these issues.

Thus, markets and government are not distinct entities. Instead, they rely heavily on each other. However, the real debate over economic policies between the conservatives and liberals is not that government sets the rules, but rather the extent to which government enters into commercial activities. Governments have no business (no pun intended) setting prices, controlling production, producing goods, or interfering with the free flow of commerce. A great deal of the distortion in any economy is the result of government departing from its principal function, which is to establish and maintain property rights. When government departs from these functions, it damages markets.

It must be admitted, however, that a considerable portion of destructive government intervention is the result of the pressure that businesses—those parties supposedly in favor of free markets—bring to bear on government in order to enhance their own private interest. These anti-competitive and anti-market forces attempt to co-opt government's role. They should be resisted on every hand.

It would be best, therefore, if everyone would recognize that the problem is not just one of government or one of markets—the problem lies in the difficulty in maintaining a proper balance between the two.

The Theory of the Public Interest

According to this theory, government needs to supply regulations that promote competition and efficient operation of markets. More efficient markets would be in the public interest. No one disagrees with this goal of government regulation. However, it may miss the point entirely. Free markets are *self-regulating* for the most part. If some business operator drops into town and sells a lot of bad goods, takes money, and leaves, the people will rightly ask for laws to prevent this from occurring. The government's job is to enforce contracts. Here, the contract was fraudulent and police action is warranted. But local businesses will often ask for government rules to prevent the entry of outsiders, arguing that the public interest will be served if public access to the shoddy goods of outsiders is restricted. Everyone agrees that government regulations should protect the public interest, but very often the regulations protect private interests instead. It is never easy to tell the difference between these two types of regulation.

The Capture Theory

If you were president and you were going to appoint someone to be head of the Atomic Energy Commission, presumably you would want a nuclear physicist. And, by the same token, who else should be on the Board of Governors of the Federal Reserve besides bankers, or the occasional professor of banking? And to run the country's Treasury in a businesslike way we surely need an accountant and businessman. Thus, directors of regulatory agencies tend to be chosen mostly from the industry being regulated.

This is like sending a fox to guard the chicken coop. A person coming from the industry is likely to bring a great deal of sympathy for the industry he is in charge of regulating into the job. Then the regulations that are imposed will tend to support the interests of the industry itself—often reducing the competitive forces that it faces rather than promoting them. When faced with problems, firms within the industry go directly to government regulators to ask for assistance, and the regulators then ask Congress for subsidies, protection, and other assistance. Congress, recognizing the voting clout of the large number of people in the industry, tends to be sympathetic. At the same time, Congress is lobbied by representatives of private associations made up of firms in the industry. It is difficult for Congress to resist such pressures. After all, members of Congress are *supposed to represent* their constituencies. When all is said and done, it appears that the regulators are largely controlled by the regulated—the central theme of the capture theory of regulation.

It is certainly not easy to develop a scheme that would undermine this circular flow of control that operates from the regulators to the regulated and back again in support of the private interests of the group. Ross Perot, in the presidential campaign of 1992, pledged to attack the lobbyist group, but it is not clear just how one might go about tackling the problem effectively.

Demand and Supply for Regulation

Another approach to understanding why there is so much government regulation is to think of regulation more or less as a commodity for which there is a demand by groups of individuals, and then think of politicians who view their jobs to be to supply those groups with what they want. This approach was suggested by George Stigler (1971).

An example of this approach to regulation at work is found in recent legislation that follows a trend set in 1968 when the Truth in Lending Act was passed by Congress. The Federal Reserve was made responsible for enforcing the rules—the Fed's Regulation Z. Under this, any bank or finance company is supposed to ensure that the borrower has been told precisely the annual percentage rate of interest on the loan and just what the finance charges will be. Credit card bills contain reams of fine print on the back, much of which is required by Regulation Z. Now banks make borrowers read and sign a statement to the effect that they have been informed properly—costly bureaucratic paperwork. Many trivial law suits have been brought because of minor oversights.

In June 1993, a *Truth in Saving* law came into effect. This requires banks to inform depositors about the rate of return on savings or time deposit accounts. Sounds simple, doesn't it? But when complications of quarterly, daily, or other compounding frequencies (no one is suggesting continuous compounding, which would require that banks explain the calculus of continuous growth rates) then the bureaucratic mess becomes recognizable. However, spokesmen for the American Association of Retired Persons (AARP) say they are happy that this legislation will prevent banks from cheating old-timers. (Does anyone know any bankers who conspire to cheat old-timers?) The costly paperwork involved will be a net burden on everybody and will raise the cost of banking services to those very people being "helped." The Congress and the regulators are the ones who should be charged with effectively cheating the retired folks. Banks will be forced to have all depositors of funds sign papers to indicate that they have been informed about the "true" return on their savings accounts. Will they have to sign a paper with each deposit? What sorts of trivial legal suits will this legislation give rise to?

Shortly after the Truth in Saving Act took effect, the Office of the Comptroller of the Currency recommended that banks obtain signed statements from customers to whom they sell mutual funds acknowledging that they understand that such mutual funds are *not* covered by the bank's deposit insurance program. Congressional committees began drafting legislation to put the recommendation into law. Here we have yet another set of papers to be read, signed, and kept in files. What happened to our commitment to "Save the Trees"?

These kinds of costly regulations make banks inefficient. Is a person stepping into a bank to assume no responsibility whatever for knowing anything about interest rates or banking? It seems not under the new world of paternalistic government in which groups of people demand care from government and politicians willingly supply it.

Rent-seeking

If business firms hire a worker, they must believe that the worker's activities will bring in at least as much revenue as required to cover wages and possibly a bit more. Applying this reasoning to the hiring of lobbyists means that firms are expected to benefit enough to pay the lobbyists' wages and make some profit. Profit that arises from protected business activities can be called rent. To analyze why people ask government to protect and expand their private interests is to analyze rent-seeking behavior (see Buchanan et al., 1980). (See the discussion on seigniorage in Chapter 5.)

Dynamic Interaction Theories of Regulation

In the example of demand and supply presented above, some consumers of banking services influenced the regulators to pass costly programs on banks. What happened to the idea that the regulators were captured? Why did the banks not persuade Congress to protect the banks from costly regulations? Any theory of regulation needs to include not just the regulated and regulators, but the consumer groups, or other private interest groups as well because there is interaction between the three (see Joskow, 1974).

A Regulatory Dialectic. Getting around regulations is a favorite hobby of lawyers and accountants. As noted in Chapter 4, when thrift institutions wanted to compete with banks and issue checking accounts on which they paid interest, they had to change the name of what amounted to a demand deposit account to a negotiable order of withdrawal. It was illegal to pay interest on a demand deposit, and still is. So the question immediately arises, how does one manage to get around the law? This question is very important when there is a lot of money to be had. Some people act illegally and become criminals. Others try to figure out what will work without offending the regulators. When their operations get large, regulators are often behind the operations, and finally enter the fray and begin regulating the new operations. The real world is replete with examples.

Thus, a dynamic process involving regulation, the introduction of new ways of avoiding regulation, the emergence of problems, the introduction of new regulation, and so on, over and over, may be called a *regulatory dialectic.* This concept was presented by Edward Kane (1977, 1991).

Sometimes this process takes a very long time to come about. When the Federal Reserve started operations in 1914, banks throughout the country would cash checks drawn on each other, but would not cash them at par or face value. Instead they would discount each other's checks, and if the check was drawn on a town far away, the discount was quite large. So the Federal Reserve, established to handle check clearing, required that its members clear checks at par value. In the 1990s, 80 years later, a huge number of small businesses have been established in the U.S. for the specific purpose of cashing checks. Fees are charged that amount to the discounting of the check's par value. Banks and businesses used to cash checks for people, but there are too few who do so now. So, a profitable business has arisen. And regulators are beginning to draft laws preventing these businesses from charging fees that they deem are "too high." Regulation, the emergence of new business to get around the regulation, and more regulation—is a never ending circle.

Regulations to Promote Competition, Stability and Efficiency

Maintaining a Balance between Competition and Failure. How do regulators promote competition and yet not let an inefficient bank fail? That is the question bank regulators ask. They do not want a bank to fail because of the *domino effect*. If a bank's depositors lose their money, then they cannot pay their bills and their suppliers cannot pay their bills either. These bills may include payments on bank loans that have come due. When they are not paid, other banks are likely to fail. If a large bank fails, and if it holds deposits of smaller banks, as it is very likely to do, then small banks fail, too, and their depositors all face the loss of funds and perhaps bankruptcy. Bank failures spread bankruptcy all around the community.

One of the reasons for the bad results of the domino effect is that there are too few banks. If regulations did not limit the number of banks, then there might be a much smaller domino effect. If banks were as numerous as restaurants, then the failure of a single bank would involve less social harm.

Social and economic stability require that banks, especially large banks, not be allowed to fail. The "too big to fail" criteria for bailing out banks smacks of unfairness, however, and hardly makes for sound economic policy. Why did the banks get "too large" in the first place? Can this situation be partially explained by restrictions on the entry of new banks into banking?

Why is it not as easy to start a bank as it is to start a restaurant? After all, there are many licenses that a restauranteur has to maintain. We do not want him serving us bad food. So, we do not want a banker who absconds with our funds, either. Requirements that a bank's employees be bonded should suffice to protect depositors from embezzlement.

But what about poor investments? Banks are greatly limited in the types of investments they can make under current regulations in the U.S. Banks are much less regulated in other countries in making investments. In this, as in other regulation faced by business in the U.S., the U.S. is unique.

It is not easy for government to maintain the delicate balance between having a competitive banking industry and protecting the banking industry sufficiently to prevent socially damaging failures.

America's Unique Attitude toward Regulation. Built on the concept of protecting private property and free enterprise, while rejecting the granting of monopoly rights and titles, U.S. legislation reflects a belief in the need to bar the usurpation of power, both political and economic, from the people. Anti-trust laws, passed in the early 1900s, reflected the spirit of the people. It is O.K. to get rich, but it is not O.K. to control vast wealth and manipulate it in a way to eliminate opposing competitive forces.

Why not organize a group of bankers and have them all get together, form a cartel, and monopolize the provision of banking services to the American public? In the U.S., cartels are not formed mainly since it is illegal to do so and there are tough penalties, including imprisonment, for engaging in such efforts even if they are unsuccessful.

Most economists recognize that even if a cartel were formed, after a few years it would be broken down by competition. In the long run the cartel would collapse. But, as Keynes wrote, in the long run we are all dead. Can anyone imagine the huge profit that would accrue to the banking industry during the several years it would take for the cartel to dissolve?

In 1973 many conservative economists predicted that the OPEC cartel would soon collapse. (Your author was one of those.) It took over ten years to happen. (Your author got tired telling students, "any time now.") Of course, it did finally weaken considerably. But the cartel's members certainly got rich. And, though weakened from age, it still survives.

A banking cartel in America would certainly survive a long time. In a sense we do have a cartel in banking operating under the Federal Reserve System, the stock of which is owned by member banks. But in this case "ownership" is almost totally irrelevant as the Congress instructs the Federal Reserve on its duties as manager of the nation's monetary controls. It also instructs other regulatory agencies that are charged with the responsibility of controlling banks and insuring bank deposits.

The economy might be served better by a competitive banking system where entry to the business of banking were open to all and regulators were not permitted to establish, through their regulations, *de facto* cartels.

Agency Costs and Information Costs. Americans do not want any business to get big enough to operate as a cartel, especially a bank. In general, American banks are not permitted to own and operate other businesses. In Greece, and most other countries in Europe, for example, banks do own apartment buildings and other properties. But banks have relations with customers who give them privileged information.

If your firm manufactured furniture, and if your bank also owned and operated a furniture manufacturing firm, would you like it if you went to this bank for a loan and had to disclose your plans for expansion to someone who was already active as your business competitor? Americans generally believe that businesses that are also bank customers should not have to compete with banks. So regulations prohibit banks from engaging in many activities.

In many contractual relations, there is a principal and an agent. The standard example from business is the owner as principal and the manager as agent. But the customer who purchases a service from a bank acts as a principal hiring an agent. There are often significant costs incurred by principals who must monitor an agent's performance. A bank is the *agent* of its customers—accepting funds for safekeeping and investing them as an intermediary. *By restricting bank activities, regulators serve to reduce agency costs.*

One major problem is that the agents almost always have more information than the principals have. The cook knows exactly what went into the sandwich, but does the customer? Banks may know that risky loans have been made to businesses, but the depositor has little knowledge of such risky transactions. If a bank holds securities that are traded in financial markets, then the depositor can look at the prices of those, and the banks may be required by accounting standards to "mark-to-market" the value of securities. *But there is no way to "mark-to-market" the value of risky business loans.* This means that *the banker will always have better information* about the soundness of the bank than the depositor.

The laws of regulation restrict those who may enter the banking business, so when someone sees a sign that says "BANK," he knows that there is a certain degree of enforced trust expected if he does business there. It is illegal to put up a sign that says bank if you do not have a license to bank. Thus, many regulations help provide the public with information.

It must be difficult to be a regulator who decides when the regulation promotes competition, when it promotes monopoly, and when it promotes economic stability.

Two Styles of Regulation: Prohibitive and Preventive

Before the 1980s, financial markets and institutions in Korea were almost completely characterized by what could be called *prohibitive* rules (see Euh and Amsden, 1990: 49). In general, banks were not allowed to do anything except what was specifically permitted by the rules. With deregulation and financial reform, the essence of change has been to give financial institutions more flexibility. This means a shift to preventive regulations— banks are permitted to do everything the rules do not explicitly prevent them from doing.

The distinction between prohibitive and preventive rules can be clarified by the idea of permission. In the case of prohibitive rules, the managers of an institution are told what they can do and they are prohibited from doing anything else, without permission. If they do something without permission they must ask for forgiveness and, as the old saying goes, it is much easier to ask for forgiveness than it is to ask for permission. If you ask for permission, permission may be denied. If you do it and ask for forgiveness, forgiveness is usually accepted—just do not do it again.

In contrast, under preventive regulation, the purpose is to prevent activities that might do harm while leaving the managers free to do whatever else they like—they have permission to do anything not explicitly against the rules. Under preventive rules, there are, understandably, far fewer rules and restrictions. Removing regulations, or deregulating and reforming, has led to a relaxation of restrictions and a movement away from prohibitive rule.

Preventive rules are typical of a free society, while prohibitive rules are more typical of an authoritarian society. The need for "financial liberalization" has been widely recognized in Japan, Korea, and Taiwan. The British influence in Hong Kong and Singapore has left those financial markets and institutions with little or no need for further liberalization, but certainly no need for more regulation.

Market Regulation

The best regulators in any exchange economy are free markets. They should be relied upon in commercial activities whenever possible. Free markets function most efficiently when there is full and free information available to all. Thus, New Zealand's new system being put into place by the Reserve Bank will be closely watched to see if it will set a precedent for other central banks in the years ahead.

The 1990 Reserve Bank Act in New Zealand gave the central bank its independence. Since then the Reserve Bank has moved aggressively to reach its goal of an economy with zero inflation. It has also accelerated its program to keep prudential regulations to a minimum.

During 1995 all the 18 banks in New Zealand will be required to provide full disclosure of their activities and positions on a regular basis. This system will replace the current system that is typical of most supervisory schemes which requires that banks supply confidential information to regulators and be judged by them. By requiring full disclosure to the public instead, it will be up to the depositors and other customers of the bank to judge the safety of their deposits in individual banks. Pressures exercised by customers in the marketplace will replace a group of government supervisors as the principal regulator of banks.

Of course, some regulatory authority will still decide precisely what information will have to be publicly disclosed by the banks. It has been suggested that the credit rating services of Moody's and/or Standard & Poors might be useful. However, the system will fail if every customer has to be told every detail of every aspect of a loan or deposit on an individual basis and sign a form to the effect that he or she understands everything disclosed.

Efficiency

Are financial markets "efficient"? There have been literally thousands of academic articles written on this question since Eugene Fama wrote his 1970 article (see Fama, 1970) arguing that financial markets were clearly efficient in the sense outlined by Harry V. Roberts: "Strong form, Semi-strong form, and weak form efficiency." These terms appear in quotation marks because they must be defined in terms that refer specifically to them and in the context that their author chose. A scientist, indeed anyone, has a perfect right to coin a term or use an existing word and define that word to suit whatever purpose it serves. The term gay, for example, means happy, but if someone defines it to mean homosexual, one cannot object to a new definition for an old word. One word may have many definitions.

The word "efficient," defined in every finance text in use today, is related to the extent to which market participants have information that is relevant to the price of a security. A market is said to have "strong form" efficiency if participants have access to *all the relevant information about the price of a security that exists*—including information that inside traders have. A market is said to have "semi-strong" efficiency if participants have access to all relevant *published* information about factors that may affect the price of a security. And the market is said to have "weak form" efficiency if participants have access only to all information about past prices of a security.

Since new information is presumed to occur randomly, security prices will move randomly. Thus, when markets are efficient, someone who chooses securities using a table of random numbers will be as successful as someone who studies the markets. (It is sometimes called the "throw the dart at the financial page" theory of stock purchase decisions. Of course, this assumes that the thrower is not a steady winning player at the local pub, but a complete novice who misses the entire board as often as he hits it.)

Financial analysts who believe in the Efficient Markets Hypothesis may feel that their activities are worthless—they cannot beat the market in results. If the price reflects all relevant information, then it is impossible to find an opportunity in an "undervalued" stock. A joke about efficient markets goes like this: two traders were walking along the street and one looks on the sidewalk and sees a $20 bill. He says, "Look, a $20 bill," and stops to pick it up. His colleague, an EMH believer, says, "Don't bother with it. If it were really a $20 bill, someone else would have already picked it up."

However, it should be remembered that financial analysts are *providers of relevant information to the market, which is presumably what makes it efficient in the first place.*

Difficulties with Relevant Information. How can anyone know whether or not market participants have information, let alone, "relevant" information? Everyone acts upon the basis of some information, some of which is relevant and a great deal of which is not. Does anyone in the market act on the basis of irrelevant information that results in sending out a price that does not reflect relevant information? Surely the answer is yes. Why, then, should the casual observer of a price believe that it reflects all relevant information?

At bottom, the problem is that "relevant information" is unobservable. Even "new information" is unobservable. Some research is focused on "announcement" effects, and many examples of such effects have been found in the data. But even if they are not found, the theory is still not rejected, it is simply said that other effects that were not observed must have offset the announcement effects.

Thus, no one ever ends up refuting the proposition that financial markets are efficient in the information-based sense. No experiment can ever reject the proposition that the market price reflects all the information that market participants have simply because it is not possible to measure all the information that they have. So, if the price takes an unexpected turn, it must be due to information market participants have, but that the research person does not have, so no rejection of the theory is possible.

Economic Efficiency

The word efficiency is well defined in economic theory. It has little to do with information related efficiency. A market is said to be efficient if no one can be made better off without someone else being worse off. If this condition holds, the allocation of resources is said to be Paretian efficient, after Vilfredo Pareto, the Italian economist who articulated the criterion in the 1920s. After all, if someone can be made better off without anyone else being made worse off, then the allocation is clearly inefficient. The paretian condition is a necessary condition, not a sufficient condition, for efficiency in the allocation of resources. (See Chapter 13 for a description of the equality of the marginal rate of time preference and its equality with the internal rate of return on investments. This is the paretian condition for efficiency.)

This definition of efficiency is different from that of the "efficient markets hypothesis" (EMH). Proponents of EMH, however, claim that if EMH does not hold, surely the markets cannot be efficient in the paretian sense—business investment and financing decisions using financial markets as sources of funds cannot lead to paretian optimal allocation of capital resources if prices of securities do not reflect all relevant information.

However, *even if prices do reflect all relevant information, this does not mean that the allocation of capital is paretian efficient*. Why? Because a considerable amount of relevant information is information about regulations that governments impose in restricting, in a variety of ways, the free flow of capital to investment projects!

Also, *even if prices do not reflect all relevant information, the allocation of capital may still be paretian efficient* in a statistically relevant sense. Decision errors are made by each and every one of us, so there will *always* be errors in capital allocations. If there were none, then there would be no bankruptcies. So, a dynamic economy will be subjected to buffeting winds, and the best that can be expected is to have prices that are flexible so that conditions of paretian efficiency will be as closely approximated as possible.

Paretian efficiency is an abstract ideal; it is a star to hitch a wagon to; it is a guide; it is also an operationally meaningful proposition that can be used in predicting real world responses to shocks to the market imposed by outside events.

In contrast, the EMH has few such qualities. It implies that financial analysis is a waste of time because market prices reflect all there is to know. All the while, various government regulations make the market inefficient in the fundamental paretian sense, so attention is taken away from important sources of market inefficiency.

A Formal Statement of the EMH and Evidence against It[†]

The EMH can be readily stated in complex mathematical form but in a manner that is easy to interpret. Thus, the EMH can be stated as:

$$P_t = E(P_t^* | \Omega_t)$$

[†]The author draws on the outline of the article by Peter Fortune (1991) for this section.

Every equation is a statement. Let us read this statement. It says that the price of a security at time t equals the term on the right-hand side of the equal sign. E indicates that we are taking about the *expected* value of the items within the parentheses. The first item there is P^*. This P represents a set of *fundamental values* of P that are all based on a set of probable states of the world. In one state of the world, P^* might be $100 with a probability of 0.25 attached to it, or $25. In another state it might be $80 with a probability of 0.40 attached to it, or $32, and so forth, for all of a set fundamental values based on probable states of the world. The expected value is the average of all values of P^*. Then the vertical line simply means "*conditional upon*," and it is followed by an omega. The omega stands for "all available information" and the subscript t means today.

To summarize, the equation reads: today's price of a security will equal the price that would be expected based on assessments of fundamental values using all information available today. It is useful to note that P^* is not a measurable variable and neither is Ω. Essentially, both variables used to determine P in this equation are unobservable. Proxies must be used whenever testing is tried.

Empirical Tests of Implications of the EMH

Tests of operationally meaningless hypotheses are never made directly. Instead, researchers draw implications from the hypothesis and usually add their own hypotheses to derive an implication. Thus, initial tests of the EMH assumed that all relevant information arrives randomly over time. If information is random and if the EMH holds, then the price of a security (or sometimes an index of security prices) should follow a random walk. These studies examined the pattern of prices over time and the nature of errors in the forecasts made by the EMH. Many studies concluded that the EMH could not be rejected by the evidence.

The EMH was widely accepted in the 1970s and most of the 1980s. But then several studies led to doubts—doubts that have grown such that now nearly all economists say that markets are not efficient, but still argue in the same breadth that it is useful to assume that markets are efficient in the EMH sense. Some textbooks, not this one, still espouse the hypothesis, while offering evidence against it.

The Small Firm Effect. Even after accounting for greater risk, small firms have returns that are higher than those for large firms. If the EMH were at work, this would not be true.

The Closed-end Mutual Fund Puzzle. When one buys shares in a mutual fund, the money is used by the fund's managers to purchase securities, and thus the size of the fund increases. If funds are withdrawn, the fund pays an amount equal to the net asset value of the shares in the fund, and the size of the fund decreases. This is the case of an open-end fund. A closed-end fund differs. A set amount of shares are purchased by the managers and a set amount of shares in the fund are sold to investors. The shares that are traded on the market have a capitalized market value. This value should add up to the value of the fund's shares that are also traded on the market. But the closed-end fund's shares almost always sell for a discount below the value of the underlying collateral. Something is keeping the EMH from working in this case. There is some arbitrage between the collateral and the shares in the fund, but not nearly enough to eliminate the discount. Why, if information is available, would the fund's value not equal at least as much as the value of its collateral? It is a puzzle.

Weekend and January Effects. There is a tendency for stocks to decline in value on Fridays and Mondays. But if new information occurs randomly, this weekend effect should not exist. Evidence also seems to show that stocks tend to do better than average during January. No one knows why.

The Value Line Enigma. The Value Line Investment Survey covers about 1,700 firms whose stock is traded on securities markets. Each stock is ranked from one to five. A rank of one indicates that the firm's stock will perform better than the market, a rank of three indicates a projection of equal-to-market performance, and a rank of five indicates below market performance is projected. After adjusting for differences in risk, it appears that on average the firms ranked one and two do perform better, while those ranked four and five do perform less well. What do the people at Value Line know that the rest of us do not? What does this imply for the "throw the dart" decision rule? It implies that the EMH does not hold.

Excess Volatility of Stock Prices. Returning to the equation expressing the EMH, let us add an error term to the right-hand side.

$$P_t = E(P_t^* | \Omega_t) + \epsilon_t$$

The epsilon stands for error in accord with statistical analysis. Statistically, in accord with the EMH assumption, the variation in market prices on the left will equal the variation in fundamental prices plus the variation in epsilon. After constructing estimates of "fundamental" prices based on a proxy constructed from dividend history, Shiller found that P^*, reflecting fundamental factors, varied *more than* the actual price P_t. If the variance of the error must be positive, as must all variances, then this, the right-hand side, is greater than the left-hand side of the equation! The equality does not hold so the EMH cannot hold. Of course, Shiller did not use the true P^* because it cannot be observed. Perhaps the variance is actually smaller on the true variable, but we will never know (see Shiller, 1991).

Speculative Bubbles and the "Greater Fool" Theory. Speculators push up stock market prices forming a "bubble" that will surely burst just as the soap bubbles do. If so, the market prices, and the index of prices, do not reflect fundamentals. Why do investors still purchase stock even though they know that a bubble is forming? One answer is that every investor believes that out there somewhere is a fool even greater than he is.

As investors continue in their foolish ways, eventually a sufficient number of players have second thoughts about the intellectual prowess of their group and the bubble bursts.

Bubbles do not burst frequently. The probability of occurrence is low. But the effect is dramatic. This is known as the peso problem: the market tends to ignore very low probability events even when they are drastic. If investors do ignore these, then EMH does not hold.

Mean Reversion in Stock Returns—the Winner's Curse and Loser's Blessing. It is quite common to hear a market player comment that he or she bought a stock and it went up and now they think they had better sell before it falls back to the price they paid. They were winners, but they face the curse of loss as the stock is likely to revert to its old average price. Statistically, it has been found that the tendency for high returns to be followed by low returns does exist, at least on stocks held for 18 months. So does the tendency of low returns to be followed by high returns—the loser's blessing (see Fama and French, 1988).

If returns on stock tend to revert to their past averages then *they do not follow a random walk.* Ergo, the EMH does not hold.

Noise Trading. Do the researchers finally give up? Not on your life. Undaunted they construct new explanations of stock price variability models that assume *irrational* behavior on the part of investors. Irrational investors are likely to follow fads in the markets and push stock prices away from that predicted by the EMH, but sophisticated investors who "know better" do not bother to arbitrage away the prices that are out of line with the fundamentals because arbitrage is expensive and not totally without risk in such cases.

A Tempest in a Teapot

Those who argue these issues at length are concerned that finding stock markets to be inefficient in the information sense will lead to a variety of suggestions for more regulation of financial markets. But there is little in the EMH or all of the sophisticated statistical tests that will assist in the formation of regulatory policy. Today's markets would be just as efficient as they are even if there had been no studies of market efficiency and no EMH. The real efficiency question that should be raised here is the allocation of resources by economists to studies of operationally meaningless propositions. Such discussions have led to a dead end, as could have been predicted using fundamentals of scientific research.

On the Failure of Banks and Thrift Institutions

In the U.S. the decade of the 1980s will be remembered for the widespread failure of financial institutions.

The thrift institutions were the first group to be hit by the tight monetary policies imposed by the Federal Reserve in a determined move to halt inflation. The principal business of thrift institutions has been the making of mortgage loans and the acceptance of savings deposits to fund them. Savings deposits could be withdrawn more or less on demand as short-term obligations that usually carry low interest rates. These low rates meant a low cost-of-funds for the thrifts. In contrast, the mortgage loans offered by thrifts were long-term obligations that typically carried higher fixed interest rates and provided revenues to the thrifts. Revenues exceeded costs and thrifts were profitable. Then the Federal Reserve's tight money policies raised short-term rates to double digit levels. This pushed the cost-of-funds up and costs exceeded revenues from mortgages. Losses prevailed in the thrift industry as well as in many other industrial sectors of the economy that were adversely affected by the costs of short-term funds.

By the mid-1980s the annual failure rates among thrifts were in the hundreds. The number of thrift institutions (savings banks and savings and loan institutions) fell from nearly 5,000 at the beginning of the decade to around 2,500 at the end of the decade.

The Federal Savings and Loan Insurance Corporation soon found that demands on its reserves, needed to pay off depositors of the failed thrifts, soon exceeded its supply. It, too, failed and was replaced by Congress as Congress grappled with the problems of providing over $200 billion to meet obligations. Congress was obligated to cover the losses because deposits of up to $100,000 were insured by the federal government.

The second group to be hit by failure was commercial banking. Damage to these institutions was delayed because their assets tend to have much shorter maturity on average than the long-term fixed rate mortgages held by the thrift institutions. Thus, they were able to raise interest rates on their short-term business loans and hold their losses down. This was so costly to businesses that had to roll over notes at higher interest rates that many of them failed.

The costs of bankruptcy and business failure could be attributed to the cost of halting inflation. Politically, the Federal Reserve could never openly admit that its anti-inflationary tight monetary policies led to widespread bankruptcy and business failure in the 1980s. But authors are not constrained by political factors.

So after a few years, the commercial banks, too, found costs-of-funds too high, and revenues from loans too low, to be profitable. Their failure rate was over 200 per year in the late 1980s. The Federal Deposit Insurance Corporation also failed in the sense that Congress had to bail it out by restructuring and refinancing it. Under the new arrangements, the Federal Deposit Insurance Corporation manages two insurance funds. One of these insures deposits of thrifts and is called the *Savings Association Insurance Fund*. The other insures bank deposits and is called the *Bank Insurance Fund*.

In 1989 Congress passed the Financial Institutions Reform, Recovery, and Enforcement Act. It established the Office of Thrift Supervision as an agency of the Treasury to supervise savings associations. In 1991 Congress passed the Federal Deposit Insurance Corporation Improvement Act. Both acts were designed to enable regulators to deal more effectively with bank and thrift failures.

Causes of Failure

It would be wrong to believe that the Federal Reserve's tight monetary policies were the single cause of bank failure. The blame must be shared by all of the regulators. The regulators being discussed here are executives of the regulatory agencies including the Federal Reserve, the Congress, the Treasury, and state legislatures.

For example, in the mid-1970s when interest rates soared and left the financial institutions unable to meet their costs, other restrictions prevented them from dealing with their situation effectively. State legislatures had placed effective ceilings on the interest rates that various banking institutions could charge. The ceiling was 8½ per cent in New York when interest rates had reached double digits. Thrift institutions could not make mortgage loans at higher interest rates. Had they been able to do so, they would have had a better cushion against the difficult years in the 1980s. Congress finally overrode state usury laws and provided some relief to the banks and thrifts, but a great deal of damage had already been done.

Regulators also tie the hands of the bank and thrift managers in choosing assets in many ways. (Capital Adequacy Requirements were discussed in Chapter 4.)

So, a myriad of regulatory constraints make it extremely difficult for persons in the business of banking to deal effectively with problem situations.

The news media has spent many lines of print and many hours of radio and television on the subject of thrifts and bank failure. Nearly all of the media's coverage concentrated on the handful of unscrupulous executives who engaged in fraudulent activities that led to losses by investors. It must be emphasized that *over 99 per cent of all banks and thrifts that failed recently were operated and managed by decent, law-abiding citizens who were trapped by government imposed rules and regulations.*

Moral Hazard

Deposit insurance, like other forms of insurance, may give rise to unethical and illegal behavior if it is too generous. For example, a person running a business with a heavy dose of fire insurance may find that the insurance gives him or her the incentive to burn the inventory and collect the insurance. Offering such incentives is referred to as moral hazard.

Some observers have suggested that insurance on bank deposits gives an incentive to bank managers to take high risks with depositor's funds. With high risks, there will be some losses and then the taker of risks is blamed for taking the risks. Such taking of risks is then called a moral hazard that follows from deposit insurance.

Consider an analogy. Suppose it is the last play of the game and you are behind by a touchdown. You throw a long pass to the end zone called a "Hail Mary" pass, and pray that somehow someone will catch it. It is a very risky play and seldom fruitful. But the quarterback is left with no other choice.

It is appropriate to view the manager of a failing thrift as in a similar situation. Such managers purchased huge volumes of risky securities that promised high yields. But the alternative, given the options they had, was to do nothing and let the institution go under. Yet such managers were often blamed for their risky actions. No one blamed the quarterback.

A New Organizational Structure for Bank Regulation

In this small space it is not possible to examine and evaluate the many changes to the regulatory structure of financial institutions in detail. There is a debate in Congress over changes in the organizational structure of financial regulation. Currently the Federal Reserve carries out examinations of banks and so does the Federal Deposit Insurance Corporation and the Comptroller of the Currency, or state bank regulators. It has been suggested that the overlap of activities is costly and unnecessary. Thus, the Federal Reserve may, in the future, be responsible for monetary policy only, and not for bank solvency. Furthermore, Congress is considering requiring that the Federal Reserve publish transcripts of the meetings of the Federal Open Market Committee, and that the General Accounting Office be given the authority to audit Federal Reserve operations. Unfortunately, there is too little space to consider these matters here.

Summary

Governments have a very difficult job. When it comes to regulation of financial institutions, those holding political power are damned if they do and damned if they don't. How do governments respond when they are faced with the necessity for regulation? That is the subject of this chapter.

Several theories of regulation were described in this chapter. Does regulation help direct financial activities toward the public interest? Do regulations promote competition, stability and efficiency? Do those who are regulated control the regulators as the capture theory suggests?

What does regulation portend for economic efficiency? Are financial markets efficient? Bank and thrift failures of the 1980s could be attributed to government failure to regulate the financial industry appropriately.

Key Terms and Concepts

The capture theory	Truth in Lending
Truth in Saving	A regulatory dialectic
Domino effect	Prohibitive vs. preventive rules
Efficient Markets Hypothesis (EMH)	Causes of thrift failure
Moral hazard	Empirical tests of EMH

Discussion Questions and Exercises

1. What are the two principal reasons for government controls over financial institutions?
2. What is the role of government in a market economy?

3. Distinguish between "government failure" and "market failure." Give examples.
4. What is the nature of the regulatory dilemma posed by the Capture Theory of regulation?
5. Explain the role played by lawyers and accountants in the dialectic theory of regulation.
6. Are there good reasons for restricting banks from entering other businesses? Discuss.
7. Distinguish between prohibitive and preventive regulations.
8. The Efficient Markets Hypothesis uses its own definition of "efficiency." Distinguish it from other meanings of the term.
9. Several studies show that the implications of the EMH do not hold, such as the weekend effect, the January effect, the Value Line Enigma, the small firm effect, and so forth. Identify each of these.
10. Closed-end mutual fund shares trade for a lower capitalization than the market value of the underlying collateral. How would someone gain by engaging in arbitrage to eliminate this difference? What steps would be involved in arbitrage?
11. Explain the greater fool theory.
12. Discuss broadly the finding that stock prices tend to fall after rising and vice versa, and that, since there is evidence of mean reversion, this indicates that stock markets are "inefficient."
13. Explain the concept of "moral hazard" and how it might relate to failures of financial institutions.
14. What are some of the reasons for the failure of so many thrift institutions in the 1980s?

References

Booth, James R., "FDIC Improvement Act and Corporate Governance of Commercial Banks," *Economic Review*, Federal Reserve Bank of San Francisco, No. 1, 1993, pp. 14–22.

Buchanan, James M., Tollison, Robert D., and Tullock, Gordon, *Toward a Theory of the Rent Seeking Society*, Texas A&M University Press, College Station, TX, 1980.

Constantinides, George M., "Habit Formation: A Resolution of the Equity Premium Puzzle," *Journal of Political Economy*, No. 98, June 1990, pp. 519–43.

Cross, Frank, "The Behavior of Stock Prices on Fridays and Mondays," *Financial Analysts Journal*, November/December 1973, pp. 67–69.

Cunningham, Thomas J., "A Liberal Discussion of Financial Liberalization," *Economic Review*, Federal Reserve Bank of Atlanta, November/December 1991, pp. 1–8.

Dawson, Steve, "Is the Hong Kong Market Efficient?" *Journal of Portfolio Management*, Spring 1992, pp. 17–20.

DeJong, David N., and Whiteman, Charles H., "More Unsettling Evidence on the Perfect Markets Hypothesis," *Economic Review*, Federal Reserve Bank of Atlanta, November/December 1992, pp. 1–13.

Dowd, Kevin, "Deposit Insurance: A Skeptical View," *Review*, Federal Reserve Bank of St. Louis, January/February 1993, pp. 14–21.

Dybvig, Philip H., "Remarks on Banking and Deposit Insurance," *Review*, Federal Reserve Bank of St. Louis, January/February 1993, pp. 21–24.

Edwards, Franklin R., and Patrick, Hugh T., eds., *Regulating International Financial Markets: Issues and Policies*, Kluwer Academic, Norwell, MA, 1992.

Engel, Charles, and Morris, Charles S., "Challenges to Stock Market Efficiency: Evidence from Mean Reversion Studies," *Economic Review*, Federal Reserve Bank of Kansas City, September/October 1991, pp. 21–36.

Euh, Yoon-Dae, and Amsden, Alice H., "Korea's Financial Reform," *Journal of Management*, College of Business Administration, Korea University, Seoul, Vol. 33, 1990, pp. 45–84.

Fama, Eugene F., "Efficient Capital Markets: A Review of Theory and Empirical Work," *Journal of Finance*, Vol. 25, No. 2, 1970, pp. 383–417.

Fama, Eugene F., and French, Kenneth R., "Permanent and Temporary Components of Stock Prices," *Journal of Political Economy*, April 1988, pp. 246–73.

Flood, Mark D., "Deposit Insurance: Problems and Solutions," *Review*, Federal Reserve Bank of St. Louis, January/February 1993, pp. 28–34.

Fortune, Peter, "Stock Market Efficiency: An Autopsy?" *New England Economic Review*, Federal Reserve Bank of Boston, March/April 1991, pp. 17–40.

Ho, Richard Y. K., "The Regulatory Framework of the Banking Sector," in Y. K. Ho, R. H. Scott, and K. A. Wong, eds., *The Hong Kong Financial System*, Oxford University Press, Hong Kong, 1991, pp. 91–118.

Huang, C. H., and Ederington, Louis H., "Variance Bound Tests of Bond Market Efficiency," *Journal of Financial Research*, Summer 1993, pp. 89–106.

Jordan, Jerry L., "A Market-based Approach to Regulatory Reform," *Economic Commentary*, Federal Reserve Bank of Cleveland, March 15, 1993.

Joskow, P. L., "Inflation and Environment Concern: Structural Change in the Process of Public Utility Regulation," *Journal of Law and Economics*, October 1974, pp. 291–327.

Kane, Edward J., "Good Intentions and Unintended Evil: The Case against Selective Credit Allocation," *Journal of Money, Credit, and Banking*, Vol. 9, February 1977, pp. 55–69.

Kane, Edward J., "Incentive Conflict in the International Regulatory Agreement on Risk-based Capital," in S. G. Rhee and R. P. Chang, eds., *Pacific-Basin Capital Markets Research*, Vol. 2, Elsevier, Amsterdam, 1991, pp. 3–21.

Lee, Charles, Shleifer, Andrei, and Thaler, Richard, "Closed-end Mutual Funds," *Journal of Economic Perspectives*, Fall 1990, pp. 153–64.

Mehra, Rajnish, and Prescott, Edward C., "The Equity Premium: A Puzzle," *Journal of Monetary Economics*, No. 15, March 1985, pp. 145–61.

Osterberg, William P., and Thomson, James B., "Making the SAIF Safe for Taxpayers," *Economic Commentary*, Federal Reserve Bank of Cleveland, November 1, 1993.

Poterba, James M., and Summers, Lawrence H., "Mean Reversion in Stock Prices: Evidence and Implications," *Journal of Financial Economics*, February 1988, pp. 27–59.

Rietz, Thomas A., "The Equity Risk Premium: A Solution," *Journal of Monetary Economics*, No. 22, July 1991, pp. 117–31.

Russell, Steven, "The Government's Role in Deposit Insurance," *Review*, Federal Reserve Bank of St. Louis, January/February 1993, pp. 3–9.

Selgin, George A., *The Theory of Free Banking: Money Supply under Competitive Note Issue*, Rowman & Littlefield, Totowa, NJ, 1988.

Shiller, Robert J., "Do Stock Prices Move Too Much to be Justified by Subsequent Changes in Dividends?" *American Economic Review*, June 1991, pp. 421–36.

Shleifer, Andrei, and Summers, Lawrence H., "The Noise Trader Approach to Finance," *Journal of Economic Perspectives*, Spring 1990, pp. 19–33.

Smith, Stephen D., and Wall, Larry D., "Financial Panics, Bank Failures, and the Role of Regulatory Policy," *Economic Review*, Federal Reserve Bank of Atlanta, January/February 1992, pp. 1–11.

Stigler, George J., "The Theory of Economic Regulation," *Bell Journal of Economics*, Vol. 2, 1971, pp. 3–21.

Syron, Richard F., "The Fed Must Continue to Supervise Banks," *New England Economic Review*, January/February 1994, pp. 3–8.

Thakor, Anjan, "Deposit Insurance Policy," *Review*, Federal Reserve Bank of St. Louis, January/February 1993, pp. 25–28.

Thomson, James B., "Using Market Incentives to Reform Bank Regulation and Federal Deposit Insurance," *Economic Review*, Federal Reserve Bank of Cleveland, 1st Quarter, 1990, pp. 28–40.

Tong, Wilson H. S., "An Analysis of the January Effect (the US, Taiwan and Korea)," in *Proceedings of the Second International Conference on Asian-Pacific Financial Markets*, City Polytechnic of Hong Kong, September 12–14, 1991, pp. 487–500.

Weil, Philippe, "The Equity Premium Puzzle and the Risk-free Rate Puzzle," *Journal of Monetary Economics*, No. 24, November 1989, pp. 401–21.

Wheelock, David C., "What have We Learned about Deposit Insurance from the Historical Record," *Review*, Federal Reserve Bank of St. Louis, January/February 1993, pp. 10–14.

Wong, Kie Ann, and Leng, Tan Chiew, "Price to Book Value Anomaly and Stock Return Seasonality: Evidence from Singapore," in *Proceedings of the Second International Conference on Asian-Pacific Financial Markets*, City Polytechnic of Hong Kong, September 12–14, 1991, pp. 438–47.

CHAPTER 16

Formulating and Implementing Monetary Policy

THIS CHAPTER BUILDS on materials covered briefly in Chapters 6 and 7 on central bank activities, and on the monetary theory presented in Chapters 12 and 13.

Monetary rules, regulations, and policies are all created by people involved in a political process. The institutional arrangements that are established to carry out policies differ within each country. However, central banks tend to look to each other for advice. The result is that many overall similarities exist amid a morass of technical differences in procedure and detail. Because of the importance of the U.S. economy in world trade, it is useful to focus on the process by which monetary policy is implemented there. Brief comparisons can then be drawn between implementation in other countries and that in the U.S.

Meetings of the Federal Open Market Committee

The Federal Open Market Committee (FOMC) is the group that has major responsibility for the implementation of monetary policy in the U.S. It consists of seven members of the Board of Governors of the Federal Reserve System plus five presidents from five of the twelve Federal Reserve Banks. One of the five presidents is on the committee all of the time—the president of the Federal Reserve Bank of New York—because that bank carries out open market operations and has greater involvement in world financial concerns than do others. Thus, the remaining four positions on the FOMC rotate among the remaining eleven Federal Reserve Bank presidents. All presidents usually attend meetings, but only the designated five are permitted to vote.

The committee meets monthly, and occasionally there is an interim meeting by telephone conference call. At regular meetings, members hear reports covering international and exchange rate developments, forecasts of economic trends, regional economic conditions, projections from econometric models, and other topics of current concern.

The FOMC Directive

After a general discussion, members of the committee are asked to vote on various concerns. Following the votes, the FOMC formulates a "directive" to the Manager for Domestic Operations of the trading desk at the New York Federal Reserve Bank. The directive includes a very brief summary of important information discussed at the meeting. These directives contain a variety of guidelines for the Manager. These take such forms as "maintain the existing degree of tightness in the federal funds market," or "keep the current conditions of restraint in place," or "foster conditions conducive to orderly reduction in the rate of inflation," and so forth. The statements are very indirect. Directives never say, "raise the federal funds rate to 4 per cent," or even mention any such specific target, although on occasion a target range is mentioned.

In spite of the indirectness of the statements made in the directive, it is quite easy for a group of economists to read the directive and place the overall emphasis as being within one of three classes: make monetary policy tighter, leave it unchanged, or make it easier. Persons who study data to uncover political influences in the making of monetary policy have classified such information in this way (see Havrilesky and Schweitzer, 1990).

Then there is a vote taken to approve or disapprove the directive. On most occasions, there will be some dissenting votes and these may be accompanied with a brief statement of the reason for disagreement with the other members of the committee.

Minutes of the meeting, including the directive, are published in the *Federal Reserve Bulletin* several weeks following the meeting. Some observers believe that the minutes should be published immediately after the meeting.

Of course, anyone in attendance at the meeting would know whether or not profit could be made from investing in securities traded by the open market desk. That is, all participants in the meeting have access to "inside information." Because of what appeared to be minor leaks of information prior to publication in newspapers in 1992 and 1993, members of Congress have complained to the Federal Reserve to control their participants. Here again, the question is how to deal with inside information. One of the best ways is to announce it so that information is no longer held "inside" but instead is available to everyone. Congress may instruct the Federal Reserve to publish the minutes right after the meeting.

A Typical Directive of the FOMC. The best way to gain an understanding of the "flavor" of a directive is to read an example. The directive for March 23, 1993, appearing in the July issue of the *Federal Reserve Bulletin* reads as follows:

At the conclusion of the meeting, the Federal Reserve Bank of New York was authorized and directed, until instructed otherwise by the Committee, to execute transactions in the System account in accordance with the following domestic policy directive:

The Federal Open Market Committee seeks monetary and financial conditions that will foster price stability and promote sustainable growth in output. In futherance of these objectives, the Committee at its meeting in February established ranges for growth of M2 and M3 of 2 to 6 percent and ½ to 4½ percent, respectively, measured from the fourth quarter of 1992 to the fourth quarter of 1993. The Committee expects that developments contributing to unusual velocity increases are likely to persist during the year. The monitoring range for growth of total domestic nonfinancial debt was set at 4½ to 8½ percent for the year. The behavior of the monetary aggregates will continue to be evaluated in the light of progress toward price level stability, movements in their velocities, and developments in the economy and financial markets.

In the implementation of policy for the immediate future, the Committee seeks to maintain the existing degree of pressure on reserve positions. In the context of the Committee's long-run objectives for price stability and sustainable economic growth, and giving careful consideration to economic, financial, and monetary developments, slightly greater reserve restraint or slightly lesser reserve restraint would be acceptable in the intermeeting period. The contemplated reserve conditions are expected to be consistent with a resumption of moderate growth in the broader monetary aggregates over the second quarter.

Votes for this action: Messrs. Greenspan, Corrigan, Boehne, Keehn, Kelley, LaWare, McTeer, Mullins, Ms. Phillips, and Mr. Stern. Votes against this action: Messrs. Angell and Lindsey.

Messrs. Angell and Lindsey indicated that their concerns about the outlook for inflation prompted them to favor an immediate move to tighten reserve conditions. In their view, such an action was desirable not only to arrest the possible emergence of greater inflation but especially to promote further disinflation. They were persuaded that monetary policy currently was overly accommodative as suggested by various indicators such as recent data on consumer and producer prices, the upswing in commodity prices, the low level of real short-term interest rates, and what in their judgment was a relatively depressed foreign exchange value of the dollar given the comparative strength of the U.S. economy and international interest rate trends.

Meetings with Congress

The Chairman of the Federal Reserve Board meets quarterly with Congress. Also, under provisions of the Humphrey-Hawkins Act, the Board must report in writing to the Congress by February 20 and July 20 of each year on its objectives and plans for the year ahead. Newspapers always cover these meetings and reports.

Minutes of Monetary Policy Meetings in the U.K.

After a lag of six weeks the first set of minutes of the regular monthly meetings of the Chancellor of the Exchequer, Mr. Kenneth Clarke, and the Governor of the Bank of

England, Mr. Eddie George, was published in April 1994. The minutes are patterned somewhat after those of the Federal Reserve. Various secretaries and advisors from the Treasury and the Bank attend the meetings to present information. Then the Governor and the Chancellor present their views about whether the Bank should change its policy posture. Only one person gets to vote—the Chancellor.

Open Market Operations: Targets and Details

Operating Targets

The open market desk supplies reserves to banks when it buys government securities. These reserves, of course, are *not* borrowed from the Fed and may be called nonborrowed reserves or unborrowed reserves.

When the Fed's discount window lends to banks, bank reserves increase and these are called borrowed reserves. If

T = total reserves

N = nonborrowed or unborrowed reserves supplied by open market purchases

B = borrowed reserves supplied to banks through the discount window

then $T = N + B$

The Federal Reserve may choose to have its operating target be any one of these three variables, or some combination of them. We will examine each of the three possibilities using graphs. The discount rate i_D and the federal funds rate i_F are measured on the vertical axis, while measures of reserves appear on the horizontal axis, in Figure 16–1.

The demand curve, D, appears in its usual falling shape. Banks want more reserves as interest rates fall. The supply curve for reserves, S, is not typical. It rises vertically above the quantity of nonborrowed reserves N. At the height of the discount rate it kinks up to the right. This portion of reserves is borrowed, B. The intersection of D and S determines i_F. The higher i_F, the greater $i_F - i_D$, and the greater the incentive for banks to take advantage of the discount window's lower cost for reserves. Hence, B increases as $i_F - i_D$ increases.

Total Reserve Targets: T* = N + B. The asterisk on the T indicates that the Fed's target is to keep total reserves constant. To see how the open market desk and the discount window respond to changes in the demand for reserves, assume that there is an increase in the demand for reserves as shown by the shift from D to D' in Figure 16–1.

Beginning at the original point, point O, the increase in demand to D' pushes interest rates up in the federal funds market. Higher interest rates encourage banks to borrow more from the Fed, and to keep these increased borrowings from leading to an increase in total reserves, the volume of nonborrowed reserves must be reduced. The reduction in N is shown by the leftward shift in the supply function from S to S'. Thus, the yield on fed funds rises from i_F to i_F'.

Since T is to be held constant, if B increases, N must decrease by an equal amount.

Figure 16–1

Total Reserves Target

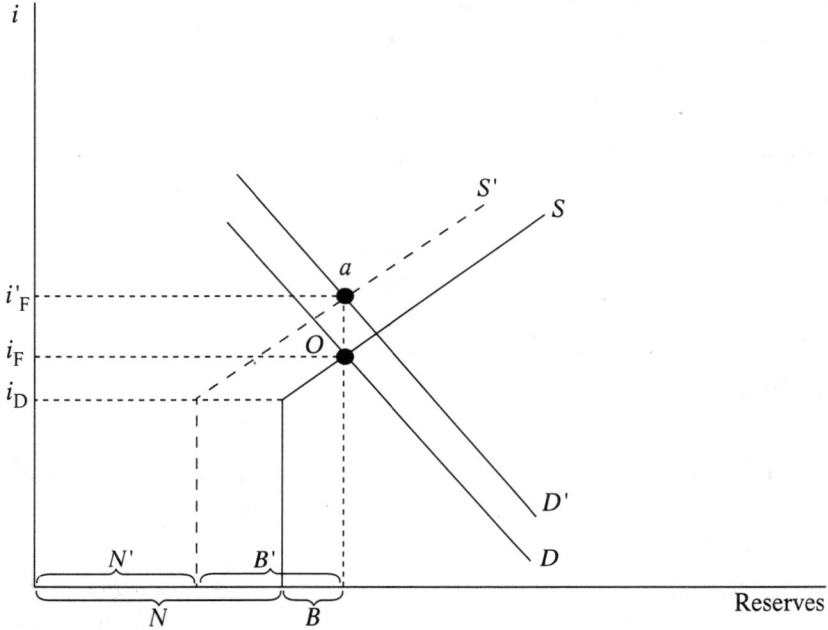

To summarize:

1. When $T^* = N + B$, there is no change in T.
2. There is a decrease in N and increase in B by equal and offsetting amounts.
3. The federal funds rate rises to a high level.

Nonborrowed Reserve Targets: T = N* + B. The asterisk on the N indicates that the Fed's target is to keep nonborrowed reserves constant. The response of the Fed will be to let B increase to accommodate an increase in T as shown in Figure 16–2.

To summarize:

1. When $T = N^* + B$ and reserve demand increases to D', the level of borrowed reserves, B, expands and the equilibrium point moves along the supply curve, S, to point b.
2. Total reserves increase an equal amount as unborrowed reserves do not change.
3. There will be some increase in the fed funds rate to i_F, but not as much increase as there would have been under total reserve targeting.

Borrowed Reserve Targets: T = N + B*. Here again the asterisk now indicates that the level of borrowing from the Fed should stay constant under a program of borrowed reserve targeting. To keep this constant, the open market desk will have to expand N as

Figure 16–2
Nonborrowed Reserves Target

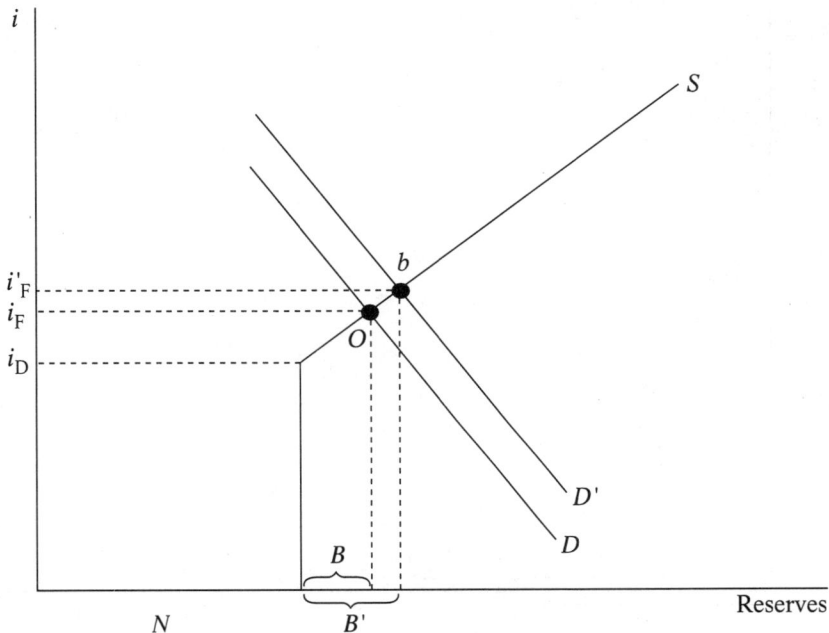

shown in Figure 16–3. This expansion results in a rightward shift in the supply of reserves from S to S'.

To summarize:

1. When $T = N + B^*$ and D increases to D' then N must increase by the full extent of the rightward shift in D so that S shifts to S'.
2. Total reserves increase the same amount as N increases, but B stays constant.
3. The federal funds rate does not increase at all in this case. Thus, targeting of a level of borrowed reserves is nearly the same as targeting the federal funds rate.

Figure 16–4 captures the results of all three operating target alternatives in one graph.

Using Supply and Demand Curves in Analysis

The examples above described the open market desk's response to and *increase in demand* for reserves under three operating targets. It should be clear that a similar set of graphs could be drawn that would show what happens if there were a *decrease in demand* instead of an increase. Furthermore, one may consider what response might follow from *shifts in the supply of reserves* because the supply itself may be affected by some outside event. For example, the supply of reserves would fall if an unexpectedly

Figure 16–3
Borrowed Reserves Target

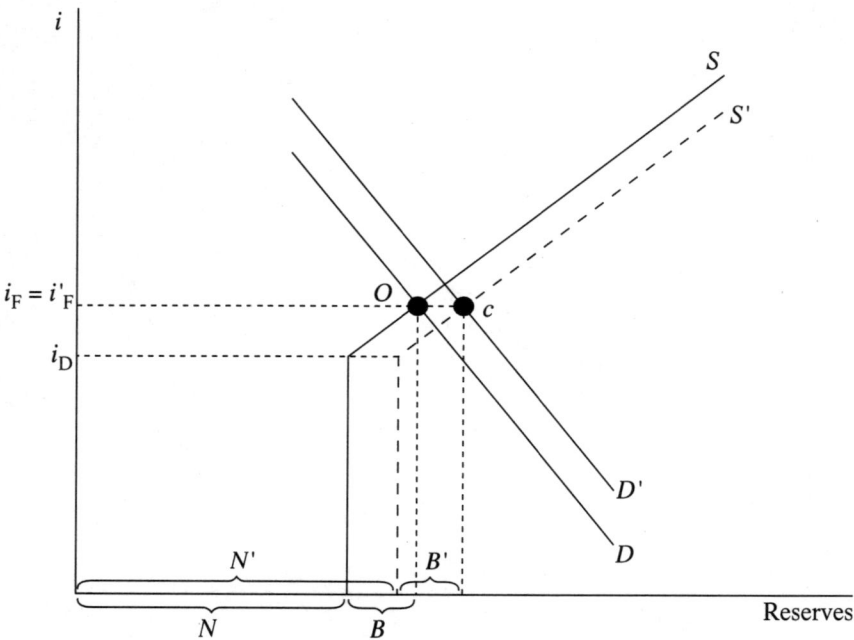

Figure 16–4
Federal Funds Rates Movements under Three Targets

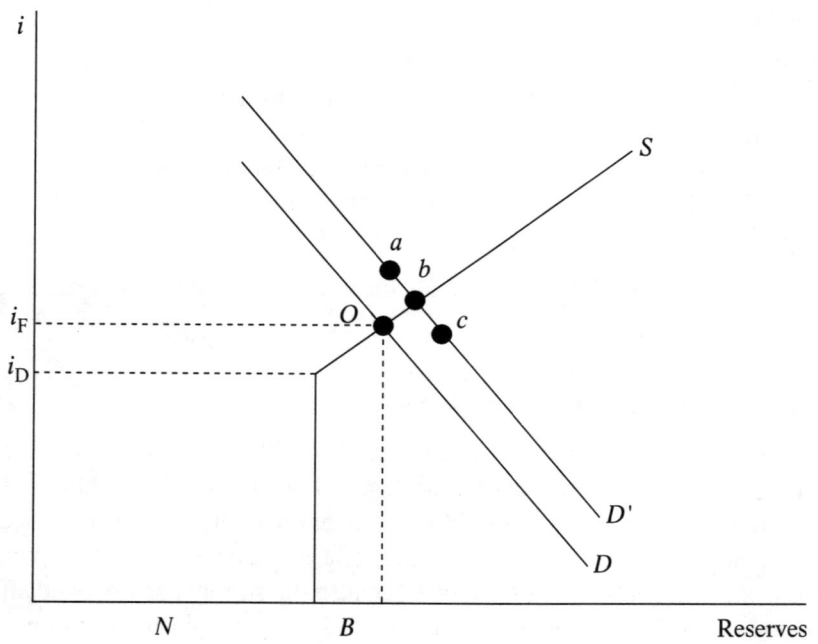

large increase in currency in circulation were to occur. Then, if the Federal Reserve kept its target on total, nonborrowed, or borrowed reserves, it would respond to the decline in reserves by replenishing the supply with an increase in nonborrowed reserves through open market purchases of securities. In other words it would "sterilize" the unwanted change is the supply of reserves. The reader may wish to draw rough graphs similar to the ones above that show the response to an increase in demand, and to interpret the response when defensive open market operations are used to offset an unwanted change in supply.

Lagged Reserve Accounting. One may imagine a graph like those in the figures in which the demand curve is vertical instead of sloping downward to the right. When the vertical demand curve is drawn slightly to the right of the vertical portion of the supply curve for reserves, the intersection showing the determination of the federal funds rate will be above the discount rate. However, if the vertical demand curve is shifted to the left, it eventually moves beyond the vertical portion of the supply curve to a position where the two curves no longer intersect. In this case, supply of reserves exceeds demand for reserves and the federal funds rate would fall below the discount rate, indeed, it would fall to approach zero.

Precisely the same result would occur if, instead of moving the demand curve to the left, the supply curve were moved to the right.

The reason for pointing this out is that, under lagged reserve accounting, the demand for reserves is vertical. It is determined by the level of deposits set earlier. So when banks face a need for reserves to meet legal requirements, there must be a sufficient amount of reserves for all of the banks. Reserves may flow from bank to bank, but like musical chairs, when the music stops and banks have to fulfill their obligation to hold reserves, there must be chairs available to sit on. Otherwise, some bank must fail. Legal reserve requirements are not imposed for the purpose of playing musical chairs with them and running some participant out of the game.

What all of this means is that under lagged reserve accounting *the federal funds rate must be above the discount rate.* It also means that the Federal Reserve must supply sufficiently small amounts of reserves with open market operations to ensure that *some banks are in a borrowed reserve position.* The system we now have, described in detail in Chapter 3, is called contemporaneous reserve accounting. The general characteristic of this system is that the demand for reserves would be downward sloping and not vertical. But the contemporaneous accounting applies to only 12 days of the 2-week accounting period. The remaining 2 days are Tuesday and Wednesday. On these days of the week the amount of reserves the banks require is fixed and the demand is vertical. On these days the federal funds rate must lie above the discount rate. Thus, the open market desk must see that reserves are limited and force banks to the discount window. If the policy requires more expansionary monetary policy, the Federal Reserve must lower the discount rate. It must do this if it is to avoid the problems arising from demand and supply curves for reserves that do not intersect on Tuesday and Wednesday.

Targeting Procedures

Definitions of terms:

T = total reserves of banks
N = nonborrowed reserves
B = borrowed reserves
S = seasonal borrowings
A = adjustment borrowings
E = extended credit borrowings
T = $N + B$, also
T = $RR + ER$
RR = required reserves
ER = excess reserves

S and A are sensitive to i_F, the federal funds rate. For a given discount rate i_D, as the rate of interest on federal funds rises, both seasonal and adjustment borrowings by banks from the federal reserve will rise, too, so that B increases as i_F rises. E is not sensitive to i_F. The interest charged on E is set higher than i_D charged by the Federal Reserve on S and A borrowings, and acts as a penalty rate on troubled banks that require extended assistance from the lender of last resort.

Total reserves target $T^* = N + B$. Here, N is a slack variable. It is adjusted to whatever level is required to keep T on track.

Nonborrowed reserves target $N^* = T - B$. Here N is both a slack variable and a target variable. To determine N one needs estimates of both T and B.

Borrowed reserves target $B^* = T - N$. Here, N is again the slack variable. B is now a target instead of an assumption or estimate as it was under nonborrowed targeting. T is estimated by forecasts of its various components.

Notice that, in each case, N is the slack or instrumental variable and that open market operations are used to bring N to its targeted amount.

With some manipulation:

$B = T - N = S + A + E$, and
$T = RR + ER$, therefore,
$S + A + E = RR + ER - N$

Letting E be estimated so that the focus is on Seasonal and Adjustment credit borrowing when the Open Market Desk is changing N, shift E to the right-hand side of the equation to show it as an independent variable. Then:

$S + A = RR + ER - E - N$

Here, estimates are made of required reserves and excess reserves that sum to total reserves, and also of extended credit borrowing. N is then adjusted by the open market desk to bring $S + A$ components of borrowing into line with the "borrowings target" or the "borrowings assumption" depending on which phrase one wishes to use.

RR used to be known in advance under lagged reserve accounting. Now, under contemporaneous reserve accounting, the open market desk's estimate of *RR* sometimes needs to be revised during the reserve period. When it is revised, the slack variable *N* must also be changed by the same amount since $S + A$ is the target.

N is affected not only by open market operations that affect the Federal Reserve's portfolio of government securities, but also by other items on the Fed's balance sheet. These other items include such things as the float, Treasury deposits, foreign deposits, currency in circulation, and so forth. These items are all estimated, too, in order to allow the managers of the open market desk to bring the government securities portfolio of the Fed into line with the borrowings target.

Summary Statement of Procedures

The Federal Open Market Committee meets, examines evidence on the state of the economy, and votes on the appropriate "degree of restraint." Degrees of restraint are identified as "more," "the same," or "less." The Manager of the Federal Open Market Desk interprets and translates this order into an amount of purchases or sales of government securities that should be made (changes in *N*) in order to meet the borrowings target $(S + A)$. If more restraint is needed, after all the various factors mentioned above are estimated, a borrowings target is placed higher than the current level of borrowings, and the appropriate *N* is established. In case the FOMC orders less restraint, *N* is changed to fit with a lower level of $S + A$ borrowings.

The overall net effect of these procedures is as follows: When shifts in money demand occur, the Fed's response is to adjust *N* to keep *B* on target, and this means accommodating the shift in demand with reserves so that interest levels are not affected. However, when a change in monetary policy is dictated by the FOMC, the manager translates the policy change into a change in the desired level of borrowings that will accompany a change in the interest rate on federal funds. A tighter policy implies setting a higher borrowings target and this implies setting a lower *N*, and the result will include higher interest rate levels.

Filling in the Blanks

The FOMC issues directives to the manager of the open market desk at the Federal Reserve Bank of New York. Members of the FOMC are asked: What do you recommend?

They are given a blue-book, like an exam book, and asked to check the blank space for example, to choose A, B, or C (or even D for none of the above!) This example is hypothetical. Assume that the discount rate is 3 per cent and the current federal funds rate is 5 per cent. Check your choice.

    _____ A. Borrowings $100 million, federal funds rate 4%
    _____ B. Borrowings $200 million, federal funds rate 5%
    _____ C. Borrowings $300 million, federal funds rate 6%

The A, B, and C represent, essentially, easier, unchanged, and tighter, monetary policies, respectively.

In other words, maintaining current monetary conditions at the implied target for borrowings of $200 million will mean an unchanged and anticipated 5 per cent level for the federal funds rate. If the target for borrowings were lowered, and if the open market desk were to expand nonborrowed reserves through open market purchases, the federal funds rate would fall to about 4 per cent and banks would reduce borrowing levels to about $100 million, as indicated by B.

If the FOMC chooses C, then the open market desk would sell securities and banks would be forced to borrow about $300 million from the Fed. This would happen when interest rates on federal funds were pushed up to the 6 per cent range as the open market desk at the New York Fed drains reserves from the banks at the direction of the FOMC.

In this hypothetical example the relation between borrowing and the federal funds rate specifies that a $100 million change in borrowings would result in a change in the federal funds rate of 1 per cent. Actual data indicates that a change in borrowing of $100 million will lead to a change of only about a quarter of a percentage point, that is, about 25 basis points (see Stevens, 1990). When the Federal Reserve decides to raise the federal funds rate by this amount, as it did on two occasions in early 1994, this would have been the result of a change in the borrowing objective of $100 million.

This example makes a reader feel that the decision-making process is mechanical. To a certain degree it certainly is. However, members of the FOMC understand that there can be shifts in the relation between borrowing and the federal funds rate. So they look at the data carefully and if a shift is indicated they may adjust the borrowing target.

Given the current outlook for economic activity in the U.S. economy, would you vote for A, B or C? If none of the above, what are your recommendations?

Open Market Churning of Accounts

The Federal Reserve *Bulletin* reports open market transactions with monthly figures. Table 16–1 is taken from the March 1994 issue. This table takes awhile to figure out, but taking the time to figure it out is worth it.

First, the reader should know that the current table was chosen simply because it was the most recently published table when this book was ready for the publisher. It appears to be representative.

At the top of the table there are data on Gross Purchases, Gross Sales, Exchanges and Redemptions of Treasury bills. Figures for the year 1992 indicate that $14.714 billion were purchased, $1.628 billion were sold, and $1.600 billion were redeemed for new issues of bills when the Treasury conducted its weekly auctions of bills. Redemptions indicate a change in holdings of the bills, as the full amount maturing was not exchanged for new issues. Redemptions reduce holdings of bills.

In the within-one-year category, there are both maturity shifts and exchanges. The categories continue showing the extent of securities trading in the longer maturity ranges.

More interesting figures are lower down in the table showing gross purchases, gross sales and redemptions of all maturities (lines 22–24). Gross purchases were $34.079 billion and gross sales were $1.628 billion. But look at the volume of "matched transactions," which are reverse repurchase agreements, and then there are repurchase agreements themselves. Altogether the total runs about $1.5 trillion in matched transactions, and another $300 billion in repurchase agreements.

But the net change in the holdings of U.S. Treasury securities by the Federal Reserve was only $20.642 billion (line 29).

The Federal Reserve does not engage in business with dealers without paying fees or spreads. The reasons given for such a large volume of transactions day in and day out is that it needs to keep bank reserves on a steady growth path, or that it needs to keep federal funds rates steady. But the irony is that banks have contracts that specify that *they* take responsibility for managing their liabilities for the purpose of maintaining reserves sufficient to pay depositor withdrawals on demand. They should be responsible if the Treasury withdraws funds. They should be prepared to provide shoppers with cash on a seasonal basis. They should meet their obligations in the face of foreign exchange needs. In short, they should take care of themselves and not rely on expenses provided by the taxpayer. There is simply no justification for this huge volume of defensive open market operations that has developed to do for banks that for which banks themselves should be responsible.

The Federal Reserve provides us, in this instance, with a beautiful example of the Capture Theory of Regulation at work. If a private broker churned your investment account as much as the Federal Reserve does its investment account held for the taxpayer, your broker would probably be put in jail. The law should provide similar penalties for those who run government.

Notice that over the year there was a net increase in security holdings by the Federal Reserve of about $20 billion. These additional reserves could have been injected into the system by having a clerk purchase about $400 million each Wednesday for 50 weeks, taking 2 weeks for vacation, and letting the banks fend for themselves (see Friedman, 1982; 1993). This would save the taxpayers a lot of money.

Intervention in Foreign Exchange Markets

By buying and holding large blocks of foreign currencies, the Federal Reserve tries to push up their market value, that is, it tries to push down the dollar's value. The Fed should stop this intervention because it has no lasting effect on the dollar's value and because it disrupts markets in foreign exchange and government securities.

Those who wish to reduce America's trade deficit point out that a low-valued dollar limits imports by making them expensive. It also stimulates exports by making them cheap. But a dollar that is depressed artificially and temporarily only serves to raise false hopes.

Continuing to raise false hopes, both the Fed and the Treasury's Exchange Equalization Fund intervened frequently over the past year. The Fed's *Bulletin* for January 1990

Table 16–1
Federal Reserve Open Market Transactions[1] (Million of dollars)

Type of transaction and maturity	1990	1991	1992	1993						
				May	June	July	Aug.	Sept.	Oct.	Nov.
U.S. TREASURY SECURITIES										
Outright transactions (excluding matched transactions)										
Treasury bills										
1 Gross purchases	24,739	20,158	14,714	349	7,280	0	902	366	1,396	5,931
2 Gross sales	7,291	120	1,628	0	0	0	0	0	0	0
3 Exchanges	241,086	277,314	308,699	26,610	24,821	35,943	27,775	31,128	25,783	27,641
4 Redemptions	4,400	1,000	1,600	0	0	0	0	0	468	0
Others within one year										
5 Gross purchases	425	3,043	1,096	0	0	0	100	411	0	0
6 Gross sales	0	0	0	0	0	0	0	0	0	0
7 Maturity shifts	25,638	24,454	36,662	4,108	4,002	0	1,497	3,074	913	5,518
8 Exchanges	-27,424	-28,090	-30,543	-4,013	-2,152	0	-5,491	-1,861	-1,566	-7,641
9 Redemptions	0	1,000	0	0	0	0	0	0	0	0
One to five years										
10 Gross purchases	250	6,583	13,118	0	0	200	1,100	2,400	0	100
11 Gross sales	200	0	0	0	0	0	0	0	0	0
12 Maturity shifts	-21,770	-21,211	-34,478	-3,652	-4,002	666	-834	-3,074	-31	-4,689
13 Exchanges	25,410	24,594	25,811	3,245	2,152	0	3,866	1,861	1,566	5,341
Five to ten years										
14 Gross purchases	0	1,280	2,818	0	0	0	500	797	0	0
15 Gross sales	100	0	0	0	0	0	0	0	0	0
16 Maturity shifts	-2,186	-2,037	-1,915	-333	0	-666	-432	0	-882	-272
17 Exchanges	789	2,894	3,532	468	0	0	1,100	0	0	2,300
More than ten years										
18 Gross purchases	0	375	2,333	0	0	0	100	717	0	0
19 Gross sales	0	0	0	0	0	0	0	0	0	0
20 Maturity shifts	-1,681	-1,209	-269	-123	0	0	-231	0	0	-197
21 Exchanges	1,226	600	1,200	300	0	0	525	0	0	0

All maturities										
22 Gross purchases	25,414	31,439	34,079	349	7,280	200	2,702	4,691	1,396	6,031
23 Gross sales	7,591	120	1,628	0	0	0	0	0	0	0
24 Redemptions	4,400	1,000	1,600	0	0	0	0	0	468	0
Matched transactions										
25 Gross sales	1,369,052	1,570,456	1,482,467	124,462	111,726	115,504	136,037	124,898	115,160	109,941
26 Gross purchases	1,363,434	1,571,534	1,480,140	123,227	113,095	117,074	135,705	122,578	112,837	112,772
Repurchase agreements										
27 Gross purchases	219,632	310,084	378,374	33,987	53,051	41,190	53,053	62,905	27,693	38,493
28 Gross sales	202,551	311,752	386,257	28,640	43,342	56,246	48,263	61,399	30,397	34,072
29 Net change in U.S. Treasury securities	24,886	29,729	20,642	4,461	18,357	-13,286	7,160	3,878	-4,099	13,283
FEDERAL AGENCY OBLIGATIONS										
Outright transactions										
30 Gross purchases	0	0	0	0	0	0	0	0	0	0
31 Gross sales	0	5	0	0	0	0	0	0	0	0
32 Redemptions	183	292	632	41	22	366	125	35	70	15
Repurchase agreements										
33 Gross purchases	41,836	22,807	14,565	2,105	2,968	3,479	2,485	9,810	3,812	2,841
34 Gross sales	40,461	23,595	14,486	2,105	2,019	4,428	2,415	7,734	5,509	2,861
35 Net changes in federal agency obligations	1,192	-1,085	-554	-41	927	-1,315	-55	2,041	-1,767	-35
36 Total net change in System Open Market Account	26,078	28,644	20,089	4,420	19,284	-14,061	7,105	5,919	-5,866	13,248

1. Sales, redemptions, and negative figures reduce holdings of the System Open Market Account: all other figures increase such holdings.

Source: *Federal Reserve Bulletin*, March 1994.

reports that U.S. monetary authorities bought nearly $6 billion in foreign currencies during August, September, and October 1989. In January 1989 the Fed held only $9.5 billion in foreign currencies. By October's end it held $29 billion in foreign currencies. The Fed's *Bulletin* for September 1994 reports that on May 4 the Fed joined eighteen other central banks to sell yen and marks. In total the Fed purchased $750 million worth of marks and $500 million worth of yen.

To understand why intervention does not work, one need only examine the mechanics of the process.

Assume the Federal Reserve intervenes to support the value of the yen against the dollar. The Federal Reserve simply enters the market for yen, buys up a sufficiently large block of yen and shocks the market into temporarily pushing up the price of yen.

Since the Fed buys yen with dollars, the supply of dollars increases as the Fed takes yen out of the economy and pumps dollars in.

In a typical intervention, the Fed gives a foreign exchange dealer a check for dollars and accepts a check for yen drawn on a Japanese bank in exchange.

The Fed deposits the yen check in a Japanese bank and holds an asset account in yen. The dealer who sold yen will collect dollars by depositing the Fed's check in a U.S. bank. Since this bank banks at the Fed, it sends the check to the Fed for deposit to its account. Bank deposits in the Fed are banks' legal reserves, and now these reserves are up. With more reserves, the banking system loans more and creates more dollars.

As more dollars are dumped into the economy, they flow from hand to hand as they are spent. Prices rise. Inflation follows. Dollars thus buy less yen, and the foreign exchange value of the dollar continues to fall.

But, inflation means that dollars also buy less goods and services at home so Americans continue to demand imports from Japan. Japanese find prices of American goods inflated and do not want to buy American exports. The trade deficit with Japan grows worse, not better.

Driving down the dollar's value through inflation fails to solve the trade deficit problem.

Policymakers know this. Therefore, to prevent inflation the Fed will "sterilize" intervention's effect on bank reserves and money.

In this example, the Fed created bank reserves when it bought yen. To remove these added reserves, the Fed must sell an equal dollar amount of something else. It sells Treasury securities to reduce reserves and "sterilize" the intervention.

Since hundreds of billions of dollars change hands in the foreign exchange markets around the world every day, it takes a billion dollar purchase to have any lasting effect in that vast market. If the Fed buys $1 billion worth of yen, it must turn around and sell $1 billion worth of Treasuries, so their prices fall.

The buying public will demand higher interest rates as an inducement to hold another billion worth of government securities on top of those already issued to finance an excessive budget deficit. Interest rates on U.S. securities will rise.

Japanese investors will want to take advantage of relatively high interest rates. To do so, they will sell yen and buy dollars. American investors will be reluctant to buy yen-dominated securities because their yields are relatively low. On both sides of the Pacific, investors will demand more dollars and fewer yen, thus pushing up the dollar's value and offsetting intervention's downward push.

In effect "sterilizing" intervention's effect on bank reserves ends up "sterilizing" intervention's effect on the dollar's value as well. Therefore, sterilized intervention simply will not affect the value of the dollar over any period longer than a few days or weeks—never long enough to cause a change in imports or exports. Not only does intervention fail to regulate the dollar's value, but it also disrupts foreign exchange markets.

If markets are to allocate scarce foreign exchange efficiently, the markets need full information. Acts of intervention by central banks serve only to muddy the waters and cloud the information usually provided by prices. They make day-in and day-out trading of foreign exchange more risky.

Increased riskiness in foreign exchange markets has two damaging effects on world economies: it makes doing business across national borders more difficult, and it diverts productive resources to risk-avoiding activities, such as trading in options and futures markets in foreign exchange.

While intervention disrupts foreign exchange markets, action taken by the Fed to "sterilize" intervention disrupts domestic government securities markets as well. It increases riskiness and clouds information in those markets. Doing business domestically becomes more risky as investors must deal with greater fluctuations in interest rates. Fewer investment projects are acceptable. Economic growth slows. More resources are diverted away from productive activities into risk-avoiding activities.

Although not recorded in dollars and cents, the damage done to both foreign and domestic economic activity by ill-conceived intervention in foreign exchange markets is, nonetheless, very real.

Responsible policymaking officials have a duty to reject intervention: it does not work, and it damages markets.

Pegging Interest Rates and the "Bills-only" Policy

Before World War II, economists paid little attention to the term structure of interest rates. They were concerned principally with the level of rates and its relation to other variables. However, Keynes's medicine for the Great Depression was concerned principally with long-term interest rates, and he suggested that they be kept low in order to stimulate investment spending. Other economists stressed the relevance of short-term interest rates and business investment in inventories. Since then the literature on the term structure of interest rates has ballooned, as is indicated by having an entire chapter in this book devoted to it.

Pegging the Yield Curve. When World War II began the Federal Reserve quickly moved to peg the interest rates on all outstanding Treasury debt at prevailing yields. The reason it acted swiftly was that people remembered the Treasury's experience with its debt issues during World War I. The Treasury had made successive issues of debt, each at slightly higher interest rates, so the market for Treasury debt soon dried up because every investor decided simply to wait for the next issue to obtain higher yields.

To prevent a repeat experience the Federal Reserve cooperated with the Treasury and "pegged" the yield curve. The Federal Reserve simply bought any securities not bought by the private sector, at prices that maintained yields at fixed levels. In doing this, large volumes of reserves were added to the assets of commercial banks, and because loans were restricted principally to firms with legal priorities for activities related to war production, the banks' excess reserves were used to purchase government securities.

During this time, the yield curve was positively sloped, with very short-term Treasury bills yielding ⅜ per cent and long-term bonds yielding 2½ per cent.

As the war continued, there were some portfolio managers who "read" the Federal Reserves' unannounced policy and began to buy only longer-term securities to "play the pattern or rates" or "ride down the yield curve" so they could obtain higher yields and capital gains as well. This meant that the Federal Reserve found itself purchasing large volumes of short-term securities.

Soon after World War II came to an end, the Federal Reserve allowed short-term rates to rise, but it retained the peg on longer-term securities. Economists generally expected a postwar recession to develop, and no one pressed the Federal Reserve to raise long-term rates.

After a slight recession in 1948–49, the economy began to boom again and, in June 1950, the war with North Korea broke out. Fortunately, Congress was in session at the time and introduced a tax increase to finance the war. This fiscal measure helped restrain the development of inflationary pressures typical of wartime economies, but Federal Reserve officials also decided that a measure of restraint on their part would be appropriate. They discussed their plans to raise long-term interest rates a bit with Treasury officials. But Treasury officials were reluctant to give up their privileged position in the securities markets. On one occasion, the Treasury appeared to agree with the Federal Reserve but then announced the issue of debt with no change in yield so the Federal Reserve was forced to purchase the unsold portion in order to ensure that the issue did not fail.

Finally, President Truman was asked to resolve the differences between the Treasury and the Federal Reserve. Usually, the Federal Reserve is treated as an independent agency of the government, but in this case the president was asked to listen to the arguments and decide which path to take—pegged low interest rates, or higher rates to deter inflation? He sided with the argument of the Federal Reserve, and one wonders what the independent Fed would have done if he had decided in favor of the Treasury argument.

In March 1951, the Treasury and Federal Reserve announced their *Accord*. Long-term interest rates were freed from the peg and began to rise.

The "Bills-only" Policy. One hurdle was over, but another was just beginning. In 1953, an ad hoc subcommittee of the Federal Open Market Committee reported on a study of the government securities market. It recommended that open market operations be confined to the market for Treasury bills, except that trading in long-term securities would take place to prevent or subdue any "disorderly conditions" that might develop among long-term issues. The bills market, it was argued, had depth, breadth, and resiliency and was, therefore, the appropriate market to use to adjust member bank reserve positions. The FOMC adopted a resolution that became known as the "bills-only" policy.

The policy, like others of the FOMC, was kept secret for a time until congressmen released it to the public. Academic economists questioned the wisdom of the policy and a debate broke out. They argued that if long-term rates needed lowering, the Federal Reserve might buy long-term securities and push them down while adding to bank reserves at the same time. If they bought only bills, pushing bill rates down, would interest rates on long-term securities stay high, or come down only marginally and slowly as pressures from an easier monetary policy trickled out to the long-end of the market? Moving the long-end would be more consistent with the Keynesian emphasis on long-term investments.

Operation Twist. The debate continued for several years, and in 1961 the Federal Reserve abandoned the "bills-only" policy briefly to engage in "operation twist." At that time, President Kennedy had just come into office and the economy was operating at what was considered to be a relatively low employment level. Thus, to promote the expansion of the economy, lower long-term interest rates were called for.

However, the balance of trade situation was deteriorating, and the U.S. was beginning to lose gold to exports. Higher interest rates, especially higher short-term interest rates, would attract foreign capital and help stem the outflow of foreign exchange reserves.

Thus, by buying long-term securities in a departure from the "bills-only" policy and putting downward pressure on long-term yields, the Federal Reserve could stimulate economic activity. At the same time, it could sell short-term securities and push short-term interest rates up in order to attract foreign exchange. The twisting of the yield curve from its positive slope into a flatter position would allow both domestic employment and foreign exchange targets to be hit at the same time. After a very brief and weak attempt to twist the curve, the Fed abandoned the "twist" effort.

Conservative academic economists believed the Fed should not engage in attempts to move interest rates around and were pleased. They also published articles attempting to verify that the "twist" effort had been a failure. But it is obviously a failure *if no attempt is made* to carry out the policy. There is no evidence to say an "operation twist" would not work if the Fed wanted to do it and took appropriate steps.

Thus, the Federal Reserve had argued persuasively for the right to move long-term interest rates around in order to promote financial stability, but then imposed a self-restricting "bills-only" policy.

The Debate Continues. As described in some detail in Chapter 14, the rational expectations approach to the theory of the yield curve says that expectations control interest rates and that changes in supplies of securities in various maturity ranges will have no effect on them. These views prevailed until the presidential campaign of 1992. The staff of the Clinton administration suggested that perhaps long-term interest rates could be reduced if the Treasury sold fewer long-term bonds. They also stated that a reduction in interest expenses for the Treasury would help reduce the deficit. The Treasury considered such a proposal and put it into effect. It will be discussed in Chapter 17. However, influenced politically by all the talk, the Federal Reserve was not about to appear uncooperative, and it began making what is called in the market a *"treasury pass,"* which means that it asked dealers to run down their prices on long-term securities to see which would be a good buy.

The following discussion is about how the Fed might deal with its open market operations more successfully.

A Broadside Approach to Open Market Operations: A Proposal

Two Immediate Impacts of Open Market Operations

Consider the first impact of open market trades on those short-term securities markets the Federal Reserve enters in carrying out policy. The initial impact, if any, would be in the short-term market itself. For example, the market supply of Treasury bills expands when the Federal Reserve sells bills out of its portfolio and dumps them into the market. If the volume of sales is sufficiently large, interest rates may rise in the Treasury bills market.

A second impact, reinforcing the first, is on the volume of bank reserves and interest rates in the federal funds market. Since reserves are drained from banks when the Federal Reserve sells bills, interest rates on interbank borrowing and lending of reserves in the federal funds market rise here, too. But tight conditions in the federal funds market may have little *direct* effect on the interest rates of short-term securities held by the consuming public. Instead, the principal *indirect* effect of a tight federal funds market on the public is that, facing a general market shortage of funds, banks must act to restrain their lending and will charge higher interest on short-term loans to business.

In addition, banks may sell Treasury bills or other short-term securities in order to acquire funds needed to meet loan demand. This action creates additional upward pressure on interest rates in the markets for short-term securities. To obtain more funds, banks may issue short-term certificates of deposit. Faced with a shortage of reserves, banks may reduce their holdings of short-term assets or they may increase their outstanding short-term liabilities. In either case, they increase the supply of short-term securities in the hands of the public.

Thus, both the direct and the indirect effects of the decision to implement a tight monetary policy force short-term market interest rates up.

Combining the Two Impacts of Open Market Operations. Now, assume that the Federal Reserve would tighten by selling long-term securities instead of short-term securities. The direct impact, if any, would be to put downward pressure on prices of long-term

securities and cause long-term interest yields to rise. The indirect impact would exert itself through bank reserves and bank lending just as described above. Thus, short-term interest rates would rise as well. The level of the yield curve—*both* the short and long ends of the curve—would be pushed up by the tightening measures taken by the Federal Reserve.

Implementing a Broadside Open Market Policy. Instead of dealing only in long-term securities, the Federal Reserve could trade in all maturity ranges of the yield curve. For example, if the Federal Reserve wishes to drain $100 million in reserves in a given operation, instead of making a sale of only one kind of maturity, the Fed might sell $40 million in Treasury bills, $30 million of three-year securities, $20 million in the five- to ten-year range, and $10 million on the 30-year bond. The goal of such a weighted set of purchases over the entire range of maturities would be to avoid putting pressure on any single portion of the yield curve.

To be more certain of the overall impact on the yield curve, however, managers at the Federal Reserve would have to consider the implications of both direct and indirect impacts on the yield curve—those arising from market operations as well as those affecting bank reserves and bank portfolio adjustments. A simple and effective broadside approach would require equal purchases in each maturity range.

To protect the viability of financial intermediaries, it is extremely important that the yield curve not be *pushed* into an inverted shape.

The yield curve can be expected to vary its shape in a dynamic economy because it is made up of a set of prices, which *respond* to changes in demand and supply conditions in order to better allocate scarce resources. It would be totally inappropriate to *interfere* with this pricing mechanism by keeping the yield curve in a set shape, such as was the policy of the Federal Reserve from 1941 to 1945. Because prices of commodities should be determined by competitive markets, central banks avoid using open market operations in those markets to control bank reserves. They should avoid securities markets too.

The problem is that, as it is carried out today, monetary policy does *not* have a neutral effect on the shape of the yield curve. Under the broadside proposal described above, central bank monetary policy would be much more likely to be more neutral, and less disruptive, in its effects on the shape of the yield curve. While some changes in shape would be expected from time to time, monetary tightening would place pressure across the entire maturity spectrum and not just at the short end.

The retention of a positively sloped yield curve would reduce extensively the tendency for tight policy operations to push banks toward bankruptcy, as occurred in the Volcker-induced economic crunch of 1980–82. Nor would an easing of monetary conditions, as in the Greenspan recession of 1991, fail to induce significant declines in long-term interest rates. Nor would the tight policy of 1994 have flattened the yield curve as it did.

Concerns about a Broadside Approach

By using Treasury bills or other short-term monetary instruments as the conduit for its open market operations, the Federal Reserve argues that it is attempting to leave the smallest possible impact on interest rate levels. It is argued that these short-term markets are very liquid and that the volume of purchases involved in open market operations do not change short-term security prices. However, the evidence showing the predicted cyclical effects on the shape of the yield curve indicates otherwise. For example, data plotted to show the difference between the yield on six-month Treasury bills and the yield on 20-year bonds as estimated from the *Treasury Bulletin* give an instructive picture. When the difference is positive, the yield curve is positively sloped with long-term rates higher than short-term rates. When the difference is negative, the yield curve is negatively sloped—often called "inverted." Tight monetary policies began in 1978 and pushed the yield curve into an inverted shape where it generally remained except for five months in 1980. From 1982 through 1986, the curve retained its usual positive slope with bill yields about two to three percentage points lower than yields on bonds. The inverted yield curve period is widely recognized as a period of tight monetary policy. Federal Reserve policies caused this inverted curve.

Would long-term interest rates be affected by the limited amount of trading in the long-term range of the market? Market makers say yes. Some argue, therefore, that the Federal Reserve should buy only bills. But we must return to the basic premise that the purpose of Federal Reserve tightening action is precisely to dampen an overly robust economy, and this goal can be achieved by monetary policies that raise interest rates. A broadside policy should bring about a rise in long-term rates, so why should one object if the long-term bond market is "thin" and sensitive to Federal Reserve sales of bonds? A thin market simply implies that interest rates can be raised, and the targeted degree of tightening can be achieved, with a smaller amount of sales *and a smaller impact on bank reserve positions*. As carried out today, the brunt of the impact of tightening is on banks, thrifts, and on the structure of depository institutions—those very institutions that democratic populations instruct their governments to protect because individuals prefer to keep their wealth in protected accounts.

An Objection Based On Consideration of Rational Expectations. Those who believe that expectations of future short-term interest rates determine long-term yields may be expected to argue that only unexpected surprises will cause yields to change, and then only temporarily and without significant impact on economic activity.

If, as those who hold to the expectations approach believe, expectations do determine interest rates, and if changes in supplies of securities in the various maturity ranges do have *no lasting effect* on the yield curve, then to operate in the long-term markets would have no impact on the yield curve. That is, there is no reason *not* to operate in the long-term end of the market. So, even if the expectations approach were correct, open market operation still might just as well take place in any one market as in any other—short or long maturities, stocks, bank assets, foreign exchange, or even commodities.

Therefore, even if one does not believe that greater stability might be forthcoming with a broadside attack across maturity sectors, there is no reason to object to using a broadside approach to the securities markets when implementing monetary policies.

A broadside approach cannot do harm, and may do a great deal of good.

The Federal Reserve should be sensitive when tight monetary conditions introduce distortions in the yield curve and in the relation between short-lived and long-lived markets. The dampening impact of a tight monetary policy can place excessive burdens on financial markets and institutions—excessive principally because the focus of actions is on short-term securities and bank reserves.

Therefore, the suggestion put forward here is that open market operations be carried out in all segments of the maturity structure of securities. A more appropriate set of changes in interest rates will follow and the structure of yields will have far less tendency to cause great difficulty for banking and thrift institutions.

Debate over Reserve Requirements

Should banks be required to hold legal reserves against deposit money withdrawal on demand—that is, against checking account money? Proposals have been made for 100 per cent reserve requirements, 0 per cent reserve requirements, and fractional reserves. Arguments for either 100 or 0 per cent are made by some economists. If banks operated like mutual funds, they would have 100 per cent reserves. If their reserves had to be held in U.S. Treasury securities, banks would earn interest on the deposit money they created. They would not make any business loans except by using other sources of funds, such as equity capital or time deposits.

Reserve requirements were discussed briefly in Chapter 3.

Monetary Policy Concerns

Choosing indicators, setting targets for monetary policy and implementing those policies, are made difficult by bureaucratic processes. Many new suggestions are put forward each day by bureaucrats who need to feel useful in their jobs. A lot less expense for the taxpayer would be necessary if a set of rules were put in place and not tampered with—permitting that the market economy handle necessary adjustments in interest rates with the efficiency for which it is well-known.

Some members of the FOMC have suggested that a good indicator of expected inflation might be the price of gold. Perhaps the Fed should try to carry out policies to stabilize it. Others say the target should be zero inflation. There is considerable merit in the idea that the Federal Reserve should target zero inflation. Some believe that, instead of moving the federal funds rate by modest amounts, the FOMC should focus on targeting the "real" interest rate, whatever that is. Others think that a good target would be the growth rate of nominal Gross Domestic Product, which is the economy's output multiplied by the price level. The result is that there are nearly as many appropriate targets as there are members of the FOMC. This result suggests that the FOMC is relying on intuition as the members rely on many different variables and do not focus exclusively on any single variable or even any package of variables.

Summary

In this chapter the mechanics of forming and implementing monetary policy were discussed. In the U.S. the principal group responsible for monetary policy is the Federal Open Market Committee made up of the seven members of the Board of Governors of the Federal Reserve System and five of the twelve presidents of the regional Federal Reserve Banks. There is a considerable amount of politics involved is selecting members of the FOMC.

The committee has set different types of operating targets in order to guide the manager of the open market account, who is a vice president of the Federal Reserve Bank of New York. The targets can be described using supply and demand curves for bank reserves. These curves are useful analytical tools.

Procedures for establishing targets involve making estimates of various accounting items that affect the volume of reserves.

The churning of the Federal Reserve's open market portfolio in order to carry out defensive open market operations has been criticized as expensive and unnecessary. Intervention in foreign exchange markets has also been criticized. Finally, the "bills-only" policy has also been criticized, on the grounds that it distorts the yield curve.

The chapter closes with mention of the question of whether or not the Federal Reserve should abandon its program of maintaining legally required reserve ratios for banks and other monetary policy concerns.

The formulation of monetary policies by the governments of the Asian Tigers will be the subject of Chapter 18.

Key Terms and Concepts

FOMC directives

Supply and demand for reserves

Churning on the open market

Pegged interest rates

The "bills-only" policy

Broadside approach

T, N, and B as operating targets

Reserve accounting

Sterilized intervention in foreign exchange markets

Operation twist

Discussion Questions and Exercises

1. Who serves on the Federal Open Market Committee and what is that committee's responsibility?
2. What sort of information is contained in the FOMC directive to the manager of the open market account? What sort of instructions does the directive contain?
3. What are the terms in the equation $T = N + B$? Which of the three may be "targeted" by the Federal Reserve? Explain.
4. Using the graphs and shifting supply and demand curves for reserves as the basis for your analysis, describe how interest rates on federal funds will respond to increases in the demand for reserves under targeting of: (a) total reserves,

(b) nonborrowed reserves, and (c) borrowed reserves. Explain again assuming a decrease in demand for reserves (leftward shift in the demand curve). Explain once more assuming unexpected shifts in the supply of reserves.

5. Explain why one would expect more volatile interest rates under lagged reserve accounting than under contemporaneous reserve accounting.

6. Why must the federal funds rate lie above the discount rate except for isolated instances?

7. Distinguish between seasonal, adjustment, and extended credit borrowings from the Federal Reserve.

8. Precisely what does it mean to say that the Federal Reserve targets borrowed reserves?

9. Discuss the pros and cons of having the Federal Reserve churning the open market account during the year in order to hold the total level of bank reserves steady.

10. Describe how central banks carry out interventions in the foreign exchange markets in order to affect exchange rates.

11. What is "sterilized" intervention in foreign exhange markets and why do central banks sterilize their actions?

12. Briefly explain what the "bills-only" policy is.

13. What was intended when the Federal Reserve experimented with "Operation Twist"?

14. Explain the concept of a "broadside approach" to open market operations.

15. Should banks be required to hold legally required reserves against their deposit liabilities, or should they simply hold reserves in amounts that are in accord with their judgment regarding their prudential responsibilities?

References

Altig, David, "An Ebbing Tide Lowers All Boats: Monetary Policy, Inflation, and Social Justice," *Economic Review*, Federal Reserve Bank of Cleveland, 2nd Quarter, 1992, pp. 14–22.

Avery, Robert B., and Kwast, Myron L., "Money and Interest Rates under a Reserves Operating Target," *Economic Review*, Federal Reserve Bank of Cleveland, 2nd Quarter, 1993, pp. 24–34.

Batten, Dallas S., Blackwell, Michael P., Kim, In-Su, Nocera, Simon E., and Ozeki, Yuzuru, "The Conduct of Monetary Policy in the Major Industrial Countries: Instruments and Operating Procedures," Occasional Paper No. 70, International Monetary Fund, Washington, DC, July 1990.

Bernake, Ben, and Blinder, Alan, "The Federal Funds Rate and the Channels of Monetary Transmission," *American Economic Review*, September 1992, pp. 901–21.

Bullard, James B., "Learning, Rational Expectations and Policy: A Summary of Recent Research," *Review*, Federal Reserve Bank of St. Louis, January/February 1991, pp. 50–58.

Cover, James Peery, "Asymmetric Effects of Positive and Negative Money-supply Shocks," *Quarterly Journal of Economics*, November 1992, pp. 1261–82.

Feinman, Joshua N., "Reserve Requirements: History, Current Practice, and Potential Reform," *Federal Reserve Bulletin*, June 1993, pp. 569–89.

Friedman, Milton, "Monetary Policy: Theory and Practice," *Journal of Money, Credit, and Banking*, February 1982, pp. 98–118.

_____, "End the Fed's Fine-Tuning," *Wall Street Journal*, September 15, 1993.

Fuhrer, Jeffrey C., "Commodity Prices, the Term Structure of Interest Rates, and Exchange Rates: Useful Indicators for Monetary Policy?" *New England Economic Review*, November/December 1993, pp. 18–32.

Greider, William, *Secrets of the Temple: How the Federal Reserve Runs the Country*, Simon & Schuster, New York, 1987.

Havrilesky, Thomas, and Schweitzer, Robert, "A Theory of FOMC Dissent Voting with Evidence from the Time Series," in Thomas Mayer, ed., *The Political Economy of American Monetary Policy*, Cambridge University Press, New York, 1990, pp. 197–210.

Hoenig, Thomas M., "China's Economic Growth with Price Stability: What Role for the Central Bank?" *Economic Review*, Federal Reserve Bank of Kansas City, 1st Quarter, 1993, pp. 5–10.

Humpage, Owen F., "Central-bank Intervention: Recent Literature, Continuing Controversy," *Economic Review*, Federal Reserve Bank of Cleveland, 2nd Quarter, 1991, pp. 12–26.

_____, "Institutional Aspects of U.S. Intervention," *Economic Reviews*, Federal Reserve Bank of Cleveland, 1st Quarter, 1994, pp. 2–19.

Judd, John P., and Motley, Brian, "Using a Nominal GDP Rule to Guide Discretionary Monetary Policy," *Economic Review*, Federal Reserve Bank of San Francisco, No. 3, 1993, pp. 3–11.

Kasman, B., "A Comparison of Monetary Policy Operating Procedures in Six Industrial Countries," *Quarterly Review*, Federal Reserve Bank of New York, Summer 1992, pp. 5–24.

Klein, Michael W., and Rosengren, Eric S., "Foreign Exchange Intervention as a Signal of Monetary Policy," *New England Economic Review*, Federal Reserve Bank of Boston, May/June 1991, pp. 39–50.

Kneeshaw, J. T., and Van den Bergh, P., "Changes in Central Bank Money Market Operating Procedures in the 1980's," Economic Paper No. 23, Bank for International Settlements, January 1989.

Leeper, Eric M., "Facing up to Our Ignorance about Measuring Monetary Policy Effects," *Economic Review*, Federal Reserve Bank of Atlanta, May/June 1992, pp. 1–16.

Meulendyke, Ann-Marie, "A Review of Federal Reserve Policy Targets and Operating Guides in Recent Decades," *Quarterly Review*, Federal Reserve Bank of New York, Autumn 1988, pp. 6–17.

———, *U.S. Monetary Policy and Financial Markets*, Federal Reserve Bank of New York, 1989.

Mitchell, K., and Pearce, D. K., "Discount Window Borrowing across Federal Reserve Districts: Evidence under Contemporaneous Reserve Accounting," *Journal of Banking Finance*, August 1992, pp. 771–90.

Morgan, Donald P., "Asymmetric Effects of Monetary Policy," *Economic Review*, Federal Reserve Bank of Kansas City, 2nd Quarter, 1993, pp. 21–33.

Nakao, Masaaki, and Horii, Akinari, "The Process of Decision-making and Implementation of Monetary Policy in Japan," Special Paper No. 198, Bank of Japan, March 1991.

Pearce, Douglas K., "Discount Window Borrowing and Federal Reserve Operating Regimes," *Economic Inquiry*, October 1993, pp. 564–79.

Poole, W., "Exchange-rate Management and Monetary-policy Mismanagement: A Study of Germany, Japan, United Kingdom, and United States after Plaza," *Carnegie-Rochester Conference Series in Public Policy*, July 1992, pp. 57–91.

Roberts, William, "What hath the Fed Wrought? Interest Rate Smoothing in Theory and Practice," *Economic Review*, Federal Reserve Bank of Atlanta, January/February 1992, pp. 12–24.

Stevens, E. J., "Seasonal Borrowing and Open Market Operations," *Economic Review*, Federal Reserve Bank of Cleveland, 2nd Quarter, 1990, pp. 29–39.

———, "Is There Any Rationale for Reserve Requirements?" *Economic Review*, Federal Reserve Bank of Cleveland, 3rd Quarter, 1991, pp. 2–18.

Thorton, Daniel L., "Targeting M2: The Issue of Monetary Control," *Review*, Federal Reserve Bank of St. Louis, July/August 1992, pp. 23–35.

Todd, Walker F., "FDICIA's Discount Window Provisions," *Economic Commentary*, Federal Reserve Bank of Cleveland, December 15, 1992.

Whitt, Joseph A., Jr., "Flexible Exchange Rates: An Idea Whose Time has Passed?" *Economic Review*, Federal Reserve Bank of Atlanta, September/October 1990, pp. 2–15.

CHAPTER 17

Implementing Fiscal and Debt Management Policies

EARLIER CHAPTERS ON interest rate theory emphasize the interdependence of the level of interest rates and the state of economic activity. Monetary policies affect both variables, and so does fiscal policy. Monetary policy implementation was discussed in the previous chapter. This chapter is devoted to fiscal policy, and its close relative, debt management.

Modern exchange economies cannot operate without government. Besides providing for the national defense and producing other public goods, governments enforce commercial contracts. That is, they set the rules under which exchanges take place. Some of the issues surrounding this role of governments were discussed in Chapter 15. All these activities of governments added together make government operations a significant force in determining the general level of economic activity. Therefore, government is also a significant force in determining conditions in financial markets.

Fiscal Policy. Fiscal policy concerns both government spending and taxing. Projected flows of spending (G) and taxes (T) comprise the government's budget B. Let $B = G - T$. When $G > T$, $B > 0$, that is, B is positive and the budget is in deficit. Projected tax collections are too low to cover projected expenditures. When $B < 0$, spending is below tax collection and the budget is in surplus. Thus, it is often the case that questions surrounding fiscal policy are couched in terms of the state of the budget.

For most governments, budget projections are one thing, while actual expenditures and tax revenues are quite another. Thus, if a spokesman says the budget deficit has been cut, it simply means that the *plan* has been changed to spend less or tax more.

Debt Management. If actual spending exceeds actual tax revenues, a government incurs a deficit and, in order to finance the excess of spending over revenue, the government must issue debt and borrow funds. If deficits occur repeatedly over the years, they build up a large volume of outstanding government debt. The way in which this debt is managed has important macroeconomic implications. If the current deficit is large, the total debt will increase, and the Treasury will have to decide what type of new debt to issue. Even if there is no deficit, and no change in the volume of current debt, previously issued debt may come to maturity and have to be refinanced. Maturities of debt issues are important. Budgetary implications of interest costs on the debt are important as well. Debt management decisions can affect prices and yields on securities in private financial markets as well as in markets for government securities.

The first part of this chapter concerns fiscal policy and the second part concerns debt management policy.

Fiscal Policy

Monetary and fiscal policy are two distinct types of policy. However, they are often discussed as if they are interrelated. Indeed, they may become interrelated if governments choose not to treat them separately.

For example, when a government collects a tax, people may complain that the government "took away our money." This may be literally true for the individuals who paid the tax, but it is not true that the amount of money in circulation has fallen. The reason is that a government will not collect a tax unless it wants to spend the revenues it collects. So, the money taken away by tax is placed back into circulation as the government spends the tax revenues. Thus, what the government has accomplished with its tax and spend activities is a diversion of *purchasing power* from the public to the government, leaving the money supply in circulation unchanged.

So, if spending and tax revenues increase and decrease together there will be no change in the volume of money in circulation. But what if government spending decreases while tax collections remain the same? In this case the government has a surplus. Will it reduce the money supply by putting cash into a vault? Probably not. In the case of the U.S., it will use the surplus to retire outstanding public debt and thereby return the cash to circulation. In the case of Hong Kong, which regularly has surpluses in revenues over expenditures, it will use the extra revenues to purchase interest-earning assets. Again, the money supply in the hands of the public, that is, in circulation, is unchanged.

If a government runs a deficit to "pump more money into the economy," does it really pump money in? No, because it first pulled the money out when it borrowed the funds to use to pump back in. No change in the supply of money occurs. Hence, government spending and taxing can move up, or down, or generate surpluses or deficits, and none of these situations will result in any changes in the quantity of money in circulation. *Tax and spend policies are separate from monetary policy.* They shift purchasing power to and from government, but do not alter the money supply.

A government may, if it wishes, combine monetary policy with fiscal policy. For example, a government may print more currency and simply spend it. The injection of additional money into circulation is a monetary action while spending by government takes resources away from the public and diverts it to use by government—a fiscal action. Similarly, a government may collect money and put it into a vault without either spending or investing it. When it does this, it engages in simultaneous monetary and fiscal policies.

Governments of Russia and China under communism did not distinguish between monetary and fiscal policy. Under their managed-economy programs, when the central government wanted to support an enterprise it simply sent along "credits." In effect, it printed and distributed money. The larger money supply stimulated spending and led to inflation.

By raising administered prices on basic commodities (thereby contributing to inflation), a communist government could collect money from the public and put it back with the central bank. The money supply would be reduced. (The real money supply, M/P, would be reduced by the inflation that increased P, but the nominal money supply, M, would also fall if government did not use it to "allocate credit.") Raising prices and causing inflation in order to reduce money supplies and stop inflation is one more anomaly that is characteristic of a centrally planned economy.

Rampant inflation plagued nearly all of the former republics of the U.S.S.R. soon after its break-up. Inflation was due, in large part, to the absence of any semblance of a monetary control system that could operate separately from a fiscal system. If the U.S.S.R. had only administered monetary and fiscal matters separately, the countries of the former Soviet Union could have coped more readily with the inflation that accompanied their move to a market economy. The rapid modernization in China has also led to inflationary periods, although inflation there was far less severe than in Russia and other former republics of the Soviet Union.

Automatic and Discretionary Fiscal Policies

Economic history provides details of fluctuations in business activity over time. Assuming upswings and downswings are bound to occur in an exchange economy, the amplitude of such swings becomes an important concern. If inflation is too high, or if a depression is too deep, the public will clamor for government interference. Thus, there will be public support for the implementation of contra-cyclical monetary and fiscal policies, and political power will go to those who promise such policies. In the interest of economic and political stability, it is useful to understand the existence of stabilizing aspects of various fiscal measures.

Automatic Stabilizers. Assume that a government has a balanced budget, $G = T$. When economic activity increases as a result of inflation, income and spending will also increase. Thus, if taxes are set on income, production or spending, then tax revenues will increase as well. If government spending does not increase to use up the increased revenues, then the budget will turn to surplus. This implies that the government absorbs purchasing power from the public, holds down the increase in spending, and restrains inflationary pressures. So, income taxes and sales taxes act to dampen the *amplitude* of inflation. Similarly, such tax collections fall in a recession and help limit the downswing in business activity.

Some spending programs imposed by government tend to increase G when an economy goes into a recession. For example, unemployment programs provide more spending on unemployment when individuals lose their jobs in a recession. Thus, G increases automatically and helps limit the fall in business activity and spending. The unemployment insurance program tends to help reduce the amplitude of the downswing in business activity. And when economic recovery begins, spending by government falls.

Thus, there are two important automatic stabilizers: income and sales taxes that provide contra-cyclical changes in T, and safety net programs, such as unemployment compensation that provide contra-cyclical changes in G.

One problem with these programs is that they only come into play *after the fact.* For example, inflation, with its adverse consequences, has to occur *before* tax collections increase. Automatic stabilizers soothe the pain of an economic difficulty, but never act to prevent it from occurring. This is the reason that economists search for appropriate discretionary fiscal policies to use in an attempt to prevent inflation and recession before they occur, thus eliminating the need for automatic policies.

Discretionary Policy. Instead of simply letting tax collections rise with inflation, it may be appropriate for government to legislate an increase in taxes in an attempt to dampen inflation. If a recession is at hand, it may be appropriate to increase government spending on public works in an attempt to stimulate economic activity. Such discretionary changes in T and G are often implemented with good intentions. Unfortunately, they have often been known for their distorting effects rather than for their stabilizing effects. The reason is usually that there is a significant time lag between the time that the need for a policy is recognized and the time the effects of the policy occur.

Policy Lags

Discretionary policy, whether monetary or fiscal policy, requires time to implement. Time lags are often described as follows: (a) *recognition lag*—the lapse of time it takes for data on the state of the economy to be collected and reported. After all, policymakers may forecast the coming inflation, but would hesitate to act until concrete evidence of it exists, (b) *implementation lag*—the time it takes to use the evidence to convince the policymakers to take action, and (c) *impact lag*—the time it takes for a newly implemented policy to take effect.

Economists often complain that, given a natural tendency for swings in business activity to occur, by the time a discretionary policy has an impact, the reason for it will have disappeared. Tax increases to dampen an inflation may not take effect until the economy is already in a recession, so the effect of the policy will be the opposite of what was intended. A spending program to stimulate an economy may finally take effect just as the economy is in a state of boom—too late to help and so late as to end up being the wrong policy at the time.

Such lags apply to the discretionary implementation of monetary as well as to fiscal policy. Indeed, the existence of these lags leads many economists to argue, persuasively, that the best alternative path for the authorities to take is a *laissez faire* (let alone) policy under which a government avoids interference, holds the money supply constant or in a steady slow growth path, keeps the budget in balance, and permits market-determined prices to provide any adjustments needed to keep the economy operating effectively.

Balancing the Budget

Economists who believe in steady money growth also believe governments should maintain balanced budgets. Proposals currently before the Congress of the U.S. include passing a constitutional amendment that requires the government to balance the budget. If the recommendation is passed by Congress, it must then be approved by two-thirds of the legislatures of the 50 states to become law. Because the federal government ran large deficits every year except one since 1961, the outstanding volume of national debt has become huge, and it appears that some political sentiment is in favor of the amendment (see Table 17–3 later).

Usefulness of Government Debt. Before everyone shouts hurray at the prospect of eliminating national debt, it would be well to reflect on its impact on economic efficiency. Government debt is free of default risk. The rate of interest on Treasury bills is viewed as the risk-free rate of interest for the purpose of valuing risky investments. Most of the money in the U.S. is non-interest-bearing government debt, and its steady growth is viewed as a necessary accompaniment to a growing and prosperous economy. In similar fashion, a steadily growing volume of outstanding interest-bearing government bonds is also a desirable accompaniment to a prosperous economy.

Of course, U.S. government debt grew too rapidly from 1965 to 1994. To limit its growth would be appropriate. But to stop its growth altogether might not be the optimal solution.

Deficits by Another Name—Debt Financing. Government debt is issued to provide the means of financing government's expenses. However, governments, both state and

Table 17–1

U.S. Budget Receipts and Outlays, Estimates for Fiscal 1994* (Billions of dollars)

Receipts		Outlays	
Individual income taxes	$ 550	National defense and	
Corporate income taxes	131	international affairs	$ 297
Social insurance taxes	462	National resources and	
Excise tax	55	environment, energy,	
Customs duties	13	general science, space	44
Estate and gift taxes	19	Agriculture, commerce,	
Miscellaneous		housing, transportation	55
Deposits of earnings by		Community development,	
Federal Reserve System	16	education, and social services	60
Other	4	Health (includes Medicare)	143
		Income and Social Security	535
		Veterans' benefits and services	38
		Administration of justice	16
		General government	14
		Net interest on debt	203
		Offsetting receipts	−37
Total	$1,250	Total	$1,354

*Figures do not add exactly because of rounding.

Source: *Economic Report of the President,* February 1994, p. 361.

Table 17–2

Federal Fiscal and Financing Operations, Fiscal 1993
(Billions of dollars)

Type of account or operation	1993
U.S. budget	
Receipts	$1,153
Outlays	1,408
Surplus or deficit	−255
Deficit financed by	
Borrowing from the public	249
Cash and monetary assets,	
decrease or increase (−)	−6
Other	0
Note:	
Treasury operating balance (level, end of period)	53
Federal Reserve Banks	17
Tax and Loan accounts	35

Source: *Federal Reserve Bulletin,* April 1994, p. A28.

local, can sell bonds to raise funds for the purpose of building roads, bridges, school dormitories, and so forth. Then, taxes can be levied to raise revenues that are then used to repay the bonded indebtedness. For example, the State of Washington has, in its constitution, a balanced budget provision. The state must balance its budget, *but* it can arrange to debt-finance a host of government-sponsored projects. That is, it can deficit spend and simply call the process debt financing. Thus, it is unlikely that a balanced budget amendment to the Constitution will result in the elimination of issues of debt by the federal government, just as it has not eliminated the sale of bonds by states.

The Rationale for Budget Deficits and Surpluses

Many years ago the idea of *fiscal finance* was promoted by the economist Abba Lerner. Lerner argued that the only reason for a government to levy a tax would be to prevent inflation and its undesirable side-effects. If an increase in government spending did not cause inflation, there would be no reason to tax the public to pay for it even if the result would be a budget deficit. Similarly, if an economy was already suffering from the disorder caused by excessive inflation, it would be appropriate to battle inflation by levying taxes to withdraw purchasing power from the general public even though the budget might already be in surplus. The point is that government spending need not necessarily be tied to government tax collections. A tax is desirable when it is needed to prevent inflation and to stabilize the price level. The deficit should be viewed as incidental to the basic concern.

Indeed, when examined on the surface, every deficit is simply the result of two distinct sets of decisions. First, spending decisions are made. These presumably reflect the needs of government and must be justified on the basis of cost and benefit. Second, taxing decisions are made. These reflect the need for government to provide stability in the level of prices and economic activity, and are not subject to cost-benefit analysis except in relation to collection and administrative costs. Thus, spending decisions are distinct from taxing decisions, and each should be justified on its own merits.

Thus appeals to government to balance the budget are essentially meaningless. An appropriate appeal to government might be to cut spending, and then to address the question—which spending should be cut? In a recession, an appeal to reduce taxes is appropriate. But, which tax is to be cut? The budget deficit or surplus is simply the result of decisions to spend and decisions to tax. If those decisions have merit, whether the budget is left in deficit or surplus is only of secondary importance. That is why most economists say that budget deficits may be an annoyance but are not a basic economic problem. Politically, however, deficits are of great importance.

It may seem strange to see governments of countries such as Taiwan, Hong Kong, and Singapore bask in the sun of public approval when their governments often run huge surpluses. Surpluses mean that they take purchasing power from the private sector and divert it to government, which uses it to build up foreign exchange reserves and strengthen its economic power. But such is political reality.

Table 17-3

Federal Government Receipts and Outlays, 1970–95* (Billions of dollars)

Fiscal year	Receipts	Expenditures	Surplus or deficit
1970	192.8	195.6	–2.8
1971	187.1	210.2	–23.0
1972	207.3	230.7	–23.4
1973	230.8	245.7	–14.9
1974	263.2	269.4	–6.1
1975	279.1	332.3	–53.2
1976	298.1	371.8	–73.7
Transition quarter	81.2	96.0	–14.7
1977	355.6	409.2	–53.6
1978	399.6	458.7	–59.2
1979	463.3	503.5	–40.2
1980	517.1	590.9	–73.8
1981	599.3	678.2	–78.9
1982	617.8	745.7	–127.9
1983	600.6	808.3	–207.8
1984	666.5	851.8	–185.3
1985	734.1	946.3	–212.2
1986	769.1	990.3	–202.8
1987	854.1	1,003.9	–149.8
1988	909.0	1,064.1	–155.2
1989	990.7	1,143.2	–152.5
1990	1,031.3	1,252.7	–221.4
1991	1,054.3	1,323.8	–269.5
1992	1,090.5	1,380.9	–290.4
1993	1,153.5	1,408.2	–254.7
1994	1,249.1	1,483.8	–234.8
1995	1,353.8	1,518.9	–165.1

*1994 and 1995 are estimates.

Source: *Economic Report of the President*, February 1994, p. 359.

Debt Management Policy

As described above, fiscal policy has to do with government spending and taxes, and the size of the budget deficit or surplus. In contrast, debt management consists of those actions of the Treasury and the Federal Reserve that affect the composition of the federal debt held by the public, in particular, the maturity structure of outstanding government debt. Monetary policy actions are those that change the amount of bank reserves rather than the maturity of the securities involved in open market operations. These definitions are somewhat arbitrary, but they help to distinguish fiscal, monetary, and debt management policies while indicating their interrelatedness.

Debt Management Operations

Both Treasury and Federal Reserve operations can change the maturity structure of the marketable component of the debt. A broadside approach to the Federal Reserve's open market operations was described in Chapter 16. The design of that approach was focused on managing open market operations to avoid impact on the yield curve. In this chapter the Treasury's debt management policies are discussed. These, too, have implications for the shape of the yield curve.

To isolate the effects of debt management, assume that total marketable government debt is constant. The Treasury can shorten or lengthen the average time to maturity of the debt by changing the mix of securities sold to the public. To shorten the debt, the Treasury may issue bills and use the funds to retire bonds. To lengthen the debt, the Treasury may replace maturing bills with longer-term securities.

The Federal Reserve also engages in debt management when it carries out an open market operation that alters the maturity structure of the publicly held debt. If the Fed were, say, to sell $500 million of long-term securities and buy the same amount of short-term securities, the reserves of banks could remain the same but the maturity of the publicly held debt would be lengthened. Alternatively, if the Fed exchanged short-term for long-term government securities, the maturity of the debt held by the public would be shortened.

The marketable component of the public debt is important for management. It consists of Treasury bills, notes, and bonds. Nonmarketable issues, those that must be held until maturity or redemption by the Treasury, include savings bonds and notes, foreign issues, and special issues. Table 17–4 shows the types of securities that made up the public debt during 1993. About two-thirds of interest-bearing public debt was marketable.

The Treasury has primary responsibility for managing the debt, and Treasury officials make day-to-day decisions concerning the marketable debt held by the public. It decides on the types and maturities of securities to be issued; the yields on coupon issues; special features such as call provisions, ownership restrictions, and allotments that might attach to these obligations; and so on.

Before turning to questions of the economic impact of the debt and appropriate debt management policy, let us look at the ownership of the debt and its maturity distribution. Table 17–4 shows that 68 per cent of the debt was held by private investors, chiefly commercial banks, individuals, and foreigners.

The maturity distribution of the marketable debt is presented in Table 17–5. Clearly, most of the marketable securities are short-term. These include bills and those notes and bonds that have been outstanding for a period of time. Some of the notes and bonds were securities whose original maturities may have been intermediate- or long-term but are now fairly close to maturity. From portfolio managers' point of view, a bond whose original maturity was, say, ten years is considered a short-term liquid instrument if it is due to mature within one or two years.

Table 17–4

Gross Public Debt of U.S. Treasury (Billions of dollars, end of period)

Type and holder	1993		
	Q1	Q2	Q3
Total gross public debt	4,230.6	4,352.0	4,411.5
By type			
Interest-bearing	4,227.6	4,349.0	4,408.6
Marketable	2,807.1	2,860.6	2,904.9
Bills	659.9	659.3	658.4
Notes	1,652.1	1,698.7	1,734.2
Bonds	480.2	487.6	497.4
Nonmarketable[1]	1,420.5	1,488.4	1,503.7
State and local government series	151.6	152.8	149.5
Foreign issues[2]	37.0	43.0	42.5
Government	37.0	43.0	42.5
Public	0	0	0
Savings bonds and notes	161.4	164.4	167.0
Government account series[3]	1,040.0	1,097.8	1,114.3
Non-interest-bearing	3.0	2.9	2.9
By Holder[4]			
U.S. Treasury and other federal agencies and trust funds	1,043.2	1,099.8	1,116.7
Federal Reserve Banks	305.2	328.2	325.7
Private investors	2,895.0	2,938.4	2,983.0
Commercial banks	310.0	305.9	306.0
Money market funds	77.7	76.2	75.2
Insurance companies	205.0	208.1	210.0
Other companies	199.3	206.1	215.6
State and local treasuries	541.0	553.9	558.0
Individuals			
Savings bonds	163.6	166.5	169.1
Other securities	134.1	136.4	136.7
Foreign and international[5]	565.5	568.2	592.3
Other miscellaneous investors[6]	698.8	717.0	720.0

1. Includes (not shown separately) securities issued to the Rural Electrification Administration, depository bonds, retirement plan bonds, and individual retirement bonds.
2. Nonmarketable series denominated in dollars, and series denominated in foreign currency held by foreigners.
3. Held almost entirely by U.S. Treasury and other federal agencies and trust funds.
4. Data for Federal Reserve Banks and U.S. government agencies and trust funds are actual holdings; data for other groups are Treasury estimates.
5. Consists of investments of foreign balances and international accounts in the United States.
6. Includes savings and loan associations, nonprofit institutions, credit unions, mutual savings banks, corporate pension trust funds, dealers and brokers, certain U.S. Treasury deposit accounts, and federally sponsored agencies.

Sources: U.S. Treasury Department, data by type of security, *Monthly Statement of the Public Debt of the United States*; data by holder, *Treasury Bulletin*.

Table 17–5

Maturity Distribution and Average Length of Marketable Interest-bearing Public Debt Securities Held by Private Investors, 1970–1993 (Millions of dollars)

End of year or month	Amount out- standing, privately held	Maturity class					Average length	
		Within 1 year	1 to 5 years	5 to 10 years	10 to 20 years	20 years and over	Years	Months
1970	157,910	76,443	57,035	8,286	7,876	8,272	3	8
1971	161,863	74,803	58,557	14,503	6,357	7,645	3	6
1972	165,978	79,509	57,157	16,033	6,358	6,922	3	3
1973	167,869	84,041	54,139	16,385	8,741	4,564	3	1
1974	164,862	87,150	50,103	14,197	9,930	3,481	2	11
1975	210,382	115,677	65,852	15,385	8,857	4,611	2	8
1976	279,782	151,723	89,151	24,169	8,087	6,652	2	7
1977	326,674	161,329	113,319	33,067	8,428	10,531	2	11
1978	356,501	163,819	132,993	33,500	11,383	14,805	3	3
1979	380,530	181,883	127,574	32,279	18,489	20,304	3	7
1980	463,717	220,084	156,244	38,809	25,901	22,679	3	9
1981	549,863	256,187	182,237	48,743	32,569	30,127	4	0
1982	682,043	314,436	221,783	75,749	33,017	37,058	3	11
1983	862,631	379,579	294,955	99,174	40,826	48,097	4	1
1984	1,017,488	437,941	332,808	130,417	49,664	66,658	4	6
1985	1,185,675	472,661	402,766	159,383	62,853	88,012	4	11
1986	1,354,275	506,903	467,348	189,995	70,664	119,365	5	3
1987	1,445,366	483,582	526,746	209,160	72,862	153,016	5	9
1988	1,555,208	524,201	552,993	232,453	74,186	171,375	5	9
1989	1,654,660	546,751	578,333	247,428	80,616	201,532	6	0
1990	1,841,903	626,297	630,144	267,573	82,713	235,176	6	1
1991	2,113,799	713,778	761,243	280,574	84,900	273,304	6	0
1992	2,363,802	808,705	866,329	295,921	84,706	308,141	5	11
1993	2,562,336	858,135	978,714	306,663	94,346	324,479	5	10

Source: *Economic Report of the President*, February 1994, Table B-86.

Economic Impact of Changes in Debt Structure

According to the segmented markets approach to the term structure of interest rates, as described in Chapter 14, changing the maturity structure of the debt may alter the maturity structure of interest rates: lengthening the debt means more long-term debt and less short-term debt. This increased supply of long-term securities should lead to higher long-term interest rates, and the reduced supply of short-term securities should lead to lower short-term interest rates if long-term securities and short-term securities are not perfect substitutes in the eyes of investors. Thus, the yield curve should be more positively sloped after a debt-lengthening operation than it was before. There is some evidence that this is the case.

Higher long-term rates dampen the willingness of business managers to engage in long-lived investment, and long-lived investment is below what it otherwise would be. Thus, lengthening the debt should help to restrict a boom in investment and dampen an overheated economy. Lower short-term rates might encourage some forms of investment, specifically investment in inventories. Most economists feel, however, that long-term investment projects are more sensitive to interest rate changes than is inventory investment. Thus, if long-term investments are significantly restricted but inventory investment does not change very much, the net effect of lengthening the maturity of the debt would be restrictive.

Another view, consistent with possible interest rate effects, is that the "liquidity" of the public's portfolio can be changed by debt management. Thus, if the Treasury shortens the debt and issues more short-term securities, these securities will, because of their liquidity, be good substitutes for money. Therefore, people will demand less money and lower their cash balances by purchasing goods (and perhaps bonds) as described by the Tobin model in Chapter 13. This will increase the velocity of money, and the increased spending will be expansionary. The reverse will occur when debt maturity is lengthened.

Thus, by changing the liquidity of the public's portfolio, not only do interest rates change, thereby indirectly changing investment spending, but spending also changes directly, as the desire to hold cash balances is affected. In these ways some economists believe that debt management can significantly affect the overall level of economic activity.

Effectiveness of Debt Management

Nearly everyone agrees that for stabilization purposes debt management policy is less "powerful" than either monetary or fiscal policy. However, it is a liquidity policy that can either support or work at cross-purposes with the other policy tools. In general, if a single policy direction is called for, it would seem best if all policy tools were coordinated, so as not to thwart each other.

If debt management were completely ineffective as a policy tool, then for stabilization purposes it would not matter whether the Treasury sold long-term or short-term securities. Because short-term interest rates have generally been lower than long-term rates in recent decades, regular issues of weekly bills keep interest charges low. Why would any lengthening of the debt be warranted?

On the other hand, if perverse management of the debt can *interfere* with monetary and fiscal policies, then it follows that it *is* a policy tool with noticeable effectiveness and should be handled accordingly. The issue, then, is largely empirical: Just how "powerful" is debt management policy? If it can readily interfere with other policies, then it must be powerful.

Is there any past experience that could give us a hint as to the strength of debt management policy? "Operation Twist" took place in 1961. The Fed bought bonds to help hold yields down in order to support the expansion of domestic economic activity.

Simultaneously, in order to mitigate balance of payments problems arising from capital outflows, the Fed attempted to raise short-term interest rates by selling T-bills in order to discourage further capital outflows and encourage capital inflows.

Did the program work? Yield differences did not respond significantly, but perhaps this was because the Treasury issued new long-term debt, while at the same time the Federal Reserve was buying long-term debt. The "experiment" was impure because other forces affected the securities markets at the same time. The appropriate question to ask is, "What would the pattern of yields have been if the Fed had not purchased those long-term securities?" Controlled experiments are required to answer questions such as this with confidence. Also, the Fed did not carry out its program aggressively. If it had increased its volume of purchases and sales, the yields would have responded appropriately. The Fed has the power to set yields if it wishes to do so. Thus, the question is less, "Is the tool powerful?" than it is "Is it used aggressively?" The power of a hammer is directly proportional to the strength of the blow!

Milton Friedman believes that small changes in maturity structure usually have only a slight effect on the demand for money. Many years ago he noted, however, that when bond prices were unpegged after the Federal Reserve-Treasury Accord of 1951, securities that formerly were effectively demand obligations became long-term securities in fact, as well as in name. This was a drastic increase in the "effective maturity" of the debt, and Friedman argued that this loss of liquidity led to an "increase in the demand for money something like 2 or 3 per cent" (see Friedman, 1959).

A more recent study by V. Vance Roley involving a statistical experiment also concluded that the maturity composition of the federal debt does indeed affect Treasury security yields and that federal debt management can possibly be used to help in stabilizing the economy (see Roley, 1978).

It is fair to conclude that debt management, if aggressively pursued, could become an effective stabilization tool.

Holding Interest Cost Down

One of the reasons that the Treasury has not pursued an aggressive contra-cyclical debt management policy is that it would probably raise the interest cost of the debt. Contra-cyclical policy calls for the issue of long-term debt during inflation when interest rates are high. In a recession, when interest rates are low, the Treasury would issue short-term debt. From the point of view of minimizing interest charges, this practice is the opposite of the one that a prudent corporate treasurer would use.

But what would a prudent corporate treasurer do with debt? To minimize interest costs to the corporation over time, the treasurer would sell long-term debt when interest rates were low in order to lock in low costs. When both long- and short-term rates were high, the Treasurer would issue short-term debt so that, when interest rates fell at a later time, the sale of long-term debt could replace short-term debt as the latter matured. This has generally been the policy of the Treasury when managed in a "business-like" approach. But such a policy of minimizing interest charges on the national debt to reduce the interest costs and the tax burden is *inconsistent* with debt management policy for stabilization.

In view of the fact that Treasury officials face inconsistent objectives—promoting economic stability on the one hand and minimizing interest cost of the debt on the other—it is little wonder that they sometimes appear erratic in moves to change the maturity of the debt.

Evaluation of the goal of holding debt service costs to a minimum shows that, in the final analysis, this goal should *not* take precedence over the goal of economic stabilization. The reasons become clear when we consider extreme cases. First, if government wished, the entire debt could be monetized. Interest-bearing debt would be withdrawn and non-interest-bearing money issued in its place. This would bring interest costs to zero, but would surely be accompanied by disastrous inflation, with all its adverse effects on economic stability.

Indeed, the size of the Treasury's operations gives it effective power to corner the market for its own securities. It could probably issue securities, depress that market, buy them back at a discount, and make money on its speculative operations. It clearly has the power to carry out such activities if Congress permitted. *It does not do so because it is not a profit-making institution.* As with all government activities, the Treasury's debt should be managed with the purpose of promoting the general welfare and not of earning profits. Having a market economy does *not* mean *government* operations should be based on a bottom line.

It was noted above that the purpose of collecting taxes is not to pay for government spending, but to divert purchasing power from the hands of the public in order to avoid inflation. In debt management there is a similar purpose. The reason for issuing long-term debt is to hold long-term interest rates higher than otherwise and hold down inflationary spending even though interest costs on the debt are not minimized.

Debt Management Techniques

Having discussed the goals of Treasury debt management, let us turn now to certain aspects of debt management techniques.

Scheduling Issues

Managers prefer to keep things orderly, and Treasury officials are no exception to this rule. Managing a total debt of $5 trillion is a problem of significant proportions, especially when a major portion of this must be "rolled over" in a year's time.

The average length of time to maturity to the total debt was about nine years in 1946. This meant that the total value of debt would have to roll over every nine years. By mid-1976, the average maturity of the Treasury's outstanding marketable debt had fallen to two years and six months—an all time low. By 1986 the average maturity had increased to five years and six months and to six years in 1990.

In the 1960s the Treasury attempted to lengthen the maturity of the debt by a program of "advance refunding," under which the Treasury offered to replace securities due to mature in one or two years with new long-term securities. By offering an attractive refunding package, the Treasury could forestall additional shortening of the debt maturity. But advance refunding had its own complexities and the experiment lasted but a few years.

Other Techniques

We can only mention a few other issues concerning debt management techniques. The Treasury sometimes auctions its securities, and sometimes offers them on a subscription basis. If it offers a subscription issue, the Fed may feel obligated to stabilize the market so that the sale will be successful. Such stabilization activity on the part of the Fed is referred to as "maintaining an even keel." Since the auction technique does not require an even-keel policy, it interferes less with the Fed's pursuit of monetary policy than a subscription offering does.

If securities are auctioned, should all awards be made at the same price—the lowest of the accepted bid prices—as in the case of a "Dutch" auction? Whether or not a Dutch auction encourages greater investor participation is a subject of debate. It was discussed at some length in Chapter 9.

Should commercial banks be allowed to credit the Treasury's Tax and Loan accounts when they purchase government securities for their own account and that of their customers? This privilege has been curtailed in recent years, and banks have paid for most of their purchases of government securities by having their reserves reduced at Federal Reserve Banks.

Currently, the Treasury sells bills at minimum amounts of $10,000. At one time it offered $1,000 bills, but commercial and savings banks argued that too many small customers were investing directly in bills and that deposits were falling because of disintermediation. What should be the denomination of Treasury issues?

Milton Friedman's rule is to keep things simple. He recommends having only two types of government securities, say a 2-year and a 20-year security. Then simply issue equal amounts of these each time new cash is needed, and roll them over as they come due. This way the general public would know what to expect. As it is, the Treasury issues a complex array of different maturities with different features that reflect those on corporate bonds. The result is a make-work program for Treasury bureaucrats that does little more than keep the investing public confused.

Politics and Debt Management

Budgetary matters are political. They are kept under wraps in autocratic societies and are explosive topics of debate in democracies. Taxing and spending decisions will sway public opinion of leaders. Budgetary deficits dominated discussions in the presidential elections in the U.S. in 1992, for example. President Reagan had lowered taxes and raised spending. Deficits, which are politically unpopular, continued under President

Bush. President Clinton raised taxes and lowered spending on many items although raising spending on others. The Clinton program was directly aimed at reducing the budget deficit with the purpose of deflecting public criticism of deficit spending programs.

Debt management concerns have taken a back seat to deficits on the political scene, but, during the national elections of 1992, the subject was raised as an important one. It even made headlines on the financial pages of newspapers. The economy had been in a recession for a year. Short-term interest rates had come down in response to monetary policies, but long-term interest rates remained high. Clinton's advisors said the Treasury should stop selling so much long-term debt. Specific reference was made to the volume of 30-year bonds issued at quarterly auctions. It was suggested that if the volume were reduced, interest rates on long-term securities might come down and help promote investment spending and economic recovery.

The Baker Treasury of the Bush administration procrastinated on the issue, but finally did take steps to reduce the volume of issues of 30-year bonds even before the Bentsen Treasury of the Clinton administration took over debt management operations in January 1993. The result—while short-term interest rates on Treasury securities remained just above 3 per cent, long-term interest rates fell from 8 per cent to below 6 per cent and remained in the neighborhood of 6 per cent until the Fed began tightening again in February 1994. President Clinton took credit for the decline in interest rates and said he believed that they helped make homes more affordable. Of course, lower interest rates left retired individuals, living on interest income, with lower incomes as well—a political liability for a president. You cannot please all the people all the time.

The discussion of a broadside approach to open market operations in Chapter 16 applies equally to a discussion of debt management. Under it, the Treasury would simplify its debt-issuing activities and would simply identify a set of securities, say 1, 5, 10, 20, and 30 years, and issue equal amounts of each whenever it needed to raise additional cash. In that way the volume of maturities in each maturity range would be changed proportionally, and the Treasury's impact on the structure of the yield curve would be distributed throughout the curve. The Treasury's actions would then have less direct effect on financial markets. Instead, the effects would be, for the most part, small and indirect. Over many years the average length of time to maturity of the outstanding federal debt would stabilize at 5.5 years, or 66 months, which is the weighted average of the six different maturities divided by two.

This discussion is about the average length of time to maturity of the *marketable* Treasury debt outstanding and privately held. This average was 125 months in 1946. It fell steadily to under 30 months in 1975. See Table 17–5 for data from 1970–93.

Debt Management Operations and Financial Markets

Treasury debt management operations are important to financial market participants for two reasons. First, newly issued government securities may be attractively priced relative to outstanding issues and thereby offer profitable investment opportunities.

Second, actions to lengthen or shorten the debt may change the pattern of interest rates in the market for government and private securities. Any such changes have important implications for the earnings of financial institutions and for the allocation of savings among sectors of the economy. We can illustrate these effects of debt management policy by tracing changes in interest rates that might accompany a particular action by the Treasury.

Suppose that the Treasury pursues a contra-cyclical policy aimed at restraining aggregate borrowing during a period of inflation. To do this, the Treasury sells bonds and redeems Treasury bills. This debt-lengthening operation is intended to reduce the liquidity of the outstanding debt and/or to raise the average level of interest rates. The success of such a program depends upon certain assumptions about the substitutability of Treasury bills for bonds and government securities for private claims.

Following the increase in Treasury bonds and the redemption of bills, bond yields would rise somewhat and bill yields would decline, if market participants view bills and bonds as imperfect substitutes. That is, bonds must be considered somewhat less liquid than bills or, for other reasons, certain groups of investors must prefer bonds to bills, or vice versa. The market will accept the new bonds but only at lower prices and higher yields. Because the amount of outstanding bills has fallen, the bill price rises and the average bill yield declines. This development, of course, implies a segmented markets theory of the term structure of interest rates.

Assuming that bond yields rise while bill yields decline, we might expect investors to adjust their portfolios. The higher yield on Treasury bonds should induce some lenders to switch out of, say, corporate bonds, municipals, or mortgages and into the Treasury issues. If they do, the yields on private securities should rise until a new equilibrium is established in the capital markets. At this new position all long-term rates should be somewhat higher than they were before the sale of bonds by the Treasury. For similar reasons there would be some downward pressure on the yields on private money market instruments, such as commercial paper and CDs. It is important to note that these portfolio changes occur only if government and private securities of the same maturity are considered fairly close, but not perfect, substitutes for one another.

Profitability of Financial Institutions and the Yield Curve

How will these changes in the structure of yields affect financial institutions? There will be different effects on various intermediaries, depending upon their individual sources and uses of funds. However, depository institutions will find their profit positions affected. When the yield curve is steep and short-term interest rates are low, the cost of funds to banks and thrifts is also low. And when long-term interest rates are high, banks and thrifts can earn high returns on their loans. Thus, a bank's profits will rise. This increased profit position of banks and thrifts was clearly evident after the recession of 1992–94 led to low short-term interest rates and long-term interest rates that were slow to fall. As short-term rates were pushed back up in 1994, bank profit positions began to weaken.

Summary

Monetary and fiscal policies are separate and distinct. However, the distinction is often blurred by the mixup that occurs when spending appears to pump money into an economy and taxing appears to take it away. To the extent that money is printed and spent simultaneously, there is a simultaneous implementation of two policies.

The only legitimate reason for a government to collect taxes is to prevent inflation that would otherwise result from government spending. A deficit itself is neither bad nor good because a deficit is the *result* of a difference between taxes and spending. Thus, any blame for a deficit should be on the shoulders of taxes and/or spending.

A Constitutional amendment to force government to maintain a balanced budget was proposed in Congress in 1994. It was defeated, but it will undoubtedly be proposed again in a few years. However, if such an amendment is passed again the federal government can adopt the strategy of many state governments that have such rules in their constitutions. They simply change their accounting procedures and have a capital budget. Then they pass legislation that provides for the debt-financing of a capital expenditure. The result is the same as deficit spending.

Some fiscal policies automatically restrain inflationary trends in an economy, and automatically stimulate a recessed economy. But the economy must be suffering from inflation or recession before the automatic effects are stimulated. Thus, they are like a thermostat. The room must get cold before the heat turns on. So the automatic stabilizers help dampen the amplitude of swings in economic activity.

The existence of a large outstanding volume of debt is, again, a *result* of government spending and taxing. The blame for it, as stated ealier, rests on spending and taxing activities. But its existence does raise important economic questions about its management. In particular, debt may be of short or long maturity. The question is whether or not borrowing short affects the economy differently than borrowing long. Since the volume of Treasury debt outstanding is very large, changing its maturity structure may affect the term structure of interest rates.

Selling more long-term debt and less short-term debt would make long-term interest rates rise and short-term interest rates fall. If higher long-term rates cause the level of long-term investment spending to decline, and lower short-term rates do not stimulate much short-term investment, the net effect of lengthening the maturity structure of the debt will be to dampen inflationary tendencies in an economy.

Unfortunately, by trying to reduce interest costs over the long run, governments may issue long-term debt and hold up long-term interest rates just when the economy is already recessed and needs to retain low long-term rates. When governments try to run their affairs like a business, rather than like a government, they can damage the economy. Thus, an attempt to reduce costs may have the effect of sustaining an even more costly recession. A government is not a business and should not be run with a focus on profit. It is one thing to hold a government's costs down by controlling them. But cost-saving activities should not result in damage to the economy that results in greater costs!

Key Terms and Concepts

$B = G - T$ Deficits and debt-financing
Automatic stabilizer   Discretionary policy lags
Broadside approach   Nonmarketable issues
Effects of debt lengthening and   Operation Twist
  shortening   Stability vs. interest cost minimizing policies

Discussion Questions and Exercises

1. Write a paragraph describing the elements of fiscal policies.
2. Is fiscal policy different from or a part of monetary policy?
3. How is the money supply controlled in communist countries?
4. Distinguish between automatic and discretionary policies. If discretionary policies worked well, would anyone need automatic policies? Explain.
5. What are the lags in monetary and fiscal policy implementation, and why are they important?
6. Are deficits a "problem"? Explain.
7. Explain the concept of "fiscal finance."
8. If debt management operations are aimed at minimizing the interest cost on the federal debt, should the debt be shortened or lengthened during periods of inflation? Explain.
9. Explain the essence of contra-cyclical debt management policy.
10. If the government wanted to introduce a steeper yield curve throughout debt management, what actions would it take? Explain how those actions would work.
11. Should the Treasury try to minimize interest costs? Why or why not?
12. Discuss some of the difficulties involved in the scheduling of Treasury debt.
13. How might a broadside approach to debt management work?
14. Describe how the imposition of a debt management stabilization policy might affect interest rates in financial markets.
15. How might a debt management policy affect the profitability of financial intermediaries? Explain.

References

Agell, Jonas, Persson, Mats, and Friedman, Benjamin, *Does Debt Management Matter?* Swedish Trade Union Institute for Economic Research (FIEF) Studies in Labour Markets and Economic Policy, Oxford University Press, Oxford, 1992.

Bartlett, Bruce, "Gimmick of Refinancing U.S. Debt," *Wall Street Journal*, January 29, 1993.

Friedman, Milton, *A Program for Monetary Stability*, Fordham University Press, New York, 1959.

Glick, Reuven, and Hutchison, Michael, "Economic Integration and Fiscal Policy

Transmission: Implications for Europe in 1992 and Beyond," *Economic Review*, Federal Reserve Bank of San Francisco, Spring 1990, pp. 17–28.

Kretzmer, Peter E., "Monetary vs. Fiscal Policy: New Evidence on an Old Debate," *Economic Review*, Federal Reserve Bank of Kansas City, 2nd Quarter, 1992, pp. 21–30.

Roley, V. Vance, "Federal Debt Management Policy: A Re-examination of the Issues," *Economic Review*, Federal Reserve Bank of Kansas City, February 1978, pp. 14–23.

CHAPTER 18

Monetary Policy in the Asian Tigers

THE DISCUSSION OF U.S. monetary and fiscal policies in Chapters 16 and 17 may serve to introduce the monetary and fiscal policies of the Asian Tiger countries. Fiscal policy is not used actively in these countries, so the discussion is devoted primarily to a description of monetary policy. Tools of control over money supplies in the Asian Tigers were described very briefly in Chapter 6, and readers may refer to those pages for a review before continuing here.

This chapter begins with a discussion of Hong Kong's monetary and fiscal policies, followed by those of Singapore. Singapore and Hong Kong are discussed together because there are important similarities stemming from their common heritage as British colonies. Brief discussions of policies in Korea and Taiwan follow.

Monetary and Fiscal Policies in Hong Kong

Followers of financial markets in any country need a steady supply of information on both monetary and fiscal developments. Governments exercise direct control over fiscal matters, but they often delegate responsibility for monetary matters to a special agency of government or to a central bank. Some governments give a great deal of independence to their central banks, while others keep their thumbs pressed down heavily on the central bank's activities. Over the years, Hong Kong has been a maverick in this regard. Its institutions that control money growth have evolved in what may be called a haphazard fashion. From the point of view of its organizational structure, responsibility for all monetary matters falls on the office of the Financial Secretary, under which is the Monetary Affairs Branch of the Hong Kong Government.

However, Hong Kong's government has had *laissez faire* economics orientation, and has "left alone" not only most activities of commercial enterprises but activities of banks as well. Not only has government stayed out of the way of business, but it has often promoted what has been called "positive non-intervention" in business affairs. (Presumably "positive non-intervention," in practice, means promoting non-intervention whenever the opportunity arises.)

This free-market orientation has served Hong Kong well, and many of its freedoms are refreshing as befits a place with the name "Fragrant Harbor." For example, there is no restriction on the free flow of currencies into or out of Hong Kong—a freedom rarely found elsewhere. In the U.S., individuals are free to bring in or take out as much currency as they like, but must register it if the sum exceeds $10,000. The objective of this registration requirement is to erect barriers to the flow of drug-related money.

Banks are free to send money into and out of the territory. And, in past years, a profit-making commercial bank, the Hongkong and Shanghai Banking Corporation, often assisted government officials in carrying out monetary policies so directly and extensively that it was often called the *de facto* central bank of Hong Kong. It issued currency and it handled the government's bank accounts. It assisted the government whenever a bank got into financial difficulty. It holds the deposits of other banks and handles interbank clearings among those banks. However, it never assumed direct control over monetary policies.

The Hongkong and Shanghai Banking Corporation was the principal bank in the cartel the government established, the Hong Kong Association of Banks. The cartel sets rates of interest that banks are allowed to pay depositors. Occasionally, the government would approach the cartel it created and request that interest rates be changed in order to pursue a monetary policy goal. In mid-1994, the cartel came under heavy criticism from consumer interest groups that argued banks were exploiting depositors because the cartel set low deposit rates. As noted in Chapter 3, the cartel's control over interest rates is scheduled to be phased out by the end of 1995.

The Exchange Fund and the Hong Kong Monetary Authority

Hong Kong's Exchange Fund was established by ordinance in 1935. Until the spring of 1993, when the Hong Kong Monetary Authority (HKMA) was established, the Exchange Fund (EF) held the foreign exchange that served to "back" the value of Hong Kong's dollar. Its operations in backing the currency were described in some detail in the discussion on seigniorage in Chapter 5. Its activities in the 1980s evolved into its current role as the principal agency responsible for monetary control under the HKMA.

Under the Exchange Fund Ordinance, the Financial Secretary is an ex-officio chairman of an Exchange Fund Advisory Committee. Other members of the committee are appointed by the Governor of Hong Kong. They are prominent members of the banking and financial community. Everyday management of the EF was delegated to the Secretary for Monetary Affairs. One part of the EF was managed by the Monetary Affairs Branch and other parts were managed by investment specialists in other countries.

The problem with this structure was that the EF became more and more involved in the exercise of monetary policies that are typical of central banks. Therefore, in February 1991, management of the EF was altered. Two divisions were established—the Monetary Management Division responsible for the development of monetary policy and the monetary system, and the Investment Division responsible for managing the assets of the fund itself in order to bring in interest earnings. The Director of the Office of the Exchange Fund reported directly to the Secretary for Monetary Affairs and undertook the responsibility and authority to make decisions regarding monetary policy actions. Then, in 1993, these parts of the Office of the Exchange Fund were transformed into the Hong Kong Monetary Authority.

Monetary Tools of the Exchange Fund

In Chapter 7 the monetary tools of control in the U.S. were described in some detail, and those used in Hong Kong were mentioned. Although there are many similarities, Hong Kong's regulation of the money supply has many unique characteristics as well.

In the few years just prior to the establishment of the HKMA, the Exchange Fund put into place all of the tools it needed to carry out central banking functions. The institutional detail reflects the historical development of monetary matters in Hong Kong. Balance sheets of the EF and the Hongkong and Shanghai Banking Corporation (HSBC) provide a convenient platform to describe modern money mechanics in Hong Kong.

The principal reason the HSBC's balance sheet is part of the platform, rather than simply any representative bank in the system, is that the Hong Kong Association of Banks (HKAB) has appointed the HSBC as the Management Bank of the Clearing House of the HKAB. Every licensed bank in Hong Kong maintains an account to use to clear checks and settle interbank transfers of funds. Large banks deal directly with the Clearing House managed by the HSBC. Other banks may use the services of a settlement bank, that is, a bank that has been authorized to clear transactions through its own account with the Clearing House on behalf of a correspondent bank. For clearing purposes, a small bank may use the services of a large bank instead of dealing directly with the clearing house.

One important note: since the HSBC managed the Clearing House, it did not have to maintain a clearing balance for itself! The clearing accounts of all other banks were on its balance sheet. It was as if the other banks had to maintain a type of reserves in the form of clearing balances with the HSBC while the HSBC was exempt from the need to do so. Furthermore, the HSBC's own operations could increase the volume of clearing balances of all banks in the system, by, for example, making a loan to another bank or purchasing an asset from someone who deposited the HSBC's check in an account in some other bank. Actions by the EF to affect the liquidity of the banking system would not necessarily have the desired effect if they were inadvertently offset by operations of the HSBC.

Because of this problem, in July 1988 the government introduced a new set of accounting arrangements between the EF and the HSBC. Under these arrangements, the EF gained control over the net clearing balance of the banks in Hong Kong. To understand how the system is structured, let us turn to balance sheet examples (Tables 18–1 and 18–2).

Table 18–1
Selected Items on the Exchange Fund's Balance Sheet

Assets	Liabilities	
Foreign currency assets	Certificates of indebtedness	
	Government coin in circulation	
	Government deposit certificates	
	Exchange Fund bills outstanding	−1,000
Hong Kong dollar assets	THE ACCOUNT of HSBC	+1,000

Table 18–2
Selected Items on the HSBC's Balance Sheet

Assets		Liabilities	
Certificates of indebtedness		Notes payable	
Foreign currency assets		HK$ deposits	
		Foreign currency deposits	
Domestic assets		Government deposits	
Loans		Exchange Fund deposits	
Mortgages			
Etc.		Interbank clearing deposits	
		Bank A	+1,000
		Bank B	
		Bank C	
		Etc.	
THE ACCOUNT at EF	+1,000	Net clearing balance	+1,000

The Exchange Fund's Balance Sheet. On the asset side appears the foreign currency denominated assets owned by the Exchange Fund. In the old days there used to be gold and silver holdings, but today most assets consist of some British government bonds, U.S. Treasury bills, certificates of deposit in U.S. banks, German securities, Japanese securities, and so forth. These assets represent a huge amount of wealth to be managed for the purpose of earning interest and bringing in funds for the Hong Kong government.

The EF also holds assets denominated in H.K. dollars. These are mostly bank deposits—time deposits on which interest is paid.

On the liabilities side there are certificates of indebtedness. These are issued to the note-issuing banks in exchange for interest-earning assets in foreign currencies. The assets that back the certificates represent the foreign exchange backing for Hong Kong's dollar. They were described in detail in Chapter 5 under the discussion of seigniorage. The reader may wish to glance back for review.

The EF also holds most of the government's budget surplus and acts as investment manager for the government. It issues the government certificates of deposit and uses the funds to buy foreign investments. As of 1994 the Hong Kong government had accumulated a budget surplus of about US$40 billion, about half of which it planned to use to construct a new airport facility.

As described in Chapter 7, the EF also issues bills for the purpose of creating a money market instrument that it can use in open market purchases and sales that will add or subtract liquidity from the banking system. These are recorded as a liability on the EF's balance sheet. Again, the reader may wish to glance back for review. Thus, the volume of EF bills outstanding is recorded in a liability account on the EF's balance sheet.

Finally, THE ACCOUNT of the HSBC is the special EF account that the HSBC must hold under the arrangements for instituting a method of control over liquidity in the banking system. This method of control and the 1,000 dollar entries appearing on the balance sheet will be explained below.

The HSBC's Balance Sheet. On the asset side appear the certificates of indebtedness that the EF gave the bank in exchange for foreign currency, or for interest-earning assets denominated in foreign currency. The bank must hold these certificates to back the notes payable it has issued, which circulate as paper money in Hong Kong. The bank also holds both foreign and domestic assets.

The last asset item is THE ACCOUNT at the Exchange Fund—the accounting item that was created especially for the purpose of enabling the EF to control the liquidity of the banking system. If the Exchange Fund were viewed as a central bank, this account would represent the HSBC's reserves held with the lender of last resort, the EF.

On the liability side the HSBC has the notes payable account, representing bank notes in circulation, along with the usual deposit accounts belonging to individuals, corporations, and the government. Some of these are denominated in foreign currencies. Also, the EF holds deposits with the HSBC.

The unusual item is the listing of interbank clearing deposits accounts. Taken in total, this group of accounts represents the Clearing House of the Hong Kong Association of Banks that is managed by the HSBC.

Finally, there is a net clearing balance representing the funds that banks hold for use in their business of transferring funds. These balances represent their reserves. Banks borrow and lend these balances, and the market for them is the interbank borrowing market. The interest rate on interbank funds fluctuates during the day. At a given time each day, as interbank trading of funds takes place, the Hongkong Inter-Bank Offered Rate (HIBOR) is struck. This rate provides the basis for setting new interest rates on floating rate notes.

The amount of funds in the net clearing balance determines whether bank reserves are "tight" or "plentiful." If they tighten during the day, the interbank rate will rise.

Maintaining Sufficient Funds in THE ACCOUNT. Under the regulations, the HSBC must maintain THE ACCOUNT with the EF at a level at least as large as the Net Clearing Balance (NCB). If it does not do so, the EF will charge the HSBC interest on the deficiency at a penalty rate. This is the equivalent of a fine levied on the HSBC should it fail to comply.

Exchange Fund Operations. By its own operations, which might be called open market operations, the EF can change the size of THE ACCOUNT *and* the Net Clearing Balance, by a given amount. It may increase both, thus providing more liquidity to the banking system, or it may decrease both and absorb liquidity. For example, on the liability side of the EF's balance sheet, along with THE ACCOUNT, we have Exchange Fund bills outstanding. Assume that the EF wishes to add liquidity and have THE ACCOUNT increase. One way to engineer an increase is to have a decrease in some other liability—a miracle of double entry accounting. Thus, the EF can increase the balance in THE ACCOUNT by decreasing the account of EF bills outstanding. It simply buys some of its own bills in the open market.

It works like this. The seller of the bills will receive a check from the EF and deposit the check in a bank. To collect the funds, the bank will then send the check to the Clearing House. The bank's reserves increase, and so will the NCB.

When the HSBC sends the check to the Exchange Fund, the EF will increase THE ACCOUNT and decrease EF bills outstanding. The level of funds in THE ACCOUNT increases along with the NCB. In this case, the *target* variable is the level of funds in THE ACCOUNT and the *slack* variable, adjusted by the EF, is the EF bills outstanding account. If the EF wishes to absorb liquidity from the interbank market, it simply reverses the operation by selling EF bills.

In general, when the EF buys something it injects liquidity, and when it sells something it absorbs liquidity.

Other Accounts as Slack Variables. Other liabilities on the EF's balance sheet, besides EF bills, can be used as slack variables. If the EF arranges with the government to hold a smaller volume of government deposit certificates, the effect is the same as if it sold EF bills. The other liability is decreased while THE ACCOUNT is increased.

Similarly, there are asset accounts on the EF's balance sheet that can be used as a slack variable for the purpose of affecting bank liquidity. If the EF buys foreign exchange from a bank, it gives the bank a check and the bank will collect by sending the check to its clearing account with the HSBC—increasing both its balance and the Net Clearing Balance by the same amount. The HSBC will send the check on to THE

ACCOUNT at the EF, and the EF will record an increase in its accounting item showing holdings of foreign assets.

Finally, the EF may take measures to alter its holdings of deposits in banks, such as the liability item named Exchange Fund deposits shown on the balance sheet of the HSBC. For example, it may sell additional amounts of EF bills and, when collecting Hong Kong dollars from the sale, instead of depositing them through THE ACCOUNT and NCB it may simply hold the proceeds in its deposit account with the HSBC. Thus, the EF's asset item will show an increase in domestic assets along with an increase in the liability item, EF bills outstanding. In this situation, had not the EF allowed its holdings of HK dollar deposits to rise, the sale of bills would not have had the effect of decreasing THE ACCOUNT.

Parallels. In the U.S. the Federal Reserve clears checks for banks and holds bank reserve deposits, while in Hong Kong the Clearing House is with the HSBC. However, THE ACCOUNT is representative of the total of bank reserves with the Clearing House. That total can be influenced by (a) the Hong Kong equivalent of open market operations by the Federal Reserve, (b) the Hong Kong equivalent of depository actions of the U.S. Treasury when managing the Treasury Tax and Loan accounts in banks and its deposits with the Federal Reserve, and (c) the Hong Kong equivalent of the authority to make loans to banks as a lender of last resort, that is, a liquidity facility that is the equivalent of a discount window. The only central bank operating mechanism that is absent in Hong Kong is a legal reserve ratio.

One additional difference in banking arrangements of the U.S. and Hong Kong is that, since the Federal Reserve does not hold deposits in commercial banks, it cannot use changes in deposits to influence liquidity as the EF can.

The Pegged Exchange Rate System

During most of the 1970s, the Hong Kong dollar was free to float on foreign exchange markets, that is, foreign currencies were traded and their prices moved up and down during the trading day. One U.S. dollar could be purchased for about HK$5.00 and the price would fluctuate. If the price rose too much, the EF could supply some additional U.S. dollars out of its reserves and stabilize the price. None of the other tools of control described above was in place. However, the government had influence over the banking cartel, which was established to control interest rates that banks could set on deposits, so there were some attempts to stabilize macroeconomic conditions by changing credit conditions. It would be most accurate to say, however, that the money supply was not under control. The EF's job was to hold and manage the foreign exchange backing for the currency issue, and to intervene in the foreign exchange market from time to time in order to stabilize exchange rates.

In 1982, the prime minister of Britain, Margaret Thatcher, visited China, and the stage was set for negotiating the return of Hong Kong to China on June 30, 1997. In the summer of 1983, the cost of U.S. dollars rose to HK$6.00. In October a speculative rise in cost pushed the exchange rate to nearly HK$9.00, indicating a dramatic fall in the value of the Hong Kong dollar on foreign exchange markets. The situation was viewed as a crisis. The government stopped trading and established a new regime of pegged exchange rates, in which the HK dollar was tied to the U.S. dollar.

Under the new terms, the EF agreed to purchase or sell U.S. dollars from any bank for HK$7.80. The EF would accept only HK dollars in the form of cash. Also, individuals could not go directly to the EF to buy U.S. currencies—only banks could deal with the EF. Thus, when large sums of cash must be counted, the banks charge fees of perhaps 1 per cent for the service. This permits the exchange rate on the open market to fluctuate between HK$7.72 to HK$7.88, about 1 per cent in value, before it becomes cost effective to deal through the bank with the EF using cash.

Exchange Rates Around the World. Most countries of the world are small. Most tie their currency to a large country's currency through some type of pegged exchange rate system. For example, the U.S. dollar circulates as currency in Panama and Liberia, and about 25 countries, mostly in Africa and the Caribbean, peg their currencies to the U.S. dollar. About 15 countries, mostly African, tie their currency to the French franc. Others tie their currency to the German mark (Estonia, for example) or British pound. About 35 countries tie their currencies to a basket of foreign currencies. Only about 25 countries permit their currencies to float freely, while another 25 "manage" the markets in which their currencies are traded—a managed-float system.

Monetary Control Under a Pegged Exchange Rate System

The volume of domestic money outstanding is not controlled under a pegged rate system. At least it is not controlled directly. During a speech in 1991, Mr. Joseph Yam, their managing director of the EF and now director of the MAHK, suggested that the new operating tools of the Exchange Fund were like an umbrella (it could be used either as a weapon or as a cover for protection from the rain). They could be used to control the money supply or they could be used to hold the pegged exchange rate in place. He argued that the government intended to use the powers of the EF to hold the pegged exchange rate in place, and not to control growth in the supply of money.

The peg has prevailed, not because it is good economic policy, but only because of fear over the return of Hong Kong to China. Defenders of the pegged system argue that removing the peg and permitting the exchange rate to float freely would cause panic, or at least a debilitating loss of confidence, given the uncertainty over the change to China's rule in 1997. If a person has Hong Kong dollars, and if these can be changed into U.S. dollars, he or she has confidence that assets can be changed to money that can be taken abroad when the time comes to leave. Of course, if a hoard of people try to sell assets at the same time, asset prices will collapse. Thus, it may turn out that confidence in the pegged exchange rate has been misplaced.

Economic Disadvantages of a Pegged Exchange Rate System

Inflexibility of Interest Rates and Exchange Rates. If a small country's exchange rate is tied to that of a large trading partner, then interest rates in the two countries must be held close to each other, too. The reason for this is quite straightforward.

A person with Hong Kong dollars can invest either at home, and earn an interest rate on local deposits or securities, or, invest in the U.S. and earn an interest rate on U.S. deposits or securities. Since the exchange rate is fixed, whenever interest rates in the U.S. fall, Hong Kong people will switch U.S. dollar holdings into Hong Kong dollar holdings. Selling U.S. dollars and buying Hong Kong dollars would put downward pressure on the HK dollar price of U.S. dollars, that is, perhaps HK$7.80 might fall to HK$7.60, reflecting a rise in the value of Hong Kong's currency. *But, since the peg sets the price at HK$7.80, this change in the foreign exchange rate cannot take place.* (As noted above, because of transactions costs it might fall to HK$7.72 before stopping.)

The only way to keep the exchange rate pegged is to force interest rates in Hong Kong to fall along with interest rates in the U.S., so as to remove the incentive to change U.S. money into Hong Kong money. (For clarification of this point, readers may wish to consult books on international finance on the topic of Interest Rate Parity and the related concept of Covered Interest Arbitrage.)

Inflation in Hong Kong. Pushing interest rates lower in Hong Kong need not be bad economic policy for Hong Kong under all circumstances. Indeed, low interest rates would be good for Hong Kong if its economy were stagnating. But it is booming. Unfortunately, the U.S. economy has been recessed and interest rates fell from 1990 to 1994. This meant that lower and lower interest rates were pressed on Hong Kong's economy just when it was in the midst of a boom—just when higher rates would have been good economic policy. For years, inflation ran at just under 10 per cent per year with no effort by the Exchange Fund to stop it by implementing restrictive monetary policies. Inflation continued through mid-1995 with no end in sight.

This is why the Exchange Fund's tools of control over the money supply are used to provide banks with liquidity and hold interest rates low—to defend the peg. The tools are not used to combat inflation. In a weak attempt to justify retaining a pegged system of exchange rates, some economists in Hong Kong even argue that inflation is good for an economy. This ancient view was thoroughly debunked by Adam Smith over 200 years ago when he successfully refuted mercantilism—the idea that exporting goods, importing gold, and inflating the economy, was the best route to prosperity.

Let the real interest rate be the nominal rate less the rate of inflation. With inflation rates of about 10 per cent per annum, and nominal interest rates on one year deposits of 3 per cent, there has been a negative real interest rate of around 7 per cent in Hong Kong for many years. Little wonder that Hong Kong's economy is overheated. You can drive a car for a few miles when it is overheated and the radiator is blowing off steam, but when the water is gone, the engine will burn what oil it has, and then seize up.

A Negative Interest Rate Scheme. As just described, the problem of negative real interest rates stems from the pegged exchange rate system. However, perhaps the most bizarre phenomenon to have emerged out of this system was the institution by government of a negative interest rate scheme—referring to negative *nominal* interest rates, let alone negative real interest rates. In 1989 nominal interest rates on bank deposits fell to less than 1 per cent. The government instituted a tax to be levied on large HK dollar deposits. Thus, the effective return on such deposits would turn out to be negative after the tax was paid, hence the name "negative interest rate scheme." The purpose was to discourage people from selling U.S. dollars and buying Hong Kong dollars to deposit in Hong Kong's banks. Laws are now in place in Hong Kong to permit the authorities to levy such taxes on deposits should the need arise (see Greenwood, Ho, and Law, 1989). In the 1970s the Swiss imposed a similar tax on foreign deposits.

The economic consequences of such a tax are straightforward. Instead of putting their funds in bank deposits where the return is negative, people will buy other assets. By 1994, housing prices rose to levels equal to those in Tokyo. Thus, through inflation, the pressure brought on by low nominal rates and negative real rates is released.

Interrelations between Exchange Rates, Interest Rates and Inflation. The hallmark of a free economy is freely fluctuating prices. There are three broad types of prices whose levels can be monitored by averages or indexes: (a) the prices of commodities as measured by indexes of inflation, (b) the prices of foreign currencies as measured by the exchange value of the local currency, and (c) the prices of funds as measured by interest rate levels. These three categories of prices are interdependently determined in free markets. Therefore, when one set of these is fixed by the authorities, the pricing system, as an adjustment mechanism used to allocate resources efficiently, is impaired.

In 1993 the HKMA, operating through the Exchange Fund, pumped money into the economy on three occasions. On the last occasion it pumped in HK$1 billion. It bought either U.S. dollars in the foreign exchange markets or Exchange Fund bills in the money market. These purchases pumped Hong Kong dollars into the economy and increased the money supply. The idea was to keep the U.S. dollar from depreciating against the Hong Kong dollar, thereby supporting the pegged rate system. But by pumping money into its economy, these actions stimulate inflationary pressure when inflation is already around 10 per cent (see Fung, 1993).

There is a rule in market economics that says that when authorities set one price, they will soon have to set another, and another, and another. Examples abound. In Hong Kong, having set the exchange rate, the authorities next had to set interest rates. Finding they are left with inflation, they then try to find some way to stop it.

To stop the escalation of housing prices, for example, restrictions were imposed on down payments for mortgage loans, raising them to 30 per cent of the purchase price in 1992, and on to 40 per cent on high-valued properties in 1993. Also, they resurrect the debunked cost-push argument that inflation is caused by labor shortages. So, they arrange programs for importing labor from China to work on construction projects. Whatever happened to the concept of positive non-intervention?

None of these special interventions into economic affairs would have been necessary if a system of monetary controls had been instituted instead of the pegged exchange rate system. Now that a system of control over money has indeed been put into place with the formation of the Hong Kong Monetary Authority, Hong Kong should dispense with its pegged exchange rate system and use its monetary controls to control money and let prices find their market levels (see Dallas, 1992; Greenwood, 1993; and Perkin, 1993).

The people of Hong Kong are unnerved by the prospect of control by China in 1997. Supporters of the pegged exchange rate suggest that China would be very angry if the peg were removed, thus adding to people's fears. The sad part is that the Chinese government and the people who will remain in Hong Kong have the most to lose if Hong Kong's inflation is not brought under control.

The Deceptive Image of Stability. The true price of anything, be it rice, labor, or foreign exchange, cannot be set by administrative fiat. If the price of rice is set too low, there will be lines of people waiting to buy rice, but the shelves will be empty, and the price to those who go home empty handed is high. A government may say they have kept the price of rice stable. There is an image of stability, but this is not the reality.

When prices are not free to fluctuate in response to market forces, the signals they should send to market participants are blotted out.

Sir Alan Walters, former chief economic advisor to Britain's prime minister, Margaret Thatcher, has been known to support the pegging of currencies for Hong Kong and for other countries such as those of the former U.S.S.R. (see Hanke and Walters, 1993). However, he argues persuasively against such a pegged system for Britain: "Pegged exchange rates promote perverse monetary policies ... There is much to be said in favor of a pegged currency, but not if it in turn magnifies an inflation and promotes a slump" (Walters, 1992). If Britain should protect its economy with a floating currency, why should Hong Kong not do so too?

Fiscal Policies in Hong Kong

The tax, spending, and welfare systems in Hong Kong have unique and interesting qualities.

Taxes. Hong Kong has the usual varieties of excise taxes on liquor, cigarettes and automobiles. It collects a variety of duties and fees, and it also has revenues from its share of ownership of the Mass Transit Railway. Also, it "owns" most of the land in Hong Kong and leases it, or sells it, to developers. Apartment owners and renters pay "rates" that represent a type of property tax.

Its principal tax on incomes is not an income tax, but a wages and salaries tax. There is no tax on interest or dividends, nor on capital gains. The tax fluctuates from time to time but it is usually a flat tax of about 15 per cent of total wage and salary income for high wage and salary employees, with allowances for those at low income levels. There is also a profits tax on net revenues of businesses. This is usually around 16 per cent. Interest expenses are deductible, but interest earnings are not taxed. Altogether, this tax structure provides strong incentives to save and invest—key ingredients to growth. America would have high saving rates, too, if it had a similar tax structure.

In spite of low tax rates, and the existence of many sources of income that are not taxed, the Hong Kong government manages to have large budget surpluses. Of course, it helps not to have a large burden of military spending.

Welfare. Unlike other governments that manage huge welfare programs—safety nets for the poor—Hong Kong finances many of its welfare programs through a huge private organization, the Jockey Club. The Club has been given a monopoly over gambling and takes a large portion of the betting at race tracks and numerous local betting parlors. Proceeds of betting are used to pay for subsidized facilities that serve members of the club, and the remainder, a huge sum, is spent on welfare services for the poor of Hong Kong and other public service projects, such as opening a new university.

Although the government does provide a wide range of social services, it usually shows a budget surplus by excluding a large volume of welfare payments to the indigent in its budget. A very large budget surplus for 1993 led the government to reduce profits and salary taxes, the airport tax and so forth. The government is now actively looking into the idea of providing a retirement scheme with pension funds, but views unfavorably the establishment of a central provident fund, such as Singapore has.

Budget Matters. Hong Kong has a goal of maintaining a balanced budget. In the spring of 1994 the government announced significant reductions in taxes as a result of an unexpectedly large increase in the budget surplus in 1993. This will create additional inflationary pressure on an already overheated Hong Kong economy. But whether or not a fiscal policy result is expansionary or contractionary does not seem to enter the government's calculations, at least not as reported in the press. Hong Kong needs a contractionary monetary policy to offset the expansionary forces that follow from its fiscal position, but this is unavailable given the pegged exchange rate system.

Monetary and Fiscal Policies in Singapore

The Minister of Finance is the chairman of a seven-person Board that governs the Monetary Authority of Singapore (MAS). The six other directors are appointed by the President of Singapore. Thus, the executive branch of government in Singapore has direct control over activities of the MAS. It is not, by any stretch of the imagination, an *independent* central banking operation.

The MAS was established in 1970 and began operating in January 1971. Its Board also has a deputy chairman, and one of the Board members is also Managing Director of the MAS and responsible for operations. To assist the Managing Director, there are three deputy directors and seven directors that oversee the departments that regulate financial institutions and implement monetary policies.

The MAS acts as banker to banks and finance companies. It imposes reserve requirements that require banks to maintain a percentage of liabilities in the form of cash with the MAS. Accounts at the MAS are used in the clearing of checks among banks and in clearing checks with government.

The MAS acts as banker for the government—holding government deposits and providing checking facilities. It also acts as the government's financial agent by issuing and redeeming government debt. It conducts regular auctions of Treasury bills and other government securities. The MAS is authorized to buy, sell, discount, and rediscount various securities—open market operations. The MAS is responsible for implementing Singapore's monetary and *exchange rate* policies.

As noted in Chapter 7, Singapore requires that banks hold reserves in the form of deposits with the MAS. Also, as supervisor of banks, the MAS has imposed a 12 per cent capital adequacy requirement—exceeding the requirement of 8 per cent recommended by the Bank for International Settlements and major countries around the world.

The only monetary matter for which the MAS is *not* responsible is the issue of currency.

The Board of Commissioners of Currency of Singapore (BCCS)

This board is what was known, historically, as a *currency board*. These institutions were typical of colonial governments. The local currency would be issued by the local government, but would be backed by holdings of foreign exchange, typically, the currency of the colonizing country. Local money could be traded for foreign exchange at a fixed rate of exchange. Thus, Hong Kong's pegged system, described above, represents a reversion to the earlier currency board type of monetary system. Singapore's board has a similar history, but has moved forward. Today's BCCS was established in 1967 and celebrated its twenty-fifth anniversary in 1992.

In colonial days, of course, gold and silver were used as money, especially in international trade. So currency boards held reserves against note issues in the form of bullion. Nowadays, they hold nearly all of the reserves, which back the local issue of currency, in the form of interest-earning assets. Indeed, in Singapore the law requires the BCCS to hold at least 30 per cent of its foreign exchange reserves in the form of "liquid" assets. These are gold, bank deposits, money at call, and treasury bills. The BCCS also holds securities issued by foreign governments and international institutions. Interest is earned on all but the holdings of gold.

Earnings on holdings of securities denominated in foreign currencies are accumulated in a currency fund income account, out of which the BCCS pays its operating expenses. Any surplus or deficit in the account is transferred to the government at the end of the financial year. This is a clear and direct example of the payment of seigniorage to the government such as was described in Chapter 5 for Hong Kong and the U.S.

Prior to 1972 the parity rate of exchange of the Singapore currency was set to that of the British pound. But when the world turned to freely fluctuating exchange rates in

1973, Singapore switched to the U.S. dollar as its intervention currency, and now will buy and sell foreign exchange, *not at a fixed rate, but at a market-determined rate.* Thus, Singapore has abandoned the fixed rate provision typical of currency boards, although it has retained "foreign exchange backing" for all outstanding currency.

It is difficult to know, however, just what it means to say that the currency is "backed" by foreign exchange when the price (value) of the backing fluctuates according to market forces, and when any buyer wishing to purchase foreign exchange with local Singapore dollars can get the same rate dealing in the foreign exchange market as that offered by the BCCS. As an institution, the BCCS is mostly symbolic.

A Basket of Currencies. As noted above the MAS is responsible for the implementation of monetary policy and for exchange rate policy. It maintains holdings of foreign exchange and mediates between banks and the BCCS regarding currency requirements. Thus, the MAS has designated a basket of different currencies of major countries, and it will buy and sell these in the local foreign exchange market in order to stabilize the value of Singapore dollars.

During the 1980s, when the U.S. dollar was falling in value against other major currencies of the world, the Singapore dollar appreciated in value. During the same period, the Hong Kong dollar—tied to the U.S. dollar by the peg—did not appreciate. Instead, it depreciated on world markets right along with the U.S. dollar.

Exchange Rate Intervention and Money Supply Control

The MAS can engage in open market operations. It can buy or sell securities and cause bank reserve positions to increase or decrease. In this sense its portfolio of securities represents an asset account that can be used as a slack variable in order to adjust a target variable—bank liquidity.

But it also has another asset account that it can, and does, use as a slack variable— its holdings of foreign exchange. (As noted in Chapter 7, Germany used its foreign exchange accounts as a slack variable for several years.) By buying foreign exchange, it can increase bank liquidity in the same way that it increases bank liquidity by buying securities.

Reinforcing Tools. Governments can stimulate economic activity by expansionary monetary and fiscal policies. They can also stimulate economic activity by encouraging exports and discouraging imports.

This latter solution usually requires direct intervention into trading relations with export subsidies or tariffs/quotas on imports. These distort relative prices and are not appropriate economic tools to use in a market economy. However, exports may be stimulated, and imports discouraged, if the country's currency falls in value.

For example, if U.S. dollars cost 1.6 Singapore dollars per unit, the exchange rate could be quoted as S$1.60/US$. By buying U.S. dollars in sufficient quantities, the MAS could push up their Singapore dollar price, for example, to S$1.80/US$. This change represents a devaluation of the Singapore dollar and an upward revaluation of the U.S. dollar. A devaluation of the Singapore dollar makes Singapore exports more attractive to Americans and stimulates exports. It also makes U.S. imports more expensive to Singaporeans, and discourages imports. Thus, a stimulus to the economy follows from an aggressive move to lower the foreign exchange value of the Singapore dollar.

But, and here's the point, buying U.S. dollars *also* adds to bank liquidity. An increase in MAS's holdings of foreign exchange is accompanied by an increase in bank deposits with the MAS. If no counter-move is undertaken to sterilize (offset) this increase in bank reserves, the increased liquidity of the financial institutions should lead to lower interest rates. Lower rates would provide a stimulus to investment spending and economic activity generally.

Thus, with the purchase of foreign exchange, both the movement in the exchange rate and the easier monetary conditions contribute to the goal of economic stimulus. Both the foreign exchange rate *and* local monetary conditions change appropriately. Since both are at work, neither one has to play a heavy-duty role in absorbing the burden of stabilization. Small changes in the exchange rate may be *supported* by small changes in bank liquidity positions. Thus, the goal can be accomplished without highly distorting shifts in either of the two sets of prices—foreign exchange and interest rates.

If economic restraint, rather than stimulus, were the goal, the appropriate action would be to sell U.S. dollars. Then the direction of all of the forces described in the example would be reversed.

Hong Kong's Folly. It is useful to point out that Hong Kong's fixed foreign exchange rate has essentially blocked the effects that could otherwise flow from permitting the rate to fluctuate and reinforce other stabilizing actions. In contrast, Singapore has implemented a system that permits flexibility in the exchange rate and freely fluctuating interest rates. The result in Hong Kong, as noted above, has been a ridiculous interest rate policy and distorting inflation. Yet many economists there still argue that the pegged exchange rate provides stability.

When Singapore's inflation rate was over 3 per cent in 1988–91, the government felt it was too high and took measures to reduce it. Hong Kong did not, and could not, with the pegged rate it has imposed upon itself. Both economies boomed. Economic prosperity simply does not require inflation.

The Central Provident Fund (CPF)

The CPF was established in 1955 in Singapore. Formed by government, its purpose is to require compulsory saving (read this as taxes) to be pooled into a fund out of which retirement benefits would be paid (read this as transfer payments to retired persons). The amount a worker and his or her employer, were each forced to "contribute" was initially 5 per cent of wages or salaries. The percentage rose from year to year until it reached 25 per cent in 1984. This was *25 per cent each, employer and employee,* but with a ceiling on the total amount of wages and salaries to which the percentage contribution applied. (In this respect the system is a great deal like the social security system in the U.S.)

The rate has been reduced since 1984, but the government has pledged that 20 per cent will be the rate over the longer run. This is significantly higher than the 7.65 per cent that the social security system of the U.S. government has set as a tax on wages to be matched by employers.

In the U.S., the huge amount of funds taxed from wages is invested in a pool of U.S. Treasury securities and thus helps fund the national debt. By contrast, in Singapore the CPF has become a huge financial intermediary. For example, early withdrawal of funds provides a source of housing finance for many individuals. Also, the government may issue special bonds for infrastructure development, including housing estates, and "persuade" the CPF to invest heavily in them. Thus, one branch of government finances another, and the government directs the flow of funds into a goal of providing housing for everyone. It is not public housing, as such, because there is a sense of private property ownership that accompanies the building of apartments and their sale to workers. But, in the end, the government persuades the public where and how it should organize its living space. It is a government-directed housing program.

Also, when newspapers report that, in Singapore, the saving rate out of income is 45 per cent, remember that such a high saving rate would not be likely if it were voluntary.

The MAS and CPF Accounts. Since the CPF is a statutory agent of government, it maintains its accounts with the MAS. Transfers into and out of the CPF account with the MAS have opposite effects on bank reserve positions. Just as the Federal Reserve undertakes defensive open market operations to offset significant changes in bank reserves brought on by changes in Treasury balances, the MAS will use defensive open market operations to offset changes in CPF accounts that deflect the level of bank reserves from its target level.

Fiscal Policy in Singapore

The government's policy is to keep a balanced budget over time, recognizing that in some years there will be deficits to be made up with surpluses in other years. In this fashion it recognizes that economic fluctuations are a normal and expected aspect of market-based economies, and that automatic stabilizers have some role to play in reducing the amplitude in economic fluctuations. Thus, in a booming economy, tax revenues will increase and may lead to a surplus in the government's budget that will help control inflationary tendencies, and so forth.

Monetary and Fiscal Policies in Korea

The Monetary Board. Monetary policy in Korea is formulated and implemented by the Monetary Board of the Bank of Korea (BOK), which was established in 1950. The Bank itself operates under the authority of Korea's Ministry of Finance, which has ultimate authority over the Bank's actions through a provision that permits the Minister to veto and overturn the Monetary Board's decisions. The Minister of Finance is the chairman of the nine-person Monetary Board, and all members of the board are appointed by the President.

The Governor of the Bank of Korea is vice chairman of the board and is appointed by the President, upon the recommendation of the Minister of Finance, to serve a four-year term. The Governor administers and directs the Bank's operations and executes monetary policy under the Board's instruction. The Bank also operates the Office of Bank Supervision and Examination.

Other members of the Board include one member recommended by the Minister of the Economic Planning Board, two members recommended by banking institutions, two members recommended by the Ministry of Agriculture and Fisheries, and two members recommended by the Ministry of Trade and Industry. In summary, various government departments are represented on the Monetary Board along with two representatives from the banking institutions being regulated.

The Bank of Korea's Operations

The BOK's Balance Sheet. A glance at the principal entries under the balance sheet accounts of the Bank of Korea indicates its activities (see Table 18–3).

These balance sheet items indicate that the Bank of Korea may use a variety of monetary tools to achieve its obligatory goal of maintaining a stable value of money by managing the money supply.

It can make loans to banks and act as a lender of last resort. In earlier years it used its authority to set the terms of loans to banks so as to direct credit flows, but, with greater liberalization of its money markets, it now uses this tool less frequently.

The BOK holds government securities that may be used in open market operations.

It imposes legal reserve requirements. In past years it changed reserve requirements frequently. For example, in May 1989, it imposed marginal reserve requirements of

Table 18–3
Selected Balance Sheet Accounts of the Bank of Korea

Assets	Liabilities
Cash	Bank notes and coin issued
Checks and bills	Reserves of banks
Loans to banks	Deposits of other financial institutions
Securities	Government deposits
Government bonds	Monetary stabilization bonds
Other loans to government	Monetary stabilization accounts
Foreign assets	Foreign liabilities

30 per cent. This policy action was withdrawn in 1990, and it has relied more heavily on open market operations since then.

It can set interest rate ceilings on various types of deposits and loans of banking institutions, but has recently moved away from direct controls.

Its current, most frequent, tool of control is the use of open market operations on its own bonds, Monetary Stabilization Bonds (MSB). These were first introduced in 1961 as a negotiable obligation of the Bank of Korea. MSB are issued and repurchased at discount rates similar to interest rates on time deposits. Dealers in stabilization bonds have been established and provisions for competitive sales to the public have been implemented.

For several years the Bank of Korea also required banks to hold funds with it in a Monetary Stabilization Account. This account was separate from the legal reserve account. Legal reserves are accounted for on a semi-monthly basis. The Monetary Stabilization Account can be varied frequently and provides the BOK with a means of affecting bank liquidity on a more frequent basis.

As of 1990 the BOK used, as a target variable, an $M2$ measure including currency in circulation, demand deposits, and time and savings deposits of banking institutions.

Fiscal Policy in Korea

Korea's fiscal policy has involved a mixture of government budget items and foreign debt. Korea's budget was in surplus from 1985 through 1990, but since then it has had deficits.

As the economy prospered through the 1980s, there were foreign exchange earnings that exceeded expenditures by significant amounts, but Korea had borrowed large sums from abroad under its overall program for economic development, and these foreign exchange earnings were used largely to retire foreign debt. Thus, the Korean government does not actively pursue spending and tax policies with a view to economic stabilization.

Monetary and Fiscal Policies in Taiwan

The Central Bank of China (CBC), Taiwan's central bank, was established on November 1, 1928 in Shanghai. In 1949, when China's government gave way to the Communist movement and moved to Taiwan, most of the functions of the CBC were delegated to the Bank of Taiwan. In July 1961, the CBC reconvened and took over central banking operations again. The Bank of Taiwan continues to operate as an important commercial bank.

In November 1979, the Executive Yuan of the government amended the Central Bank of China Act and placed the Ministry of Finance and the CBC on an equal and parallel footing. That is, the CBC is not under the authority of the Ministry of Finance. But it is under the authority of the executive branch of government. The Ministry of Finance does have a department of Monetary Affairs with broad responsibility over financial markets.

Monetary Controls

Major policy tools used by the Central Bank of China include legal reserve requirements, open market operations, and lending to commercial banks as a lender of last resort.

The major money market instruments through which open market operations take place are Treasury bills, commercial paper, banker's acceptances, commercial acceptances, and negotiable certificates of deposit. Also, government bonds, corporate bonds, and bank debt that originated with longer maturities, but that has less than one year remaining to maturity, may be traded in the money markets.

Before 1978 foreign exchange trading was carried out at fixed rates of exchange—pegged to the U.S. dollar. But Taiwan discovered that exchange rate fluctuations interfered with internal policy objectives. Therefore, from 1979 to 1989, foreign exchange rates floated under a system where five banks associated with the Foreign Exchange Trading Center set new forward exchange rates each day against the U.S. dollar within a limited range. Beginning in April 1989, all transactions above US$10,000 were freely determined in the foreign exchange markets.

Liberalization of Financial Matters. During the 1980s, the government took many small steps to liberate financial markets and institutions and to replace government mandated controls with market determined systems. Its policy position was to take one step at a time, but continue to move forward. In June 1991, it authorized 15 new licenses for private banks to begin competition with the 16 banks already operating, 13 of which were government owned.

When the banking system was dominated by government-owned banks, it was a simple matter to push interest rates up or down by using moral suasion—government simply told the banks what to do, and they did it. But with a competitive market in banking, interest rates can be pressured to move indirectly by BOC operations that affect bank liquidity.

International Markets. In 1984 Offshore Banking Units (OBU) were introduced in Taiwan. These are similar in many regards to Asian Currency Units in Singapore—divisions of banks that borrow and lend in foreign currencies. The OBUs in Taiwan were authorized to borrow and lend all currencies other than the New Taiwan (NT) dollar. Foreign exchange banks set up OBUs, as did nonresident firms. Transactions with resident firms were restricted. Profits of OBUs were made tax exempt in order to encourage development of the market.

By 1989 the market had grown to such an extent that it could support the introduction of a call loan market in foreign currencies. The market grew rapidly and loans with maturities ranging from overnight to six months were developed in U.S. dollars, Deutschemarks, and Japanese yen. In London there is the London Interbank Offered Rate, LIBOR, and now there is also HIBOR, SIBOR, and TIBOR, for Hong Kong, Singapore, and Taipei (not Taiwan). These rates are set for the purpose of establishing interest rates on floating interest rate securities.

Interactions among Markets. There have been several occasions in which the CBC has attempted to deal with foreign exchange fluctuations and domestic interest rate policies simultaneously. As one of the most financially successful of the Asian Tigers, Taiwan has prospered from the huge volume of sales it has made to the U.S. It has had export surpluses for many years, and built up foreign exchange reserves of over US$85 billion by 1993. During this process, there was pressure for the value of the NT dollar to appreciate against the U.S. dollar.

On occasion, for example, the CBC attempted to hold back the rising value of the NT dollar so that exports would be maintained. So it bought U.S. dollars and supplied Taiwan dollars. But the CBC's purchases added liquidity to the banking system and held down interest rates. The CBC attempted to offset this effect on bank liquidity by offsetting sales of securities in the open market to "sterilize" the effect of the foreign exchange transactions. In Chapter 16 there is a discussion of the futility of sterilized foreign exchange intervention.

In the end, when export surpluses led to a strong currency and, at the same time, overheated economic activity, the currency was allowed to appreciate, and interest rates to rise, both of which tended to function as stabilizing adjustments for a prosperous economy. In this regard, the monetary authorities in Taiwan have been somewhat slower to adjust their system of controls, but have followed the spirit of Singapore's system.

Fiscal Policy in Taiwan

From 1950 through the 1960s, the government's budget was greatly in deficit, and in the 1970s the deficit was replaced with a huge surplus. Expanding the size of the government sector with a variety of social welfare programs, and a larger percentage of GDP devoted to government spending, the huge surplus disappeared and the government's budget has been more or less balanced since then.

A large balance of trade surplus in the 1980s led to an excessive accumulation of foreign exchange holdings. This has led the Taiwanese to remark, in casual conversations, that the people of Taiwan are up to their knees in money. The government's problem is, what to do with it? The result is that the government has drawn up plans for expansive infrastructure development programs of all sorts.

Government spending increases tend to be inflationary. However, to the extent that government spends foreign exchange reserves in order to increase imports for use in infrastructure construction, the increased imports hold down domestic demand to levels below what it would be if imports did not increase. However, even if imports do restrain the size of the multiplier effect of spending by government, the multiplier effect is still positive.

Consequently, the government's development of the economy's infrastructure is bound to be inflationary. It may seem ironic, but having a lot of wealth does not always mean that it can be spent without adverse consequences. However, with the adjustment mechanism of the pricing system at work through freely fluctuating exchange rates, and with free market determination of interest rates, a deliberate, slow, and steady plan for making good use of the excessive levels of foreign exchange reserves can be fruitfully developed without undue economic instability.

Summary

The monetary system in Hong Kong has a very unique quality because it has a pegged exchange rate system. This system has an interface with monetary conditions, and has many implications for the carrying out of monetary policy. The recently established Monetary Authority of Hong Kong has put into place all of the tools of monetary control that central banks around the world use, but is applying those tools to maintain a pegged exchange rate system. Unfortunately, supporting the pegged system prevents the Exchange Fund from undertaking appropriate measures to rein in Hong Kong's inflationary economy.

Singapore and Hong Kong have a common heritage and have been influenced by western economics. Korea and Taiwan, in contrast, kept much greater government control over their economies than did Singapore and Hong Kong. All four, in varying degree, have shown such successful economic growth rates that they have become known as the Four Asian Tigers. All four have had authoritarian governments. On paper, Singapore's government seems more democratic than the others, but for practical purposes, it has a single party system.

Along with economic growth, financial institutions in the economies of Korea and Taiwan have been liberalized. They are moving more and more closely to the free market structures that characterize the economies of Hong Kong and Singapore.

Key Terms and Concepts

Hong Kong Exchange Fund
Hongkong and Shanghai Banking
   Corporation
Negative interest rate scheme
Board of Commissioners of Currency
   of Singapore
Bank of Korea activities

Hong Kong Monetary Authority
THE ACCOUNT
Pegged exchange rates
Monetary Authority of Singapore
Basket of currencies
Central Provident Fund
Bank of China activities

Discussion Questions and Exercises

1. Briefly describe the role of the Hongkong Shanghai Banking Corporation as operator of the Clearing House.
2. How is THE ACCOUNT of the Exchange Fund related to the Net Clearing Balance with the Hongkong and Shanghai Banking Corporation?
3. What are the principal accounts on the Exchange Fund's balance sheet? What does each represent?
4. What are the principal accounts on the HSBC's balance sheet?

5. What accounting items might the Exchange Fund treat as slack variables in implementing a monetary policy?
6. Briefly describe the pegged exchange rate system of Hong Kong.
7. How do exchange rates vary under the pegged system?
8. Which economy might you have greater confidence in, one with a pegged exchange rate, or one with an established commitment to monetary control? Explain briefly Hong Kong's situation.
9. Explain the relation between interest rate levels and the exchange rate of a currency.
10. What is required if Hong Kong is to introduce an anti-inflationary monetary policy?
11. Briefly describe Hong Kong's negative interest rate scheme.
12. What are the effects of price-fixing arrangements generally, and fixing the price of foreign exchange specifically?
13. Describe the unique status of gambling on horse races in Hong Kong.
14. Describe the types of taxes the government of Hong Kong levies, and those it does not levy. Would this tax structure encourage or discourage investment? Why?
15. Briefly describe the activities of the Monetary Authority of Singapore.
16. The Central Provident Fund is an important financial intermediary in Singapore. Briefly describe its activities.
17. In what respects is the Board of Commissioners of Currency of Singapore a "currency board" in the classic sense? How do its operations today differ from those of earlier days?
18. Explain how intervention in the foreign exchange markets by central banks affects bank liquidity—the case of Singapore. Contrast this result with Hong Kong's folly.
19. What is the objective of Singapore's fiscal policy, and how is it carried out?
20. In Korea, what are Monetary Stabilization Bonds, and what function do they serve? How are these like Exchange Fund bills in Hong Kong?
21. Who controls the Central Bank of China in Taiwan?
22. What has Taiwan done to liberalize its financial system in recent years?

References

Annual Reports, Monetary Authority of Singapore, various issues.

Annual Reports and Accounts, Board of Commissioners of Currency of Singapore, various issues.

Cha, Baekin, "Hong Kong's Inflation: A Macroeconomic View," Technical Report No. 93–2, Asia-Pacific Financial and Forecasting Research Centre, City Polytechnic of Hong Kong, July 1993.

Chen, Mu-Tsai, "The Financial System and Financial Policy in the Republic of China," *Economic Review*, International Commercial Bank of China, July–August 1990, pp. 1–19.

Currency Notes, Board of Commissioners of Currency of Singapore, various issues.

Dallas, Pauline, "Call for Flotation of Hongkong Dollar: Exchange Rate Floor to Halt Depreciation," Interview by Rosa Ocampo, *South China Morning Post,* March 11, 1992.

Euh, Yoon-Dae, and Amsden, Alice H., "Korea's Financial Reform," *Journal of Management,* College of Business Administration, Korea University, Seoul, Vol. 33, 1990, pp. 45–84.

Euh, Yoon-Dae, and Baker, James C., *The Korean Banking System and Foreign Influence,* Routledge, London, 1990. (Of special interest is Chapter 7: "The Financial Systems of Korea and Taiwan: A Comparative Analysis.")

Fieleke, Norman S., "The Quest for Sound Money: Currency Boards to the Rescue?" *New England Economic Review,* Federal Reserve Bank of Boston, November/December 1992, pp. 14–24.

Fung, Noel, "$1 Billion Injected to Save US Dollar Peg," *South China Morning Post International Weekly,* October 16–17, 1993, p. 1.

Greenwood, John G., "Pros and Cons of the Currency Peg," *South China Morning Post International Weekly,* October 23–24, 1993, p. 11.

Greenwood, John G., Ho, Y. K., and Law, C. K., "Forum on the Negative Interest Rate Scheme," *Hong Kong Economic Papers,* Hong Kong Economic Association, No. 19, 1989, pp. 67–78.

Hanke, Steve H., and Walters, Sir Alan, "Back to the Future," *Forbes,* November 8, 1993, p. 298.

Ho, Y. K., Scott, Robert Haney, and Wong, K. A., eds., *The Hong Kong Financial System,* Oxford University Press, Hong Kong, 1991.

Korea, Bank of, *The Financial System in Korea,* Republic of Korea, December 1990.

Kroszner, Randall, "Alternative Approaches to Banking in Hong Kong," *HKCER Letters,* Hong Kong Centre for Economic Research, Chinese University of Hong Kong, September 1990.

Monthly Statistical Bulletin, Bank of Korea, Republic of Korea, various issues.

Monthly Statistical Bulletin, Monetary Authority of Singapore, various issues.

Moreno, Ramon, "Monetary Control Without a Central Bank: The Case of Hong Kong," *Economic Review,* Federal Reserve Bank of San Francisco, Spring 1986, pp. 17–37.

———, "Monetary Lessons of Hong Kong," *Weekly Letter,* Federal Reserve Bank of San Francisco, September 7, 1990.

———, "Pegging, Floating, and Price Stability: Lessons from Taiwan," *Weekly Letter,* Federal Reserve Bank of San Francisco, September 11, 1992.

Moreno, Ramon, and Yin, Norman, "Exchange Rate Policy and Shocks to Asset Markets: The Case of Taiwan in the 1980's," *Economic Review,* Federal Reserve Bank of San Francisco, No. 1, 1992, pp. 14–34.

Perkin, Ian K., "Short-term Cure has Outlived Usefulness," *South China Morning Post International Weekly,* October 23–24, 1993, p. 11.

"The Role of the Interest Rate Agreement," *Hong Kong Economic Indicators,* Standard Chartered Bank, No. 78, October 1990.

Saavalainen, Tapio, "Estonia Stabilizes Economy through a Currency Reform," *IMF Survey*, International Monetary Fund, December 14, 1992, pp. 381–84.

Scott, Robert Haney, *Saving Hong Kong's Dollar*, University Publisher and Printer, Hong Kong, 1984.

————, "Money Supply Control and the Peg to the U.S. Dollar," *Hong Kong Economic Papers*, Hong Kong Economic Association, No. 22, 1992, pp. 53–71.

Shieh, Samuel C., "The Role of the Central Bank in Economic Development: The R.O.C.'s Taiwan Experience," *Economic Review*, International Commercial Bank of China, November–December 1990, pp. 1–11.

Singapore, Monetary Authority of, *The Financial Structure of Singapore*, 3rd Edition, 1989.

Taiwan, Central Bank of China, *Financial Institutions in Taiwan, the Republic of China*, Taipei, Taiwan, August 1993.

Tan, Chwee Huat, *Financial Markets and Institutions in Singapore*, 6th Edition, Singapore University Press, Singapore, 1990.

Walters, Alan, "Pegging the Culprit in Economic Slump," Letters to the Editor, *Wall Street Journal*, August 31, 1992.

Walters, Alan, and Hanke, Steve H., "Currency Boards," *Working Papers in Economics*, No. 281, Johns Hopkins University, April 1992.

Yam, Joseph, "The Development of Monetary Policy in Hong Kong," in *Monetary Management in Hong Kong: The Changing Role of the Exchange Fund*, Chartered Institute of Bankers, Hong Kong, July 1991, pp. 54–83.

Zurlinden, Mathias, "The Vulnerability of Pegged Exchange Rate: The British Pound in the ERM," *Review*, Federal Reserve Bank of St. Louis, September/October 1993, 41–56.

Author Index

Abken, Peter A., 252, 318
Agell, Jonas, 384
Aiyagari, S. Rao, 297
Altig, David, 363
Amsden, Alice H., 158, 209, 338, 408
Anderson, Gary A., 229
Anderson, Torben Juul, 252
Avery, Robert, 85, 363

Bacon, Kenneth H., 85
Bae, Kee Hong, 209
Baker, James C., 62, 158, 408
Barber, Joel R., 229
Bartlett, Bruce, 384
Basham, Michael E., 209
Batten, Dallas S., 61, 158, 363
Baum, C. F., 318
Baumol, W. J., 209, 297
Becketti, Sean, 85, 229, 252
Belongia, Michael T., 318
Berger, Allen, 85
Berger, George S., 85
Bernake, Ben, 363
Bernanke, Ben S., 318
Bhattacharya, A. K., 229
Blackwell, Michael P., 61, 363
Blinder, Alan, 363

Boemio, Thomas R., 184
Booth, James R., 337
Booth, Richard A., 209
Breeden, Richard C., 85
Brunner, Allan D., 62
Buchanan, James M., 337
Bullard, James B., 363
Bykhovsky, Michael, 229

Cagan, L. D., 229
Campbell, John Y., 319
Cargill, Thomas F., 10
Carmichael, Jeffery, 183
Carriero, N. J., 229
Caskey, John P., 85
Cha, Baekin, 407
Chan, David Y. K., 252
Chang, Chun-Hao, 229
Chen, Mu-Tsai, 62, 158, 183, 407
Chen, S. M., 158
Cheng, Yan-leung, 209
Cheung, Y. L., 209
Cheung, Yin-Wong, 252
Chin, H. W., 229
Ciotti, Glenn J., 209
Clarke, Robert L., 85
Constantinides, George M., 337

Cooper, S. Kerry, 10
Cover, James Peery, 364
Cross, Frank, 337
Culp, Christopher, 184
Cunningham, Thomas J., 337

Dallas, Pauline, 408
Damodaran, Aswath, 252
Davis, K. T., 86
Dawson, Steve, 337
Dawson, Steven M., 209
DeJong, David N., 337
Derosa, Paul, 229
Dickey, David A., 297
Dowd, Kevin, 338
Drake, P. J., 158
Dufey, Gunter, 10
Dybvig, Philip H., 338

Edwards, Franklin R., 338
Edwards, Gerald A. Jr., 184
Effros, Robert C., 37
Emery, Robert F., 184
Engel, Charles, 338
English, William B., 62
Espinosa, Marco, 158
Euh, Yoon-Dae, 62, 158, 209, 338, 408
Evanoff, Douglas D., 62
Evans, John S., 10

Fabozzi, Frank J., 10, 229
Fama, Eugene F., 85, 338
Feinman, Joshua N., 364
Ferri, Michael G., 10
Ferson, Wayne E., 318
Fieleke, Norman S., 408
Fisher, Irving, 274, 297
Flood, Mark D., 338
Fortune, Peter, 338
Fraser, Donald R., 10
Freer, Jim, 229
French, Kenneth R., 338
Friedman, Benjamin, 384
Friedman, Milton, 209, 364, 384
Froot, Kenneth R., 319
Fuhrer, Jeffrey C., 364
Fung, Noel, 408
Furlong, Frederick, 85

Garfinkel, Michelle R., 158

Ghose, T. K., 62
Giddy, Ian, 10
Gilbert, R. Alton, 133, 252
Gilkeson, James H., 229
Gillis, John G., 209
Glick, Reuven, 384
Glick, Steven L., 209
Gonczy, Anne Marie, 10
Goodhart, Charles, 133
Goodman, Laurie, 229
Greenwood, John G., 408
Gregory, Deborah, 209
Greider, William, 364

Hafer, R. W., 319
Hahn, Thomas K., 184
Hamid, Akhtar, 37
Hanke, Steve H., 408, 409
Harper, Ian R., 183
Hasan, Rikky, 252
Haubrich, Joseph G., 85, 229
Havrilesky, Thomas, 364
Hayre, Lakhbir, 229
Hein, Scott E., 319
Henning, C. N., 10
Ho, Y. K., 10, 11, 62, 159, 209, 338, 408
Hoenig, Thomas M., 364
Holder, Christopher L., 85
Homer, Sidney, 297
Horii, Akinari, 365
Hsu, Paul S., 209
Huang, C. H., 338
Humpage, Owen F., 364
Hutchison, Michael, 384

Ip, Y. K., 252
Iqbal, Zubair, 37
Israilevich, Philip R., 62

Jackson, William D., 274
Jansen, Dennis W., 297
Jao, Y. C., 159
Jegadeesh, Narasimhan, 209
Jereski, Laura, 229, 253
Johnson, Dudley W., 113
Johnson, Hazel J., 10
Johnson, Verle B., 133
Jones, C. P., 11
Jordan, Jerry L., 338
Joskow, P. L., 338

Judd, John P., 364

Kahn, Mohsin S., 37
Kane, Edward J., 85, 338
Kapner, K. R., 253
Kasman, B., 159, 364
Kavanagh, Barbara, 184
Keeley, Michael, 85
Keeton, William R., 85
Kidwell, David S., 10
Kim, In-Su, 61, 363
Kim, Wang-Woong, 159
King, Robert G., 10
Klein, Michael W., 364
Kneeshaw, J. T., 159, 364
Knight, Frank H., 253
Koekijk, Kees G., 318
Kohn, Meir, 10
Konstas, Panoz, 229
Kopcke, Richard W., 210
Kretzmer, Peter E., 385
Kroszner, Randall, 408
Kwag, Dae-Hwan, 253
Kwast, Myron L., 363

Laderman, Elizabeth S., 85
LaRoche, Robert K., 184
Law, C. K., 408
Lee, Charles, 338
Lee, S. Y., 159
Lee, Wan Deok, 159
Leeper, Eric M., 364
Leng, Tan Chiew, 339
Levine, Ross, 10
Levingston, Steven E., 274
Levonian, Mark E., 85
Lewis, M. K., 86
Liu, Lawrence S., 209
Livingston, Miles, 209
Lui, Y. H., 184, 210

Madura, Jeff, 10
Mankiw, N. Gregory, 319
Marino, Vivian, 86
Marriott, Dean, 86
Marshall, John F., 253
Mayer, Martin, 210, 253
McCartney, Scott, 253
Mehra, Rajnish, 338
Meulendyke, Ann-Marie, 364, 365

Meyer, Paul A., 10
Miller, Sam Scott, 210
Mirakhor, Abbas, 37
Miron, Jeffrey A., 319
Mitchell, K., 365
Modigliani, Franco, 10
Moreno, Ramon, 408
Morgan, Donald P., 365
Morris, Charles, 85, 253, 338
Motley, Brian, 364
Mougoue, M., 319
Murvat, Sardad Khan, 37

Nakao, Masaaki, 365
Neumann, Manfred J. M., 113
Newberger, Jonathan A., 86
Ng, Lilian K., 252
Ng, Linda F., 252
Nichols, Dorothy M., 10
Niederhoffer, Victor, 253
Nocera, Simon E., 61, 363

Osterberg, William P., 338
Ozeki, Yuzuru, 61, 363

Park, Kieth K. H., 210
Patrick, Hugh T., 338
Pearce, D. K., 365
Peek, Joe, 229
Perkin, Ian K., 408
Persson, Mats, 384
Pesando, James E., 319
Peterson, Richard L., 10
Pigott, William, 10
Plourde, Andre, 319
Poindexter, J. C., 11
Poole, W., 365
Post, Mitchell A., 184
Poterba, James M., 339
Powell, Jerome H., 210
Pozdena, Randall J., 62, 85
Prescott, Edward C., 338
Price, David W., 113
Pulliam, Susan, 229

Reinhart, Vincent, 210
Rietz, Thomas A., 339
Roberds, William, 113
Roberts, Dan J., 252
Roberts, William, 365

Roh, Choong-Hwan, 184
Roley, V. Vance, 385
Rose, Peter S., 10, 11
Rosengren, Eric S., 210, 364
Russell, S., 113, 319, 339

Saavalainen, Tapio, 409
Scarlata, Jodi G., 253
Schoenholtz, Kermit L., 319
Schweitzer, Robert, 364
Scott, Robert Haney, 10, 11, 62, 113, 159,
    210, 297, 319, 408, 409
Scott, William L., 11
Seater, John J., 319
Selgin, George A., 339
Selwyn, Susan M., 210
Sharpe, Antonia, 229
Shieh, Samuel C., 159, 409
Shiller, Robert J., 319
Shleifer, Andrei, 338, 339
Siconolfi, Michael, 210
Simmons, Katerina, 253
Simons, Katerina, 210
Smith, Adam, 274
Smith, Bruce D., 297
Smith, D. J., 229
Smith, Gary, 11
Smith, Stephen D., 229, 339
Sprenkle, Case M., 113
Srinivasan, Aruna, 62
Stevens, E. J., 62, 133, 159, 365
Stewart, Ian, 210
Stigler, George J., 339
Stowe, David W., 210
Summers, Bruce J., 86
Summers, Lawrence H., 339
Syron, Richard F., 339

Tan, Chwee Huat, 62, 159, 409
Terpstra, Robert H., 210, 253
Thakor, Anjan, 339
Thaler, Richard, 338

Thies, C. F., 318
Thomson, James B., 229, 338, 339
Thorton, Daniel L., 158, 297, 365
Thygerson, Kenneth J., 11
Titman, Sheridan, 209
Tobin, James, 297
Todd, Walker F., 365
Tong, Wilson H. S., 339
Tyson, James L., 86

Van Agtmael, Antoine W., 210
Van den Bergh, P., 159, 364
Von Bohm-Bawerk, Eugen, 274

Wachtel, Paul, 85
Wall, Larry D., 339
Wallace, Neil, 297
Walters, Alan, 408, 409
Wartzman, Rick, 253
Weil, Philippe, 339
West, Donald A., 113
Wheelock, David C., 339
White, Lawrence J., 86
Whiteman, Charles H., 337
Whitt, Joseph A. Jr., 365
Wilcox, James A., 11, 229
Wong, Gordon W., 253
Wong, Kai-tai, 209
Wong, Kie Ann, 10, 11, 62, 159, 210, 339,
    408

Yam, Joseph, 409
Yamashita, Takeji, 184, 210
Yin, Norman, 408
Yip, Ying K., 319
Yun, Yuo-Jin, 210

Zazzarino, Mike, 229
Zenios, S. A., 229
Zuckerman, Laurence, 210
Zurlinden, Mathias, 409

Subject Index

Agency bonds, 191
   government agency, 192
   spreads of yields on, 192
Agency costs, 326
American Association of Retired Persons, 323
American Express, 67
American Stock Exchange, 201
Announcement effects, 329
Arkansas Best Corporation, 239
Armored car services, 65
Asian Currency Unit (ACU), 58
Asian dollar market, 171
Asian Tiger countries, 8, 12
   financial derivatives in, 249
   gross domestic product data, 33
   money markets in, 176
   saving rates in, 259
Auctions, 187
   Dutch, 188, 189
Automatic Transfer System (ATS)
   accounts, 65, 68, 91

Bacon, Kenneth H., 80, 85
Bagehot, Walter, 161
Baker, James C., 55, 62
Balancing the budget, 370

Bank America, 173
Bank of China, 97, 154
Bank of Credit and Commerce, 48, 115
Bank of Credit and Commerce
   International, 48
Bank of East Asia, 115
Bank of England, 115, 148
Bank of France (Banque de France), 117, 143, 173
Bank Holding Company Acts of 1956, 40
Bank holiday, 47, 64
Bank Insurance Fund, 334
Bank of Japan, 150
Bank of Korea, 55, 56, 154, 401
   monetary stabilization bond, 154
Bank runs, 48
Bank of Taiwan, 59
Banker's acceptances, 6, 167
Banking Act of 1933, 1935, 64
Banking corporations, 39
   in Asian Tiger countries, 81
   balance sheets, 41
   branch offices, 39
   correspondent banks, 114
   income statements, 41

Banks, 63
  bank on not having to pay, 48
  are they special, 63
Banque de France, *see* Bank of France
Barclays bank, 172
Barclays de Zoete Wedd Investment
    Management Limited, 242
Barclay's Share Price Index (New Zealand),
    240
Barter, 13
Base money, 134
Basham, Michael E., 190
Basis in futures markets, 237
Basket of currencies in Singapore, 399
Basle Agreement, 76
Baumol, William J., 195, 209, 279
Becketti, Sean, 63
Bills-only policy, 356
Board of Commissioners of Currency of
    Singapore, 155, 398
Bohm-Bawerk, Eugen von, 258
Bond formulas, 256
Borrowing, 129
  adjustment, 129
  extended credit, 130
  seasonal, 129
Brassage, 96
Breeden, Richard C., 80, 85
Bretton-Woods Agreement, 239
Broadside approach to open market
    operations, 358
  concerns about, 359
  implementing, 359
  objection based on rational expectations,
    360
Brunner, Allan D., 45, 62
Buchanan, James M., 324, 337
Budget deficits, 370
  constitutional amendment, 370
Bull and bear bonds, 204
Bundesbank, 145
Bush, George, 381

Call loans, 218
Call provisions, 193
Callable bonds, 218
Capital, 20
Capital adequacy ratios (CARs), 75
  concerns over, 78
  Tier I and II capital, 76

  Weighted risky assets, 77
Capital markets, 6, 185
Capital value, 24
Capture theory, 322
Cash flow yields, 221
Cash management bills, 161
Central bank, 116
  functions of, 116
Central Bank of China, 59, 156, 403
Central Provident Fund, 400
Certificates of Accrual on Treasury
    Securities (CATS), 191
Certificates of deposit (CDs), 65, 166
Certificates of indebtedness, 98
Chase Manhattan Bank, 171
Check cashing stores, 80, 325
Chen, M. T., 182, 183
Chicago Board of Trade, 239, 248, 321
Chicago Mercantile Exchange, 239, 250
Chung-Hsin Bills Finance Corporation (in
    Taiwan), 182
Chung-Hua Bills Finance Corporation (in
    Taiwan), 182
Churchill, Winston, 170
Churning of accounts, 350
Ciotti, Glenn J., 196, 209
Circular flow diagram, 17
Citibank, 49, 167
Clearing house of the Hong Kong
    Association of Banks, 388
Clinton, William, 381
Collateralized Mortgage Obligations
    (CMOs), 217, 222
Commercial banking, 64
Commercial paper, 6, 169
  in Hong Kong, 180
Commercial real estate mortgages, 224
Commodities Trading Ordinance, 249
Competitive bids, 163
Comptroller of the currency, 39, 323
Constant prepayment rate assumption, 219
Contemporaneous reserve accounting, 52
Continental Illinois Bank of Chicago, 167
Convertible bonds, 193
  warrants, 193
Correspondent banking, 114
Counterfeiters, 100
Credit cards as a substitute for money, 281
Credit enhancement, 169
Credit risk, 78

Culp, Christopher, 179, 184
Currency, 91
   circulating in Guangdong, 98
   missing, 111
   outside the U.S., 101
Cut-throat competition, 47, 64

Dallas, Pauline, 396, 408
Dealer market, 186
Debt
   is also an asset, 14
   and usury, 14
Debt financing, 370
Debt management, 367, 374
   during 1992 U.S. election, 381
   broadside approach to, 374
   effectiveness of, 377
   and profitability of financial institutions,
     382
Deficits, 370
Demand deposits, 91
Demand and supply
   for funds, 2, 264
   for securities, 3
   shifts in, 264
Deposit insurance, 70
Depository Institutions Act of 1982, 69
Depository Institutions Deregulation
   and Monetary Control Act of 1980,
   50, 68
Depth, breadth, and resiliency, 187
Derivatives, 6
Deutsche Bundesbank, 145
Discount rate, 162
   on Treasury bills, 162
Disintermediation, 23, 217
Duke, Paul Jr., 171
Dutch auction, 188, 189, 380

Economic efficiency, 329
Edgeworth box diagram, 289
Efficiency, 328
Efficient Markets Hypothesis (EMH), 329
Einstein, Albert, 314
Empirical tests of EMH, 331
   closed-end mutual fund puzzle, 331
   excess volatility of stock prices, 332
   greater fool theory, 332
   loser's blessing, 333
   mean reversion, 333

   noise trading, 333
   small firm effect, 331
   speculative bubbles, 332
   value line enigma, 332
   winner's curse, 333
English, William B., 45, 62
Environmental Protection Agency, 248
Equation of exchange, 276
Euh, Yoon-Dae, 55, 62
Eurocurrencies, 171
Eurodollars, 170
   creation of, 172
   Kundsen's example, 172
   rate spread in, 176
Exchange Equalization Fund, 351
Exchange Fund, 57, 153, 387
   THE ACCOUNT of, 391
   advisory committee, 387
   balance sheet, 389
   bills, 179
   foreign currency reserves, 97
   investment division, 388
   monetary management division, 388
   monetary tools, 388
Expected inflation, 266

Fable of the Talents, 17
Fama, Eugene F., 63, 85, 328, 333, 338
Federal Accounting Standards Board, 78
Federal Deposit Insurance Corporation
   (FDIC), 130, 334
Federal Deposit Insurance Corporation
   Improvement Act, 79, 130, 334
Federal Financing Bank, 164
Federal funds, 6, 54, 165
   borrowed, 124
   net purchased, 122, 123
Federal Home Loan Bank, 216
Federal Home Loan Mortgage Corporation
   (FHLMC), 216
Federal Housing Administration (FHA),
   212
Federal National Mortgage Association
   (FNMA), 215, 239
Federal Open Market Committee, 129, 142,
   186, 340
   directive, 341, 349
Finance paper, 169
Financial derivatives, 6
Financial intermediaries, 7

Financial markets, 5
   futures contracts, 7
   for loans and securities, 5
   money markets, 6
   primary and secondary, 5
   religious and cultural influence, 15
Financial Times Stock Exchange Index
   (Footsie 100), 240
Fiscal finance, 372
Fiscal policy, 366
   automatic and discretionary, 368
   policy lags, 369
      implementation and impact, 370
      recognition, 369
   separate from monetary policy, 367
Fisher effect, 267
Fisher, Irving, 267, 287
Fisherian time-preference model, 287
Float, 118
Floaters, 223
   inverse floaters, 223
Floating rate notes, 165
Flow of funds analysis, 24
Food stamps, 105
Foreign stock index futures contracts, 240
Fortune, Peter, 330n, 338
Forward market and futures market, 233
Four Asian Tigers, xi
Four asset model, 284
Fractional reserve banking system, 71
Franklin Savings Association of Ottawa,
   Kansas, 238
French, Kenneth R., 333, 338
Friedman, Milton, 189, 279, 351, 378, 380
Froot, Kenneth R., 314, 319
Fungible, 105
Furlong, Frederick, 63, 85
Futures markets, 233
   basis in, 237
   commodities futures, 233
   contracts, 234
      arbitrage, 241
      foreign stock index, 240
      futures contract prices, 241
   financial futures, 233
   foreign exchange futures, 233
   futures exchange, 234
   Hang Seng Stock Index, 240
   Hong Kong Futures Exchange, 240
   interest rate futures, 233
   options on futures contracts, 238
   taxes on gains and losses on contracts,
      239
   Treasury bill futures, 233

Garn-St Germain Act of 1982, 50, 69
Gillis, John G., 196, 209
Giro payments system, 82
Glass-Steagall Act of 1933, 40, 47, 64, 68
   restrictions, 70
Glick, Steven L., 209
Global bonds, 196
Global Positioning System (GPS), 321
Gold Exchange of Singapore, 250
Goldsmith-Nagan, 314
Government debt, 185
Government failure, 321
Government National Mortgage Association
   (GNMA), 239
Government securities dealers, 162
Greenwood, John G., 395, 396, 408
Gross domestic product, 20

Hang Seng Bank, 240
Hang Seng Stock Index, 240
Hang Seng Stock Index futures contract,
   240, 249
Hanke, Steve H., 396, 408
Haubrich, Joseph G., 225, 229
Havrilesky, Thomas, 341, 364
Hedging bets, 232, 304
Hedging losses, 239
Ho, Y. K., 395, 408
Hoarding, 261
   dishoarding, 261
Holding period, 257
   yield on, 312
Homer, Sidney, 275
Hong Kong Association of Banks, 45, 179,
   249, 387, 388
Hong Kong Commodity Exchange Limited,
   249
Hong Kong Interbank Offered Rate
   (HIBOR), 179, 249
Hong Kong Monetary Authority, 57, 76,
   153, 387
Hongkong and Shanghai Banking
   Corporation, 76, 96, 152, 153, 387
   THE ACCOUNT, 390
Hong Kong, Stock Exchange of, 76, 205

Hong Kong's folly, 400
Hsu, Paul S., 207, 209
Hume, David, 276
Humphrey-Hawkins Act, 342
Hyperion Capital Management, Inc., 224

Immediately available funds, 165
Income bonds, 193
Indifference curves, 287
Information costs, 326
Inner reserves, 76
Insider trading, 195
Insurance in small towns, 65
Interest only securities, 223, 224
Interest rate, 2, 255
Interest rate risk, 78
Intermediaries, 7
    financial, 7, 23
Internal rate of return, 292
Internal revenue service, 239
International Banking Facilities, 171
International Business Machines (IBM), 248
International Monetary Fund, 117
International Monetary Market (IMM), 239
International Reciprocal Trade Association,
    13
Interstate banking, 40
Intervention in foreign exchange markets,
    351
Inverse floaters, 224
    risk of, 224
Investment, 20
    financial, 22
    real, 22
Investment banking, 64
Investment Finance Companies (in Korea),
    180
Investment opportunity curve, 292
Iqbal, Zubair, 16
Isaac, William M., 80, 85
Islamic banking, 16
Islamic law, 15

Jackson, William D., 270, 274
JASDAQ, 204
Jereski, Laura, 224, 229, 239, 253
Jockey Club, 397
Johnson, Lyndon, 213
Joskow, P. L., 324, 338
Junk bonds, 195

Kane, Edward, 324, 338
Kansas City Board of Trade, 239
Keeley, Michael, 63, 85
Keynes, John Maynard, 278
Keynes's medicine for the Great
    Depression, 355
Kidwell, David S., 85
Korean Exchange Bank, 56
Korean Stock Exchange, 205

Lagged reserve accounting, 52
Lagrangian multiplier, 295n
Law, C. K., 395, 408
Legally required reserves, 49, 55
Lender of last resort, 115, 148–49
Lerner, Abba, 372
Leverage, 44
Leveraged buy-outs, 195
Levingston, Steven E., 269, 274
Levonian, Mark E., 79, 85
Linked securities, 193, 204
Liquidity, 23
    measures of, 94
    preference, 279
    premium, 304, 311
        as risk premium, 311
        as term premium, 311
Liquidity requirements, 56
    in Hong Kong, 56
Liquidity reserves, 55
Little old lady of Threadneedle Street, 115
Loanable funds, 259
Local improvement district bonds, 197
Lombard rate, 146
London Discount Market Association, 148
London Interbank Offered Rate (LIBOR),
    176, 223
London International Financial Futures
    Exchange (LIFFE), 239
Loran navigation system, 321
Love of money, 13
Ludvig, Eugene, 80
Lui, Y. H., 180, 184, 204

Major Market Index, 240
Malaysian Stock Exchange, 206
Mankiw, N. Gregory, 313, 319
Marginal rate of time preference, 288
Maria's Bakery, 48
Marino, Vivian, 80, 85

Market's forecast, 315
  accuracy of, 315
Marshall, Alfred, 259
Mass Transit Railway, 180, 194, 396
McCartney, Scott, 238, 253
McCulloch, James W., 197
McCulloch vs. Maryland, 197
McFadden Act of 1927, 40
Mercantilism, 394
Merchant Banking Corporation Act
  (Korea), 181
Mericurrency, Merimarks, Meriyen, 172
Merrill Lynch, 191
Michaelson and Morley, 314
Midland Bank, 76
Mirakhor, Abbas, 16
Modern Money Mechanics, xii, 84
Monetary Affairs Branch, 387
Monetary Authority, Hong Kong, *see*
  Hong Kong Monetary Authority
Monetary Authority of Singapore, 58, 155,
  206, 399
Monetary base, 134
Monetary Control Act of 1980, 50, 53, 130
Monetary policy, 142
  four steps in, 142
  in Hong Kong, 386
  in Korea, 401
  separate from fiscal policy, 367
  in Singapore, 397
  in Taiwan, 403
Monetary stabilization bond in Korea, 180,
  403
Money
  correlation with gross domestic product,
    90
  creation, 70
    by Money Market Mutual Funds, 73
    by thrifts, 73
    tools of control over, 125
  definition of, 88
  functions of, 88
  love of, 13
  measurement of, 90
    in Asian Tigers, 105
    in Hong Kong, 103
  Quantity Theory of, 277
  transfer payment systems
    checking, 82
    giro, 82

Money market deposit (MMD) accounts,
  69, 91, 166
Money Market Mutual Funds, 65, 68, 91
Money markets, 6, 160
Money multiplier, 134
Moody's, 167, 194, 217, 328
Moral hazard, 335
Moral suasion, 131
Morris, Charles, 63, 85
Mortgages, 211
  adjustable rate, 213, 216
    caps on, 214, 216
    rates tied to indexes, 214
    risks on, 214, 216
  deductible interest on, 211
  fixed rate, 213
  graduated payment, 215
  negative amortization, 214
  reverse payment, 215
  roll over, 214
Municipal bonds, 197
  general obligation, 197
  revenue, 197
  taxes on, 197
Murry, Alan, 171
Muslim law, 16
Mutual savings banks, 64

NASDAQ, 204
National Banking Act of 1863, 39, 40
Negative interest rate scheme, 395
Negotiable certificates of deposit, 8, 65,
  167, 179, 181
Negotiable Orders of Withdrawal (NOW
  accounts), 65, 66, 68, 91
Neoclassical theory, 259
New York Stock Exchange, 201
New York Stock Exchange Composite
  Index, 240
New Zealand's Reserve Bank Act, 328
Nikkei Index, 240
Note issuing banks, 96
Notional principal, 247

Office of Thrift Supervision, 238, 334
Offshore banking units in Taiwan, 404
OPEC cartel, 326
Open Market Investment Committee, 128
Open market operations, 127, 343
  broadside approach to, 358

Open market operations (*continued*)
    defensive and dynamic, 127
        in Japan, 151
    discovered by accident, 128
    targets, 343
    two immediate impacts of, 358
Operation twist, 357, 377
Options, 7, 243
    American and European, 244
    on futures contracts, 238
    value of, 244
Options Exchanges, 244
    American Stock Exchange, 244
    Chicago Board of Options Exchange,
        244
    New York Stock Exchange, 244
    Philadelphia Stock Exchange, 244
Orders to pay, 168
Osaka Index, 240

Paribus Investment (Asia), 204
Park, Kieth K. H., 207, 210
Partial equilibrium analysis, 283
Participation certificates, 216
Pegged exchange rate system, 392
    disadvantages of, 394
    inflation, 394
    monetary control under, 393
Pegging the yield curve, 355
People's Bank of China, 59
People's Republic of China, 59
Perkin, Ian K., 396, 408
Perpetuity, 255
Peterson, Richard L., 85
Planned Amortization Classes (PACs), 223
Pollution rights (market for), 248, 321
Positive non-intervention, 387
Post office, 164
Postal savings system, 81
Powell, Jerome H., 190, 210
Prepayment problem, 218
    assumptions, 219
Present value, 4
Price, David W., 110, 113
Price fixing, 395
Prices of securities, 4
Prices and yields, 4, 255
    inverse relation, 4
Principal only securities, 223
Public interest, theory of, 322

Public Securities Association (PSA), 221
    PSA standard prepayment assumption,
        221
Pulliam, Susan, 224, 229

Quantity Theory of Money, 277

Rate of return, 292
Real Estate Mortgage Investment Conduits
    (REMICs), 222
Regulation D, 49, 165
Regulation Q, 47, 65
Regulations, 325
    America's attitude toward, 326
    prohibitive, 327
    to promote competition, 325
Relevant information, 329
Rent-seeking, 324
Rental income, 212
    implicit in Greece, 212
Repurchase agreements, 6, 91, 122, 144,
    165
Repurchase contracts, 144
    as borrowing, 144
    interest rate tender, 147
    volume tender, 147
Repurchase tender offer, 144
Required reserve ratio, 127
    changing, 130
Required reserves, 49
Reserve maintenance periods, 55
Reserve requirements, 50
    interest on, 69
    in Korea, 55
    management of, 118
    in other countries, 54
    in Singapore, 58
    in Taiwan, 58, 59
    target and slack variables, 120
Reserves, 124
    borrowed, 124
    excess, 124
    factors affecting, 140
    legal, 124
    nonborrowed, 124
    total, 124
Resolution Trust Corporation, 238
Retained earnings, 257
Revolving underwriting facility, 180
Ricardian equivalence, 266

Risk and uncertainty, 230
Risks in finance, 231
   capital risk, 231
   default risk, 231
   foreign exchange risk, 232
   inflation risk, 231
   reinvestment risk, 232
Roberts, Harry V., 328
Roh, Choong-Hwan, 180, 181, 183
Roley, V. Vance, 378, 385
Roosevelt, Franklin D., 47, 64
Russian dollar deposits, 170

Salomon Brothers, 189, 191
   trading scandal, 189
Saving, 20
   supply of, 291
Savings Association Insurance Fund, 334
Savings and loan associations, 64
Schultz, George, 189
Schweitzer, Robert, 341, 364
Scott, Robert Haney, 316
Sears, 67
Securities and Exchange Act of 1939, 64
Securities and Exchange Commission, 189, 196, 203, 217
Securities and Exchange Law (in Taiwan), 207
Securities and Futures Commission (in Hong Kong), 76
Securities Trading Automated Quotations System (STAQS), 202
Seigniorage, 96
   on checking accounts, 99
   in Hong Kong, 97
   in the U.S., 96
Selgin, George A., 320, 339
Selwyn, Susan M., 201, 210
Separate Trading in Registered Interest and Principal of Securities (STRIPS), 191
Shanghai Stock Exchange, 202, 203
Shenzhen Stock Exchange, 202, 203
Short sales, 243
Siconolfi, Michael, 189, 210
Simon, William, 189
Singapore, Board of Commissioners of Currency of, 156, 398
Singapore International Monetary Exchange (SIMEX), 250

Singapore, Stock Exchange of, 206
Slack variable, 120, 127, 348, 391
Smith, Adam, 258, 259, 394
Special drawing rights, 117
Sprenkle, Case M., 111, 113
Stability in Hong Kong, 396
   deceptive image of, 396
Standard Chartered Bank, 49, 154
Standard & Poor's, 167, 194, 217, 328
Standard & Poor's 500 Index, 240
Sterilized intervention, 354
Stewart, Ian, 206, 210
Stigler, George, 323
Stock Exchange of Hong Kong, 76, 205
Stock Exchange of Singapore, 206
Stock formula, 257
Stock market index futures contracts, 239
Stock market popularity, 201
Subordinated bonds, 193
Supply of saving, 291
Student loan program, 111
Swap markets, 245
   currency swaps, 245
   fake dollar swaps, 245
   interest rate swaps, 245
   notional principal, 247
   "plain vanilla", 246

Taiwan Stock Exchange, 206
Taiwan Tracker Fund, Limited, 242
Taiwanese up to their knees in money, 405
Target variable, 120, 391
Targeted Amortization Classes (TACs), 223
Tax anticipation bills, 161
Tax break on homeownership, 218
Tax and loan accounts, 122
Term premium, 314
Term structure of interest rates, 299, 376
   segmented markets approach, 306, 376
Terpstra, Robert H., 241, 253
Thatcher, Margaret, 392, 396
Thomson, James B., 225, 229
Thoreau, Henry, 258
Three Tier Banking System, 57
Thrift industry, 213
   victims of high interest rates, 213
Tier I and II capital, 76
Tight money conditions, 125
Tobin, James, 279, 284
Tobin's Q, 195

Tools of control over money creation,
    125, 142
  in the Asian Tigers, 152
  in France, Germany, U.K., 143
  in Japan, 150
  moral suasion, 131
Transactions costs, 24
Treasury bills, 6, 161
  as a substitute for money, 281
Treasury-Federal Reserve Accord, 356, 378
Treasury Investment Growth Receipts
  (TIGRs), 191
Treasury not a profit-making institution,
  379
Treasury tax and loan accounts, 122
Truman, Harry S., 356
Truth in Lending Act, 323
Truth in Saving law, 323
Tyson, James L., 80, 86

unit banking system, 40
U.S. League of Savings Institutions, 218
Usury, 47
Usury and debt, 14
  Fable of the Talents, 17

Value Line Stock Index, 240
Van Agtmael, Antoine W., 207, 210

Veterans Administration (VA), 213
Volcker, Paul A., 64

Walt Disney, 193
Walters, Sir Alan, 396, 408
Wartzman, Rick, 239, 253
Washington Public Power Supply System
  (WPPSS), 200
Weighted risky assets, 77
West, Donald A., 110, 113
Wicksell, Knut, 278
Wong, Kie Ann, 205, 210
World Bank, 248
World Financial Markets, 54

Yam, Joseph, 393
Yankee bonds, 203
Yankee CDs, 167
Yield, 2
Yield curves, 299
  expectations approach to, 306
  inverted, 300
  normal, 300
  segmented markets approach to, 303
Yun, Yuo-Jin, 205, 210

Zero coupon bonds, 190
Zuckerman, Laurence, 205, 210

International Book Distributors Ltd

DESPATCH NOTE

Campus 400, Maylands Avenue, Hemel Hempstead, Herts, HP2 7EZ
Tele: 01442 881900   Telex: 824455   Fax: 01442 882099
Registration: London 714518   VAT No: GB 490 5885 08

INVOICE No	279792
ACCOUNT No	131140
DATE/TAXPOINT	8/03/97
DUE DATE	8/03/97

W/H ORDER NO	P091659 SML
W/H PICK NOTE	0

DELIVERY METHOD
SECURICOR OMEGA STAN

PAGE No	1
TRACKING No	5574928 ED

INVOICE ADDRESS
TONY JOHNSTON
FREE ISSUES

DELIVERY ADDRESS
DR SIMON HAYES
DEPT OF ECONOMICS
UNIVERSITY OF NEWCASTLE UPON
TYNE

NE1 7RU

HP2 7EZ
INTERNAL

Payments
Barclays Bank PLC
11 Bank Court
Hemel Hempstead
Herts HP1 1BX
Sort Code: 20 39 07   Swift: BARCGB22
£ GDP A/c 80605573 $ USD A/c 48001300

Or
Girobank PLC
Bootle
Merseyside
GIR 0AA
A/c 490-6357

Mail Payments to:
International Book Distributors Ltd
P.O. Box 591
Hemel Hempstead
Herts
HP2 4YU

SPECIAL INSTRUCTIONS

THESE BOOKS ARE SUPPLIED UNDER THE TERMS & CONDITIONS DETAILED OVERLEAF

Customer Reference	Back Order Date	SBN	Quantity Ordered	Quantity Supplied	Quantity B/Ordered	Title	Edition Binding	Author
	EX B/O	0131920898	1	1	0	MONEY FINANCIAL MARKETS &	01 P	SCOTT
	Total		1	1	0			
	Total Weight	1.00						

DR SIMON HAYES

FREE SUPPLY - NO CHARGE.

ANSWER CODES
* OS Out of Stock   * NP Not yet Published
* NE New Edition in Preparation   * RP Re-Printing
* OO On Order Abroad
OP Out of Print   AB Publication Abandoned
RR Rights Restricted
* Indicates order recorded for supply when stock
available unless your instructions are to the contrary.

INTERNATIONAL BOOK DISTRIBUTORS LTD TERMS AND CONDITIONS OF SALE

1. GENERAL

(A) In these Conditions 'The Company' means International Book Distributors Limited and, where applicable, any other company which is part of the Simon & Schuster Group or any third party for whom International Book Distributors provides a contracted service. 'The Customer' means the person, firm or company placing an order with The Company.

(B) All orders are accepted and goods supplied subject to the following Terms and Conditions which shall govern the contract and cannot be altered by The Customers' Terms of Purchase. No addition to or variation from these Terms and Conditions shall be binding on The Company unless it is in writing and signed by a duly authorised representative of The Company.

(C) Goods must not be sold to the general public before their publication date, namely that date in respect of any of the goods which is shown on the invoice or despatch documentation or which The Company otherwise indicates as the first day they may be sold to the general public.

2. ORDERS

(A) The Company reserves the immediate right, at any time (without prejudice to any other remedy) to terminate the agreement constituted by these Conditions or to cancel any uncompleted order or to suspend delivery in the event that any amounts payable by The Customer are overdue or there is any breach by The Customer of any of its obligations under these Conditions or for any other reason which at the discretion of The Company justifies such action.

(B) Prices are subject to change without prior notification (before or after goods are invoiced, in the latter case only as a consequence of pricing or invoicing error).

We reserve the right to charge any extra costs incurred by The Company in meeting The Customer's order requirements.

(C) Any orders outstanding with The Company after the termination or expiry of a distribution agreement between The Company and the publisher concerned will be transferred to the publisher's new distributor together with any money paid in advance of despatch of the order for cash sales. (Alternatively The Company will refund such monies paid in advance to The Customer depending on the distribution agreement).

3. DELIVERY AND RISK

(A) Goods will be delivered to the delivery address shown on The Company's invoice or to the Customer's designated Shipper or Agent and, if none is shown, to the person to whom the invoice is addressed/despatched. Any delivery dates are given as estimates only and in no circumstances shall The Company be liable for any loss whatsoever suffered or caused through late delivery or non-delivery. Neither The Company nor its carriers are obliged to provide loading or unloading facilities on delivery.

(B) The risk of loss and/or damage (but not title) to goods supplied by The Company shall pass to The Customer when they are delivered to The Customer or other person to whom The Company has been authorised by The Customer to deliver the goods, whether expressly or by implication, and The Company shall not be liable for the safety of the goods thereafter. (Accordingly The Customer should insure the goods thereafter against such risks as may be commercially prudent).

(C) Any damage to the goods in transit, or shortages in the goods delivered must be notified to the relevant carrier within 10 days of receipt (packing and contents to be held for inspection). On no account will claims be considered if notified outside this period.

4. RETURNS

(A) Prior written authorisation for returned goods must be obtained. Returns will only be considered at its discretion by The Company within 12 months of supply. Returns permission must be requested from the publisher of the goods in question. Authorisation will be subject to the returns conditions and policies imposed by the publishers concerned which are in addition to and terms and conditions set out herein. Authorisation by a publisher's representative does not confer automatic credit for returns if the returns conditions and policies are not adhered to.

(B) ISBN and full details of the books requested to be returned must be provided within 3 months of the publication of a new edition provided such returns are within 12 months of original supply. If this is not possible, the minimum information required is the month and year of supply. Failure by The Customer to provide correct information will delay the processing procedure. The Customer reserves the right to refuse to credit any goods returned by The Customer where no evidence of purchase is provided.

(C) Subject to the provisions of this paragraph 4, old editions may be returned within 3 months of the publication of a new edition provided such returns are further made within 12 months of original supply.

(D) Unauthorised returns will, at The Company's discretion, be sent back to The Customer at The Customer's risk and expense, or be credited at a reduced rate or subject to the imposition of some other penalty.

(E) Goods returned from exhibitions must be listed and packed separately with the complete number of parcels stated. Invoice numbers must always be quoted for these returns.

(F) Defective and incorrect supplies should be returned immediately quoting the relevant invoice number and the reason for return.

(G) All parcels returned by The Customer should be clearly marked as returned goods and should be enclosed with the full details showing the reason for the return. Only complete books may be returned and not title pages unless otherwise authorised in advance by The Company, in writing.

(H) The Company will not accept books back for credit unless they are in mint condition, and the titles within are not out of print.

(I) The Company advise that all returns should be delivered by a carrier who can provide proof of delivery. The Company is not liable for any returns lost in transit. All returns should be securely packed to ensure safe arrival. Returns remain the responsibility and property of The Customer until receipt in The Company's warehouse. The Customer is liable for any shortages or damages during transit. All returns are made at The Customer's expense and accordingly The Company will not accept any charges levied by shipping/transport agents.

(J) The Company will not give returns permission for software or books specially ordered from our USA offices and special price deals.

(K) A copy of the Authorised Returns Note must be returned with the books.

5. TITLE

(A) Notwithstanding any other provision of these Conditions, the ownership of all goods supplied pursuant to these Conditions shall remain vested in The Company (which reserves the right to dispose of them) until The Customer has received payment in full of all debts owing by The Customer to The Company.

(B) In the event that payment is overdue in whole or in part or upon the commencement of any act or proceedings in which The Customer's solvency is involved, The Company may without prejudice to any of its other rights recover or resell the goods, or any of them and may enter upon The Customer's premises by its servants or agents for that purpose. The Customer agrees to pay The Company all costs of repossession.

(C) Where The Customer sells the goods, prior to acquiring the ownership of them, all money received from such sale shall be held by The Customer as trustee for The Company until all sums due to The Company from The Customer have been duly paid.

6. PAYMENT

(A) Payment terms are as agreed by The Customer and The Credit Manager in writing. Time is of the essence with respect to The Customer's obligations hereunder. Payment may not be withheld, or delayed by The Customer for unauthorised returns or otherwise without the prior written agreement of The Company.

(B) The Company reserves the right to charge interest on overdue amounts accruing on a daily basis from the date payment is due until the date of actual payment both before and after judgement. The rate of interest charged will be equal to 3% above Barclays Bank plc base rate from time to time in force.

7. LIABILITY

(A) The Company shall be liable for death or personal injury resulting from negligence of The Company, its servants or agents (but not independent contractors) while acting in the course of their employment by The Company.

(B) The Company does not make or give any warranty, representation or undertaking as to the quality of the goods, their correspondence with description or fitness for purpose, that the goods are not defamatory, injurious, obscene, unlawful or in breach of copyright or in any other manner whatsoever.

(C) Save as and to the extent provided by these Conditions, The Company shall not in any circumstances be liable to The Customer or any successor or assignee of The Customer in respect of any loss of whatsoever nature occurring to The Customer arising from the supply of goods or from non-delivery, delayed delivery, damage to or loss of the goods arising out of any act or omission by The Company (including negligence) or any cause not within The Company's control including (without limitation) fire, flood, accident, strike, riot, lock-out, trade dispute, industrial action, terrorism, nuclear accident, war, insurrection, act or restraint of Government.

8. TERMINATION AND GENERAL

(A) The agreement constituted by these Conditions shall terminate forthwith if any order is made for the bankruptcy of or an effective resolution is passed for the winding-up of The Customer or if The Customer being a company is unable to pay its debts within the meaning of Section 123 of the Insolvency Act 1986, or any statutory re-enactment or modification thereof, or makes a composition with creditors or if a supervisor, receiver, administrator, administrative receiver or other encumbrancer takes possession of or is appointed over the whole or any part of the assets of The Customer.

(B) If the agreement between The Company and a publisher expires or is terminated for any reason The Company may terminate the agreement constituted by these Conditions forthwith or at any time thereafter in relation to the goods supplied by that publisher.

(C) The termination of the agreement constituted by these Conditions shall not affect any rights or obligations of the parties arising prior to such termination.

(D) All contracts under these Conditions shall be governed by and construed in accordance with the laws of England and all disputes shall be submitted to the exclusive jurisdiction of the English courts.